Annual Review of United Nations Affairs

2006/2007

Volume V

Edited by
Joachim Müller
and
Karl P. Sauvant

Oceana®
NEW YORK

OXFORD
UNIVERSITY PRESS

Oxford University Press, Inc., publishes works that further Oxford University's objective of excellence in research, scholarship, and education.

Published by Oxford University Press, Inc.
198 Madison Avenue, New York, New York 10016

ISSN: 0066-4340

ISBN: 978-0-19-537076-8 (2006/2007, Volume V)

Note to Readers:

This publication is designed to provide accurate and authoritative information in regard to the subject matter covered. It is based upon sources believed to be accurate and reliable and is intended to be current as of the time it was written. It is sold with the understanding that the publisher is not engaged in rendering legal, accounting, or other professional services. If legal advice or other expert assistance is required, the services of a competent professional person should be sought. Also, to confirm that the information has not been affected or changed by recent developments, traditional legal research techniques should be used, including checking primary sources where appropriate.

(Based on the Declaration of Principles jointly adopted by a Committee of the American Bar Association and a Committee of Publishers and Associations.)

SUMMARY TABLE OF CONTENTS

TABLE OF CONTENTS VOLUME V

CHAPTER 7

Selected Reports of Intergovernmental Bodies, Expert Groups and the United Nations Secretariat *(continued)*

CHAPTER 7

Selected Reports of Intergovernmental Bodies, Expert Groups and the United Nations Secretariat *(Continued)*

F. Middle East

1. Report of the Secretary-General on the implementation of resolution 1701 (2006), for the period 11 to 17 August 2006 (S/2006/670)

I. Introduction

1. In paragraph 17 of its resolution 1701 (2006) of 11 August 2006, the Security Council requested that I report to it within one week on the implementation of the resolution. The present report is submitted pursuant to that request.

2. In its resolution 1701 (2006), the Council called upon the United Nations to assume a broad range of political, humanitarian and military responsibilities. Intensive work is proceeding on all fronts. The present report, however, focuses primarily on the steps taken and measures urgently required to consolidate the cessation of hostilities, in particular the withdrawal and deployment of forces in southern Lebanon and the rapid reinforcement of the United Nations Interim Force in Lebanon (UNIFIL). It also provides an assessment of the humanitarian situation and the action being taken by the United Nations to address it.

3. As concerns the political situation, I intend to submit to the Security Council by mid-September 2006, in connection with paragraph 10 of resolution 1701 (2006), a more comprehensive report on significant developments, and to provide an update on the implementation of all the relevant provisions of the resolution. That report will be informed by the mission to the region of my Special Envoys, Terje Roed-Larsen and Vijay Nambiar, whom I dispatched on 18 August 2006. The aim of the mission is to provide full support to the process of implementation of Council resolution 1701 (2006). I acknowledge the respective invitation and request from the Council, contained in paragraphs 9 and 10 of resolution 1701 (2006), that I support efforts to secure from the parties as soon as possible agreements in principle on the principles and elements for a long-term solution, and that I develop, in liaison with relevant international actors and the concerned parties, proposals on the implementation of those principles. To this end, the mission will also initiate a process of consultation with the Governments of Israel and Lebanon and will report back directly to me on those matters.

II. Cessation of hostilities

4. I am greatly relieved to inform the Security Council that, as of the writing of the present report, the parties are generally complying with the cessation of hostilities called for in paragraph 1 of resolution 1701 (2006).

5. As indicated in my letter dated 12 August 2006 to the President of the Security Council (S/2006/647), the cessation of hostilities went into effect at 0500 hours GMT on 14 August, which was the date and time mutually agreed to by the Prime Ministers of Israel and Lebanon in discussions with me following the adoption of the resolution.

6. I wrote to both Prime Ministers on 12 August to confirm the agreement. I also conveyed to them the expectation that, once the cessation of hostilities came into effect, the parties would cease firing into the territory of, or at, the other party, with any type of weapon from

the ground, air or sea, and that no force should occupy or seek to take control of any additional territory from the other. In addition, I urged the parties to make every effort, in the interest of the civilian population on both sides, to continue to consolidate the cessation of hostilities and to move swiftly to convert it into a lasting ceasefire, in cooperation with UNIFIL, through the measures prescribed in resolution 1701 (2006).

7. On 12 August, the Government of Lebanon announced its acceptance of resolution 1701 (2006). On 13 August, the Government of Israel announced that it would act according to its obligations as outlined in the resolution.

8. Meanwhile, some of the heaviest fighting of the month-long conflict occurred during the 48-hour period prior to the cessation of hostilities coming into effect. Israel Defense Forces (IDF) intensified shelling and aerial bombardment across Lebanon. Hizbollah launched a barrage of rockets into northern Israel. The two sides exchanged heavy fire on the ground, in particular in the area of Bayyadah, Al Jibbayn and Tayr Harfa in the western sector, and Mays al Jabal and Markaba in the central sector.

9. In the midst of the escalation of fighting in the final hours leading up to the cessation of hostilities, UNIFIL personnel endured 85 IDF-fired artillery shells impacting directly inside several positions, 35 in the area of Tibnin alone, in addition to 10 air-to-ground rockets and 108 artillery rounds landing in the immediate vicinity of these and other United Nations positions, including the UNIFIL headquarters in Naqoura. UNIFIL very fortunately did not suffer casualties but a number of positions sustained significant material damage. The mission strongly protested to IDF command throughout the period in question.

10. UNIFIL also strongly protested to the Lebanese authorities one incident of a Hizbollah-fired rocket impacting directly inside a UNIFIL position in the area of Ghanduriyah. The impact caused material damage but no casualties.

11. On the heels of this intensive fighting, the guns on all sides fell silent at 0500 hours GMT on 14 August, as agreed.

12. UNIFIL personnel emerged from shelters immediately to carry out intensive patrolling. The patrolling continued into the night, throughout its area of operation and in the "Tyre pocket" up to the Litani river, to assess the situation on the ground and to monitor the cessation of hostilities. UNIFIL also resumed air patrols over the area along the Blue Line the following day.

13. UNIFIL has reported only a handful of isolated violations of the cessation of hostilities since it came into effect. In one incident on 15 August, UNIFIL learned that IDF and Hizbollah had exchanged fire in the area of Haddathah in the central sector. It immediately dispatched patrols to the scene, to find the dead bodies of four Hizbollah members, which were later taken away in an ambulance. In another incident on 16 August, an IDF tank positioned on the Israeli side fired one round across the Blue Line into Lebanese territory towards the village of Markaba in the central sector. There was no response from the other side and the situation in the area remained calm. UNIFIL observed one to four Israeli violations of Lebanese airspace daily. On 17 August 2006, a group of 100 armed elements in vehicles crossed into one of the sectors vacated by IDF near Al Qalay in the Marjayoun area and moved to the south. Also on 17 August, UNIFIL reported shepherds having crossed the Blue Line in the Shab'a farms area. UNIFIL strongly protested these incidents to both sides.

III. Deployment of the Lebanese Armed Forces together with the United Nations Interim Force in Lebanon and withdrawal of Israeli Forces

14. The implementation of paragraph 2 of resolution 1701, which calls on the Government of Lebanon and UNIFIL to deploy their forces jointly throughout the south and for the Government of Israel to withdraw all of its forces from southern Lebanon, in parallel, is vital for enabling the cessation of hostilities to hold.

15. I am pleased to report that both parties have made constructive efforts to uphold their obligations in this regard. A significant first step was taken on 14 August just hours after the cessation of hostilities came into effect, when the two sides responded positively to a request from the UNIFIL Force Commander, Major-General Pellegrini, to jointly meet with him to coordinate their deployment and withdrawal plans, respectively. Major-General Dekel represented the Israeli Defense Forces and Major-General Shehaitly represented the Lebanese Armed Forces. The tripartite meeting, which was held at the UNIFIL position at the Ras Naqoura border crossing, was the first of its kind in over a decade.

16. At that and a subsequent meeting held on 16 August, the Lebanese side confirmed its desire and intention to deploy its forces to the south as quickly as possible, with the assistance of UNIFIL, to extend its authority in areas vacated by withdrawing Israeli forces. UNIFIL currently supports this deployment effort by the Lebanese Armed Forces, which involves three light infantry brigades, one armoured brigade and one armoured regiment.

17. For its part, the Israeli side provided information marked on a map of the areas occupied by its forces north of the Blue Line, encompassing 16 pockets/sectors. The Israeli side expressed its desire to withdraw its forces from all of the sectors as quickly as possible. IDF has provided maps showing mines and unexploded ordnance in the sectors from which it is withdrawing.

18. By mutual agreement, it was decided that a phased approach, by groups of sectors at a time, would be the most appropriate course of action. As per the understandings reached, in the first phase IDF vacated three sectors on 16 August. UNIFIL confirmed the withdrawal, established checkpoints and immediately commenced patrolling those areas. At the time of the writing of the present report, the Lebanese Armed Forces have deployed more than 1,500 troops, with vehicles of the 6th, 10th and 11th brigades, in the three sectors from which the Israel Defense Forces have withdrawn. UNIFIL checkpoints are now in place for monitoring the second phase withdrawal of the Israel Defense Forces from two additional sectors on 18 August. UNIFIL verification of the withdrawal is being carried out. The Lebanese Armed Forces plan to deploy additional units into the three sectors, as well as deploy their forces into the two additional sectors on 19 August. Contrary to the understanding of the 14 August meeting, whereby IDF would withdraw from the remaining sectors in the third phase on 16 August, Israel indicated that the withdrawal from the remaining sectors would not be carried out in one stage. On 17 August, IDF presented a revised map dividing the remaining 11 sectors into up to four subsectors, from which withdrawal would take place on a step-by-step basis.

19. A third tripartite meeting was scheduled to be held on 20 August in order to agree upon the next sectors to be handed over, taking into account security, logistical and humanitarian considerations. The intention is to swiftly proceed in this methodical manner, convening tripartite meetings to coordinate and reach mutual agreement on each set of movements in

advance, until the full withdrawal of Israeli forces and the full deployment, with support from UNIFIL, of Lebanese Armed Forces north of the Blue Line is complete. It would be premature to predict an exact date by which time that will occur, but it seems that all sides are working constructively towards that goal.

20. The initial phase of the deployment of the Lebanese Armed Forces to the south has shown that significant support is required to carry out the process quickly and effectively. The requirements conveyed to the UNIFIL Force Commander include petrol, oil, spare parts, bottled water, tentage items, personal kits, small arms ammunition, camp items, generators, tyres, batteries, prefabricated office accommodation stores and a wide range of communication equipment. I urge Member States in a position to do so to support requests from the Government of Lebanon in addressing those requirements so as to avoid any delays in the tactical deployment of the Lebanese Armed Forces. For its part, UNIFIL is already providing as much support as it can within its limited means.

IV. Reinforcement of the United Nations Interim Force in Lebanon

A. Concept of operations, force requirements and rules of engagement

21. A reinforced UNIFIL, as called for in paragraph 11 of resolution 1701 (2006), is a vital part of the package to enable the full deployment of the Lebanese Armed Forces to the south and, in parallel, the full withdrawal of the Israeli forces from Lebanon; monitor compliance with the cessation of hostilities; help ensure humanitarian access to civilian populations and the voluntary and safe return of displaced persons; and establish conditions conducive to concluding a permanent ceasefire agreement and help to implement it. In meeting those and related objectives outlined in resolution 1701 (2006), UNIFIL would be making an essential contribution to enable the Government of Lebanon to extend its authority over all of its territory.

22. As admirably and courageously as the men and women of the currently 2,000-strong UNIFIL have performed throughout this crisis, they will not be able to do much more without a rapid and massive injection of additional forces. To that end, since the adoption of the resolution I have been in contact with leaders around the world to appeal for contributions to UNIFIL. Within hours, the Department of Peacekeeping Operations of the United Nations Secretariat initiated contact with military counterparts in the permanent missions in order to informally exchange views on the concept of operations, new force requirements and revised rules of engagement. The approach has been to seek and incorporate the views of potential contributors to the force so as to arrive at arrangements that will give them maximum confidence in their participation.

23. At a formal meeting of current and potential troop-contributing countries chaired by the Deputy Secretary-General on 17 August, Member States generally reacted positively to this approach to reinforce UNIFIL. At that meeting, the Department of Peacekeeping Operations presented a detailed briefing on the concept of operations, force requirements and revisions to the rules of engagement. All current contributors to UNIFIL, the United Nations Disengagement Observer Force and the United Nations Truce Supervision Organization (UNTSO), all members of the Security Council, all participants at the Rome Meeting held on 26 July and additional countries that had indicated interest to participate in the force were invited to attend. In total, some 70 countries were in attendance. Copies of the presentation

were made available to participants after the meeting. This information should facilitate decision-making in capitals in the days ahead.

24. As the briefing at the meeting of troop-contributing countries and the documents made available already make clear, the most urgent need will be to reinforce UNIFIL, between 17 August and 2 September, with up to 3,500 additional personnel, consisting of the following capabilities: three mechanized infantry battalions; one light reconnaissance battalion; one engineer battalion (combat); one engineer battalion (construction); two signal companies; one military police company; one headquarters company; and a maritime unit for patrolling the coastline. Those requirements do not yet take into account any additional needs that may be identified as a result of further requests for UNIFIL assistance by the Lebanese Armed Forces as their deployment to the south continues.

25. The main effort of the first wave of additional forces will be to reinforce the military capabilities of the existing UNIFIL, with special attention to rear area security and security of the lines of communication, as well as to support the handover by IDF to the Lebanese Armed Forces of occupied locations in southern Lebanon, while preventing attempts by forceful means to disrupt the process. Deployment would be focused on establishing a presence in the Tyre pocket and supplementing existing positions held by the Indian and Ghanaian battalions. A detailed list of potential tasks flowing from this main effort has been shared with potential troop-contributing countries.

26. We have also shared with potential troop-contributing countries a draft of the concept of operations and of the new robust rules of engagement, which are being revised to cater to the additional tasks and authority assigned to UNIFIL in resolution 1701 (2006). The most significant revisions pertain to the authorization of the use of force consistent with paragraph 12 of resolution 1701 (2006).

27. Assuming that the cessation of hostilities continues to hold and that there is no significant change in the situation on the ground, a second wave of reinforcements, consisting of up to an additional 3,500 forces, would be required in theatre between 3 September and 5 October. The following capabilities would be required: three mechanized infantry battalions; two light reconnaissance battalions; one engineer battalion; two signal companies; one helicopter unit for observation and reconnaissance; one helicopter unit for medium-lift capacity; one military police company; one level II hospital; one logistics battalion; and two sector headquarters and headquarter companies. The main effort of the second wave would be to assist the Lebanese Armed Forces in the achievement of full operational capacity.

28. A third and final wave of reinforcements, consisting of up to an additional 3,000 troops, will be required to arrive in theatre between 5 October and 4 November. The following capabilities will be required: two mechanized infantry battalions; one gendarmerie battalion; and one cartographic section. The main effort of UNIFIL, at that time should remain focused on assistance to the Lebanese Armed Forces in the achievement of full operational capacity, as well as verifying and monitoring the compliance of the parties with all relevant provisions of resolution 1701 (2006).

29. In summary, our hope would be for the full strengthening of UNIFIL called for in paragraph 11 of resolution 1701 (2006) to have been completed within less than 90 days of the resolution's adoption. In the event that another Security Council resolution is adopted mandating UNIFIL with significant new and additional tasks, additional forces could be

required up to, or above, the authorized strength of 15,000 troops, consistent with paragraph 16 of resolution 1701 (2006).

30. It must be understood, however, that the phases of deployment and disposition of UNIFIL troops may need to be adjusted as circumstances dictate. The concept of operations and force requirements shared with the troop-contributing countries on 17 August were developed within an extremely short time frame, against the backdrop of a fragile cessation of hostilities and a fluid situation on the ground. Adherence to the deployment time frame, as described above, will depend on the required capabilities being made available by Member States, as requested.

B. Commitments to date

31. A number of commitments were confirmed at the meeting of troop-contributing countries on 17 August. Some of these commitments were, however, made subject to parliamentary approval. The Department of Peacekeeping Operations will work closely with these and other countries that have indicated an interest to contribute to UNIFIL, to expedite the initial deployment of a coherent and balanced force of up to 3,500 all ranks, and to ensure that the concept of operations and the rules of engagement are fully understood and supported. While the commitments made were encouraging, further commitments are urgently needed, in particular as regards enabling units.

C. Logistics support

32. UNIFIL has established a rear UNIFIL administrative headquarters in Cyprus with facilities provided by the United Nations Peacekeeping Force in Cyprus (UNFICYP). This headquarters is carrying out routine administration in finance, personnel and procurement on behalf of the mission and is coordinating movement of personnel and material to Naqoura by sea and air. Two MI-8 helicopters and a chartered medium-size logistic ship (*MV Kiriaki*) are now in Cyprus to provide rapid movement of personnel, medical evacuation and resupply. Preparations are being made to use facilities in Cyprus for the transit of troops and equipment to Naqoura, if direct deployment through Lebanese airports and ports is not practicable owing to congestion and the state of disrepair of roads and bridges.

33. A logistics planning team will arrive in Cyprus during the weekend of 19 and 20 August to travel to Naqoura to assist the mission in developing a logistic concept for support of the expanded force. Plans are advanced for the deployment of strategic deployment stocks from the United Nations Logistics Base to southern Lebanon.

D. Flexibility in administrative arrangements to ensure rapid deployment

34. The expansion of UNIFIL will require extensive and immediate augmentation of the support infrastructure and sustainment capabilities of the current mission. To facilitate this and the rapid deployment of the additional troops, I have granted the Secretariat, on an exceptional basis, a degree of flexibility in the application of administrative processes governing the assignment of human resources, the deployment of contingents, the extension and increase in the value of support contracts, delegations for financial management and procurement, and utilization of exigency provisions within the Financial Regulations and Rules of the United Nations and the Staff Rules. In this respect, I have written to the President of the General Assembly, informing Member States of the extraordinary

measures in place to enable the efficient and effective implementation of resolution 1701 (2006).

35. Under the measures described above, deployment of contingents will be fast-tracked, waiving the requirement for pre-inspections and the signing of a memorandum of understanding in advance. Contingents will deploy based on broad agreement of the composition of the force provided through load lists and the conditions under which the contingent will be sustained in the mission area. I have also given approval for the use of letters of assist with troop-contributing countries to facilitate the strategic lift of contingents and their equipment, where the costs are reasonable based on experience with current commercial rates. Small numbers of gratis personnel will be deployed for limited periods to facilitate military planning by the troop-contributing countries without the requirement for the two-month notification of all Member States. I request the understanding of Member States of the necessity for these special arrangements.

36. To facilitate the rapid build-up of civilian support staff, I have waived the requirement for advertisement of the post when a lateral transfer at the same level and post nomenclature is involved. As appropriate, these personnel will retain existing delegations of authority, pending completion of the formal designation process, which will follow in due course. I have also authorized relief from the present three-month limit on temporary deployment of civilian staff. General temporary assistance provisions will be used to augment planning staff at Headquarters and in the field.

37. In addition, immediate provision is being made to increase the not-to-exceed level of existing commodity contracts (i.e., for fuel, rations, water and accommodation) of UNIFIL and UNFICYP (which will provide some logistics support to UNIFIL), as well as increasing the not-to-exceed level of global systems contracts in support of both missions.

38. While the exact nature of support to assist the deployment of Lebanese Armed Forces in southern Lebanon is not known at this time, I have authorized the use of letters of assist with non-UNIFIL troop-contributing countries to provide support to the Lebanese Armed Forces, where it is prudent to do so.

E. Headquarters support structures

39. The scope and complexity of military tasks to be performed by UNIFIL may require further strengthening of the Military Division of the Department of Peacekeeping Operations. A military cell, dedicated to UNIFIL, drawing on the existing resources of the Military Division and augmented by officers from key troop-contributing countries, will be needed to provide military guidance at the strategic level.

F. Financial aspects

40. Immediate steps have been taken to provide additional funding for the expansion of UNIFIL. I have sought the concurrence of the Advisory Committee on Administrative and Budgetary Questions to enter into commitments not to exceed $50 million to meet the most immediate and essential preparatory steps to constitute a planning team, conduct strategic lift of the additional forces and initiate procurement actions for necessary goods and services, including additional requirements for air transportation, naval transportation, facilities and infrastructure. A further request for additional commitment authority will be sought within the next few weeks to cover the period from August 2006 until the end of

March 2006, pending the submission of the detailed budget for the expansion of UNIFIL for the period 11 August 2006 to 30 June 2007. This additional financing request will be submitted to the General Assembly, through the Advisory Committee, for consideration during the regular part of its sixty-first session.

41. I would also like to inform the Advisory Committee that, in addition to the immediate requirement of $50 million indicated above, the appropriation for UNIFIL for the period 1 July 2006 to 30 June 2007 in the amount of $97,579,600, as approved by the General Assembly in its resolution 60/278 of 30 June 2006, shall be used flexibly to meet the requirements of the expanded UNIFIL.

V. Humanitarian assistance for security measures, Government of Lebanon security measures and mine action

A. General humanitarian situation

42. The month-long hostilities have had a traumatic impact on the civilian population in Lebanon. Almost 1 million people have been displaced, about 1,200 are recorded dead and thousands injured, the majority of them women and children. The number of fatalities continues to rise as the cessation of hostilities allows more bodies to be recovered. The damage to essential infrastructure, residential housing and the economy is severe. An estimated 15,000 apartments have been destroyed and 140 bridges hit. Initial assessments, for example, indicate that in the villages of Ghanduriyah and Zibqin more than 60 per cent of residential housing has been destroyed.

43. The announcement of the cessation of hostilities, however, has prompted an immediate and massive movement of displaced populations returning to their home communities. It is estimated that despite numerous cautionary messages from the Government of Lebanon and international aid organizations, 400,000 people, including 107,000 who have returned from the Syrian Arab Republic, have returned to the southern suburbs of Beirut and other areas further south. The almost 800 public institutions, schools and buildings temporarily occupied by up to 150,000 displaced persons are now virtually empty, thereby significantly easing the stress on host communities.

44. The key priorities for the humanitarian community during this immediate post-ceasefire phase are: (a) providing assistance along routes of return and to home communities, including shelter materials; (b) securing sustained access for humanitarian convoys and speedy aid distribution to the most vulnerable; (c) addressing prevailing security risks for relief workers and returnees, primarily owing to the proliferation of unexploded ordnance; and (d) carrying out repairs to basic infrastructure, such as water pumps.

45. An oil spill into the Mediterranean Sea of at least 15,000 tons of heavy fuel has spread along 150 kilometres of the coast, following the bombing by IDF of an oil storage depot at Jiyeh, south of Beirut, on 13 and 15 July, leaving an immediate severe impact on the fishing community and the tourism sector and potential long-term consequences for public health owing to an increased risk of cancer. Efforts to clean up the spill got under way with the cessation of hostilities. On 17 August, a high-level meeting was convened by the International Maritime Organization and the United Nations Environment Programme in Athens, to finalize an international assistance action plan. The $64 million plan will assist the authorities in Lebanon with the clean-up of coastal oil pollution and is geared towards preventing

any damage to neighbouring countries. Several countries and other partners have also pledged personnel, training and equipment for the clean-up.

46. The hostilities also claimed the lives of 170 Israelis, including 52 civilians killed by rocket fire. More than 600 civilians were injured. Between 300,000 and 500,000 Israeli civilians either fled their homes or remained in shelters during the conflict. Since the cessation of hostilities, residents of the north have begun to return en masse to their homes. The Government of Israel reports extensive damage to private properties, hospitals and schools, as well as to more than 60,000 acres of forest and open fields by fires created by rocket fire. The Government is responding with an emergency aid package for northern towns and villages, and UNSCO has invited the Israeli authorities to approach the United Nations if they require assistance to support those efforts.

B. Humanitarian action

47. Throughout the hostilities, in particular in the south of Lebanon, persistent security concerns and widespread infrastructure damage owing to ongoing combat operations severely limited access to vulnerable civilian populations by humanitarian agencies, including the United Nations, the International Committee of the Red Cross, the Lebanese Red Cross and non-governmental organizations.

48. The absence of hostilities itself has greatly improved the frequency and quantity of humanitarian assistance. Within 96 hours of the cessation of hostilities, 20 convoys totalling 118 trucks have been dispatched to locations in the south, including Saida, Tyre, Rmaish and Marjayoun, and various locations in the Bekaa valley, despite increasingly congested roads owing to the stream of returns. A first United Nations vessel delivered relief goods and fuel to the port of Tyre for onward distribution into the south and a more regular naval shuttle between Beirut and Tyre is envisaged. A twice-weekly passenger service has commenced from Cyprus to Beirut.

49. Humanitarian agencies have also provided food, water, medicines, blankets and other shelter materials to returnees at border crossings and en route. In home communities, the United Nations convoys have delivered fuel for generators and water pumps, food and bottled water. The United Nations is also setting up tented camps in return locations in the south to provide temporary shelter until houses can be repaired. Winterization kits are being procured to allow returnees to refurbish "one warm room" during the upcoming winter months. The United Nations is also providing medicines and medical equipment to hospitals across the south, establishing a capacity that will allow for 120,000 emergency operations and instant medical assistance to the war-wounded and sick. Rapid needs assessments are under way, including on infrastructure damage, housing, and unexploded ordnance, in close cooperation with the Government of Lebanon. The first unexploded ordnance clearance operations are already taking place, in parallel with the continuing public information campaigns by the Government of Lebanon and United Nations agencies. In areas still not accessible to humanitarian agencies, including Al Hinniyah, Zibqin, Bint Jbeil, Kafra and Bayt Leif, UNIFIL has distributed food and water. UNIFIL has also engaged in medical evacuations of the war-wounded from villages near the Blue Line.

C. Sixty-day plan

50. It is expected that United Nations humanitarian response efforts will peak during the next 60 days and then gradually evolve into a recovery and reconstruction response,

coordinated by the Government of Lebanon. A three-stage humanitarian action plan lays out a concept of decentralized humanitarian operations in close proximity to target populations, primarily returnees. The already existing humanitarian hubs in Beirut and Tyre are being further strengthened and additional hubs have been established in Saida, Tripoli and Zahle. The United Nations and its partners will move significant stocks of supplies into those hubs for onward distribution into the most affected areas. Decentralized security operations linked to the humanitarian hubs will ensure safety and security of humanitarian staff. Emergency infrastructure repairs through the Lebanese Armed Forces, private initiatives and UNIFIL will support the enhanced humanitarian response on the ground.

D. Remaining obstacles

51. Despite significant progress within the first days of the cessation of hostilities in reaching people previously cut off from aid supplies, massive access problems remain the key obstacles to further accelerating the humanitarian response. The enormous damage to most road and bridge infrastructures leading to the south merits lifting the continuing sea and air blockade on Lebanon as soon as possible, within the terms of Council resolution 1701 (2006). In view of the speed and scale of return movements, obtaining full and unrestricted access to all means of transportation on the most direct route will be critical for the successful delivery of assistance by the United Nations, its partners and the Government of Lebanon.

E. Government of Lebanon security measures

52. In response to paragraphs 6 and 14 of resolution 1701 (2006), the Government of Lebanon has initiated changes in security personnel and procedures at Rafiq Hariri International Airport and has established a new security coordination committee. I have also learned of the arrival in Beirut during the weekend of 19 and 20 August of international experts who have been asked by the Government of Lebanon to provide technical assistance and professional assessment of security procedures at border crossings.

F. Mine action and unexploded ordnance

53. The conflict resulted in considerable unexploded ordnance contamination south of the Litani River and in areas in the north and east of the country. The widespread contamination of unexploded ordnance and mines has already led to maiming injuries and deaths among returnees to the South. Initial assessments of the Mines Advisory Group, a United Kingdom non-governmental organization, indicated that unexploded ordnance contamination in Lebanon was on a far higher scale than that identified in Iraq after the end of the war in 2003. Bombs, missiles, rockets, mortars, cluster bomblets and other sub-munitions litter routes, housing and the debris that must be cleared for reconstruction to commence. In the days since the cessation of hostilities went into affect, reports of civilian casualties, most notably from cluster bomblets and sub-munitions, have already been reported. The contamination presents a significant obstacle to humanitarian efforts and a threat to men, women, boys and girls returning to their homes and daily activities.

54. The United Nations Mine Action Team, coordinated by the United Nations Mine Action Service, is supporting the existing structures within the Government of Lebanon and civil society, specifically the National Demining Office and the National Mine Risk Education Steering Committee. The first response to protect civilians has included mine/unexploded

ordnance risk education in Lebanon and, for refugees in the Syrian Arab Republic, unexploded ordnance safety training for humanitarian workers operating in affected areas and the imminent deployment of explosive ordnance disposal and battle area clearance teams to support humanitarian efforts. Those teams will bolster the response of Lebanese Armed Forces engineers and the Mines Advisory Group, a non-governmental organization. These activities will be coordinated by the Mine Action Co-ordination Centre—South Lebanon, located in Tyre, under the guidance of the United Nations Mine Action Service. I urge Member States to provide contributions to the Voluntary Trust Fund for Assistance in Mine Action to ensure that all of those vital activities can be realized.

55. The UNIFIL mine-clearance efforts are focused on the clearance of contamination in observation posts, patrol bases and other Mission facilities to ensure the safety of mission personnel and prepare for the expansion of UNIFIL. As the United Nations Mine Action Service deploys assets, it will coordinate with UNIFIL assets to ensure the most effective use of resources. With the deployment of the expanded UNIFIL, it is essential that the engineering units requested to reinforce UNIFIL possess explosive ordnance disposal capacity.

VI. Observations

56. I am encouraged by the positive first steps that have followed the coming into effect of the cessation of hostilities. However, I would caution that the situation is still very fragile. I call on all parties to do their utmost to ensure that the cessation of hostilities holds and to transform it into a durable ceasefire.

57. I would stress that continued support for prompt humanitarian action and reconstruction is an essential element in solidifying the situation. As larger areas of the south along the Blue Line become accessible, the humanitarian aid effort will need to accelerate to ensure that the basic needs of the civilian population for shelter, food and medical assistance can be met. Preparations for longer-term stabilization and development assistance, in coordination with and supported by the Government of Lebanon, need to be accelerated to ensure a speedy recovery process.

58. I welcome the efforts of the Government of Lebanon to enhance its security procedures at its airports, harbours and border crossings. I would encourage the Government of Lebanon to take advantage of other available expertise to put in place the necessary arrangements. I look forward to the reopening of Lebanon's airports and harbours. I would also stress that Lebanon's neighbours have a duty to implement paragraphs 14 and 15 of resolution 1701 (2006).

59. I very much welcome the significant and historic step by the Government of Lebanon to deploy the Lebanese Armed Forces to the south of the country while IDF continues its withdrawal. I note in particular the Lebanese national consensus, involving all parties, which led to the deployment of the Lebanese Armed Forces to the south. I have also been pleased with the strong Lebanese consensus in support of the enhanced role of UNIFIL.

60. I strongly appeal to Member States to reinforce UNIFIL on an emergency basis, as called for in resolution 1701 (2006) and by the parties. I would stress that the most urgent requirement is to provide UNIFIL with an additional 3,500 personnel, along the lines outlined in the present report, by 2 September. The Secretariat has done its part in seeking and

incorporating the views and concerns of potential troop-contributing countries in the development of the force concept of operations and rules of engagement. It is now up to Member States to do their part in translating expressions of interest into the immediate provision of actual troops on the ground.

61. A reinforced UNIFIL is not going to wage war on any of the actors in the theatre. It is not expected to achieve by force what must be realized through negotiation and an internal Lebanese consensus. Nor can a reinforced UNIFIL be a substitute for a political process. That political process, however, will need the kind of help, assistance and confidence that only a robust peacekeeping presence can provide, in support of the Government of Lebanon and its efforts to exercise its authority effectively throughout its territory.

62. I call on both the Government of Lebanon and the Government of Israel to work resolutely towards a long-term solution and a permanent ceasefire. I have been in close touch with the Prime Ministers of Lebanon and Israel, respectively, as well as key leaders in the region and internationally. I also look forward to hearing back from the mission that is currently in the region.

63. While one of the immediate triggers of the crisis was the abduction of Israeli soldiers, their unconditional release is only one of the many measures still to be taken and the painful compromises that will have to be made by both sides in the interests of peace for the peoples of Lebanon and Israel. In this context, although it is a separate issue, the Security Council has stated that it is mindful of the sensitivity of the issue of the prisoners and has encouraged efforts to urgently settle the issue of the Lebanese prisoners detained in Israel.

64. I call on all States in the region to support and encourage the parties to take the right steps to solidify the cessation of hostilities and develop a framework for the permanent solution to which the peoples of the region have aspired for so long.

65. Finally, I would like to express my gratitude to my representatives in the region, Alvaro de Soto and Geir O. Pedersen, to the UNTSO Chief of Staff, Major-General Clive Lilley, and to all United Nations staff in the region for their dedication, perseverance and commitment to peace and security. The UNIFIL Force Commander, Major-General Alain Pellegrini, and all the men and women of UNIFIL and the Observer Group Lebanon deserve a special tribute for their courage and bearing during the hostilities, when they were exposed to extreme danger.

2. Report of the Secretary-General on the Implementation of Resolution 1701 (2006), 12 September 2006 (S/2006/730)

I. Introduction

1. The present report is my second report on the implementation of Security Council resolution 1701 (2006). It follows my report of 18 August 2006 (S/2006/670), which focused on steps taken until that date, and measures required to consolidate the fragile cessation of hostilities. The present report provides a more comprehensive assessment of the political situation, in addition to an update on all steps taken to implement resolution 1701 (2006). I submit the former in response to paragraphs 8, 9 and 10 of the resolution.

2. In its resolution 1701 (2006), the Council sets out the following principles and elements on which a permanent ceasefire and long-term solution would be based:

(a) Full respect for the Blue Line by both Lebanon and Israel;

(b) Security arrangements to prevent the resumption of hostilities, including the establishment between the Blue Line and the Litani River of an area free of any armed personnel, assets and weapons other than those of the Government of Lebanon and of the United Nations Interim Force in Lebanon (UNIFIL);

(c) Full implementation of the relevant provisions of the Taif Accords and of Security Council resolutions 1559 (2004) and 1680 (2006), which require the disarmament of all armed groups in Lebanon so that, pursuant to the Lebanese Cabinet decision of 27 July 2006, there will be no weapons or authority in Lebanon other than that of the Lebanese State;

(d) No foreign forces in Lebanon without the consent of its Government;

(e) No sales or supply of arms and related materiel to Lebanon except as authorized by its Government;

(f) Provision to the United Nations of all remaining maps of landmines in Lebanon in Israel's possession.

The Council also highlighted the delineation of the international borders of Lebanon, especially in those areas where the border is disputed or uncertain, including in the Shab'a Farms area, and the establishment of diplomatic relations between the Syrian Arab Republic and Lebanon as important steps. Additional matters to be addressed include the unconditional release of the captured Israeli soldiers and the issue of the Lebanese prisoners detained in Israel.

II. Background

A. Outcome of the war

3. As of 31 August 2006, official Lebanese figures showed that 1,187 people had died and 4,092 had been injured in Lebanon as a result of the conflict. Many of these victims were children. The Office for the Coordination of Humanitarian Affairs estimates that one million Lebanese were displaced between 12 July and 14 August, with some 735,000 seeking shelter within Lebanon and 230,000 outside; this included the secondary displacement of

approximately 16,000 Palestinian refugees. The cessation of hostilities on 14 August triggered a massive and speedy return of internally displaced persons and refugees back to their areas of origin. According to the Office of the United Nations High Commissioner for Refugees (UNHCR), within days of the ceasefire some 90 per cent of those displaced in Lebanon during the hostilities—around 900,000 or one quarter of the population—returned to their homes or were staying nearby. At the end of August, it was estimated that between 100,000 and 150,000 people remained internally displaced.

4. In Lebanon, the Office for the Coordination of Humanitarian Affairs estimates that the conflict caused physical damage amounting to $3.6 billion, including the destruction of 80 bridges, 600 km of roads; 900 factories, markets, farms and other commercial buildings; 31 airports, ports, water- and sewage-treatment plants, dams and electrical plants; and 25 fuel stations. Unemployment is currently as high as 75 per cent in some parts of the country. An estimated 15,000 homes were destroyed.

5. On the Israeli side, from 12 July until 14 August, 43 Israeli civilians and 117 Israeli Defense Forces (IDF) soldiers were killed. In addition to large numbers of people treated for shock and anxiety, 33 Israelis were wounded seriously and 68 moderately. During that time, 3,970 rockets landed in Israel, 901 of them in urban areas; 300,000 residents were displaced and more than a million were forced to live for some of the time in shelters, according to official Israeli figures.

6. Since the cessation of hostilities went into effect, the nature of the humanitarian response in Lebanon has seen a rapid transition to early recovery activities and short-term intervention to provide assistance to the large numbers of returnees. The revised United Nations flash appeal, launched in Stockholm on 31 August, has put the emphasis on the clearance of mines and unexploded ordinance, emergency health and education needs, and water and sanitation, with the vast part of project implementation to take place in the coming six weeks. As of 31 August, 30 to 50 per cent of households in conflict-affected areas remained in need of food assistance; 120,000 people in southern Beirut and 30,000 in schools and other public institutions also needed food assistance, although immediate demands have thus far been largely met.[1] Humanitarian activities were and continue to be coordinated through clusters led by United Nations agencies and partners and delivered via humanitarian hubs (Tyre and Saida).

7. Immediately following the cessation of hostilities, the Government of Lebanon, with the full support of the United Nations system, civil society and international institutions, launched a series of preliminary needs assessments and developed a strategy to address early recovery needs, which laid the basis for longer-term reconstruction. The strategy was presented at the international donor conference held in Stockholm on 31 August, along with the United Nations revised flash appeal. More than $900 million was pledged at the meeting to support the Government's short-term efforts.[2]

8. In Israel, the existing well developed infrastructure of bomb shelters meant that displacement remained relatively limited. Many affected Israeli civilians moved southwards and were cared for by relatives or friends. As a result, the humanitarian situation has remained under control. Following the cessation of hostilities, the Government pledged to make the rehabilitation of Haifa and the north a central goal of Israel's priorities for the near future. On 20 August, the Cabinet decided to establish a special Committee for Strengthening Haifa

and the North; Israel's Chief Coordinator for the Reconstruction of Public Infrastructure in the North told ministers that damaged schools would be repaired by the start of the school year on 3 September. The Government has also paid compensation to business owners and families and opened treatment centres for those suffering from shock.

B. United Nations missions to the region

9. Since the crisis in the Middle East erupted with the outbreak of hostilities between Hizbollah and Israel on 12 July, I have maintained regular contact with the Prime Ministers of Lebanon and of Israel, as well as other relevant actors and concerned parties. I have also despatched a number of high-level missions to the region.

10. Given the importance of implementing Security Council resolution 1701 (2006), I decided to visit the region myself. I attended the extraordinary ministerial-level meeting of the European Union in Brussels on 25 August, and travelled to Lebanon, Israel, the Occupied Palestinian Territory, Jordan, the Syrian Arab Republic, the Islamic Republic of Iran, Qatar, Saudi Arabia, Egypt, Turkey and Spain in subsequent days, meeting Heads of State, Heads of Government, Foreign Ministers and other senior officials. In addition, I kept in close contact by telephone with those senior officials and the representatives of other concerned parties and relevant actors throughout my mission. I discerned broad support for the implementation of resolution 1701 (2006) and was encouraged by the general commitment to restoring security and stability across the Middle East. I am pleased to note that my efforts appear to have contributed to securing the commitments of several troop-contributing countries to help stabilize the situation as part of UNIFIL, and to lifting the full aerial and sea blockade Israel had imposed on Lebanon.

III. Implementation of Security Council resolution 1701 (2006)

A. Respect for the Blue Line

11. In paragraph 4 of its resolution 1701 (2006), the Council reiterated its strong support for full respect for the Blue Line. In paragraph 8 of the same resolution, the Council also affirmed full respect for the Blue Line as one of the principles and elements of a permanent ceasefire and long-term solution. As I have outlined in a number of reports to the Council, both sides in the past have failed to respect the Blue Line. Since it was drawn by the United Nations in 2000, the Blue Line has remained tense, with violations from both sides.

12. Since my previous report of 18 August (S/2006/670), the parties have largely complied with the cessation of hostilities. UNIFIL has, however, observed numerous minor incidents and violations in its area of operation between the Litani River and the Blue Line. These have primarily been ground violations related to the fortifying of IDF positions and the technical fence. IDF has also continued to resupply and rotate troops inside Lebanon. UNIFIL has taken particular note of daily Israeli air incursions over Lebanese air space. From the Lebanese side, shepherds have resumed their practice of crossing the Blue Line in the Shab'a farms vicinity. There has been little visible activity by Hizbollah in the UNIFIL area of operations, other than some reported attempts to salvage equipment from its previous positions and transport it northwards.

13. On the whole, the ground violations have not been of an offensive and hostile character and the parties seem determined to uphold the agreement. There was, however, one severe violation of the cessation of hostilities, when Israeli forces carried out a raid in eastern

Lebanon on 19 August. The assessment that the parties seem generally determined to uphold the cessation of hostilities converges with the fact that both the Government of Lebanon and the Government of Israel have assured me of their commitment to fully respect the Blue Line. In order to aid the parties in honouring their obligation to respect the Blue Line in its entirety, UNIFIL intends to place visible markers on the ground along its full length.

B. Security arrangements

14. On 27 July, the Government of Lebanon decided "to extend its authority over its territory through its own legitimate armed forces, such that there will be no weapons or authority other than that of the Lebanese State". This decision provides the necessary basis for the establishment of an area free of any armed personnel, assets and weapons between the Blue Line and the Litani River, as one of the elements of a permanent ceasefire set out in paragraph 8 of Security Council resolution 1701 (2006). Both the Government of Israel and the Government of Lebanon have expressed their agreement with this principle to me. UNIFIL is now assisting the Lebanese Armed Forces (LAF) in taking steps towards the establishment of this area following a full withdrawal of IDF from Lebanese territory.

15. Concerning security arrangements to prevent the resumption of hostilities, the Government of Lebanon, in its Cabinet decision of 27 July, called "on the United Nations, in cooperation with the relevant parties, to undertake the necessary measures to once again put into effect the Armistice Agreement signed by Lebanon and Israel in 1949, and to ensure adherence to the provisions of that agreement, as well as to explore possible amendments to or development of the said provisions, as necessary". IDF, for its part, suggested that UNIFIL set up a tripartite body, modelled after the current tripartite coordination mechanism, to address security matters on a long-term basis. UNIFIL has asked the parties to provide more detailed suggestions in writing, on the basis of which UNIFIL will prepare a draft proposal for consideration by the Governments of Lebanon and Israel.

16. On the ground, significant progress continues to be made as regards the gradual withdrawal of Israeli forces and the deployment of LAF. UNIFIL continues to coordinate a gradual IDF withdrawal from and LAF deployment into south Lebanon. Since my previous report of 18 August (S/2006/670), senior officers of IDF and LAF have met with the Force Commander of UNIFIL on six occasions to facilitate this process through the procedures and plan of withdrawal agreed in mid-August. IDF has divided the occupied area into 16 sectors and sub-sectors, and had vacated 9 of these by 7 September, with withdrawal from the others projected before the end of September 2006. In total, IDF to date has vacated approximately 65 per cent of the area it occupied when the cessation of hostilities went into effect. UNIFIL established checkpoints and carried out intensive patrolling to verify that there was no IDF presence in these locations, and LAF deployed in the vacated areas after a 24-hour period. On 31 August, LAF deployed for the first time along the eastern part of the Blue Line and has now established some permanent positions there.

17. A general understanding has been reached that IDF will completely withdraw from Lebanese territory once UNIFIL strength is increased to 5,000 troops and the Lebanese Army is ready to deploy at the full strength of 15,000 troops. According to Lebanese military authorities at the time of preparation of the present report LAF supported by UNIFIL had deployed close to 10,000 troops south of the Litani River. I expect this process to be

completed in the coming weeks, which would further stabilize the situation. The blueprint for the induction of LAF in south Lebanon, as presented by the Lebanese Army Command, envisions four brigades in the areas between the Blue Line and the Litani River, and another brigade and two battalions in reserve north of the Litani River.

18. A planning and coordination mechanism has been established between UNIFIL and the Lebanese Ministry of Defence and Army Command to ensure ongoing effective cooperation on deployment and joint activities. In addition, a high-level security coordination mechanism has been created, at my behest, with the participation of, on the Lebanese side, the Prime Minister, the Minister of Defence, the Minister of the Interior, the Commander of LAF, the head of the Internal Security Forces and my Personal Representative for Lebanon, as well as the UNIFIL Force Commander. LAF has also established a liaison cell in Tyre to interact with the various UNIFIL units and headquarters branches on the ground. I expect this liaison cell to co-locate with UNIFIL headquarters in Naqoura once IDF withdraws from the area.

19. UNIFIL and IDF have also taken steps to ensure effective liaison, primarily to address security matters following the withdrawal. A small UNIFIL liaison office is being set up in the headquarters of the IDF Northern Command, and talks are ongoing about the establishment of a UNIFIL office in Tel Aviv for liaison and coordination with the IDF headquarters and Ministry of Defence.

20. The past several weeks have seen significant progress in the augmentation of UNIFIL. A contingent from France of 224 troops, primarily engineers, has been deployed and commenced operations. An Italian Joint Landing Force of 858 with armoured vehicles and equipment arrived on 3 September and is currently positioned in the area of Frun, awaiting the completion of their accommodations for deployment to Marakah.

21. As of 8 September, UNIFIL troop strength was 3,085 all ranks, with contributions from Belgium, China, France, Ghana, India, Ireland, Norway, Poland and Spain. These are supplemented by 53 United Nations Truce Supervision Organization (Observer Group Lebanon) military observers. A French battalion of some 882 troops with vehicles and equipment is scheduled to arrive in Beirut on 12 September and will be deployed to its area of operation in the general sector of Bint Jubayl as soon as possible. A Spanish mechanized infantry battalion of some 850 troops plus the command elements for a sector headquarters are to depart Spain for Lebanon in the next few days. This will bring the total number of troops on the ground to almost 5,000. A second wave of troops is scheduled to arrive in Lebanon by mid-October. Italy has pledged to deploy another battalion and support element, Nepal a battalion, Indonesia a battalion and Ghana an additional 250 troops to enhance its current contribution. Turkey and Finland have pledged to deploy multi-role engineer companies and Belgium a level II hospital.

22. The UNIFIL area of operation has expanded to include the Tyre pocket in addition to its pre-conflict positions. The Observer Group Lebanon military observers have reoccupied their patrol bases, with the exception of patrol base Khiyam, which will have to be rebuilt following the IDF shelling of the base during the hostilities.

23. Planning for the longer-term augmentation of the civilian operations and support of UNIFIL has commenced. A Department of Peacekeeping Operations planning team returned from Lebanon on 5 September and, following consultations with the relevant

departments, the Department will in the coming weeks finalize a staffing table. I will be reporting to the Council separately on the longer-term requirements and financial aspects for the expanded UNIFIL. To meet the immediate and essential requirements for the expansion of UNIFIL, concurrence was granted on 18 August by the Advisory Committee on Administrative and Budgetary Questions (ACABQ) to enter into commitments not to exceed $50 million. Additional commitment authority will be sought from the General Assembly during the regular part of its sixty-first session to cover the period 1 July 2006 to 31 March 2007.

24. As indicated in my last report, a military cell dedicated to UNIFIL, drawing on the existing resources of the Military Division and staffed by officers from key troop-contributing countries, will be established to augment the Department of Peacekeeping Operations headquarters. The military director of this cell, reporting to the Under-Secretary-General for Peacekeeping Operations, will act as the focal point for the provision of military advice on UNIFIL, working in close coordination with the Assistant Secretaries-General for Operations and Mission Support and the Military Adviser. On behalf of the Under-Secretary-General for Peacekeeping Operations and consistent with his political direction, the director of this cell will provide strategic military guidance and direction to the UNIFIL Force Commander. The Department of Peacekeeping Operations is at present consulting with Member States to develop the structure and size of the strategic cell, which will be funded through the UNIFIL budget. The UNIFIL Force Commander, as head of mission, will continue to exercise operational authority in the field on my behalf and to exercise operational control over the military units assigned to UNIFIL. Force Commander Alain Pellegrini will remain in office until 17 February 2007 and will then be replaced by an Italian Force Commander.

C. Disarming armed groups

25. In its resolution 1701 (2006), the Security Council envisaged the full implementation of the relevant provisions of the Taif Accords and of its resolutions 1559 (2004) and 1680 (2006), which require the disarmament of all armed groups in Lebanon so that, pursuant to the Lebanese cabinet decision of 27 July 2006, there will be no weapons or authority in Lebanon other than that of the Lebanese State. Both the Government of Lebanon and the Government of Israel concur with this principle of a permanent ceasefire and a long-term solution.

26. I have provided details on the status of Lebanese and non-Lebanese militias in my previous reports on the implementation of Security Council resolution 1559 (2004) and will provide a further update in my fourth semi-annual report in October 2006. I remain convinced that the disarming of Hizbollah and other militia should take place through a political process that will lead to the full restoration of the authority of the Government of Lebanon so that there will be no weapons or authority other than its own. The national dialogue has not managed so far to achieve a consensus on a political process and timeline for the full disarming of Hizbollah in the sense of an integration of its armed capacity into the Lebanese Armed Forces. I expect that the Government of Lebanon, pursuant to its decision of 27 July 2006, will define such a political process.

27. The agreement reached in the national dialogue on the arms of Palestinian militias outside Palestinian refugee camps has been recognized as a significant and important step. But its implementation within the six-month period stipulated by the national dialogue (which ended on 26 August) has not yet been realized.

D. Foreign forces

28. In resolution 1701 (2006), the Security Council envisaged that no foreign forces should be in Lebanon without the consent of its Government as an element underpinning a permanent ceasefire and long-term solution. As I have previously reported, to the best of the ability of the United Nations to ascertain it, the only foreign forces currently deployed in Lebanon are either those serving under the banner of UNIFIL or IDF troops whose full withdrawal I anticipate to take place in the coming week, as UNIFIL strength reaches 5,000 troops.

E. Arms embargo

29. In paragraph 14 of its resolution 1701 (2006), the Council called on the Government of Lebanon to secure its borders and other entry points to prevent the entry into Lebanon of arms or related material without its consent. The Council has asked UNIFIL "to assist the Government of Lebanon, at its request", in its efforts to implement this provision. It further decided, in paragraph 15 of the same resolution, that all States should take the necessary measures to prevent, by their nationals or from their territories or using their flag vessels or aircraft, the sale or supply to any entity or individual in Lebanon of arms and related materiel of all types, and the provision to any entity or individual in Lebanon of any technical training or assistance related to the provision, manufacture, maintenance or use of such items, except if authorized by the Government of Lebanon or UNIFIL. The imposition of such an arms embargo is fully consistent with the Lebanese Cabinet decision of 27 July 2006 that there shall be no weapons or authority in Lebanon other than that of the Lebanese State and is a measure that is inherently part of the security arrangements preventing a resumption of hostilities, as envisaged in Security Council resolution 1701 (2006). In this context, I also note the provision of paragraph 15 of the same resolution and I urge all Member States to fully comply with it.

30. Both the Government of Lebanon and the Government of Israel are in agreement with this element underpinning a permanent ceasefire and a long-term solution. Indeed, the United Nations has devoted considerable efforts to putting in place the necessary arrangements for such an embargo.

31. I note the assurances given to me by the President of the Syrian Arab Republic that, while the Syrian Arab Republic objects to the presence of foreign troops along the Syrian Arab Republic-Lebanese border, the Syrian Arab Republic would undertake all necessary measures to implement in full paragraph 15 of resolution 1701 (2006). President Assad also told me that the Syrian Arab Republic would increase the number of border guards deployed and enhance their capacity through the provision of additional training and the supply of materiel, such as vehicles. He further said that the Syrian Arab Republic would be willing to establish liaison mechanisms with LAF, Lebanese border police and international personnel providing technical assistance to the Lebanese in order to set up an effective interdiction regime. President Assad also affirmed that the Syrian Arab Republic would be willing to establish, where possible, joint border patrols and control points with the Lebanese authorities. I have further been informed that the President has in the meantime requested the SAR military to deploy one additional battalion to the land border with Lebanon, and has indicated willingness to accept assistance from Germany.

32. The Lebanese authorities have meanwhile undertaken a variety of steps to enforce their monopoly on the control and legitimate use of force throughout Lebanon's territory. In order to enhance coordination among the concerned branches of the Lebanese security establishment, a high-level coordination mechanism has been established, as I have described above.

33. In a letter dated 5 September, the Commander of the Lebanese Armed Forces, General Michel Sleiman, informed Force Commander UNIFIL General Alain Pellegrini about measures taken by LAF to secure the borders and prevent unauthorized and illegitimate entry of arms and related materials into Lebanon. He specified that some 8,000 troops had been deployed along Lebanon's land border with the Syrian Arab Republic, and that similar measures had been taken along the 200 km of the coastline in order to secure the maritime border. He also provided maps indicating the deployment of the Army in these areas. The LAF Commander invited UNIFIL, including a team of experts, to visit these positions and suggest appropriate steps for improving the efficacy of these measures through the use of modern technology and training for the troops. He also inquired whether the United Nations could assist in providing LAF with the assets and equipment that could help in accomplishing this mission. In a letter dated 6 September, the Minister of Interior and Municipalities invited UNIFIL to visit Beirut International Airport to take stock of the existing security systems and procedures as well as the enhancements to airport security that have been or are being put in place.

34. In response to these letters, Germany, on a bilateral basis, has sent a small team of experts to provide technical assistance and review the measures put in place by the Lebanese authorities, offering advice on what is needed for their improvement. UNIFIL is dispatching its own team of military, police, customs and border experts to augment these efforts.

35. The Lebanese Council of Ministers decided on 4 September to task the Army to exercise control of the Lebanese territorial waters in the context of paragraph 14 of Security Council resolution 1701 and, in that regard, to call on the support and technical assistance of UNIFIL. On that basis, the coordination and planning team engaged in discussions with the Lebanese military authorities and troop-contributing countries in order to define operational and coordination procedures for such maritime operations. On 6 September, in accordance with the decision of the Council of Ministers, Prime Minister Siniora wrote to me to request the assistance of the United Nations in securing Lebanon's maritime border and maritime entry points into Lebanon. He specifically asked whether UNIFIL "could provide a naval task force that would help prevent the unauthorized entry of arms or related material by sea into Lebanon, until such time that [Lebanon's] naval and security forces are able to fulfil these tasks on their own". While acknowledging that Lebanon's "current naval capabilities are too limited to effectively patrol Lebanon's 200 kilometres of coastline", the Prime Minister noted that United Nations maritime surveillance would be undertaken "in close coordination with the Lebanese Navy and armed forces". Prime Minister Siniora further wrote that it would be important that such maritime assistance "also include technical training of Lebanon's naval and other security personnel and, hopefully, the provision at a later date of marine and other equipment to upgrade Lebanon's capacity for effective and independent coastal monitoring and control".

36. In response to the request by Prime Minister Siniora, UNIFIL will establish a naval component that is projected to be in place within the coming weeks. Until all necessary

arrangements are made and the UNIFIL maritime component can be deployed, interim measures have been put in place. Italy has agreed to lead an interim maritime task force on a bilateral basis with the Government of Lebanon, maintaining close coordination with UNIFIL, comprised of naval assets contributed by France, Greece, Italy and the United Kingdom on a non-reimbursable basis. At the same time, the Department of Peacekeeping Operations is working on an urgent basis with Member States to plan, generate and deploy a maritime task force to UNIFIL to support the Lebanese naval and security forces. A large maritime element presents a new challenge for a peacekeeping operation and will require a degree of flexibility, including as regards arrangements for the reimbursement of contributing Member States. It is expected that the maritime force will comprise at least four frigates forming an outer screen for maritime surveillance and interdiction operations. A screen of smaller vessels, in particular corvettes and fast patrol boats able to intercept suspect vessels, will be deployed closer inshore and operate in close cooperation with LAF.

F. Land mines and cluster bombs

37. In its resolution 1701 (2006), the Security Council envisaged that all remaining maps of landmines in Lebanon in Israel's possession be provided to the United Nations in order to enable a permanent ceasefire and long-term solution. IDF has been handing over some maps to UNIFIL as it withdraws from particular locations. The Israeli authorities have assured UNIFIL that all relevant maps of landmines and unexploded ordnance in their possession will be handed over on completion of the withdrawal.

38. I wish to emphasize the danger that unexploded ordnance represents and the harm that has been caused by such materiel. The extent of contamination south of the Litani River from unexploded ordnance, namely from cluster bomblets and sub-munitions, has become clearer since my last report and unexploded ordnance clearly presents a significant challenge to the implementation of resolution 1701 (2006). As of 8 September 2006, the United Nations Mine Action Coordination Centre, in conjunction with the Lebanese national demining office, have identified 451 individual cluster strike locations, each containing up to hundreds of individual bomblets or sub-munitions. That number is an increase of 25 per cent over the past two weeks and is expected to grow further. According to the Centre, an estimated 90 per cent of all cluster bombs were discharged between the time of the adoption of Security Council resolution 1701 (2006) on 11 August and the actual cessation of hostilities on 14 August.

39. While IDF has provided some maps to UNIFIL regarding cluster strikes, they are not specific enough to be of use to operators on the ground. I expect that Israel will provide further detailed information to UNIFIL regarding the exact location, quantity and type of cluster munitions utilized during the conflict. In addition to cluster munitions, unexploded bombs, rockets, mortars and other ordnance also litter the south and areas in the north and east of Lebanon. I am sad to report that three Lebanese military engineers were killed when an unexploded bomb they were neutralizing detonated. The contamination poses a serious threat to the deployment of the Lebanese Armed Forces and the enhanced UNIFIL Force whose mission is to assist them. Unexploded ordnance has been found inside UNIFIL bases, along patrol routes and in proposed locations for the expanded deployment. The humanitarian impact of these explosive remnants of war on civilians has resulted in at least 14 deaths and 57 injuries. The vast majority of these casualties have been young men and boys. In addition to the threat to human lives, unexploded ordnance poses an obstacle to the

return of displaced families, access to housing and agriculture activities affecting the livelihoods of the population of southern Lebanon.

40. The United Nations Mine Action Team continues to assist the national demining office, other branches of the Government of Lebanon and United Nations and NGO humanitarian actors to mitigate the threat. Lebanese military engineers, teams from the non-governmental organization Mines Advisory Group and teams provided through the Swedish Rescue Services Agency are on the ground clearing unexploded ordnance. In addition, under the United Nations Framework for Mine Action Planning and Rapid Response, the United Nations Mine Action Service has contracted and deployed five explosive ordnance disposal teams, five battle area clearance teams and three technical survey teams. Additional capacity in explosive ordnance disposal and battle area clearance are already planned and should be deployed in the coming weeks. These efforts have already resulted in the destruction of over 15,000 individual cluster munitions as well as hundreds of other unexploded ordnance. Unexploded ordnance awareness for returning populations has been provided by the national committee for mine risk education, supported by the United Nations Children's Fund, and unexploded ordnance safety training for aid workers and mission staff has also been provided by the United Nations Mine Action Service in Beirut and Tyre. All of this has been made possible by the enthusiastic response by donors to the mine action components of the flash appeal and early recovery proposal through the Voluntary Trust Fund for Assistance in Mine Action and bilaterally. While the response has been encouraging, more is needed in the coming months and years to ensure that the threat is fully neutralized.

41. While coordinated with the humanitarian efforts above, I would like to mention specifically the response within UNIFIL. The first reinforcements of French troops included military engineers, who along with the existing Chinese capacity have been securing UNIFIL facilities. Additional clearance capacity has been promised by troop-contributing countries and should be deployed in the coming months. As these capacities come online, they will be able to address the implicit mandate contained in Security Council resolution 1701 (2006) to protect UNIFIL and other mission personnel as well as the explicit mandate to facilitate the provision of humanitarian assistance. Based on funding requested and capacity, it is estimated that it will take well over a year to clear the cluster bomblets.

G. Delineation of borders

42. In its resolution 1701 (2006), the Security Council emphasized the importance of the extension of the control of the Government of Lebanon over all Lebanese territory. The Council also requested me to develop proposals for the delineation of the international borders of Lebanon, especially in those areas where the border is disputed or uncertain, including by dealing with the Shab'a Farms area.

43. I have previously noted the repeated statements by representatives of the Government of the Syrian Arab Republic that the Shab'a farms area is Lebanese and not (Israeli-occupied) the Syrian Arab Republic territory, as determined by the United Nations on the basis of the Blue Line, and my caveat that the determination by the United Nations of the status of the Shab'a Farms is without prejudice to any border delineation agreement between the Syrian Arab Republic and Lebanon. I have previously called on both Governments to urgently take steps in keeping with international law to reach such an agreement. I have also noted

Lebanon's readiness to deal with this issue and urgently called for the cooperation of the Syrian Arab Republic.

44. It is important to emphasize that the issue of the Shab'a Farms area continues to be put forward—in contradiction to the repeated resolutions of the Security Council—to justify the existence and activities of Hizbollah insofar as militant activity across the Blue Line is concerned. In light of the Syrian Arab Republic statements indicating that the Shab'a Farms area is Lebanese, clarifying the status of the area is likely to facilitate the Government of Lebanon's efforts to fully implement the relevant provisions of the Taif Accords and of Security Council resolutions 1559 (2004), 1680 (2006) and 1701 (2006). A permanent solution of this issue, however, remains contingent upon the delineation of the border between the Syrian Arab Republic and Lebanon.

45. I am encouraged by my talks with the Governments of the Syrian Arab Republic and Lebanon on this issue and note that the Lebanese remain committed to the agreement they reached in their national dialogue earlier in 2006. I also note that President Assad informed me that the Syrian Arab Republic was prepared to go ahead with the delineation of its border with Lebanon and that he was ready to meet with Prime Minister Siniora at any time to discuss all issues of common interest. I reiterate my strong expectation of speedy steps towards an agreement on the delineation of the border as an important means to help fully restore the sovereignty, territorial integrity and political independence of Lebanon in fulfilment of Security Council resolution 1701 (2006).

46. In this context, I have taken careful note of an alternative path, suggested by the Government of Lebanon, to achieve progress on clarifying, in particular, the status of the Shab'a Farms. In his Seven Point Plan, Prime Minister Siniora proposed that, together with an immediate and comprehensive ceasefire, agreement would be declared on a number of elements, including a commitment from the Security Council to place the Shab'a Farms area and the adjacent Kafr Shuba hills under United Nations jurisdiction until border delineation and Lebanese sovereignty over them are fully settled. Implementation of such a measure would still require the determination of the precise geographic scope of the Shab'a Farms area, which I have previously identified as an essential element to be addressed in a letter I sent to Prime Minister Siniora on 5 June 2006 regarding his question about the possible steps to be undertaken, from the perspective of the United Nations, for the sovereignty of the Shab'a Farms area to be transferred from the Syrian Arab Republic to Lebanon. I am now studying carefully the complicated cartographic, legal and political implications of such an approach and will revert to the Council in due course.

H. Establishment of diplomatic relations

47. I wish to note the assurances given to me by President Assad that the Syrian Arab Republic is prepared to establish normal diplomatic relations between the Syrian Arab Republic and Lebanon and that he is ready to meet at any time with Prime Minister Siniora to discuss all issues of common interest. Prime Minister Siniora has informed me that he stands ready to meet with the President of the Syrian Arab Republic at any time to discuss such issues according to an agreed agenda. I reiterate my expectation of the early initiation of a process between the two countries, based on an agreed action agenda, which will eventually lead to the establishment of full diplomatic relations. President Assad informed me

that he considered this a sovereign decision, and that the details and timing must be worked out between the Syrian Arab Republic and Lebanon.

I. Captured soldiers and prisoners

48. The unconditional release of the captured Israeli soldiers and the issue of the Lebanese prisoners detained in Israel are both of vital importance. I have made these issues a top priority during my efforts over the past weeks. My discussions in the region, in particular with the Government of Israel, the Government of Lebanon and Lebanese Speaker of Parliament Nabih Berri, have impressed on me that resolution of these issues is an inherent necessity. I have also been made to understand that all relevant parties are open to a discussion of the issues at stake.

49. I also wish to note that in his Seven Point Plan, Prime Minister Siniora suggested that, together with an immediate and comprehensive ceasefire, agreement would be declared on a number of elements, including an undertaking to release the Lebanese and Israeli prisoners and detainees through the International Committee of the Red Cross.

50. I have raised humanitarian issues, in particular the release of the Israeli soldiers captured by Hizbollah, with the Governments of the Syrian Arab Republic and the Islamic Republic of Iran. I have been encouraged by their support of my calls for the release of captured soldiers and prisoners.

51. I have appointed an experienced facilitator specifically tasked to address these vital issues. Because of the nature of such efforts, I am not at liberty to outline in detail how the release of the captured and of prisoners may be accomplished. I do look forward to reverting to the Council on this matter at the earliest opportunity.

J. Blockade

52. A further element that had to be addressed owing to its inherent relevance in the short term was the comprehensive aerial and maritime blockade Israel imposed on Lebanon with the eruption of hostilities on 12 July. Throughout recent weeks, the revocation of the blockade was naturally a key interest of the Government of Lebanon, in particular given its harmful effects on the Lebanese economy. The Government of Israel had justified the blockade as a necessary measure to ensure the maintenance of the arms embargo sanctioned by the Security Council in paragraph 15 of its resolution 1701 (2006).

53. Along with the issue of captured soldiers and prisoners, I saw the goal of ending the blockade as another top priority during my efforts in recent weeks. I am pleased to report that Israel fully lifted the aerial blockade on 6 September and the maritime blockade on 7 September, after my discussions with all concerned parties led to a consensus on the necessary security arrangements to ensure sufficient and uninterrupted maintenance of the arms embargo imposed under resolution 1701 (2006). I have reported on these measures in more detail above.

54. I now look forward to the imminent deployment of the United Nations naval task force off the Lebanese coast to assist the Lebanese authorities in securing the maritime border and in replacement of the interim maritime task force currently in operation.

IV. Observations

55. Once again, part of the Middle East is emerging from the aftermath of war, destruction and crisis. A tragic 34-day conflict has thrown the region back into the instability that

prevailed for decades. In its aftermath, much work must be done and much of it, sadly, must be re-done. I have spoken to the Council about how the Lebanese and Israeli peoples were brutally dragged back into war and confrontation. I reiterate the previous commitment of the United Nations to support Lebanon and the Lebanese people as they move forward. I also wish to assure the Israeli people that the United Nations is committed to their security and well-being, along with that of all other peoples in the region. Security, stability and comprehensive peace remain the overarching goals. As I have outlined in the present report, a start has been made. But many other steps are required.

56. I am pleased to note that in Lebanon itself, the Government, in reflection of a true national consensus, has decided in clear terms that there can only be one source of law, order and authority. I commend the Government and Prime Minister Siniora for their decision and their efforts. I am also greatly encouraged by the statements made to me by relevant parties, including the Syrian Arab Republic and the Islamic Republic of Iran, during my mission to the region and expect their further tangible cooperation. No State in the region or elsewhere would tolerate the existence of armed groups which challenge the State's monopoly on the legitimate use of force throughout its territory. Indeed, many of Lebanon's neighbours and other concerned actors have taken strict measures to ensure the prevalence of the State. It is my hope that they will extend their full cooperation in implementing the relevant measures, as is requested of them in Security Council resolution 1701 (2006).

57. In this context, I urge all States to channel their humanitarian assistance, economic recovery and the wider political and economic reconstruction to the Government of Lebanon. More broadly, the economic reconstruction and recovery of Lebanon will require significant sustained support and assistance from the international community.

58. While short-term measures are currently being put in place in a variety of ways to ensure that the cessation of hostilities is converted into a permanent ceasefire, a sustainable long-term solution can only be implemented on the basis of inclusive political processes, domestically in Lebanon as well as in the wider region, as recognized in Security Council resolution 1701 (2006). At the same time, I wish to note that permanent respect of the Blue Line can only be expected to be sustainable if, on the Lebanese side, security arrangements are put in place to prevent the resumption of hostilities, including the establishment between the Blue Line and the Litani River of an area free of any armed personnel, assets and weapons other than those of the Government of Lebanon or UNIFIL. In addition, all forces other than the regular Lebanese Armed Forces must be disarmed, as envisaged in Security Council resolution 1701 (2006). At the same time, on the Israeli side, over-flights must cease completely.

59. I welcome the troop contributions to date and the commitments by Member States to support and reinforce UNIFIL. I take special note of the willingness of the Governments of Italy and France to step forward and take leading roles, and the European commitments overall, as well as those of Asian and African Member States. As a result of these contributions, UNIFIL will have a truly diverse character, which is evidence of the international community's deep commitment to seeing peace reign in the Middle East. A fully resourced UNIFIL is within reach and I count on Member States to rapidly honour their pledges to provide all necessary troops and equipment. I also wish to express my gratitude specifically to Spain, Germany, the United Kingdom and Jordan for their assistance to United Nations missions over the past month.

60. In order to prevent a resurgence of violence and bloodshed the underlying causes of conflict in the region must be addressed. Other crises cannot be ignored, especially in the Occupied Palestinian Territory, as they are all interlinked. Until the international community insists on a just, lasting and comprehensive peace in the Middle East, any one of these conflicts has the potential to erupt and engulf the entire region.

61. I will continue my efforts to pursue the full implementation of Security Council resolution 1701 (2006) and other relevant resolutions and will report to the Council at regular intervals.

---

[1] Concerns also remain as to the possible impact of the shortage of some essential drugs and the effects of the interruption of general, reproductive, vaccination and child health services; a United Nations assessment of more than 400 health facilities in conflict-affected areas found that 26 per cent of all facilities were not functioning due to physical damage, lack of staff or lack of accessibility. A large number of schools were also damaged or destroyed. Initial United Nations inter-agency field assessments in the south show local communities have set schooling as a priority since without major efforts the school year will be jeopardized.

[2] To date, $92.3 million has been committed against the $96.5 million required under the revised Lebanon flash appeal, with an additional $13.4 million in pledges also recorded. While the initiatives under the Government of Lebanon's early recovery strategy are implemented over the next 4 to 6 months, the Government will also finalize a number of in-depth social and economic impact assessments and develop its long-term reconstruction programme on the basis of the economic and social reform agenda it had prepared before the conflict.

3. Fourth Semi-annual Report of the Secretary-General to the Security Council on the implementation of Security Council Resolution 1559 (2004), 19 October 2006 (S/2006/832)

I. Introduction

1. The present report is my fourth semi-annual report to the Security Council on the implementation of resolution 1559 (2004).

2. In the six months since my last report, of 19 April 2006 (S/2006/248), Lebanon witnessed first political standstill, then severe deterioration and prolonged instability.

3. Lebanon's National Dialogue reconvened on 28 April and 16 May 2006 to discuss the two remaining issues on its agenda, the Lebanese presidency and the arms of Hizbollah, amidst an increasingly tense political climate both domestically and with regard to Lebanese-Syrian relations.

4. On 1 and 2 June 2006 protests and clashes erupted after a television programme appeared to parody the Secretary-General of Hizbollah, Hassan Nasrallah. Youths from the southern suburbs of Beirut blocked the road to the airport with burning tyres and engaged in clashes with youths from the north-eastern suburbs.

5. In this context, the National Dialogue met on 8 June 2006; in the session, Lebanese political leaders agreed on a written code of conduct stipulating that they would refrain from attacking each other, in order to decrease the rising political and sectarian tension. On 29 June, the National Dialogue convened for the last time to date and adjourned, having reached no further agreements.

6. On 12 July, hostilities erupted between Israel and Hizbollah after Hizbollah launched an unprovoked attack across the Blue Line, abducting two Israeli soldiers and killing several others. I have outlined the course of events and effects of the conflict elsewhere in my reports on the implementation of resolution 1701 (2006) (S/2006/670 and S/2006/730), which was adopted on 11 August 2006 and led to a cessation of hostilities that has remained in effect since 14 August.

7. A tense political climate has continued to prevail in Lebanon. In its midst, in a worrying return to last year's climate of frequent assassinations and terrorist acts, a senior Lebanese security official survived an assassination attempt while driving on a road in south Lebanon on 5 September. Four of his aides and bodyguards were killed in the attack and five were wounded.

8. In the early morning hours of 15 October, six Lebanese civilians were hurt when three rockets were launched into a building in downtown Beirut, close to both United Nations headquarters and the Grand Serail which houses the Prime Minister's offices. This disconcerting incident followed two other attacks which had not caused any casualties, with similar rocket launchers and with hand grenades against police stations in Lebanon. In the aftermath of the latest attacks, the Government of Lebanon has expanded the presence of the Internal Security Forces in Beirut by 800 men.

II. Implementation of resolution 1559 (2004)

9. Since the Council adopted resolution 1559 (2004) on 2 September 2004, there has been considerable progress towards its full implementation. In April 2005, the full withdrawal of Syrian troops, military assets and military intelligence apparatus was achieved. Shortly afterwards, free and fair legislative elections were conducted in Lebanon (see S/2005/673). In my last report, I stated that with the agreements reached in the Lebanese National Dialogue, significant further progress towards the full implementation of resolution 1559 (2004) had been made.

10. Additional progress has been made in recent months with the significant and historic deployment of the Lebanese Armed Forces in the south of the country for the first time in three decades. Moreover, Lebanese troops have taken up positions along the eastern part of the Blue Line for the first time ever, and have deployed in significant numbers along Lebanon's border with the Syrian Arab Republic. These steps represent important progress towards the full extension of the Government of Lebanon's control over all Lebanese territory and the fulfilment of the requirements of resolutions 425 (1978) and 1559 (2004) and the Taif Accords.

11. However, resolution 1559 (2004), and in particular its provisions calling for the disbanding and disarmament of all Lebanese and non-Lebanese militias and the strict respect of the sovereignty, territorial integrity, unity, and political independence of Lebanon under the sole and exclusive authority of the Government, has yet to be implemented in full.

A. Withdrawal of foreign forces deployed in Lebanon

12. In my report on the implementation of resolution 1701 (2006) of 12 September 2006 (S/2006/730), I stated that to the best of the ability of the United Nations to ascertain, the only foreign forces currently deployed in Lebanon were those serving under the banner of the United Nations Interim Force in Lebanon (UNIFIL). Israeli troops, who had entered Lebanon in the course of the recent conflict, returned beyond the Blue Line on 1 October 2006, with the exception of their deployment in the divided village of Ghajar. I expect this presence to end shortly in the context of a trilateral discussion on security arrangements for the village.[1]

B. Sovereignty, territorial integrity, unity and political independence of Lebanon

1. Syrian intelligence apparatus and activity in Lebanon

13. The Government of Lebanon has stated to me that its efforts to consolidate its full control over all security services continue. Allegations have at times been made, including by the Government of Lebanon, that there continues to be Syrian intelligence activity in Lebanon.[2]

2. Establishment of mutual diplomatic representation

14. Subsequent to my last report on the implementation of resolution 1559 (2004), the Security Council adopted its resolution 1680 (2006) of 17 May 2006, which encouraged the delineation of borders between the Syrian Arab Republic and Lebanon and the establishment of full diplomatic relations and representation.

15. I have stated my expectation of the early initiation of a process between Lebanon and the Syrian Arab Republic, based on an agreed action agenda, which will eventually lead to

the establishment of full diplomatic relations.[3] I reiterate my expectation in the light of the Council's position, as expressed in resolutions 1680 (2006) and 1701 (2006). Steps towards the establishment of diplomatic relations between the Syrian Arab Republic and Lebanon would significantly contribute to the stability of the region.

3. Delineation of the border

16. In addition to its call contained in resolution 1680 (2006) on the Government of the Syrian Arab Republic to respond positively to the request made by the Government of Lebanon to delineate their common border, the Council again emphasized the importance of the extension of the control of the Government of Lebanon over all Lebanese territory in its resolution 1701 (2006).

17. In the context of the general need for a delineation of the Syrian-Lebanese border, the Government of Lebanon has informed me that Syrian border police maintained sand barriers and positions inside Lebanese territory in several locations during the last six months. The Government of Lebanon further informed me that there were mobile positions, some of which were also manned by Syrian border police on occasion. The apparent uncertainty over the border in the areas concerned highlights, once again, the need for a comprehensive border delineation agreement between Lebanon and the Syrian Arab Republic, in the best interest of both countries.

18. As regards delineation of the border in the Shab'a Farms area, Prime Minister Siniora enquired in a meeting between us on 21 April 2006 as to possible steps to be undertaken, from the perspective of the United Nations, for the sovereignty of the Shab'a Farms to be transferred from the Syrian Arab Republic to Lebanon. I responded to the Prime Minister in a letter dated 5 June 2006. Prime Minister Siniora and I have discussed the matter further, including when I visited Beirut during my recent mission to the region and in connection with the Government of Lebanon's seven-point plan.

19. In the light of Syrian statements indicating that the Shab'a Farms area is Lebanese and considering the alternative path suggested by the Government of Lebanon in its seven-point plan, I continue to investigate carefully the complicated cartographic, legal and political implications of such an approach and will revert to the Council in due course.[4] In the meantime, I wish to reiterate my urgent call on the Syrian Arab Republic and Lebanon to undertake the necessary steps to delineate their common border, in fulfilment of resolutions 1559 (2004), 1680 (2006) and 1701 (2006). Such steps would significantly contribute to the stability of the region.

4. Israeli violations of Lebanese sovereignty and territorial integrity

20. Subsequent to my last report on the implementation of resolution 1559 (2004) (S/2006/248), persistent and provocative Israeli air incursions, occasionally reaching deep into Lebanese airspace and generating sonic booms over populated areas, continued to be a matter of serious concern (see S/2006/560). The Government of Israel has continued to maintain its claim that such overflights are carried out for security reasons.

21. Israeli overflights have also continued since the cessation of hostilities between Israel and Hizbollah went into effect on 14 August 2006. I expect that such air incursions and violations of Lebanese sovereignty, which stand in contradiction to resolutions 425 (1978) and 1559 (2004) as well as resolution 1701 (2006) itself, will cease fully.

22. The recent hostilities between Israel and Hizbollah saw an extended period of time in which Israel violated Lebanese sovereignty and territorial integrity. With resolution 1701 (2006), a cessation of hostilities has been established, which both parties have by and large abided by, as I have reported in my report on the implementation of resolution 1701 (2006) (S/2006/730).

23. The Government of Lebanon has also informed me of another alleged violation of Lebanese sovereignty by Israel.[5]

C. Extension of Lebanese Government control over all Lebanese territory

24. In my last report on the implementation of resolution 1559 (2004), I noted that a number of serious incidents had emphasized the necessity for the Government of Lebanon, through its regular security and armed forces, to extend its control over all its territory, in order to maintain quiet along the Blue Line. As I stated, the Government of Lebanon, as the sole legitimate authority vested with a monopoly on the use of force throughout its territory, had to do more to exercise its control accordingly.

25. During the hostilities, the Lebanese Government reaffirmed its determination to extend its control over all of Lebanon's territory and to establish its monopoly on the legitimate use of violence. Prime Minister Siniora's seven-point plan envisaged that the Lebanese Government would extend its authority over its territory through its own legitimate armed forces, such that there will be no weapons or authority other than that of the Lebanese State as stipulated in the Taif Accords. The Lebanese Council of Ministers adopted the seven-point plan as the official position of the Government of Lebanon on 27 July 2006. On 7 August 2006, the cabinet again reaffirmed its commitment and decided to send 15,000 Lebanese soldiers to the south simultaneously with the withdrawal of the occupying Israeli forces beyond the Blue Line. The Council of Ministers also confirmed its readiness to accept UNIFIL support, if needed, in order to facilitate the deployment of the Lebanese army troops in the context of the implementation of the seven-point plan.

26. I wish to welcome again the significant and historic step taken by the Government of Lebanon to deploy the Lebanese Armed Forces to the south of the country. In addition to the first deployment of the Lebanese Armed Forces in the south in three decades, Lebanese troops have taken up positions along the eastern part of the Blue Line for the first time ever. As I have previously reported, a significant number of Lebanese troops have also been deployed along the Lebanese border with the Syrian Arab Republic.[6]

27. Since the cessation of hostilities came into effect in Lebanon on 14 August 2006, renewed reports of intercepted arms shipments have been brought to my attention; such shipments would stand in contradiction to the arms embargo imposed by resolution 1701 (2006). I will endeavour to comply with my reporting requirements on the implementation of resolution 1701 (2006), as expressed in paragraph 17 of that resolution, with regard to possible reports of arms shipments. I also call on all Member States, particularly Lebanon's neighbours, to ensure full compliance with the arms embargo imposed by paragraph 15 of resolution 1701 (2006).

D. Disbanding and disarmament of Lebanese and non-Lebanese militias

28. I continue to believe that disarmament must take place through a political process that will lead to the full restoration of the authority of the Government of Lebanon. If the

ultimate purpose of disarmament is the establishment of a strong Lebanese State for all inhabitants of Lebanon, as the Taif Accords stipulated, then the disarming and disbanding of all remaining militias must be realized in such a way that it strengthens, rather than weakens, the central authorities. It is a definitional requirement of the state to enjoy a monopoly on the legitimate use of force throughout its territory. In that context, it is important that all neighbouring States abide by the arms embargo, as called for in resolution 1701 (2006).

1. Palestinian militias

29. The National Dialogue's decision to disarm Palestinian militias outside the camps has not been implemented within the six-month deadline, which ended on 26 August 2006. The National Dialogue, in its session on 16 May 2006, had decided to establish a committee tasked with following up on the implementation of its agreement.

30. I expect that the Government of Lebanon, pursuant to its decision of 27 July 2006, according to which there should be no weapons or authority other than that of the Lebanese State as stipulated in the Taif Accords, will further define a political process and a clear timeline for the full disarmament of Palestinian militias in Lebanon. I call for the issue to be settled as early as possible. I also call on all donors to support the efforts of the Government of Lebanon and of the United Nations Relief and Works Agency for Palestine Refugees in the Near East (UNRWA).

31. There have been a number of incidents underlining the importance of the eventual full disarmament of Palestinian militias in Lebanon over the past six months. On 17 May 2006, the Lebanese Armed Forces and the Palestinian militia Fatah-Intifada, which is headquartered in Damascus and maintains a number of bases on Lebanese territory, engaged in clashes after an army patrol approached a newly established Fatah-Intifada position in eastern Lebanon and came under fire. A Lebanese Armed Forces soldier and a Palestinian militant later died from wounds sustained in the subsequent exchanges of fire; another Lebanese soldier was detained for several hours before he was released. The Lebanese Armed Forces eventually took over the base; the Palestinian militants implicated in the incident were later arrested.

32. On 26 May 2006, a leader of the Palestinian Islamic Jihad was assassinated together with his brother in southern Lebanon by a car bomb. A major escalation occurred two days later along the Blue Line, when at least eight rockets were launched across the Blue Line into Israel (see S/2006/560). The Palestinian Islamic Jihad initially claimed responsibility, but later retracted its assertion. Israel retaliated with air strikes against Lebanese bases of the Damascus-based Popular Front for the Liberation of Palestine-General Command (PFLP-GC); a subsequent major exchange across the Blue Line also involved Hizbollah and escalated into the firing of rockets and missiles across the Blue Line by Hizbollah and the Israel Defense Forces. Later the same day, the Lebanese Armed Forces sent equipment to clear rubble at a PFLP-GC base but were denied entry to the base. Also the same day, PFLP-GC leader Ahmad Jibril said in an interview with a Lebanese newspaper that his group coordinated all of their military action with Hizbollah, also stating his opposition to the disarmament of Palestinian militias in Lebanon.

33. Despite these incidents, I took positive note of the reopening of the representative office of the Palestine Liberation Organization (PLO) in Lebanon on 15 May 2006. I have

continued my dialogue on the issue of the Palestinian militias in Lebanon with the Chairman of PLO, Mahmoud Abbas, who has assured me of his full support for the restoration of the Lebanese Government's monopoly on the use of force throughout its territory.

2. Hizbollah

34. With regard to the armed component of Hizbollah, I wish to recall once again Prime Minister Siniora's address to the Council of 21 April 2006 (S/PV.5417) and the consensual decision of the Lebanese in the Taif Accords.[7] The National Dialogue extensively discussed the issue of Hizbollah's arms earlier this year, but did not reach agreement. Hizbollah continued to limit the authority of the Government of Lebanon, especially in areas close to the Blue Line.

35. The eventual disarmament of Hizbollah in the sense of the completion of its transformation into a solely political party, consistent with the requirements of the Taif Accords, is a key element in ensuring a permanent end to the hostilities and a critical provision to be realized in the implementation of resolution 1701 (2006) and in the full restoration of Lebanon's sovereignty, territorial integrity and political independence. A number of specific measures to further this purpose are enumerated in resolution 1701 (2006) and are in the process of being implemented, in particular the establishment between the Blue Line and the Litani River of an area free of any armed personnel, assets and weapons other than those of the Government of Lebanon and of UNIFIL, which would constitute an important step towards the disarming of all militias in Lebanon.

36. I expect that the Government of Lebanon, pursuant to its decision of 27 July 2006, according to which there should be no weapons or authority other than that of the Lebanese State as stipulated in the Taif Accords," will further define a political process and a clear timeline for the full disarmament of Hizbollah in the sense of the completion of its transformation into a solely political party. I call for the disarmament of all Lebanese and non-Lebanese militias to be settled as early as possible.

37. I note that Hizbollah, through its representatives in the Lebanese Council of Ministers, agreed to the cabinet decision of 27 July 2006.[8] At the same time, I have taken note of further statements by Hizbollah representatives that stand in contradiction to Security Council resolution 1559 (2004).

38. In this context, I note again that a dialogue with parties other than the Lebanese authorities is indispensable in order to realize the implementation of the mandate contained in resolution 1559 (2004) to disarm and disband all Lebanese and non-Lebanese militias. I expect to continue my dialogue with such parties, in particular with the Governments of the Syrian Arab Republic and the Islamic Republic of Iran, which maintain close relations with Hizbollah.

39. Against this background, I wish to reiterate my call on all parties with the ability to influence Hizbollah to support its transformation into a solely political party, consistent with the requirements of the Taif Accords, as a means to achieve the full disarmament of all Lebanese and non-Lebanese militias. I also reiterate my call to all Member States, particularly Lebanon's neighbours, to ensure compliance with the arms embargo imposed by paragraph 15 of resolution 1701 (2006), which is a measure facilitating the full implementation of the relevant provisions of the Taif Accords and of resolutions 1559 (2004) and 1680 (2006), which require the disarmament of militias in Lebanon.

E. Presidential election process

40. The issue of the Lebanese presidency was discussed in several rounds of the National Dialogue until the participants in the National Dialogue "agreed to disagree" on the subject in their seventh round of consultations. In this context, I also recall Prime Minister Siniora's address to the Security Council on 21 April 2006.[9]

III. Observations

41. Over the past two years, there has been considerable progress towards the full implementation of resolution 1559 (2004). The Syrian Arab Republic has withdrawn its troops, military assets and military intelligence apparatus. Free and fair legislative elections have been conducted. The Lebanese National Dialogue manifested further progress. In the past few months, there has been additional progress with the extension of the Government's control over Lebanese territory, in particular in the south and along the border with the Syrian Arab Republic. However, resolution 1559 (2004), and in particular its provisions calling for the disbanding and disarmament of all Lebanese and non-Lebanese militias and the strict respect of the sovereignty, territorial integrity, unity and political independence of Lebanon under the sole and exclusive authority of the Government, has yet to be implemented in full.

42. In the past six months, Lebanon has suffered a severe setback. Instead of making further strides towards completing its political transformation and reaping the economic rewards of political progress, Lebanon confronts challenges of a magnitude unseen since the end of the civil war. Moreover, since the end of the hostilities, a tense political climate has prevailed, with manifold challenges confronting the Lebanese in their quest to reconstruct their country, their polity and their economy.

43. The United Nations remains committed to supporting Lebanon, its Government and its people as they face the enormous task of recovering the momentum on the path to consolidating the Lebanese State as an authority of the people, by the people, for the people.

44. I would like to express my thanks to all countries that have already provided assistance to the Lebanese, be it in the form of troop contributions to UNIFIL, bilateral technical aid, or through financial support. Such assistance will continue to be needed as the Lebanese once again embrace their fate of economic and political reconstruction. I also emphasize that all such assistance should be lent in ways that contribute to the consolidation of the Government's monopoly on the use of force throughout its territory.

45. In the months ahead, much remains to be done. With the adoption of resolutions 1680 (2006) and 1701 (2006) and with repeated Lebanese cabinet decisions to extend the Government's authority over all Lebanese territory, a new framework has been established for the full implementation of all provisions of resolution 1559 (2004). A catalogue of measures has been laid down that constitute a road map for the full implementation of resolution 1559 (2004). The Government of Lebanon, with significant international support, is undertaking important steps that will help it to fully implement resolution 1559 (2004). Achieving this goal, however, continues to depend on both the Lebanese and on the cooperation of parties other than the Lebanese.

46. In the months ahead, Lebanon will have to engage again in a truly national and inclusive dialogue. The disarming and disbanding of Lebanese and non-Lebanese militias, which lies

at the heart of the political transformation Lebanon has been undergoing and is a necessary element to complete, at long last, Lebanon's consolidation as a sovereign and democratic State, can only be achieved through an inclusive process that addresses the political and economic interests of all Lebanese and of those living in Lebanon.

47. It is my deep hope that the opportunities born from conflict will be seized upon and that Lebanon may once again rise from the ashes of destruction and war. I emphasize once again in this context that Hizbollah's transformation into a solely political party, consistent with the requirements of the Taif Accords, is a key element in ensuring a permanent end to hostilities and in the full restoration of Lebanon's sovereignty, territorial integrity and political independence.

48. For the purpose of achieving this goal, on the path towards the greater objective of consolidating the Lebanese State, it is indispensable that all parties who have influence in Lebanon support a constructive political process. I note in this context that the cooperation of outside parties is explicitly called for in resolutions 1559 (2004), 1680 (2006) and 1701 (2006), and I join these calls.

49. The establishment of full diplomatic relations between Lebanon and the Syrian Arab Republic and their delineation of the shared border, including, in particular, in the Shab'a Farms area, through a bilateral agreement would constitute significant steps towards promoting peace and security in the region. Mindful of the importance of border delineation to the Lebanese, I am expeditiously working to establish in full the cartographic, legal and political implications of the approach suggested in Lebanon's seven-point plan and will revert to the Council. I also wish to call for the Syrian Arab Republic and Lebanon to address in their bilateral contacts the issue of Lebanese detainees in Syrian custody.

50. I reiterate my call on all parties and actors to support Lebanon's reconstruction and political transformation and to urgently take all enabling measures to this end, as outlined in the Taif Accords and in resolutions 1559 (2004), 1680 (2006) and 1701 (2006).

51. I will continue my efforts for the purpose of the full implementation of these and all other relevant Security Council resolutions pertaining to the restoration of the territorial integrity, full sovereignty and political independence of Lebanon and the achievement of a just, lasting and comprehensive peace throughout the entire Middle Eastern region, consistent with all relevant Security Council resolutions.

---

[1] I have previously reported on the otherwise complete withdrawal of Israeli forces from all Lebanese territory, in full compliance with this aspect of resolution 425 (1978), and on the full withdrawal of all Syrian troops, military assets and the military intelligence apparatus from Lebanon, in full compliance with this aspect of resolution 1559 (2004). The Security Council has endorsed my conclusions in both respects.

[2] The Syrian Government stated in a letter to me dated 24 April 2006 that it would "like to reaffirm once again that all its troops, military assets and security apparatus withdrew from Lebanon on 26 April 2005" (S/2006/259, annex).

[3] In my report on the implementation of resolution 1701 (2006) of 12 September 2006 (S/2006/730), I noted the assurances given to me by President Assad and reiterated my expectation of the early initiation of a process between the two countries, based on an agreed action agenda, which would eventually lead to the establishment of full diplomatic relations. I must recall in this context the statements made by the representative of the Government of the Syrian Arab Republic in the

Security Council after Prime Minister Siniora's address on 21 April 2006 (S/PV.5417) and in the letter addressed to me from the Government of the Syrian Arab Republic of 24 April 2006 (S/2006/259).

4 According to the seven-point plan, the Security Council might place the Shab'a Farms area and the adjacent Kafr Shuba hills temporarily under United Nations jurisdiction until border delineation and Lebanese sovereignty over them are fully settled in accordance with international law.

5 The Lebanese Government asserted to me that the assassination of an official of the Palestinian Islamic Jihad in Lebanon on 26 May 2006 had been carried out by an intelligence network operating under the instruction of Israel. A press release from the Lebanese delegation, dated 21 June 2006, stated that the Department of Intelligence of the Lebanese Armed Forces had uncovered a terrorist network working for Israel. One of the alleged members of the network, the press release further asserted, had admitted to several assassinations carried out in Lebanon at the behest of Israeli security services, including that of 26 May 2006. The Israeli Government has denied these claims.

6 As outlined in my last report on the implementation of resolution 1701 (2006) (S/2006/730), I continue to believe that the imposition of an arms embargo, which is fully consistent with the Lebanese cabinet decision of 27 July 2006 that there should be no weapons or authority in Lebanon other than those of the Lebanese State, is a necessary measure given the history of arms traffic bound for Lebanese and non-Lebanese militias. I also emphasized the need for the Syrian Arab Republic, in particular, to help enforce the provisions of paragraphs 14 and 15 of resolution 1701 (2006), given that it shares the sole land border with Lebanon that is generally open to traffic.

7 Prime Minister Siniora repeated in his address that "the future role of Hizbollah's weapons in defending Lebanon is a matter of national debate. That debate will be carried out in the context of a strategy agreed upon by all Lebanese concerning how best to defend Lebanon, against the backdrop of the provisions of the Taif Accords of 1989, United Nations resolutions regarding Lebanon and the continued occupation of the Shab'a Farms, as well as the long history of incursions and violations of Lebanese territory by Israel. Reconciling those considerations with the natural obligation of the State to be the sole provider of security to all its citizens and residents, and the right of the State to have a monopoly over arms and to exercise its full authority throughout the country, is a major challenge to be addressed in the period ahead."

8 I have also taken note of the statements by Hizbollah Secretary-General Hassan Nasrallah in his address to a major rally in southern Beirut on 22 September 2006 that "we are not saying that our weapons will remain forever. It is not logical for these weapons to remain forever. There is bound to be an end to them".

9 Prime Minister Siniora stated that "the majority in parliament considers the extension of President Lahoud's term in September 2004 for three more years to have been the result of interference and coercion by Syria—which had great influence over the Lebanese parliament at that time—against all of the advice discouraging such heavy-handed interference" (S/PV.5417).

4. Letter dated 1 December 2006 from the Secretary-General addressed to the President of the Security Council, 1 December 2006 (S/2006/933)

I have the honour to submit a factual update to my report of 12 September 2006 on the implementation of Security Council resolution 1701 (2006) (S/2006/780), in particular on the operations of the United Nations Interim Force in Lebanon (UNIFIL) and other relevant United Nations activities. In doing so, I have noted and welcome the continuing commitment of the Government of Lebanon and the Government of Israel to all aspects of the implementation of Security Council resolution 1701 (2006).

I. Respect for the Blue Line

Since my report of 12 September 2006, the military and security situation in the UNIFIL area of operation has further stabilized. The cessation of hostilities was maintained and there were no serious incidents or confrontations. Nevertheless, UNIFIL observed and reported air violations by Israeli jets and unmanned aerial vehicles on an almost daily basis. On 31 October and again on 16 November, UNIFIL recorded a total of 14 such overflights on each day. A number of these took the form of mock air attacks above the headquarters of the French battalion of UNIFIL located in the general area of Frun. In another instance, two Israeli jets flew within two nautical miles of a French ship that is part of the Interim Maritime Task Force. The Government of Lebanon has protested the overflights as a serious violation of Lebanese sovereignty in contravention of resolution 1701 (2006). Israel, however, maintains that they are not violations but a necessary security measure and its Minister of Defence has linked them to the return of two Israel Defense Force (IDF) soldiers captured by Hizbollah on 12 July and full respect for the arms embargo established in paragraphs 14 and 15 of resolution 1701 (2006). While mindful of the Israeli motivations to continue their air incursions into Lebanese airspace, I would note that such violations of Lebanese sovereignty, which stand in contradiction to resolution 1701 (2006) and other relevant resolutions, undermine the credibility of both UNIFIL and the Lebanese Armed Forces (LAF) and compromise overall efforts to stabilize the situation in the south and efforts to build trust and confidence generally.

UNIFIL observed and recorded a number of minor ground violations of the Blue Line by the IDF and Israeli civilian construction workers who were repairing the technical fence and from the Lebanese side by local shepherds. On one occasion Lebanese protesters crossed the Blue Line in the area of the Shab'a Farms, but the LAF, after being notified by UNIFIL, quickly intervened and persuaded them to return to the Lebanese side.

II. Security arrangements

Israel continued to withdraw its forces from southern Lebanon, in coordination with UNIFIL. The IDF retain a presence only in the northern part of the village of Ghajar. Given the specific status of the village of Ghajar, which is divided by the Blue Line, UNIFIL is working with the LAF and the IDF to finalize the withdrawal of the IDF from the remaining area inside Lebanon and set up temporary security arrangements for the part of the village of Ghajar inside Lebanese territory.

In parallel with the withdrawal of Israeli forces, Lebanon deployed, in coordination with UNIFIL, four brigades of its armed forces throughout the south in the areas vacated by the IDF, including along the Blue Line. The deployment of the LAF throughout the south for the first time in decades down to the Blue Line is a most notable achievement and a key stabilizing factor. The LAF, assisted by UNIFIL, have taken some specific steps to ensure that the area between the Litani River and the Blue Line is free of armed personnel, assets and weapons other than those of the Government of Lebanon and those of UNIFIL. Specifically, the LAF have established a considerable number of permanent positions and checkpoints and commenced patrols. The LAF have also demonstrated a high degree of cooperation with UNIFIL and have responded promptly to its requests.

The UNIFIL mechanism for liaison and coordination with the LAF and the IDF has been very effective in addressing military and security issues, especially through the periodic meetings of the UNIFIL Force Commander with senior representatives of the LAF and the IDF. This is a key element of UNIFIL efforts to foster stability in southern Lebanon and continues to provide an essential forum for negotiation of matters requiring the cooperation of all three parties, such as the Israeli withdrawal from Lebanon and temporary security arrangements for the northern part of Ghajar village. UNIFIL is engaged in discussions with the LAF and the IDF on means to further enhance liaison and coordination.

UNIFIL and the LAF have seen sporadic evidence of the presence of unauthorized armed personnel, assets and/or weapons. On one occasion, a UNIFIL demining team was challenged by two Hizbollah personnel in combat uniform carrying AK47 rifles. UNIFIL notified the LAF, who arrested three suspects the following day. Since early September, there have been 13 instances where UNIFIL came across unauthorized arms or related materiel in its area of operation. The two most noteworthy were the discovery of 17 Katyushas and several improvised explosive devices in Rachaya El-Foukhar and, in the general area of Bourhoz, of a weapons cache consisting of seven missiles, three rocket launchers and substantial amounts of ammunition. On all of these occasions, UNIFIL informed the LAF, who took prompt action either to confiscate or destroy the materials. In the area between the Litani River and the Blue Line, there are, in addition, Palestinian armed elements largely confined to the refugee camps.

The Interim Maritime Task Force, under the lead of the Italian Navy, operated in support of the Lebanese Navy to secure Lebanese territorial waters until 15 October, when the UNIFIL Maritime Task Force became operational. The latter has questioned and confirmed the identity of some 950 ships, detecting one suspicious boat, which, when searched, was found to be smuggling cigarettes, and rendering assistance to one vessel in distress. As with the ground forces, cooperation between the LAF and the UNIFIL Maritime Task Force, and the Interim Maritime Task Force before it, has been of a high standard.

The Lebanese authorities reported that they had undertaken a variety of measures to secure their borders and entry points in order to prevent the illegal entry into Lebanon of arms and related materiel. However, the United Nations continues to receive reports of illegal arms smuggling across the Lebanese-Syrian border, but has not been able to verify such reports.

Since my last report, I dispatched a team of border police experts as requested by the Government of Lebanon to review the measures put in place and to assess the need for technical assistance. The team reviewed the security measures and arrangements at Beirut International Airport, seaports in Beirut and Tripoli, and a few smaller ports along the coast, as well as the main land border and entry points between Lebanon and the Syrian Arab Republic. Significant deficiencies were found in equipment and in training and in coordination among the four different government services responsible for the borders, as well as in compliance with some basic border security standards. The team was, however, able to confirm that the Lebanese authorities had taken initial steps to improve border security and control, including most notably the implementation of an effective integrated approach to security at the airport. I also note the presence of some 8,000 LAF troops all along Lebanon's land border with the Syrian Arab Republic.

The Government has instructed the head of the Internal Security Forces to establish a committee to review the systems in place at all border entry points and make recommendations for their improvement. That committee's preliminary findings and recommendations conform in most respects to those of the United Nations assessment team. After analysing the findings of the assessment team, the United Nations will share its observations with the Government of Lebanon. It is my understanding that the Government is also awaiting further recommendations from a German team of experts, which has been providing technical advice and assistance to the Lebanese authorities on a bilateral basis.

It is plain, however, that there is a need for bilateral assistance to the Government in order to enhance its border security capabilities. I would request that further specialized equipment and technical know-how, which has been requested by the Government of Lebanon, be provided. The provision of such assistance would be a useful confidence-building measure.

III. Deployment of the United Nations Interim Force in Lebanon

Following the decision of the Security Council to supplement and enhance the UNIFIL force in numbers, equipment, mandate and scope of operations, a phased deployment was planned and has largely been implemented in the area of operation between the Litani River and the Blue Line.

The first phase involved a rapid response deployment, reinforcing UNIFIL troops on the ground for the purpose of stabilizing the security situation and facilitating the withdrawal of the IDF from Lebanon and the concomitant deployment of the LAF throughout the south. Battalions from France, Italy and Spain deployed into the area of operation by 15 September, joining the battalions already in place from Ghana and India, and increased the overall strength of UNIFIL to over 5,000. Italy and Spain each deployed marine infantry units to facilitate this early entry, which were later relieved in place with regular army units. Upon the completion of the first phase in mid-October, five battalions were fully deployed and operational. In addition, France has deployed one engineer unit and Belgium and Luxembourg have deployed a level-2 hospital and an engineering unit. Italian air resources were strengthened with the deployment of a UH1 helicopter, bringing the total number of helicopters to five.

The support requirement placed on the limited resources of UNIFIL has been exacerbated by the rapid flow of deployment into the area of operation and the difficulties associated with the acquisition of land, which is the responsibility of the host Government, to accommodate the incoming troops.

Responsibility for maritime operations was handed over to the UNIFIL Maritime Task Force on 15 October, under the operational control of the UNIFIL Force Commander. The Task Force consists of four frigates, 10 corvettes/fast patrol boats supported by organic helicopters and two logistics support ships with hospital facilities.

The second phase of the augmentation of UNIFIL is now under way, and involves the further deployment of four mechanized infantry battalions from France, Indonesia, Italy and Nepal and one infantry unit each from Malaysia and Qatar. The French composite battalion is assuming the role of quick reaction force. Finland, Ireland and Turkey have deployed engineer units and another is expected from Portugal. China will deploy one level-2 hospital, in addition to its existing engineering company. The Dominican Republic and the United Republic of Tanzania are expected to deploy military police companies.

As at 28 November, UNIFIL troop strength was 10,480 all ranks (see annex). The completion of the augmentation is expected in December, when UNIFIL force strength will reach approximately 11,500 ground troops, 1,750 naval personnel and 51 military observers from the United Nations Truce Supervision Organization. With the deployment by the LAF of four brigades to south Lebanon, these numbers are deemed to be sufficient to execute the mandate.

The regular UNIFIL supply chain was recently re-established, thus enabling the Force to discontinue the air/sea bridge between Cyprus and Lebanon, which had been in place to maintain UNIFIL operability during the IDF naval and air blockade.

Structure

Command of UNIFIL in the field is exercised by the Force Commander, who is also head of the mission. My intention is to assign to the Deputy Force Commander the additional function of deputy head of the mission as a United Nations staff member. The Chief of Staff will assist the Force Commander in planning and controlling the conduct and employment of all military components. Two sector headquarters, West and East, have been established in Tibnin and Marjayoun, respectively. Each of the sectors is commanded by a brigadier general and will consist of four mechanized infantry battalions and a signal company. In addition, a quick reaction force will be based in Frun. UNIFIL air assets, provided and operated by Italy, are based at the Force headquarters. The UNIFIL Maritime Task Force is operating in Lebanese territorial waters. UNIFIL will have six engineering units, as well as two level-2 hospitals and one level-1 hospital. A UNIFIL office for coordination and joint planning with the LAF, the Ministry of Defence and other relevant Lebanese authorities is being set up in Beirut.

Another UNIFIL office will be established in Tel Aviv for liaison and coordination with IDF headquarters, the Ministry of Defence and other relevant Israeli authorities. A UNIFIL liaison office, based in the IDF Northern Command, is fully operational. The Office of Political Affairs, comprising also civil affairs and public information, is being augmented within the Force headquarters and will staff the liaison offices and also deploy at the sector level. The Strategic Military Cell for UNIFIL has been established at United Nations Headquarters and is operational.

The administrative and logistics component is being significantly reinforced in order to provide adequate and sufficient support to the Force. Troop-contributing countries were requested to deploy on a self-sufficiency basis for periods of from 15 to 60 days. Significant resources will continue to be required in the areas of engineering, transport and movement control, communications, supply and medical and administrative support.

Financial aspects

By its resolution 60/278 of 30 June 2006, the General Assembly appropriated to the Special Account for UNIFIL the amount of $93.5 million gross, equivalent to $7.8 million per month, for the maintenance of the Force for the period from 1 July 2006 to 30 June 2007. Pursuant to Security Council resolution 1701 (2006), concurrence was granted by the Advisory Committee on Administrative and Budgetary Questions to enter into commitments not to exceed $50 million to meet the most immediate and essential requirements for the expansion of UNIFIL following the recent hostilities in July and August 2006. In addition, the Advisory Committee has been informed that the UNIFIL appropriation for the period from 1 July 2006 to 30 June 2007 as approved by the Assembly in its resolution 60/278, will be used flexibly to meet the requirements of the expanded UNIFIL.

Pending submission of the detailed budget for the expansion of UNIFIL for the period from 1 July 2006 to 30 June 2007, a request for commitment authority will be submitted to the General Assembly for its consideration during the regular part of its sixty-first session. The detailed budget for that period for the expanded UNIFIL will be submitted for consideration by the Assembly during its first resumed session, in March 2007.

IV. Other issues

Captured soldiers and prisoners

I continue to make the unconditional release of the captured Israeli soldiers and the issue of the Lebanese prisoners detained in Israel a top priority. The facilitator appointed by me specifically to address these vital issues is currently engaged in an intensive effort with all parties to reach a resolution.

I underline my firm expectation that the necessary degree of respect for the provisions of resolution 1701 (2006) and compassion for the fate of the victims will prevail. I consider it a basic moral obligation for at least humanitarian gestures to be made with the shortest delay possible.

Landmines and cluster bombs

Since my last report, the full scope of contamination from unexploded cluster munitions has come to light. As at 20 November, the National Demining Office, the LAF and the United Nations Mine Action Coordination Centre South Lebanon have recorded 822 cluster bomb strike sites, an 80 per cent increase since I last reported. Civilian casualties have increased to 152 as at 24 November. Of those 152 civilian victims, 17 were killed and 135 injured. The joint efforts of the teams working under the Mine Action Coordination Centre, the LAF engineering units and the UNIFIL troops have resulted to date in the clearance of more than 60,000 cluster bomblets.

Israel has yet to provide UNIFIL with the detailed firing data on its use of cluster munitions that I referred to in my previous report. The provision of this data, which would be in keeping with the spirit of Protocol V of the Convention on Prohibitions or Restrictions on the Use of Certain Conventional Weapons Which May Be Deemed to Be Excessively Injurious or to Have Indiscriminate Effects, which came into force recently, would significantly assist operators on the ground to mitigate the threat to innocent civilians. I reiterate my expectation for the provision of these data.

I would note that Israel confirmed in a letter dated 14 November 2006 from its Chargé d'Affaires that it had handed over to the United Nations all pre-2000 minefield records available for southern Lebanon and the area north of the Litani River.

However, I regret to inform you that four deminers working for the United Nations mine clearance programme in south Lebanon have been injured over the past few days, after they stepped on Israeli-manufactured anti-personnel mines near the village of Deir Mimas. As this area was considered safe prior to the conflict, there is the possibility that new anti-personnel landmines were laid during the recent conflict. While investigations on those incidents are still ongoing, I want to reiterate that the United Nations condemns the use of all anti-personnel mines and calls upon any party that laid such mines during the recent conflict to provide information as to where they have been laid to prevent similar tragic incidents occurring in the future.

Delineation of borders

Further to the Council's request to me in paragraph 10 of its resolution 1701 (2006) to develop proposals for delineation of the international borders of Lebanon, especially in those areas where the border was disputed or uncertain, including by dealing with the Shab'a Farms area, I have appointed a senior cartographer to assume the lead on reviewing relevant material and developing an accurate territorial definition of the Shab'a Farms area. The cartographer is in the process of conducting such an exercise for the purpose of any further diplomatic activity that could be carried out by the United Nations as regards this issue. I am heartened to note that both Lebanon and Israel have indicated their readiness to cooperate in this exercise.

A permanent solution of this issue remains contingent upon the delineation of the border between Lebanon and the Syrian Arab Republic, in fulfilment of resolutions 1559 (2004), 1680 (2006) and 1701 (2006). At the same time, and in view of the repeated Syrian statements indicating that the Shab'a Farms area is Lebanese, I continue to take careful note of the alternative path suggested by the Government of Lebanon in its seven-point plan, namely, placing the Shab'a Farms under United Nations jurisdiction until permanent border delineation and Lebanese sovereignty over them is settled. The United Nations looks forward to reporting further on this matter in early 2007.

I should be grateful if you would bring this information to the attention of the members of the Security Council.

(*Signed*) Kofi A. **Annan**

Annex
United Nations Interim Force in Lebanon: countries providing military ground and naval contingents, as at 28 November 2006

Country	*Ground*	*Naval*	***Total***
Belgium	368	—	**368**
Bulgaria	—	130	**130**
China	190	—	**190**
Denmark	—	80	**80**
Finland	203	—	**203**
France	1 608	—	**1 608**
Germany	—	1 113	**1 113**
Ghana	661	—	**661**
Greece	—	225	**225**
India	670	—	**670**
Indonesia	360	—	**360**
Ireland	163	—	**163**
Italy	2 068	—	**2 068**
Luxembourg	2	—	**2**
Nepal	226	—	**226**
Norway	—	134	**134**
Poland	321	—	**321**
Portugal	143	—	**143**
Spain	1 290	—	**1 290**
Sweden	—	41	**41**
Turkey	262	232	**494**
Total	**8 535**	**1 955**	**10 490**

5. Report of the Secretary-General on the United Nations Disengagement Observer Force (for the period from 10 June 2006 to 1 December 2006), 4 December 2006 (S/2006/938)

I. Introduction

1. The present report gives an account of the activities of the United Nations Disengagement Observer Force (UNDOF) during the past six months pursuant to the mandate contained in Security Council resolution 350 (1974) and extended in subsequent resolutions, most recently resolution 1685 (2006) of 13 June 2006.

II. Situation in the area and activities of the Force

2. During the period under review the ceasefire in the Israel-Syria sector was maintained and the UNDOF area of operation remained generally quiet except in the Shab'a Farms (area 6), which experienced activity originating from the area of operation of the United Nations Interim Force in Lebanon (UNIFIL), described in my reports on UNIFIL. In particular, between 12 July and 14 August 2006, rockets originating from the UNIFIL area of operation hit close to UNDOF installations, destroying one United Nations unmanned watchtower. Also, unidentified elements operating from the UNDOF area of separation detonated an explosive along the A-Line and destroyed a small portion of the technical fence.

3. UNDOF supervised its area of separation by means of fixed positions and patrols to ensure that military forces of either party were excluded from it. The Force also carried out fortnightly inspections of equipment and force levels in the areas of limitation. Liaison officers from the party concerned accompanied the inspection teams. As in the past, both sides denied inspection teams access to some of their positions and imposed restrictions on the Force's freedom of movement. From 12 July to 14 August 2006, the Force temporarily restricted its patrolling and inspection activities in areas 4, 5 and 6, adjacent to the UNIFIL area of operation. Israeli national customs officials continued to operate at the Israel Defense Forces (IDF) post at the UNDOF crossing gate between the Israeli-occupied Golan and the Syrian Arab Republic.

4. The Force continued to assist the International Committee of the Red Cross with the passage of persons through the area of separation. During the past six months, UNDOF assisted in the crossing of 727 students, 1,009 pilgrims and 6 civilians, provided protection at one wedding and facilitated the passage of a body for burial. In addition, the Force assisted in the handover from the IDF to the Syrian authorities of three Syrian civilians who had crossed into the Israeli-occupied Golan.

5. In the area of operation, especially in the area of separation, mines continued to pose a threat to UNDOF personnel and local inhabitants. Owing to the age of the mines and their deteriorating explosives, this threat has increased. UNDOF continued to carry out operational mine clearance. UNDOF remained available to support the United Nations Children's Fund in activities to promote mine awareness among the civilian population.

6. The Force Commander and his staff maintained close contact with the military authorities of Israel and the Syrian Arab Republic. Both sides generally cooperated with the Force in the execution of its tasks.

7. As at 15 November 2006, UNDOF comprised 1,025 troops, from Austria (372), Canada (2), India (190), Japan (30), Nepal (2), Poland (334) and Slovakia (95), respectively. A total of 15 personnel were employed by Japan as a national support element. In addition, 83 military observers from the United Nations Truce Supervision Organization (UNTSO) assisted the Force in carrying out its tasks. A map showing the deployment of the Force is attached to the present report.

III. Financial aspects

8. By its resolution 60/277 of 30 June 2006, the General Assembly appropriated the amount of $39.9 million gross, equivalent to $3.3 million gross per month, for the maintenance of the Force for the period from 1 July 2006 to 30 June 2007. Should the Council decide to extend the mandate of the Force beyond 31 December 2006, as recommended in paragraph 13 below, the cost of maintaining the Force will be limited to the amounts approved by the Assembly.

9. As at 30 September 2006, unpaid assessed contributions to the UNDOF special account for the period from the inception of the Force to 30 September 2006 amounted to $30.2 million. Total outstanding assessed contributions for all peacekeeping operations as at the same date amounted to $2,080.2 million. As at 31 October 2006, amounts owed to troop contributors totalled $2.4 million. Reimbursement of troop- and contingent-owned equipment costs have been made for the period up to 31 August and 31 March 2006, respectively, in accordance with the quarterly payment schedule.

IV. Implementation of Security Council resolution 338 (1973)

10. The Security Council, when deciding in its resolution 1685 (2006) to renew the mandate of UNDOF for a further period of six months, until 31 December 2006, also called upon the parties concerned to implement immediately its resolution 338 (1973), and requested the Secretary-General to submit, at the end of the period, a report on developments in the situation and the measures taken to implement that resolution. The search for a peaceful settlement in the Middle East, and in particular the efforts undertaken at various levels to implement resolution 338 (1973), was dealt with in the report of the Secretary-General on the situation in the Middle East (A/61/298) submitted pursuant to General Assembly resolutions 60/40 and 60/41.

V. Observations

11. The situation in the Israel-Syria sector has remained generally quiet. UNDOF, which was established in May 1974 to supervise the ceasefire called for by the Security Council and the agreement on disengagement between Syrian and Israeli forces of 31 May 1974, has continued to perform its function effectively, with the cooperation of the parties.

12. Nevertheless, the situation in the Middle East is tense and is likely to remain so, unless and until a comprehensive settlement covering all aspects of the Middle East problem can be reached. I hope that determined efforts will be made by all concerned to tackle the problem in all its aspects, with a view to arriving at a just and durable peace settlement, as called for by the Security Council in its resolution 338 (1973).

13. Under the prevailing circumstances, I consider the continued presence of UNDOF in the area to be essential. I therefore recommend that the Security Council extend the

mandate of the Force for a further period of six months, until 30 June 2007. The Government of the Syrian Arab Republic has given its assent to the proposed extension. The Government of Israel has also expressed its agreement.

14. In making this recommendation, I must draw attention to the shortfall in the funding of the Force. At present, unpaid assessments amount to some $30.2 million. The sum represents money owed to the Member States that contribute the troops who make up the Force. I appeal to all Member States to pay their assessments promptly and in full and to clear all remaining arrears.

15. In conclusion, I wish to pay tribute to Lieutenant General Bala Nanda Sharma and to the men and women serving with UNDOF and UNTSO. They have performed with efficiency and devotion to duty the important tasks assigned to them by the Security Council. I take this opportunity to express my appreciation to the Governments contributing troops to UNDOF and to those which provide the UNTSO military observers assigned to the Force.

6. Report of the Secretary-General on the Middle East, 11 December 2006 (S/2006/956)

Introduction

1. As my term as Secretary-General nears its end, I would like to review the situation in the Middle East. Rather than summarize all the developments of the past ten years, I wish to focus on the attempts of the international community and the parties to reach a negotiated political solution to the enduring and painful conflicts that have bedevilled the region.

2. Today, the Middle East faces grim prospects, and is more complex, fragile and dangerous than it has been for many years. The various unresolved but increasingly interconnected conflicts in the region both feed and feed off a growing sense of estrangement between peoples of different faiths, with consequences throughout the world. Overall, the instability that prevails in the Middle East is the greatest regional challenge to international peace and security, and needs to be addressed far more thoroughly than it has been to date.

3. The failure to achieve a just and comprehensive solution to the long-festering Arab-Israeli conflict remains the major underlying source of frustration and instability in the region. Other, more recent, conflicts have been shaped by this failure, although they have inevitably taken on a dynamic of their own. I have addressed a number of these conflicts in other reports. However, I am convinced that the search for stability in Iraq, Lebanon and elsewhere will be greatly served by a concerted effort to address the legitimate aspirations of Israelis, Palestinians, Syrians and Lebanese to achieve two independent and secure States of Israel and Palestine; an end to the occupation of Arab land both in the Occupied Palestinian Territory and the Golan Heights; and the comprehensive, just and lasting peace in the Middle East referred to in Security Council resolution 1701 (2006) and many other resolutions. A regional approach is needed to resolve the various crises and conflicts in the Middle East today, not least because progress in each arena is to a large extent dependent on progress in others.

The post-Oslo era

4. When I began my tenure as Secretary-General on 1 January 1997, Israelis and Palestinians were engaged in the implementation of the Oslo Accords of 1993, which had led to the establishment of the Palestinian Authority in 1994. This period witnessed continuing negotiations, gradual Israeli withdrawal from some parts of the West Bank and Gaza Strip and the growth of the Palestinian Authority. Under the terms of the Oslo Accords, the international community supported a process that involved step-by-step actions to build confidence and establish a basis from which to move towards resolution of all final status issues (Jerusalem, refugees, settlements, security arrangements, borders and relations and cooperation with other neighbours).

5. The period immediately following 1993 was one of hope and new beginnings. However, two developments illustrated the weakness of the political will of both parties, and the low level of trust between them. On the Israeli side, settlements continued to be expanded and Israeli control over land, borders and Palestinian movement was consolidated, with frequent and widespread closures, and some targeted killings. On the Palestinian side, there

was early evidence that the goal of building strong and transparent institutions would not be achieved easily. There was also the inability to tackle directly and firmly the phenomenon of armed resistance, which increasingly took the form of acts of terrorism. In combination, these phenomena weakened the basic tenet of a settlement in the Middle East: ending the occupation that began in 1967 on the basis of the principle of "land for peace" in accordance with Security Council resolution 242 (1967). The assassination in 1995 of Prime Minister Yitzhak Rabin, who so clearly recognized that to attain peace it is necessary to negotiate not with one's friends but with one's enemies, was a tragic setback for the peace process.

6. For understandable reasons, the framers of the Oslo Accords felt that it was impossible to define end goals that would have come close to satisfying the concerns of both peoples at that time, and a gradualist approach was thought to be necessary. However, with the benefit of hindsight, certain aspects of the Oslo Accords have been identified as problematic. Some people believed that the actual implementation of the steps to be taken by the parties was supposed to be sequential rather than parallel—meaning that a failure of one party or spoiler could, and often did, derail the process. Importantly, there was no monitoring mechanism involved, either for settlement expansion or for violence. In addition, the Oslo Accords lacked a clearly defined end goal, and did not spell out where the parties would be at the end of the process. In consequence, the deeply divisive issues of final status were left undefined, and, as was feared by both parties, became hostages to the creation of facts on the ground.

7. There were some successes, including the Hebron Protocol and the Wye River agreement. However, the extent of the erosion of the Oslo peace process was made painfully clear with the failure of the Camp David peace talks and the outbreak of the second intifada in September 2000 following the contentious visit of Ariel Sharon to the Al-Haram al-Sharif/Temple Mount in East Jerusalem. The Palestinian Authority failed to rein in violence against Israeli civilians, or to confront militant groups. Moreover, despite major achievements in service provision, the Authority had also failed to institute reform and a transparent and accountable system of governance, and was weakened within by widespread allegations of corruption. For its part, Israel resorted to heavy force, increased extrajudicial killings, reoccupation of areas under Palestinian self-rule, and the confinement of the Palestinian President to his compound for two years. Israeli settlement activity continued, while the concepts of unilateralism and separation emerged and became popular. Israel began the construction of the barrier inside the West Bank that departed significantly from the 1967 line and was declared illegal by an advisory opinion of the International Court of Justice. The Mitchell report of 2001 cited the underlying causes of the conflict to be the divergent expectations created by the Oslo process and the failure of both parties to recognize the grievances of the other, specifically the humiliation and suffering of Palestinians caused by continued occupation, and the fear felt by Israelis at continued violence and terrorism.

The Quartet and the road map process

8. Concerned by these stark trends, I invited representatives of the European Union, the Russian Federation and the United States of America for a discussion. Our consultation laid the ground for the establishment of the Quartet. On 10 April 2002, the Government of Spain, representing the rotating Presidency of the European Union, High Representative

for the Common Security and Foreign Policy Javier Solana, Secretary of State Colin Powell, Foreign Minister Igor Ivanov and myself began our discussions of what later became "A performance-based road map to a permanent two-State solution to the Israeli-Palestinian conflict" (S/2003/529, annex), or in short, the road map.

9. The framework for the road map was based on relevant Security Council resolutions, and the process was given impetus by two important developments. First, in March 2002, the Security Council explicitly endorsed the two-State solution in its resolution 1397 (2002). Secondly, the Council of the League of Arab States adopted the Arab Peace Initiative, the initiative of then Saudi Crown Prince Abdallah, in Beirut the same month. In it, the members of the League affirmed that achieving a just and comprehensive peace was their strategic choice and goal, asked for a complete Israeli withdrawal to the 1967 borders and a "just solution" to the refugee problem, and called for the establishment of an independent Palestinian State with East Jerusalem as its capital. All of this was to be in exchange for full recognition of Israel. Two months later, on 24 June, the commitment of the international community to a two-State solution was further consolidated when President Bush stated his vision for "two States, living side by side in peace and security", and went on to say that "this means that the Israeli occupation that began in 1967 will be ended through a settlement negotiated between the parties, based on United Nations resolutions 242 (1967) and 338 (1973), with Israeli withdrawal to secure and recognized borders". Since then, these elements, together with the road map, have defined our common vision for an end to the Israeli-Palestinian conflict.

10. Formally presented to the parties on 30 April 2003, the road map outlined a three-phase plan aimed at achieving a final and comprehensive settlement of the Israeli-Palestinian conflict on the basis of a goal-driven and performance-based approach. The Quartet members shared a broad vision of the outcome of the peace process, and the group's combination of legitimacy, political strength and financial power was intended to provide a robust push for implementation of steps by the parties to achieve this shared goal. In addition to Security Council resolutions, the Quartet drew inspiration from the Arab Peace Initiative.

11. The road map was intended to re-energize the peace process by addressing the perceived weaknesses of Oslo while retaining its broad political outline. It defined the endgame as two States and the end of occupation (though without taking a clear stance on the border of the future Palestinian State); instituted a strict and clearly delineated parallelism; added a precise time frame for each phase of the process; and specified that a monitoring mechanism would be established to provide a means of enforcement. The Palestinian side endorsed the road map; the Israeli endorsement came with important reservations.

12. In phase I of the road map, both parties were asked to commit to and implement certain basic steps, or obligations: an end to terror and incitement; reform of Palestinian Authority institutions and security forces; a freeze on all settlement activity and the dismantlement of settlement outposts; and ceasing all actions that undermined trust. Phase II (June-December 2003) was to be a transition phase focused on Palestinian institution building, and called for the convening of a first international conference to launch a process leading to the creation of an independent Palestinian State with provisional borders and a comprehensive regional peace process. In phase III (2004-2005), a second international conference would endorse the agreement on an independent Palestinian State with provisional borders and begin a process leading to a settlement of final status issues. The phases would be

completed when the parties reached a final and comprehensive permanent status agreement and Arab States established full normal relations with Israel.

13. Phase I has regrettably yet to be completed, and indeed, developments over the past year have largely eroded previous gains. In order to again move forward, we need to examine honestly the sources of past and current failure, for which both parties and the international community must share responsibility.

14. Probably the greatest Palestinian shortcoming was not to do more to consolidate internal security and directly challenge the use of terrorism against Israeli civilians. President Arafat did not use his power and legitimacy to undertake serious reform of the security sector. More recently, following the Israeli withdrawal from the Gaza Strip, the Palestinian Authority could have used that opportunity to assert its control over militant groups then outside the Palestine Liberation Organization and the Authority. The failure to confront such groups, even within the framework of the negotiated ceasefire, contributed to the situation we face now in which militant groups persistently fire rockets from Gaza into Israel. Since the election of Hamas, moreover, the Palestinian Authority security forces have been fractured along political lines, and have been unable either to contain factional violence or to stop attacks against Israelis.

15. It is important to note that the Palestinian Authority's unwillingness or inability to undertake comprehensive institutional reform, and the public perception of pervasive corruption, was a major reason why the leadership lacked the necessary support for security reform, and indeed, one factor in the faltering of both the Oslo and road map processes and the electoral defeat of Fatah earlier this year. Many of the material benefits that accrued from the peace process reached only the elites and those close to political decision-makers, not the broad populace. Yet without broad socio-economic progress, there cannot be sustained political progress. Another factor was the Palestinian public's lack of trust in the political process with Israel, and the erosion in their belief that they would ever be allowed an independent and viable State.

16. During its first phase, the road map also called on Arab States to cut off all forms of support for groups engaging in terrorism. Many Arab countries, especially Egypt and Jordan, have engaged heavily in efforts to build up the Palestinian Authority's security capacity. However, the security weaknesses of the Authority have been compounded by the interventions of some regional parties, and the increasingly close relationship that some militant Palestinian groups appear to have with the Syrian Arab Republic and the Islamic Republic of Iran, in particular.

17. Israel's military actions in the West Bank and Gaza have frequently involved excessive or disproportionate use of force, causing heavy civilian casualties while also damaging Palestinian infrastructure and institutions. While Israel has a right to defend itself against terrorism and other forms of violence, which do so much damage to prospects for peace, Israel's methods of doing so have also done their share of damage to those prospects.

18. However, Israel's central failure lay in not halting its settlement enterprise, even though this is a clear phase I obligation under the road map. The continuation and even consolidation of Israeli settlements and related infrastructure on occupied land are the main reasons for the mistrust and frustration felt by ordinary Palestinians, which often find their outlet in violence of one form or another.

19. In the period that I have served as Secretary-General, the number of Israeli settlers living in the West Bank (excluding East Jerusalem) has grown from 140,000 to 240,000. The settler population of East Jerusalem grew during this period from approximately 160,000 to 190,000. The area formally controlled by the settlements, according to Israeli law, now encompasses some 40 per cent of the West Bank (excluding East Jerusalem). In a welcome development, the Government of Israel withdrew all settlements from the Gaza Strip and four settlements in the West Bank in August 2005. However, during the year following this disengagement, West Bank settlements grew by 3,000 more people than had moved out of Gaza. Indeed, according to official Israeli figures, more than 1,000 settlers a month took up residence in the Occupied Palestinian Territory during 2005, a rate that appears to be continuing. In total, in the decade and a half after the Oslo Accords, Israel more than doubled its physical presence in the West Bank through settlements—a policy that was implemented under Labour, Likud and Kadima Governments. This remains the single biggest impediment to realizing a viable Palestinian State with territorial contiguity. Just as Israelis are dismayed that terrorism continued after Oslo and the Israeli disengagement from the Gaza Strip, Palestinians are dismayed when they see prospects for a viable Palestinian State disappearing and the entrenchment of the occupation.

20. The use of violence on both sides and the continuation of settlement activity have been the key factors in the failure to move beyond phase I of the road map. Equally critical, however, has been the unwillingness of the Quartet to use its authority to push both parties forward. We must admit our own weaknesses, and we have been too hesitant in emphasizing those very elements that most distinguished the road map from the Oslo process—parallelism, monitoring and clear end goals. It is no surprise that today we find ourselves once again deadlocked.

21. In the past year, a further problematic factor was added. In September 2005 the Quartet encouraged the Palestinian Authority to take its own decision regarding participation in the forthcoming legislative elections. But after the victory of Hamas in those elections, which were held in January 2006, the members of the Quartet were faced with a dilemma. Hamas, having agreed to join that political process, was at best ambivalent about, and at worst rejected, the two-State solution. In the light of the new Government's failure to commit to the Quartet principles of 30 January, donors' legal obligations and political priorities led to a significant shift in funding to Palestinians during the past year: although funding has actually increased, the channels of funding have shifted away from the Palestinian Authority. This shift, combined with Israel's refusal to hand over value added tax and customs revenues it collects on behalf of the Palestinian Authority (an obligation under agreements reached in the Oslo framework), has largely caused the immense financial difficulties facing the Authority and contributed to the decline of Palestinian institutions.

22. The Hamas-led Palestinian government has still not reacted constructively to the call of the international community to review its stance and accept the basic principles of the peace process. Although the President of the Palestinian Authority and the Palestine Liberation Organization remain committed to the principles of the peace process, and the Palestinian Authority government claims that it does not object to President Abbas negotiating with Israel (provided the outcome is submitted to the approval of a reformed Palestine Liberation Organization, the Palestinian Legislative Council or a referendum), Israel believes that his scope to negotiate a final status agreement is limited by the disparate

visions of the elected government and the Palestinian Legislative Council, on the one hand, and the Palestinian Authority President and the Palestine Liberation Organization, on the other, concerning such an agreement. The continued equivocation of the Hamas-led government ill serves the aspirations of the Palestinian people. At the same time, Hamas is able to tap into a widely felt Palestinian sentiment that the Palestine Liberation Organization and the previous Palestinian Authority obtained too few achievements as a result of their negotiations with Israel. Dialogue between, and compromises on the part of, both main Palestinian parties are clearly in the interests of the Palestinian people as a whole.

The current situation

23. At the time of writing, efforts to form a Palestinian national unity government appear to have stalled. However, a precarious and imperfect ceasefire is in place in Gaza, and tentative feelers have been put out regarding the possibility of resumed Israeli-Palestinian dialogue, as well as broader regional dialogue. The ceasefire follows a period of political deadlock and spiralling violence that has had serious consequences for civilians on both sides, with Palestinian militants firing rockets from Gaza into Israel, and massive Israeli military operations and targeted killings that have led to several hundred Palestinian deaths this year, at a rate that has increased significantly since June 2006. Negotiations under Egyptian auspices are continuing for the release of the Israeli soldier captured at that time. Prime Minister Olmert recently announced that he would consider a prisoner exchange of 1,400 Palestinian prisoners, including lawmakers and officials seized by Israel after Corporal Gilad Shalit's capture. There are an estimated 9,000 Palestinians currently in detention in Israel, a matter of burning concern for the Palestinian population. The release of some of them and also the Israeli soldier would be a very positive development.

24. I have consistently condemned the firing of rockets and suicide bombings by Palestinians, and fully acknowledge Israel's right to self-defence. I do not condone terrorism in any form and condemn it unequivocally. But I stress with equal conviction that Israel's right to self-defence must be carried out in accordance with international law. The repeated phenomenon of large numbers of civilian casualties from Israeli military operations is not acceptable. Israel's excessive use of force exacerbates existing resentments and fuels those who advocate hatred, be they in the region or elsewhere.

25. Political deadlock and the security situation have combined to undermine the efforts undertaken by James Wolfensohn as the Quartet's Special Envoy. A year ago, on 15 November 2005, the Agreement on Movement and Access was concluded. Implementation of this agreement, intended to promote peaceful economic development and improve the situation in the Gaza Strip, has been limited, with Israel citing security concerns: despite the stationing of European Union observers, the Rafah crossing between Gaza and Egypt has been open for only 58 per cent of scheduled opening hours over the past year and for only 9 per cent since June. This year, Palestinians have been allowed to export on average only 14 truckloads of produce per day, a tiny fraction of minimum export levels needed to prevent further decline of the Palestinian economy and suffering of the population. No Palestinian worker has been allowed to cross at Erez to access jobs in Israel since March 2006, and no progress has been reported on bus or truck convoys between Gaza and the West Bank. Similarly, there has been no progress reported on plans to build the Gaza seaport and airport. One year after signing the agreement, the Government of Israel has still not presented its plan to reduce internal closure measures inside the West Bank. In fact, the

total number of obstacles has increased from 400 a year ago to 542 today, stifling still further Palestinians' efforts to lead normal daily lives.

26. Given the complexity of the situation, continuing high levels of tension and the steep decline in Palestinian living standards since 2000, the United Nations presence on the ground continues to be of key importance. United Nations peacekeeping operations in the region—the United Nations Truce Supervision Organization, the United Nations Disengagement Observer Force and the United Nations Interim Force in Lebanon (UNIFIL)—play a crucial role in helping to maintain regional security. The United Nations provides considerable assistance to meet the basic needs of Palestinians throughout the region.

27. The United Nations Relief and Works Agency for Palestine Refugees in the Near East (UNRWA) is a major asset through which the international community supports some 4.3 million Palestine refugees in the region. For 56 years, it has delivered vital services to them, helping to raise their educational and health status to among the highest levels in the region. Investment by UNRWA in the skills and self-reliance of the refugees has enabled many to pursue productive careers in their communities and host countries, in the Arab Gulf and in the West. The Agency serves as a vital antidote to the poverty and deprivation which come with conflict and occupation. I note with concern that the Agency continues to be seriously underfunded, and that its budget shortfall this year of over $100 million is the greatest ever.

28. The Office of the United Nations Special Coordinator for the Middle East Peace Process has, since 1994, been present on the ground to enhance the involvement of the United Nations system during the transition process and to strengthen inter-agency cooperation. In 1999, with the permission of the General Assembly and informing the Council, I designated the Special Coordinator as my Personal Representative to the Palestine Liberation Organization and the Palestinian Authority, and also for discussions with the parties and the international community in all matters related to the peace process. In 2006, I further strengthened the Office of the Special Coordinator by designating a Deputy Special Coordinator who acts as Humanitarian and Resident Coordinator to consolidate United Nations leadership on aid policy and common operational issues. This appointment also builds on the work of the Office for the Coordination of Humanitarian Affairs since 2003, which has considerably sharpened our picture of the humanitarian problems caused by restrictions on movement and access, the barrier and settlement activity.

29. I am proud of the work that my United Nations colleagues perform in assisting Palestinians and working with all parties towards a lasting peace. It is with some regret that I note that the United Nations role as aid provider has become more important to Palestinians during the past year, as living conditions have deteriorated sharply and parts of the Palestinian Authority have almost ceased to function. The importance of using my good offices in helping to resolve crises and propose ways forward has also been very clear to me throughout my term as Secretary-General, not least during the Lebanon crisis this summer.

Lebanon

30. My tenure as Secretary-General underlined the special role that the United Nations has developed in Lebanon, a role that has grown even more intense, especially over the past two years. Our engagement signals the Organization's enduring commitment to Lebanon's stability, unity, sovereignty, territorial integrity and political independence. In May 2000,

Israel withdrew its last troops from southern Lebanon after more than 20 years of occupation and in fulfilment of its obligations under resolution 425 (1978). With the help of my good offices and intense shuttle diplomacy, a line of withdrawal known as the Blue Line was delineated, which both Israel and Lebanon accepted and committed themselves to respecting (though Lebanon expressed its reservations regarding the conformity of the Line in the area known as the Shab'a farmlands). The Security Council endorsed the position I took in my report of 22 May 2000 (S/2000/459), which set out the demarcation line to confirm the Israeli withdrawal, and stated that "the adoption of this line for the practical purpose of confirming the Israeli withdrawal from Lebanon in compliance with resolution 425 (1978) is without prejudice to any internationally recognized border agreement that Lebanon and the Syrian Arab Republic may wish to conclude in the future". The Security Council has since repeatedly endorsed the Blue Line and called on both parties to respect it.

31. The period just after the Israeli withdrawal was one of hope for Lebanon with the promise of reconstruction in the south. This followed the rebuilding of the capital, Beirut, renewed investment in the country and the return of a significant portion of the Lebanese diaspora. However, between October 2000 and the beginning of the past summer's full-scale and devastating conflict between Hizbollah and Israel, the Blue Line witnessed sporadic, limited exchanges of fire in the Shab'a farmlands area and elsewhere, periods of tense calm but also of intense conflict and loss of life on both sides. Of particular concern was the capture and killing by Hizbollah of three Israeli soldiers, whose bodies were not returned until January 2003, in the Shab'a farmlands area in October 2000 and the capture, in July 2006, of two soldiers who unfortunately remain in captivity and whose release is essential.

32. This latter event precipitated a tragic conflict that took too long to stop. Israel's ground invasion into southern Lebanon and the bombardment of large parts of the country killed an estimated 1,200 Lebanese and injured over 4,000, killed four United Nations military observers, created nearly a million internally displaced people and destroyed a large part of the country's infrastructure. Over 140 Israelis, 43 of them civilians, were killed and over 100 injured, many by Hizbollah attacks against population centres in northern Israel, using rockets secured by or provided to the movement without the approval of the Government of Lebanon. Further sources of tension include reports of weapons supplies to Hizbollah, as well as continued Israeli overflights in violation of Lebanon's sovereignty and territorial integrity, and in contradiction of resolutions 1559 (2004) and 1701 (2006). The latter resolution, painstakingly negotiated and passed a full month after the hostilities began, was the framework for United Nations efforts to secure a cessation of hostilities, to be underpinned by a stronger UNIFIL. This expanded UNIFIL, however, was intended to buy time, not substitute, for progress on the political track both within Lebanon and also between Lebanon and its neighbours.

33. The past two tumultuous years in Lebanon's history have illustrated the vulnerabilities of the Lebanese State to both external influences and internal political divisions, and their potential to ignite conflicts old and new. Throughout this period, the involvement of the United Nations has been considerable. Within the domestic context, the extension of President Lahoud's mandate signalled for many in Lebanon the beginning of a political division between those who openly opposed the presence and role of the Syrian Arab Republic in Lebanon and those who were perceived as having a pro-Syrian approach. The Security Council's adoption of resolution 1559 (2004) was in keeping with its commitment

to support Lebanon's sovereignty and territorial integrity, which led, five years after the Israeli withdrawal, to the Syrian withdrawal in the spring of 2005 from Lebanon. The adoption of the resolution was followed by the assassination in Beirut of former Prime Minister Rafik Hariri and 22 others in February 2005. The Security Council has followed up on developments since, including the subsequent assassinations and assassination attempts against political figures and key figures in the Lebanese media. It requested the United Nations to set up the International Independent Investigation Commission and most recently to agree with the Lebanese authorities on the statutes for a special tribunal for Lebanon to try the perpetrators of these crimes.

34. I have reported in my letter of 1 December 2006 (S/2006/933) on the most recent progress that has been made and the outstanding challenges related to the implementation of Security Council resolution 1701 (2006). I would note here only the historic achievement of the deployment of the Lebanese army in the area south of the Litani River and along the Blue Line and the crucial role that an expanded UNIFIL is now playing in helping the Lebanese army to ensure that the area is "free of armed personnel, assets and weapons other than those of the Government of Lebanon and those of UNIFIL". I would also note the considerable achievement of the establishment of the UNIFIL Maritime Task Force to assist the Lebanese navy in securing its territorial waters. However, I fully recognize the limitations of peacekeeping activities and stress the importance of ensuring the right political context in which those activities can be most effective. The period following the Israeli withdrawal from southern Lebanon till the outbreak of hostilities in the summer of 2006 illustrates the limits to the monitoring and peacekeeping capabilities of UNIFIL, especially when operating in a difficult political environment and with limited mandates and resources. Hizbollah's arms build-up during this period was a continuing cause for concern, as are reports that these efforts may have continued.

35. I am deeply concerned at the present time about prospects for the stability and independence of Lebanon. The serious political crisis which the country is now experiencing illustrates the need for continued efforts to assist the country. Lebanon remains hostage to its own difficult history. Since the end of the civil war and the signing of the Taif Accords in 1989, Lebanon has remained mired in an incomplete political transformation that has not seen further progress away from the instinct for confessionalism. The Lebanese themselves, especially now, bear much of the responsibility for ensuring the country does not slide deeper into tension and providing a way forward based on a degree of national consensus on key issues. In this regard, I am disappointed that the various rounds of high-level talks, which started with the National Dialogue in February 2006, have not led to agreement among Lebanon's leaders. I also note that despite the Taif Accords and the agreement achieved in the Dialogue regarding the question of Palestinian weapons outside the camps and living standards, there has been little progress achieved in implementing these decisions to date. Furthermore, I continue to advocate a mechanism to address the question of disarmament of Hizbollah's weapons, whether by resuming the National Dialogue or within the existing institutions of the State. Serious progress on these issues in accordance with resolution 1701 (2006) is one of the principles for a permanent ceasefire and a long-term solution.

36. Outside parties too, especially those in the region, have a responsibility to play a positive role in ensuring Lebanon's stability, independence, sovereignty and territorial integrity.

The Syrian Arab Republic and the Islamic Republic of Iran in particular have much influence on Lebanese parties, which I expect them to exert in a constructive way. The Syrian Arab Republic also has a role to play in enabling Lebanon's full assertion of its sovereignty by agreeing to delineate the joint border between the two countries and by meeting its verbal commitment to the establishment of formal diplomatic relations with Lebanon.

37. Given its history, and perhaps also because of its small size and geography, Lebanon has been inextricably bound with more powerful forces, whether immediate neighbours or colonial or regional powers. Its mosaic of cultures and confessional groups has been both a strength, giving it unique attributes within the region, and a weakness, allowing for these to be manipulated into lines of conflict. I would warn that as the region has affected Lebanon, so instability within Lebanon, and a return to the dark days of the 1970s and 1980s, can have a further destabilizing affect on the region as a whole.

Golan Heights

38. During my tenure, there was no movement towards handover of the Israeli-occupied Golan Heights to the Syrian Arab Republic in return for peace between the Syrian Arab Republic and Israel. I was disappointed that the last serious attempt by the United States to negotiate a solution to this long-standing issue ended in failure in 2000.

39. Some 20,000 Israeli settlers live in the Golan Heights, alongside an Arab population of about 18,400. The Golan Heights is fully incorporated into the Israeli legal, administrative and social service delivery systems. The Arab population is generally unable to travel to the Syrian Arab Republic to visit family members and has, over time, experienced increasing limits on land use owing to Israeli zoning restrictions. But the Arab population suffers neither the deep insecurity nor the economic deprivation and restrictions on movement which characterize life in the Occupied Palestinian Territory, and for their part, Israelis have faced little violence emanating from this territory. This must not, however, lead the international community into complacency about the need to resolve this problem—indeed, the failure to do so just because the situation on the ground is calm sends entirely the wrong message.

40. As with the peace treaties between Israel and Egypt in 1979, and Israel and Jordan in 1994, a sustained effort must be made to achieve a negotiated settlement between Israel and the Syrian Arab Republic based on resolutions 242 (1967) and 338 (1973). For as long as the principle of land for peace that underlies those resolutions is not implemented between these two countries, there can be no comprehensive regional peace. Israel and some other countries continue to view the Syrian Arab Republic as a supporter of militant groups in Lebanon and the Occupied Palestinian Territory that seek to carry out attacks against Israel. For its part, the Syrian Arab Republic points to Israeli Government statements which declare the Golan Heights to be an inseparable part of Israel. Israel has recently rejected the notion of resumed negotiations with the Syrian Arab Republic, despite statements of President Assad raising this prospect. It is clear that the parties must think anew about their approach to this vital issue, which is so intrinsically connected to progress on other tracks in the Middle East peace process.

Observations

41. As Secretary-General, I have been conscious of the enormous responsibility that rests on the United Nations to contribute to the resolution of the Arab-Israeli conflict. I have also

been acutely aware of the difficulties associated with doing so, some of which stem from the polarization of the membership on the conflict and the consequent range of positions taken by different principal and intergovernmental organs. One side perceives itself as being singled out for unfair criticism; the other regards the Organization as ineffective in ensuring compliance with its resolutions. Accusations of double standards are regularly made in both directions, and each with some justification.

42. In my view, until the Member States match their professions of concern with a concerted effort to empower the United Nations to make a strategic difference, I am convinced that other forums will be sought to ensure effective multilateral engagement on the conflict. The formation of the Quartet and my participation in it embody this conviction.

43. Unfortunately, however, as I leave office, I am concerned that the divisions which have often paralyzed the United Nations itself now also increasingly inhibit the capacity of the Quartet (and its regional partners) to play the beneficial role which it could do were it to act with determination and consistency. We therefore find ourselves at a crossroads, with increasing frustration—both in the region and in the international community at large—at the Quartet's regrettably limited effectiveness, matched by the apparent lack of any alternative mechanism at present. Since it is my conviction that, ultimately, the solution will only be achieved by direct negotiations between the parties, facilitated and sustained by effective multilateral engagement, this is a source of deep concern which I would urge Member States to reflect on. The observations which follow are designed to point the way towards realizing more effective multilateral engagement.

44. The Quartet retains its relevance because of its combination of legitimacy, political strength and economic influence. As for the road map, it is still the reference point around which any effort to re-energize a political effort on the Israeli-Palestinian track should be centred. It remains the only document of recent years accepted—albeit with substantial reservations by Israel—by Palestinian and Israeli leaderships alike, by the Arab States, and by the Security Council. The Prime Minister of Israel has recently reiterated that he sees a return to the road map as a way forward, and the Palestinian President is committed to it. Nevertheless, to be meaningful, its shortcomings will need to be addressed urgently.

45. To restore a sense of faith in the practicability of the road map, it is crucial that its sponsors, the Quartet members, act together to create the conditions for re-energizing the Israeli-Palestinian peace process. The Quartet must also find a way to institutionalize its consultations with the relevant regional partners, building on the Arab Peace Initiative and the constructive spirit in which the 21 September 2006 ministerial meeting of the Security Council was held. The Quartet should also engage the parties directly in its deliberations, as it announced that it would do on 20 September 2006.

46. Under the revitalized stewardship of the Quartet, it should therefore be possible to look again at the road map with a view to restating its basic goals, principles and end destination; identifying priority action items in the security arena and in the economic, humanitarian and institution building realms; addressing the political issues and political negotiations; and updating its timetable. The Quartet should consider the need for greater clarity at the outset regarding the parameters of an end-game deal. It will also need to tackle openly the road map's premise of parallelism and monitoring: it is hard to see the consolidation of progress as we move forward without serious and systematic independent monitoring on the ground.

47. To retain its validity, the Quartet also needs to be open to new ideas and initiatives from within the region and outside it, and from State and non-State actors alike. Equally, it has to match the responsibility entrusted to it to oversee this process with a method of work that is systematic, even-handed and proactive rather than reactive, and ensures common messaging to the parties.

48. There are also a number of issues that I believe should be addressed by the Quartet and the international community. Politically, we need a policy to address the dilemma posed by Hamas as constructively as possible to stem the growing trend towards disintegration of Palestinian society, by renewing support for Palestinian institutions, promoting efforts to achieve unity among Palestinian factions on basic principles of the peace process, and persuading Israel not to pursue any policy which damages institutions or deprives Palestinians of democratically elected and therefore legitimate leaders. We must recognize that the postponement of a settlement has taken a social and political toll, and that countercurrents to the previously widely accepted notion of a two-State solution have grown and acquired greater cogency. Forging an internal Palestinian consensus once again around a two-State solution should be seen as a process rather than an event, one that should be encouraged and nurtured. This could be considerably quickened by a credible effort between the parties and from the international community to re-energize the political process.

49. Similarly, the international community needs to find constructive responses to the challenge posed by democratic choices made by the peoples of the region. Whatever some might think of the actual results, it is undeniable that the legislative elections that brought Hamas to power last January were remarkably transparent, free and fair by the standards of most of the Arab world. Support for the democratic aspirations of the peoples of the region is something the international community must do more to sustain. For their part, victorious parties, even radical ones, need to acknowledge that with power comes responsibilities, including acceptance that the legitimacy and rights of others need to be respected too, and that the previous decisions and agreements reached by the governments to which they have been elected cannot be ignored or put aside without serious consequence.

50. One immediate priority is to work to devise new ways of protecting Palestinian and Israeli civilians, as suggested in the Security Council and mentioned recently by the General Assembly: the monitoring foreseen in the road map can help to ensure far greater accountability. The international community cannot shepherd a process that tolerates the blatant abuse of human rights and international law by all parties. The United Nations High Commissioner for Human Rights, on a recent visit to Israel and the Occupied Palestinian Territory, found that human rights abuses were systematic, chronic and widespread. I agree with her that the rule of the law should not be contingent on peace. I also agree that there is a pressing need for mechanisms for the protection of civilians, and hope that possible mechanisms such as international observers will be further explored, with the strong backing of the Quartet and the Council.

51. I would urge the Quartet and the Council to explore the feasibility of consolidating the current Gaza ceasefire within an international framework. As in Lebanon earlier this year, the parameters of the political framework for a permanent solution are clear, but the political will to advance it is not sufficient. In order to halt the current violence and open a space

for negotiations, a stronger international role is required. Elements for this role could include:

(a) To consolidate the current Gaza ceasefire by working with the parties to define its parameters and rules;

(b) To work to extend the ceasefire to the West Bank;

(c) To promote unconditional and open-ended talks between the Prime Minister of Israel and the President of the Palestinian Authority;

(d) To work with the parties to secure their agreement to the deployment of international observers to monitor the ceasefire;

(e) To establish with the parties a mechanism for the protection of civilians;

(f) To monitor consistently the actions of the parties to implement existing commitments and agreements and ensure that the results of this monitoring are systematically acted upon;

(g) to ensure that the political framework for negotiations is updated and credible, including clear parameters for the settlement of final status issues, so that the end goal of the process is visible to all concerned.

52. In this regard, I urge the members of the Security Council and the Quartet to consider viable options that would be acceptable to both parties, as I am convinced that an active and systematic third party role is indispensable. Israel has traditionally been suspicious of such roles. However, the record shows that an international presence on the ground has been a key feature of nearly every modus vivendi reached between Israel and its adversaries. The Israeli-Syrian border would not be stable without the peacekeepers of the United Nations Disengagement Observer Force. The situation in Hebron, tense and dangerous as it is, would be even worse without the Temporary International Presence in Hebron. The full disengagement from Gaza would not have been achieved had the European Union not stepped forward to monitor the Rafah crossing. The Israeli-Hizbollah war of 2006 would probably have come much sooner and been still more explosive had UNIFIL not been present, and would not have been ended without a reconfigured UNIFIL to help implement Security Council resolution 1701 (2006), whose full implementation is in the interest of all States in the region. In my years as Secretary-General, I have noticed a growing Israeli awareness that third-party roles on the ground can serve Israeli as well as Arab interests. As there is a common interest in achieving a two-State solution, so there should be a common awareness that this will not happen without a stronger third-party role on the ground.

53. The challenge of how to pursue a comprehensive regional approach to the conflict must also be tackled. Ultimately, we are dealing with the Arab-Israeli conflict, not that between Israel and the Palestinians alone. The region and its concerns need to be fully addressed, as an ultimate peace will be between Israel and its neighbours, although progress on one track should not be held hostage to progress on another. I would like to remind the Syrian Arab Republic that it must pursue policies that demonstrate its commitment to peace and stability in the region, in particular with its immediate neighbours. I equally remind Israel that comprehensive regional peace cannot be achieved without a return of the Golan Heights to the Syrian Arab Republic.

54. I note that many have suggested the possibility of convening an international conference, along the lines of that held in 1991 in Madrid, so that the full regional dimensions of the conflict can be addressed. This idea must now be explored again. The resuscitation of the regional track of the peace process, which is an inherent element of the road map, is in the interests of all. We must work to ensure that the conditions are right and that the foundations for trust and successful negotiations are laid through meaningful gestures.

55. As I leave office, it is a matter of deep personal regret that peace in the Middle East has not been achieved. The need for the international community to engage with the main parties and finally reach a settlement of the fundamental Middle East problem—a settlement whose inevitable contours we know so well—is even more pressing today than it was 10 years ago.

7. Report of the Secretary-General on the Implementation of Resolution 1701 (2006), 14 March 2007 (S/2007/147)

I. Introduction

1. The present report is submitted in response to the request of the Security Council, in its statement by the President of 12 December 2006 (S/PRST/2006/52), to report on a quarterly basis on the implementation of resolution 1701 (2006), notably on further progress made towards the achievement of a permanent ceasefire and a long-term solution. This is the third report of the Secretary-General on the implementation of that resolution, and it follows the letter of 1 December 2006, which was a factual update on the implementation of resolution 1701 (2006) (S/2006/933), in particular on the operations of the United Nations Interim Force in Lebanon (UNIFIL) and other relevant United Nations activities. The present report provides a comprehensive assessment of the steps taken to implement resolution 1701 (2006).

2. I am pleased to report that the overall commitment by the Government of Israel and the Government of Lebanon to Security Council resolution 1701 (2006) remains strong. I am also encouraged by the major strategic changes that have been made in the area south of the Litani River, including the near full deployment of a strengthened UNIFIL and the deployment of the Lebanese Army. I am also encouraged by the absence of any positions other than those of the Lebanese Armed Forces and UNIFIL along the Blue Line. However, the present report is submitted against the background of an acute and continuing political crisis in Lebanon and mounting Israeli concerns about the unauthorized transfer of arms across the Lebanese-Syrian border. I am concerned that there has not been greater progress on key issues that are vital to the achievement of a permanent ceasefire and a long-term solution, such as the captured Israeli soldiers and the Lebanese prisoners, the Shab'a Farms and the halting of Israeli overflights. I am also distressed by the continuing danger posed to Lebanese citizens in the south of Lebanon owing to the use of cluster bombs by the Israeli Defense Force during the 2006 conflict.

II. Implementation of Security Council resolution 1701 (2006)

A. Respect for the Blue Line

3. Since the letter of the Secretary-General addressed to the President of the Security Council (S/2006/933), the military and security situation in the UNIFIL area of operations has been generally stable. However, the cessation of hostilities was breached by a serious incident along the Blue Line on 7 February 2007.

4. On 7 February, the Israeli Defense Force informed UNIFIL of its intention to cross the Israeli technical fence that night, near the Lebanese village of Maroun Al-Ras, to clear a number of suspected mines identified north of the fence on Israeli territory. The Lebanese Armed Forces pointed out through UNIFIL that, should the Israeli Defense Force cross the technical fence during the night, it would be difficult to ensure that no violation of the Blue Line would occur. The Lebanese Armed Forces stressed that they would not accept the planned Israeli night-time operation and would open fire should it be conducted.

They proposed the action be suspended until the following day. The UNIFIL Force Commander urged restraint and emphasized to the Lebanese Armed Forces that such an action would constitute a breach of the cessation of hostilities and a violation of resolution 1701 (2006). While acknowledging the security concerns of Israel, the Force Commander also urged the Israeli Defense Force to suspend its action and to resolve the matter by relaying its concerns through UNIFIL liaison channels and the holding of an urgent tripartite meeting. In the meantime, UNIFIL deployed two platoons to the area to establish a buffer zone between the Lebanese Armed Forces and the Israeli Defense Force, and later increased its strength to a company of mechanized infantry, reinforced by a tank platoon and supported by artillery, with another mechanized infantry company in reserve close by.

5. Despite the Force Commander's appeals, the Israeli Defense Force proceeded with the operation that night. The Lebanese Armed Forces at first fired warning shots after the Israeli Defense Force had made an opening in the fence, and then intensified fire, thus breaching the cessation of hostilities agreement, towards the bulldozer of the Israeli Defense Force, which had passed through the fence but was still on the Israeli side of the Blue Line. The Israeli Defense Force responded by firing a round. While the UNIFIL Force Commander, through his contacts with the parties, was able to negotiate a ceasefire, the bulldozer and accompanying excavator subsequently violated the Blue Line when carrying out earthworks to clear the suspected mines.

6. The Force Commander convened a tripartite meeting with senior representatives of the Israeli Defense Force and the Lebanese Armed Forces on 12 February and presented them with a report on the incident by UNIFIL. The report concluded that both parties had violated resolution 1701 (2006) by their actions that night. It recommended that the Blue Line be visibly marked in sensitive areas, that the agreed coordination and liaison arrangements be brought into force, and called on the parties to make use of the tripartite coordination mechanism in order to avoid similar incidents in the future.

7. That serious violation of resolution 1701 (2006) came only two days after the Israeli Defense Force had taken unilateral action to destroy other suspected improvised explosive devices detected near the Blue Line at the same location. On that occasion, the Israeli Defense Force informed UNIFIL of the devices but, before UNIFIL and Lebanese armed forces patrols could arrive at the scene, the Israeli Defense Force opened fire, detonating one device and causing two others to burn out. Subsequently, a UNIFIL team established that the devices were located some metres north of the Blue Line and that Israeli rounds had therefore violated the line and entered Lebanese territory. As a result of that action, evidence was destroyed and it was not possible to determine whether the devices were new.

8. Subsequent to the two incidents described above, UNIFIL reported an increased level of tension along the Blue Line. There have been several reports that Israeli and Lebanese soldiers on either side of the line have aimed weapons at each other in the area of Fatima Gate. Most recently, on 2 March, a Lebanese youth approached the Blue Line next to United Nations position 8-33 and, despite warnings from UNIFIL, started digging in the ground on the Lebanese side adjacent to the Blue Line. After warning the boy several times, the Israeli Defense Force fired one warning shot and, in violation of resolution 1701 (2006), forced the boy at gunpoint to cross the Blue Line into Israel, where he was taken into custody. He was released to UNIFIL personnel later in the day.

9. I am concerned by all violations of the Blue Line, which also constitute violations of resolution 1701 (2006). Throughout the period under review, UNIFIL continued to report Israeli air violations of the Blue Line by overflights of jets and unmanned aerial vehicles. Incursions into Lebanese airspace continue on an almost daily basis. UNIFIL reported a significant increase in Israeli air violations in February and at the beginning of March; on some days, more than 10 Israeli overflights were reported in its area of operations. The Government of Lebanon continues to protest the overflights as a serious violation of Lebanese sovereignty and of resolution 1701 (2006), while the Government of Israel continues to maintain that the overflights are a necessary security measure that will continue until the two abducted Israeli soldiers are released and the measures established in paragraphs 14 and 15 of resolution 1701 (2006) are implemented. On 21 February, UNIFIL reported 10 Israeli overflights in its area of operations. On the same day, the Lebanese Armed Forces opened anti-aircraft fire near Tyre.

10. On a number of occasions, UNIFIL also reported the presence of hunters with rifles, as well as a number of minor ground violations of the Blue Line from the Lebanese side, mainly by local shepherds. I would remind the parties that any crossing of the Blue Line, whether planned or inadvertent, endangers the precarious calm that prevails in southern Lebanon.

11. I am pleased to report that both parties have now agreed to the UNIFIL proposal to visibly mark the Blue Line in sensitive areas, particularly in locations where there is a significant distance between the line and the Israeli technical fence. UNIFIL is engaged with the Lebanese Armed Forces and the Israeli Defense Force to initiate the process of erecting markers at selected points, in close coordination with both parties, in order to prevent inadvertent violations. Regular Lebanese patrols along the Blue Line have also contributed to providing better security and preventing violations by civilians on a number of occasions. The Lebanese Armed Forces have also enhanced control of Lebanese territorial waters south of Naqoura to prevent violations of the buoy-line by local fishermen.

B. Security arrangements

12. The Israeli Defense Force continues to maintain a presence north of the Blue Line inside Lebanese territory through its control of the northern part of Ghajar village. UNIFIL has been engaged with the Israeli Defense Force and the Lebanese Armed Forces in order to finalize temporary security arrangements for northern Ghajar, which would facilitate the withdrawal of the Israel Defense Forces from the area. While the arrangements have been approved by the Government of Israel, the Government of Lebanon has suggested an amendment to the text, which is under consideration.

13. There have been no significant changes in the deployment of the Lebanese Armed Forces inside the UNIFIL area of operations since the letter of the Secretary-General of 1 December to the President of the Security Council. There are three Lebanese brigades (two light infantry and one heavy infantry) deployed along the Blue Line, and another brigade in the area of Tyre. The Lebanese Armed Forces maintain a total of 142 positions in the UNIFIL area of operations, of which 45 are along the Blue Line. A total of 114 of the Lebanese positions are checkpoints. On 5 December 2006, a UNIFIL patrol came across a significant number of mortar shells and rockets in the general area of Kafr Shuba and informed the Lebanese Armed Forces. The following day, a UNIFIL patrol revisited the

area and discovered five booby-trapped or mined obstacles, apparently newly laid, in the same location. UNIFIL dismantled the obstacles and the Lebanese Armed Forces confiscated the ammunition.

14. UNIFIL continues to assist the Lebanese Armed Forces in ensuring that the area between the Blue Line and the Litani River is free of any armed personnel, assets or weapons other than those of the Lebanese Armed Forces and UNIFIL. The mission received no reports of unauthorized armed personnel in the area during the period under review, except for local hunters and Palestinian armed elements, who are largely confined to the refugee camps. On a number of occasions, however, UNIFIL came across abandoned unauthorized arms, ammunition or related material in its area of operations south of the Litani River. On all such occasions, UNIFIL informed the Lebanese Armed Forces, which took action to confiscate or to destroy the material. The Lebanese Armed Forces and UNIFIL carried out coordinated operations in the Kafr Shuba area and in Wadi Zibquin with the aim of locating and clearing unauthorized arms, ammunition and mines. The Lebanese Armed Forces continue to monitor and control entry points into the area between the Litani River and the Blue Line through permanent checkpoints and patrols. Joint efforts by the Lebanese Armed Forces and UNIFIL have not detected illegal transfers of arms to the area south of the Litani River.

15. However, in public pronouncements, Hizbullah has claimed that it is strengthening its capacity and rebuilding its armed presence. On 16 February 2007, the Secretary-General of the organization, Sayyed Nasrallah, declared that Hizbullah fighters were present in southern Lebanon, although UNIFIL had no evidence of the presence of Hizbullah armed elements south of the Litani River. He further claimed that not only did Hizbullah have plenty of weapons, but that it also had the right to transport its arms within the country in order to combat Israel. On a number of occasions, Hizbullah also publicly criticized the Lebanese authorities for seizing a truckload of its rockets, rocket launchers and mortars on 8 February on the outskirts of Beirut, and demanded that the Lebanese army hand back the weapons, which it described as "arms of the resistance". Such statements are an open admission of activities that constitute a direct violation of provisions of resolution 1701 (2006) that were accepted by Hizbullah last year.

16. During the reporting period, the UNIFIL Maritime Task Force hailed and confirmed the identity of over 2,000 ships, bringing the total number to over 3,000 since the Task Force was established. It detected 10 suspicious vessels, which were inspected by Lebanese naval or customs officials on arrival in port. No illegal arms were discovered. The Task Force also assisted two vessels in distress, and participated in search and rescue operations that saved the lives of 18 seamen. Effective arrangements have been put in place between the Task Force and the Lebanese Navy with regard to access to Lebanese territorial waters, the conduct of boarding and inspections, communications and reporting procedures.

17. The UNIFIL liaison and coordination mechanism with both the Israeli and Lebanese armed forces has been generally effective in addressing all military and security issues. The Force Commander holds regular tripartite meetings with senior representatives of both parties. As witnessed following the incident of 7 February, the mechanism has become instrumental in addressing critical security matters and is now a key element in the mission's efforts to foster stability in southern Lebanon.

18. The Lebanese Armed Forces, which are estimated to total some 55,000 military personnel, have, according to resolution 1701 (2006), a significant number of essential tasks to carry out, including the maintenance of peace and security in southern Lebanon in cooperation with UNIFIL, and helping to secure the country's land and maritime borders. However, the country's ongoing political crisis has also required the Lebanese Armed Forces to deploy in Beirut and in other areas of the country to ensure internal security. These additional tasks have put considerable strain on the Forces, whose entire army corps is currently deployed, and have sometimes limited their ability to carry out the tasks required under resolution 1701 (2006).

19. It has become clear in recent weeks that the Lebanese Armed Forces are facing considerable capacity problems, which have had an impact on their ability to respond quickly to some UNIFIL requests, including coordinated search operations. UNIFIL has received a number of requests for equipment from the Lebanese Armed Forces, including, for example, night-vision goggles, which the mission is not currently able to provide. Representatives of both the Government of Lebanon and the United Nations have been approaching potential donors on this issue. I note that several interested partners have already made some contributions and I would urge others to come forward and assist the Lebanese Armed Forces to carry out their obligations under resolution 1701 (2006).

20. While acknowledging the capacity problems of the Lebanese Armed Forces, I have also noted that on some recent occasions their units have shown a certain reluctance to respond to requests from UNIFIL, including when conducting coordinated search operations. In each case, however, UNIFIL and the Lebanese Armed Forces were able to agree on a tactical approach that allowed joint operations to go forward. The Prime Minister, the Minister for Defence and the Lebanese Armed Forces Commander have reassured the UNIFIL Force Commander that the Lebanese forces are determined to work closely with UNIFIL and, given the good cooperation that the mission has received since 2006, I am confident that the Lebanese Armed Forces are committed to carrying out their obligations under resolution 1701 (2006).

21. It should also be noted that there have been a number of incidents when UNIFIL patrols have faced stone throwing, mainly by local youths. The Lebanese Armed Forces have taken action to prevent such isolated incidents and in some cases have detained the perpetrators. Municipal authorities in a small number of towns and villages raised concerns about some UNIFIL activities in their areas, in particular patrolling with heavy vehicles. However, in general, local authorities and residents have been well disposed to the mission, which endeavours to carry out its mandated tasks with sensitivity and minimum disruption to the local community. I welcome the public statements that leaders from all political factions have made promoting good relations between the local residents and UNIFIL.

22. While coordination and liaison between UNIFIL and the Israeli Defense Force have been generally good, the UNIFIL Force Commander was unable to establish direct contact with senior Israeli Defense Force representatives for much of the time during the incidents along the Blue Line in February 2007, contravening agreed arrangements. It is of critical importance that the Israeli Defense Force ensures that an officer, of appropriate rank and authority, can be contacted at all times by the UNIFIL Force Commander, so that any future incidents arising along the Blue Line can be quickly resolved before they escalate.

C. Disarming armed groups

23. Given the considerable military presence of the Lebanese Armed Forces and the United Nations Force south of the Litani River, senior commanders of both forces believe it would be very difficult for unauthorized armed personnel to establish any new military capacity in that area. At the same time, unarmed personnel, suspected of being affiliated to Hizbullah, have been observed monitoring UNIFIL activities at various points throughout its area of operations, at times taking photographs and filming.

24. There have, however, been a number of reports of activities conducted by armed elements north of the Litani River, outside the UNIFIL area of operations. The reports have not been denied by either the Government of Lebanon or Hizbullah. Armed elements, suspected of being members of Hizbullah, have been observed constructing new facilities in the Bourrhoz region, just north of the Litani River. With regard to activities outside the UNIFIL area of operations, it should be noted that the Lebanese authorities and armed forces have primary responsibility for preventing any hostile or armed action being launched from within Lebanese territory.

25. However, the stated position of the Commander of the Lebanese Armed Forces is that the forces apply the same rules in adjacent areas north of the Litani River as in the area to its south, and that they would prevent any armed actions from being carried out by unauthorized armed elements in either region.

26. A further update on the status of Lebanese and non-Lebanese militias will be provided in my fifth semi-annual report on the implementation of Security Council resolution 1559 (2004), due in April 2007. It should be noted that, with reference to paragraph 10 of resolution 1701 (2006) and the issue of disarmament, I have already proposed, in my report of 12 September 2006 on the implementation of resolution 1701 (2006) (S/2006/730), that the disarming of Hizbullah and other militia should take place through a political process that would lead to the full authority of the Government of Lebanon so that there would be no weapons or authority than its own. I am still waiting for the Government of Lebanon, further to its decision to adopt the Seven-Point Plan, to define such a political process.

D. Arms embargo

27. Over the past few weeks, the Government of Israel has provided a series of detailed intelligence briefings to senior United Nations representatives that indicate serious breaches of the arms embargo across the Lebanese-Syrian border. The briefings included a specific example of a reported arms shipment to Hizbullah early in January across the Lebanese-Syrian border. The date, exact times and names of places of the incident were reported to United Nations officials.

28. Israel claims that hundreds of such shipments, including short- and longer-range rockets, anti-tank and anti-aircraft defence systems, have crossed the Lebanese-Syrian border since the end of the 2006 conflict.

29. With regard to Israeli charges of weapon smuggling across the Lebanese-Syrian border, Lebanese authorities have requested that evidence be provided to allow experts to verify the allegations. Some senior Lebanese officials have denied the Israeli allegations.

30. While the Lebanese authorities, in their workplan to control all the country's borders, acknowledge that much remains to be done to strengthen their border-control capacity and

modernize their current systems, they also point out the progress that has already been achieved in this regard and the plans and projects under way to further improve that capacity. A joint security committee, headed by the Director-General of General Security, and comprising representatives of the Lebanese Armed Forces, Customs Authorities, Internal Security and General Security, has been established to monitor and control all Lebanese international borders, liaise with international partners providing assistance and implement applicable laws and regulations.

31. The Syrian Arab Republic has indicated, most recently in the letter of its Permanent Representative dated 1 March 2007, that it has taken all measures required on its borders to prevent smuggling between its territory and Lebanon. Its Permanent Representative has also informed senior United Nations representatives that, since the commitment to deploy an additional battalion and take other measures made by President Assad to the Secretary-General in September 2006, the Syrian Arab Republic has doubled its border guards and increased its patrols along its border with Lebanon. The Syrian Arab Republic also alleges that Israel is sending weapons to some Lebanese groups in order to affect the situation in Lebanon negatively. It has not however provided any evidence in support of that allegation.

32. Further to the request contained in the statement of the President of the Security Council dated 12 December 2006 (S/PRST/2006/52) inviting me to pursue further a technical and independent assessment of the situation along the Lebanese-Syrian border, a United Nations team of border police experts made a second visit to Lebanon late in the reporting period. The team sought feedback from relevant Lebanese authorities on the report provided to the Government concerning the findings of the first assessment mission, and to evaluate progress made since the visit conducted in September 2006.

33. The team was encouraged by the commitment of representatives of the relevant border security agencies to fully implement its findings. There has been some effort to improve cooperation and coordination between headquarters and field levels in all four agencies concerned. However, the lack of critical equipment and basic training for Customs and other officials continues to hamper efforts to properly secure the Lebanese land border with the Syrian Arab Republic. On the maritime border, the recent donation of 10 small patrol boats by the United Arab Emirates should also be welcomed. While they alone will be insufficient to fully monitor and patrol Lebanese territorial waters, the boats will provide an important new capacity to the Lebanese Navy once they are fully operational.

34. The Lebanese authorities informed the team that they accepted the findings of the report with regard to equipment, methods, capacity and training. The next phase is for the border security agencies to fully implement the enhancements while seeking the necessary bilateral assistance. Bilateral assistance to the Government of Lebanon to help enhance those capabilities will continue to be critical. I welcome and am encouraged by the work of a team from Germany that has been working closely with relevant Lebanese officials to launch a pilot project on the northern part of the Lebanese-Syrian border, as well as devising training programmes and delivering equipment. I would like to thank the Government of Germany, the Government of the United Arab Emirates and other donor countries for their crucial ongoing assistance in this regard.

35. The team has suggested a follow-up mission in four to six months to allow the Government of Lebanon adequate time to implement the improvements.

E. Land mines and cluster bombs

36. The extent of contamination from unexploded ordnance, namely from cluster bomblets and sub-munitions, has become clearer since the letter of the Secretary-General to the President of the Security Council (S/2007/933). The United Nations Mine Action Coordination Centre, in conjunction with the Lebanese national demining office, has identified an additional 32 individual cluster strike locations. As at 27 February 2007, a total of 854 cluster bomblet strike locations had been recorded. The contamination covers more than 34 million square metres, some of which had been cleared from mines and unexploded ordnance prior to the 2006 conflict.

37. Each strike location contains hundreds of individual bomblets or sub-munitions. As at 22 February, the humanitarian toll of these explosive remnants of war on civilians amounted to 22 deaths and 159 injuries. In the past two months, UNIFIL battalions experienced five accidents, in which five members of the ordnance removal team—four from the Belgian battalion and one from the China battalion—were injured in a series of unfortunate demining and cluster bomb incidents.

38. While the above numbers are alarming, there has been a decrease in the number of victims per day, which can be attributed to the joint efforts of the clearance capacities contracted and bilaterally funded by the Lebanese Armed Forces, UNIFIL and the United Nations. As at 25 January 2007, approximately 10 per cent of the contaminated area had been cleared, through the location and destruction of 103,010 unexploded cluster munitions. In addition to cluster munitions, unexploded bombs, rockets, mortars and other ordnance also litter the south and areas to the north and east of Lebanon.

39. Despite repeated United Nations efforts to receive detailed information from the Israeli Defense Force regarding the exact location, quantity and type of cluster munitions utilized during the conflict, I regret to report that Israel has not yet provided UNIFIL with these data. While I acknowledge receipt of Israeli maps of mines laid until the withdrawal of the Israeli Defense Force from southern Lebanon in 2000, I reiterate my request, as contained in my previous reports, for Israel to provide detailed data on its use of cluster munitions to the United Nations as soon as possible.

F. Captured soldiers and prisoners

40. The return of the two Israeli soldiers abducted by Hizbullah on 12 July 2006 and a solution of the question of Lebanese citizens detained in Israel have been the focus of further intense efforts made by the facilitator appointed by my predecessor to handle these issues.

41. Hizbullah publicly rejected the concept of an immediate and unconditional release of the two Israeli soldiers at an early stage, insisting instead on the release of large numbers of detainees in Israel beyond the framework of resolution 1701 (2006). There were also prohibitive demands with regard to proof that the two Israeli soldiers were alive.

42. On the Israeli side, I note that the Lebanese citizens captured by the Israeli Defense Force during the 2006 conflict have all been visited by the International Committee of the Red Cross and have been able to write letters to their families. I also note the readiness to solve the very few Lebanese cases, on condition that Hizbullah honours its obligations.

43. More recently, a conceptual framework has been developed which should lead the way to an agreement on an exchange of information and several gestures of humanitarian significance. Against that background, I hope Hizbullah will allow the facilitator to see the two abducted Israeli soldiers very soon.

44. In his contacts with Hizbullah, the facilitator has emphasized my firm expectation that a solution for the release of the two soldiers will be found soon, on the basis of restraint in demands, moderation and compassion for the victims of the recent conflict. Not least in view of the international standing of Lebanon, I have urged Hizbullah leaders to avoid disproportionate demands and protracted bargaining that cannot be considered adequate in the face of the humanitarian urgency of the cases and the clear message of resolution 1701 (2006).

45. I will inform the Security Council immediately in the event of any major developments in this area.

G. Delineation of borders

46. A permanent solution to the issue of the delineation of borders remains contingent upon the delineation of the border between the Syrian Arab Republic and Lebanon, in fulfilment of resolutions 1559 (2004), 1680 (2006) and 1701 (2006). In this regard, the Secretary-General has noted the repeated statements of representatives of the Syrian Arab Republic made over the past year that the Shab'a Farms area is Lebanese. Such statements constitute a new legal reality, as outlined in more detail in the third and fourth semi-annual reports of the Secretary-General on the implementation of resolution 1559 (2004). At the same time, I note in particular the alternative path suggested by the Government of Lebanon in its Seven-Point Plan, namely placing the Shab'a Farms under United Nations jurisdiction until a border is permanently delineated and Lebanese sovereignty over them is settled.

47. In December 2006, I noted in my letter to the President of the Council that a senior cartographer had been engaged to examine the geographical definition of the Shab'a Farms area. Over the past months, the cartographer has been reviewing all available material.

48. The Government of Lebanon has submitted a comprehensive collection of papers in support of its claim to the Shab'a Farms area, including over 150 property deeds, cadastral maps of two villages, a general administrative map and a map on which a "proposed State limit" is depicted. Summary assessments included with the papers, covering the period from the end of Ottoman rule to the present time, cite decrees, settlements of land-use disputes, legal opinions, and the proceedings of joint Lebanese-Syrian boundary committees. Furthermore, they also take account of documents and sketch maps recently found in the diplomatic archives located in Nantes, France, which attest to the long history of the Lebanese identity of the Shab'a Farms. The Government of Lebanon contends that the 1920 intra-mandate line that defined the boundary between Lebanon and the Syrian Arab Republic in this region was drawn with scant knowledge of the geographical realities; the resulting status has been perpetuated ever since.

49. In the recent attempts to define the Shab'a Farms area, it should be noted that many of the documents being examined, including the above-mentioned diplomatic correspondence, were not previously available.

50. The cartographer is in the process of classifying and analysing the documentation verifying and recompiling information that could be considered evidence of a boundary in the

Shab'a Farms area. While good progress has been made, some papers have not been translated. In addition, further amplification has been requested of Lebanon, and a similar call for any relevant material has been made to the Syrian Arab Republic. I also look forward to cooperation with Israel.

III. Deployment of the United Nations Interim Force in Lebanon

51. In response to the decision by the Council in its resolution 1701 (2006) to supplement and enhance the numbers, equipment, mandate and scope of operations of UNIFIL, the mission continued its phased deployment during the reporting period. With the second phase of deployment complete, as at 20 February, the total number of military personnel had reached 12,431, from 29 contributing countries. A current total of 10,479 ground troops operate in two established sectors: Sector West, based in Tibnin, and Sector East, based in Marjayoun. The total UNIFIL naval personnel now number 1,772. It is with regret that I report that, on 7 March, a UNIFIL armoured personnel carrier carrying four Belgian soldiers had an accident in the Kafr Hammam area. Two of the peacekeepers died immediately and a third one died later in hospital. The fourth sustained serious injuries and has been repatriated.

52. The mission continues to recruit civilian staff. As at 8 February, staff strength totalled 473 (163 international and 310 national staff) of an authorized maximum of 1,078 staff (390 international and 688 national staff). The increased staff strength is reflected across all civilian functions of the mission, particularly in the critical area of mission support.

53. The Office of Political Affairs, which now comprises civil affairs, public information, and an office for joint planning and coordination, was also augmented during the period under review. Civil affairs teams have been deployed in both sectors of the mission: the Sector East team, co-located with the civil-military cooperation cell in Marjayoun, and the Sector West team, currently operating from UNIFIL headquarters in Naqoura. Civil affairs is working closely with the civil-military cooperation cells; activities focus on relations with local communities and confidence-building measures. The military public information cell is now fully integrated into the public information office, and the office for joint planning and coordination with the Lebanese Armed Forces, the Ministry of Defence and other relevant authorities, is now fully operational in Beirut. At the same time, a number of UNIFIL staff officers are also based with the Israeli Defense Force at Northern Command headquarters, and the mission is seeking an agreement with the Government of Israel to establish a small office in Tel Aviv.

54. On 2 February 2007, Major General Claudio Graziano (Italy) took over the command of UNIFIL from Major General Alain Pellegrini (France). I would like to commend General Pellegrini for his outstanding contribution to the work of UNIFIL, and especially for his exemplary performance during the hostilities of summer 2006 and his subsequent role in overseeing the recent augmentation of the mission.

IV. Observations

55. I note and welcome the continued commitment by both the Government of Israel and the Government of Lebanon to the implementation of resolution 1701 (2006). I also note the commitment of the Syrian Arab Republic to the implementation of the resolution, as stated in its identical letters to me and the President of the Security Council dated 1 March 2007.

56. In Israel, there is growing criticism that resolution 1701 (2006) has not addressed the issues of most concern to Israelis, namely the return of its captured soldiers and reported arms movements to and within Lebanon. I would urge the Government of Israel to continue to work to implement all aspects of the resolution, without selectivity. I call on the Government of Israel, once again, to review its policy of flights over Lebanese airspace, which are a continuing violation of resolution 1701 (2006), and most urgently to provide the United Nations with all information on cluster munitions fired during the 2006 conflict.

57. The Prime Minister of Lebanon has expressed his country's frustration with the continuing Israeli overflights, the rising civilian toll caused by Israeli cluster bombs and the slow progress on the issue of the Shab'a Farms. In Lebanon, I welcome the support to UNIFIL and to resolution 1701 (2006) that has been expressed publicly by all Lebanese parties. However, the persistent political crisis in the country is now overshadowing the implementation of the resolution. I call on all Lebanese parties to recommit themselves to the principles of the Seven-Point Plan of the Government of Lebanon. An understanding which incorporates the principles of no rearmament of unauthorized groups, and no movement of arms other than with the consent of the Lebanese Armed Forces, should also be encouraged, especially in the current volatile security environment in the country. Such an understanding would reflect a broad-based Lebanese determination to both the letter and the spirit of resolution 1701 (2006).

58. The Lebanese Armed Forces have made significant and commendable strides towards fulfilling their obligations under resolution 1701 (2006), and I have been greatly encouraged by the cooperation and assistance provided by their highest-ranking leaders. Recognizing that the armed forces face considerable capacity problems and shortages of manpower and equipment, I call on the international community to provide relevant, timely and necessary bilateral assistance to the Government of Lebanon, to support the Lebanese Armed Forces working with UNIFIL to carry out its mandated tasks. In this regard, it should be noted that the Lebanese Armed Forces are the peacekeeping partner of UNIFIL, and the success of UNIFIL is tied to the capacities and capabilities of the Lebanese Armed Forces.

59. While the Government of Lebanon and its armed forces have provided crucial support to UNIFIL, and the Government of Israel and its armed forces have helped to facilitate the mission's new mandated tasks, both parties can do more to ensure the successful implementation of this aspect of resolution 1701 (2006). I urge both parties to commit themselves fully to furthering close liaison and coordination arrangements with UNIFIL, especially through full participation and information-sharing at tripartite meetings.

60. I welcome the efforts made by the Government of Lebanon to extend its authority over its territory through its own legitimate armed forces, and encourage the Lebanese Armed Forces to continue to provide full and timely assistance to UNIFIL. In order to facilitate the swift withdrawal of remaining Israeli Defense Force personnel from Lebanese territory, I call on both parties to approve the temporary security arrangements for northern Ghajar.

61. The incidents along the Blue Line early in February were regrettable and could have been avoided. In the current atmosphere of fragile peace, both parties have a responsibility to avoid provocative actions likely to cause tension to escalate along the Blue Line. I am also concerned by the reported activities of unauthorized armed elements outside of the

UNIFIL area of operations. I recall that the successful implementation of resolution 1701 (2006) depends upon the full implementation of the relevant provisions of the Taif Accords and of resolutions 1559 (2004) and 1680 (2006), which require the disarmament of all armed groups in Lebanon.

62. The information provided by Israeli military sources to senior United Nations representatives on alleged breaches of the arms embargo across the Lebanese-Syrian border was more detailed than that previously shown to the United Nations. While the information was substantial, its authentication requires independent military assessment.

63. Confidence-building measures to strengthen the Lebanese-Syrian border regime are highly recommended and urgently needed. The ongoing bilateral assistance provided by the Government of Germany is a welcome step in helping the Government of Lebanon to enhance its border security capacities. Technical assistance, training and equipment to improve Lebanese border security, other than that provided by Germany, has been slow to arrive.

64. I am encouraged that Lebanese authorities continue to commit themselves to full cooperation with the United Nations team of border police experts and to bilateral assistance programmes. It will clearly take some time for this initiative to progress. I call upon Member States and relevant regional organizations to redouble their efforts in support of the Government of Lebanon in this regard. In considering further steps to ensure the full implementation of paragraph 15 of resolution 1701 (2006), including the arms embargo, the Council may wish to consider supporting an independent assessment mission to monitor the border.

65. I would also strongly urge all Member States, in particular the Syrian Arab Republic, other regional States and the Islamic Republic of Iran to do all they can to ensure that the provisions of resolution 1701 (2006) are fully respected. In this regard, in August 2006, I noted the measures that the Syrian Arab Republic committed itself to taking on its side of the border with Lebanon and further measures of which it has informed me.

66. The Shab'a Farms area remains a key issue in the implementation of resolution 1701 (2006). There is no alternative but to move forward on the issue with due diligence. The full cooperation of Lebanon, the Syrian Arab Republic and Israel in particular is required in assisting the senior cartographer to review relevant material and develop an accurate territorial definition of the Shab'a Farms area. I am pleased by the good progress that has been made by the senior cartographer and intend to report more fully in the next report on the implementation of resolution 1701 (2006), due in June, when I expect the technical work to be completed. In the meantime, I wish to reiterate the urgent call on the Syrian Arab Republic and Lebanon to take the necessary steps to delineate their common border, in fulfilment of resolutions 1559 (2004), 1680 (2006) and 1701 (2006).

67. I am concerned by a growing threat to the presence of the United Nations in Lebanon from extremist Islamist groups, which have reportedly found safe haven in Palestinian refugee camps. This presence in Palestinian camps has been reportedly strengthened in the period under review. In order to meet this threat, assistance to the Lebanese Armed Forces and other relevant security forces is urgently required.

68. We need to be fully aware that challenging work remains ahead for the implementation of resolution 1701 (2006). Both parties could do more to further its implementation. Maintaining the momentum is the responsibility of the Lebanese, the Government of Israel, regional countries and other Member States. If there is no progress on core issues such as the prisoners, the Shab'a Farms area, Israeli overflights and enforcement of the arms embargo, progress on resolution 1701 (2006) will be severely tested in the months to come.

8. Fifth Semi-annual Report of the Secretary-General on the Implementation of Security Council Resolution 1559 (2004), 7 May 2007 (S/2007/262)

I. Introduction

1. The present report is my fifth semi-annual report to the Security Council on the implementation of resolution 1559 (2004).

2. In the past six months, Lebanon has continued to witness prolonged political uncertainty, with the issue of the creation of a special tribunal for Lebanon in the context of the work of the International Independent Investigation Commission moving increasingly centre stage.

3. Political consultations among Lebanese leaders to resolve their differences began on 6 November 2006. Amidst their collapse, the Shiite members of the Cabinet resigned from the Government on 11 November. A further minister resigned on 13 November. Tension rose further with the approval of a draft statutory agreement on the special tribunal with an international character on 13 November, and then the finalized statutory agreement on 25 November by the remaining members of the Cabinet.

4. The opposition, consisting of Amal, Hizbullah and the Free Patriotic Movement, as well as President Lahoud, have maintained that the Cabinet no longer enjoys constitutional legitimacy. The Government continues to meet and function, since it continues to enjoy the support of a parliamentary majority. In addition, the Government maintains that since the Prime Minister never formally accepted the resignations submitted to him, they are not valid. In the context of an intensifying debate over the constitutional legitimacy of the remaining Cabinet, supporters of Hizbullah, Amal, and the Free Patriotic Movement began staging a sit-in at the Prime Minister's office in downtown Beirut from 1 December, which endures to the present day.

5. The demonstrations have on occasion led to violent clashes between supporters of the opposition forces and those of the Government. Early in December, one person was killed in the context of such clashes. On 23 January 2007, 3 people were killed and over 100 injured when a general strike was called and the country left in paralysis. Two days later, as donors assembled in Paris and pledged their assistance to Lebanon's reconstruction effort after the war of last summer, clashes at a Beirut university campus turned violent, leaving 4 people dead and over 150 injured. Renewed clashes also occurred in rural parts of the Beqaa Valley in February.

6. A variety of parties and actors have undertaken commendable efforts to mediate between the opposing sides in Lebanon. The laudable visits and efforts by the Secretary-General of the League of Arab States and a praiseworthy initiative pursued by the Kingdom of Saudi Arabia laid the foundations for talks between the leader of the parliamentary majority, Saad Hariri, and the Speaker of Parliament, Nabih Berri, in early to mid-March. The crisis is yet to be resolved, however, and the standoff that paralyses Lebanon continues.

7. Twice in the last four months, petitions signed by a majority of the members of Parliament and expressing their support for the holding of a parliamentary session to ratify the establishment of the international tribunal have been submitted to me. Parliament has not met since the end of the fall session, and is yet to launch its regular spring session deliberations, which formally began on 22 March 2007, as the Speaker has not called for the convening of the assembly. Against this background, the Prime Minister, Fouad Siniora, sent me a letter dated 10 April, requesting that in the light of the "paralysis" of the Lebanese Parliament, the Security Council "examine alternative ways and means that will ensure the establishment without delay, of the special tribunal for Lebanon, which is essential for the safeguarding of liberties and deterring further political assassinations".

8. On 21 November 2006, the Industry Minister, Pierre Gemayel, the scion of one of Lebanon's most prominent political families, was assassinated by gunmen in Beirut. On 13 February 2007, three people were killed when two buses were successively bombed near the village of Bikfaya. Seventeen people were injured. The members of the Security Council condemned these acts and, on both occasions, reaffirmed their previous calls upon all parties concerned to cooperate fully and urgently for the full implementation of all relevant resolutions concerning the restoration of the territorial integrity, full sovereignty and political independence of Lebanon, in particular resolutions 1559 (2004), 1595 (2005), 1636 (2005), 1664 (2006), 1680 (2006) and 1701 (2006). My predecessor and I also condemned these atrocities.

9. While a tense calm continues to prevail in Lebanon, the month of March saw an increase in the reported number of security threats and bomb scares. On 26 April, two young men were found dead, three days after having disappeared in a southern Beirut neighbourhood. There have been allegations that the incident may have been linked to sectarian tension.

II. Implementation of resolution 1559 (2004)

10. In the aftermath of the last report, of 19 October 2006, on the implementation of resolution 1559 (2004) (S/2006/832), further progress has been achieved to consolidate the arrangements established by resolution 1701 (2006).[1] Such progress is relevant to the achievement of strict respect of the sovereignty, territorial integrity, unity, and political independence of Lebanon under the sole and exclusive authority of the Government, as called for in resolution 1559 (2004).

11. However, the provisions of resolution 1559 (2004) calling for the disbanding and disarmament of all Lebanese and non-Lebanese militias and the strict respect of the sovereignty, territorial integrity, unity, and political independence of Lebanon under the sole and exclusive authority of the Government, as well as the Council's support for a free and fair electoral process in Lebanon's presidential election conducted according to Lebanese constitutional rules devised without foreign interference or influence, remain to be implemented in full.

A. Sovereignty, territorial integrity, unity and political independence of Lebanon

12. In reaction to my most recent report, of 14 March 2007, on the implementation of resolution 1701 (2006) (S/2007/147), the Council adopted a presidential statement on 17 April (S/PRST/2007/12), in which it reiterated its full support for the legitimate and democratically elected Government of Lebanon, called for full respect of the democratic institutions

of the country, in conformity with its constitution, and condemned any effort to destabilize Lebanon. The Council further called upon all Lebanese political parties to show responsibility with a view to preventing, through dialogue, further deterioration of the situation in Lebanon, and reaffirmed its strong support for the sovereignty, territorial integrity, unity, and political independence of Lebanon within its internationally recognized borders and under the sole and exclusive authority of the Government of Lebanon.

13. In the context of the enduring political standoff and of widespread allegations that illegal arms trafficking is taking place clandestinely via the Syrian-Lebanese border, the 14 March alliance, which represents the majority faction in Parliament, released a statement on 16 January 2007, in which it asserted that "forces directly affiliated with Syrian intelligence are bringing in new shipments of weapons and distributing them in sensitive areas of Lebanon, especially in the western Beqaa and Reshaya and some areas of Mount Lebanon". The statement continued by drawing "the attention of the Arab League and the United Nations to such non-stop practices by the Syrian regime in Lebanon". The Government of the Syrian Arab Republic has repeatedly denied any involvement in arms trafficking or any intelligence activity in Lebanon, and has pointed to its efforts and full cooperation in enforcing the weapons embargo imposed by resolution 1701 (2006). President Assad also informed me during our meeting in Damascus on 24 April that the Syrian Arab Republic is willing to work with the United Nations on all matters relating to peace and stability in the region, also reaffirming the commitment of the Syrian Arab Republic to the full implementation of resolution 1701 (2006) and to enhance consultations with the United Nations in that regard.

14. Regrettably, the expectation of the early initiation of a process between Lebanon and the Syrian Arab Republic, based on an agreed action agenda, which will eventually lead to the establishment of full diplomatic relations, as expressed in the last report (S/2006/832) and in fulfilment of the relevant provisions of resolution 1680 (2006), has not yet been met. I have urged President Assad to establish diplomatic relations with Lebanon, and he reconfirmed his readiness in principle to establish relations with Lebanon. At the same time, the Syrian Arab Republic has reiterated its position to me that the establishment of mutual diplomatic representation is a bilateral matter. I continue to believe that the establishment of formal diplomatic relations would be an important measure to affirm the strict respect for Lebanon's sovereignty, territorial integrity, and political independence. As was stated in the last semi-annual report (ibid.), steps towards the establishment of diplomatic relations between the Syrian Arab Republic and Lebanon would significantly contribute to the stability of the region.

15. The affirmation of Lebanon's sovereignty, territorial integrity and political independence also continues to be inextricably linked with the delineation of the border it shares with the Syrian Arab Republic. Steps towards delineating in full the border between Lebanon and the Syrian Arab Republic would also significantly contribute to the stability of the region.

16. The Government of the Syrian Arab Republic, in its letter to the Security Council of 20 March 2007, reaffirmed its position that the question of the demarcation of borders between the Syrian Arab Republic and Lebanon is a bilateral matter that relates to State sovereignty and must be solved by agreement between the Syrian and Lebanese Governments. The Syrian Arab Republic has also informed me, latest in my meeting with President Assad

on 24 April, that it is willing to resume meetings of the Syrian-Lebanese commission on the borders and that it agrees to begin a process of delineation, proceeding from north to south. I welcome President Assad's agreement to reactivate the Border Committee with Lebanon.

17. It is my view that the delineation and demarcation of the Lebanese-Syrian border is indeed a bilateral matter that can only be settled through a bilateral agreement between the two parties. As concerns the majority of the length of the Lebanese-Syrian border, there are no impediments to the early commencement of such a process. I now look forward to the early reconvention of the bilateral Border Committee, as President Assad has committed, and the conclusion of a border agreement, which would also prove an important and useful vehicle to address the stated concerns of the members of the Security Council over allegations and reports of illegal arms transfers across the border, in violation of Lebanon's sovereignty and of resolutions 1559 (2004) and 1701 (2006).

18. With regard to the Shab'a Farms, the Syrian Arab Republic has also informed me in its letter of 20 March 2007 that "Israeli withdrawal from the area is essential, it being understood that the border will be demarcated following complete Israeli withdrawal from the occupied Syrian Golan". Previously, the Syrian Arab Republic had indicated to me its concurrence—consistent with the statements of a number of its senior officials that the Shab'a Farms are to be considered Lebanese—with the Lebanese seven-point-plan, which envisages placing the Shab'a Farms under United Nations jurisdiction until permanent border delineation and Lebanese sovereignty over them is settled. The third semi-annual report, of 19 April 2006, on the implementation of Security Council resolution 1559 (2004) (S/2006/248) had noted that it appeared "that there exists a consensus on the general need to delineate the Lebanese-Syrian border". This position on a need for a delineation of the border was reaffirmed by the Security Council in its resolution 1680 (2006).

19. In this context, I also reiterate the position that while a permanent solution of this particular issue remains contingent upon the delineation of the border between the Syrian Arab Republic and Lebanon, in fulfilment of resolutions 1559 (2004), 1680 (2006) and 1701 (2006), and its eventual demarcation on the ground, I have also taken note of the Government of Lebanon's seven-point-plan and the approach suggested in it. Accordingly, I continue my work to examine the geographical definition of the Shab'a Farms, as outlined in my report of 14 March 2007 on the implementation of resolution 1701 (2006) (S/2007/147).

20. As I also wrote in my recent report, Israeli air violations of the Blue Line, through Israel Defense Force jet and unmanned aerial vehicle overflights, continue on an almost daily basis. The Government of Israel continues to maintain that the overflights are a necessary security measure that will continue until the two abducted Israeli soldiers are released and respect for the full arms embargo, established in paragraphs 14 and 15 of resolution 1701 (2006), is implemented. The Government of Lebanon continues to protest the overflights as a serious violation of Lebanese sovereignty and a violation of resolution 1701 (2006), and has argued in a recent letter to the Security Council of 4 April 2007 that Israeli overflights should not be linked to the enforcement of the arms embargo.

21. Mindful of the potential repercussions of continued regular violations of Lebanese sovereignty through Israeli overflights, I have, as I reported in my briefing to the Security Council on my trip to the Middle East on 5 April, asked the Government of Israel to halt its

policy of overflights, which are a violation of Lebanese sovereignty and of resolutions 1559 (2004) and 1701 (2006). I continue to expect that such air incursions and violations of Lebanese sovereignty will cease fully.

22. The Government of Lebanon has also asserted, in its letter to the members of the Security Council of 4 April 2007, that Israel's continued occupation of the northern part of Ghajar constitutes another breach of the Blue Line. As such, Israel's presence in Ghajar would constitute a violation of Lebanese sovereignty. The issue is being dealt with through the tripartite meetings convened by the Force Commander of the United Nations Interim Force in Lebanon (UNIFIL), and I am confident that a solution to the ongoing divergence of views can be found in due course. The same applies to Israeli violations of Lebanese sovereignty and territorial integrity that have occurred in the context of incidents along the Blue Line in February and March 2007. I continue to have full confidence that the tripartite meeting mechanism convened by the UNIFIL Force Commander can be utilized to satisfactorily address such incidents.

B. Extension of Lebanese Government control over all Lebanese territory

23. Under the conditions of the ongoing political crisis in Lebanon, the Government is restricted in its ability to extend its authority over all Lebanese territory. The Government's constitutional legitimacy itself has been called into question by the opposition. A resolution of the crisis, through dialogue and consensus, is a necessary precondition for the extension of Lebanese Government control over all Lebanese territory and the exertion of the Government's monopoly on the legitimate use of the force.

24. In response to my recent report on the implementation of resolution 1701 (2007) (S/2007/147), the Security Council has, while commending the steps taken by the Government of Lebanon to exercise its monopoly on the use of force throughout its territory, taken note with concern of reported activities of unauthorized armed elements outside of the UNIFIL area of operations and has reiterated its call for disbanding and disarming of all militias and armed groups in Lebanon.

25. I highlighted in my recent report the laudable efforts and achievements of the Government of Lebanon and the Lebanese Armed Forces to extend the Government's control over all Lebanese territory. The Lebanese Armed Forces, in particular, have played a commendable role in recent months in their efforts to establish the Government's monopoly on the legitimate use of force.

26. However, I have also outlined that the Lebanese Armed Forces are under considerable strain and thus limited in their ability to fully discharge their responsibilities. I reiterate my call on donor countries to come forward and help the Lebanese Armed Forces meet their obligations under resolution 1701 (2006) and as concerns the extension of the Government of Lebanon's control over all of Lebanon's territory and the establishment of the democratically elected Government's monopoly on the legitimate use of force throughout Lebanon, in fulfilment of the provisions of resolution 1559 (2004). As I told the Security Council in my recent briefing on my trip to the region on 5 April, the Government of Lebanon has indicated that it would be willing to consider further technical assistance, training and equipment, including, on a bilateral basis, to enhance the capabilities of its forces to better monitor its borders. The Government of Lebanon also has informed me that it has taken a series of measures to curb illegal arms activities. To that end, 8,000 troops

were deployed along the eastern and northern borders with the Syrian Arab Republic. Furthermore, the Government of Lebanon has reassured me again that it views the matter of border control and the prevention of the illegal entry of arms as vital issues of national security.

27. I have been provided with detailed information related to an extensive number of illegal crossing points between the Syrian Arab Republic and Lebanon, many of which are said to be used for smuggling, mostly of fuel, cement, and stolen vehicles by both Lebanese and Syrian nationals. The United Nations is in no position to verify such information. The indication, however, suffices to underline the necessity of a full delineation of the Syrian-Lebanese border and of improvements in the monitoring of the border.

28. While the Government of Lebanon has made considerable progress in asserting its authority, there remains concern as to the continued challenge posed to the legitimate authorities by militias. In particular, in my recent report (S/2007/147), I noted with concern the activities of Hizbullah and other militias outside of the UNIFIL area of operations. In addition, there have been reports of arms shipments and arms trafficking, which I also outlined in that report. Any form of illegal transfer of arms does not only stand in contradiction to resolution 1701 (2006), it also inherently undermines the authority of the State and its monopoly on the legitimate use of force, and thus contravenes resolution 1559 (2004). I have received information from Israel on arms trafficking. This information has been detailed and substantial, as outlined in my recent report. In addition, I have also received reports from other Member States detailing that illegal transfers of arms do occur. According to such reports, some weapons produced outside the region arrive via third countries and are brought clandestinely into Lebanon through the Syrian-Lebanese border. Such transfers are alleged to be taking place on a regular basis.

29. Against that background, I emphasized the importance of preventing illegal movement of arms into Lebanon in my recent talks with President Assad in Damascus. The Syrian Arab Republic has consistently denied reports of illegal arms trafficking through the Syrian-Lebanese border, except for individual incidents, as manifested in the Syrian seizure of a truck bearing Iraqi number plates in which there were contraband weapons that were on their way to Lebanon, as outlined in the letter of the Syrian Arab Republic to the Security Council of 20 March 2007. I have also received a number of photographs showing the contraband weaponry captured in that incident.

30. I join the call of the Security Council, expressed in its recent presidential statement (S/PRST/2007/12), on the Government of the Syrian Arab Republic to take further measures to reinforce controls at the Syrian-Lebanese border, emphasizing that under the given circumstances, its cooperation to enforce the arms embargo imposed by resolution 1701 (2006) is an indispensable element in enabling the exertion of the Lebanese Government's control over all of its territory. Having taken note of the letter of the Syrian Arab Republic to the Security Council dated 20 March 2007 and the information contained therein that the Syrian Arab Republic had apprehended a truck with Iraqi number plates which was carrying contraband weapons, I continue to view both the delineation of and strict control of the Lebanese-Syrian border, from both sides, as critically important.

31. Accordingly, I continue to develop a framework for the evaluation of the situation along the border and to intend to dispatch at the earliest, in close liaison with the Government of

Lebanon, an independent mission to fully assess the monitoring of the border. In accordance with the presidential statement of 17 April, I will keep the Council informed on my contacts with the Government, and report back to the Council in due course on its findings and recommendations in this regard.

32. I have also taken note of the assertion by the Syrian Arab Republic, which I referred to in my report of 14 March 2007 (S/2007/147) as well as mounting media speculation, that Israel is sending weapons to some Lebanese groups. Some reports have also asserted that other parties from the region and outside it are engaged in such weapons transfers. I have not been provided with any evidence to support such claims. At the same time, I cannot but be concerned over the disconcerting nature of all such reports, allegations and speculation, which illustrate that the authority of the State of Lebanon throughout its territory and its monopoly on the legitimate use of force is far from uncontested and assured.

33. In my recent report, I also referred to my concern over a growing threat from extremist Islamist groups, who have reportedly found safe haven in Palestinian refugee camps, to the presence of the United Nations in Lebanon. The presence and reportedly growing strength of such groups stands in direct contradiction to resolution 1559 (2004) and is deeply disconcerting, threatening not only the United Nations presence, but also undermining the Government of Lebanon's exertion of authority and its monopoly on the use of force throughout its territory. In the aftermath of the twin bus bombings of 13 February 2007, the Internal Security Force arrested a number of members of the Fatah al-Islam group, most of whom were Syrian nationals. Lebanese officials have informed me of their belief that Fatah al-Islam, which shares ideological tenets with Al-Qaida, is provided with funds by the Damascus-headquartered Fatah-Intifada militia and is composed primarily of Syrian nationals and Palestinians ordinarily resident in the Syrian Arab Republic, though there are also Lebanese and members of other nationalities among its activists. Fatah al-Islam is believed to number between 200 and 250 members and to be under the leadership of a Jordanian-Palestinian wanted for questioning in connection with the murder of a United States diplomat in Amman in 2001. The Government of the Syrian Arab Republic has written, in a letter to the President of the Security Council dated 26 March 2007, that it categorically denies accusations directed against it by some Lebanese authorities of coordination between Syrian bodies and Fatah al-Islam. The Syrian Minister of the Interior has asserted that the group is connected to Al-Qaida and had contacts with the former leader of Al-Qaida in Mesopotamia, Abu Musab al-Zarqawi. According to the Government of the Syrian Arab Republic, the Jordanian-Palestinian leader of Fatah al-Islam served three years in prison until 2006 and is wanted for renewed arrest in the Syrian Arab Republic. The Government of the Syrian Arab Republic also repeated in its letter that it regrets these accusations and affirmed that it condemns all crimes and continues to stand by Lebanon in order to strengthen stability and security therein.

34. I further note that extension of the Government's control over all Lebanese territory also remains contingent on a resolution of the continued Israeli presence in the northern part of Ghajar. The issue continues to be discussed through the tripartite meeting channel, and I expect it to be resolved in accordance with the Security Council's recent presidential statement.

C. Disbanding and disarmament of Lebanese andnon-Lebanese militias

35. As I have stated previously, it is my belief that the disarmament of Lebanese and non-Lebanese militias must take place through a political process that will lead to the full

affirmation of the authority of the Government of Lebanon throughout all of its territory. Such a political process presupposes, in the first instance, dialogue and a spirit of cooperation between the various political forces in Lebanon. As such, resolution of the ongoing political crisis in Lebanon—which primarily revolves around the question of the international tribunal and the establishment of a national unity Government—is a necessary precondition for such a far-reaching political process.

36. At the same time, the enforcement of the arms embargo imposed by resolution 1701 (2006) and the cooperation of parties outside Lebanon, in particular the Syrian Arab Republic and the Islamic Republic of Iran, remain a key ingredient in ensuring that such a political process can proceed and is not undermined by parties and groups extending their political power through the acquisition of arms. I stated in Damascus on 24 April that the Syrian Arab Republic should support the disbanding and disarming of all armed groups in Lebanon, consistent with its commitment to the implementation of resolution 1701 (2006).

37. In recent months, there has been no discussion among Lebanese political leaders about such a political process leading to the disbanding and disarmament of Lebanese and non-Lebanese militias. On the contrary, in the context of the enduring crisis, there have been mounting reports and increasing media speculation that a variety of Lebanese groups are expanding their existing weapons arsenals or are reacquiring a weapons capacity.

38. In the context of the prolonged political crisis that has paralysed Lebanon, fears have frequently been voiced that even the uneasy interim status quo maintained in the aftermath of the civil war—under which most Lebanese political groupings, except for Hizbullah had given up their armed capacities—may unravel, lead to widespread rearming and thus raise the spectre of a renewed confrontation among the Lebanese. The United Nations has not been able to investigate in-depth the empirical basis for such fears. I am deeply concerned, however, that the existing public and media discourse—whether based on evidence or speculative—may in fact accelerate, if not prompt, a domestic arms race in Lebanon, with unforeseeable consequences.

39. I have noted above and in my recent report (S/2007/147) the assertion put forward by the Syrian Arab Republic that some Lebanese groups are receiving arms from Israel. There has also been media speculation that Israel and other parties inside and outside the region are providing weaponry to groups aligned with the 14 March movement. The United Nations has not received any evidence substantiating such claims.

40. The Government of Lebanon has informed me that, on 21 December 2006, Lebanese security forces raided homes of a number of members of the Syrian Socialist Nationalist Party in northern Lebanon, discovering a considerable amount of weaponry and explosives of different types. The Lebanese authorities also made this information public. The head of the Party released a statement, according to which the raid had been politically motivated and the weapons found had been remnants from Lebanese resistance against the Israeli occupation in the 1980s.

41. The Government of Lebanon has also informed me that, on 3 March 2007, Lebanese customs authorities apprehended a private car in the Mt. Lebanon area, seizing 25 new Kalashnikov rifles, as well as six boxes containing 700 bullets each and 50 chargers. This information was also made public in Lebanon.

42. As concerns the Palestinian militias in Lebanon, there has been no progress or action towards the disarming and disbanding of such groups. My Special Representative has continued his dialogue with the representative of the Palestine Liberation Organization in Lebanon, who is also in close contact with the Lebanese authorities on all issues of mutual concern.

43. As I outlined in my report of 14 March 2007 (S/2007/147), Hizbullah has claimed that it is strengthening its capacity and rebuilding its armed presence, that it is present in southern Lebanon, close to the Blue Line, and that it has plenty of weapons and asserts the right to transport its arms within the country in order to combat Israel. Israel has also frequently asserted that Hizbullah is rebuilding its presence and infrastructure in south Lebanon and that it continues to receive weaponry through the Syrian-Lebanese border. I also outlined in that report that UNIFIL received no reports of unauthorized armed personnel in the area during the period under review, except for local hunters and Palestinian armed elements, who are largely confined to the refugee camps. In addition, I wrote that joint efforts by the Lebanese Armed Forces and UNIFIL have not detected illegal transfers of arms to the area south of the Litani River.

44. As I have referred to in my recent report, on 8 February 2007, Lebanese authorities intercepted a truck containing rockets, rocket launchers and mortars in an east Beirut suburb. The Government of Lebanon has now informed me that the truck had originally been seized by Lebanese customs officials on the Beirut-Damascus highway between Shtoura and Dahr al-Baydar in Lebanon, and had then been transferred for a detailed search to Beirut. The customs officials found a significant number of mortars, mortar shells, rockets and flares in the truck. In a statement released to the media, Hizbullah acknowledged that "a truck carrying ammunition for the resistance from the Beqaa to the south" had been seized, and demanded that "the concerned authorities must return the truck and the ammunitions to the resistance". Such activities would constitute a violation of resolutions 1559 (2004) and 1701 (2006).

45. The Government of Lebanon has further informed me that on 2 March 2007, three persons were captured by the Lebanese authorities with three Strella missiles in the vicinity of Nabatieh. The incident also stands in contradiction to the provisions of resolution 1559 (2004).

46. Hizbullah has accused other groups of stockpiling weapons in secrecy, and has publicly acknowledged remaining an armed militia, in defiance of resolution 1559 (2004).

47. In other public addresses, Nasrallah appeared to reject the notion that Hizbullah was a "state within a state," drawing into question the very authority of the Lebanese State. He also appeared to condition the disarmament of his group ("the solution to the resistance issue") on the establishment of "a strong state and a strong army". In this context, I recall the observations, made in previous reports on the implementation of resolution 1559 (2004) (S/2005/673 of 26 October 2005 and S/2006/248 of 19 April 2006), that in implementing the 1989 Taif Agreement, the majority of Lebanese militias merged into the Lebanese Armed Forces during the 1990s, in accordance with the Taif Agreement's provision that the "disbanding of all Lebanese and non-Lebanese militias shall be announced", and that "the militias' weapons shall be delivered to the Government of Lebanon within a period of six months", beginning with the ratification of the Agreement. I note that the establishment of a strong State and a strong army logically follows, rather than precedes, the disarming and

disbanding of militias, the integration of their military capacities into the regular armed forces, and their commitment to participate in the democratic political process.

48. Against this background, I also emphasize the importance of cooperation by regional parties that maintain ties with Hizbullah. The full implementation of the arms embargo imposed by resolution 1701 (2006) is an indispensable element in decreasing the tension and conflict potential that currently exists in Lebanon and in paving the ground for the disarming and disbanding of all Lebanese and non-Lebanese militias. It is also an obligation imposed by the Security Council's resolutions on all Member States.

49. I also reiterate once again the call on all those parties with the ability to influence Hizbullah to support its transformation into a solely political party, consistent with the requirements of the Taif Agreement, as a means to achieve the full disarmament of all Lebanese and non-Lebanese militias.

50. The eventual disarmament of Hizbullah in the sense of the completion of its transformation into a solely political party, consistent with the requirements of the Taif Agreement, is a key element in ensuring a permanent end of the hostilities and a critical provision to be realized in the implementation of resolution 1701 (2006) and in the full restoration of Lebanon's sovereignty, territorial integrity and political independence. In addition, it is my firm conviction that rivalry and antagonism between different factions in Lebanon must finally be channelled into a framework of political competition, rather than continuously imply the risk of an escalation into armed confrontation. The disarmament and disbanding of all militias in Lebanon will be an important step in this regard.

D. Presidential election process

51. The issue of the Lebanese presidency is now once again becoming a prominent political issue in Lebanon. Since the adoption of resolution 1559 (2004) in September 2004, regrettably, there has been no free and fair electoral process in Lebanon's presidential election conducted according to Lebanese constitutional rules devised without foreign interference or influence. In its presidential statement of 30 October 2006 (S/PRST/2006/43), the Security Council noted again with regret that some provisions of resolution 1559 (2004) had yet to be implemented, including free and fair presidential elections conducted according to the Lebanese constitutional rules, without any foreign interference and influence.

52. The parliamentary majority represented by the 14 March alliance continues to maintain that President Lahoud's continued presence in office is illegitimate. I have also taken note of the recent petition signed by 70 members of Parliament in favour of a parliamentary session to ratify the statutory agreement on the international tribunal for Lebanon, in which signatories justified their resort to a petition with reference to "the position of the President of the Republic, whose mandate was extended in contravention of Security Council resolution 1559 (2006), and who continues in his attempt to obstruct the constitutional prerogatives of the legitimate government of Lebanon".

53. In the coming months, the extended term of President Lahoud will be coming to an end. A new president will have to be elected, in an electoral process that should be free and fair and be conducted according to Lebanese constitutional rules devised without foreign interference or influence, in accordance with resolution 1559 (2004). Such an election will also help revive the ordinary and constitutional political process in Lebanon.

III. Observations

54. Since the report of 19 October 2006 on the implementation of resolution 1559 (2004) (S/2006/832), further progress has been achieved to consolidate the arrangements established by resolution 1701 (2006), which provides an enabling framework for Lebanon's stabilization and its return onto the path towards reasserting its sovereignty, territorial integrity, and political independence, which the country had been pursuing prior to last summer's war. To date, however, resolution 1559 (2004) has not yet been implemented in full.

55. The prolonged political crisis and uncertainty that has haunted Lebanon over the past few months illustrates that the provisions of resolution 1559 (2004) remain as relevant as they were when the resolution was first adopted. Since September 2004, Lebanon has undergone a momentous transition, in partnership with the United Nations. Most importantly, the country elected a Government that continues to enjoy democratic legitimacy bestowed on it by a process of free and fair parliamentary elections, under the supervision of international monitors. However, the transition has not yet been completed, and indeed, has suffered tremendous setbacks.

56. The enduring standoff also demonstrates that Lebanon is in need of a comprehensive and, most importantly, consensual political framework, as manifested in the Taif Agreement. This framework also necessitates the renewed support and engagement of all relevant external parties and supporters of Lebanon. Without it, and without an end to the stifling crisis, Lebanon will not be able to make much further progress towards reasserting its sovereignty, territorial integrity, and political independence, or to sustain such progress in the long term. I have taken positive note of the assurances I have received from President Assad and other senior Syrian officials during my talks in Damascus on 24 April, and look forward to their realization in practice.

57. On the domestic level, a resolution of the current crisis will have to encompass discussion of and agreement on the issue of the Lebanese presidency. In the first report, of 1 October 2004, on the implementation of resolution 1559 (2004) (S/2004/777), the belief was stated that "Governments and leaders should not hold on to office beyond prescribed term limits". The divisive issue of President Lahoud's extended term in office will soon no longer be of relevance. What will be of relevance, however, is that the process of the presidential election will be free and fair, be conducted according to Lebanese constitutional rules devised without foreign interference or influence, in accordance with resolution 1559 (2004).

58. Neither the current political crisis in Lebanon nor the overall implementation of all provisions of resolution 1559 (2004) is a purely domestic matter. As has long been the case, the fate of Lebanon remains tied up with broader regional trends and concerns. On one level, this relates to the Arab-Israeli conflict and efforts to attain a just, comprehensive and lasting peace for all peoples in the region. On another level, this relates to the full implementation of not just resolution 1559 (2004), but also resolutions 1680 (2006) and 1701 (2006), as well as, insofar as it is relevant, resolution 1747 (2007).

59. Most importantly, the subject of the allegations that illegal arms trafficking is taking place clandestinely via the Syrian-Lebanese border needs to be addressed, since any form of weapons smuggling inherently undermines the authority of the Government and its monopoly on the legitimate use of force. I was and remain concerned over the extent and detail of the reports. I call on all relevant parties, in particular the Governments of the

Syrian Arab Republic and of the Islamic Republic of Iran, to ensure the full implementation of resolutions 1559 (2004) and 1701 (2006).

60. In this context, I reiterate my belief that the establishment of formal diplomatic relations between the Syrian Arab Republic and Lebanon and the delineation of the Syrian-Lebanese border are essential measures to affirm the strict respect for Lebanon's sovereignty, territorial integrity, and political independence of Lebanon and enable the full implementation of all provisions of resolution 1559 (2004). I expect that the Syrian Arab Republic and Lebanon, in the context of a resolution of the current political crisis in Lebanon, will make progress towards a bilateral agreement on these elements. With regard to the Shab'a Farms, I am continuing my work to examine the geographical definition of the area. I also wish to call for the Syrian Arab Republic and Lebanon to address in their bilateral contacts the issue of Lebanese detainees in Syrian custody.

61. I have noted the diverse allegations coming from various sides and parties as concerns illegal arms trafficking and the possible arming of a variety of Lebanese and non-Lebanese groups. All these are of great concern. I am deeply worried that the political crisis in Lebanon may be deepened and exacerbated by the allegations and related speculation. Most importantly, fears of and speculation fuelling a process of widespread rearmament of political groups in Lebanon have raised the spectre of return to Lebanon's darkest days. This must not happen.

62. Hizbullah's arms continue to pose a key challenge to the Government's monopoly on the legitimate use of force and all efforts to reassert Lebanon's sovereignty, territorial integrity and political independence. I reiterate my conviction that the disarmament of Lebanese and non-Lebanese militias must take place through a political process, which in the first instance depends on a resolution of the current political crisis and the establishment of dialogue and consensus on a number of the most pressing issues. At the same time, the full implementation of the arms embargo imposed by resolution 1701 (2006) is an indispensable element in decreasing the tension and conflict potential that currently exists in Lebanon and in paving the ground for the disarming and disbanding of all Lebanese and non-Lebanese militias. All regional parties concerned, in particular the Syrian Arab Republic, must lend their support to this process. I note positively in this regard my conversation with President Assad on the relevant issues.

63. In addition, the domestic and regional political process must also return to addressing the issue of the Palestinian militias, in accordance with the agreements reached in last year's national dialogue.

64. All regional and extraregional parties are called upon to provide all necessary support. With the efforts to implement in full resolution 1701 (2006), much progress has been achieved. I thank all troop contributors to UNIFIL, all providers of bilateral technical assistance, and all donor countries. I also wish to commend the Lebanese Armed Forces, in particular, for the important role they have played in recent months in their efforts to establish the Government's monopoly on the legitimate use of force and extend its authority throughout all of Lebanon's territory.

65. I reiterate my call on all parties and actors to support Lebanon's reconstruction and political transformation, and to urgently take all enabling measures to this end, as outlined in the Taif Agreement and in resolutions 1559 (2004), 1680 (2006), and 1701 (2006).

66. I will continue my efforts for the purpose of the full implementation of these and all other relevant Security Council resolutions pertaining to the restoration of the territorial integrity, full sovereignty, and political independence of Lebanon and the achievement of a just, lasting and comprehensive peace throughout the entire Middle Eastern region, consistent with all relevant Security Council resolutions, especially resolutions 242 (1967) and 338 (1973).

[1] See the letter to the President of the Security Council of 1 December 2006 (S/2006/933) and my report of 14 March 2007 on the implementation of Security Council resolution 1701 (2006) (S/2007/147).

9. Report of the Secretary-General on the United Nations Disengagement Observer Force (for the period from 2 December 2006 to 6 June 2007), 5 June 2007 (S/2007/331)

I. Introduction

1. The present report gives an account of the activities of the United Nations Disengagement Observer Force (UNDOF) during the past six months pursuant to the mandate contained in Security Council resolution 350 (1974) and extended in subsequent resolutions, most recently resolution 1729 (2006) of 15 December 2006.

II. Situation in the area and activities of the Force

2. During the period under review the ceasefire in the Israel-Syria sector was maintained and the UNDOF area of operation remained generally quiet. UNDOF supervised the area of separation by means of fixed positions and patrols to ensure that military forces of either party were excluded from it. The Force also carried out fortnightly inspections of equipment and force levels in the areas of limitation. Liaison officers from the party concerned accompanied the inspection teams. UNDOF monitored increased patrolling of the area between the ceasefire line and the technical fence by the Israel Defense Forces (IDF). As in the past, both sides denied inspection teams access to some of their positions and imposed restrictions on the Force's freedom of movement. Israeli national Customs officials continued to operate at the IDF post at the UNDOF crossing gate between the Israeli-occupied Golan and the Syrian Arab Republic.

3. The Force continued to assist the International Committee of the Red Cross with the passage of persons through the area of separation. During the past six months, UNDOF assisted in the crossing of 33 students and one bride. Between 26 February and 30 April, UNDOF also facilitated the transfer of 6,946 tons of apples through the area of separation from the Israeli side to the Syrian side. In addition, the Force assisted in the handover from IDF to the Syrian authorities of one Syrian civilian who had crossed into the Israeli-occupied Golan.

4. In the area of operation, especially in the area of separation, mines continued to pose a threat to UNDOF personnel and local inhabitants. Owing to the age of the mines and their deteriorating explosives, this threat has increased. UNDOF continued to carry out operational mine clearance. UNDOF remained available to support the United Nations Children's Fund in activities to promote mine awareness among the civilian population.

5. The Force Commander and his staff maintained close contact with the military authorities of Israel and the Syrian Arab Republic. Both sides generally cooperated with the Force in the execution of its tasks.

6. As at 31 May 2007, UNDOF comprised 1,047 troops, from Austria (378), Canada (2), India (190), Japan (30), Poland (352) and Slovakia (95). A total of 15 personnel were employed by Japan as a national support element. In addition, 85 military observers from the United Nations Truce Supervision Organization (UNTSO) assisted the Force in carrying out its tasks. A map showing the deployment of the Force is attached to the present report.

III. Financial aspects

7. By its resolution 60/277 of 30 June 2006, the General Assembly appropriated the amount of $39.9 million for the maintenance of the Force for the period from 1 July 2006 to 30 June 2007. The proposed budget for UNDOF for the financial period commencing 1 July 2007 amounting to $39.6 million, equivalent to $3.3 million per month, is currently under consideration by the General Assembly. Should the Council decide to extend the mandate of the Force beyond 30 June 2007, as recommended in paragraph 12 below, the cost of maintaining the Force would be limited to the monthly amounts approved by the General Assembly.

8. As at 31 March 2007, unpaid assessed contributions to the UNDOF special account for the period from the inception of the Force to 31 March 2007 amounted to $20.8 million. Total outstanding assessed contributions for all peacekeeping operations as at the same date amounted to $1.8 billion. As at 31 March 2007, amounts owed to troop contributors for UNDOF totalled $1.1 million. Troop and contingent-owned equipment costs have been reimbursed for the periods up to 28 February 2007 and 31 December 2006, respectively, in accordance with the quarterly payment schedule.

IV. Implementation of Security Council resolution 338 (1973)

9. The Security Council, when deciding in its resolution 1729 (2006) to renew the mandate of UNDOF for a further period of six months, until 30 June 2007, also called upon the parties concerned to implement immediately its resolution 338 (1973), and requested the Secretary-General to submit, at the end of the period, a report on developments in the situation and the measures taken to implement that resolution. The search for a peaceful settlement in the Middle East, and in particular the efforts undertaken at various levels to implement resolution 338 (1973), was dealt with in the report of the Secretary-General on the situation in the Middle East (A/61/298) submitted pursuant to General Assembly resolutions 60/40 and 60/41.

V. Observations

10. The situation in the Israel-Syria sector has remained generally quiet. UNDOF, which was established in May 1974 to supervise the ceasefire called for by the Security Council and the agreement on disengagement between Syrian and Israeli forces of 31 May 1974, has continued to perform its function effectively, with the cooperation of the parties.

11. Nevertheless, the situation in the Middle East is tense and is likely to remain so, unless and until a comprehensive settlement covering all aspects of the Middle East problem can be reached. I hope that determined efforts will be made by all concerned to tackle the problem in all its aspects, with a view to arriving at a just and durable peace settlement, as called for by the Security Council in its resolution 338 (1973).

12. Under the prevailing circumstances, I consider the continued presence of UNDOF in the area to be essential. I therefore recommend that the Security Council extend the mandate of the Force for a further period of six months, until 31 December 2007. The Government of the Syrian Arab Republic has given its assent to the proposed extension. The Government of Israel has also expressed its agreement.

13. In making this recommendation, I must draw attention to the shortfall in the funding of the Force. At present, unpaid assessments amount to some $1.1 million. The sum represents money owed to the Member States that contribute the troops who make up the Force. I appeal to all Member States to pay their assessments promptly and in full and to clear all remaining arrears.

14. In conclusion, I wish to pay tribute to Major General Wolfgang Jilke and to the men and women serving with UNDOF and UNTSO. They have performed with efficiency and devotion to duty the important tasks assigned to them by the Security Council. I take this opportunity to express my appreciation to the Governments contributing troops to UNDOF and to those which provide the UNTSO military observers assigned to the Force.

10. Report of the Secretary-General on the Implementation of Resolution 1701 (2006), 28 June 2007 (S/2007/392)

I. Introduction

1. The present report is the fourth report of the Secretary-General on the implementation of resolution 1701 (2006), notably on efforts towards the achievement of a permanent ceasefire between Israel and Lebanon and a long-term solution based on the principles and elements outlined in paragraph 8 of the resolution. It provides a comprehensive assessment of the steps taken to implement resolution 1701 (2006) since my quarterly report issued on 14 March 2007 (S/2007/147).

2. The present report is being issued as we approach the first anniversary of the conflict that took place during the second quarter of 2006 between Hizbullah and Israel. On 12 July 2006, eight Israeli soldiers were killed and two soldiers, Eldad Regev and Ehud Goldwasser, were abducted and are still being held by Hizbullah. The event precipitated Israeli military reprisals on the same day and Hizbullah rocket fire into northern Israel, igniting a conflict that ultimately led to the deaths of nearly 1,200 Lebanese and 160 Israelis, the destruction of much of Lebanon's infrastructure and severe damage to the economies of both countries. The present report highlights both continuing progress in the implementation of resolution 1701 (2006) and areas of concern, which to date, have not led to the establishment of a permanent ceasefire and a long-term solution as envisioned in the resolution. I am encouraged by the significant deployment of the Lebanese Armed Forces and of the United Nations Interim Force in Lebanon (UNIFIL) in the area south of the Litani River, both of whose activities aim to ensure that the area is free of any unauthorized armed personnel, assets and weapons and that there continue to be no positions other than those of the Lebanese Armed Forces and UNIFIL along the Blue Line. This constitutes a strengthening of the security arrangements aimed at preventing the resumption of hostilities in the area between the Blue Line and the Litani River. I am also pleased to report that there remains an enduring commitment by the Government of Lebanon and the Government of Israel to resolution 1701 (2006).

3. I am deeply concerned, however, that Lebanon remains in the midst of a debilitating political crisis and faces ongoing attacks aimed at destabilizing and undermining its sovereignty, territorial integrity and independence. During the reporting period, the country witnessed fighting between militants from the Fatah al-Islam group and the Lebanese security forces, the worst internal fighting since its civil war, which lasted from 1995 to 1990; a series of bomb explosions in and around Beirut, the latest of which killed Walid Eido, a member of the Lebanese Parliament, and nine others on 13 June; and a bomb attack on 24 June against UNIFIL that killed six peacekeepers serving with the Spanish contingent. In addition, the firing of Katyusha rockets from southern Lebanon into northern Israel on 17 June by unknown elements was the most serious breach of the cessation of hostilities since the end of the war. Such incidents pose a direct challenge to both the new security arrangements in southern Lebanon and to the stability of the country as a whole.

4. Against this background, I am concerned that continued implementation of resolution 1701 (2006) may face recurring difficulties. Greater progress is necessary on key issues

that are central to the achievement of a permanent ceasefire and a longer-term solution, such as the release of the abducted Israeli soldiers and of the Lebanese prisoners, the enforcement of the arms embargo, the halting of Israeli air violations of Lebanese sovereignty and the Shab'a Farms issue.

II. Attack against the United Nations Interim Force in Lebanon

5. As the present report was being finalized, on 24 June, a Spanish battalion patrol was hit by an explosion on the main road between the towns of Marjayoun and Khiam. The initial investigation confirmed that the explosion was caused by a car bomb. Six UNIFIL personnel serving with the Spanish contingent were killed, and two others were injured. No one has claimed responsibility for the attack.

6. The Lebanese political leadership, including Prime Minister Siniora, condemned the attack and expressed condolences to UNIFIL and to the Governments of the nations concerned. Hizbullah also denounced the attack, stating that it only hurt the people of Lebanon. The Government of Lebanon has established a high commission to investigate the attack and an investigation by UNIFIL is also under way.

7. I am deeply saddened and condemn in the strongest possible terms that terrorist attack against soldiers who had gone to Lebanon in the name of peace. I urge the Government of Lebanon to bring to justice those responsible as swiftly as possible.

8. In recent months, there have been a number of threats against UNIFIL from militant groups. UNIFIL has put in place a number of mitigation measures to ensure the safety and security of its military and civilian personnel and of its installations. It has reinforced its installations throughout its area of operations south of the Litani River and in Beirut and has implemented enhanced security procedures for all of its military and civilian personnel. Once the investigation into the 24 June attack is concluded, security arrangements will be further adjusted, if and as necessary, to mitigate the potential for such incidents in the future. At the same time, all measures will continue to ensure that mandated activities are conducted without hindrance, while taking due care of the prevailing security environment.

III. Implementation of Security Council resolution 1701 (2006)

A. Respect for the Blue Line

9. The military and security situation in the UNIFIL area of operations has been generally stable since my report of 14 March 2007 (S/2007/147). However, in the most serious breach of the cessation of hostilities and violation of the Blue Line since the end of the conflict in 2006, three Katyusha rockets were launched from the area of El Aadeisse in south Lebanon on 17 June 2007. Despite very rudimentary launching mechanisms, two of the rockets landed in the Israeli town of Kiryat Shemona, causing minor damage but claiming no casualties. The attack was carried out by unidentified perpetrators. A group under the name Jihadi Badr Brigades-Lebanon branch claimed responsibility; however, its claim could not as yet be verified. Immediately after the attack occurred, Hizbullah denied any responsibility or knowledge of the attack and issued a press statement to that effect.

10. The Lebanese Armed Forces quickly deployed to the area, along with units from UNIFIL and deactivated a fourth rocket that had failed to fire. No suspects were found at the site.

11. Subsequent to the attack, the Lebanese Armed Forces deployed additional personnel in the area, established a number of new checkpoints and detained over 200 persons for investigation. UNIFIL has also increased its patrolling activities in the area, working in close coordination with the Lebanese Armed Forces and the UNIFIL Force Commander and maintaining open lines of communication with the army senior commanders on both sides. The Prime Minister of Lebanon, the Speaker of the Parliament and the Lebanese Armed Forces promptly issued statements strongly condemning the attack.

12. UNIFIL was also in close contact with the Israel Defense Forces immediately after the incident occurred to urge Israel to exercise maximum restraint. Israel has so far refrained from taking retaliatory action.

13. I would like to commend the Lebanese Armed Forces, the Israel Defense Forces and UNIFIL for the way in which they handled the incident. It shows that, with appropriate coordination and liaison arrangements in place, it is possible to prevent such incidents from escalating. However, the fact that as yet unidentified elements were able to execute the attack from southern Lebanon is deeply troubling and underlines the need to further strengthen security arrangements, which are being put in place by the Lebanese Armed Forces, together with UNIFIL.

14. The situation along the Blue Line remains tense and fragile. On a number of occasions, the Israel Defense Forces and the Lebanese Armed Forces patrols have aimed weapons at each other across the Blue Line. In each instance, UNIFIL has acted promptly to dispatch a patrol to the scene to calm the situation and prevent confrontation. A number of ground violations by both sides have also raised tensions. On 28 May, the Israel Defense Forces violated the Blue Line by approximately 60 metres in the vicinity of United Nations position 4-31, with a tank and earthworks machinery. The Israel Defense Forces subsequently stated that the exact location of the Blue Line at the spot was unclear and that the violation had occurred inadvertently. A number of minor violations have also occurred on the Lebanese side, predominantly by shepherds and hunters. On two occasions, individuals who crossed the Blue Line were detained by the Israel Defense Forces and released hours later. Inadvertent crossings are a particular concern in the Shab'a Farms region where there is rough terrain and no Israeli technical fence. The Force Commander of UNIFIL has urged both parties to act with restraint and refrain from activities that contribute to tension along the Blue Line.

15. The ground violations highlight the importance of visibly marking the Blue Line in sensitive areas, in particular where there is a considerable distance between the Blue Line and the Israeli technical fence. In my report dated 14 March, I noted that both parties had orally agreed to the UNIFIL proposal to mark the Blue Line. After further intensive discussions in tripartite meetings on the issue, the Government of Lebanon has officially accepted the UNIFIL proposed technical process for marking the Blue Line, while the Government of Israel has sought clarifications. I urge both parties to move forward expeditiously with UNIFIL on the proposal, which, if fully implemented on the ground, would build trust, decrease tension and significantly contribute towards a reduction in incidents and inadvertent violations of the Blue Line.

16. UNIFIL has reported a significant increase in Israeli air violations, through jet and unmanned aerial vehicle overflights of Lebanese territory. These violations occur on an almost daily basis, frequently numbering between 15 and 20 overflights, and even reaching

32, in a single day. The Government of Lebanon continues to protest the overflights as a serious violation of Lebanese sovereignty and of resolution 1701 (2006). The Government of Israel maintains that they are a necessary security measure that will continue until its two abducted soldiers are released and the measures set out in paragraphs 14 and 15 of resolution 1701 (2006) are implemented in full. Notwithstanding the essential requirement to fully implement all provisions of resolution 1701 (2006), Israeli overflights not only constitute repeated violations of that and other relevant Security Council resolutions; they also undermine the credibility of both UNIFIL and the Lebanese Armed Forces in the eyes of the local population and negatively affect efforts to stabilize the situation on the ground.

B. Security and liaison arrangements

17. The Force Commander of UNIFIL continues to hold regular tripartite meetings with senior representatives of the Lebanese Armed Forces and the Israel Defense Forces, in which critical security issues are addressed. Steady progress has been made on a number of key areas through this forum, which is essential to UNIFIL efforts to foster stability and prevent incidents across the Blue Line.

18. I am pleased to report that the liaison and coordination arrangements, referred to in my previous report, were accepted by both parties and came into force during the period under review, following written notification of acceptance from the Lebanese Armed Forces and the Israel Defense Forces. The arrangements stipulate that both the Lebanese Armed Forces and the Israel Defense Forces must ensure that an officer at the rank of General, or his deputy, can be contacted at all times by the UNIFIL Force Commander so that any incident can be quickly resolved before it escalates. As noted above, the benefits of having strong coordination and liaison arrangements became clear during the incident of 17 June, where the Force Commander was able to establish and maintain a continuous exchange with senior-level officers of the Israel Defense Forces and of the Lebanese Armed Forces. UNIFIL is in the process of establishing a hotline between the Force Commander and his counterparts in the Lebanese Armed Forces and Israel Defense Forces.

19. The Israel Defense Forces remain in control of the northern part of Ghajar village, north of the Blue Line inside Lebanese territory, although they do not maintain a permanent military presence. Discussions on the issue of temporary security arrangements for northern Ghajar continue in tripartite meetings, and both parties indicate that they are committed to reaching an agreement with UNIFIL, which would facilitate Israeli withdrawal from the area. However, the duration of the temporary security arrangements still remains a point of contention. The UNIFIL Force Commander is actively engaged with both sides in an attempt to overcome the obstacle and finalize the arrangements. I am concerned that further delay in resolving the issue may contribute to increasing tensions along the Blue Line. It should be recalled that, as long as the Israel Defense Forces remains in northern Ghajar, Israel will have yet to complete its withdrawal from southern Lebanon in accordance with its obligations under resolution 1701 (2006).

20. The existing planning and coordination mechanism between UNIFIL and the Lebanese Army Command remains instrumental for coordinating activities on the ground. Collaboration between UNIFIL and the Lebanese Armed Forces and Lebanese Navy has been further strengthened through coordinated exercises and training initiatives during the reporting period. Liaison officers of the Lebanese Armed Forces are detached in the

UNIFIL headquarters Joint Operation Centre and Naval Operation Centre, in both sector headquarters and in all infantry battalions. While UNIFIL maintains two officers at the Israel Defense Forces Northern Command headquarters in Zefat, agreement has yet to be reached between the Government of Israel and the United Nations on establishing a civilian-led integrated UNIFIL liaison office in Tel Aviv.

21. The Lebanese Armed Forces maintain four infantry brigades south of the Litani River, operating 145 positions. Efforts are under way to increase and fortify the 47 Lebanese Armed Forces observation towers and positions along the Blue Line. The Lebanese Armed Forces monitor and control entry into the UNIFIL area of operations across the Litani River through permanent checkpoints and patrols. They have also requested UNIFIL assistance in building a military road parallel to the Blue Line in order to improve monitoring capabilities. Construction of that road is contingent upon the marking of the Blue Line.

22. UNIFIL continues to implement its mandate to assist the Lebanese Armed Forces in ensuring that the area between the Blue Line and the Litani River is free of unauthorized armed personnel, assets, weapons, infrastructure or related materiel. To that end, UNIFIL carries out more than 400 patrols per day throughout its area of operations, night surveillance on suspected activities by armed elements and operations in open areas. In addition, UNIFIL troops stop any individual if they have reason to suspect any activity in violation of resolution 1701 (2006).

23. Coordinated operations undertaken by the Lebanese Armed Forces and UNIFIL during the period under review have led to the discovery of abandoned arms, ammunition, explosive devices, bunkers and related infrastructure. The most significant discoveries were an ammunition dump and 17 rockets in the vicinity of El Fardeis, a cave with 100 mortar bombs in the vicinity of Mazraat Islamiye, two rocket launchers in Rchaf, a cave containing mines, mortars and detonators in the Kafr Shouba area and a weapons and ammunitions cache containing an anti-tank recoilless gun with two rocket launchers and ammunition in the same general area. The Lebanese Armed Forces destroy or confiscate all arms and ammunition found south of the Litani River.

24. With the exception of two very disturbing incidents, which occurred at the end of the reporting period, namely, the 17 June rocket attack on Kiryat Shemona and the 24 June attack on UNIFIL, UNIFIL has neither discovered, nor received reports of, armed elements inside its area of operations, other than those within Palestinian refugee camps and local hunters. At the same time, the Lebanese Armed Forces and UNIFIL have not detected any illegal transfers of arms south of the Litani River. However, the two recent attacks, as well as the continuing weapons discoveries by UNIFIL and the Lebanese Armed Forces, clearly indicate that there are still weapons in the UNIFIL area of operations and persons prepared to use them. This underlines the importance of the activities of the Lebanese Armed Forces and UNIFIL to ensure that the area becomes free of any armed personnel, assets and weapons, which will require more time to achieve. UNIFIL and the Lebanese Armed Forces have very strict security controls in place, including a significant number of positions, Lebanese Armed Forces checkpoints and UNIFIL road and open area patrols. In addition, as a consequence of the two attacks, the Lebanese Armed Forces are now taking additional security steps to address the situation in any suspected areas and UNIFIL will support their efforts.

25. The Government of Israel continues to claim that Hizbullah is rebuilding its military capacity primarily north but also south of the Litani River. UNIFIL, in collaboration with the Lebanese Armed Forces, stands ready to immediately investigate any such claims or alleged violations of resolution 1701 (2006) once the necessary specific information and evidence has been received. Hizbullah continues to have strong support among the local population and maintains a significant non-military presence. Suspected members have continued to closely monitor UNIFIL activities throughout the period under review, including through the taking of photographs and filming.

26. The UNIFIL Maritime Task Force, in collaboration with the Lebanese Navy, continues to enhance control of Lebanese territorial waters to prevent entry into Lebanon of unauthorized arms or related materiel by sea. Since my last report, the Maritime Task Force has hailed more than 3,000 ships. The identities of all vessels were checked and confirmed, and 25 suspicious vessels were inspected by Lebanese naval and customs officials on arrival in port. No attempts to smuggle weapons were reported. I am grateful to the Government of Germany for donating two naval vessels to the Lebanese Navy, which will represent a significant step in building its naval capacity and assisting Lebanon to assume increased responsibility for securing its sea boundaries.

27. I regret to report that there have been several occasions during the reporting period when actions by Israel Defense Forces personnel have endangered their own security and that of United Nations personnel. In an incident on 30 April, a fast patrol boat of the Israel Defense Forces approached a UNIFIL Maritime Task Force frigate at high speed and on a collision with the frigate and did not respond to the frigate's radio communication. The frigate was only able to avoid collision by rapidly and significantly reducing speed. On two other occasions, Israeli aircraft flew at low altitude over Maritime Task Force frigates in contravention of established procedures. In a meeting between the Maritime Task Force Commander and his Israeli Navy counterpart, the Israel Defense Forces reassured UNIFIL that they would adhere to the operational arrangements between the Israel Defense Forces and the UNIFIL Maritime Task Force.

28. Relations between UNIFIL and the local population have continued to develop, especially through the work undertaken by the UNIFIL Civilian-military cooperation units and civil affairs teams. The implementation of quick-impact projects is proving to be a critical instrument for assisting local communities. The Force Commander has also initiated a series of meetings with community leaders throughout the UNIFIL area of operations, which have further helped to build trust and confidence as well as broaden the understanding of the UNIFIL mandate within local communities. Nevertheless, UNIFIL patrols have faced a number of isolated stone-throwing and other incidents, mainly by local youths. The Lebanese Armed Forces have taken a proactive role in preventing and addressing those incidents and in some cases have detained the perpetrators.

C. Disarming armed groups

29. A number of reports have indicated an increase in activities conducted by armed elements north of the Litani River, where the Lebanese authorities and the Lebanese Armed Forces have sole security responsibility. Suspected Hizbullah armed elements are alleged to be constructing new facilities in the Bekaa valley, including command and control centres and rocket launching capabilities, and conducting military training exercises. The reports have not been refuted by Hizbullah.

30. In identical letters dated 12 June from the Chargé d'affaires a.i. of the Permanent Mission of Lebanon to the United Nations addressed to me and to the President of the Security Council (S/2007/348-A/61/953), the Government of Lebanon provided detailed information, collected by the Lebanese Armed Forces, on the activities of Palestinian armed elements and groups outside the Palestinian refugee camps based in Lebanon. A comprehensive update on the status of Lebanese and non-Lebanese militias has also been provided in my most recent semi-annual report (S/2009/262) and in a briefing in June on the implementation of Security Council resolution 1559 (2004).

31. Specifically, we have been informed by the Government of Lebanon that the Popular Front for the Liberation of Palestine-General Command and Fatah-Intifada have reinforced their posts throughout the country following the attacks launched by Fatah al-Islam against the Lebanese Armed Forces in northern Lebanon. The information provides details of reinforcements of the Popular Front for the Liberation of Palestine-General Command in areas such as Jubayla and Ain el-Bayda outposts, where about 100 members wearing military uniforms similar to those of the Lebanese Armed Forces have been deployed. In the Qussaya outpost, the group has installed eight rocket launchers (12- and 40-barrel) and directed them towards the Rayak airport. The information also outlines how Fatah-Intifada has reinforced its posts in Wadi al-Asswad, Balta, Helwa and Deir el-Achayer. Their number is estimated at about 500 men equipped with sophisticated weaponry, including rockets, mortars, anti-tank guns (106 mm recoilless gun and B10 gun) and anti-aircraft guns.

32. It is widely believed in Lebanon, including by the Government, that the strengthening of Fatah-Intifada outposts and those of the Popular Front for the Liberation of Palestine-General Command could not have taken place without the tacit knowledge and support of the Government of the Syrian Arab Republic. The Prime Minister of Lebanon has recently stated publicly that the outposts have been reinforced with munitions, arms and fighters by the Syrian Arab Republic. The Government of the Syrian Arab Republic has denied such assertions as misleading. It should be noted that the Lebanese national dialogue involving all major Lebanese political parties, which was held in April and May 2006, agreed that Palestinian armed groups outside the Palestinian camps should be disarmed within six months. I expect the support of the Government of the Syrian Arab Republic on that particular issue.

33. In addition, the Government of Lebanon provided us with information on the recent seizure of a truckload of Grad rockets, mortars and ammunition for automatic rifles and machine guns. The truckload, which belonged to Hizbullah, was seized on 5 June 2007 at a checkpoint of the Lebanese Armed Forces at Douriss near Baalbek in east Lebanon's Bekaa valley. According to the Government of Lebanon, the arms were being moved within the country. There seems to be an emerging consensus in Lebanon that the incident is similar to the one that took place on 8 February 2007, which was documented in my most recent report to the Council on implementation of resolution 1701 (2006) (S/2007/147).

34. The reports are disconcerting and a cause of great concern and constitute a clear violation of both the letter and spirit of Security Council resolution 1701 (2006) as well as resolution 1559 (2004).

35. With reference to paragraph 10 of resolution 1701 (2006) and the issue of disarmament, I continue to believe that the disarmament of Hizbullah and other militia should be

conducted through a Lebanese-led political process that will lead to the full restoration of the authority of the Government of Lebanon in all its territory so that there will be no weapons or authority other than its own.

36. The Government of Lebanon maintains that the question of Hizbullah arms and the arms of other militias remains open and in the centre of the political debate. However, no progress on the issue has been made. The ongoing political crisis continues to prevent the parties from discussing national dialogue issues or making progress on the Government's seven-point plan, which was adopted on 27 July 2006.

D. Arms embargo

37. Further to the update I have provided in relation to possible breaches of the arms embargo in my fifth semi-annual report on the implementation of Security Council resolution 1559 (2004) (S/2007/262), I have received further disturbing information from the Government of Lebanon. The Government of Lebanon has informed me that on 6 June 2007, four truck carriers, each carrying two vehicles mounted with 40-barrel rocket launchers (a total of eight rocket-launchers) were seen by the Lebanese Armed Forces heading from Al-Kafeer in the Syrian Arab Republic across the Lebanese-Syrian border to Idriss Fortnress and then on to an outpost of the Popular Front for the Liberation of Palestine-General Command in Jabal al-Maaysara.

38. For its part, the Government of Israel continues to allege significant breaches of the arms embargo across the Lebanese-Syrian border, which it states, pose a serious strategic threat to the security of Israel and its citizens. It has claimed that the transfer of sophisticated weaponry by the Syrian Arab Republic and the Islamic Republic of Iran across the Lebanese-Syrian border, including long-range rockets (with a range of 250 miles), anti-tank and anti-aircraft defence systems, occurs on a weekly basis, enabling Hizbullah to rearm to the same levels as before the past year's war or beyond. It has not provided any further specific evidence to back up those claims.

39. The Government of the Syrian Arab Republic has denied any involvement in effecting breaches of the arms embargo. In its identical letters to me and the President of the Security Council dated 4 May 2007, it provided a table listing weapons and ammunition smuggled into the Syrian Arab Republic from Lebanon, which have been confiscated by the Syrian security forces during the period from 26 April 2005, the date of the withdrawal of the Syrian army from Lebanon, to 4 May 2007. Through its identical letters to me and the President of the Security Council dated 11 May 2007, and subsequently, the Syrian authorities have informed me of their support for the meetings of the regional governors on either side of the Lebanese-Syrian border to agree to measures to halt smuggling and unauthorized movements across the border. The Government of the Syrian Arab Republic has informed us that it has recently requested technical border assistance from European Governments including the provision of equipment for the border and the training of Syrian border guards.

40. The Government of Lebanon has stated to me that it has a vital interest in controlling its borders to prevent the smuggling of arms, munitions and personnel into its territory. It has repeated its request that any information about illegal smuggling of arms or persons in the possession of any third country be shared with the Government of Lebanon directly, if possible, or, alternatively, through the United Nations. It has informed me that the Lebanese Armed Forces have maintained their positions along its border with the Syrian

Arab Republic. In addition, the Government of Lebanon has informed me that the various security crises throughout the reporting period have placed a huge strain on the Lebanese Armed Forces, which have now been called upon to perform such various but critical tasks as fighting militants in the Nahr el-Bared refugee camp; internal security; traditional territorial defence; and anti-smuggling activities. In that context, the Government of Lebanon has made it clear that the control of its northern and eastern borders is a responsibility shared both by the Syrian Arab Republic and by Lebanon, in accordance with paragraph 15 of resolution 1701 (2006).

41. Pursuant to the statement of the President of the Security Council of 17 April 2007, in which the President encouraged me to establish an independent team to fully assess the monitoring of the Lebanese-Syrian border and to report thereon before submission of the present report, I am pleased that the Lebanon Independent Border Assessment Team has completed its work and has now submitted its report. In my view, this is a crucial report, which provides a professional and detailed technical evaluation of the difficult situation along the entire Lebanese-Syrian border. I note in particular the recommendations to improve, urgently and in the longer term, Lebanese capacities to secure the border regime along Lebanon's border with the Syrian Arab Republic. The report clearly shows that, in addition to the valuable assistance being provided by the German pilot project along the northern border and the proposals for Lebanese integrated border management, further international assistance is urgently required to enhance Lebanese capabilities and to ensure that there are no breaches of the arms embargo.

E. Land mines and cluster bombs

42. In southern Lebanon, clean-up of the estimated 1 million unexploded cluster munitions continues. Since my previous report to the Security Council, an additional 50 new cluster bomblet strike locations have been identified by the United Nations Mine Action Coordination Centre-South Lebanon. As of 31 May 2007, 904 cluster bomblet strike locations have been recorded, contaminating an area of up to 36.6 million square metres.

43. As a result of the joint efforts of the Lebanese Armed Forces, 22 UNIFIL teams and 75 United Nations contracted and bilaterally funded clearance teams operating under the coordination of the United Nations Mine Action Coordination Centre-South Lebanon, 28 per cent of the surface and 15 per cent of the subsurface of the 36.6 million square metres have been cleared, and 117,872 of an estimated 1 million unexploded cluster munitions have been neutralized.

44. While there has been a decrease in the number of casualty figures in recent months, there have been 22 additional incidents among civilians since my previous report, with one person killed and 21 injured. Since the cessation of hostilities came into effect, a total of 203 civilians have been injured (180) or killed (23) as a result of cluster munitions. I regret to have to report that, despite a number of attempts by United Nations senior officials to obtain information regarding the firing data of cluster munitions utilized during the conflict in the second quarter of 2006, Israel has yet to provide that critical data. I call on the Government of Israel once again to provide the information to the United Nations.

F. Abducted soldiers and prisoners

45. Despite major efforts of the facilitator and the flexibility of Israel beyond the framework of Security Council resolution 1701 (2006), implementation of the humanitarian aspects of the resolution has not yet been possible.

46. Controversial issues raised by Hizbullah require sustained and complicated efforts for reaching a solution. Progress is therefore slow, but continues. The situation unfortunately is aggravated by Hizbullah's persistent refusal to provide proof that the two soldiers are alive. Worries are thus increasing about their fate. I share deeply the anxiety of the families and call again on Hizbullah to reconsider this posture, which contradicts basic humanitarian values.

47. Despite difficulties, both sides request further United Nations facilitation efforts in order to overcome the remaining obstacles. In that regard, Hizbullah expressed its hope that a compromise be found prior to the next report to the Security Council to be submitted in September 2007. Israel is still ready to show flexibility with regard to the Lebanese prisoners. Against this background, I still hope that a solution can be found soon on the basis of moderation and of strict restraint in demands, in compliance with resolution 1701 (2006).

G. Delineation of borders

48. My representatives and I have continued to stress to the Government of the Syrian Arab Republic and the Government of Lebanon the importance of the final determination of their common borders for peaceful coexistence and good neighbourliness. Bilateral agreement on the borders would present a permanent solution to the issue of delineating Lebanon's international boundaries with the Syrian Arab Republic in fulfilment of resolutions 1680 (2006) and 1701 (2006). The Government of the Syrian Arab Republic has insisted, as stated in more detail in my semi-annual reports on the implementation of resolution 1559 (2004), that the demarcation of the borders is a bilateral matter. However, no movement has been reported by the Government of the Syrian Arab Republic on reactivating the Lebanese-Syrian border committee, suggested by President Assad at his most recent meeting with me on 24 April 2007.

49. Specifically, as regards the Shab'a Farms, the Government of the Syrian Arab Republic, while agreeing with the Lebanese position in maintaining that the Shab'a Farms are Lebanese, has conveyed to me its view that a resolution of the issue would be possible only after a peace treaty with Israel has been concluded. I would encourage the Government of the Syrian Arab Republic to reconsider this policy, which is in contradiction of resolutions 1680 (2006) and 1701 (2006). At the same time, I continue to investigate the cartographic, legal and political implications of the alternative path suggested by the Government of Lebanon in its seven-point plan, namely placing the Shab'a Farms under United Nations jurisdiction until a boundary is permanently delineated.

50. I am pleased to report that, based on the best available information, the senior cartographer has made solid progress towards a provisional determination of the geographical extent of the Shab'a Farms area. The Government of Lebanon has submitted to us new and useful material. I hope the Council will understand the subsequent need to discuss the cartographer's findings with the relevant parties. Israel has indicated its willingness to agree to my request to enable the cartographer to visit the area in the next few weeks. I look forward to delivering a detailed report on the conclusions of his work and on our discussions with the relevant parties, including with the Government of Israel, the Government of Lebanon and the Government of the Syrian Arab Republic, in my next report on the implementation of resolution 1701 (2006).

IV. Deployment of the United Nations Interim Force in Lebanon

51. Since my previous report, UNIFIL strength has increased as planned. The total number of military personnel, as of 19 June 2007, now stands at 13,313. That number includes 11,113 UNIFIL ground troops deployed in two sectors, with headquarters in Tibnin and Marjayoun, and 2,000 personnel serving in the Maritime Task Force, in addition to 179 staff officers at UNIFIL headquarters in Naqoura and 21 national support elements. UNIFIL is assisted in its tasks by 51 military observers of the United Nations Truce Supervision Organization. Twenty-nine staff officers serve with the Strategic Military Cell based at United Nations Headquarters. With the planned deployment of approximately 340 troops from the Republic of Korea in July, UNIFIL strength will reach approximately 13,700 military personnel from 30 troop-contributing countries. UNIFIL troops have reached a high level of operational readiness, which allows them to react promptly to incidents throughout its area of operations. The civilian component has also continued to strengthen across all components of the mission. As of 5 June 2007, UNIFIL civilian staff strength totalled 706 (254 international and 452 national staff).

52. The mission is carrying out an expansion and refurbishment programme of its Naqoura headquarters to ensure adequate facilities for all personnel, in full compliance with minimum operating security standard requirements. UNIFIL will also refurbish the Naqoura port that borders UNIFIL headquarters to provide improved maritime access to UNIFIL, resulting in better security for UNIFIL in a crisis situation, and to support the Lebanese Armed Forces and local civilian maritime activities.

V. Observations

53. Almost one year has passed since hostilities erupted in southern Lebanon in July 2006. The swift and effective deployment of a significantly expanded peacekeeping force has helped to establish a new strategic military and security environment in southern Lebanon. I am grateful to the 30 troop-contributing countries that make up the new UNIFIL. The speed with which they responded to resolution 1701 (2006) and the activities that their troops undertake on a daily basis have been critical in preventing a recurrence of hostilities across the Blue Line. At the same time, we must recognize the immense and historic contribution of the Lebanese Armed Forces in helping to stabilize the situation in southern Lebanon. Over the past 10 months, the Lebanese Armed Forces and UNIFIL have developed a partnership that has achieved a number of key objectives contained in the resolution and has helped to maintain the cessation of hostilities.

54. The 17 June rocket attack from southern Lebanon against Israel constitutes a serious breach of the cessation of hostilities. The attack did not come entirely as a surprise since hostile groups have publicly voiced their opposition to the implementation of resolution 1701 (2006). In order to address the threat, it is important that all parties maintain their strong commitment and continue to show determination to respect the cessation of hostilities agreement and implement all provisions of the resolution.

55. As I have done in previous reports, I urge the international community to provide relevant, timely and necessary bilateral assistance and support to the Lebanese Armed Forces to help it implement its obligations under resolution 1701 (2006). For the Government of Lebanon to extend its authority and exercise full sovereignty, it is crucial that it has credible and legitimate armed forces capable of ensuring security and stability over all its territory.

There is a risk that the current fighting in Nahr Al-Bared refugee camp and the volatile situation in other camps may lead to additional shortages of resources and could negatively affect the ability of the Lebanese Armed Forces to carry out its obligations under resolution 1701 (2006). While appreciating the considerable difficulties faced by the Lebanese Armed Forces at the current time, I appreciate the Government's pledge to maintain the army's high visibility and close coordination with UNIFIL in southern Lebanon. The rocket attack on 17 June and the attack against UNIFIL one week later only serve to underline the importance of maintaining the highest degree of vigilance.

56. I also appreciate the support of the Government of Israel and of the Israel Defense Forces for UNIFIL. In this connection, I note especially the words of appreciation expressed to me and other United Nations personnel by a number of senior Israeli political and military officials, and their acknowledgement of the new strategic realities created by the deployment of UNIFIL and the Lebanese Armed Forces in southern Lebanon. I welcome the decision of the Government of Israel not to retaliate following the rocket attack on 17 June. I regret, however, that the Israel Defense Forces continue with almost daily flights over Lebanese territory and, once again, I call upon the Government of Israel to cease the air violations.

57. With reference to paragraph 6 of resolution 1701 (2006), I am pleased to report that the international community has continued to provide assistance for the reconstruction and development of Lebanon. Through the conference held in Stockholm, which focused on emergency assistance and rehabilitation, and more recently, through the Paris III process, Lebanon has received substantial international financial support. However, updated information related to donor commitments and disbursement figures highlight the importance for all donors to fulfil their pledges of financial assistance and reconstruction programmes.

58. As noted above, as well as in previous reports, Israel has yet to provide detailed firing data that would give the exact location, quantity and type of cluster munitions utilized during the conflict in the second quarter of 2006. The provision of such information to UNIFIL would greatly assist the United Nations Mine Action Coordination Centre in its efforts to clean up the estimated 1 million unexploded cluster munitions. While the Lebanese Armed Forces, the United Nations and the bilaterally funded teams are making progress, it will take until 2008 to clear the estimated 36.6 million square metres contaminated by the cluster munitions. Continuing deaths and injuries to Lebanese civilians caused by those munitions, not to mention the loss of agricultural production in affected areas, only increases the local population's antagonism towards Israel. I again urge Israel to provide detailed data on its use of cluster munitions to the United Nations as soon as possible.

59. I am disturbed by the persistent reports pointing to breaches of the arms embargo along the Lebanese-Syrian border. Such reports constitute a major impediment to the establishment of the permanent ceasefire and long-term solution envisaged in resolution 1701 (2006). While a complete sealing of the border may not be possible, I am concerned that the Lebanon Independent Border Assessment Team concludes in its report that the Lebanese-Syrian border is not sufficiently secure and that Lebanese capabilities are lacking. I also note the observation contained in the report that the potential already exists to significantly improve the border security regime and that the Government of Lebanon could do more with existing capabilities. I would recommend that the Government of Lebanon implement the findings of the report in full. Further to the recommendations of the Lebanon Independent Border Assessment Team, I would again call upon Member States and relevant regional

organizations to provide the urgently needed technical assistance, training and equipment that the Government of Lebanon requires to strengthen the border security regime along its border with the Syrian Arab Republic, and to ensure the full implementation of paragraph 15 of resolution 1701 (2006), including the arms embargo.

60. The Syrian Arab Republic, other regional States and the Islamic Republic of Iran have a particular responsibility to ensure that the provisions of resolution 1701 (2006) related to the arms embargo are fully respected. The Syrian Arab Republic, in particular, has a shared responsibility in controlling its borders with Lebanon and in implementing paragraph 15 of resolution 1701 (2006), including in safeguarding against breaches of the arms embargo. In this regard, I urge the Syrian Arab Republic to do more to control its border with Lebanon and I look forward to specific proposals from the Syrian authorities in time for the next quarterly report on the implementation of resolution 1701 (2006), which is due in September. I have taken note of the Syrian Arab Republic's expressed willingness to consider working with European Governments on improving border security. I welcome this development. I also welcome and would encourage, as suggested by the Government of Lebanon, the establishment of a mechanism also including the Government of the Syrian Arab Republic and the European Union or the United Nations, which would aim to improve technical facilities and arrangements along Lebanon's border with the Syrian Arab Republic.

61. As I stated in my previous report, border delineation, including in the Shab'a Farms area, remains a key issue in the implementation of resolution 1701 (2006). In that regard, I am disappointed that no further progress has been made between the Government of Lebanon and the Government of the Syrian Arab Republic in determining their common borders. I call again on the Syrian Arab Republic to take the necessary steps with Lebanon to delineate their common border in accordance with resolutions 1680 (2006) and 1701 (2006). It should be recognized that joint Lebanese-Syrian boundary committees demonstrated good collaboration and agreement on boundary procedures during the 1960s. It is suggested that with the assistance of the United Nations a joint boundary commission could be re-established.

62. I would like to commend the senior cartographer on his work, to date, on developing an accurate territorial definition of the Shab'a Farms area. I believe the provisional determination of the geographical extent of the Shab'a Farms area based on the best information available, provides a good basis on which to move the issue forward. I would note the cooperation that the Government of Lebanon has given to the senior cartographer in his work and would urge Member States, in particular the Syrian Arab Republic, to provide any relevant documentation in their possession and other assistance. In this regard, I am pleased that the Government of Israel has agreed to a visit by the senior cartographer to the Shab'a Farms area. I am hopeful that further discussions on the area, including on its territorial definition, with the Governments of Israel, Lebanon and the Syrian Arab Republic will strengthen a diplomatic process aimed at resolving this key issue in accordance with the relevant provisions of resolution 1701 (2006). Progress on the issue, however, cannot be separated from the principles and elements required for the permanent ceasefire and long-term solution identified in resolution 1701 (2006).

63. I am concerned by the activities of armed elements and groups and the challenges they pose for the stability and independence of Lebanon and for the implementation of resolution 1701 (2006). The appalling attack on 24 June against UNIFIL is only the latest

example of the threat that they pose. I am very concerned for the safety and security of all United Nations personnel based in Lebanon. Further assistance to the Government of Lebanon and its security forces is required to ensure that, as stated in its seven-point plan, it can extend its authority over its territory through its legitimate armed forces and that there are no weapons or authority other than that of the Government of Lebanon.

64. As we move towards the one-year anniversary of the hostilities that erupted in 2006, I regret that we have not been able to arrive at a permanent ceasefire between Israel and Lebanon. I also regret that further progress has not been made in obtaining the release of the abducted Israeli soldiers and on such issues as halting Israeli violations of Lebanese airspace. However, I am hopeful that a long-term solution can be found, in particular, if we further consolidate the strategic change that has occurred in southern Lebanon; strengthen the security regime along Lebanon's border with the Syrian Arab Republic; and make further progress on the issue of Shab'a Farms. Above all, I would call on Lebanon, Israel and key States such as the Syrian Arab Republic and the Islamic Republic of Iran, as well as the international community, to support the implementation of all aspects of resolution 1701 (2006). At a time of heightened regional instability and tension, resolution 1701 (2006) remains a vital element in helping to settle issues of critical importance to international peace and security. We must not lessen our commitment to implementing the resolution fully. At the same time, we must remain committed to the achievement of a just, lasting and comprehensive peace in the region.

65. As the Security Council is aware, the UNIFIL mandate will expire on 31 August 2007. On 25 June, the Lebanese Council of Ministers requested the renewal of the mandate. On the same day, during my meeting with Prime Minister Siniora in Paris, I received a letter requesting the Council to extend the mandate for a further period of one year, without amendment. In that regard, I intend to submit a letter to the Council during the month of August requesting that it consider the renewal of the mandate.

66. In concluding, I want to pay tribute to all United Nations military and civilian personnel serving in these difficult circumstances in Lebanon. I want to express my heartfelt condolences to the Government of Spain and the families of the six peacekeepers killed in the past weekend. I would add that the terrorist attack against UNIFIL will not deter the United Nations from carrying out its Security Council-mandated activities. Rather, it redoubles our commitment to ensuring that resolution 1701 (2006) is fully implemented by all parties and that the larger United Nations goals of peace, stability and justice in the Middle East are achieved. In this regard, it will be critical at the current time to maintain the full capacities of UNIFIL in order to preserve stability in its area of operations south of the Litani River.

G. Sudan

1. Report of the Secretary-General on Children and Armed Conflict in the Sudan, 17 August 2006 (S/2006/662)

Summary

The present report has been prepared in accordance with the provisions of Security Council resolution 1612 (2005). It is presented to the Council and its Working Group on Children and Armed Conflict as the second country report from the monitoring and reporting mechanism referred to in paragraph 3 of that resolution. The report, which covers the period from May to July 2006, specifies incidents of grave child rights abuses, indicative of the nature and trend of systematic violations in the Sudan. The report focuses specifically on the killing and maiming of children, their recruitment and use as soldiers, grave sexual violence, abductions and denial of humanitarian access to children, and indicates that these violations continue in the Sudan largely unabated. The report explicitly identifies parties to the conflict who are committing grave abuses, including the Sudanese Armed Forces, the Sudan People's Liberation Army, the Popular Defence Forces, the Sudan Liberation Army, the White Army, the Janjaweed militia, the Lord's Resistance Army and Chadian opposition forces. The report stresses that individual commanders of the numerous armed forces and groups in the Sudan bear responsibility for the commission of grave violations by their forces, but that the Government of National Unity and the Government of Southern Sudan are also directly accountable for the commission of violations by individuals within their command structures. This government accountability is critical as groups are incorporated into the legally regulated armed forces under government control.

The report highlights action plans and other programme responses in place to address violations against children, and contains a series of recommendations with a view to securing strengthened action for the protection of war-affected children in the Sudan.

I. Introduction

1. The present report, prepared in accordance with the provisions of Security Council resolution 1612 (2005), covers the period from 1 May to 15 July 2006. The incidents of violations cited for the reporting period serve to illustrate the nature and trend of continuing child rights violations in the Sudan. The report identifies parties to the conflict responsible for several categories of grave violations, including the killing and maiming of children, the recruitment and use of children in armed forces and groups, abductions, sexual violence, attacks on schools and hospitals and denial of humanitarian access to children. The report also highlights the plans of action and programme responses that have been undertaken to halt violations and strengthen child protection.

II. Political, military and social developments in the Sudan

Situations of armed conflict and peace processes

2. The Sudan is a vast country with many local histories of violence: in the south, in the transitional areas that straddle the border between north and south, in Darfur and the east. The country's conflicts are closely linked to acute imbalances in the distribution of wealth

and services along regional, ethnic and class lines. Many years of war have served to exacerbate these imbalances and have resulted in significant militarization of the society.

3. Three different peace processes are under way in the Sudan, with two separate peacekeeping missions in place. The Comprehensive Peace Agreement of 9 January 2005 covers the southern Sudan, eastern Sudan and the transitional areas, and the United Nations Mission in the Sudan (UNMIS) is supporting its implementation. The Darfur Peace Agreement of 5 May 2006 covers the conflict in Darfur, and the African Union Mission in the Sudan (AMIS) is supporting its implementation. In eastern Sudan, the Government and the Eastern Front, a coalition of local rebel groups, signed a declaration of principles for the resolution of the eastern conflict on 19 June 2006 in Asmara. However, access to eastern Sudan remains problematic, which has translated into a critical lack of information on child rights violations in the east for this report.

4. There are two separate governments in place in the Sudan. The Comprehensive Peace Agreement established the Government of National Unity (referred to as the Government in this report), with enhanced representation for southern Sudan. It also established a separate Government of Southern Sudan with its own budget, constitution, laws, army and ministries. The Government of Southern Sudan will keep these powers until a referendum in 2011, in which the people of southern Sudan will decide whether to become an independent State or remain part of a unified Sudan. The Comprehensive Peace Agreement established a set of ceasefire monitoring institutions supported by UNMIS, and requires the Government's Sudanese Armed Forces to leave southern Sudan by 2007. Recruitment of children is a breach of the Comprehensive Peace Agreement.

5. The Darfur Peace Agreement established new security and ceasefire institutions supported by AMIS. However, it did not create significant new political institutions for Darfur, but permitted representation of Darfur rebel forces in the Government pending elections. It established new initiatives to address problems related to access to land, compensation for victims of the conflict and a Darfur-Darfur dialogue conference. Recruiting and using children is a breach of the Darfur Peace Agreement, which also includes provisions for the protection of minors who come into contact with the law and the immediate release of all boys and girls under 18 years of age from armed forces and groups. Overall, the Darfur Peace Agreement has not led to an increase in security in Darfur as a significant number of rebel groups did not sign the Agreement.

Armed forces and groups operating in the Sudan

6. The considerable number of armed forces and groups in the Sudan makes it difficult to establish specific responsibility for grave violations of children's rights. The Sudan has three legally regulated armed forces: the Sudanese Armed Forces are the regular Government military and currently operate throughout the country; the Sudan People's Liberation Army (SPLA) is the regular military force of the Government of Southern Sudan; and, the Popular Defence Force is an armed force linked to the ruling party of northern Sudan and to armed groups raised from rural ethnic groups. A fourth group, the Joint Integrated Units, composed of units from SPLA and the Sudanese Armed Forces, was established by the Comprehensive Peace Agreement to form the nucleus of a unified army if the southern Sudan decides against independence in the referendum scheduled for 2011.

7. In addition to these legally regulated forces, there are numerous non-legal forces operating in the Sudan. During the civil war in southern Sudan and the transitional areas, the Sudanese Armed Forces used non-legal militias to control territory. The Comprehensive Peace Agreement refers to these non-legal militias as other armed groups. There were over 50 such groups brought together under the South Sudan Defence Forces (SSDF), an umbrella organization that was nominally led by Major General Paulino Matiep of the South Sudan Unity Movement (SSUM) but was effectively under the control of the military intelligence division of the Sudanese Armed Forces.

8. The Comprehensive Peace Agreement required the other armed groups to join either the Sudanese Armed Forces or SPLA by 9 January 2006. Most have done so, but the incorporation remains partial and inadequate. Some have not incorporated which has perpetuated instability in their areas of control. Decades of war in southern Sudan have distorted and militarized society. Thus, pastoralist communities have been obliged to maintain defence forces to protect livestock. For instance, the White Army, linked to the Lou clan of the pastoralist Nuer ethnic group, is made up largely of males aged 15 to 20 years, with some much younger. These forces were sometimes used by larger groups to carry out military tasks, and although they were not directly remunerated, they were permitted to loot. This has exacerbated the development of livelihood strategies based on looting in southern Sudan. In situations of limited economic opportunity such alternative forces have also served as a magnet for children who have been demobilized from larger forces but have failed to reintegrate into society.

9. The Lord's Resistance Army (LRA) has its origins in the conflict in northern Uganda, but operated in southern Sudan for many years, initially with the support of the Sudanese Armed Forces. The Uganda People's Defence Forces, the regular army of Uganda, conducted operations inside the Sudan aimed at defeating LRA. The Government of Southern Sudan is currently sponsoring talks between LRA and the Government of Uganda in an effort to bring an end to this long-standing conflict.

10. The Darfur Peace Agreement classifies six different categories of armed forces or groups as parties to the Darfur conflict. The main groups are the Sudanese Armed Forces, and the two rebel movements that participated in the peace talks in May, namely, the Sudan Liberation Army (SLA) and the Justice and Equality Movement (JEM). In addition, the Darfur Peace Agreement refers to militias aligned to the main parties ("other armed groups"), foreign (or Chadian) militias, the Popular Defence Force and the Janjaweed. Both the Janjaweed and the Popular Defence Force in Darfur are drawn from ethnic groups whose leaders are close to the Government, and paragraph 315 of the Darfur Peace Agreement explicitly links the Popular Defence Force and the Janjaweed. Elsewhere, the Agreement declares the Janjaweed a separate illegal group. This ambiguity makes it more difficult to hold groups accountable for violations. As in southern Sudan, distinctions between legal and non-legal militias are blurred, which also undermines the possibility of holding armed groups responsible for child rights violations.

11. Responsibility for the actions of the Janjaweed is particularly important to clarify for the purpose of this report. Janjaweed are irregular forces whose core constituency is often linked to landless camel-pastoralist ethnic groups. Because these ethnic groups are native Arabic-speaking, and some of their neighbours speak African languages in addition to Arabic, they are often called "Arabs". Throughout their existence they have been linked to

the Government security apparatus and the loosely organized but legally regulated Popular Defence Force. The Government, by signing the Darfur Peace Agreement, has committed itself to neutralizing the Janjaweed. In June 2006, the Government presented AMIS with a plan to neutralize the Janjaweed, but the plan was not linked to time lines or outcomes agreed to in the Agreement. No steps to implement the plan have been taken thus far, apart from one demobilization ceremony in Kass, Southern Darfur on 23 June 2006, where 150 weapons were collected. The Janjaweed are widely perceived as the main security problem in Darfur.

Responsibility for recruitment and use of children

12. The numerous armed forces and groups that are parties to the conflict in the Sudan have a long history of using children for military purposes. My report on children and armed conflict of February 2005 (A/59/695-S/2005/72) listed five armed groups that recruit or use children: the Janjaweed, JEM, SSUM, SLA and SPLA. In 2005, both the Janjaweed (based in Darfur) and SSUM (based in Khartoum and southern Sudan) were aligned with the Government and effectively controlled by its security forces. SLA and JEM were engaged in armed rebellion against the Government, and SPLA had just signed a peace agreement with the Government. There is still credible evidence that all these groups continue to recruit or use children, in addition to other groups aligned with the Government and with rebels or peace partners that were not mentioned in my earlier report. However, it should be noted that some of them have since changed their relationship with the Government. SSUM joined SPLA on 9 January 2006; the SLA faction led by Minni Minawi (referred to in this report as SLA (Minawi)) has entered into a peace agreement with the Government; and, as I noted above, the Government has committed itself to neutralizing the Janjaweed. The Government's seriousness in meeting this commitment needs to be scrutinized if it is to distance itself from responsibility for Janjaweed attacks. SSUM and many of the other armed groups in the Government-aligned SSDF recruited children through 2005. There are credible reports that SSUM and the other armed groups from SSDF which were incorporated in SPLA in January continued to recruit children after their incorporation, in contravention of SPLA rules. The Commander in Chief of SPLA and First Vice President of the Sudan, Salva Kiir, wrote to these other armed groups in April 2006 requiring them to stop child recruitment. Child recruitment remains a practice deeply rooted in southern Sudanese military culture.

13. When other armed groups recruit and use children, the responsibility for that practice rests with individual commanders of those groups. However, the Government and SPLA also bear a direct responsibility when individuals within their command structures recruit children. This responsibility of the Government must be stressed, particularly in the present context of shifting alliances and arrangements in the Sudan.

III. Grave violations of children's rights

Recruitment and use of children in armed forces and groups in southern Sudan and in Khartoum

The following groups are responsible for recruitment and use of children:

- *Sudanese Armed Forces*

- *Sudan People's Liberation Army (SPLA)*
- *White Army*

14. During the reporting period there was evidence to show that both the Sudanese Armed Forces and SPLA were responsible for recruiting and/or using children, and that children were used in the White Army ethnic militias.

15. There were confirmed reports of child recruitment between May and July 2006 in Khartoum, Jonglei and Bahr al-Ghazal. It is not clear whether this constitutes an increase or reduction in recruitment because trends are difficult to follow owing to access restrictions and other factors. It is clear that thousands of children are still associated with armed forces in southern Sudan, awaiting demobilization. Some of them were used in conflict between May and July 2006. Responsibility for the recruitment and use of these children lies with the Sudanese Armed Forces and SPLA.

16. Recruitment continues to be widespread because the war in southern Sudan created a plethora of Government-aligned militias or other armed groups. These militias were not parties to the Comprehensive Peace Agreement, but the Agreement required them to negotiate their incorporation into the Sudanese Armed Forces or SPLA. It has been reported that militias start recruitment drives before incorporation in order to bolster their numbers and strengthen their negotiating power, and that many children are caught up in the recruitment drives. Although all other armed groups were supposed to have incorporated by 9 January 2006, some major groups are still negotiating with both parties and have continued to recruit children. In addition, several million people, most of them children, have been displaced from southern Sudan conflict zones to the north. These young Southerners want to return home and participate politically and economically, having long been excluded from such participation. Militia groups recruiting in Khartoum are seen as groups with effective power to return people to the south and to offer jobs in an environment of severely limited employment opportunities.

17. The following specific incidents were confirmed during the reporting period:

(a) In June, reports from Jonglei State in southern Sudan confirmed that SPLA, the White Army, a local "other armed group" and the Sudanese Armed Forces were recruiting and using children. Reports indicated that some recently demobilized children who had not been reunited with their families were among those recruited. On 22 June 2006, in Pulchoul, Jonglei, children aged 12 and over were given the option of joining SPLA or returning to civilian life;

(b) In Nasser, Upper Nile State, on 16 May 2006 there were confirmed reports that the Sudanese Armed Forces, SPLA and the new Joint Integrated Units were all involved in recruiting children. Recent serious incidents of fighting in Jonglei have seen the direct involvement of children, with reports of hundreds of White Army members killed, many of them children. Also in May 2006, child soldiers were seen in a newly incorporated unit of the Sudanese Armed Forces near Nasser, and there were reports of approximately 50 uniformed and armed SPLA soldiers aged 14 to 16 in the same area. One 14-year-old was a bodyguard to the SPLA commissioner;

(c) In May 2006, SPLA attacked the White Army and an armed group in Motot, Jonglei State, killing 113 White Army youth;

(d) At the beginning of May 2006, 14 young soldiers (believed to be under 18 years old) from the Sudanese Armed Forces unit of Lieutenant Colonel Thomas Thiel in Abyei were interviewed by United Nations staff, and in June child soldiers associated with the unit were identified in Abyei town;

(e) On 7 June 2006, there were confirmed reports that commanders from southern Sudan were actively recruiting children in Khartoum.

Recruitment and use of children in armed forces and groups in Darfur

The following groups are responsible for recruitment and use of children:

- *Sudan Liberation Army (SLA) (Minawi faction)*
- *Janjaweed militias*
- *Chadian opposition forces*
- *Camel police*

18. During the reporting period, evidence indicated that SLA (Minawi) and Chadian opposition forces were responsible for recruiting and/or using children, as were the Janjaweed militias, which may still be under the control of the Sudanese Armed Forces. Young persons under the age of 18 years were also recruited into the legally regulated camel police.

19. It is estimated that thousands of children are still associated with armed forces and groups in Darfur and were actively involved in conflict between May and July 2006. The security situation, access limitations, the delayed implementation of the peace agreement and the complexity of monitoring mechanisms in Darfur make it very difficult to monitor the recruitment and use of children. Therefore, while most of the following incidents are linked to SLA (Minawi), this may reflect the fact that this group controls large and relatively accessible territory:

(a) There were confirmed reports from Shangil Tobay, Northern Darfur, on 5 May 2006, that SLA (Minawi) had abducted and recruited children and young men;

(b) In May 2006, armed boys aged 15 to 17 were seen near the offices of SLA (Minawi) in Gereida, Southern Darfur. SLA (Minawi) denied that they were soldiers but local leaders contradicted this in interviews with United Nations staff. SLA (Minawi) commanders were observed forcibly recruiting boys in Gereida in May 2006, and many child soldiers were also seen in Gereida at the end of June 2006;

(c) G19, a breakaway faction of SLA (Minawi) that rejects the Darfur Peace Agreement, claimed in interviews at the beginning of June that SLA (Minawi) had abducted 108 children for use as soldiers on 10 May 2006, confirming community reports to this effect;

(d) On 29 June 2006, six armed boys aged 15 to 17 were observed in the forces of SLA (Minawi) at Tabet, Southern Darfur. An SLA official claimed that the children joined SLA voluntarily because they were separated from their families;

(e) On 15 May 2006, interviews by United Nations staff of people displaced after Janjaweed attacks on villages near Kutum, Northern Darfur, confirmed that there were many armed child soldiers among the Janjaweed militiamen who attacked them;

(f) A 17-year-old Tama boy was abducted by Chadian opposition forces from Geneina, Southern Darfur on 24 May 2006. This is indicative of the ongoing problem of abduction of youth from the Tama ethnic group for recruitment to the Chadian opposition;

(g) In June 2006, in Western Darfur there were reports of many boys less than 18 years old recruited into the camel police, a force used to mediate and control disputes between pastoralists and farmers;

(h) There are reports that students in Darfur towns are obliged to carry out military service in the Sudanese Armed Forces in order to sit for secondary school examinations. On 3 June 2006, some of these students were seen in Nyala, Southern Darfur, and there were reports in May of the deaths of two students during military training in Southern and Western Darfur.

Recruitment and use of children in armed forces and groups in eastern Sudan

20. Although there were confirmed reports that the Eastern Front recruited many children and youths in 2005, during the reporting period no cases of recruitment or use of children were reported in eastern Sudan. This may be related to access restrictions.

Abductions in southern Sudan

21. There is a long history of unresolved abductions during the protracted conflict in southern Sudan. There are thousands of documented cases of women and children abducted for forced labour or forced sex by Popular Defence Force militias constituted from northern ethnic groups operating in southern Sudan. Abductions of women and girls for forced marriage are also reported among southern ethnic groups, and for LRA abduction is the main recruitment strategy for soldiers and sexual companions.

22. Although there were few reports of abductions during the reporting period, several cases are being monitored by United Nations police in southern Sudan on the basis of complaints made to police by girls.

23. Between May and July 2006, there were confirmed reports of abduction of children in Jonglei State. It has been difficult to ascertain the exact numbers or responsible parties owing to access restrictions.

Abductions in Darfur

The following groups are responsible for abduction of children:

- *Janjaweed militias*
- *Sudan Liberation Army (SLA) (Minawi faction)*
- *Sudanese Armed Forces*

24. During the reporting period evidence indicated that paramilitary units of the Sudanese Armed Forces and allied militias, as well as SLA (Minawi), abducted children. Janjaweed militias, which may still be under control of the Sudanese Armed Forces also carried out abductions.

25. Girls are frequently abducted for short periods for forced sex, and children are forced to carry goods and property that have been looted from villages during attacks. In these

cases, the children are often released some distance from their villages and become lost or "separated" children when they return home to find that their families have fled. Many abductions are also linked to recruitment. Between May and July 2006, 18 cases of abduction were reported to the United Nations. The abductions specified below were carried out by different armed forces and groups, including Janjaweed militias:

(a) A baby was among 15 people confirmed as abducted when Janjaweed attacked Dito village in Southern Darfur on 1 May 2006;

(b) AMIS confirmed reports by the local community that two boys were abducted in an attack by Janjaweed militiamen on Abuderesa camp, Southern Darfur, on 21 June 2006;

(c) Sixteen armed men on camels believed to be Janjaweed militiamen abducted a woman and her 12-year-old son from Shag Al-Nil village, Northern Darfur, on 11 June 2006;

(d) A source linked to G19 claimed that SLA (Minawi) had abducted 108 children on 10 May 2006 for use as fighters, corroborating reports by local community;

(e) Six armed men in SAF uniform abducted a 13-year-old boy from Wadi Saleh, West Darfur, on 26 May 2006 while he was collecting wood with his father;

(f) On 13 June 2006, while collecting firewood, a teenage girl and three other women were abducted and beaten near Hara village by two men suspected to be members of pro-Government militias, approximately three kilometres from Kabkabiya, North Darfur;

(g) An unknown militia abducted a girl while she was collecting firewood near Kalma camp, South Darfur on 1 May 2006;

(h) In May 2006, seven children abducted by an unknown armed group from Shangil Tobay, North Darfur, were released after AMIS intervention;

(i) On 21 June 2006, two boys were abducted when an unknown militia attacked Abu Deresa IDP Camp to loot cattle;

(j) On 28 June 2006, two women together with a 13-year-old boy were abducted from Kundesha village, South Darfur by unknown militia.

Abductions in eastern Sudan

26. During the reporting period no abductions were reported in eastern Sudan. This may be related to access restrictions.

Killings of children in southern Sudan

The following groups are responsible for killing of children:

- *Sudan People's Liberation Army (SPLA)*
- *Sudanese Armed Forces*
- *White Army*

27. During the reporting period evidence indicated that the Sudanese Armed Forces, SPLA and the White Army were responsible for killing of children. Some of these children were killed while participating in hostilities.

28. During the reporting period, 38 children were killed. However, it has been difficult to determine the full extent of child deaths in clashes in Jonglei State because of access restrictions. It is confirmed that some children died while participating in hostilities against SPLA, while others were killed in local inter-ethnic conflicts. Specific incidents were confirmed as follows:

(a) Thirty-three children were killed in fighting in Ulang and Akobo (Jonglei State) between the White Army and SPLA between 24 April 2006 and 15 May 2006;

(b) A young girl was killed in retaliatory cattle raiding between the Dinka Aguok and Apuk clans in Gogrial county, Northern Bahr al Ghazal State, on 11 June 2006;

(c) A young Dinka boy was among three people killed in an attack on Gumbo village, Central Equatoria State, on 21 June 2006. The attackers were reported to belong to the Sudanese Armed Forces;

(d) Clashes between different Dinka clans linked to cattle looting in Koch county, Unity State, on 8 July 2006 resulted in the deaths of three children and six adults.

Killings of children in Darfur

The following groups are responsible for killing of children:

- *Sudan Liberation Army (SLA) (Minawi faction)*
- *Popular Defence Force*

29. Over 51 children were reported killed between May and July 2006. However, these reports did not cover all of the areas of fighting in Darfur. Many reports of civilian deaths are not age-disaggregated. For example, 46 civilians were killed when SLA (Minawi) attacked villages around Tawilla in Northern Darfur on 5 July 2006, with many of the casualties reported to have been children. Other specific incidents were reported as follows:

(a) SLA (Wahid) (a breakaway faction of SLA led by Abdul Wahid) reported that SLA (Minawi) forces killed several children on their way to school on 5 July 2006 at the village of Dalil, Northern Darfur; the report was later confirmed by child protection staff. Displaced people in El Fasher interviewed by the United Nations later reported that 16 children had been killed;

(b) Two Popular Defence Force soldiers killed a 14-year-old boy in Kass, Southern Darfur, on 9 May 2006. The soldiers were arrested by police and compensation has been paid to the boy's family;

(c) Two boys, aged 13 and 16, were killed when police opened fire on displaced persons demonstrating against the Darfur Peace Agreement in Abu Shouk camp, El Fasher;

(d) Two boys from an Arab ethnic group, aged 15 and 17, were killed in Sirba, Western Darfur, by unknown men on 7 June 2006. As a result, Janjaweed groups blocked the Sirba area to humanitarian workers on 8 June 2006;

(e) A local leader in Gereida reported that 150 children were missing after attacks on villages around Gereida in March 2006 by Government-allied militias. By the end of May 2006, 30 of the children had been found dead in different locations between Joughana and Gereida. In addition, five children displaced by that attack died of malnutrition in Gereida.

Killings of children in eastern Sudan

30. No killings of children were reported in eastern Sudan. This may be related to access restrictions.

Sexual violence in southern Sudan

31. No cases of sexual violence by members of armed groups were reported between May and July 2006. Several cases dating from April are being dealt with by the courts in southern Sudan, and are being monitored by UNMIS child protection advisers.

Sexual violence in Darfur

The following groups are responsible for sexual violence against children:

- *Sudanese Armed Forces*
- *Janjaweed militias*

32. Renewed conflict in Darfur may have drawn attention away from the continuing practice of ethnically targeted sexual violence against girls and women, particularly in areas of displaced populations. Grave sexual violence against girls and women in Darfur continues to worsen. During the reporting period, United Nations personnel were following up on a series of 20 cases in Gereida and near Kalma camp (Southern Darfur) of girls being attacked late at night and rendered unconscious through the use of neck piercing, strangulation and/or drugs before being raped. Many of these attacks are reportedly carried out by uniformed men.

33. Reports over the past year have shown that girls are over-represented in reports of sexual violence: a report from the Office of the United Nations High Commissioner for Human Rights last year indicated that 40 per cent of victims were under 18 years of age. There is evidence to suggest that sexual exploitation and abuse have increased in Darfur since the break-out of internal fighting.

34. There are several reasons for the particular vulnerability of girls to sexual violence, including the fact that the displaced and impoverished families of Darfur often rely heavily on child labour and income to survive. Thus, many girls are involved in water carrying or in firewood collection for domestic use or commercial charcoal production, and become easy targets when they leave densely populated camps. Girls have been targeted in inter-ethnic conflicts as a deliberate form of humiliation of a group, and as a means of ethnic cleansing. Rape has been used to force displacement. It is reported that wherever AMIS firewood patrols are established there is a noticeable impact on the safety and security of girls collecting wood or water.

35. Many women and girls who have been raped do not report such attacks for fear of stigmatization. The police continue to deny knowledge of any pattern of abuse and claim a lack of resources and capacity to deal with cases of sexual violence. However, it is more often

than not a matter of lack of will to deal with such cases. Where cases have been successfully prosecuted, convicted rapists have received relatively light sentences. For example, a central reserve policeman found guilty of raping a 10-year-old girl in Western Darfur was sentenced to three years and 100 lashes. An important precedent was set during the reporting period with the acquittal of a 17-year-old girl who had killed a man who was attempting to rape her in March 2006. Although the Sudan's Criminal Act grants an unconditional right of self-defence in cases of rape, and although the girl had reported the rape to the police before it was realized that her assailant had died, she was held in prison for three months until her acquittal on 3 June 2006.

36. Four cases of sexual violence by members of armed groups were confirmed between May and July 2006. The sexual attacks listed are indicative and were carried out by forces linked to the Government:

(a) On 24 May 2006, a group of about 25 armed men in SLA uniforms threatened, beat and robbed six separate groups of women and girls in Hajar Jalanga, Western Darfur. A 15-year-old girl was sexually assaulted;

(b) Women and girls displaced from villages near Kutum, Western Darfur, stated on 15 May 2006 that Janjaweed militias attempted to rape girls, and that the attackers targeted particularly girls under 18 years old. They cited the attempted rapes as the reason for their decision to leave the villages;

(c) On 25 June 2006, men from unknown militias near Tawilla, Northern Darfur, attacked the villages of Abu Senit and Jonjona. Two girls and a woman were raped;

(d) On 11 June 2006, two men used a knife to sexually assault a young girl in Western Darfur.

Sexual violence in eastern Sudan

37. No cases of sexual violence against children were reported from eastern Sudan. This may be related to access restrictions.

Attacks on schools and hospitals

The following group is responsible for attacking schools:

- *Lord's Resistance Army (LRA)*

38. One attack on an educational facility was reported in southern Sudan between May and July 2006: LRA attacked the Arapi Regional Teacher Training Institute near Juba, Central Equatoria State, on 23 May 2006.

Denial of humanitarian access in southern Sudan

39. Inter-ethnic conflict in parts of southern Sudan continued to hamper humanitarian access in some locations. However, there have been no reports of denial of humanitarian access by armed groups between May and July 2006.

Denial of humanitarian access in Darfur

The following parties are responsible for denial of humanitarian access:

- *Government of National Unity*

- *Sudanese Armed Forces*

40. Humanitarian access worsened between May and July 2006 with the upsurge in violence that followed the peace agreement. Specific incidents were reported as follows:

(a) The Government suspended all United Nations activities in Darfur from 25 to 27 June 2006, after UNMIS allowed a humanitarian official who is linked to SLA (Wahid) to travel on one of its aircraft. Exceptions were granted for the World Food Programme and the United Nations Children's Fund (UNICEF), but the activities of UNMIS, the Office for the Coordination of Humanitarian Affairs, the United Nations Population Fund and the Office of the United Nations High Commissioner for Refugees were affected;

(b) On 6 June 2006, SLA (Wahid) reported that the Sudanese Armed Forces checkpoint at Kass, Northern Darfur, had denied access to trucks carrying food into areas under their control; the report was confirmed by humanitarian personnel;

(c) Three cases were reported in Western and Southern Darfur in May of hijacking of humanitarian convoys to loot commodities by armed men believed to be affiliated to Government militias;

(d) People from ethnic groups or areas who believed that they were being overlooked in food distributions, obstructed food distribution to other areas. For instance, a group of unconfirmed identity stopped a food convoy in the Mershing area of South Darfur on 2 May 2006.

Denial of humanitarian access in eastern Sudan

The following party is responsible for denial of humanitarian access:

- *Government of National Unity*

41. Government-imposed access restrictions on United Nations agencies in eastern Sudan in March 2006 continued through July 2006. The Government believes that there should be no role for UNMIS in eastern Sudan unless a United Nations role is agreed to by parties to a possible future peace agreement there. This disagreement has led to administrative restrictions for United Nations humanitarian agencies including expulsions of international staff and detention of national staff. Food assistance for about 110,000 refugees and internally displaced persons was suspended in March but resumed in June 2006; it was blocked again and resumed once more in July. UNHCR protection activities for the refugee population were suspended. In addition, the Government banned activity by the United Nations and international non-governmental organizations in the rebel enclave of Hamesh Koreib, affecting a population of about 70,000. The Government allows access to one local organization, and will permit a United Nations assessment of an outbreak of acute diarrhoea in the enclave. Over half the population of eastern Sudan is children. Acute malnutrition and mortality rates for children in eastern Sudan are significantly higher than those in Darfur.

IV. Dialogue and action plans to redress violations of children's rights

42. Serious violations of children's rights are seldom prosecuted in the Sudan, but new peace agreements create ceasefire institutions that have powers to make binding or partially binding recommendations on the parties to prosecute violators of children's rights. In southern Sudan, UNMIS child protection advisors have been using the Ceasefire Joint

Military Committee and its seven subsidiary Area Joint Military Committees to engage the Sudanese Armed Forces and SPLA in dialogue on abuses against children and problems in releasing children from military units, particularly those newly incorporated from other armed groups. Child protection advisers have presented evidence of child recruitment to the Committees and have developed and begun to implement child protection workplans for them, including dissemination of Security Council resolution 1612 (2005) and training on child protection for field commanders. This training is specifically aimed at field commanders who have recently incorporated from other armed groups, who are most likely to recruit children. In May and June 2006, an UNMIS child protection adviser acted as an observer on a joint military investigation of an attack on unarmed soldiers and their families. The investigation found a local Sudanese Armed Forces commander, Lieutenant Colonel Thomas Thiel, responsible. It also found both the Sudanese Armed Forces and SPLA responsible for recruitment of children and recommended prosecutions.

43. The Ceasefire Commission is a body within the AMIS peacekeeping operation that was instituted in 2004 with powers similar to those of the Ceasefire Joint Military Committee. It has not yet used those powers to address violations of children's rights. The Darfur Peace Agreement instituted a new set of localized ceasefire institutions called ceasefire subcommissions to be deployed in each AMIS sector. These local institutions, a vital mechanism for dialogue and action to address children's rights violations in a timely way, have not yet been established. However, it should be noted that local AMIS military commanders have acted decisively to resolve abductions of children during the reporting period.

44. Other forums and mechanisms for dialogue with armed groups have been established by United Nations staff. UNICEF has been discussing with the SLA Minawi and Wahid factions the need to end recruitment of children and to release children who are still in armed groups after the signing of the Darfur Peace Agreement. UNICEF discussed the possibility of helping SLA to release and reintegrate children, making it clear that it wants all boys and girls associated with SLA (Minawi) to return to their families. This includes not only children carrying guns, but also children associated with non-combatant roles. SLA (Minawi) committed itself to facilitating the work of UNICEF and providing full support for the release and reintegration of children associated with the armed groups. Follow-up has been complicated by recent internal fighting within the SLA (Minawi) faction. SLA (Wahid) has not signed the Darfur Peace Agreement, but UNICEF also approached them to discuss the release of children from their forces, and they have been equally willing to collaborate. In late July, UNICEF will train representatives from both SLA factions on child rights and start registering children for future reintegration programmes. UNMIS child protection advisers have urged field commanders from SLA (Minawi), SLA (Wahid) and local militias in Northern and Southern Darfur to end child recruitment.

45. The United Nations and AMIS have engaged in dialogue with the Government of the Sudan on the issue of sexual violence in Darfur. This engagement has involved police and legal institutions as well as local and national structures for the protection of civilians, including a committee of the Joint Implementation Mechanism set up to implement the 2004 agreement between the United Nations and the Government to end the crisis in Darfur. However, the problem of sexual violence is still far from resolution, and the Government needs to commit greater attention, resources and will to curb sexual violence.

46. It is important to note that the ability of the United Nations to initiate and engage in dialogue with armed groups on grave child rights violations is often hindered by access restrictions.

V. Follow-up and programmatic response to violations

47. The Sudan has ratified the Convention on the Rights of the Child and its Optional Protocol on the Involvement of Children in Armed Conflict, but has not yet introduced legislation criminalizing the recruitment and use of child soldiers. UNICEF is working with various Government institutions to harmonize Sudanese legislation with the Convention and its Optional Protocols.

48. During the reporting period, UNICEF jointly with the Darfur State Governments and the National Council for Child Welfare organized a child protection workshop in Nyala. The workshop reviewed an independent situation analysis of child protection in Darfur, commissioned by UNICEF, which identified a number of risks and vulnerabilities that children face in Darfur such as recruitment by armed groups and forces, child labour, sexual and gender-based violence, abandonment of babies, separation from families and psychosocial distress as well as early marriage and female circumcision. The workshop led to an agreement to develop reintegration services for children involved in the military and street children including psycho-social support, vocational training and catch-up education, and an awareness campaign for protection of those children and others at risk of female circumcision, early marriage and sexual abuse and exploitation. It also agreed on proposals for legal reforms focusing on a number of areas including the age of the child, the age of criminal responsibility and the age of marriageability; support to the police for recording and maintaining data on crimes against children; and training of police officers and judges in child-friendly procedures for dealing with children in contact with the law.

49. The UNMIS child protection adviser has worked systematically to ensure that the mission mainstreams children's concerns across all components—civilian, military and police—particularly to support monitoring, reporting and response on grave child rights violations. For example, the UNMIS child protection section liaises closely with the United Nations police, who have over 700 personnel deployed in southern Sudan and the transitional areas. The United Nations police have now established a Gender and Child Protection Unit of over 30 officers who regularly monitor police stations and prisons and follow cases of serious crimes against children, including sexual violence, killings and abduction. They also develop training for police and legal officials on child protection.

Children's disarmament, demobilization and reintegration in Khartoum, the transitional areas and southern Sudan

50. The Comprehensive Peace Agreement obliged its signatories to demobilize all children in their ranks by July 2005. One year later, approximately 1,000 children have been released, all of them in southern Sudan and the transitional areas. One reason for the delay is the routine denial by the Sudanese Armed Forces of the presence of children in their units. However, the Sudanese Armed Forces have accepted evidence presented at the Ceasefire Joint Military Committee that there are children in unincorporated other armed groups and in other armed groups newly incorporated into the Sudanese Armed Forces in southern Sudan. The Sudanese Armed Forces say that there are approximately 19,000 soldiers in these units, and it is estimated that a significant number of them are under 18 years old.

Responsibility for demobilizing these children lies with the Northern Sudan Disarmament, Demobilization and Reintegration Commission, a civilian body established under the Comprehensive Peace Agreement. The Commission has just completed registration and provided reinsertion support to special needs groups of other armed groups aligned with the Sudanese Armed Forces. Similar programmes still have to be carried out in southern Sudan where disarmament, demobilization and reintegration is to be done by the Southern Sudan Disarmament, Demobilization and Reintegration Commission. Both the northern and the southern Commissions fall under the umbrella of the National Disarmament, Demobilization and Reintegration Coordination Council. The Council has taken important steps in policy development and planning, with the support and participation of UNMIS and UNICEF. It has organized capacity-building for local non-governmental organizations and at the end of May 2006 hosted a first coordination meeting among government and non-governmental counterparts.

51. SPLA has long acknowledged that it has child soldiers in its ranks and has made a high-level commitment to ending recruitment and use. Since 2001, it has carried out child demobilization activities with varying degrees of success. Since the signing of the Comprehensive Peace Agreement, responsibility for children's disarmament, demobilization and reintegration lies with the Southern Sudan Disarmament, Demobilization and Reintegration Commission. It released more than 960 children and returned them to their families. There are still challenges in ensuring that reintegration programmes are effective. Reintegration can fail if family tracing is inadequate or if schools are not accessible to children. Ensuring adequate resourcing for child disarmament, demobilization and reintegration programmes over time continues to be a challenge.

Children's disarmament, demobilization and reintegration in Darfur

52. The government of Northern Darfur State recently announced the release of prisoners of war, some of whom reportedly are children. UNICEF has been working with the Ministry of Social Welfare and the National Disarmament, Demobilization and Reintegration Coordination Council to ensure programming for their reintegration.

53. Funding is generally available for children's disarmament, demobilization and reintegration in the context of the Comprehensive Peace Agreement, but not for the children's disarmament, demobilization and reintegration required by the Darfur Peace Agreement. Once the outcomes of the Darfur child protection workshop have been turned into a plan of action, this will provide a fund-raising platform for a comprehensive protection programme for children affected by the conflict in Darfur.

VI. Recommendations

54. I call upon all parties to the conflict, without further delay, to comply with the resolutions of the Security Council on children and armed conflict by entering into dialogue with the United Nations for the preparation and implementation of concrete and time-bound action plans to halt the grave child rights violations for which they have been cited, including commitment to the release of children associated with their forces and prioritization of disarmament, demobilization and reintegration programmes for children.

55. I am deeply concerned over the continued lack of access in many areas of the Sudan for child protection activities, particularly in the east, and reiterate the call to all parties to

ensure unhindered and safe humanitarian access to children, denial of which is considered a grave violation against children.

56. I strongly urge the leaders of the Government of National Unity and the Government of Southern Sudan to take steps to end child recruitment and use and to take immediate steps to implement effective, well-resourced and well-monitored programmes to release children from armed forces, safely return them to families and places of origin and provide the services needed to reintegrate them into ordinary life. The current peace processes in Darfur and southern Sudan offer a real opportunity for the leaders of the Sudan to end the practice of recruitment and use of children once and for all.

57. The Government of National Unity bears direct responsibility for child recruitment and use in the Sudanese Armed Forces and all aligned forces, and must act to end this practice immediately. I strongly urge the Government to take appropriate legislative steps to criminalize the recruitment and use of children, as required by the Optional Protocol to the Convention on the Rights of the Child on the Involvement of Children in Armed Conflict, which the Government ratified last year. I call upon the Government also to meet its commitment to investigate and prosecute any individuals for commission of grave violations against children, beginning with its commitment to prosecute Lieutenant Colonel Thomas Thiel for the attack on an unarmed convoy in March 2006, which led to the deaths of two children.

58. I strongly appeal to the Government to take all necessary measures to neutralize the Janjaweed as stipulated in the Darfur Peace Agreement, and stress that the Government's seriousness in meeting this particular commitment should be scrutinized if it is to distance itself from responsibility for violations committed by the Janjaweed.

59. The Government of Southern Sudan bears direct responsibility for the recruitment and use of children in SPLA and must act to halt recruitment and release all children from its forces without delay. I urge the Government of Southern Sudan also to rigorously investigate and prosecute those responsible for committing grave violations against children.

60. I call upon the relevant national disarmament, demobilization and reintegration authorities to undertake without delay an audit of children in the Government's forces in southern Sudan and in Darfur, to ensure that the many children in southern Sudan who have recently been incorporated into the Sudanese Armed Forces are not released from the military without adequate support to return to their families and reintegrate into normal life.

61. I stress the need for SLA (Minawi) and SLA (Wahid) in Darfur to make good on their commitments in the Darfur Peace Agreement and in previous accords to end the recruitment and use of children, and I call upon other armed groups in Darfur to enter into or renew commitments in this regard. I stress the need for all the parties to work with disarmament, demobilization and reintegration authorities and the Task Force on Children and Armed Conflict to develop action plans to release children and return them safely to their communities.

62. All armed forces and armed groups, as well as other actors such as United Nations entities, the African Union and non-governmental organizations should take appropriate steps to address the special vulnerabilities and needs of girls associated with the armed forces and groups, particularly as regards their protection, release and reintegration into

communities. In this regard, I call on the international community to provide adequate long-term resources for such interventions.

63. I am deeply concerned about the increase in sexual violence against girls and women, particularly in Darfur, and stress the urgent need for national authorities to rigorously investigate and prosecute responsible parties and to put in place measures for the protection of girls and women who are more vulnerable, especially among internally displaced populations.

64. I am also concerned over reports of systematic abduction and kidnapping of children, particularly in Darfur, and urge both the Government and the rebel movements in Darfur to act without delay to stop this practice. I call upon the Government to rigorously investigate and prosecute all those who commit this violation, which is also a crime under Sudanese law.

65. I affirm the special role and responsibility of peacekeepers in efforts to bring an end to the commission of grave violations against children in situations of armed conflict, and urge UNMIS and AMIS to play a proactive supporting role in the implementation of Security Council resolution 1612 (2005) and other Council resolutions on children and armed conflict, particularly as regards monitoring and reporting on grave violations and the provision of systematic training for peacekeeping personnel in child rights and protection. In this regard, I commend and welcome the strong support that AMIS has given to the implementation of resolution 1612 (2005), and I call upon the military observers and civilian police of AMIS to continue to work with the police and armed forces and groups to monitor and report on violations against children, including child recruitment, and to use the ceasefire institutions established by the Darfur Peace Agreement to bring an end to such violations.

66. My Special Representative for Children and Armed Conflict plans to conduct a mission to the Sudan in the near future. I encourage a delegation of the Security Council Working Group on Children in Armed Conflict also to undertake a mission to the Sudan as soon as possible.

2. Report of the Secretary-General on the Sudan, 12 September 2006 (S/2006/728)

I. Introduction

1. The present report is submitted pursuant to paragraph 11 of Security Council resolution 1590 (2005), in which the Council requested me to keep it regularly informed of the progress in implementing the Comprehensive Peace Agreement, respect for the ceasefire and the implementation of the mandate of the United Nations Mission in the Sudan (UNMIS). The report also provides an assessment of the overall situation in the country since my previous report to the Council, dated 23 June 2006 (S/2006/426).

II. Implementation of the major elements of the Comprehensive Peace Agreement

2. When I attended the inauguration of the presidency of the Government of National Unity and the signing of the Interim National Constitution in Khartoum on 9 July 2005, I called on the National Congress Party (NCP) and the Sudan People's Liberation Movement (SPLM) to fulfil their obligations under the Comprehensive Peace Agreement promptly and completely. One year later, the parties are in the process of implementing some of the security arrangements set out in the Agreement, while there has not been much progress in respect of their power—and wealth-sharing obligations. Indeed, the parties continue to contest the interpretation of several aspects of the Agreement, and have neglected other commitments.

3. UNMIS and the wider United Nations system have continued to play a key role in support of the implementation of the Comprehensive Peace Agreement. In accordance with its Security Council mandate, the peacekeeping Mission has provided good offices and political support to the parties, monitored and verified their security arrangements and offered assistance in a number of areas, including governance, recovery and development.

4. Overall, the parties' efforts to implement the security provisions of the Comprehensive Peace Agreement have reduced the likelihood of future conflict. The continuing redeployment of the Sudan Armed Forces (SAF) from southern Sudan is generally on schedule, although the Sudanese People's Liberation Army (SPLA) has accused SAF forces of concentrating around oilfields in the region bordering between the north and the south, rather than redeploying further north. In the months ahead, it will be crucial for the transfers of military command to take place in all areas in southern Sudan.

5. In its meeting held on 4 July, the Ceasefire Joint Military Committee, created under the Comprehensive Peace Agreement, established that SPLA had completed its redeployment from eastern Sudan. The redeployment of 5,672 troops out of a declared strength of 8,763 was verified by UNMIS. The troops unaccounted for were considered to have abandoned SPLA. The completion of the redeployment marked an important milestone in the implementation of the Agreement, as well as the end of the UNMIS monitoring mandate in the east of the country. UNMIS subsequently commenced its withdrawal from that region.

6. Comprehensive Peace Agreement security mechanisms, such as the Ceasefire Joint Military Committee and the Area Joint Military Committees, are largely functioning as

intended, investigating violations and resolving disputes through discussions. These mechanisms played a significant role in the peaceful resolution of a number of incidents that could have triggered wider conflict, notably, the March ambush of an unarmed convoy north of Abyei, and the August clash between off-duty SPLA and SAF officers in the Rubkona market in Unity State, in which eight civilians and three soldiers were killed.

7. However, southern Sudan is still suffering from insecurity due to the presence of other armed groups, communal violence and forced disarmament campaigns. While SPLA has absorbed much of the former Southern Sudan Defence Forces (SSDF), other armed groups remain a major threat throughout southern Sudan. The proliferation of small arms has contributed to the loss of hundreds of lives in communal clashes over land, water and grazing rights. An SPLA operation intended to disarm the rogue White Army in Jonglei in May sparked serious armed clashes. The parties have fallen well behind schedule on the incorporation of other armed groups into their forces. The Other Armed Groups Collaborative Committee met for only the second time, in Juba on 5 August, agreeing, however, that the parties would alternately chair regular meetings in the future. While each party has provided the Ceasefire Joint Military Committee with a list of aligned other armed groups, their actual alignment status, composition and location remain vague.

8. Also, the formation of Joint Integrated Units has been slow. The parties are approximately 18 months behind schedule on this important aspect and are unlikely to meet the 1 October 2006 deadline for the completion of co-location, training and deployment of the Units. At the same time, the parties have taken the first step of co-locating such units in Juba, Torit and Khartoum. However, in order for the Units to be truly effective and for them to fill security gaps left by SPLA and SAF redeployments, they need additional training, as well as budgetary and material support. Much also remains to be done in the area of integrating the units and defining their command structures.

9. At meetings of the Ceasefire Political Commission and through the Joint Defence Board, both parties have identified the need and expressed their desire for international support for the establishment of Joint Integrated Units. In order to advance the issue, UNMIS has invited them to submit a formal request to the international community. In addition, on 9 August the UNMIS Force Commander convened a meeting with representatives of embassies in Khartoum to discuss areas in which the international community can assist in training for the Units. For its part, the Government of Southern Sudan will require substantial international assistance to restructure, train and equip SPLA while developing the administrative capacity to support a modern army. Some SPLA soldiers have not been paid for many months, which has led to isolated clashes and instances of insubordination. Comprehensive Peace Agreement-mandated troop reductions will also require international support for a disarmament, demobilization and reintegration effort.

10. International support will also be important for the reform of the rest of the Sudanese national security sector. The Comprehensive Peace Agreement requires the parties to adopt a National Security Act to govern the National Security Service and create a National Security Council charged with implementing reforms. The UNMIS mandate includes helping the parties restructure the Sudanese police service with support from bilateral and multilateral assistance programmes. The parties have made little progress at the national level, however. While key security agencies are reviewing draft amendments to the existing National Security Act, no proposals have been released for public comment.

11. Despite some positive signs on the security side, the parties are well behind schedule in implementing the power- and wealth-sharing aspects of the Comprehensive Peace Agreement, where there is little progress to report. In the key area of oil, they continue to disagree on whether the National Petroleum Commission, on which both parties are represented, should be an advisory or a decision-making body, on the nature of its relationship with the Ministry of Energy and Mining and on its participation in oil contract negotiations. In this regard, the Ministry needs to display further transparency to ensure fairness and accuracy in oil-revenue calculations.

12. The related north-south border issues have proved similarly contentious. While the Technical Ad Hoc Border Committee met once during the reporting period, it has not yet commenced substantive work on border delineation, and was delayed by the onset of the rains. This task is urgent because the lack of an agreed delineation of the north-south border hinders or confuses obligations relating to military redeployment, the distribution of oil revenues, Joint Integrated Unit formation and, eventually, the referendum to confirm the unity of the Sudan or allow the secession of the south.

13. Similarly, the parties have made no progress on implementing the Protocol on the Resolution of the Conflict in the Abyei Area, since NCP rejected the Abyei Boundaries Commission report issued in July 2005. Meanwhile, the failure of the presidency to appoint a local Executive Council or Abyei Area Council has left the people of that region largely without formal policing, public sanitation and health services. Abyei remains a serious potential flashpoint with regard to implementation of the Comprehensive Peace Agreement.

14. The parties' difficulty in reaching decisions and compromises has slowed implementation in a number of other areas. The Ceasefire Political Commission has proved unable to resolve a number of issues on its agenda, including restrictions imposed on UNMIS freedom of movement north of Abyei town and the status of disputed redeployment assembly areas. At a meeting convened in May to address contentious issues including Abyei, the NCP-SPLM joint leadership chose instead to refer the issues to the presidency, which has yet to deliver its decisions. In August, the parties established a new layer of joint committees, and the issue of Abyei is now in the hands of a subcommittee of the NCP-SPLM Joint Political Committee.

15. Altogether, the parties have so far failed to give other obligations under the Comprehensive Peace Agreement sufficient priority, despite the fact that the joint Government continues to function. Hardly any action has been taken to start preparing for national elections, originally scheduled for mid-2008, but deferred to mid-2009 by the Interim National Constitution.

16. Few of the commissions called for in the Comprehensive Peace Agreement function as originally intended. The National Constitutional Review Commission, charged with reviewing national legislation, has not met this year. The National Assembly has passed only one act establishing a commission, and the National Constitutional Review Commission did not review that act as required by the Comprehensive Peace Agreement. Legislation necessary to establish the National Human Rights, Civil Service, Land and Electoral Commissions is still pending. However, there are encouraging signs of the National Assembly emerging as a vibrant forum for broad political dialogue. During the second session, parliamentarians from a wide variety of political parties held intensive discussions on a number of national issues and issues related to the Comprehensive Peace Agreement.

17. The parties have also fallen behind schedule in implementing the legislative reform agenda required by the Comprehensive Peace Agreement. The National Assembly concluded its three-month second session in July without passing any legislation related to the Agreement. At its next session, the National Assembly is expected to consider critical draft legislation on electoral issues, political parties and the national security sector. However, the parties have not yet released drafts for public discussion. Those laws will have a major effect on the future of the country.

18. The Assessment and Evaluation Commission continues to monitor implementation through its plenary and four working groups, which focus on power-sharing, wealth-sharing, security and the three areas dealt with separately in the Comprehensive Peace Agreement Protocols, i.e. Abyei, Southern Kordofan and Blue Nile. On 16 August, UNMIS joined the Assessment and Evaluation Commission at its eleventh plenary meeting as an ex officio member, and was welcomed by the parties and other international members of the Commission. However, the parties have not displayed sufficient interest in the Commission, nor are they yet fully utilizing the mechanism to advance the peace process.

19. For its part, SPLM is facing the natural challenges of transforming itself from a liberation movement into an inclusive political party and government that reflect the diversity of the peoples of southern Sudan. Its Interim Political Bureau, charged with overseeing internal party reform, was endorsed in April 2006 in Rumbek, and the second party convention was expected to be convened before the end of the year.

20. During the early stages of the reporting period, the Lord's Resistance Army (LRA) continued to attack civilians and destabilize the area along the Sudan's borders with Uganda and the Democratic Republic of the Congo. Military efforts have so far failed to eliminate it as a threat, in part because of coordination difficulties among the affected states. Following an extended effort of the Government of Southern Sudan, the Government of Uganda and LRA launched talks in Juba on 14 July, mediated by the Government of Southern Sudan. The negotiators face a number of complex and contentious issues, but the current talks are unprecedented. In Juba, on 26 August, the Government of Uganda and LRA signed a cessation of hostilities agreement that requires LRA members to assemble at two designated points in southern Sudan.

III. Implementation of the mandate of the United Nations Mission in the Sudan

Political support and reconciliation

21. In accordance with paragraph 3 of Security Council resolution 1590 (2005), UNMIS continued to provide good offices and political support in several areas to help implement the Comprehensive Peace Agreement and resolve other conflicts in the Sudan. In southern Sudan, UNMIS used its good offices to help restore calm in a number of volatile situations, including the clashes caused by the forced disarmament campaign in Jonglei and the Rubkona market incident. Starting on 11 August, UNMIS convened several emergency meetings of the Area Joint Military Committee to secure a halt to the fighting between the SPLA and the SAF-aligned Pangak Peace Force in sector III (Malakal). Also, UNMIS liaison and good relations with most commanders of SAF, SPLA and other armed groups proved crucial in de-escalating the tense situation in Upper Nile State. More broadly, UNMIS continues to perform an important early warning role throughout southern Sudan, identifying and acting to defuse intercommunal tensions.

22. UNMIS has monitored the Eritrean-mediated talks between the Sudanese Government and the Eastern Front, which began in Asmara on 13 June. The parties decided not to involve other international actors in the talks at this stage, and did not take up the UNMIS offer of technical and expert support for the negotiations. Eritrea's role in the talks also confirms the warming of relations between Eritrea and the Sudan; on 12 June, the Presidents of the Sudan and Eritrea met for the first time in more than five years.

23. UNMIS also assisted in efforts to implement and build support for the Darfur Peace Agreement. The Mission continued to persuade the non-signatory groups to support the Agreement, and participated in the work of the African Union (AU)-led Joint Commission and Ceasefire Commissions. The United Nations organized six workshops in Nyala and El-Fashir to explain the Darfur Peace Agreement, targeting a wide range of stakeholders, including the African Union Mission in the Sudan (AMIS), civil society organizations, women's groups and traditional leaders. UNMIS also provided its good offices to promote discussions between AMIS and internally displaced persons in Zalingei, allowing the latter to express their concerns and the former to resume patrol activities in the camps.

24. During the reporting period, UNMIS support for AMIS increased substantially in line with the additional tasks and responsibilities that AMIS has assumed under the Darfur Peace Agreement. AMIS developed a new concept of operations, which the AU Peace and Security Council approved on 27 June. UNMIS also responded to AU requests for assistance relating to communications, logistics, transportation, public information and humanitarian issues. The United Nations and AU are currently formulating a support package for AMIS to enhance its capability and help it to implement its mandated tasks. However, the position of the Sudanese Government with regard to Security Council resolution 1706 (2006) and transition of peacekeeping responsibilities in Darfur from AU to the United Nations has been very negative. The United Nations will continue to engage Khartoum on this very important issue.

Military deployment and activities

25. UNMIS has now deployed almost all of its expected total of 9,880 military personnel. As at 4 September, 8,727 troops, 695 military observers and 186 staff officers drawn from 61 countries had taken up their duties in the Sudan.

26. With the completion of SPLA redeployment to the south, UNMIS Redeployment Coordination Headquarters, based in Kassala, had fulfilled its tasks in eastern Sudan, and its drawdown was initiated on 1 August. While Redeployment Coordination Headquarters staff officers from Nepal and Germany will be repatriated, the Nepalese infantry company will deploy to another United Nations peacekeeping operation, and military observers have been reassigned to sectors in the South. At a farewell ceremony held on 29 July, the Wali of Kassala stressed that United Nations agencies could continue their humanitarian work in the region unhindered. I would like to take this opportunity to recognize the important role of the Redeployment Coordination Headquarters in the implementation of the Comprehensive Peace Agreement in eastern Sudan.

27. In recent months, UNMIS has bolstered its presence and security in Equatoria. As the Council will recall, the Mission is mandated to help protect civilians facing an imminent threat within its areas of deployment and capabilities. With respect to LRA, the role of UNMIS is currently limited to coordination and information-sharing with the Sudanese

authorities, other affected Member States and the United Nations Organization Mission in the Democratic Republic of the Congo, as described in my report of 29 June 2006 (S/2006/478).

28. Regrettably, the Sudanese customs service in Port Sudan and Khartoum delayed for extended periods the release of a wide range of items, including food rations. It had held some major communications equipment since February and generally clears United Nations stores and supplies at an extremely slow pace, creating significant logistical obstacles to the operation of UNMIS forces. UNMIS has protested many times, and at many levels, to the Government about this issue. The situation has now slightly improved; however, UNMIS communications equipment has yet to be released.

29. In the meantime, customs delays and rain-related road closures have increased the reliance of UNMIS on air and water transport. The Russian, Indian and Pakistani military aviation units are now fully deployed and operational, but are not yet cleared by the United Nations Secretariat for night operations. The force riverine unit has proved effective in deploying joint monitoring teams and force protection elements along the Nile within its operational range of 100 kilometres from its base. On 17 August, unidentified gunmen fired at a boat belonging to the United Nations riverine unit, which was transporting a joint monitoring team near Malakal. Two Indian soldiers and one SAF national monitor were injured. I am very concerned about this instance of deliberate targeting of UNMIS personnel, which UNMIS considers a serious violation of the ceasefire.

30. As at 4 September, UNMIS had chaired 35 meetings of the Ceasefire Joint Military Committee. Despite slow progress on a number of issues, the Committee continues to provide a useful forum for open and results-oriented discussion. After a long delay, both parties have now submitted to the Committee information on the structure of their respective forces. Upon completion of analysis of those data, the information may significantly assist in the monitoring and verification of SAF and SPLA strength and disposition of forces.

Disarmament, demobilization and reintegration

31. Although the Northern and Southern Sudan Disarmament, Demobilization and Reintegration Commissions have been set up to lead and implement the interim disarmament, demobilization and reintegration programme, overall progress in the implementation and preparation of the multi-year disarmament, demobilization and reintegration programme has been slow. The Commissions continued to need capable and motivated staff, as well as adequate budgets for their operations, in order to boost their capacities. However, the absence of some key decision-making national bodies, particularly the National Council for Disarmament, Demobilization and Reintegration Coordination, continued to limit the authority of the Commissions.

32. In the course of June, the SPLA forced civilian disarmament campaign met with some violent resistance in Jonglei State. In response, UNMIS, together with the United Nations Development Programme (UNDP) led efforts to support the civilian disarmament programme in Akobo county, in order to promote non-coercive disarmament. UNMIS also resumed training support for 420 SPLA data collectors for the registration of SPLA troops, and has offered similar training support to SAF for the other armed groups aligned with it. In the meantime, 650 demobilized child combatants from SPLA were reunified with their families.

33. During the reporting period, the Northern Sudan Disarmament, Demobilization and Reintegration Commission, with the support of UNMIS, demobilized and provided reinsertion support to 122 women and disabled ex-combatants from SAF-aligned other armed groups.

Electoral assistance

34. Security Council resolution 1590 (2005) mandated UNMIS to provide guidance and technical assistance to the parties to support their preparations for and conduct of elections and referendums provided for by the Comprehensive Peace Agreement. During the reporting period, UNMIS completed an initial assessment of electoral legislation and initiated discussions with parliamentarians, National Electoral Commissioners, the Registrar for Political Parties, political party leaders and civil society representatives. Recruitment for the UNMIS Electoral Unit is ongoing. The Unit will provide capacity-building and sustainable technical assistance to the National Electoral Commission, serve as focal point for electoral matters and coordinate international assistance to the electoral process.

Police

35. As at 1 September, UNMIS had deployed 666 United Nations police officers from 42 countries, who are currently stationed at 21 team sites, representing over 90 per cent of the authorized strength. Following agreement with the Southern Sudan Police Service (SSPS), United Nations police officers are now working alongside the local police leadership in the areas of Juba and Kadugli.

36. On the recommendation of UNMIS, SSPS established the Police Development Committee in May to formulate policy and coordinate capacity-building efforts. The Inspector-General of Police chairs the Committee, which includes representatives of SPLM, the Government of National Unity and international agencies. Also, with UNMIS support, the Committee has drafted a framework and action plan for community policing in Juba. The UNMIS police component has drafted a code of conduct for the Sudan police, which is awaiting approval, and is prepared to play a leading role in SSPS officer training, providing an initial pool of 34 trainers for this purpose. SSPS has also approved an UNMIS proposal to develop a system intended to identify and register all SSPS personnel and issue each with an identification card. The implementation of this project began in June with the registration of senior SSPS officials, and as at 1 September almost 2,000 police officers had been registered. At the national level, UNMIS and other United Nations agencies are planning to begin human rights training for Government of National Unity police in Khartoum in September 2006. In the meantime, the Mission will continue its discussions with the Government of National Unity to identify other opportunities to assist the police in northern Sudan.

Human rights

37. The parties made little progress in establishing human rights commissions called for in the Comprehensive Peace Agreement. On 27 June, President Kiir of southern Sudan issued a decree naming five members of the Southern Sudan Human Rights Commission, though the Commission itself does not yet formally exist. President Kiir asked the designated Commissioners to collaborate in finalizing the necessary legislation. In response to this development, UNMIS organized a workshop for the designated Commissioners to familiarize

them with relevant human rights issues. At the national level, however, the National Assembly did not consider a draft act to establish the National Human Rights Commission before its three-month recess, which began in July. During the reporting period, UNMIS organized a workshop with the Advisory Council for Human Rights in which civil society groups called for amendments to the draft act, and another one with the National Assembly's Human Rights Standing Committee on international human rights treaties to which the Sudan is a party. In August, in cooperation with the Khartoum State police, UNMIS organized a series of workshops on human rights and law enforcement aimed at introducing and promoting international human rights standards within the national police force.

Rule of law

38. During the period under review, UNMIS assisted the Government of Southern Sudan authorities in preparing a training programme for corrections staff in southern Sudan, and in Rumbek, from 18 to 27 July, trained 100 Government of Southern Sudan corrections officers in the United Nations standard minimum rules for the treatment of prisoners. On 26 July, UNDP and UNMIS trained 250 police officers in Juba on the topic "Rule of law principles and the criminal justice chain". The Government of Southern Sudan has requested UNMIS to co-locate corrections experts in major prisons in order to provide advice and training to local staff. UNMIS will need to second 25 prison experts from Member States to meet that request. UNDP has also conducted capacity-building activities for national rule-of-law institutions and actors, including the organization of three study tours for members of the National Judicial Services Commission. Through the Government of Southern Sudan Budget Sector Working Group, UNMIS and UNDP helped the Government to plan and budget for rule-of-law institutions up to 2009.

Public information

39. UNMIS Radio started broadcasting in Juba on 30 June. The new station, Miraya ("Mirror") FM, broadcasts continuously and airs news bulletins in English, Arabic and Juba Arabic, which are updated three times per day. The Government of Southern Sudan has approved the roll-out of Miraya FM throughout southern Sudan, and UNMIS now plans to complete coverage of the largest population centres in southern Sudan by the end of the year. However, the Khartoum authorities continued their opposition to UNMIS Radio broadcasting in the North, despite the obligation under the status-of-forces agreement to allow it to broadcast countrywide.

40. In July, UNMIS attended the Joint Media Commission's first meeting since August 2005. The meeting discussed dissemination of the Comprehensive Peace Agreement, including by using UNMIS materials for print, radio and television. However, no concrete decisions were taken. UNMIS obtained buildings for outreach centres in Kadugli and Malakal and is negotiating for outreach centres in Juba and Khartoum. UNMIS also continued to support AU in its efforts to disseminate the Darfur Peace Agreement in Darfur through workshops, website support and the production of radio programmes.

Humanitarian assistance

41. The humanitarian situation in southern Sudan remains stable and has led to increased activity and optimism among the international aid community. Between January and early June this year, international assistance contributed to the construction or repair of 370 kilometres

of road. This in turn has supported the return of over 10,000 refugees to southern Sudan and the delivery of food aid to 3 million people, as well as polio immunization for 4.8 million children. While activities are temporarily restricted by seasonal rains at the moment, they are expected to resume at normal levels by October or November.

42. In Darfur, however, the humanitarian situation has deteriorated sharply since the signing of the Darfur Peace Agreement on 5 May. Where reliable access exists, the humanitarian community continues to deliver a strong multisectoral programme, helping to maintain the gains in health, nutrition, water and sanitation that it has achieved since August 2004. However, reduced access in other areas, increased violence towards humanitarian actors and a weakening of the position of AMIS are beginning to reverse these hard-won humanitarian gains. During the reporting period, humanitarian access reached its lowest levels since 2003 (below 60 per cent). Populations are suffering from both the increased instability and violence and the diminished ability of humanitarian workers to reach them. Perceptions of AMIS partiality have reduced the confidence of internally displaced persons in the AU Mission, leading to reduced security as AMIS withdrew from several camps. Humanitarian needs are likely to increase in the short term, as displacements have reduced planting this season, leading to a much-diminished harvest in November.

43. The Government continued to restrict humanitarian access in Kassala, Red Sea and Gedaref States. While bilateral arrangements have facilitated access for some agencies, further restrictions were being imposed towards the end of August. Access for humanitarian personnel in Abyei improved, despite ongoing restrictions on the movement of UNMIS monitors. The lack of a civil administration in Abyei continued to delay the transition from humanitarian assistance to recovery programmes, increasing the risk of a humanitarian crisis.

Protection of civilians

44. During the reporting period, police in Northern Sudan carried out raids on camps for internally displaced persons, relocation sites and squatter areas around Khartoum. Such raids are regularly accompanied by violence, abuse and extortions. On 16 and 17 August, authorities evicted some 12,000 internally displaced persons in Dar Assalam, south of Khartoum, and demolished about 3,500 houses in a day. Reports suggest that authorities killed and injured an unknown number of internally displaced persons during the operations. UNMIS, which to date has been denied all access to the area, is pressing for immediate high-level Government measures to address the needs of the relocated populations and to prevent further abuses. In this connection, I would like to remind the Sudanese authorities of the willingness and capability of United Nations agencies and partners to assist them in planning the relocation process for communities, including the proper preparation of sites and provision of services.

45. In southern Sudan, enhanced cooperation between agencies and UNMIS helped ensure coordinated responses to protection issues arising from ongoing insecurity. For example, when civilians were attacked and looted in Jonglei by militia members resisting forcible disarmament, UNMIS rapidly deployed inter-agency assessment teams from Malakal and Juba.

46. The inclusion of children in armed forces in the Sudan remains a grave concern, as described in my report to the Security Council of 17 August (S/2006/662). In Southern Sudan, child soldiers are most often associated with other armed groups.

Returns

47. During the reporting period, returns to the three areas (Abyei, Southern Kordofan and Blue Nile) and the south dwindled as the rains made many roads impassable; small numbers of returnees are still arriving by barge. However, the returns are likely to resume on a large scale in October. The Government of Southern Sudan intends to organize the return of as many as possible of the 680,000 people who are already registered with State authorities to return. In response to the ambitious plans of the Government of Southern Sudan, the United Nations provided technical support for organized returns to ensure they are conducted according to international standards. Providing effective and timely reintegration and recovery assistance to communities in areas with large numbers of returnees remains a critical challenge.

48. In Darfur, the security situation did not allow for returns. Instead, UNMIS activities focused on preparedness for return contingencies, enabling agencies to respond effectively should the situation change. Existing mechanisms, particularly agreements with the Government, will remain central tools for ensuring that any returns that take place do so under conditions of voluntariness, safety and dignity.

Mine action

49. Landmines and unexploded ordnance continue to constitute a major threat to the population in many parts of the Sudan, as well as to United Nations staff and humanitarian personnel operating on the ground. However, UNMIS mine action teams have made major progress in demining activities and mine education. To date, 7 million square metres of suspected dangerous areas have been cleared, and some 2,100 anti-personnel mines, over 900 anti-tank mines and some 270,000 pieces of unexploded ordnance and small-arms ammunition have been destroyed. UNMIS and the United Nations Children's Fund have provided mine-risk education to more than 834,000 people. UNMIS has provided briefings on landmine safety to over 2,400 staff working with the Mission or other United Nations agencies and non-governmental organizations, while 179 staff have been trained as trainers.

50. UNMIS mine action teams prioritized the clearing of humanitarian routes in the Nuba Mountains, Juba, Rumbek, Wau, Yei, Malakal, Ed Damazin and Darfur. Over 1,200 kilometres of roads have been verified or cleared for emergency deployment and aid delivery. The road from Kadugli to Fama, closed for 16 years, can now be reopened. However, as these efforts have come to a halt during the rainy season, the focus has shifted to the recruitment and training of deminers. Three UNMIS demining contingents from Egypt (Kadugli), Kenya (Wau) and Bangladesh (Juba), have commenced operations. Pakistani units have been issued with provisional accreditation and are awaiting deployment to Kurmuk by the end of August. Cambodian units in Malakal are going through in-country training for final accreditation and are expected to be fully operational by the end of the rainy season.

51. The National Mine Action Authority, launched in March 2006, met for the first time in August and approved the National Mine Action Strategic Framework. UNMIS has supported and implemented several national capacity-development activities of the Authority, including an eight-week training course for Joint Integrated Demining Unit personnel and seven national mine-action capacity-development courses to develop the technical and managerial skills of national and international mine-action staff.

Economic recovery and reconstruction

52. The economy continues to grow rapidly, while inflation remains subdued. Real GDP growth is projected at 12 per cent for 2006, strengthened by higher oil receipts and buoyant activity in the non-oil sector. However, a decrease in oil production during the first half of the year caused both the fiscal and the external current account balances to deteriorate. Average inflation fell from 8.5 per cent in December 2005 to 6.4 per cent in June 2006. The favourable inflation performance is reflected in lower food prices, among other indicators. Unfortunately, most private-sector gains remain confined to Khartoum, and benefits are reaped primarily by the elite and higher income earners. The United Nations, the World Bank and the African Development Bank initiated the Darfur Joint Assessment Mission under the Darfur Peace Agreement in The Hague on 21 and 22 June. The Joint Assessment Mission is designed to provide rapid implementation in relation to urgent needs, and better planning and coordination of longer-term development requirements, based on the identified needs of Darfurians. However, the escalation of violence in Darfur severely impeded the work of the Mission.

53. Donor support continues to lag behind needs with respect to humanitarian requirements. By the end of August 2006, donor pledges met only 56 per cent ($896.5 million) of identified humanitarian work-plan requirements. With respect to recovery and development, while donor commitments lagged, participants at the first Sudan Consortium meeting in March 2006 agreed that a principal challenge has been the slow disbursements of paid-in contributions through the multi-donor trust funds. The World Bank structure and administration of the trust funds have proved ill-suited to meet immediate post-conflict requirements. This has been compounded by the fact that the capacity of the Government of Southern Sudan is still nascent. Since the Oslo conference, approximately $430 million of the $2.6 billion needed for post-conflict reconstruction, as identified by the Joint Assessment Mission, has been committed. With respect to the multi-donor trust funds, less than $12 million had been disbursed for programming by the end of July 2006.

Gender

54. While some progress has been made in opening space for discussion of gender issues since the signing of the Comprehensive Peace Agreement, many challenges to the political and economic empowerment of women in the Sudan remain. UNMIS began drafting a training manual for women candidates for the national elections, and began working with police officers in Southern Kordofan on improving sensitivity to victims of gender-based violence. Within UNMIS, the Gender Unit distributed copies of Security Council resolution 1325 (2000) and the Secretary-General's bulletin on special measures for protection from sexual exploitation and sexual abuse (ST/SGB/2003/13).

HIV/AIDS

55. The UNMIS HIV/AIDS Unit continued providing voluntary counselling and testing services, induction courses and HIV sensitization for peacekeeping contingents in the sectors. The Unit also trained 32 SPLA HIV/AIDS change agents in Rumbek as part of the National Disarmament, Demobilization and Reintegration Programme. In addition, awareness training reached some 1,200 SPLA members, and about 1,000 internally displaced persons in Lologo way station, in Juba. The Unit assisted the Sudan National AIDS Programme in drafting a project proposal for HIV/AIDS awareness among SAF members.

Conduct and discipline

56. The UNMIS Conduct and Discipline Unit continues to be engaged in active prevention, enforcement and outreach activities to ensure that all Mission personnel comply with the United Nations code of conduct for the Sudan. All new staff now receive extensive induction training on the code of conduct and on sexual exploitation and abuse. During the reporting period, UNMIS also launched a public information strategy on United Nations standards of conduct and developed and implemented a standard operating procedure for reporting misconduct. As a result of an investigation, one staff member was dismissed for sexual exploitation in connection with an incident that occurred in 2005. As at 28 August, 33 similar cases were under active investigation; in 8 of those cases, reports are being awaited from the Office of Internal Oversight Services.

Status-of-forces agreement

57. There is a major concern about several apparent breaches of the Government's commitments under the status-of-forces agreement. During the reporting period, SAF personnel continued to prevent UNMIS movement north of Abyei, restricting the United Nations monitoring to only 20 per cent of the sector, which is also in violation of the Government's obligations under the Comprehensive Peace Agreement. At the same time, the Government continues to arrest and detain national UNMIS staff, in violation of the Convention on the Privileges and Immunities of the United Nations and the status-of-forces agreement. The obstacles to clearing UNMIS materiel through customs and the refusal to allow UNMIS Radio to broadcast in northern Sudan are also in breach of obligations under the status-of-forces agreement.

IV. Observations

58. One year after the inauguration of the Government of National Unity, the parties have made progress, albeit on a limited scale, in carrying out their commitments under the Comprehensive Peace Agreement. While they are observing their security commitments reasonably well, the implementation of several other major provisions of the Agreement has fallen behind schedule. Disappointingly, the implementation of the provisions of the Agreement appears to be selective. The parties have not been able to resolve some important contentious issues, and little progress has been made in the crucial areas of power- and wealth-sharing which together form the cornerstone of the Agreement, including in respect of Abyei, oil revenues, the north-south border and other armed groups. In addition, the parties have so far done too little to begin preparing for national elections. They should be reminded that none of the commitments enshrined in the Comprehensive Peace Agreement are optional. The parties must meet all their obligations promptly and fully.

59. While various ceasefire bodies envisaged in the Comprehensive Peace Agreement are working well, the ongoing restrictions imposed on the activities of UNMIS monitors in and around Abyei constitute a clear violation of the Agreement. This is of particular concern because the inability of UNMIS to operate properly in northern Abyei only heightens suspicions between the parties. It is also unacceptable that the Ceasefire Political Commission has failed to reach a political compromise on this pivotal issue. I urge that body to resolve the matter expeditiously.

60. The deliberate attack by unidentified armed men on a joint monitoring team on 17 August near Malakal is particularly alarming. The Ceasefire Joint Military Committee

is investigating the incident, including the allegations about the involvement of other armed groups. I call on the two parties to ensure that the perpetrators of the crime are identified and held to account, and that no such incidents occur in the future.

61. The people of the Sudan have high expectations of peace dividends under the Comprehensive Peace Agreement. To date, those expectations have not been met. The United Nations has expanded humanitarian activities and increased recovery interventions considerably, with only limited resources at its disposal. However, accelerated implementation of recovery and development programmes, in particular through multi-donor trust funds, will be critical in order to help build public support for the peace, especially in the south and the three areas. At the same time, donors will need to make good on the commitments they made at the Oslo pledging conference in 2005. I renew my call to the international community to fulfil its pledges in a timely and effective manner.

62. The implementation of the Comprehensive Peace Agreement is entering a new and challenging phase. In the months ahead, the parties must make substantial progress on the difficult tasks related to security-sector reform, police reform and restructuring, preparing for the return of internally displaced persons, the national census and future elections, while continuing active and determined disarmament, demobilization and reintegration programmes to reduce the scourge of small arms. I call on the international community to support the Sudanese people as they confront these new challenges, and to lend financial, technical and political assistance to the implementation of the Comprehensive Peace Agreement agenda.

63. It is clear that implementing the Comprehensive Peace Agreement remains a daunting challenge. There can be no harvest without planting; and if the international community wishes the Sudan to reap the harvest of a durable peace by the end of the interim period envisaged in the Agreement, everything possible should be done to perform the task of planting the seeds of sustainable peace and development.

64. The Sudan's own history confirms that peace is indivisible. The progress that is being made in the talks on eastern Sudan is encouraging, and I hope that they will lead to a full and lasting agreement. However, efforts to implement the Comprehensive Peace Agreement will prove inadequate until durable peace also comes to Darfur. Conversely, the Comprehensive Peace Agreement remains the bedrock on which the Darfur Peace Agreement, however unsteady it may appear now, could be built. The people and the leaders of the Sudan, with the active support of the international community, must tend to both if the country is to finally emerge from conflict and instability.

65. I sincerely hope that the leaders of the Sudan are fully aware of the possible consequences of their negative reaction to the generous proposals of the international community with regard to Darfur, which are based on the Darfur Peace Agreement and the joint position of the African Union and the United Nations concerning the strengthening of AMIS and the transition to the United Nations. There cannot be a lasting solution in Darfur through coercion and violence. The United Nations is therefore prepared to seek the political path, as was agreed by the Sudanese themselves at Abuja. I am ready to continue to engage all parties involved in order to pursue this path. The Security Council has a key role to play in this process, but its effectiveness will depend on its ability to speak and act in complete unity. Ultimately, however, the leaders in Khartoum bear full responsibility for the route they may finally choose.

66. In conclusion, I wish to thank my Special Representative and all United Nations staff for their tireless efforts to help bring peace to the people of the Sudan. In this context, I recommend that the Security Council renew the mandate of UNMIS for a period of 12 months, until 24 September 2007.

Annex
Military and police strength as at 27 August 2006

	Military component									
	Observers		*Troops*		*Staff officers*		*Total*		*Civilian police*	
Country	*Female*	*Male*	*Female*	*Male*	*Female*	*Male*	*Female*	*Male*	*Female*	*Male*
Argentina									0	11
Australia	0	6			3	6	3	12	2	8
Austria						2		2		
Bangladesh	0	23	0	1 501	0	26	0	1 548	3	26
Belgium	0	4					0	4		
Benin	0	7					0	7		
Bolivia	0	15					0	15		
Botswana	0	5					0	5		
Bosnia									1	1
Brazil	0	24					0	24	0	3
Burkina Faso	0	7					0	7		
Cambodia	0	15	0	135	0	1	0	151		
Canada	2	23			1	5	3	28	0	2
China	0	15	7	428		8	7	451	2	13
Croatia					0	3	0	3		
Denmark					0	6	0	6		
Ecuador	0	20					0	20		
Egypt	0	21	16	780		19	16	820		
El Salvador	0	5					0	5	1	5
Fiji	0	8					0	8	0	5
Finland					0	2	0	2	0	2
Gabon	0	10					0	10		
Gambia									4	15
Germany	0	34			0	3	0	37	0	4
Ghana									6	35
Greece	0	4			0	2	0	6		
Guatemala	0	8					0	8		

	Military component									
	Observers		*Troops*		*Staff officers*		*Total*		*Civilian police*	
Country	*Female*	*Male*	*Female*	*Male*	*Female*	*Male*	*Female*	*Male*	*Female*	*Male*
Guinea	0	16					0	16		
India	0	26	4	2 571		25	4	2 622	1	29
Indonesia	0	13					0	13		
Jamaica									2	5
Jordan	0	15			0	8	0	23	0	10
Kenya	0	10	32	786		6	33	802	1	20
Kyrgyzstan	3	7					3	7	0	1
Malawi	0	7			0	1	0	8		
Malaysia	0	10			0	3	0	13	0	10
Mali	0	15					0	15		
Mongolia	0	2					0	2		
Mozambique	0	3					0	3		
Namibia	0	10					0	10	0	1
Nepal	2	8	2	221		4	4	233	1	54
Netherlands	1	13				2	1	15	2	10
New Zealand	0	2			0	1	0	3		
Nigeria	0	8					0	8	4	45
Norway	1	19				7	1	26	0	4
Pakistan	0	22	0	1 542	0	23	0	1 587	0	44
Paraguay	0	10					0	10		
Peru	0	17					0	17		
Philippines	0	20					0	20	0	55
Poland	0	2					0	2		
Republic of Korea	0	7					0	7		
Republic of Moldova	0	2					0	2		
Romania	0	12					0	12		
Russian Federation	0	15	0	120	0	2	0	15	0	13
Rwanda	0	18	0	254	0	2	0	274	0	20
Samoa									0	17
Sri Lanka	0	6					0	6	0	23

Continued

	Military component									
	Observers		*Troops*		*Staff officers*		*Total*		*Civilian police*	
Country	*Female*	*Male*	*Female*	*Male*	*Female*	*Male*	*Female*	*Male*	*Female*	*Male*
Sweden	0	3			0	1	0	4	0	8
Thailand	1	14					1	14		
Turkey					0	4	0	4	0	28
Uganda	0	10					0	10	2	17
Ukraine	0	13					0	13	1	23
United Kingdom					0	3	0	3		
United Republic of Tanzania	1	19					1	19	0	3
Uruguay									0	2
United States of America									2	5
Vanuatu									0	6
Yemen	0	20					0	20	0	3
Zambia	0	15	13	315		7	13	338	0	19
Zimbabwe	2	19					2	19	0	26
Total per gender	**13**	**682**	**75**	**8 653**	**4**	**182**	**92**	**9 516**	**41**	**625**
Total	**695**		**8 727**		**186**		**9 608**		**666**	

3. Monthly Report of the Secretary-General on Darfur, 26 December 2006 (S/2006/764)

I. Introduction

1. The present report is submitted pursuant to paragraphs 6, 13 and 16 of Security Council resolution 1556 (2004), paragraph 15 of Security Council resolution 1564 (2004), paragraph 17 of Security Council resolution 1574 (2004), paragraph 12 of Security Council resolution 1590 (2005), and paragraph 11 of Security Council resolution 1706 (2006). It covers the month of August 2006.

II. Insecurity in Darfur

2. During the reporting period, the overall situation in Darfur deteriorated considerably. The decision of the Government of the Sudan to deploy a large number of military troops to Darfur signals its apparent determination to pursue a military solution to the crisis in the region.

3. The signatories of the Darfur Peace Agreement signed on 5 May 2006 maintained the ceasefire towards each other through the reporting period. However, during the same period, serious violence flared between Darfur Peace Agreement signatories and non-signatories, in breach of the Agreement and 17 December 2004 N'Djamena ceasefire obligations. The 19 August ambush of an African Union fuel convoy, which took place at Kuma, claimed the lives of two peacekeepers, and attacks against humanitarian actors continued unabated. Banditry was rampant across most of Darfur. Militia groups continued to attack civilians and internally displaced persons, and internally displaced person camp security remained very precarious, with an alarming surge in violence towards women and girls. The region is again descending into a vicious cycle of violence.

4. On 28 July, the Sudanese Armed Forces, reportedly assisted by Janjaweed militia, clashed with Darfur Peace Agreement non-signatory forces in the Jebel Moon area of Western Darfur. On 18 August, unknown assailants believed to belong to non-signatory groups attacked a Sudanese Armed Forces camp at Goz Mino, killing three Sudanese Armed Forces soldiers. On 24 August, another armed group ambushed a convoy of the Government of the Sudan near Abu Soroug in Western Darfur, killing the Assistant Commissioner of Kulbus and six others. Government-affiliated militia also repeatedly attacked villages near Jebel Marra between 17 July and 2 August, killing 12 civilians and looting over a thousand cattle.

5. In the meantime, the Government of the Sudan and Minawi troops of the Sudan Liberation Movement (SLM) attacked National Redemption Front (NRF) forces north of El Fasher throughout the reporting period. In particular, fighting erupted between the NRF and Sudanese Armed Forces and SLM-Minawi forces on 28 July around Kulkul, 60 kilometres north of El Fasher; and resulted in the capture of Kulkul by Sudanese Armed Forces on 6 August. The same day, NRF forces attacked and captured Sayeh village, 90 kilometres north-east of El Fasher. On 28 August, Sudanese Armed Forces and NRF forces reportedly resumed fighting west of Kulkul with aerial bombing from government aircraft. Sudanese Armed Forces captured Abu Sakin and Kulkul from the NRF on 28 August, and Um Sidir on 31 August, while introducing additional troops to Northern Darfur. In early September,

Sudanese Armed Forces also moved a considerable number of forces north of El Geneina along the Chad border and north from Kordofan into the Sayeh area.

6. In the meantime, the Sudanese Armed Forces has reportedly deployed aircraft to Northern Darfur for reconnaissance, logistics support and bombing raids. Reports indicate that a government aircraft bombed Hassan village near Kulkul on 29 July, killing at least one civilian and injuring seven others. Villagers from Gosh Marakh, Um Hashab, and Yonka reported bombings in their areas between 30 July and 1 August. A Government of the Sudan Antonov aircraft crash-landed at El Fasher airport on 7 August; NRF fighters claimed to have crippled it with ground-fire around Sayeh. At the 9 August Ceasefire Commission meeting held in El Fasher, the Justice and Equality Movement (JEM) alleged that the Sudanese Armed Forces was using white helicopters and aircraft in support of their ground forces. On 28 and 29 August, reports were received that aircraft had bombed areas near Tura, Sayeh, and Um Sidir, and that the attacks resulted in a number of civilian casualties.

7. As mentioned in paragraph 3 above, on 19 August, a group of armed men in 15 vehicles ambushed an African Union Mission in the Sudan (AMIS) convoy of 12 fuel tankers near Kuma, 80 kilometres north-east of El Fasher. The AMIS protection force resisted and called for reinforcements. In the heavy fighting that followed, the AMIS force killed 12 attackers, while 2 AMIS soldiers were killed and 3 wounded.

8. Armed robbery of humanitarian vehicles and convoys grew increasingly brazen over the reporting period, continuing a recent trend. On 31 July, two armed men stole an international non-governmental organization vehicle in the Abu Shouk internally displaced person camp in Northern Darfur. On 24 August, two United Nations agency trucks disappeared between Tawila and Kabkabiya. On 15 and 16 August, armed men hijacked and stole three vehicles of the International Committee of the Red Cross (ICRC) near El Fasher; on 30 August, the ICRC confirmed the death of one of their drivers. That death adds to the growing death toll of humanitarians in Darfur; 12 died in July and August alone.

9. Throughout Darfur, bandits looted non-governmental organization vehicles and stole cash and communications equipment from passengers and drivers. On 29 July, 6 armed men ambushed a 29-truck United Nations humanitarian convoy between Habila and El Geneina and robbed the drivers. On 3 August, unknown assailants attacked and looted a United Nations truck carrying food south of Nyala. On 25 August, 3 armed men ambushed a 7-truck food convoy and robbed the drivers.

10. Raids on commercial traffic also continued. On 2 August, a group of armed men attacked and robbed a bus travelling from El Fasher to Nyala, killing 7 passengers and injuring 12. On 11 August, 4 armed men attacked a 21-truck commercial convoy south of Nyala and robbed the drivers. On 17 August, 10 armed men on horseback ambushed 2 trucks on the way to Gereida market, killing 1 and injuring 6 people before looting the trucks and robbing the passengers.

11. Also in Northern Darfur after capturing Korma town on 5 July from the Abdul Wahid faction of the Sudan Liberation Army (SLA), SLA-Minawi elements, who are now allied with the government forces on the ground, attacked nearby villages, looting livestock and killing at least 100 civilians. Those and other clashes resulted in almost 20,000 internally displaced persons arriving in Northern Darfur camps in July. Displaced persons reported indiscriminate killing, rape and abduction. Villagers who remained in place reported

SLA-Minawi harassment, beatings, and intimidation; some reported that SLA-Minawi and Zaghawa fighters told them to leave their villages for the internally displaced person camps. SLA-Minawi elements also harassed people trying to return to their villages, while also extorting money and confiscating documents.

12. Security in internally displaced person camps remained very precarious, especially where AMIS was unable to deploy or patrol. AMIS is operating in some internally displaced person camps, but camp leaders have warned the mission to stay away from others. Internally displaced person communities have increasingly splintered along communal lines into pro- and anti-Darfur Peace Agreement groups. In Shangil Tobayi camp, reports indicate that armed men harassed and robbed internally displaced persons after enquiring about their ethnicity. On 10 August, a Fur internally displaced person was shot dead in Kalma camp, sparking clashes between Fur and Zaghawa internally displaced persons in which two were seriously injured. An AMIS platoon intervened and remained in the camp overnight to ease tension. On 12 August, AMIS organized a reconciliation meeting between community leaders from the two groups. On 9 August, Civil Affairs Officers of the United Nations Mission in the Sudan (UNMIS) arranged discussions between AMIS and internally displaced persons in Zalingei, allowing internally displaced persons to express their concerns and AMIS to resume some patrols.

13. The militarization of some internally displaced person camps continued unabated over the reporting period. SLA-Minawi soldiers harassed internally displaced persons in the camps around El Fasher, especially Zam Zam camp. On 13 August, an international non-governmental organization medical team was forced to leave Kalma camp when assaulted by two armed men. On 23 August, SLA-Abdul Wahid troops harassed civilians in Otash camp in Southern Darfur.

14. Rumours of poisoning have hindered water supply and vaccination efforts in camps across Darfur. On 20 July, the rumours apparently prompted an angry crowd of internally displaced persons to beat to death three employees of the government Department for Water and Environmental Sanitation in Hassa Hissa camp near Zalingei. Internally displaced persons have challenged and threatened vaccination and sanitation workers in camps across Darfur.

15. Various militia groups continued to operate with impunity throughout Darfur, attacking villages, stealing livestock and harassing internally displaced persons. Some have settled in cleared villages near Zalingei and are cultivating the land.

16. Relations between Chad and the Sudan improved considerably over the reporting period. Under a 26 July agreement signed in N'Djamena, both countries agreed to create a political commission to follow up on the implementation of the agreement. Furthermore, they agreed to establish a mixed military commission to monitor the situation along common borders, as well as deploy a mixed military force to Bahai, Tiné, Koulbous, Khor Baranga, Amdjereme, Adré, Adé, Modoina, El Geneina, Tissi and Amdoukoum. Chad and the Sudan normalized diplomatic relations on 8 August.

17. However, Chadian armed opposition groups remained active in Western Darfur. On 11 August, suspected Chadian armed opposition group members harassed villagers in Chichir and Korgi. On 12 August, armed men stole cattle from Geilu village, before crossing the border into Chad.

18. On 23 August, Chadian officials reportedly arrested seven JEM leaders in N'Djamena, but released them the same day. On 28 August in Khartoum, the Foreign Minister of Chad stated that his Government intended to hand over 17 JEM and 30 SLA-Abdul Wahid leaders to the African Union.

III. Human rights and protection

19. The killing and suffering of civilians during attacks on villages and internally displaced persons make clear that combatants are not distinguishing between civilian and military targets.

20. Sexual and gender-based violence increased dramatically throughout Darfur since my last report. Militia forces continued to attack female internally displaced persons when they left the confines of their camps to undertake income-generating activities, such as gathering grass, fruit and firewood. Around Kalma camp, such attacks increased from 10 per month to almost 10 per day by mid-July. On 23 July, a group of several hundred armed militia raped 21 women north of Kalma camp; the next day, another 17 women were raped in the same location. Several internally displaced women and girls, including two girls collecting grass adjacent to a Sudanese Armed Forces camp near Tawila internally displaced person camp, alleged that government personnel had attacked them. In Northern Darfur, fleeing internally displaced persons reported that various armed groups were targeting women and girls believed to support rival factions.

21. Government authorities appear unable or reluctant to address the wave of sexual violence. The local government in Southern Darfur has downplayed sexual assaults and linked them to general criminal activity in the camps.

22. The United Nations Special Rapporteur on the Human Rights Situation in the Sudan, Dr. Sima Samar, visited the Sudan from 11 to 17 August. She is extremely disturbed by the critical human rights situation in the region and the signs that there will be a further deterioration in the coming months if action is not taken to protect civilians from attacks and end the conflict through peaceful means. In discussions with senior government officials, she raised concerns about the killings of civilians, rape, torture and displacement.

23. On numerous occasions during the reporting period, authorities obstructed United Nations human rights officers in the performance of their duties, in breach of government obligations under the status-of-forces agreement. On 15 August, the Humanitarian Aid Commission prevented an UNMIS helicopter from taking off from Nyala airport. On 17 August, Sudanese National Intelligence and Security Service officers prevented a United Nations agency staff member from boarding a helicopter in the same airport. Also on 17 August, the Sudanese National Intelligence and Security Service briefly detained a United Nations agency driver in El Geneina. The Sudanese National Intelligence and Security Service continues to regularly restrict UNMIS access to Darfur detention facilities.

IV. Humanitarian situation

24. Continued fighting, attacks on humanitarian workers, official obstruction, together with the arrival of the difficult rainy season have hampered humanitarian efforts. United Nations agencies now have considerably less access to affected populations than in late 2004 and most of 2005.

25. Once again, Darfur is becoming an increasingly difficult and very dangerous environment for humanitarian workers. The World Food Programme indicated that it could not reach 350,000 beneficiaries in August, up from 290,000 in June. Direct attacks on humanitarian operations have forced many organizations to suspend all but the most essential operations. The World Health Organization has reported that 40 per cent of the people of Northern Darfur are now without basic health care as a result. The vaccination rate has declined from 90 per cent in 2005 to 20 per cent in 2006.

26. Widespread instability and insecurity have had a substantial impact on agriculture and food security. Fighting near Tawila, Korma, Jebel Moon, and Jebel Marra has forced local farmers to flee during the few weeks available for planting the sorghum and millet upon which thousands depend for their sustenance. Although humanitarian agencies have distributed seeds, this year's harvest will be a poor one because of continued insecurity, which makes maintaining and harvesting crops difficult.

27. Heavy seasonal rains have also hindered humanitarian efforts and brought additional health threats. Flooded roads in Southern Darfur have forced some non-governmental organizations to postpone activities. Community health experts fear that flooding may contaminate drinking water, and cholera outbreaks have already been confirmed in Western Darfur. Acute watery diarrhoea has claimed eight lives in Monroe internally displaced person camp alone, including four children under the age of five.

V. Implementation of the Darfur Peace Agreement

28. In spite of the efforts of the wider international community and major African Union and United Nations initiatives, no additional signatories joined the Darfur Peace Agreement during the reporting period. Implementation of the Agreement is well behind schedule, and the inability of Darfur Peace Agreement mechanisms and arrangements to halt the continuing violence has undermined the credibility of the Agreement.

29. Delegations from the Government of the Sudan and the international community visited Abdul Wahid in Asmara during the reporting period in unsuccessful attempts to persuade him to sign the Darfur Peace Agreement. Abdul Wahid did not entirely reject the Agreement, but he called for amendments or additions to satisfy his four political demands: a role in reviewing the Janjaweed disarmament; a national Vice-Presidency position for Darfur; more compensation; and the merging of the three Darfur states into one region.

30. At the same time, Abdul Wahid's authority has reportedly been challenged by several influential commanders. On 28 July, one of them, Ahmed Abdul Shafi Bassey issued a press statement claiming that the SLM Military Council and Field Command had dismissed Abdul Wahid. On 18 August, Ahmed Abdul Shafi Bassey announced plans for an "All Sudan Liberation Movement/Army Conference" to clarify the leadership and organizational structure. Abdul Wahid's position and strength within the Sudan Liberation Army remain unclear.

31. In addition to the Abdul Wahid faction of the SLA, the "anti-Darfur Peace Agreement bloc" consists of the G19 and the JEM, elements of which formed the National Redemption Front in June 2006. The G19 is a group of former SLA-Abdul Wahid commanders and their followers, who were disaffected with Abdul Wahid's negotiating positions at Abuja.

32. The JEM has taken the toughest line against the Darfur Peace Agreement, and appears to be executing its threat to resist the Agreement following the conclusion of the Abuja

negotiations. However, the JEM has also been splintered; the JEM-Wing for Peace has reportedly become a partner to the Darfur Peace Agreement, and some JEM commanders in Jebel Moon have eschewed further intra-rebel violence.

33. The NRF has rejected the Darfur Peace Agreement. It is currently the most ethnically diverse of the rebel groups, and includes significant Fur, Marsalis, and Zaghawa contingents. The NRF was founded by Justice and Equality Movement chief Dr. Khalil Ibrahim, Sudan Federal Democratic Alliance (SFDA) chief Ahmed Ibrahim Diraige, former SLA Deputy Chair and G19 leader Khamis Abdalla Abakar, and Dr. Sharif Harir of the SFDA.

34. On 8 June, several groups signed a Declaration of Commitment to the Darfur Peace Agreement. In its 27 June Communiqué, the African Union Peace and Security Council recognized them as "partners in the peace process", and the Joint Commission invited them to participate in its meetings. The Darfur Peace Agreement signatories, however, have opposed any significant role or benefits for non-signatories, and the African Union and the parties have yet to develop a plan for including them in the Darfur Peace Agreement implementation process.

35. At the Joint Commission's second meeting, on 3 August, the chairman of the Ceasefire Commission presented a report listing 60 separate ceasefire violations. Upon learning that the Ceasefire Commission had not considered the report, however, the Joint Commission Chairman referred all 60 violations back to the Ceasefire Commission for investigation.

36. The Ceasefire Commission is meeting regularly, but has been largely incapacitated by disagreements over the non-Darfur Peace Agreement signatories' role and the relationship between the N'Djamena and Darfur Peace Agreement ceasefire commissions. On 13 August, AMIS notified the Ceasefire Commission Chairman that it had decided to remove SLA-Abdul Wahid and JEM representatives from the Ceasefire Commission and from AMIS sites.

37. The Ceasefire Commission currently has a backlog of 92 alleged ceasefire violations. Sub-Ceasefire Commissions have now been formed and are functioning, but some lack representation from Darfur Peace Agreement parties and Declaration of Commitment signatories. At the 30 August meeting, the Ceasefire Commission discussed 15 violation reports forwarded by the Sub-Ceasefire Commissions.

38. The parties have also missed several security-related deadlines. The parties have yet to create the Transitional Darfur Regional Authority, which in turn rendered it impossible to meet the 15 June deadline for establishing the Darfur Security Arrangement Implementation Committee; nor has AMIS been able to establish the Joint Logistics Coordination Committee, which was due on 21 May. Also, the African Union has yet to complete the demarcation of areas of control, buffer zones and demilitarized zones; produce a final map indicating the parties' respective areas of control and redeployment zones; or develop a patrol plan for monitoring the buffer zones (all of which were to be complete by 22 June). Also in accordance with the Darfur Peace Agreement, the Government had to restrict Janjaweed activity to designated areas by 20 July, but that deadline has not been met. On 23 June, the Government submitted to the African Union its plan to disarm the Janjaweed. The disarmament plan was tabled for discussion at the Ceasefire Commission on 17 July, and UNMIS sent preliminary comments on the plan to the African Union Ceasefire Commission on 26 July.

39. In relation to power-sharing, the Northern and Southern Darfur state assemblies convened emergency sessions to amend their interim State Constitutions, increasing ministerial and assembly seats as required by the power-sharing provisions of the Darfur Peace Agreement. On 7 August, Minni Minawi was sworn in as Senior Assistant to the President, the fourth-highest position in the National Executive, and as Transitional Darfur Regional Authority Chairman. On 12 August, AMIS opened the African Union Darfur Peace Agreement Implementation Office in Khartoum, which will provide workspace to SLM-Minawi, SLM-Free Will, JEM-Wing of Peace representatives, the African Union Darfur Peace Agreement Implementation team, and the Preparatory Committee for the Darfur-Darfur Dialogue and Consultation. On 9 September, Minni Minawi announced the formation of seven committees for the implementation of the Darfur Peace Agreement, as a first step towards the implementation of the Agreement prior to the formation of the Transitional Darfur Regional Authority, and confirmed that the structures of the interim authority for Darfur would include the parties who signed the Declaration of Commitment. In addition to the delays in establishing the Transitional Darfur Regional Authority, a number of other important power-sharing deadlines have been missed, including in finalizing senior government and civil service appointments (as required by 15 June), and in establishing the Darfur Assessment and Evaluation Commission (as required by 14 August).

40. In wealth-sharing, the Joint Assessment Mission has begun preparatory work to identify urgent and longer-term recovery and development needs. The Joint Assessment Mission team includes 40 Sudanese and international experts drawn from the United Nations, non-governmental organizations, donors, and academic institutions, and includes both Sudanese and international experts. It was deployed to Nyala in early August, and conducted field visits, focused group discussions, and interviews with key stakeholders in Southern Darfur. Escalating violence, however, significantly impeded its assessment work.

41. The parties have made limited progress on the other Darfur Peace Agreement wealth-sharing provisions. They have yet to establish the Darfur Reconstruction and Development Fund or the Darfur Rehabilitation and Resettlement Commission (both were required, according to the Agreement, by 15 June), or a Compensation Commission (expected by 15 July). None of the Darfur state legislatures have established state land commissions, which according to the Darfur Peace Agreement were to be created immediately.

42. At the same time, the African Union has not yet appointed its nominee to chair the Preparatory Committee for the Darfur-Darfur Dialogue and Consultation. However, the African Union has been engaging the parties, constituents and the international community on an informal basis. At the same time, UNMIS and AMIS are collaborating on Darfur Peace Agreement and Darfur-Darfur Dialogue and Consultation public outreach efforts, and held several workshops in July and August. Those activities, however, remain limited to Darfur's largest towns; the current security environment precludes major outreach efforts in smaller communities and internally displaced person camps.

43. On 2 August, President Bashir sent me the Plan of the Government of the Sudan for the Restoration of Stability and Protection of Civilians in Darfur, as promised in our discussions on 2 July at the African Union Summit in Banjul, Gambia. I replied to President Bashir on 25 August, welcoming the fact that the plan identified a number of areas for United Nations support to the peace process in Darfur, including to the Darfur-Darfur Dialogue and Consultation and humanitarian operations, but indicating my concern that the

Government's plan did not indicate a willingness on the part of the Government to agree to the transition from AMIS to a United Nations peace operation in Darfur.

44. In my response, I also expressed my serious concern over the deployment of a large number of Sudanese Armed Forces troops to Darfur, in the light of the provision in the Darfur Peace Agreement against the deployment of "additional military forces into Darfur by the Government of Sudan without the consent of the Ceasefire Commission". Any offensive military action by the Sudanese Armed Forces in Darfur would also contravene Security Council resolutions 1590 (2005) and 1591 (2005), which emphasize that there can be no military solution to the conflict in Darfur.

VI. United Nations support to the African Union Mission in the Sudan

45. As of 1 September, AMIS had a total of 7,200 personnel, comprised of 783 military observers and staff officers, 1,425 civilian police, 12 Ceasefire Commission personnel, and a protection force of 4,980.

46. Throughout July and August, UNMIS responded to numerous requests from the African Union for assistance. The United Nations technical staff have assisted AMIS staff in establishing telephone and information technology networks, while the UNMIS civil-military coordinator has trained AMIS personnel on humanitarian issues. At the same time, UNMIS logistics experts briefed AMIS personnel on asset management systems.

47. During the reporting period, with the assistance of the international community, the African Union has begun developing a public information campaign to promote the Darfur Peace Agreement. In that context, UNMIS provided additional public information support to AMIS through the printing of full texts of the Darfur Peace Agreement in English and Arabic, as well as the editing, translation and printing of a summary of the Agreement. Those information products are being disseminated in all areas of Darfur.

VII. Security Council resolution 1706 (2006)

48. On 31 August, the Security Council in its resolution 1706 (2006) decided, without prejudice to its existing mandate and operations as provided for in resolution 1590 (2005), and in order to support the early and effective implementation of the Darfur Peace Agreement, that the mandate of UNMIS shall be expanded by up to 17,300 international military personnel and by an appropriate civilian component, including up to 3,300 police personnel and up to 16 Formed Police Units, and that it shall deploy to Darfur. In the resolution the Security Council also reaffirmed its strong commitment to the sovereignty, unity, independence and territorial integrity of the Sudan and expresses United Nations determination to work with the Government of National Unity to assist in tackling the problems confronting the Sudan. In the resolution, the Security Council invited the consent of the Government of National Unity for the deployment to Darfur of the expanded UNMIS force.

49. In a number of public statements, the Government of the Sudan has rejected in very strong terms the decision of the Security Council with regard to the transition from the African Union to a United Nations peace operation. The adoption of resolution 1706 (2006) was welcomed by senior members of the Sudan People's Liberation Movement and the Darfur rebel groups, as well as northern opposition parties. Demonstrations in support of and against Security Council resolution 1706 (2006) were seen throughout Darfur.

50. On 29 August, in Nyala, several thousand students staged a demonstration against a possible transition from AMIS to a United Nations operation; the Wali of Southern Darfur State presented a memorandum of rejection from the Students Union of Southern Darfur to the UNMIS Head of Office. On 1 September 2006, about 3,000 people demonstrated in El Fasher stadium in support of the transition. On 2 September, at least 1,000 demonstrators presented a letter of protest against Security Council resolution 1706 (2006) to the United Nations office at El Fasher. On 3 September, two students were killed when riot police broke up demonstrations in favour of resolution 1706 (2006) in El Fasher. Numerous demonstrations sponsored by the Government were also held in various towns in the region against the implementation of the resolution. On 3 September 2006, students and government officials held a demonstration against the resolution in El Geneina, and handed a note to the Head of the Office for the Coordination of Humanitarian Affairs there. On 5 September 2006, in Nyala, the representatives organized a demonstration against the resolution, including several thousand students. The demonstration turned violent when students began throwing stones at passing vehicles and United Nations offices and international non-governmental organization compounds. The United Nations requested the government police on 4 September to increase protection of United Nations properties but the requests went largely unanswered.

51. Government officials and their allies appear to be encouraging public sentiments opposing a United Nations transition, often using threatening anti-United Nations language, in violation of the status-of-forces agreement. During the reporting period, President Bashir and Vice-President Taha made remarks, including threatening armed resistance and other violence against the United Nations if Security Council resolution 1706 (2006) is implemented, and even promising to open special camps to train fighters who would violently resist the presence of United Nations peacekeepers in Darfur.

VIII. Observations

52. The grave violations of international human rights law and humanitarian law, which continue to be committed with impunity by the Sudanese Armed Forces, militia, and rebel factions in Darfur, are unacceptable. In that connection, I deplore in the strongest terms the 19 August attack that killed two AMIS soldiers and injured three others. That attack and many others perpetrated in recent weeks can only render the environment in Darfur more dangerous for AMIS peacekeepers, humanitarian workers and ultimately for the people of Darfur, whom the international community has undertaken to assist and help to protect. I extend my heartfelt sympathies to the families of the AMIS soldiers killed.

53. It has now been three months since the Darfur Peace Agreement was signed. However, instead of reconciliation and building of trust, we are witnessing intensified violence and deeper polarization. The region is again on the brink of a catastrophic situation. The latest decision of the Government to seek a military solution and bring more and more troops to the region, coupled with the fighting among armed groups, shows utter disregard for the Darfur Peace Agreement. Signatories and non-signatories alike continue to violate their obligations under the Darfur Peace Agreement and the N'Djamena Ceasefire Agreement. The international community is gravely concerned by reports of government military air support during attacks on civilian populations and by the movement of further military assets into Darfur. I call on all parties in the strongest terms to halt the violence and uphold their obligations to protect civilians.

54. I appeal strongly to those with influence over the groups which have not signed the Darfur Peace Agreement to put pressure on them to adhere to the spirit of the ceasefire and to join the peace process. They must know that the violent pursuit of political goals is not acceptable, and all parties must be reminded that the measures to address the crisis in Darfur need to be consistent with the decisions of the African Union Peace and Security Council and the Darfur Peace Agreement.

55. I am also very concerned about the obstruction of United Nations personnel by government authorities in Darfur. That action is in direct contravention of the Government's obligations under the status-of-forces agreement. I call on the Government to ensure that all local authorities in Darfur are reminded of their obligations under the status-of-forces agreement.

56. The Darfur Peace Agreement is a historic document for the Sudan and sets a challenging implementation timetable. The parties and the African Union, assisted by the international community, should redouble their implementation efforts. In that context, the international donors should offer all appropriate political, material and financial support to those seeking to implement the Darfur Peace Agreement in good faith. The parties should urgently overcome the Ceasefire Commission impasse. That important body must meet regularly and it must be made more inclusive so as to fully investigate reported ceasefire violations.

57. At the same time, it is essential to work to broaden political and popular support for the Darfur Peace Agreement. The Sudanese authorities and the international community must continue their efforts to persuade other parties to sign. Equally important will be broadening public support for the Darfur Peace Agreement through initiatives such as the Darfur-Darfur Dialogue and Consultation and the speedy implementation of the compensation mechanisms. The Darfur-Darfur Dialogue and Consultation should commence as a matter of urgency, and be as broadly inclusive as possible.

58. Darfur is at a critical stage. Insecurity in this troubled region is at its highest levels and humanitarian access is at its lowest levels since 2004. Unless security improves, the world is facing the prospect of having to drastically curtail an acutely needed humanitarian operation.

59. With the number of actors and combat zones multiplying, AMIS is also facing difficulty in carrying out its mandate with regard to the protection of the civilian population and the implementation of the Darfur Peace Agreement. On 20 September, the African Union Peace and Security Council took a very important step by extending the mandate of the African Union operation until 31 December 2006. The mandate extension and the endorsement of a new Concept of Operations for AMIS are welcome developments. The continued presence of a strong AMIS in Darfur has a vital role to play in protecting civilians and improving a deteriorating security situation until a United Nations operation can be put in place, with the consent of the Government of the Sudan. Once again, I call on the African Union's partners to ensure that the extension of the AMIS mandate by the Peace and Security Council is matched by the rapid and generous provision of the resources that are required for the African Union force to continue its work until the end of its mandate.

60. The Government of the Sudan must also be aware that there can be no military solution to the Darfur conflict. I remain strongly convinced that a United Nations multidimensional operation, in accordance with Security Council resolution 1706 (2006), would be the most

appropriate political approach to achieving lasting and sustainable peace in Darfur, and that only such a truly international and impartial operation, with adequate resources and capacity, and with strong African participation, can effectively support the implementation of the Darfur Peace Agreement.

61. As the Security Council has recognized, the transition to a United Nations operation will not be possible as long as the Government of the Sudan refuses its consent. Once again, therefore, I urge the Government of the Sudan to embrace the spirit of the African Union and United Nations decisions, to give its consent to the transition, and commit itself to the political process. Governments and leaders who are in a position to influence the events must also make themselves heard and redeem the solemn pledge made in September 2005, when the General Assembly agreed that Governments have a "responsibility to protect" vulnerable civilians from genocide, ethnic-cleansing, and gross and systematic violations of human rights. The Security Council is expected to play a very special role in this regard, by demonstrating unity of action. There must be a clear, strong and uniform message from the Security Council and the international community about the consequences of rejecting international assistance for the suffering people of Darfur and for failing to exercise the responsibility to protect. In the meantime, the situation in Darfur is becoming more desperate by the day. The United Nations, and I personally, will spare no effort to continue to seek a just, peaceful and urgent solution to this major man-made tragedy of the twenty-first century.

4. Monthly Report of the Secretary-General on Darfur, 8 November 2006 (S/2006/870)

I. Introduction

1. The present report is submitted pursuant to paragraphs 6, 13 and 16 of Security Council resolution 1556 (2004), paragraph 15 of Council resolution 1564 (2004), paragraph 17 of Council resolution 1574 (2004) and paragraph 12 of Council resolution 1590 (2005). It covers the month of September 2006.

II. Insecurity in Darfur

2. September witnessed an increase in violence in Darfur. Fighting between the signatories and non-signatories of the Darfur Peace Agreement intensified with the Government of the Sudan using aerial bombardment in attacks against villages controlled by the National Redemption Front (NRF) and G19 rebel groups. Tensions between Darfur Peace Agreement signatories also increased, for the first time. Militia attacks have also significantly increased, in particular in Southern Darfur, targeting civilian populations and internally displaced persons while tensions increased among rebel groups. During the reporting period, African Union Mission in the Sudan (AMIS) peacekeepers were also targeted more often, especially in Northern Darfur, while attacks on humanitarian workers continued unabated.

3. The ceasefire between the Minni Minawi faction of the Sudan Liberation Movement/Army (SLM/A) and the Government of the Sudan held generally throughout Darfur in September. However, several incidents indicated that tensions exist between these two signatories of the Darfur Peace Agreement. On 22 September 2006, SLM-Minawi forces accompanying the rebel leader beat up two Military Intelligence officers of the Government of the Sudan at the Nyala airport. This was the fourth in a series of such incidents in Nyala. On 28 September, a clash erupted between SLM-Minawi bodyguards and police officers of the Government of the Sudan in Omdurman, Khartoum, sparked by the detention of an SLM-Minawi soldier. In retaliation for the arrest of their comrade, SLM-Minawi members raided a nearby police station and took several police officers hostage. Reports suggest that at least one person was killed in the ensuing shoot-out.

4. For the first time since the signing of the Darfur Peace Agreement, one signatory accused the other of breaching the ceasefire agreement. On 30 August, an SLM-Minawi spokesperson accused the Government and the Janjaweed militia of random killing in Southern Darfur from 28 to 30 August, including the torching of around 13 villages south of Nyala.

5. Meanwhile, fighting between Darfur Peace Agreement signatories and non-signatories continued. On 28 August, the Sudanese Armed Forces (SAF) launched an aerial and ground offensive against NRF forces in the Kafod and Abu Sakin area, 60 kilometres north of El Fasher, and captured Um Sidir on 31 August. On 11 September, NRF forces recaptured Um Sidir, forcing an SAF retreat towards Mellit, 60 kilometres north-east of El Fasher.

6. Heavy fighting was also reported in Southern Darfur between 10 and 13 September when SAF troops in dozens of vehicles, assisted by hundreds of militia and aerial support, launched an offensive against Darfur Peace Agreement non-signatory groups in Eastern

Jebel Marra, attacking over a dozen villages. NRF forces moving southwards into the Jebel Marra reportedly supported the non-signatory groups in Eastern Jebel Marra.

7. In Southern Darfur, on 24 August, an armed group attacked the SAF garrison at Songo, 265 kilometres south of Nyala. Reports suggest that a former SLM-Minawi commander conducted the attack, which killed 10 and wounded 15, in retaliation for militia attacks on villages near Buram.

8. The aerial bombardment of villages in Northern Darfur, similar to patterns of warfare observed at the height of the conflict in 2004, has been particularly disturbing. On 28 and 29 August, reports were received that Government of the Sudan Antonov aircraft had bombed areas near Tura, Sayeh and Um Sidir, Northern Darfur. On 10 September, Government aircraft bombed several villages 20 kilometres south-west of Tawila. After NRF forces re-captured Um Sidir, SAF aircraft commenced aerial bombardment of that village and Hashaba North on 12 September. On 19 September, during ongoing fighting between SAF and NRF, Antonov planes reportedly bombed the NRF-controlled villages of Anka and Amarai, about 50 kilometres north-west of Um Sidir.

9. September saw increasing tension between and within rebel groups supporting the Darfur Peace Agreement in Southern Darfur. On 1 September, a group of Massalit SLM-Minawi soldiers attacked their Zaghawa comrades in Gereida. Three persons were reportedly killed and three injured. Senior SLM-Minawi commanders as well as the King of Gereida intervened to resolve the issue. Tensions heightened again on 28 September, when an unidentified armed group attacked the SLM-Minawi headquarters near Gereida, Southern Darfur, during the visit of senior leaders of the rebel group, killing 10 and injuring 20. In September, tensions rose between SLM-Minawi (mainly Zaghawa) and SLM-Free Will (mainly Birgid) in Muhajirya, Southern Darfur, after SLM-Free Will members were assaulted and detained. On 1 and 2 October, armed clashes killing dozens were reported there between SLM-Free Will and SLM-Minawi.

10. Armed banditry and looting targeting humanitarian and commercial traffic also continued to be a major source of insecurity and an indicator of the lawlessness prevailing in Darfur. On 6 September, armed men looted a commercial truck east of Zalingei. On 13 September, bandits abducted a United Nations agency truck carrying 17 metric tons of commodities near Abdel Shakur. The driver and truck were released on 15 September. On 20 September, three armed men looted two commercial trucks near Um Kardouz, about 18 kilometres from Nyala.

11. SAF soldiers have also been accused of robbery and looting. On 30 August, SAF soldiers robbed villagers in Kornoi, Northern Darfur, of their belongings and money. When one woman refused to hand over her blanket, the soldiers assaulted her. On 1 September, SAF soldiers looted the health centre, pharmacy and the guesthouse of an international non-governmental organization (NGO) in Hashaba North, Northern Darfur, after its staff had been killed in crossfire. On 9 September, SAF soldiers reportedly destroyed relief food in international NGO distribution centres in Sanihaye village, east of Um Sidir.

12. Peacekeepers of the African Union (AU), in particular in North Darfur, were targeted frequently during September. On 3 September, 12 armed men disarmed an AU team on a firewood patrol near the camp for internally displaced persons (IDPs) in Kassab, Northern Darfur, stealing their vehicles and other equipment. On 4 September, armed men in five

pick-up vehicles ambushed an AMIS patrol on its way from Tina to Kutum, Northern Darfur. On the same day, five armed men opened fire on AU personnel guarding the AU civilian police station in the Kassab IDP Camp. On 11 September, in Western Darfur, five unknown gunmen fired nine shots at AU soldiers on duty at the AMIS borehole, north of the AMIS group site at Masteri village, Western Darfur.

13. Violence against humanitarian personnel continued throughout September. On 1 September, a national stall member of the International Rescue Committee died in Hashaba, Northern Darfur, in crossfire between the NRF and Government forces. This was the twelfth aid worker killed in Darfur since the signing of the Darfur Peace Agreement. On 5 September, students in Nyala attacked United Nations offices and compounds of international non-governmental organizations during an anti-United Nations demonstration organized by the Trade Union Workers, injuring one security guard.

14. Hijacking and armed robbery of humanitarian vehicles has also become commonplace in Darfur. On 7 September, three armed men stopped two international non-governmental organization vehicles south of Zalingei, beating the NGO staff and stealing cash.

15. On 28 August, about 100 armed militia from several different tribes, including the Habaniya and Falata, attacked and looted several villages south of Buram, including Al Amoud Al Akdar and Hadak, destroying shops, a graining mill and a water tank, and burning houses. The same day, militia also attacked the village of Gueghin. On 30 August, the SLM-Minawi accused the Government of the Sudan of being involved in the attack. On 9 September, militia returned to Al Amoud Al Akdar and attacked the population, which had gathered to meet a joint AU/United Nations team coming to assess an earlier attack, which took place on 28 August.

16. Despite the agreement of 26 July and the resumption of diplomatic relations between the Sudan and Chad on 8 August, fighting between Chadian armed opposition groups and the Chadian regular forces (FANT) continued in September. On 16 September, Chadian armed opposition group rebels and FANT clashed in Jebel Merfain, 70 kilometres northwest of El Geneina, on the Chadian side of the border. The groups were reinforced from Western Darfur on 19 September and engaged in heavy clashes with FANT forces on the same day in Jebel Merfain. The Chadian armed opposition groups reportedly captured 60 Chadian soldiers and numerous tanks and vehicles in the attack.

III. Human rights and protection

17. The Government of the Sudan military campaign in Northern and Southern Darfur is taking its toll on the civilian population. The large-scale attacks by militia groups on villages south of Buram, Southern Darfur, between 28 August and 9 September, which were referred to above, resulted in dozens of people killed and injured, and thousands displaced. Many of the newly displaced find little safety in IDP camps owing to the presence of militias and armed groups around and within the camps. Sexual and gender-based violence in Darfur targeting IDP women also continued. Government authorities have curtailed Sudanese citizens' right to protest and have restricted the movement of United Nations staff in violation of the status-of-forces agreement.

18. The sustained military campaign in Northern and Southern Darfur against non-signatories has resulted in indiscriminate killings and other grave abuses against civilians, including

death, injury, rape and displacement. When a plane dropped bombs around the market and the school in Hillet Hajar, Northern Darfur, on 2 September, many of the villagers fled to the mountains to hide. Since May, the attacks have forced thousands to flee their villages to seek refuge in already overstretched IDP camps or isolated rural areas. Some 50,000 people have been displaced in the last four months, with villages in the countryside effectively emptied following aerial bombardments. Since mid-August, at least 12 people have died because of lack of medical services in camps in Tawila, Northern Darfur.

19. The militia attacks on villages near Buram described above led to the death and displacement of civilians, including the separation of children from their families. Militia surrounded, looted and set fire to villages, killing scores of civilians. In the area of Seiseban alone, witnesses reported that militia killed 75 civilians, including women and children as they were trying to escape the attack. Some 2,500 people fled their villages, and around 5,000 who were unable to escape are trapped in the area and hiding in the mountains.

20. The threat of armed militia around and within IDP camps severely restricted freedom of movement of internally displaced persons and hindered their ability to enjoy an adequate standard of living. On 31 August, militiamen killed a shepherd grazing his cattle two kilometres south of Gereida, Southern Darfur, and attacked IDP women fetching firewood in the same area. On 11 September, two uniformed men shot a male IDP in El Geneina and stole personal belongings, while on 20 September, a male IDP was beaten and robbed by five men, two of whom were in uniform outside El Geneina.

21. The presence of armed groups within IDP camps such as ZamZam and Abou Shouk in Northern Darfur makes the camps increasingly militarized and insecure. There are widespread and persistent reports of violence against civilians in camps, including murder, physical attack, rape and armed robbery. On 12 September, 10 armed men entered the Tawila IDP Camp, Northern Darfur, and stole the animals of IDPs at gunpoint. AU peacekeepers followed the gunmen and returned their fire, killing one and wounding another.

22. Attacks on female IDPs by armed militia outside the camps were recurrent. On 3 September, in camps in El Geneina, Western Darfur, four Massalit IDP women were physically assaulted and fired at by armed men in uniform. On the same day, in Gereida, Southern Darfur, four Massalit IDP women were surrounded by 60 armed men in uniform, who beat the women and raped two of them. The increase in insecurity and military conflict has exacerbated the already persistent practice of targeting women and girls with sexual violence. While the State Committees on Gender-Based Violence in Darfur could provide a potential forum to address these violations, the unwillingness of the authorities to recognize the pervasiveness of this problem and their continued efforts to cast doubt on reported incidents have only further burdened the victims of sexual violence and prevented an adequate Government response.

23. Government responses to demonstrations in early September illustrated intolerance for the public expression of dissenting views. On 3 September, Government forces broke up a peaceful gathering at El Fasher University using firearms, tear gas and electric batons; at least one student died and 19 were injured. On 8 September, in El Geneina, a religious leader was detained overnight by Sudanese Military Intelligence for allegedly urging people to demonstrate in favour of the United Nations in Darfur during his Friday sermon. The Government's use of excessive force and other repressive mechanisms to respond to

internal dissent contravenes the provisions of the Interim National Constitution guaranteeing freedom of peaceful assembly and expression and respect for human rights.

24. In violation of their obligations under the status-of-forces agreement, Government authorities repeatedly stopped United Nations staff at checkpoints and, in some cases, obstructed them from performing their mandated duties. On 18 September, a national security officer stopped a United Nations Mission in the Sudan (UNMIS) team in Nyala. The staff were taken to the local national security office and released only after United Nations security officers intervened.

IV. The humanitarian situation

25. The insecurity, banditry and fighting which have characterized the reporting period continued to prevent access to populations in need of humanitarian assistance. The targeting and killing of humanitarian workers, the hijacking of humanitarian vehicles as well as the insecurity caused by clashes between armed groups forced humanitarians to suspend operations. In Northern Darfur alone, the World Food Programme (WFP) reported that 355,000 people went without food aid during July and August. Humanitarian action is proving to be more challenging as fighting continues, the number of factions increases, lines of command fragment and frontlines multiply.

26. Humanitarian access, already at its lowest in August since 2004, is still severely limited, with road travel outside urban centres becoming more difficult. Operations depend increasingly on expensive air transport. South of Nyala, Southern Darfur, humanitarian organizations have no access to the newly displaced because of ongoing insecurity. On 16 September, an international NGO evacuated seven international and 16 national staff members from Muhajirya back to Nyala owing to the unpredictable security situation. Large parts of Jebel Marra, an estimated population of more than 100,000, are inaccessible because of militia attacks. The impact on civilians can only be estimated since no humanitarian assessments can be undertaken in recently attacked areas. Humanitarian organizations suspended activities around Tawila, as the risk of hijacking and harassment became unacceptably high. In less than a month, five vehicles belonging to humanitarian organizations have been taken at gunpoint in the area. One humanitarian aid worker was killed in Hashaba North, Northern Darfur. As a result, more than 80,000 persons have been deprived of basic health services and access to water. Up to 1,000 IDPs have sought refuge at the IDP camp close to AMIS in Tawila. Food distribution continued, but the camp is lacking in other basic services. Other IDPs sought refuge in areas which were unreachable for humanitarian operators.

27. Notwithstanding these difficulties, humanitarian actors continue to provide assistance to some 2.6 million conflict-affected people. Health, nutrition, food aid, and water and sanitation programmes continue. Agencies and Government of the Sudan counterparts worked together to control a cholera outbreak with 1,025 cases in Southern Darfur alone. In September, WFP and partners distributed food to some 130,000 people in Mellit, Malha, Sayah and Kutum in Northern Darfur. As food distribution was carried out, one vehicle was stolen in Kutum. Those areas had not been reached since May and are prone to food insecurity.

28. The moratorium on bureaucratic procedures for aid agencies to operate in Darfur remains in place and facilitates the work of over 14,000 humanitarian personnel. However, the moratorium is applied inconsistently. Unreasonable delays in obtaining visas, customs

clearance for relief items and recruitment of Sudanese staff persist. This results in a waste of time and resources that could be better spent on vulnerable populations.

29. The new agreement between the Government and the Norwegian Refugee Council (NRC) allowing it to serve as Camp Coordinator of Kalma Camp in Southern Darfur, signed in May, has been suspended. This is the sixth time that NRC activities in Kalma have been suspended. The Government has also blocked access for NRC staff to Kalma as well as other parts of Southern Darfur where they have operations.

V. Implementation of the Darfur Peace Agreement

30. No new parties joined the Darfur Peace Agreement in September while efforts to reconcile the SLM factions continued. The already weak pro-Darfur Peace Agreement bloc is further threatened by frictions between and within rebel groups. While some progress has been achieved on the Darfur-Darfur Dialogue and Consultation, Darfur Peace Agreement implementation is significantly lagging behind; almost all deadlines set out in the Agreement have been missed so far.

31. In September, both the signatories and civil society organizations stepped up efforts to bolster the peace process. The Zaghawa Native Administration, in coordination with Minni Minawi, spearheaded an initiative aimed at reconciling the SLM-Minawi and some G19 commanders in Northern Darfur. Representatives of the Native Administration met G19 commanders in Gira, Northern Darfur, on 15 September. Talks reportedly also commenced between SLM commanders in Eastern Jebel Marra and the Southern Darfur State authorities.

32. At the same time, in September the fragility of the rebel groups and alliances was demonstrated, which further complicates efforts to consolidate political support for the Darfur Peace Agreement. On 23 and 24 September, local media reported frictions within the leadership of the SLM-Free Will. While Secretary General Eissa Basi of SLM-Free will issued a statement on 22 September relieving the Chairman of SLM-Free Will, Abdul Rahman Moussa, of his duties, a number of elements within the faction issued statements on 23 September rejecting the move. Moreover, recent conflicts within the SLM-Minawi faction in Gereida and between SLM-Minawi and SLM-Free Will in Muhajirya appear to divide the pro-Darfur Peace Agreement parties along ethnic lines.

33. During September, the Ceasefire Commission remained largely inactive. It was unable to address the ongoing military confrontations, nor did it move forward with the implementation of Darfur Peace Agreement security provisions such as the disarmament of the Janjaweed. Following the exclusion of the non-signatories from the sub-Ceasefire Commission level in August, the Commission also decided to exclude observers, including the United Nations, at the sub-Ceasefire Commission level. In September, the Commission held five of its biweekly meetings while three were cancelled. It discussed 8 of the remaining 77 violation reports forwarded by the sub-Ceasefire Commissions and referred 2 to the Joint Commission. The Joint Commission, scheduled to meet monthly, has not met since the beginning of August.

34. On 26 August, following amendments in the Northern and Southern Darfur State Constitutions, the State Legislative Council in Western Darfur amended the State Constitution to allow for representation of pro-Darfur Peace Agreement groups in the

executive and legislative branches of the State. The pro-Darfur Peace Agreement groups will gain the position of the Deputy Governor, two ministers, two commissioners, two executive directors, the Deputy Chairman of the State Legislative Council and 21 members in the State Legislative Council. The Government also increased National Congress Party (NCP) membership in the State Legislative Council by four; NCP will still retain the absolute majority of seats. The Wali of Western Darfur has approved the amendments and they are awaiting endorsement from the Ministry of Justice in Khartoum.

35. Meanwhile, the Darfur Joint Assessment Mission continued its assessments through mid-September, but it has only been able to access parts of Darfur. The teams have now reconvened in Khartoum to prepare preliminary draft cluster reports based on existing work. Early findings confirm the enormous impact that the conflict has had on the lives and livelihoods of the people of Darfur. Despite the efforts of the humanitarian community, both international and national, basic services are badly overburdened or non-existent.

36. In September, the AU Darfur Peace Agreement Implementation Team in Khartoum commenced work on the Darfur-Darfur Dialogue and Consultation and circulated to key partners for comments a strategy paper on it, which outlines the main priorities of the Darfur-Darfur Dialogue and Consultation. The African Union has named Abdul Mohamed (Ethiopia) as the Chairman of the Preparatory Committee of the Darfur-Darfur Dialogue and Consultation and requested other members of the Preparatory Committee to finalize their Committee nominations. The Government of the Sudan, the League of Arab States and the United Nations have nominated their representatives. Consultations are currently under way on the appointment of the Chairperson of the Darfur-Darfur Dialogue and Consultation.

VI. United Nations support to the African Union Mission inthe Sudan

37. On 20 September, the AU Peace and Security Council (PSC) extended the mandate of the African Union Mission in the Sudan for three months and approved a new concept of operations to fulfil its Darfur Peace Agreement responsibilities. The AU PSC also called on the United Nations and other partners to support AMIS. Pursuant to this and previous PSC decisions of 10 March and 15 May 2006, the United Nations and the African Union have agreed on a package of immediate United Nations support to AMIS with a view to strengthening its efforts to implement the Darfur Peace Agreement. The support package includes logistical and material support, military staff support, advisory support to civilian police, as well as civilian support in the areas of mine action, public information and support to Darfur Peace Agreement implementation. The objective of this support is to immediately enhance the management of AMIS through a proactive advisory role by United Nations staff. These staff will be fully dedicated to supporting AMIS and co-located with AMIS throughout Darfur. In this respect it will be critical for AMIS to provide protection to those deployed as part of the support package.

38. Chairperson Konaré of the AU Commission and I wrote to President al-Bashir on 22 September outlining the main features of the support package and requesting the President's personal support for its implementation. On 3 October, President al-Bashir responded giving his personal support for the assistance package. I subsequently replied to that letter stressing that the United Nations and the African Union would proceed in full transparency with this initiative. I also stressed that any staff deployed as part of United

Nations support to AMIS would be covered by the current status-of-forces agreement between the Government of the Sudan and the United Nations concerning UNMIS.

VII. Observations

39. Five months after the signing of the Darfur Peace Agreement, violence has increased again in Darfur. I am gravely concerned about the Government's apparent attempt to find a military solution to the crisis, which runs counter to previous Security Council resolutions and the Sudan's commitments to the Darfur Peace Agreement. Thousands of Sudanese Armed Forces troops have been deployed to the area in clear violation of the Darfur Peace Agreement and Security Council resolution 1591 (2005).

40. I particularly deplore the use of aerial bombardment by Government forces, which fails to distinguish civilians from combatants and is in breach of resolution 1591 (2005) and international humanitarian law.

41. I note that Darfur Peace Agreement signatories continue to violate their obligations under the Agreement and non-signatories under the N'Djamena Ceasefire Agreement. I call on all parties to halt the violence, uphold their obligations under the various agreements and work towards a political solution for the conflict in Darfur.

42. I condemn in the strongest terms the attack by militia on defenceless civilians south of Buram, Southern Darfur, which underscores the prevailing lack of security. I urge the Government to move forward with its commitment to disarm the Janjaweed militia, who continue to pose a serious threat to the lives and livelihoods of IDPs and the civilian population at large.

43. AMIS continues to carry out its important work in this very difficult environment, while still facing serious resource shortages. The United Nations will continue to implement, as rapidly as possible, the agreed package of support for AMIS. While this support should give a boost to the AU Mission, it is not a replacement for an increase in the size and an augmentation of the capabilities of the current force in Darfur, which would be required to effectively implement the security provisions of the Darfur Peace Agreement and to put the AU Mission in a position to make a broad contribution to an improvement in the security situation in the region.

44. Even as efforts to strengthen AMIS continue, it is important to reiterate that a comprehensive and lasting resolution to the crisis will come only through a broad-based political settlement, which will require the complete commitment of the Government and the rebel movements. This settlement will be achievable only if discussion and dialogue replace the bombings, attacks and counter-attacks of the last two months.

45. The suffering of the Darfurian population has lasted far too long. The gains made in 2005 in controlling malnutrition and mortality, and in the provision of services, are coming under strain with humanitarian needs expected to increase. Humanitarian aid workers continue to attempt to reopen routes, negotiate safe passage for aid convoys, fill in emerging gaps, and advocate for the respect of humanitarian principles, but their valiant efforts are undermined by violence targeted at them. Twelve aid workers have lost their lives since the Darfur Peace Agreement was signed—more than in the previous two years. An overall trend is developing where humanitarian aid is being targeted for violence.

46. I condemn these killings and strongly appeal to all parties to stop the violence, to respect humanitarian principles, and to allow humanitarian actors to provide much-needed assistance and monitor protection concerns without being subject to harassment, looting and killing.

5. Monthly Report of the Secretary-General on Darfur, 28 December 2006 (S/2006/1041)

I. Introduction

1. The present report is submitted pursuant to paragraphs 6, 13 and 16 of Security Council resolution 1556 (2004), paragraph 15 of resolution 1564 (2004), paragraph 17 of resolution 1574 (2004) and paragraph 12 of resolution 1590 (2005). It covers the period from 1 October to 10 December 2006.

II. Insecurity in Darfur

2. During the reporting period, the security situation in Darfur remained extremely volatile with both the Government and non-signatories of the Darfur Peace Agreement continuing their relentless pursuit of a military solution to the crisis in disregard of that Agreement and the N'Djamena Humanitarian Ceasefire Agreement. The situation was complicated by continued tensions within and among the belligerent rebel factions, and also aggravated by tribal conflicts, particularly in Southern Darfur. Clashes were reported among groups supporting the Darfur Peace Agreement in both Northern and Southern Darfur. Meanwhile, Chadian armed opposition groups based in Darfur resumed attacks deep inside Chadian territory. There were also reports of Darfur rebel groups receiving weapons from within Chad. Throughout the region, militia attacks on civilians increased, while attacks on humanitarian workers and African Union (AU) personnel dramatically reduced humanitarian access to populations trapped by the conflict.

3. Military confrontations between the Government of the Sudan (GoS) and non-signatories of the Darfur Peace Agreement reached new heights in October and November, and spread to areas outside Northern Darfur. On 3 October, Janjaweed militias supported by Sudanese Armed Forces (SAF) helicopters attacked positions of the Group of 19 (G19)/ National Redemption Front (NRF) in Malagat, Northern Darfur. In retaliation, NRF attacked an SAF post in Karyare, close to the Chadian border, on 5 October. The combined rebel forces reportedly took control of Karyare on 7 October, with SAF suffering a large number of casualties. Government aircraft subsequently bombed the rebel-held town. NRF claimed to have seized dozens of vehicles and captured hundreds of SAF soldiers in the battle. Twelve seriously wounded SAF soldiers were evacuated to El Fasher, while 77 injured soldiers and rebels arrived at a hospital in Bahia, Chad.

4. On 12 and 13 October, SAF attacked rebel positions in Kulbus, Western Darfur. My Special Representative visited Northern Darfur from 16 to 18 October and appealed to G19 and NRF commanders to cease attacks, citing the holy month of Ramadan as an opportunity to halt the spiralling violence. He obtained verbal pledges from the rebel commanders that they would act only in self-defence. SAF continued its attacks, with an aerial bombardment of suspected NRF hideouts north of Kulbus on 17 October. As security deteriorated, 18 humanitarian staff were evacuated from Kulbus to El Geneina. On 18 October, the Government bombed areas east of Birmaza in Northern Darfur.

5. While the signatories of the Darfur Peace Agreement respected the ceasefire towards each other in October, tensions between the parties escalated and minor incidents were

reported, reflecting the fragility of their alliance and lack of discipline among their forces. On 10 October, the Minawi faction of the Sudan Liberation Movement (SLM) and Government soldiers engaged in a firefight in El Fasher, causing at least three civilian casualties. The following day, Government soldiers attempted to raid a house occupied by SLM-Minawi soldiers in El Fasher. A series of security incidents was also reported in Nyala, between SLM-Minawi soldiers and Government security forces.

6. Fighting among rebel groups and tribal tensions in areas controlled by parties supporting the Darfur Peace Agreement further hampered implementation of the fragile peace agreement. During the reporting period, clashes resumed between SLM-Minawi and the breakaway faction of that rebel group, SLM-Free Will, in Muhajirya, Southern Darfur, when SLM-Minawi repulsed an attack by approximately 300 SLM-Free Will forces on 23 October. Meanwhile, tensions further increased in Gereida, Southern Darfur, between the Zaghawa-dominated SLM-Minawi and the local Massalit population, which formerly supported SLM-Minawi. Following the 28 September attack on the SLM-Minawi headquarters near the town, members of the Massalit tribe in Gereida revolted against the SLM-Minawi forces, protesting the recent increase in attacks on civilians. During his visit to the area from 3 to 5 October, my Special Representative was told that lack of discipline in the SLM-Minawi forces had resulted in the increase of banditry in the area. On 9 and 10 October, shooting incidents were reported near Gereida, leaving one person dead and others wounded. As a result of this insecurity in Gereida, the Department of Safety and Security relocated seven United Nations staff members and 70 from international non-governmental organizations from Gereida to Nyala.

7. Also in October, armed militias continued to attack civilians with impunity. On 8 and 11 October, armed elements on camels and vehicles burned down several villages near the Shadad camp for internally displaced persons, 70 kilometres south of El Fasher. When the villagers tried to escape to the camp, the militia opened fire on them. The militia members reportedly used the farms of the displaced villagers to graze their animals.

8. On 29 October, several hundred Arab militia members, wearing military uniforms and armed with machine guns and rocket-propelled grenades, attacked the villages of Gebasesh, Hijlija, Siberia and Goze Mino in Western Darfur. The attackers looted livestock and killed at least 52 people, including many children and elderly people. Rebels from SLM and the Justice and Equality Movement (JEM) later engaged the attackers, allegedly killing 21 militia members. Government forces from a nearby SAF post did not intervene to stop the attack.

9. Banditry continued unabated in Darfur over the reporting period. On 8 October, bandits on horses and camels ambushed two commercial buses, near Kass, Southern Darfur, killing the drivers and seriously injuring two passengers. On 9 October, three men ambushed a truck on the Nyala-Kubum road. The attackers killed the driver and injured two others. On 11 October, SLM Abdul Shafi rebels reportedly robbed the drivers of three commercial trucks 100 kilometres west of Tawila.

10. Hijacking and armed robbery of humanitarian vehicles has continued. On 2 October, five armed men ambushed two vehicles belonging to non-governmental organizations, 11 kilometres south of Nyala. While the second vehicle managed to escape, the attackers beat the driver of the first vehicle and stole his money. On 11 October, two vehicles belonging to

non-governmental organizations were stopped by eight militia members at Goussa Shark, 35 kilometres north of Nyala. The attackers stole money, a satellite phone and other valuables. In the same period, four aid workers were attacked between Zalingei and Nertiti by a dozen armed men who beat them and threatened to kill them. The perpetrators sexually harassed one female staff member. On 15 October, five men stole a vehicle belonging to an non-governmental organization and a satellite phone at the Dorti camp for internally displaced persons.

11. During the reporting period, AU forces continued to face harassment and movement restriction by rebel groups. On 4 October, 140 SLM-Minawi troops held an African Union Mission in the Sudan (AMIS) patrol hostage in Thabit for two hours for escorting representatives of SLM-Abdul Shafi through controlled areas by SLM-Minawi. The patrol was allowed to proceed to Zam Zam after the SLM-Abdul Shafi representatives surrendered five satellite phones. On 16 October, two SLM-Minawi commanders and the traditional chief (*Umda*) of Labado demanded that AMIS vacate its team site in Labado, Southern Darfur, within 24 hours, accusing AMIS of being partial. AMIS returned the following day after the SLM commanders apologized.

12. In a more recent and particularly alarming development, there were serious clashes between Janjaweed forces and the Minni Minawi faction of SLA in El Fasher on 4 December. As a result, some 135 non-essential United Nations staff were relocated to Khartoum the following day. Both AMIS and the United Nations Mission in the Sudan (UNMIS) were put on high security alert during and immediately after the clashes.

13. The situation in Western Darfur has deteriorated considerably over the past month, with increased banditry and ambushes on the roads especially to the north of El Geneina along the Chad-Sudan border. Three cars were hijacked in November, two within El Geneina itself, where a curfew was imposed. On 9 December, a group of 30 heavily armed men attacked a commercial truck carrying medical and non-food items between Kondobe and Sirba: 22 people died and several others were injured. In protest, the local community held in Sirba the helicopter sent by AMIS to investigate the incident.

III. Regional issues

14. The reporting period saw a grave deterioration in bilateral relations between Chad and the Sudan, marked by the attack on an SAF post in Karyare mentioned in paragraph 3 above and a new offensive against the Government of Chad by Chadian armed opposition groups based in Darfur.

15. On 22 and 23 October, a recently formed Chadian rebel group, the Union of Forces for Democracy and Development (UFDD), presumably based in Darfur, briefly captured the towns of Goz Beida and Am Timam before retreating to positions outside the towns. The Chadian National Armed Forces (FANT) pursued the rebels, which provoked additional violent clashes on 29 October in Chad close to the Sudanese border. Both sides reportedly suffered high casualties, including the death of the FANT Deputy Chief of Staff. Chad also accused the Sudanese air force of bombing the towns of Bahai, Tine, Karyare and Bamina along its eastern frontier, an accusation denied by the Government of the Sudan.

16. In a further escalation of violence, UFDD attacked and took control of the town of Abéché, situated approximately 900 kilometres east of N'Djamena, on 25 November. According to the UFDD leader, former Defense Minister Mahamat Nouri, 22 rebels and

140 Government soldiers were killed in the battle. The Government of Chad retook the town of Abéché after a day of fighting. In response to the situation, the Government of Chad extended a state of emergency in N'Djamena and several areas in the east for an additional six months.

17. As Abéché serves as the base for dozens of relief organizations, the recent event considerably undermined the delivery of aid to populations in need. The number of Sudanese refugees in Chad has grown to more than 234,000. There are also 47,000 refugees from the Central African Republic and 90,000 internally displaced persons. Already, the World Food Programme (WFP) and the Office of the United Nations High Commissioner for Refugees (UNHCR) have reported that about $1.5 million worth of aid intended for refugees was looted in Abéché during the events of 25 and 26 November.

18. On many occasions, Chadian rebel groups were reported to have crossed the border with the Sudan. The Government of Chad is said to have strengthened its security presence around the capital, as rebel spokesmen continue to threaten future attacks.

19. In another worrying development, the Central African Republic accused the Sudan of supporting rebels in the country after a small group called the Union of Rallied Forces captured the town of Birao, near the border with Chad and the Sudan. The Sudan rejected the accusation. Chad reportedly said it was sending troops to the Central African Republic to help fight rebels.

IV. Human rights and protection

20. Persistent high levels of insecurity, particularly in Southern Darfur, continued to force substantial numbers of civilians to flee their villages and leave their cultivated farmlands. The additional military presence in towns increased the threat of abuse of the civilian population by armed groups. Attacks in and around camps for internally displaced persons continued, and violence against women and girls remained a concern. Overall, courts in Darfur have made little progress in addressing the abuses.

21. Fighting among rebels and tribal clashes in Muhajiriya and Gereida, Southern Darfur, displaced large numbers of civilians. Up to 10,000 internally displaced persons abandoned their camps in and around Muhajariya to seek refuge near the AMIS group site. While many later returned, renewed tensions on 23 October again forced approximately 2,000 persons to seek refuge near the African Union mission. Five combatants and one civilian were killed during the clashes and more than 150 houses were burned down. Gereida now has the largest concentration of internally displaced persons in the region, numbering more than 120,000. Thousands of other displaced are scattered in the bush, where humanitarian access is extremely limited.

22. As fighting intensifies in Darfur, civilians invariably bear the brunt of the conflict. In Northern Darfur, ongoing military clashes between NRF and SAF and aerial bombardments continue to affect the rural population. The extent of civilian casualties is largely unknown, owing to lack of access for security reasons. As populations flee to inaccessible areas, they become increasingly vulnerable.

23. Reports of violence in and around internally displaced persons camps persisted in October. On the night of 4 October, two internally displaced persons were killed in Kalma camp by a group of 10 to 15 armed men. On the same day, suspected Falata tribesmen attacked 12 internally displaced persons collecting firewood near Yasin camp, Southern

Darfur. The attackers abducted one of the internally displaced persons and took away livestock. On 14 October, a displaced male was killed by militia members outside Abararas camp, Southern Darfur.

24. In Gereida, civilians who were previously attacked by pro-Government militias are now subjected to both militia and rebel attacks. Fatalities, injuries and dozens of new cases of severe abuse of civilians by SLM-Minawi combatants have been reported in October, including abduction, rape, harassment and torture. There has also been an upsurge in the number of cases of gender-based violence. Of additional concern are reports that SLM-Minawi is preventing women from reporting incidents of sexual violence to AMIS.

25. An increasing number of rapes has been recorded in five internally displaced persons camps in Western Darfur and in the Abu Shouk and Al-Salaam camps, Northern Darfur, while violence targeting women and girls was reported in Kebkabiya and Kutum. As cases of sexual and gender-based violence persist, courts in Darfur continue to move slowly in prosecuting them. In addition, there is a recurring failure of defendants and key witnesses to appear before the court, particularly with respect to cases against Government actors. In Western Darfur, two rape trials were adjourned by the Geneina General Court on 1 and 2 October owing to the repeated non-appearance of the defendants, including a People's Defence Forces member and an ISAF soldier. The head of the Geneina local police, who was required to present evidence, was also absent from the 1 October hearing. According to the judge, the court has unsuccessfully requested the presence of this police official for over a year.

26. Government authorities continue to restrict the free movement and activities of United Nations staff, in breach of the Government's obligations under the status-of-forces agreement. On 15 October, national security authorities prevented two United Nations staff members from boarding a United Nations flight to Nyala on the grounds that they required "permits" from the Government's humanitarian assistance coordination office. In Western Darfur, contrary to the status-of-forces agreement, the coordination office is now demanding that all United Nations personnel, with the exception of UNMIS personnel, carry travel permits. Meanwhile, the Governor of Northern Darfur continues to assert that he "has not received orders" from Khartoum to apply the status-of-forces agreement, and as such will only issue travel permits in line with past agreements.

V. Humanitarian situation

27. Although humanitarian operations in Darfur continue to be seriously hampered by security incidents and access restrictions, gains continue to be made in all life-saving sectors, as shown in the September 2006 food security and nutrition survey. The survey indicated stable malnutrition and mortality rates with respect to the previous year. Additional financial resources, however, will be required in the coming months to maintain the current levels of assistance.

28. The shifting of front lines, the further fragmentation of armed groups and their unclear chain of command further complicate safe humanitarian access to many of the 3.8 million people now affected by conflict in Darfur. Moreover, frequent banditry makes road travel increasingly hazardous for humanitarian workers. The United Nations regularly assesses the local security situations and attempts to secure routes and negotiate safe passage for aid convoys, while advocating for the respect of humanitarian principles. These efforts, however, are becoming ever more difficult.

29. Despite manifold constraints, the humanitarian community has been able to implement the bulk of its programmes and safeguard humanitarian standards. In September, WFP and its partners distributed food to almost three million people, although 195,000 people could not be reached as a result of fighting and road banditry in Northern Darfur. The United Nations Children's Fund (UNICEF), WFP and the Food and Agriculture Organization of the United Nations (FAO) successfully completed their annual Darfur emergency food security and nutrition survey in September (see para. 27 above). Preliminary results show that overall malnutrition rates remained statistically unvaried and below the emergency threshold, with global acute malnutrition at 13.1 per cent and severe acute malnutrition at 2 per cent. The situation in Northern Darfur remains problematic, however, with global acute malnutrition at 16 per cent, which is above the emergency threshold of 15 per cent. Mortality rates dropped from 0.48 per 10,000 per day in 2005 to 0.36 in 2006. Food aid will remain necessary in 2007 as 70 per cent of the conflict-affected population is still considered food insecure. Only 51 per cent of the surveyed households have cultivated land this year, the same proportion as in 2005. The success of the harvests and the ability to monitor them will depend on the prevailing levels of insecurity during the coming months.

30. In Western Darfur, an outbreak of acute watery diarrhoea, was abated by various preventive measures such as chlorination of water points and accelerated distribution of soap and hygiene education. During the rainy season, activities to control the outbreak of vector-borne diseases such as malaria and yellow fever have also been stepped up.

31. In response to the influx of tens of thousands of new internally displaced persons in several camps, the humanitarian community has extended water and sanitation services, upgraded health services and increased food distributions. Overall, 73.3 per cent of affected populations in Darfur now have access to safe water, up from 62.5 per cent last year. Insecurity and road conditions have somewhat delayed the distribution of non-food items, but commercial trucks have been able to supply shelter and other materials to the most needy groups in internally displaced persons camps, schools, clinics and orphanages.

32. Over the last two months, Sudanese authorities have been increasingly limiting humanitarian space in Darfur. The national security service prevented three non-governmental organizations from working in Southern Darfur. The Norwegian Refugee Council (NRC) received two letters from the Government of the Sudan expelling the organization from Darfur and requiring it to hand over all material assets to the Government prior to its departure. While the international community has objected to the confiscation of humanitarian property by the Government, NRC has declared that it will withdraw from Darfur. Humanitarian agencies are scrambling to fill the massive void left by the organization's expulsion.

VI. Implementation of the Darfur Peace Agreement

33. The implementation of the Darfur Peace Agreement virtually stalled during October and November. While efforts to broaden the support base of the Agreement continued, they were overshadowed by continued fighting on the ground. Some progress has been made in preparing the Darfur-Darfur Dialogue and Consultation and improving the efficiency of the Ceasefire Commission. Power- and wealth-sharing commitments, however, remained largely unaddressed.

34. A number of initiatives, both by Sudanese and international actors, were undertaken to broaden the support base of the Darfur Peace Agreement. However, efforts are hampered

by the increased fragmentation of rebel groups, slow implementation of the Agreement and lack of coordination. There were indications that both parties to the Agreement could accommodate some of the demands of the non-signatories.

35. October and November also saw very limited progress in the implementation of the security protocol of the Darfur Peace Agreement. On 17 October, SAF, SLM-Minawi and JEM-Wing for Peace submitted to the Ceasefire Commission information on territorial positions they claimed. The AMIS Force Commander stated that positions would be verified and compared to those given in May during the Abuja negotiations. The Force Commander rejected the Government's demand that non-signatories be removed from AMIS premises, stating that the door of dialogue must remain open. The Government's plan to disarm the Janjaweed has been referred to the Joint Commission with comments from the Ceasefire Commission. However, the next Joint Commission meeting has yet to be scheduled.

36. There was virtually no progress on power-sharing in October. The President of the Sudan issued decrees establishing four pursuant to the Darfur Peace Agreement institutions: the Transitional Darfur Regional Authority, the Technical Ad Hoc Border Commission, the Darfur Rehabilitation and Resettlement Commission and the Compensation Commission. However, SLM-Minawi claimed that the decrees were inconsistent with certain aspects of the Agreement and sent them back to the Presidency for revision.

37. On wealth-sharing, the Darfur Joint Assessment Mission concluded the current stage of its work with a consolidation of the technical teams' field work. The mission cannot be completed at this stage because of insecurity in Darfur and the refusal of major Darfurian groups to join the Darfur Peace Agreement.

38. The hosting by SLM-Minawi on 16 October of a day-long forum in Khartoum in anticipation of the Darfur-Darfur Dialogue and Consultation was seen as a positive development. The forum, attended by a broad cross-section of approximately 500 Darfurians as well as SLM-Free Will and senior representatives of the National Congress Party (NCP) and the Sudan People's Liberation Movement (SPLM) represents the first significant effort by the Darfur Peace Agreement signatories to jointly reach out to civil society. Discussions were frank, demonstrating the potential for the Dialogue and Consultation to catalyse stakeholders to take forward a sustainable peace process.

39. During the last week of November, Salim Ahmed Salim, Special Envoy of the AU Commission Chairperson, met Sudanese officials as well as non-signatories to the Darfur Peace Agreement to broaden support for the peace process in Darfur. Subsequently, the officer in charge of UNMIS and Mr. Salim held bilateral consultations on steps to be taken to reinvigorate the political process under a joint AU/United Nations umbrella and agreed to form a working-level team to prepare for the resumption of talks early in January 2007. The team has also been mandated to consult with Darfur Peace Agreement signatories, non-signatories and other local actors and to stress the importance of an immediate cessation of hostilities, the need for a commitment to a ceasefire and the mechanisms created by the Darfur Peace Agreement and the need to complement the new political talks with a credible Darfur-Darfur Dialogue and Consultation.

VII. United Nations support to the African Union Mission in the Sudan

40. The United Nations and the African Union have agreed on a package of immediate United Nations support to AMIS. This "light support package" includes logistical and

material support, 105 military staff officers, 33 police advisers and 48 civilians to assist AMIS in the areas of mine action, public information and support for Darfur Peace Agreement implementation. The support package is intended to immediately enhance the operations of AMIS through a proactive advisory role by United Nations staff. On 3 October, President Bashir expressed his support for the assistance package. In October, only nine United Nations police advisers and nine military staff officers could be deployed to Darfur, in the light of the Government's restriction on United Nations military and police personnel travelling to Darfur while wearing blue berets.

41. UNMIS has acquired land and has started to move equipment to El Fasher. Delivery of the full package was further delayed in November by the Government's initial insistence that a "protocol" on United Nations assistance to AMIS be negotiated. However, during a meeting with the Assistant Secretary-General for Peacekeeping Operations on 12 November, President Bashir agreed that the current status-of-forces agreement is sufficient, and that a tripartite AU-United Nations-Government of the Sudan mechanism be created to facilitate the implementation of United Nations support for AMIS.

42. In a further positive development, a memorandum of understanding on United Nations support to AMIS was signed in Addis Ababa on 25 November by the AU Commissioner for Peace and Security, and the Officer in Charge of UNMIS.

43. Consultations on the longer-term "heavy" United Nations support package for AMIS, which includes substantial air assets, significant military and police advisory capacity, civilian support for the implementation of the Darfur Peace Agreement and a range of United Nations enabling capabilities, were conducted during the first week of December in Addis Ababa. The United Nations and the African Union jointly identified the contents of the proposed package, which is being shared with the Government of the Sudan. In the light of the dramatic situation on the ground, it is my intention to proceed with the implementation of both support packages without delay.

44. On 16 November, I co-chaired a high-level meeting in Addis Ababa with the Chairperson of the AU Commission, Alpha Oumar Konaré. This meeting, which was attended by the Government of the Sudan, several United Nations Member States, the European Union, the League of Arab States and a number of African countries who currently provide troops to AMIS, had the objective of identifying concrete steps to be taken to improve the current situation, notably to re-energize the peace process, establish a strengthened ceasefire and delineate the way forward for peacekeeping in Darfur.

45. With regard to the political process, the meeting produced an understanding that only a negotiated settlement, and not a military solution, could bring the conflict to an end. The meeting also agreed that the existing Darfur Peace Agreement would remain at the heart of any settlement, but would have to be made more inclusive, and that the Darfur-Darfur Dialogue and Consultation had a key role to play in complementing the Darfur Peace Agreement.

46. The Addis Ababa consultation also concluded that various efforts to bring non-signatories on board had to be brought under one umbrella, and that the African Union and the United Nations—calling on international partners for support whenever appropriate—were best positioned to lead the process. On that basis, it was agreed that, as a next step, the African Union and the United Nations would soon convene a meeting of non-signatories, the

Minawi faction of SLM and the Government to address and resolve outstanding issues by the end of the year.

47. The discussions in Addis Ababa confirmed the critical importance of an agreement by all parties to cease hostilities immediately and welcomed the recent decision to empower the AMIS Force Commander to create direct links with non-signatories, which will give him greater scope to move the parties away from violence and towards negotiations.

48. Some progress was also made, at least on paper, on the way forward for peacekeeping in Darfur. Using a non-paper I had circulated before the meeting as the starting point for our discussions, a number of basic principles were clarified, starting with the essential requirement for a logistically and financially sustainable force, which would be able to contribute to the restoration of security and protection of civilians in Darfur through the implementation of security aspects of the Darfur Peace Agreement.

49. With regard to the financing, I expressed my willingness to propose to the appropriate bodies that the United Nations provide all required funding for peacekeeping in Darfur. However, I qualified this proposal, noting that it was unlikely to receive support unless the United Nations were also put in a position to provide some form of management support and accountability mechanisms for the operation.

50. The meeting in Addis Ababa also confirmed the hope that a peacekeeping force in Darfur could be predominantly African in nature, with troops, as far as possible, sourced from the continent. To complement those troops, the meeting confirmed that the United Nations would provide backstopping and command and control structures for an expanded peacekeeping presence in Darfur. I explained to the meeting that this provision would be indispensable for the troop and police contributors which the United Nations would probably approach to provide the necessary specialist support and enabling functions, since these contributors would provide personnel and assets on the basis of the United Nations having in place standard support structures and mechanisms and clear command and control arrangements. There was also agreement that the regional security situation would have to be taken into account.

51. In addition to these basic principles, the meeting took a number of decisions with regard to the material steps to be taken to strengthen AMIS in Darfur. The meeting concluded that the United Nations would continue to implement the previously agreed "light support package" for AMIS in collaboration with the African Union and in full cooperation with the Government of the Sudan; that the "heavy support package", or phase two, would be taken forward and that the existing tripartite (United Nations-AU-Government of the Sudan) mechanism established to take forward the light package would also facilitate implementation of the heavy package; that an AU-United Nations hybrid operation would subsequently be established, led by a Special Representative and commanded by a Force Commander who would both be jointly appointed by the United Nations and the African Union; and finally, that I should, as previously mentioned, propose to the appropriate bodies that the United Nations provide all required funding for peacekeeping in Darfur.

52. The hybrid operation discussed in Addis would, in principle, reflect the recommendations I made in my report of 28 July to the Council on peacekeeping in Darfur (S/2006/591). That is, it would be comprised of up to 17,000 troops and 3,000 civilian police, as well as formed police units, whose numbers will be determined at a later date.

53. The conclusions of the 16 November high-level consultations call for a stronger, more capable, better financed peacekeeping operation, benefiting from the best of AMIS and also the experience and resources of the United Nations. The added value could include both funding and the identification and deployment of capabilities and troops which may not be available among AU member States; unified AU-United Nations leadership; and also the day-to-day backstopping, support and guidance from the Department of Peacekeeping Operations.

54. However, as the discussion in Addis Ababa took place, the Foreign Minister of the Sudan stated that his Government would consult internally on two elements of the plan for the way forward regarding peacekeeping in Darfur, namely the troop ceiling and the joint appointment of the Special Representative and the Force Commander, and that the Government would shortly revert to me with its views.

55. Subsequently, on 30 November, the AU Peace and Security Council convened a meeting at the level of Heads of State and Government, and endorsed the conclusions of the 16 November meeting.

56. During the open segment of the Peace and Security Council meeting, the Government of the Sudan distributed a document entitled "Position of the Government of Sudan regarding outstanding issues raised during the consultative meeting in Addis Ababa on the third phase". This paper expressed the following views of the Government with respect to the outstanding matters arising from the 16 November meeting in Addis Ababa.

57. With regard to the senior leadership of a hybrid operation, the Government asserted that the "Special Envoy" would be jointly appointed by the African Union and the United Nations, and would be "an African acceptable to the Government of the Sudan". During the meeting, President Bashir supplemented this position by insisting that the Force Commander of a hybrid operation would be appointed by the African Union only.

58. With respect to command and control, the Sudanese document took the position that these command and control were the sole responsibility of the African Union, although command could be enhanced by "applying United Nations systems and structures as well as United Nations advisers", provided that their ranks were junior to those of African commanders.

59. On the size of the force, the Sudanese paper referred this issue to the tripartite mechanism established to facilitate implementation of the first two phases.

60. Finally, the Sudanese document proposed that non-signatories be given a time frame to sign on to the Abuja agreement, after which they would be subject to sanctions imposed by the African Union and the United Nations.

61. These proposals broadly echoed a 28 November letter which President Bashir had sent me on these same subjects.

62. Having considered the Sudanese paper, and the remarks of the Government of the Sudan, the United Nations and the League of Arab States, which had participated as observers during the initial portion of the meeting, the Peace and Security Council issued its communiqué of 30 November. The communiqué endorsed the conclusions of the 16 November

high-level consultations and, with respect to the hybrid operation, reflected the Peace and Security Council decisions that:

- The Special Representative shall be jointly appointed by the Chairperson of the AU Commission and the Secretary-General
- The Force Commander of a hybrid operation, who should be an African, shall be appointed by the Chairperson of the AU Commission in consultation with the Secretary-General
- The hybrid mission shall benefit from United Nations backstopping and command and control structures and systems
- The size of the force for the hybrid operation shall be determined by the African Union and the United Nations, on the basis of factors on the ground and requirements for effectively discharging its mandate.

63. The Peace and Security Council also decided to extend the mandate of AMIS, which expires on 31 December 2006, for six months, subject to review by the Council and the availability of financial resources.

64. The Peace and Security Council appealed to the United Nations to "consider providing logistical and financial support to the Mission, as envisaged in the conclusions of the Addis Ababa consultation". In the meantime, the Council appealed to partners of the African Union to provide required logistical and financial support to AMIS.

65. On 3 December, the Council of Ministers of the Sudan, under the chairmanship of President Bashir, endorsed the Peace and Security Council communiqué of 30 November. I welcome the communiqué of 30 November and the commitment to implementing the Addis Ababa conclusions. The Secretariat has started to work intensively with UNMIS and the African Union in order to turn the results of Addis Ababa and Abuja into concrete results. The United Nations and the African Union have identified their respective participation in the tripartite mechanism; UNMIS and the African Union are in ongoing dialogue on the work of the preparatory committee for the Darfur-Darfur Dialogue and Consultation; and United Nations and AU teams are at this moment working together in Addis Ababa to finalize the heavy support package. The time has come, however, for the Government of the Sudan to remove all restrictions, both operational and political, imposed on the implementation of the two packages, and allow it to be delivered without delay.

VIII. Observations

66. Another two months have passed without bringing a breakthrough to the crisis in Darfur. The tragedy in this beleaguered region has been raging for three years now, and still the population remains subject to attacks, villages continue to be destroyed, killings, human rights abuses and brutality are perpetrated against innocent people and impunity is rampant. The conflict is increasingly spreading over the Sudanese borders, threatening to engulf the whole region in war. It is urgent that we take action to prevent further violations, including by bringing to account those responsible for the massive human rights abuses that have already been committed. It is essential that the Security Council send a clear and united message to warn all concerned that the current situation is unacceptable and will not be allowed to continue.

67. In addition, and as Council members are aware, in a letter dated 22 October 2006, the Government of the Sudan declared terminated the mission of my Special Representative in the Sudan. I deeply regret this decision, which has further complicated the search for expeditious solutions to the Darfur crisis.

68. Efforts to consolidate the support base for the Darfur Peace Agreement can only succeed if they are coordinated, inclusive and transparent. The main stumbling block, however, remains the belief of both the Government and the non-signatories of the Darfur Peace Agreement that they can alter the situation militarily. As my Special Representative told the Security Council on 27 October, recent clashes indicate that the Government of the Sudan continues to support a military solution to the conflict. I deplore the Government's use of aerial bombardments that fail to distinguish civilians from combatants, in breach of Security Council resolution 1591 (2005) and international humanitarian law.

69. The continued rejection, made under claims of sovereignty, of the deployment of United Nations troops in support of the AMIS operation results in the perpetuation of the attacks and abuses, which can no longer be tolerated. The time has come to lift all impediments, operational and legal, for United Nations assistance to the African Union, and to reaffirm the public declaration to cooperate with the African Union and the United Nations. We all should be guided by the sense of urgency this issue requires.

70. The most recent spate of violence and the persistent attacks on innocent civilians by armed militias are of particular concern. On 8 October, the United Nations High Commissioner for Human Rights issued a report detailing brutal militia attacks on civilians in Buram in late August and early September. The High Commissioner called for an investigation into the attacks. I support this recommendation, and likewise encourage the Government to establish an independent national inquiry and bring to justice those responsible. Accountability of the perpetrators is a key step in bringing an end to such attacks.

71. I strongly urge all warring parties to immediately refrain from using violence against civilians, to respect humanitarian principles and to allow humanitarian actors to provide the much-needed assistance without hindrance. All parties should guarantee safe passage for relief workers and lift all operational restrictions. The Sudanese authorities should also extend the Darfur moratorium for a further 12 months when it expires in January 2007. This is a critical step for humanitarian organizations to be able to carry out their life-preserving work.

72. Donor support has been crucial to humanitarian efforts in Darfur. Not only have donors' contributions enabled the continuation of programmes in all life-saving sectors, they have also allowed the resumption of some activities such as the food-for-education programme. It is my hope that such financial support can be ensured in the coming year not only to sustain the current level of assistance but also to allow for contingency planning in case the situation worsens.

73. I deeply regret that the upsurge in violence along the Chad-Sudan border has reversed the diplomatic progress the Sudan and Chad had achieved through the signing of the 26 July agreement in Tripoli. The Governments of the Sudan and Chad should refrain from any action that might have a destabilizing impact on the region and return to political dialogue.

74. In the meantime, progress, however limited, has been made on the Ceasefire Commission under the leadership of the African Union. The United Nations will do everything possible to

assist the AMIS leadership by supporting its efforts to make the ceasefire regime more effective through inclusiveness, credible investigations, accountability and implementation of the key security provisions of the Darfur Peace Agreement, by enhancing the capacities of AMIS through the support package, and by participating in the Ceasefire Commission and the Joint Commission. I encourage AMIS to convene a meeting of the Joint Commission at the earliest opportunity and look forward to its outcome. In the meantime, AMIS should continue to enjoy the financial, logistical and political support of the international community.

75. It is of critical importance to capitalize on the Abuja meeting of 30 November. I intend to reiterate to President Bashir the commitment of the United Nations to implementing, without further delay, the steps agreed to at the high-level meeting in Addis Ababa on 16 November and later confirmed by the AU Peace and Security Council at its 30 November meeting. Given the recent alarming deterioration of the security situation in Darfur, the first priority must be to establish a ceasefire and to give impetus to the political process. These are critical conditions for any meaningful peacekeeping work.

76. The time has come to turn declarations into actions in order to achieve progress towards our crucial goal: bringing an end to the violence in Darfur, and restoring to its people the right to live a normal life, free of fear, with hope for a better future.

6. Report of the Secretary-General on Darfur, 25 January 2007 (S/2007/42)

I. Introduction

1. The present report is submitted pursuant to paragraph 11 of Security Council resolution 1590 (2005), in which the Council requested me to keep it regularly informed of progress in implementing the Comprehensive Peace Agreement, respect for the ceasefire and the implementation of the mandate of the United Nations Mission in the Sudan (UNMIS). The report also provides an assessment of the overall situation in the country since the previous report to the Council, dated 12 September 2006 (S/2006/728).

II. Implementation of the major elements of the Comprehensive Peace Agreement

2. Two years after the Comprehensive Peace Agreement was signed on 9 January 2005, implementation has not progressed as effectively as was hoped. While the basic constitutional framework envisaged in the Agreement is in place, some of the political and security institutions are functioning, and the National Congress Party (NCP) and the Sudan People's Liberation Movement (SPLM) have continued to assert their commitment to full implementation; in reality, both parties have proved reluctant to take the difficult steps required to move towards sustainable peace, and critical aspects of the Agreement remain well behind schedule. Of central concern, the principles of the Agreement related to political inclusion and "making unity attractive" have yet to be fully upheld, and much remains to be done if the parties are to achieve their ambitious goals set out in the Machakos Protocol and in subsequent protocols.

Security aspects

3. The period under review witnessed the most serious violation of the ceasefire since 2002. In Malakal, Upper Nile, heavy fighting between elements of the Sudanese Armed Forces (SAF) and the Sudan People's Liberation Army (SPLA) from 27 to 30 November killed at least 150 people, including civilians. The conflict erupted after a long-running dispute over the commissionership of a county in neighbouring Jonglei State triggered a series of skirmishes between the SPLA Joint Integrated Unit contingent and SAF-aligned other armed groups. Fighting then escalated into a full-scale confrontation between SPLA forces and SAF. The UNMIS-chaired Ceasefire Joint Military Committee played a key role in bringing the fighting to a halt, and the parties subsequently withdrew to their pre-conflict positions. While the city remains tense, Joint Integrated Unit forces involved in the fighting have been rotated out of the area, and a buffer zone is being monitored by joint patrols, including UNMIS observers.

4. Redeployment of the parties' armed forces continues, although delays in the formation of Joint Integrated Units are now holding up the redeployment of SPLA forces from the transitional areas, originally to have been completed in the second quarter of 2007. With the SAF redeployment deadline of 9 July 2007 approaching, both parties face considerable challenges if redeployment is to be accomplished as agreed in the Comprehensive Peace Agreement. Both parties continue to maintain a substantial armed presence in sensitive oil-rich areas, including Upper Nile, and the 1 January 1956 border area remains highly militarized.

5. On 18 November, President Al-Bashir called for better cooperation between NCP and SPLM on security matters, particularly the problem of other armed groups, and stressed the need for the Joint Integrated Units to function in order to secure the border areas and oil installations. The failure to integrate other armed groups into existing military structures and to create functioning Joint Integrated Units, as required under the Comprehensive Peace Agreement, has left the parties facing a growing security problem, where militia violence as witnessed in Malakal can easily erupt and spiral out of control.

6. Elsewhere in Southern Sudan, unidentified armed men, allegedly belonging to SAF-aligned militia groups, were also held responsible for attacks on arterial roads outside Juba in October and December, killing some 75 people.

7. At the same time, recent months have witnessed increased instability in Northern and Southern Kordofan States, where civilian discontent has led to strike action, and attacks by armed militia groups and tribal violence represent a growing security threat. While some of the violence has spilled over from neighbouring Darfur, tribal disputes and other armed group activities further fuel tensions. For example, in the area of Meiram, south of Abyei, clashes between SPLA forces and SAF related to the integration of erstwhile other armed groups resulted in the displacement of approximately 2,000 people.

8. Efforts to resolve the problem posed by other armed groups remain stymied by mistrust between the parties, as reflected in the state of the Other Armed Groups Collaborative Committee. While its members met regularly during the reporting period, it remained mired in disputes over its rules of procedure, and there is as yet no plan to deal with armed militia groups that are aligned with SAF but that are reluctant to redeploy north of the 1 January 1956 border by 9 July 2007.

9. At the same time, the formation of Joint Integrated Units continued to be delayed, owing in part to a lack of logistical support for moving troops, a shortage of working and living accommodations and irregular and insufficient budgetary assistance. Efforts by the Joint Defence Board to agree to a single doctrine and training programme have foundered, partly over cultural and religious differences. In several areas, poorly disciplined Joint Integrated Unit elements were responsible for deteriorating security. Disputes over the payment of salary arrears to SPLA members of Joint Integrated Units triggered demonstrations in Juba on 9 December. While the presidency should take the steps necessary to provide a regular budget to the Units, there is also a need for bilateral donors to step forward and assist the Units to perform the security functions envisaged in the Comprehensive Peace Agreement and for the parties to be open to such assistance.

10. More positively, the Ceasefire Joint Military Committee and Area Joint Military Committees played an important role during the reporting period, helping to de-escalate tension between forces on the ground. This was critical during the Malakal crisis, during which the Ceasefire Joint Military Committee convened emergency sessions, on 29 November and 3 December, facilitating an immediate ceasefire and withdrawal of forces. The body, which is chaired by UNMIS, has proved to be a highly effective forum for frank discussion between the parties, as well as the mechanism for resolving military violations of the Comprehensive Peace Agreement. I commend the Chairman of the Committee and its members for the positive role the mechanism is playing.

Political aspects

11. During celebrations marking the second anniversary of the Comprehensive Peace Agreement in Juba on 9 January, President Al-Bashir and First Vice-President Kiir publicly aired their grievances over the failures of each other's party to implement key aspects of the Agreement. The accusations traded are a direct result of the parties' lack of success in effectively using the joint mechanisms set up in the Agreement to resolve contentious issues. I am hopeful, however, that this open stocktaking might revitalize the two leaders' determination to overcome their difficulties, and I very much welcome the strong commitment of both leaders to the Agreement.

12. Some welcome progress was made on the legislative agenda. The National Constitutional Review Commission drafted several important bills for consideration by the National Assembly, including those required to establish the long-overdue National Human Rights Commission and National Civil Service Commission. Other critical commissions, including the National Electoral Commission and the Commission for the Protection of the Rights of non-Muslims in the National Capital, also have yet to be established.

13. The National Assembly has now passed a political parties law and the National Civil Service Commission Act. Meanwhile, consultations on a draft elections bill are at an early stage, and the work of the Population Census Council has also been proceeding slowly. More must be done to accelerate the work of the Council, whose national census is critical not only for the electoral process, but also for long-term development planning.

14. The Southern Sudan Legislative Assembly has approved a number of bills relating to the criminal code. However, commissions on land, the civil service, human rights, anti-corruption, relief and rehabilitation and disarmament, demobilization and reintegration have yet to be formally established, although commissioners have been appointed to many of them. While six southern states signed their constitutions into law during the reporting period, the Ministry of Justice of the Government of National Unity declared the moves unconstitutional. Meanwhile, in Southern Kordofan State, the presidency resolved a lengthy deadlock over the draft constitution, which was eventually signed into law in December.

15. There are particular concerns over the slow progress of the technical ad hoc border committee, which is supposed to demarcate the 1 January 1956 border between north and south. The committee has completed its review of maps and started work with local communities; it has not, however, begun physical demarcation. Consensual demarcation of this border would go a long way to resolving a number of potentially serious Comprehensive Peace Agreement problems, including the redeployment of military personnel, the distribution of oil revenues, the formation of Joint Integrated Units and, later, preparations for elections.

16. The Abyei issue remains extremely contentious and has been referred to a joint high political committee of the parties. However, despite appeals to the presidency for guidance, no progress has been made. On 9 January 2007, First Vice-President Kiir appealed to the Intergovernmental Authority on Development (IGAD), as well as the IGAD Partner's Forum, to assist the parties in implementing the Protocol on the Resolution of the Conflict in the Abyei Area.

17. On the ground in Abyei, a temporary relaxation of freedom-of-movement restrictions has made the entire region accessible to the United Nations. This has assisted its monitoring

efforts and humanitarian activities, as well as inter-tribal negotiations and other reconciliation activities. I urge the authorities to continue to allow the Mission and all United Nations personnel to carry out their important tasks throughout the region.

18. The Ceasefire Political Commission met on 28 September and 9 November, although without the full participation of its international members. The Commission has failed to gain traction as a decision-making body, and it has rarely been able to resolve issues referred to it by the Ceasefire Joint Military Committee. Meanwhile, the Assessment and Evaluation Commission also met regularly during the reporting period and received special briefings from the Central Bank on disarmament, demobilization and reintegration, legislative transformation and the work of the border committee.

Wealth-sharing aspects

19. On the wealth-sharing agenda, the parties reached agreement on rules of procedure for the National Petroleum Commission. They also agreed to establish an independent technical secretariat of the Commission, which should help to ensure complete impartiality concerning the distribution of oil revenues. However, increasing concerns arose regarding the displacement of populations in areas of oil exploration. Provisions of the Comprehensive Peace Agreement, requiring consultation with and compensation of populations affected by resource exploitation are not systematically understood or enforced in Southern Sudan, with serious consequences for human rights and environmental protection.

20. A new national currency was launched on 9 January, marking the second anniversary of the signing of the Agreement. The new Sudanese pound will initially be distributed in Southern Sudan, replacing the multiple currencies currently in circulation. This is a big step forward, and I congratulate both parties on this achievement.

21. The roll-out of the new national currency will have an important impact on economic recovery and reconstruction. Donor support will be critical to making this effort a success. Assistance will be especially required to sensitize the public and to support the timely and efficient distribution of the new currency.

III. Implementation of other peace processes in the Sudan

22. On 14 October, the Eritrean-mediated talks between the Sudanese Government and the Eastern Front rebel movement culminated in the signing of the Eastern Sudan Peace Agreement. So far, implementation has progressed slowly, due in part to the failure of the Eastern Front to present a list of nominees for the posts allocated to it under the Agreement. However, the state of emergency was lifted in Kassala State and Red Sea State one week after the signing, and the Agreement was passed into law by the National Assembly on 6 November. Its incorporation into the Constitution is pending discussions between NCP and its allies regarding the allocation of parliamentary seats.

23. Peace talks between the Government of Uganda and the Lord's Resistance Army (LRA) continued sporadically under the mediation of the Government of Southern Sudan. The Juba talks led to an extension of the ceasefire until 28 February 2007. However, late in the reporting period, LRA made it clear that it would no longer accept the Government of Southern Sudan as mediator and wished to relocate the talks. I regret this delay. I am, however, confident that my Special Envoy for the LRA-affected areas, former Mozambican President Chissano, will play an important role in assisting the parties to this conflict to

resolve their bitter 20-year struggle. I strongly urge the parties to remain committed to finding a peaceful solution quickly.

24. As noted in the report on the latest events in Darfur (S/2006/1041), the security situation in the region remains extremely volatile, as civilian populations continue to be targeted in violation of international humanitarian and human rights law. In recent months, tens of thousands of people have been forced to flee their homes, and the total number of internally displaced persons has reached its highest level since the conflict flared up in 2003. While fighting has continued amid shifting factional allegiances, efforts to conclude local ceasefire arrangements were undermined by continued aerial bombardment of rebel positions by the Government. Violence also surged along the Chad-Sudan border, as Chadian armed opposition groups launched attacks from Darfur into Chad. Meanwhile, implementation of the Darfur Peace Agreement made only halting progress.

25. UNMIS is currently working to finalize the implementation of the "light support package" of assistance to the African Union Mission in the Sudan (AMIS). The first part of a three-phase approach that will culminate in a hybrid African Union/United Nations mission in Darfur, the package includes United Nations military and police advisory personnel, as well as material and equipment for AMIS. On 26 December, the tripartite mechanism established by the United Nations, the African Union, and the Government of National Unity to facilitate implementation of the three-phase approach resolved several outstanding issues, including the attire of United Nations military and police personnel deployed under the light support package, who will wear their national uniforms, blue berets and African Union armbands.

26. The United Nations and the African Union held a final round of consultations in Khartoum from 18 to 20 January to finalize the "heavy support package", the second step of the three-phase approach. The package, which includes a range of force enablers, three formed police units, civilian personnel and mission support items, was transmitted to President Al-Bashir on 24 January in separate letters from African Union Chairperson Konaré and the Secretary-General. It is expected that the tripartite mechanism will also facilitate the implementation of this package. The African Union and the United Nations held additional consultations from 22 to 24 January on their hybrid operation. The consultations focused on the basic requirements of the operation, including its essential characteristics such as mandate, force size and command and control arrangements.

IV. Implementation of the mandate of the United Nations Mission in the Sudan

Political support and reconciliation

27. As part of its good offices mandate to help resolve ongoing conflicts in the Sudan, UNMIS worked with politicians and local communities in Southern Sudan to promote the Comprehensive Peace Agreement and the Southern Sudan Interim Constitution. Peace and reconciliation efforts continued, especially following tensions in Juba, Rumbek and Malakal. In Abyei, UNMIS undertook a three-day helicopter peace mission with Misseriya and Dinka Ngok traditional leaders to promote peaceful coexistence along nomadic migration routes. In the peace process between the Government of Uganda and LRA, UNMIS provided aviation support to Cessation of Hostilities Monitoring Team patrols as well as flights to the assembly areas for the parties or associated individuals when necessary.

28. UNMIS also remained actively engaged in the efforts to find a political solution to the conflict in Darfur (see S/2006/1041). Further to the high-level discussions held in late November in Addis Ababa, UNMIS and the African Union are working to chart a course to re-engage the non-signatories to the Darfur Peace Agreement in the political process. UNMIS has also held events throughout Darfur to disseminate the Agreement and plan for the Darfur-Darfur Dialogue and Consultation. Meanwhile, my new Special Envoy, Jan Eliasson, visited the region, and will be working closely with the African Union over the coming weeks and months to move the peace process forward.

Military deployment and activities

29. As at 10 January, 94 per cent of mandated UNMIS military personnel (9,322 out of a total of 9,831) had been deployed, including 579 United Nations military observers, 181 staff officers and 8,514 troops from troop-contributing countries. While team sites have now been established throughout the Mission's area of operations, planning is under way to set up three additional sites at Raga in Western Bahr Al Ghazal, Talodi in Southern Kordofan and Baw in Blue Nile State. In line with the Security Council's request to reduce the military component, taking into account progress made on the ground, UNMIS has now fully withdrawn the Nepalese component that had been based in eastern Sudan, and is also adjusting its number of military observers from 750 to 625.

30. The military component continues its monitoring and verification activities throughout its area of operations. The increased tension where other armed groups continue to operate and the growing number of violent clashes has stretched the force in some areas, especially where additional team sites have been established. The force has increasingly played a proactive arbitration and humanitarian role in resolving other armed group and ethnic clashes in the Malakal region and elsewhere. It also provided river transport and escort for a Government of Southern Sudan investigative and reconciliation committee having the task of resolving an intra-tribal dispute in Jonglei State.

31. At the same time, the military component has been undertaking civil-military cooperation tasks in support of local communities, including the building and equipping of a medical clinic, the construction and grading of roads and the building of ablution facilities. With the start of the dry season, temporary repairs to sections of the Ed Damazin-Dindirou-Kurmuk road by UNMIS force engineering assets assisted in the return of refugees from Ethiopia. Wherever possible, local labour is trained to carry out such tasks, enabling individuals to gain vocational training and experience.

Disarmament, demobilization and reintegration

32. The parties have made some progress on the planning of disarmament, demobilization and reintegration programmes. The National Council for Disarmament, Demobilization and Reintegration Coordination, decreed by the presidency in February 2006, finally met in December. It requested the submission of a comprehensive disarmament, demobilization and reintegration programme for the north and the south, and started to give much-needed attention to the problem of the armed militia. The Council is key to creating a favourable political and operational environment for disarmament, demobilization and reintegration. It should now establish appropriate eligibility criteria for entry into the programme and oversee the ongoing registration of members of SAF and SPLA.

33. There continues to be modest progress in the interim disarmament, demobilization and reintegration programme, focusing on special groups (women, children and the disabled). During the reporting period, 211 children were demobilized and reunited with their families, the majority of which are enrolled in school and benefit from community-based child protection network programmes. Continued national and international support is required to strengthen the northern and southern Sudan Disarmament, Demobilization and Reintegration Commissions in order to better implement the interim programme and plan for the next phase of the programme focusing on SAF, SPLA and the other armed groups.

34. In planning for the main disarmament, demobilization and reintegration programme, UNMIS supported the Disarmament, Demobilization and Reintegration Commission in the pre-registration of 60,477 soldiers and members of other armed groups for voluntary disarmament, demobilization and reintegration. This included 22,026 regular SAF soldiers, 17,000 members of the Popular Defence Forces, 5,000 disabled soldiers and 16,451 members of other armed groups aligned with SAF. In the south, SPLA continues to finalize its list of combatants. Once the lists have been completed, UNMIS will assist the two Disarmament, Demobilization and Reintegration Commissions in verifying the numbers. Eventual acceptance into the disarmament, demobilization and reintegration programme needs to be based strictly on properly formulated eligibility criteria established by the National Council. Proper vetting during the planning stage will yield significantly better results when the disarmament, demobilization and reintegration programme commences.

Electoral assistance

35. With the midterm elections set for 2008 or 2009, UNMIS is starting to build its capacity to meet the technical assistance requirements in support of electoral preparations. As noted above, the requisite electoral legislation remains to be passed. The Mission's electoral activities have thus far focused on tracking and monitoring progress in developing the legal framework for elections, particularly the draft elections law, rules for the registration of political parties and the establishment of the National Electoral Commission, as required by the Comprehensive Peace Agreement. A mechanism for coordination of international assistance was established in early December, which will aim to identify areas of cooperation and optimize resource allocation among donors and international partners.

Police

36. As at 5 January, UNMIS had deployed 662 United Nations police officers from 44 countries, who are currently stationed at 19 team sites, representing 93 per cent of the authorized strength.

37. UNMIS continued to support the development of the Southern Sudan Police Service, working with the newly established Police Development Committee (PDC), including through the registration of police officers. During the reporting period, the Mission began to implement its strategy of co-locating its police advisers with local police forces. By early December, 74 United Nations police advisers were based at 27 local police stations in Southern Sudan, and additional advisers were located at 8 police stations in the transitional areas, proactively assisting local counterparts to perform their duties and carrying out on-site training activities. Senior United Nations police advisers were also attached to senior Southern Sudan Police Service officers responsible for planning. UNMIS is widening its community policing programmes, including within transit camps for internally displaced persons.

38. The Mission has also worked to deepen its engagement with the police service in northern Sudan. In December, UNMIS, the United Nations Development Programme (UNDP) and the police service signed a letter of collaboration enabling the provision of police training in northern Sudan. The Government of National Unity Ministry of Interior also agreed to establish a Police Development Committee to coordinate cooperation with United Nations police and donors. Detailed training needs and requests to donors can now be discussed in the Police Development Committee forum, and the Governments of Norway and Denmark have already offered assistance. As noted in previous reports, other donors are strongly urged to come forward to assist in this critical aspect of the UNMIS mandate.

Human rights

39. UNMIS continued active human rights monitoring during the reporting period. Particular human rights abuses occurred during the hostilities in Malakal, when SAF, its allied armed groups and SPLA failed to discriminate between combatants and non-combatants and used disproportionate violence resulting in a high toll on civilians. Meanwhile, chronic concerns over the proliferation of weapons, the continuing existence of other armed groups, weak command and control among armed elements and a lack of rule of law added to the insecurity, which continues to expose civilians to unnecessary and unpredictable violence.

40. Particular concerns surround the displacement of civilians associated with oil development. An UNMIS analysis of the impact of oil exploration found that companies were employing environmentally unsound methods. Hazardous waste is regularly dumped into civilian water supply areas, while roads to oil installations destroy farmland and livelihoods. At the same time, commitments under the Comprehensive Peace Agreement relating to consultation and compensation for land confiscation and displacement are not being implemented.

41. UNMIS continued to support the formation of human rights mechanisms provided for in the Agreement and held a number of workshops over the reporting period. In Southern Sudan, UNMIS supported commissioners appointed to the Southern Sudan Human Rights Commission, including in the development of enabling legislation and an annual budget and in strategic planning. Work was adversely affected by the expulsion of a staff member in October.

Rule of law

42. UNMIS continued to support parties, parliamentarians and civil society engaged in law reform, including through the organization of workshops and seminars. In that connection, UNMIS supported a seminar on parliamentary oversight of the security sector ahead of the upcoming debate on a new security bill and provided technical assistance in the drafting of the Khartoum State children's bill. The Mission also provided substantive advice to the drafting of the prison services bill for Southern Sudan. UNDP continued to provide capacity-building support to legal professionals, including paralegals, lawyers, police, prosecutors, judges and prison service personnel.

43. In response to a request by UNMIS, the Governments of Ghana and Kenya have offered to assist in training Southern Sudan prison staff in Accra and Nairobi. In November, UNMIS initiated the establishment of a Prisons Development Committee in Juba to provide policy

direction to prison officials regarding reform in Southern Sudan. In collaboration with Government of Southern Sudan authorities, the Mission has started registering all staff of the Prisons Service of Southern Sudan and is providing training on minimum standards for the treatment of prisoners and on basic prison management.

Public information

44. UNMIS Radio (Miraya/Mirror FM) continued to build listenership in the south. Repeater stations are now operating in Wau and Malakal. Miraya FM is also producing programmes on the Comprehensive and Darfur Peace Agreements for rebroadcast on some state radio stations in the south, in Southern Kordofan and, in cooperation with AMIS, in Darfur. The United Nations station is also assisting southern state radio stations through quick-impact projects and technical advice. Plans to boost listenership through short-wave radio and via a website with audio capability are ongoing. However, despite regular meetings with the Government, UNMIS still has no agreement to broadcast.

45. UNMIS has continued to provide public information support to AMIS with the loan of staff and equipment, website support and presentations on the Darfur Peace Agreement. This support will build with the recruitment of additional public information staff within the light support package. In the south, regular CPA presentations and workshops with community leaders on the Comprehensive Peace Agreement have continued, along with United Nations police and military training in the dissemination of information on the Agreement. In the north, in spite of positive interaction with some individuals and universities on issues pertaining to the Agreement and the role of UNMIS in the country, there remains an overall reluctance on the part of northern institutions and individuals to embrace the United Nations message.

Humanitarian assistance

46. The 2007 United Nations and partners' workplan was launched in Geneva on 14 December. The workplan focuses on continued support for the implementation of the Comprehensive Peace Agreement, expanded recovery and development activities, an increased emphasis on reintegration initiatives for returning populations and the continued provision of humanitarian assistance. The total cost of assistance is some $1.26 billion for humanitarian activities and $560 million for recovery and development. Relative to 2006, the workplan reflects an increased focus on the delivery of an assistance package for the reconstruction and economic development of the Sudan.

47. In October, violence along roads east of Juba in Southern Sudan severely impeded access for aid workers. The clashes in Malakal in November led the United Nations to relocate temporarily 230 non-essential United Nations and non-governmental organization personnel. Civilian displacement also occurred and, although many people have returned, some civilians still seek help to move north. Humanitarian agencies rapidly undertook the disposal of bodies, the provision of water points and chlorine and the restocking of hospital medicine and supplies in the aftermath of the ceasefire.

48. In Darfur (see S/2006/1041), humanitarian access was significantly curtailed and aid workers were increasingly targeted. Because of ongoing fighting, humanitarian staff frequently had to be relocated temporarily, and organizations' operational capacities and access to populations were seriously reduced. However, mortality rates in Darfur have dropped for the second consecutive year, and malnutrition rates remain under control.

Protection of civilians

49. As noted above, widespread insecurity continued to adversely affect civilian protection. During the fighting in Malakal in November, UNMIS personnel worked to identify and refer emergency needs of the civilian population and to establish casualty figures and damage assessments. Elsewhere, the reporting period saw rising tensions within ethnic and tribal communities and placed at-risk civilian populations out of the reach of humanitarian assistance. Protection staff provided early warning and analysis of those issues and forged joint responses with agencies and non-governmental organizations through protection working groups.

50. Children continue to be associated with armed forces and groups. United Nations field teams identified scores of child soldiers in the ranks of the Pibor Defence Forces in Jonglei State and in the Southern Sudan Defence Forces in Upper Nile State. Targeted efforts to sensitize stakeholders in the affected areas were stepped up in Pibor. Child protection staff facilitated the release of children in Wau and remain on standby as efforts to demobilize children in Bentiu proceed. Meanwhile, despite assurances to the former Emergency Relief Coordinator that it would release its considerable number of women and children, the Lord's Resistance Army has shown no sign of doing so. Work was adversely affected by the expulsion of a staff member in October.

51. The situation in Darfur diverted valuable protection resources from the chronic problems in Southern Sudan and the transitional areas. In Darfur, advocacy on protection issues has been ill received by the local authorities, and dialogue has become increasingly confrontational, as witnessed in particular by the ejection of the Norwegian Refugee Council. As non-governmental organizations reduced their protection activities, joint United Nations protection working groups sought to maintain accurate reporting and identify alternative channels for assistance.

Returns

52. The start of the dry season in November marked the beginning of the 2006/07 return season. In an unprecedented development, the Government of National Unity, the Government of Southern Sudan, UNMIS and the United Nations country team agreed to a single joint plan for the organized return of some 200,000 internally displaced persons. By December 2007, the three parties aim to return 150,000 people from Khartoum and other northern states and a further 48,000 people from other locations to Southern Sudan and Blue Nile State. In a demonstration of the seriousness of their commitment, the Government of National Unity and the Government of Southern Sudan have together contributed $51 million towards the operation, $24 million of which has already been allocated by the Government of Southern Sudan. This operation is seen by all parties as a significant step forward.

53. In greater Khartoum, the United Nations pursues its efforts to monitor the conditions of internally displaced persons through community-based mechanisms, specific assessments and dialogue with the competent authorities. In Darfur, as the dry season begins, state authorities have begun to apply pressure on the United Nations to begin returns. This year the context in Darfur makes returns even less appropriate than in 2006. However, the United Nations continues to engage the Government and has agreed to jointly assess areas to which returns may be feasible, in accordance with existing policies.

Mine action

54. Landmines and unexploded ordnance continue to present a major threat to the population in many parts of the Sudan, as well as to United Nations and non-governmental organization personnel operating on the ground. Although severely hampered by rains at the beginning of the reporting period, UNMIS mine action teams have made steady progress. Over 9.5 million square metres of suspected dangerous areas have been cleared, as well as some 2,500 anti-personnel mines, 1,000 anti-tank mines and some 500,000 pieces of unexploded ordnance and small arms ammunition. UNMIS and the United Nations Children's Fund provided mine-risk education to more than 950,000 people. UNMIS provided briefings on landmine safety to over 6,200 Mission staff, agencies and non-governmental organizations and trained more than 200 staff as trainers.

55. UNMIS mine action teams continued to work on roads and in communities that have been prioritized in the Nuba Mountains, Juba, Rumbek, Wau, Yei, Malakal, Ed Damazin, Darfur and Kassala. For the first time, a United Nations mine action team was able to survey the roads around Hameshkoreib in eastern Sudan after the SPLA withdrawal and identified several dangerous areas for further clearance. All five UNMIS demining contingents from Bangladesh, Cambodia, Egypt, Kenya and Pakistan have commenced operations. Demining activity, which is a prerequisite for further development activities in the Sudan, requires continuous support from the international community.

Economic recovery and reconstruction

56. Economic recovery and reconstruction is a critical activity in Southern Sudan and the transitional areas. The United Nations has increased its programming significantly in support of Government counterparts and local actors, including through the multi-donor trust fund for Southern Sudan. The trust fund has approved projects worth $235.3 million to support Government capacity-building, reform of the judiciary, health, education, water and sanitation, infrastructure development, livestock and the census. There are also projects planned for support for the states, agriculture, the rule of law, HIV/AIDS programmes and private sector development. Although progress in the transitional areas has been slower, the World Bank reports that over 40 per cent of total national multi-donor trust fund project commitments are earmarked for those areas ($38 million out of about $90 million total). Specific programmes focusing on capacity-building and basic social services for Southern Kordofan and Blue Nile States are currently under development.

57. Although the delivery of these and other peace dividends has been offset by slower than expected disbursement through the multi-donor trust funds, the achievements made so far in Southern Sudan give cause for optimism. These include an expansion of markets and an increase in trade, with a significant reduction in the cost of basic items in key locations, such as Juba. The opening of roads has also led to an increased movement of people and investment in the private sector in Southern Sudan. There has also been significant progress in establishing key Government functions and bodies, although functions relating to payroll, procurement and treasury systems have yet to become fully operational. The roll-out of the new national currency in 2007, which will focus in the initial stages on the south, will give a further boost to private sector development. Overall, economic indicators relating to growth, inflation and foreign direct investment remain strong.

58. Further to the signature of the Eastern Sudan Peace Agreement, the 2007 United Nations and partners' workplan includes a focus on recovery and development of the eastern states, including alignment with priorities set out in the Agreement and the Government's five-year plan. Progress in Darfur with respect to the joint assessment mission came to a halt because of the prevailing insecurity. The assessment mission will be concluded when conditions improve.

Gender

59. In connection with the upcoming elections in 2008-2009, the Gender Unit initiated an assessment of the technical support needs of prospective women candidates from political parties in both the north and the south. In Southern Sudan, UNMIS has been promoting implementation of the 25 per cent quota for women stipulated in the Southern Sudan Interim Constitution. The Unit is also strengthening dialogue and cooperation with the AMIS gender office. In Darfur, UNMIS continues to advocate for effective mechanisms to prevent and respond to gender-based violence. Training activities targeting mission personnel and national partners were also undertaken, including for police personnel of the Government of Southern Sudan. The Unit also conducted activities to mark the sixth anniversary of the adoption by the Security Council of its resolution 1325 (2000).

HIV/AIDS

60. The HIV/AIDS Unit conducted further training of HIV/AIDS peer educators, bringing the total number of trained educators to 154, and sensitized 2,000 peacekeepers. Voluntary confidential counselling and testing services were offered to 70 Mission personnel. Through its six regional HIV committees, the Unit helped to sensitize some 61,690 members of the uniformed services and the general population in the Sudan in 2006. UNMIS also organized workshops throughout the Mission area marking World AIDS Day.

Conduct and discipline

61. During the reporting period, 29 new cases of misconduct were reported to the conduct and discipline team, two of which were classified as serious misconduct and referred to the Office of Internal Oversight Services (OIOS) for investigation. Delays in reporting the outcome of OIOS investigations need to be addressed to build confidence and avoid impunity. The conduct and discipline team also continued its activities to ensure that all Mission personnel complied with the United Nations code of conduct for the Sudan. Newly deployed civilian staff, military observers and police personnel received briefings on United Nations standards of conduct and the United Nations policy of zero tolerance for sexual exploitation and abuse. UNMIS, United Nations agencies and international non-governmental organizations began a joint assessment of southern communities' perceptions and risk factors conducive to misconduct.

62. At the end of the reporting period, allegations of sexual exploitation and abuse were levelled at UNMIS personnel in Juba. I wish to make clear that I will not tolerate this behaviour within the United Nations. The zero-tolerance policy, meaning zero complacency and zero impunity, will be strictly enforced. I pledge that all allegations will be followed up systematically by relevant United Nations mechanisms, working with local authorities and other partners, including troop-contributing countries, to ensure that this kind of behaviour is rooted out wherever it exists. When necessary, strong disciplinary

action will be taken. In this connection, I would call upon all peacekeeping partners, including members of the press, to come forward with any information they may have in their possession to help us deal with the problem.

Civilian staffing

63. UNMIS continues to face serious problems in recruiting and retaining well-qualified international and nationally recruited staff members. The Mission carried out aggressive recruitment campaigns for international and national staff with the assistance of Department of Peacekeeping Operations recruitment teams, as well as staff temporarily assigned from other missions. As a result, civilian staff strength rose to 827 international staff (out of a total of 1,139 posts), 2,229 national staff (out of a total of 3,342 posts) and 177 United Nations Volunteers (out of a total of 231 posts).

V. Challenges in mandate implementation

64. UNMIS continues to face considerable challenges in carrying out its mandate and daily tasks. Since its inception, the Mission has had to operate in an atmosphere of opposition on the part of some political forces to the multidimensional mandate given to it by the Security Council in its resolution 1590 (2005). The Government's overall attitude towards the Mission has been considerably amplified as a result of the intense discussions that have unfolded over recent months concerning a possible United Nations peacekeeping role in Darfur. UNMIS regularly faces bureaucratic obstacles from the authorities, an alarming number of crises and forced evacuations from its offices in Darfur and in Southern Sudan, a latent terrorist threat and multiple mission support and logistical problems due in part to the difficult environment in which the Mission operates, as well as the increasing demands supporting its growing role in Darfur.

65. On 22 October, the Government informed my predecessor that it had decided to "terminate" the mission of Special Representative Jan Pronk and requested him to leave the Sudan within 72 hours. The United Nations strongly protested that decision and made it clear that only the Secretary-General could decide on the tenure of his Special Representatives. The unfortunate episode amplifies the imperative to resolve existing issues through dialogue and consultation. Mr. Pronk later returned to the Sudan for a short farewell visit prior to the expiration of his contract at the end of the year.

66. There are other concerns about the commitment to the letter and spirit of the agreement that governs relations between the Mission and the Sudanese authorities. On 26 September, two staff members, while monitoring demonstrations at Khartoum University, were detained and threatened, and United Nations equipment was confiscated by unidentified security personnel. They were subsequently declared personae non gratae and required to leave the Sudan. I specifically appeal to the Government of National Unity to allow those two staff members back into the country in a spirit of good faith and understanding.

67. Meanwhile, recurring restrictions on local freedom of movement hindered the work of both UNMIS, in parts of its area of operations south of Khartoum, and other United Nations and non-governmental organization partners in Darfur, which were often not authorized to operate without travel permits from the authorities.

68. At the same time, delays in clearing UNMIS materiel through customs continued to create serious problems for the Mission, which have occasionally left the military component

short of vital rations and communications equipment. Despite frequent discussions with the Government, no lasting solution to this problem has been found.

69. In the context of the intense international focus on Darfur, as well as the daily challenges faced by UNMIS on the ground, the Mission has at times found it difficult to assist the parties to the Comprehensive Peace Agreement in carrying out their considerable commitments. The sheer size of the country, as well as the lack of transport and communications infrastructure on the ground, have stretched United Nations support mechanisms and require the decentralization of some functions from Khartoum to the regions. I have initiated preliminary steps in that direction by appointing a senior official who will be responsible for coordinating all Mission activities in Southern Sudan and representing the Head of Mission on a day-to-day basis with the Government of Southern Sudan. The implications of this decentralization, which would delegate increased levels of authority to the field, will be met from existing resources for the immediate period. Any future changes having an impact on current administration and support structures will be reflected in future reports to the Security Council and subsequent budgetary submissions.

VI. Financial implications

70. The General Assembly, by its resolution 60/122 B, appropriated the amount of $1,079,534,400, equivalent to $89,961,200 per month, for UNMIS for the period from 1 July 2006 to 30 June 2007. Should the Security Council decide to extend the mandate of UNMIS beyond 30 April 2007, the cost of maintaining the Mission until 30 June 2007 would be limited to the amounts approved by the Assembly.

71. As at 31 October 2006, unpaid assessed contributions to the Special Account for UNMIS amounted to $524.0 million. The total outstanding assessed contributions for all peacekeeping operations as at that date amounted to $2,541.8 million.

72. Reimbursement of troop- and contingent-owned equipment costs have been made for the period up to 31 October 2006, in accordance with the payment schedule.

VII. Observations

73. While the parties have achieved significant progress in implementing the Comprehensive Peace Agreement, much remains to be done if they are to establish an inclusive and constitutional democracy in which unity is made attractive to voters in Southern Sudan. On the second anniversary of the Agreement, I am concerned that the "spirit of Naivasha", which resulted in a historic agreement two years ago, has been somewhat elusive, especially in recent months, and that the consensus created by the accords has been overshadowed by distrust and uncertainty.

74. The recent crisis in Malakal is a reminder that the hard-won Agreement is not yet stable or self-sustaining, but needs constant encouragement. Mistrust between the parties remains a serious obstacle, potential spoilers still exist and the war in Darfur has diverted international attention and support from implementation of the Agreement. In the context of rising tensions in the region, peace in Southern Sudan needs renewed and sustained attention. The coming year should be a year of increased focus on the Agreement to protect the gains made so far and to give the Sudan a stable basis on which to move forward. I pledge my personal commitment to this goal.

75. In that regard, there is a critical nexus of security issues where progress is required if peace is to hold in 2007. By 9 July, SAF must complete its redeployment north of the 1 January 1956 border. While redeployment of SPLA is predicated on the formation of Joint Integrated Units, this is now behind the schedule set out in the Agreement. The parties need to resolve this issue and keep to their redeployment commitments. Importantly, the redeployment targets do not apply only to regular forces, but also to other armed groups aligned with the parties.

76. The violence in Malakal underscored not only the need for other armed groups to be integrated as a matter of priority, but also that Joint Integrated Units do not yet function as the foundation of a possible future national army and as guarantors of security and stability. The need to ensure security around sensitive areas, including oil installations, is particularly pertinent. Unfortunately, there remains an acute security dilemma for both parties over the management of strategic areas. There is significant risk that what happened in Malakal could happen in other areas of Southern Sudan.

77. Both parties must cease using militias as proxy forces and make the integration of other armed groups a top priority. Building on the commitment to a joint solution agreed during President Al-Bashir's visit to Juba in November 2006, the parties should establish the ad hoc incorporation and reintegration committees provided for in the Agreement and work in earnest through the Other Armed Groups Collaborative Committee and the National Council for Disarmament, Demobilization and Reintegration Coordination for the integration or demobilization of all armed militias. As noted in paragraph 33 above, international support for the disarmament, demobilization and reintegration mechanisms will continue to be critical to implementation.

78. Equally urgent is the agreement of a joint doctrine and training programme for Joint Integrated Units. As the Sudanese Armed Forces depart Southern Sudan, the ability of the Units to provide security will be critical. If the Units are not integrated, professional and well regulated, they risk becoming part of the problem rather than part of the solution. The Joint Defence Board has previously requested help from the international community to develop the Joint Integrated Units. The Comprehensive Peace Agreement also specifically states that the parties would call upon the international community to provide technical, material and financial support to assist in forming and training the Units. I call upon Member States with experience and expertise in security sector reform to urgently second experts to assist UNMIS in this area, working with the Joint Defence Board to develop an integrated programme of assistance.

79. I urge the parties to begin in earnest the demarcation of the 1 January 1956 border and to agree the status of Abyei. It must be recognized that if the border issue is not resolved expeditiously, it might be difficult to verify full redeployment in July 2007. Where it is required, the international community should provide financial and technical support to the technical ad hoc border committee.

80. The commitment of both parties to develop professional and accountable police services in line with the Comprehensive Peace Agreement is a most welcome sign. The Police Development Committee in Southern Sudan and the newly created Police Development Committee in the north are important forums that bring together the respective police experts from the Sudan, the United Nations, non-governmental organizations and representatives of donor countries. I encourage the Committees to work energetically to identify

training and logistical needs and urge donors to liaise closely with them to ensure that capacity-building assistance to the police is well coordinated and targeted.

81. Some of the central institutions within the Comprehensive Peace Agreement need to be more effective than they have been so far. One such institution is the Assessment and Evaluation Commission, which has a critical oversight function over the Agreement and has been given the task of supporting the parties in their commitment to "make unity attractive". Equally, the Ceasefire Political Commission must function more effectively, and the parties should use the planned review of its activities to revitalize this important forum in 2007. It is recognized that UNMIS could play a more prominent role within the Assessment and Evaluation Commission, and I intend to actively support this. So too should the broader international community, and especially those countries with an interest in Sudanese peace and development, become more active in both Commissions, as well as outside their framework.

82. Despite the public airing of disagreements during the celebrations marking the second anniversary of the Agreement, there seems to be a generally improved partnership in recent weeks between NCP and SPLM, which has enabled progress on important areas, like the National Petroleum Commission. I am concerned, however, that the parties still appear reluctant to tackle resolutely difficult issues in the institutions provided for in the Agreement, preferring instead to resort to informal discussions. If the Agreement is to take deeper root, more must be done to improve transparency in political decision-making and to improve the capacity of all parties to participate in the political process. Donor support in building the capacity of political parties and parliamentary institutions will also remain essential.

83. It is time to begin the process of ensuring that conditions are in place for a free and fair electoral process, expected in 2008 or 2009. The enactment of electoral legislation and the establishment of the Electoral Commission are long overdue. I hope that the parties will move forward rapidly with the creation of the Commission, which will then need the political, financial and technical support of donors to prepare for the polls.

84. Two years after the signing of the Agreement, it is particularly crucial to provide tangible benefits of peace to the people of the Sudan. In its resolution 1590 (2005), the Security Council urged rapid delivery of an assistance package for the reconstruction and economic development of the Sudan. In practice, progress has been slower than expected, especially in Southern Sudan. I welcome the discussions now under way with the Government of Southern Sudan and other key stakeholders to establish a "second window" for the multi-donor trust fund for Southern Sudan, which would be administered by the United Nations and which would emphasize expeditious implementation in areas of urgent need. At the same time, the wider exploitation of resources in Southern Sudan must be carried out responsibly, so that accelerating economic development results in a genuine peace dividend for the population at large.

85. International concern with the situation in Darfur in the past two years has, understandably, diverted significant attention, as well as human and financial resources, away from implementation of the Comprehensive Peace Agreement. In this respect, Darfur is not just a human tragedy, it also reflects negatively on the central precept of the Agreement, that Sudanese unity should be made attractive to Southern Sudanese voters. A swift, peaceful resolution to the conflict in Darfur could go a long way towards restoring trust between the parties to the Agreement. Conversely, the longer the conflict drags on, the harder it will be to persuade the Southern Sudanese that their best interests lie within a united Sudan.

86. It is also crucial to remember that the Agreement is the bedrock and foundation of all subsequent agreements, including the Darfur Peace Agreement. Therefore, sustained international support for this complex Agreement will be indispensable. I am convinced that 2007 should be a year of renewed support and engagement on the Agreement. As a centrepiece, I fully support the recent announcement by IGAD that it, as sponsor and mediator of the Agreement, plans to convene a major meeting to assess implementation of the Agreement in July 2007.

87. While calling for additional support for the Agreement, I request that both parties continue to give their full support to the United Nations in its efforts to assist them in implementing the Agreement. As I begin my term as Secretary-General, I want to assure both parties that the Organization will remain an entirely impartial arbiter, committed to bringing peace and development to all the Sudanese people. In return, I ask for fairness from both parties, for dialogue and mutual understanding and for a commitment to assist the United Nations in carrying out its mandated role.

88. In conclusion, I wish to thank all United Nations personnel in the Sudan for their tireless service in support of the Agreement and for helping to resolve the conflict in Darfur. Thanks to their efforts, the United Nations is ready to further assist the Sudanese people and authorities in implementing their historic agreements.

Annex 1
Military and police component as at 31 December 2006

	Military component									
	Observers		*Staff officers*		*Troops*		*Military subtotal*		*Civilian police*	
Country	*Male*	*Female*	*Male*	*Female*	*Male*	*Female*	*Male*	*Female*	*Male*	*Female*
Argentina	—	—	—	—	—	—	—	—	11	—
Australia	5	1	5	4	—	—	—	—	8	2
Bangladesh	22	—	29	—	1 499	—	1 550	—	18	1
Belgium	5	—	—	—	—	—	5	—	—	—
Benin	7	—	—	—	—	—	7	—	—	—
Bolivia	15	—	—	—	—	—	15	—	—	—
Bosnia and Herzegovina	—	—	—	—	—	—	—	—	1	1
Botswana	5	—	—	—	—	—	5	—	—	—
Brazil	14	—	—	—	—	—	14	—	3	—
Burkina Faso	7	—	—	—	—	—	7	—	—	—
Cambodia	15	—	1	—	135	—	151	—	—	—
Canada	14	1	6	1	—	—	20	2	2	—
China	14	—	11	—	428	7	453	7	7	2
Croatia	—	—	5	—	—	—	5	—	—	—
Denmark	10	—	6	—	—	—	16	—	2	—
Ecuador	20	—	—	—	—	—	20	—	—	—
Egypt	18	—	22	—	781	15	821	15	2	—
El Salvador	5	—	—	—	—	—	5	—	4	1

Continued

Country	Military component								Civilian police	
	Observers		Staff officers		Troops		Military subtotal			
	Male	Female	Male	Female	Male	Female	Male	Female	Male	Female
Fiji	8	—	—	—	—	—	8	—	4	3
Finland	—	—	2	—	—	—	2	—	2	—
Gabon	6	—	—	—	—	—	6	—	—	—
Gambia	—	—	—	—	—	—	—	—	—	4
Germany	31	—	4	—	—	—	35	—	5	—
Ghana	—	—	3	—	—	—	3	—	35	6
Greece	4	—	2	—	—	—	6	—	—	—
Guatemala	8	—	—	—	—	—	8	—	—	—
Guinea	14	—	—	—	—	—	14	—	—	—
India	21	—	26	—	2 576	4	2 623	4	26	2
Indonesia	13	—	—	—	—	—	13	—	—	—
Jamaica	—	—	—	—	—	—	—	—	3	2
Jordan	12	—	7	—	—	—	19	—	21	—
Kenya	5	1	11	—	780	32	796	33	18	2
Korea	7	—	—	—	—	—	7	—	—	—
Kyrgyzstan	6	3	—	—	—	—	6	3	1	—
Malawi	6	—	1	—	—	—	7	—	—	—
Malaysia	8	—	3	—	—	—	11	—	10	—
Mali	14	—	—	—	—	—	14	—	—	—
Moldova	2	—	—	—	—	—	2	—	—	—
Mongolia	2	—	—	—	—	—	2	—	—	—
Mozambique	2	—	—	—	—	—	2	—	—	—
Namibia	9	—	—	—	—	—	9	—	1	—
Nepal	8	2	5	—	—	—	13	2	49	1
Netherlands	7	—	2	—	—	—	9	—	6	—
New Zealand	2	—	1	—	—	—	3	—	—	—
Nigeria	13	—	5	1	—	—	18	1	50	3
Norway	17	—	9	—	—	—	26	—	4	—
Pakistan	23	—	20	—	1 538	—	1 581	—	42	—
Paraguay	6	—	—	—	—	—	6	—	—	—
Peru	12	—	—	—	—	—	12	—	—	—
Philippines	6	—	—	—	—	—	6	—	56	—
Poland	2	—	—	—	—	—	2	—	—	—
Romania	12	—	—	—	—	—	12	—	—	—
Russian Federation	15	—	3	—	120	—	138	—	11	—
Rwanda	15	—	7	—	254	—	276	—	24	—
Samoa	—	—	—	—	—	—	—	—	17	—
South Africa	—	—	1	—	—	—	1	—	—	—
Sri Lanka	—	—	—	—	—	—	—	—	13	1
Sweden	3	—	2	—	—	—	5	—	9	1

Country	Military component									
	Observers		*Staff officers*		*Troops*		*Military subtotal*		*Civilian police*	
Country	*Male*	*Female*	*Male*	*Female*	*Male*	*Female*	*Male*	*Female*	*Male*	*Female*
United Republic of Tanzania	9	—	2	—	—	—	11	—	2	—
Thailand	14	1	—	—	—	—	14	1	—	—
Turkey	—	—	4	—	—	—	4	—	28	—
Uganda	9	—	—	—	—	—	9	—	17	2
Ukraine	8	—	—	—	—	—	8	—	21	1
United Kingdom	—	—	3	—	—	—	3	—	—	—
United States	—	—	—	—	—	—	—	—	7	2
Uruguay	—	—	—	—	—	—	—	—	2	—
Vanuatu	—	—	—	—	—	—	—	—	6	—
Yemen	16	—	—	—	—	—	16	—	3	—
Zambia	15	2	7	—	303	39	325	41	21	—
Zimbabwe	13	2	2	—	—	—	15	2	25	8
Total per gender	**579**	**13**	**217**	**6**	**8414**	**97**	**9200**	**111**	**597**	**45**
Total	**592**		**223**		**8511**		**9311**		**641**	

7. Monthly Report of the Secretary-General on Darfur, 23 February 2007 (S/2007/104)

I. Introduction

1. The present report is submitted pursuant to paragraphs 6, 13 and 16 of Security Council resolution 1556 (2004), paragraph 15 of Council resolution 1564 (2004), paragraph 17 of Council resolution 1574 (2004) and paragraph 12 of Council resolution 1590 (2005). It covers the months of November and December 2006, and January 2007.

II. Insecurity in Darfur

2. The security situation in Darfur has been characterized by increased violence during the reporting period. Sudanese Government forces supported by armed militia engaged in clashes with Darfur Peace Agreement non-signatory forces, especially in Northern and Southern Darfur. In their ongoing efforts to flush out non-signatory combatants, the Government of the Sudan intensified aerial bombardment of non-signatory forces positions, including civilian targets. Tension also persisted along the Sudan-Chad border. Humanitarian organizations and the African Union Mission in the Sudan (AMIS) suffered harassment and attacks, while theft and carjackings of their vehicles reached new heights in November and December.

3. The reporting period was also marked by clashes between Government forces supported by armed militia and the National Redemption Front (NRF) coalition. The clashes occurred in both Northern and Southern Darfur: in Birmaza, Sani Hayi, Umm Sidr, Sayah, Gubba, Dobo (Northern Darfur), Abu Jabre and Adilya (Southern Darfur). On 15 November, soldiers of the Sudanese armed forces and armed militia, supported by helicopter gunships, attacked several villages in the Birmaza area, killing at least three civilians, torching dozens of houses and destroying four rub halls of an international non-governmental organization (NGO).

4. The Group of 19 (G19) faction of NRF retaliated by attacking Sudanese armed forces and militia forces in several places, including Sani Hayi and Umm Sidr, and attacking Government property, including the oil installations at Abu Jabre on 26 November, which led to heavy clashes between rebels and the Sudanese armed forces. On 4 and 5 December, Government helicopter gunships and an Antonov aircraft bombed the Adilya area (Southern Darfur) in an attack on NRF forces. On 16 December, Government forces and G19 members clashed in Sayah (Northern Darfur). Nine G19 members were killed and seven of their vehicles were destroyed. On 20 December, armed militia and Government forces launched a combined ground and air strike against a joint force of the G19 group, Sudan Liberation Movement (SLM)-Abdul Shafi and the Justice and Equality Movement (JEM) in Gubba (Northern Darfur). In addition, they launched aerial bombardments on G19 strongholds of Hashaba and Anka (Northern Darfur) on 11 and 21 December, killing eight civilians.

5. Hostilities also broke out between armed militia and SLM-Minawi. On 3 and 4 December, members of SLM-Minawi and armed militia clashed at the El Fasher marketplace. Eight people, including one civilian, were killed in the ensuing violence and looting. On 5 December, one student was killed and two others injured by armed militia in the Al Mudarig

area close to El Fasher. On 6 and 7 December, schoolboys and other citizens protested the killing at demonstrations in El Fasher, which culminated in the burning of a tent that served as a classroom in a school in El Fasher.

6. Much of the violence targeted innocent civilians, in contravention of existing ceasefire arrangements and international law. On 18 November, forces of the Government of the Sudan and armed militia attacked and burned a significant portion of the village of Buli (Western Darfur), where more than 10,000 internally displaced persons had found refuge, and looted several villages between Rowata and Bul Bul (Western Darfur). Dozens of civilians were killed and thousands displaced in the attacks. Armed militia also attacked and torched villages, causing the death of many civilians. On 2 December, five civilians were killed and many more displaced in attacks on Abu Sakeen (Northern Darfur), in which 50 houses were burned. On 4 December, armed militia attacked the settlements of Shagbuba, Bunglawy, Um Serena and Hashaba (Northern Darfur), leading to the death of two civilians. On 5 and 6 December, Government aircraft bombarded Shagbuba with ground support from armed militia and killed five civilians. On 9 December, armed men on horseback attacked a commercial vehicle convoy carrying people and medical and other supplies near Runju Runju in the Sirba area (Western Darfur). The truck was hit by a rocket-propelled grenade, and the people in the truck were shot at by the horsemen. Thirty-one civilians, including five schoolteachers, were killed in the attack.

7. On 19 December, an armed group attacked returnees in Arwa (Western Darfur) and looted 150 cows and 300 sheep. Five returnees were killed and eight injured in the attack, after which the perpetrators fled across the border to Chad. The incident occurred in the wake of the signing of a letter of understanding on 13 December, between the Office of the United Nations High Commissioner for Refugees (UNHCR) and the International Organization for Migration, which provides a framework for cooperation between the two organizations to help Sudanese refugees and internally displaced persons to return to their homes.

8. Tension along the Sudan-Chad border remained high during the reporting period. On 25 November, Chadian armed opposition groups, allegedly the Rally of Democratic Forces (RFD) and the Union of Forces for Democracy and Development (UFDD), crossed the Sudanese border into Chad and captured the eastern Chadian town of Abéché, but were pushed back by the Chadian armed forces on the following day. The incident occurred soon after the summit held on 21 November 2006 in Tripoli, where the Sudan and Chad met under a Libyan peace initiative that included Egypt, Eritrea and the Central African Republic. On 28 November, Chad declared itself in a "state of war" with the Sudan over the latter's alleged support of Chadian rebels. On 12 December, fighting between Chadian armed opposition groups and the Chadian armed forces at Armankul (Western Darfur) resulted in displacement of the local population.

9. More than 24 humanitarian vehicles were carjacked or stolen in the period under review. On 7 December, three vehicles belonging to an international NGO were stolen in Khor Abeche (Southern Darfur). On 9 December, an international NGO vehicle was taken at gunpoint near Azerni (Western Darfur), while, on 11 December, three international NGO vehicles were stolen at gunpoint near Muhajariya (Southern Darfur) by armed men on camelback. On the same day, a United Nations agency vehicle that had been donated to the local Department of Health was stolen at gunpoint by Arab militiamen near the Krinding II internally displaced person camp (outside Geneina town). On 12 December, three armed

men carjacked an international NGO vehicle near Ardemata (in Geneina town) and abducted the two staff members who were in it. The carjackers then drove the vehicle some distance from Ardemata, sold it to another party and released the staff members. Two international NGO vehicles were stolen in El Geneina (Western Darfur) in separate incidents on 13 and 14 December. On 18 December, armed men attacked two international NGO compounds in Gereida (Western Darfur) and brutally assaulted and raped two international NGO staff. The perpetrators also stole 12 vehicles, along with mobile and satellite phones, laptops and other electronic communication equipment.

10. International NGO staff continued to be harassed by armed groups, while armed militia and Government forces also hindered humanitarian aid delivery. On 7 December, a group of armed men forcefully entered an international NGO complex in Khor Abeche and physically assaulted several of the organization's staff members. On 18 December, an international NGO ambulance and its Government police escort vehicle were ambushed near Khorbomba (Western Darfur) and one staff nurse was shot in the leg.

11. Government attacks on humanitarian personnel also occurred over the reporting period. On 19 January, local police and security officials raided the compound of an international NGO in Nyala and arrested 20 people, including five staff members of United Nations agencies and a number of AMIS and NGO staff. Those arrested, including United Nations staff, were subjected to physical assault and verbal abuse by the Nyala police during their arrest and detention. One female United Nations staff member was sexually abused during the arrest and several sustained serious injuries, some of which required urgent medical treatment.

12. Armed banditry continued during November and December. On 15 November, armed men looted trucks carrying World Food Programme (WFP) supplies near Kutum (Northern Darfur). On 2 December, armed militia and Government forces attacked the villages of Hilat Amar Jadeed and Lamena (Northern Darfur) during a scheduled food distribution. In Hilat Amar Jadeed, soldiers and armed men looted food and supplies and severely wounded three persons. In Lamena, witnesses reported that Sudanese Government soldiers shot at civilians, resulting in the death of at least three persons and the injury of five more, including two children.

13. Attacks on AMIS personnel, property and installations have also increased. The situation was particularly serious in Northern and Western Darfur, where internally displaced persons and civilians attacked AMIS personnel. The following locations were targeted: the Zam Zam internally displaced person camp post on 5 December, and the AMIS headquarters near El Geneina airport on 10 December, which resulted in the death of three civilians. On 10 December, an AMIS vehicle carrying two AMIS military personnel was carjacked in El Fasher. The whereabouts of the two abducted AMIS personnel are still unknown. Two other AMIS vehicles were stolen in December: one in El Fasher on 14 December, the other in Khor Abeche on 15 December. AMIS investigations were also hindered by civilians upset by the prevailing insecurity and violence. In one instance, the AMIS investigation team that went to Sirba on 9 December to inquire into the Runju Runju incident was detained overnight by local civilians. The killing of an AMIS civilian police officer during the hijacking of an AMIS vehicle in Northern Darfur on 1 February also underscored the increasingly dangerous environment in Darfur.

III. Human rights and protection

14. Security in and around internally displaced person camps continued to remain precarious, with killings, looting and harassment of internally displaced persons and gender-related crimes against female internally displaced persons. Concurrently, the number of displaced persons arriving at the internally displaced person camps increased because of the attacks. In addition, Government authorities continued to restrict the freedom of movement of United Nations personnel.

15. Violence persisted in internally displaced person camps and against internally displaced persons. On 5 December, two groups of internally displaced persons clashed in the Kalma camp (Southern Darfur), and one internally displaced person was shot dead and two others were injured. On 8 December, armed militia shot dead three internally displaced persons from the Shangil Tobayi camp (Northern Darfur), after stealing their cattle. On 19 December, armed men shot and wounded an internally displaced person at the El Sherif camp (Southern Darfur), following an attempt to steal his cattle the previous day. In a related incident, again on 19 December, armed men attacked some men in the Otash internally displaced person camp (Southern Darfur) and stole their money.

16. Female internally displaced persons faced harassment, assault and rape by members of various armed factions. On 13 November, three female internally displaced persons were raped at the Kalma camp (Northern Darfur) and, on 14 November, one woman was raped in the Tawilla camp (Northern Darfur). On 25 November, two female internally displaced persons were attacked close to the Mornei camp (Western Darfur) by three armed men who also raped them.

17. Civilians also continued to be displaced as a result of the ongoing violence. The clashes in Northern and Southern Darfur during November displaced approximately 22,000 people. The attacks on Abu Sakeen and Armankul also led to a large displacement of the local population. On 4 December, residents of Kullo (Northern Darfur) had to evacuate to the internally displaced person camp at Tawilla (Northern Darfur), following attacks on their village by SLM-Minawi members who claimed the land for themselves.

18. United Nations staff also continued to be hindered in their work by restrictions imposed by Government authorities, in violation of the status-of-forces agreement. On 16 November, upon landing in Kornoi (Northern Darfur), a group of United Nations staff were searched and questioned by the Sudanese armed forces. On 13 December, a United Nations agency team was prevented from travelling to the Zam Zam internally displaced person camp without a humanitarian assistance coordination travel permit, and on 20 December, national security officials prevented a United Nations vehicle, with UNMIS personnel, from proceeding from El Fasher to Mallit on the same grounds. Again, on 20 December, a United Nations helicopter flight that was scheduled to transport people from El Fasher to Fanga (Northern Darfur) was refused permission because the aircraft was based in Kadugli, not in El Fasher.

IV. Humanitarian situation

19. Humanitarian aid access declined steeply in November and December owing to widespread insecurity and the theft of an unprecedented number of aid vehicles. The frequent attacks and harassment also led to the relocation of a large number of humanitarian aid workers.

20. In November, 95 per cent of the roads in Western Darfur were unusable for security reasons. In December, only two roads were certified safe for United Nations and international NGO movement in and around the El Geneina area (Western Darfur). Among the closed roads were the vital Abu Surug-Geneina commercial road and the road to Um Kher. Due to the prevailing insecurity, humanitarian organizations were unable to assess the humanitarian situation in Birmaza and Jebel Marra (Western Darfur). The theft of aid vehicles further restricted the mobility of humanitarian workers.

21. Due to the prevailing insecurity, over 400 humanitarian workers were relocated on 11 separate occasions, which affected humanitarian and emergency aid delivery to around 850,000 conflict-affected people. On 5 December, following the violence in El Fasher, 52 humanitarian aid staff, along with 82 United Nations personnel, were relocated to Khartoum. The day after the theft of vehicles on 7 December from an international NGO compound in Khor Abeche, 11 of its staff members were relocated to Nyala. Following an attempted break-in at the International Committee of the Red Cross (ICRC) compound in Kutum (Northern Darfur) and the resultant shooting, 32 ICRC, international NGO and United Nations agency staff were relocated to El Fasher the following day, 8 December. Three international NGOs temporarily relocated 30 staff members on 9 December from Al Daien (Southern Darfur) to Nyala, due to the prevailing tensions in the area. On 19 December, 71 international NGO and NGO members were relocated to Nyala following the attack, theft and harassment of staff in two international NGO compounds in Gereida the previous night.

22. There have been 28 such relocations since the signing of the Darfur Peace Agreement on 5 May 2006, which has impacted humanitarian aid to the affected populations. Notably, the largest single relocation in December from Gereida has affected humanitarian support to the Gereida camp, which is the largest internally displaced person camp in Darfur, with over 130,000 inhabitants. By November, the number of people in need of humanitarian assistance had risen to around 4 million, representing roughly two thirds of the Darfur population. On 20 November, the Southern Darfur authorities expelled the international NGO Norwegian Refugee Council, claiming its reports of rape cases in the Kalma camp were inflated. That significantly reduced humanitarian aid activities in Southern Darfur.

23. Despite these daunting challenges, humanitarian aid workers have persisted in their effort to deliver humanitarian aid to those in need and to carry on developmental activities.

24. As a result of the ongoing conflict, 70 per cent of the war-affected population in Darfur is now dependent on external food aid and agencies like WFP that continue to deliver food aid to over 2.6 million people every month. Around 92 per cent of the target population in Darfur has been inoculated against polio. As a result of the efforts of the United Nations Children's Fund over the reporting period, 9,500 people will get access to potable water in internally displaced person camps in Southern Darfur. The maintenance of water schemes in another eight Southern Darfur internally displaced person camps during December benefited more than 130,000 internally displaced persons. Primary school enrolment in Darfur increased from 47 per cent to 63 per cent during 2006.

V. Implementation of the Darfur Peace Agreement

25. During the reporting period, high-level consultations on Darfur took place in Addis Ababa on 16 November, which my predecessor co-chaired with the Chairperson of the African Union Commission, Alpha Oumar Konaré. Preparatory work for the convening of a conference of non-signatories and rationalization of the various initiatives to broaden the base of the Darfur Peace Agreement are ongoing. In December, further progress was made to reinforce the ceasefire mechanism, including the creation of a second chamber of the Ceasefire Commission for non-signatories.

26. The Security Council has already been apprised of the conclusions of the Addis Ababa deliberations of 16 November. The discussions resulted in a clear agreement that only a negotiated political settlement could bring the conflict in Darfur to an end. The meeting also concurred that the Darfur Peace Agreement would remain at the heart of any settlement but would need to be made more inclusive, and that the Darfur-Darfur Dialogue and Consultation has a key role to play in complementing the Darfur Peace Agreement. The meeting further concluded that the political process should be all-inclusive. The conclusions recognized that the current proliferation of initiatives must be streamlined and brought under one umbrella. To that end, the conclusions indicated that the United Nations and the African Union were best positioned to lead this process and called on international partners for support whenever appropriate.

27. The Council will recall that, pursuant to the Addis Ababa and Abuja agreements of November 2006, my predecessor appointed Jan Eliasson, former Swedish Minister for Foreign Affairs and former President of the General Assembly, as the Secretary-General's Special Envoy for Darfur, with the objective of re-energizing the political process. In agreement with African Union Commission Chairperson Konaré, he will undertake this challenging task in full partnership with African Union Special Envoy Salim Ahmed Salim. To help establish this close working relationship, I met with Mr. Salim and Mr. Eliasson in New York in early January to discuss the situation in Darfur and their future collaboration. During his stay in New York, Special Envoy Eliasson received briefings at the Secretariat and held consultations with representatives of a large number of Member States, including members of the Security Council.

28. I subsequently dispatched my Special Envoy to Addis Ababa to meet with the African Union leadership and discuss the joint African Union-United Nations endeavour to re-energize the political process. Special Envoy Eliasson then visited the Sudan from 9 to 12 January. During his stay in the Sudan he held talks with President Bashir and other officials of the Government of National Unity. The Special Envoy also met with Presidential Assistant Mini Minawi, who is the head of the SLM faction that signed the Darfur Peace Agreement on 5 May 2006. The initial response of the Sudanese Government to Special Envoy Eliasson's mission was positive. President Bashir acknowledged the futility of pursuing a military option to resolve the Darfur issue and declared the Government's preparedness to enter into peace talks on Darfur on the basis of the Darfur Peace Agreement. Special Envoy Eliasson also visited El Fasher, where he received briefings from local UNMIS and AMIS leadership. He also met some representatives of the non-signatories to the Darfur Peace Agreement, as well as internally displaced person representatives. Throughout his consultations, Special Envoy Eliasson emphasized the need for the level of violence to decrease, so as to allow the political process to move forward.

29. From 29 to 30 January, I attended the African Union summit in Addis Ababa. Special Envoy Eliasson joined me in meetings on the situation in Darfur with key African member States. African Union Commission Chairperson Konaré and I agreed that our Special Envoys would visit the Sudan from 11 to 17 February. During that visit they would continue discussions with Government officials and non-signatory field commanders on the ground in Darfur.

30. With regard to strengthening ceasefire mechanisms, the Joint Commission meeting held on 12 November in Addis Ababa approved the establishment of a "second chamber" to the Ceasefire Commission. This second chamber provides a forum for AMIS to hold discussions with Darfur Peace Agreement non-signatories and impress upon them their obligation to abide by pre-Darfur Peace Agreement ceasefire obligations and to facilitate humanitarian access in their areas of control. On 24 December, the second chamber held its first meeting in El Fasher, which was attended by representatives of the Sudanese Government, SLA-Abdul Wahid and JEM, as well as AMIS and the United Nations. At the meeting, which was chaired by the AMIS Force Commander (who is the Chairman of the Ceasefire Commission), all parties welcomed the establishment of the mechanism. On 15 December, a high-level Joint Commission meeting in Addis Ababa emphasized the importance of the urgent disarmament of armed militia and other effective measures to address the issue of violence in Darfur. It also addressed ceasefire violations and took measures to ensure accountability by signatories and non-signatories alike.

31. In a related development, on 27 December, members from the three non-signatory parties, the SLM-Abdul Wahid, SLM-Abdul Shafi and G19, announced their merger into one movement known as the SLM-Non-Signatory Factions. They also announced a cessation of hostilities unless attacked and reiterated their commitment to the N'Djamena Ceasefire Agreement. The Birmaza area in Northern Darfur, where their meeting took place, was bombed, however, two days after the meeting.

VI. United Nations support to the African Union Mission in the Sudan

32. The three-phased United Nations support package proposal was taken forward at the African Union Peace and Security Council (PSC) meeting held in Abuja on 30 November, when PSC endorsed the United Nations support package for AMIS and extended the mandate of AMIS for a further six months, from 1 January 2007.

33. To clarify some aspects regarding the implementation of the Addis and Abuja agreements, my predecessor wrote to President Bashir on 19 December. That letter was delivered by Ambassador Ahmedou Ould-Abdallah, who visited Khartoum as my predecessor's envoy. On 23 December, pursuant to his visit, the Government of the Sudan confirmed its acceptance of the three-phased approach to peacekeeping in Darfur.

34. The Council will recall that the first phase calls for a small number of advisers to join AMIS: 105 staff officers, 33 civilian police advisers and 48 civilian staff in both substantive and support areas. The plan also calls for the provision of some assets to AMIS: 8 fly-away kits, 36 global positioning systems, 360 night-vision goggles, 36 armoured personnel carriers and some equipment for use in public information campaigns. Deployment of these personnel and assets is well under way, but must now be accelerated. There are currently a total of 81 military and police officers deployed to Darfur under the "light support package".

35. The second phase—or "heavy" package—of United Nations support to AMIS was finalized during a second round of consultations undertaken in Addis Ababa between the African Union and United Nations teams on 20 and 21 January. During the discussions, it was agreed that the United Nations will provide a number of critical enabling capabilities to AMIS totalling 2,250 military personnel, including personnel dedicated to providing static camp protection; 3 formed police units and 301 individual police advisers, for a total of 721 civilian police; and 1,136 civilian personnel to undertake substantive tasks related to the implementation of the Darfur Peace Agreement (civil affairs, humanitarian affairs, public information, etc.) and provide support to administrative and management structures. The heavy package will also include equipment and support required for AMIS to reorganize its present structure from eight sectors to three.

36. The military capabilities include: one transport unit; four engineering units; one signal unit and one logistics unit; one level 2 hospital unit and one level 3 hospital unit; one reconnaissance unit providing three fixed-wing aircraft; one aviation unit providing six light tactical helicopters; and one aviation unit providing six utility helicopters. In accordance with the AMIS concept of operations, the six light tactical helicopters would act as force multipliers and assist in the protection of civilians at risk, AMIS and United Nations personnel, as well as equipment, installations and assets.

37. The police component of the heavy package envisages the deployment of three formed police units to complement AMIS civilian police in performing its tasks, which include: (a) protecting civilians and vulnerable communities under threat of violence, as well as United Nations and African Union personnel and facilities; (b) maintaining a 24-hour presence in internally displaced person camps; (c) performing escort duties (collection of firewood, grass and water); and (d) conducting confidence-building patrols.

38. Darfur has until recently been largely free of the threat of landmines; however, a rise in civilian casualties owing to landmines and unexploded ordnance has been registered, with four deaths and 11 injuries reported in just the first few weeks of 2007. Reports in early February also indicated that landmines may have been transported to El Geneina for use along the border with Chad and possibly on roads. AMIS has also reported unexploded ordnance in close proximity to scarce water sources and along patrol routes, posing a threat to civilians and AMIS peacekeepers. For these reasons, the second phase of United Nations support to AMIS will include a mine action component that will focus on information gathering, surveying routes used by AMIS and the local population, and explosive ordnance disposal.

39. Due to the evolving security situation in Darfur and the changes in the mandate and concepts of operations of AMIS, the requirements for the second phase of United Nations support to AMIS are significantly greater than those envisaged in the report of the former Secretary-General dated 28 July 2006 (S/2006/591). These requirements have been identified jointly by the United Nations and the African Union and, in accordance with the Addis Ababa and Abuja decisions of November 2006, reflect the deployment of the heavy package in anticipation of a hybrid African Union-United Nations peacekeeping operation.

40. An indicative preliminary breakdown of the financial implications of the second phase of United Nations support to AMIS by main categories of expenditure is provided in the annex to the present report. Following the Council's endorsement of the second phase of

United Nations support to AMIS, I intend to revert to the General Assembly to obtain authorization for the financing of this second phase.

41. African Union Commission Chairperson Konaré and I sent the details of the heavy support package to President Bashir on 24 January. While President Bashir reaffirmed in his letter dated 23 December 2006 to my predecessor the readiness of the Government of the Sudan to start immediately, through the tripartite committee, the implementation of the Addis Ababa conclusions and Abuja communiqué, I have asked the President to reiterate in writing his acceptance of the heavy support package. Thus far, the President has not responded.

42. All aspects of the hybrid operation, or the third and final phase of the three-phased approach, will be finalized in close consultation with the African Union. In the meantime, specialists from the African Union Commission and the United Nations met in Addis Ababa from 22 to 24 January with the objective of determining the basic framework of the hybrid operation. In particular, the consultations focused on the basic features of the mandate of the hybrid operation, force size, command and control arrangements, and force generation and funding requirements. These consultations produced a common understanding of the essential characteristics of the hybrid operation, providing a platform for joint African Union-United Nations efforts to finalize all related operational plans.

43. In December, the tripartite committee mechanism, consisting of representatives of the Sudanese Government, the African Union and the United Nations, began functioning. The mechanism was set up to facilitate the implementation of United Nations support to AMIS. It met in Khartoum three times during the reporting period. At the last meeting on 26 December, the Sudanese Government accepted that United Nations personnel deployed to assist AMIS in Darfur would wear United Nations blue berets and AMIS armbands.

44. While efforts to implement the three-phased approach continue, it will be critical that the current partners maintain their financial support to AMIS throughout the remainder of the AMIS mandate.

VII. Observations

45. The increase in violence and tension in Darfur during the months of November, December and January stretched the capacity of AMIS to the limit. The timely extension of the AMIS mandate needs to be followed by appropriate funding and staffing from the international community to enable it to function effectively. I appeal to donors to provide urgent support in all areas related to the Mission's continued operations and agreed expansion by two battalions. In addition, I appeal to Member States for urgent contributions of human resources and equipment needed for the United Nations light and heavy support packages for AMIS, in order to make possible the delivery of timely and effective reinforcements to AMIS. Of particular importance will be the enabling units described in section VI above.

46. I welcome the establishment of the second chamber of the Ceasefire Commission and the declaration of cessation of hostilities by some non-signatory groups as steps in the right direction. However, these declarations must be implemented on the ground and matched by reciprocal actions by all parties, in particular the Government of the Sudan. It is also critical that all armed militia be disarmed for the effort to succeed. I encourage the parties to use the second chamber mechanism as a means to facilitate a negotiated and inclusive political settlement to the crisis.

47. As long as violence and attacks continue in Darfur, the efforts to reach a political settlement will not succeed. I therefore call upon all parties to agree to and implement a cessation of hostilities and commit to the resumption of peace talks on the basis of the Darfur Peace Agreement. I also ask them to cooperate fully with my Special Envoy for Darfur and with the Special Envoy of the African Union in their joint efforts to facilitate a sustainable political solution.

48. I am distressed by the deteriorating humanitarian and security situation on the ground. All parties must cease violent attacks on civilians. I particularly deplore the aerial bombings by Sudanese Government forces, which have expanded to new areas since 16 January, resulting in more civilian casualties and suffering. When my Special Envoy visited Khartoum in early January, President Bashir affirmed that there can be no military solution to the conflict and reiterated his Government's commitment to a political process. In fulfilment of that commitment, I urge the Government to put an end to the aerial bombings and to take immediate action to hold accountable the perpetrators of attacks against civilians.

49. The violence of the last three months has had a further negative effect on humanitarian aid access and delivery in Darfur. The high levels of risk confronting humanitarian organizations in their day-to-day activities are becoming critical and may jeopardize the humanitarian presence in Darfur. This reinforces the urgent need for a ceasefire and an effective political process. I welcome the decision of the Government of the Sudan to extend the moratorium on restrictions for humanitarian work in Darfur by another year from February 2007. However, its "fast track" regulations must be put into practice to allow unhindered humanitarian access and to avoid the continuation of attacks and other incidents that perpetuate the killing, displacement and general insecurity in the Darfur region. At the same time, I view the 19 January incident in Nyala, in which local police and security officials arrested and physically abused international humanitarian staff, as unacceptable, and call on the Government to ensure that the perpetrators will be held accountable.

50. During my attendance at the African Union summit in Addis Ababa on 29 and 30 January, I had the opportunity to discuss a range of issues of common interest to the United Nations and the African Union with a number of African Heads of State, including African Union Commission Chairperson Konaré. I stressed that I regard Darfur as an issue of the highest priority.

51. In my meetings with Chairperson Konaré, we discussed the urgency of obtaining a cessation of hostilities and reinvigorating the peace process in Darfur. To this end, we considered how the work of our Special Envoys for Darfur, Jan Eliasson and Salim Ahmed Salim, could best be coordinated. I stressed to Chairperson Konaré that the United Nations intends to collaborate fully with the African Union in our efforts to put the peace process back on track, and that it was important to build upon the work that the African Union has already done in that regard. We agreed that Special Envoys Eliasson and Salim would work closely together. We also agreed that they would travel to Khartoum and Darfur from 11 to 17 February, in order to hold talks with Government officials and non-signatories of the Darfur Peace Agreement.

52. In Addis Ababa, I also had the opportunity to meet and hold frank discussions with President Bashir. While our views clearly differed on the gravity of the security situation in Darfur, the President reaffirmed his Government's agreement to the three-phased approach

endorsed by the 16 November high-level meeting in Addis Ababa and the meeting of the African Union Peace and Security Council on 30 November in Abuja. I view this as positive and intend to strongly encourage President Bashir to uphold his commitment.

53. We also discussed at length the final phase of the three-phased approach, or the joint African Union-United Nations hybrid operation. I reiterated the United Nations position in this regard, making it clear that it was essential to have a joint command and control structure acceptable to United Nations Member States contributing troops and police to the operation. I pointed out that United Nations financing may not otherwise be forthcoming. I also reiterated my predecessor's commitment to strive to maintain the African character of the hybrid operation as much as possible. However, I stressed that we would have to consider offers from other troop- and police-contributing countries if there was not sufficient African capacity. I look forward to receiving from the Government of the Sudan a confirmation of their readiness to implement both the heavy package of United Nations support to AMIS and the hybrid African Union-United Nations operation. In the meantime, the United Nations is proceeding with the preparatory work to implement these plans.

54. In conclusion, I appeal, in the strongest possible terms, to the Government of the Sudan and the other parties to desist from further hostilities, which destabilize the entire region and render peace an increasingly distant prospect. All parties must submit to dialogue and negotiation, and commit themselves to a non-military solution to the devastating conflict in Darfur.

Annex
Financial implications of the second phase of United Nations support to the African Union Mission in the Sudan

1. Further to paragraph 40 of my report on Darfur above, I wish to inform the Security Council that, based on the preliminary estimates of requirements for the full deployment of military personnel, United Nations police, formed police units and civilian personnel, the financial implication for the second phase of support that the United Nations could offer to the African Mission in the Sudan (AMIS) amounts to some $287.9 million on a full cost basis for a six-month period.

2. This preliminary projection of $287.9 million for the second phase of United Nations support to AMIS for a six-month period provides for a full deployment of 2,250 military personnel, 301 United Nations police and 3 formed police units, with each unit comprising of 140 formed police personnel. The projection also provides for the full deployment of 383 international and 561 national personnel, as well as 192 United Nations volunteers. Main items under operational costs in this preliminary projection of the second phase include: 1,147 units of prefabricated facilities and $60.1 million for various construction services provided under facilities and infrastructure; the acquisition of 511 units of light, medium and heavy vehicles provided under ground transportation; six-month rental of four aircraft (Let 410), six utility helicopters (MI-17) and six tactical helicopters (MI-25); the acquisition of various communications, information technology and medical equipment; and a $6.9 million provision for mine detection and mine clearing services.

3. An indicative preliminary breakdown of the financial implications for the second phase of United Nations support to AMIS is provided, for information purposes only, in the table below.

Table
Preliminary cost estimates for the second phase of United Nations support to the African Union Mission in the Sudan for a six-month period

(THOUSANDS OF UNITED STATES DOLLARS)

Category	*Cost estimates*
Military and police personnel	
Military observers	—
Military contingents	50 870.8
United Nations police	6 117.1
Formed police units	9 786.0
Subtotal	**66 773.9**
Civilian personnel	
International staff	29 982.8
National staff	4 143.8
United Nations Volunteers	5 402.2
Subtotal	**39 528.8**
Operational costs	
General temporary assistance	—
Government-provided personnel	—
Civilian electoral observers	—
Consultants	—
Official travel	323.4
Facilities and infrastructure	97 464.2
Ground transportation	18 249.9
Air transportation	23 710.3
Naval transportation	—
Communications	16 151.6
Information technology	9 952.3
Medical	4 769.4
Special equipment	1 101.8
Other supplies, services and equipment	9 951.5
Quick-impact projects	—
Subtotal	**181 674.4**
Gross requirements	**287 977.1**
Staff assessment income	3 683.9
Net requirements	**284 293.2**
Voluntary contributions in kind (budgeted)	
Total requirements	**287 977.1**

8. Report of the Secretary-General on the Sudan, 17 April 2007 (S/2007/213)

I. Introduction

1. The present report is submitted pursuant to paragraph 11 of Security Council resolution 1590 (2005), in which the Council requested that it be kept regularly informed of progress in the implementation of the Comprehensive Peace Agreement, respect for the ceasefire and implementation of the mandate of the United Nations Mission in the Sudan (UNMIS). The report also provides an assessment of the overall situation in the country since my previous progress report to the Council, dated 25 January 2007 (S/2007/42).

II. Implementation of the major elements of the Comprehensive Peace Agreement

2. During the period under review, the parties continued to make some, albeit limited, progress in the implementation of the Comprehensive Peace Agreement, including welcome steps towards the redeployment of Sudanese Armed Forces (SAF) from Southern Sudan. However several key issues, including the status of Abyei and the management of other armed groups, remained unresolved. There are increasing concerns about the timeline for elections scheduled for 2009, the disarmament, demobilization and reintegration programme and the demarcation of the 1 January 1956 border, which remain well behind schedule.

Security aspects

3. At the same time, the security situation in the UNMIS area of operations remained generally stable. The town of Malakal, which was the scene of heavy fighting in November 2006, has been calm but tense. In parts of Upper Nile State and the transitional areas there were several civil disturbances, related mainly to the non-payment of public sector salaries. Looting and ambushes perpetrated by rogue elements continued along arterial roads around Juba. On 26 January 2007, a United Nations peacekeeper was killed in an attack on a humanitarian demining team near Magwit, Eastern Equatoria. Elsewhere in Equatoria, reported activities of the Lord's Resistance Army (LRA) in March continued to undermine security.

4. Redeployment of the parties' armed forces is at a critical stage. Recently, SAF made visible progress in withdrawing from Southern Sudan, moving troops out of the conflict-prone district of Phom al-Zeraf in Upper Nile State and redeploying an air defence unit out of the Malakal area. However, to meet the 9 July deadline for their departure from Southern Sudan, SAF still has to complete its redeployment from Malakal and other important locations, including the oil-rich Bentiu area, where it has retained a concentration of forces. Meanwhile, the redeployment of the Sudan People's Liberation Army (SPLA) from Southern Kordofan and Blue Nile States has yet to begin.

5. While both parties have asserted their commitment to meeting the redeployment timelines set out in the Comprehensive Peace Agreement, the process is under pressure because of lengthy delays in implementing other security arrangements specified in the Agreement. According to the Comprehensive Peace Agreement, redeployment targets may be met

through the actual movement of forces, the transfer of troops into Joint Integrated Units or demobilization. According to those criteria, SAF has now redeployed 71 per cent of its forces; however, SPLA remains seriously concerned about the number of forces remaining in Southern Sudan, including former militia members now assigned to Joint Integrated Units. SPLA also questions the status of some 7,747 "voluntarily demobilized" soldiers, who continue to receive SAF salaries pending absorption into the much-delayed demobilization and reintegration programme.

6. Although there has been progress in the formation of Joint Integrated Units, delays in this area continue to undermine the fulfilment of the security protocol. SPLA redeployment is contingent upon the establishment of Joint Integrated Units, which so far have reached 77 per cent of their total projected strength, with 30,112 troops assigned out of the anticipated 39,000. In some areas, the two components of the Joint Integrated Units are co-located and have established good working relations, but in others, designated forces remain in their assembly areas some distance from the planned sites. Progress in this area has been especially slow in Southern Kordofan and Blue Nile States, owing partly to the severe logistical problems of SPLA. Overall, SPLA remains suspicious of SAF military intelligence activity within the units, while SAF argues that SPLA should accelerate its own redeployment to keep pace with the formation of Joint Integrated Units.

7. In a significant development, in February the parties agreed on a common military doctrine and code of conduct for the Joint Integrated Units, which the joint operational headquarters in Juba will now translate into practical activity. This offers some hope for the much-needed integration of the units, which to date have remained functionally divided, with each side retaining its own administration and command and control mechanisms.

8. In a related issue, the integration of other armed groups aligned with the parties also remains problematic. A number of groups formerly aligned with SAF have shifted their allegiance to SPLA and remain in Southern Sudan, while others have been absorbed into the SAF component of the Joint Integrated Units. Many are expected to undergo disarmament, demobilization and reintegration, the planning for which is progressing slowly. To overcome distrust, the parties must develop a joint strategy for managing other armed groups and for allowing the transparent verification of their numbers, which has so far proved challenging.

9. In sector 6 of UNMIS operations (which includes the disputed area of Abyei), the reporting period saw renewed shifts of allegiance among non-incorporated armed groups in Meiram and Debab. The overall heavy military presence in this area remains a source of concern, particularly as both parties reimposed restrictions on UNMIS movements on 28 February, affecting the Mission's monitoring and verification ability.

10. At the same time, the Ceasefire Joint Military Committee has worked effectively to tackle the security issues in its regular meetings. Meanwhile, the Ceasefire Political Commission met on 25 January for the first time since early November 2006 and agreed to hold a special session on security problems, including those related to other armed groups, redeployments and Joint Integrated Units. This meeting was held on 5 March; however the agenda item on Joint Integrated Units has twice been postponed. Overall, there remains a need for high-level political engagement to advance the security agenda.

Political aspects

11. While political parties are beginning to focus on preparations for the midterm elections, envisaged in the Comprehensive Peace Agreement to take place in 2009, development of the legislative framework and other prerequisites for the vote are well behind schedule. The National Constitutional Review Commission is now preparing for consultations on a draft elections law. Planning for the national census, which will determine the drawing of constituency boundaries, remains mired in budget difficulties. The pilot census project is now due to be completed by the end of April.

12. The most important piece of legislation passed during the reporting period was the Political Parties Act, which regulates the registration, operations and dissolution of political parties. The National Constitutional Review Commission held wide-ranging consultations with opposition parties and civil society, but the opposition National Democratic Alliance walked out of final discussion in protest of a clause allowing for the dissolution of political parties. The National Congress Party then introduced an amendment adding further requirements for party registration, and the bill was passed in the absence of the National Democratic Alliance. Opposition parties continued to voice concerns about the commitment of both Comprehensive Peace Agreement partners to a free and fair environment for elections.

13. The period under review witnessed some progress in the establishment of other CPA institutions. The National Civil Service Act and the National Civil Service Commission Act were enacted, and members of the Commission for the Protection of the Rights of Non-Muslims in the National Capital were appointed by presidential decree. At the same time, some key CPA-related legislation has yet to be put before the legislature, in particular the new National Security Act and the National Police Act. Meanwhile, the technical border committee expects to present its final report to the Presidency by October.

14. Meanwhile, the parties continue to reiterate their commitment to their partnership. On 25 March, the National Congress Party/SPLM Joint High Political Committee established a subcommittee to prepare a strategy for their partnership and to tackle contentious issues including Abyei, the performance of certain Comprehensive Peace Agreement commissions and the integration of other armed groups. Meanwhile, the SPLM Interim National Council met in Yei from 8 to 12 February, for the first time since the death of First Vice-President John Garang, in July 2005, and reasserted its commitment to make unity attractive. SPLM also decided to relocate its national headquarters from Juba to Khartoum, as part of a plan to revitalize its national and international network of offices.

15. At the Government of Southern Sudan level, President Salva Kiir continued to appoint and reassign personnel in the Government of Southern Sudan and southern state governments, which are now established but facing serious capacity constraints. A lack of qualified personnel continues to hinder the development of the judiciary in particular.

16. President Kiir also launched a major anti-corruption campaign. A number of senior officials, including the Minister of Finance, were relieved of their posts to answer charges of embezzlement and bribery, including the alleged embezzlement of $60 million transferred to the SPLM by the National Congress Party shortly after the signing of the Comprehensive Peace Agreement.

17. In both Southern Kordofan and Blue Nile States, newly established government structures gained some traction. Southern Kordofan State appointed a new constitutional Government on 27 February, replacing a caretaker administration. The terms of the incumbent governors in both States are likely to be extended until 1 July. While the two states have recently made some gains in the implementation of the Comprehensive Peace Agreement, SPLM-controlled areas within them remain administratively separate, with their own educational and police systems, in contravention of the Comprehensive Peace Agreement.

18. In Abyei, the absence of a civilian administration continued to complicate the search for durable peace. The Abyei Development Committee, a civil society group, which took control of a former civilian administration office on 14 January, continued its ad hoc operations despite its lack of legal status. The visit of President Omer al-Bashir to Southern Kordofan State and to Misseriya areas of sector 6 in early March and to Blue Nile State later in the month raised hopes of progress in developing those marginalized regions.

Wealth-sharing aspects

19. At the second Sudan Consortium meeting, held from 19 to 21 March, both the Government of Southern Sudan and the Government of National Unity gave an optimistic account of progress achieved in implementing the wealth-sharing provisions of the Comprehensive Peace Agreement. In reality, however, there has been little movement since the previous reporting period. While the joint technical committee on oil meets regularly to calculate oil revenues and shares, the lack of transparency continues to create mistrust, with both the Government of Southern Sudan and oil-producing states maintaining that they are not receiving their full entitlements. Meanwhile the National Petroleum Commission has not met in full session since 2005. Concerns remain about the severe impact of oil exploration on the population, including environmental degradation and lack of compensation for the displaced.

20. The Fiscal and Financial Allocation and Monitoring Commission also continued to face challenges in fulfilling its mandate to ensure the prompt and transparent allocation and transfer of funds to the lower levels of Government. Without strong political support, the Commission has found it difficult to generate change in the existing mechanisms for allocating resources, including the states' support fund, which should have been dissolved after the signing of the Comprehensive Peace Agreement.

III. Implementation of other peace processes in the Sudan

21. Implementation of the Eastern Sudan Peace Agreement, signed in October 2006, has stagnated, owing largely to internal power struggles within the leadership of the Eastern Front. A split among Beja factions of the Front prevented it from presenting a list of nominees for the posts allocated to it under the Agreement. The Eastern Front leadership has now requested mediation by the Government of Eritrea to help resolve the abiding conflict among the Beja factions. For its part, the Sudanese Government continued to express optimism about the implementation of the Agreement and has begun preparations for the disarmament and integration of former Eastern Front combatants.

22. Peace talks between the Government of Uganda and the Lord's Resistance Army remained suspended, with the latter rejecting the mediation of the Government of Southern

Sudan and saying it did not feel secure enough to resume talks in Juba. Meanwhile, the Cessation of Hostilities Agreement between the two sides expired on 28 February. My Special Envoy for the LRA-affected Areas, Joaquim Chissano, played an active role in the efforts aimed at restarting the talks, meeting with key stakeholders during his visit to the region in February and March. Talks are now expected to resume in April with an expanded mediation team, including observers from the Democratic Republic of the Congo, Kenya, Mozambique, South Africa and the United Republic of Tanzania.

23. In January UNMIS began transferring personnel and equipment to the African Union Mission in the Sudan (AMIS) under the "light support package" of assistance. As at 10 April, 37 military staff officers had been deployed (of 105 foreseen in the Agreement), as had 32 police advisers (of 33) and 23 civilian staff (of 48 projected). With the exception of medical and public information equipment and armoured personnel carriers, the logistical and material support provided for in the package was handed over on 11 January. The deployment of an additional 19 military and 19 civilian personnel who have been identified and recruited is pending the construction of office facilities and living accommodations that are compliant with United Nations safety and security standards in Darfur. This is a very serious issue, which UNMIS is currently attempting to address. There is also an outstanding requirement for contributions from Member States of 44 staff officers and 36 armoured personnel carriers. The tripartite committee continued to meet to facilitate the implementation of the package. The major barrier to the full implementation of the light support package, however, remains the lack of security in the face of inadequate infrastructure in Darfur.

24. The African Union and the United Nations completed consultations on the "heavy support package" of assistance on 21 January, and a joint report was transmitted to the Government of the Sudan on 24 January. The response on 6 March from President Al-Bashir challenged key provisions of the heavy support package. Details regarding the package, as agreed upon by the African Union and the United Nations, were communicated to the Government of the Sudan by the Secretary-General and the Chairperson of the African Union Commission in identical letters addressed to President Al-Bashir on 24 January. In his response, dated 6 March, President Al-Bashir accepted some aspects of the package and expressed reservations with regard to others, in particular as they related to the Darfur Peace Agreement, and he proposed further discussions to address them. As agreed during the mini-summit on Darfur held in Riyadh on 28 March, a technical consultative briefing was held by the United Nations and the African Union with the Government of the Sudan in Addis Ababa on 9 April in order to reiterate the rationale behind joint African Union/United Nations plans with regard to command and control, force generation, funding and other contentious issues and to finalize agreement on the heavy support package. The agreement on the heavy support package for AMIS was finalized at the meeting, with the exception of tactical/armed helicopters. Subsequent to a 12 April Security Council briefing on the outcome of the Addis Ababa meeting, the Permanent Mission of the Sudan to the United Nations, in a note verbale to the Secretary-General dated 16 April, confirmed the Government's approval of the helicopter component of the heavy support package. Following Security Council authorization of the deployment of the heavy support package, appropriate steps will be taken to seek the commitment authority required to cover its cost, which is estimated to be $287.9 million.

25. With regard to the African Union/United Nations hybrid operation, the agreed terms of reference for the joint special representative and a framework containing agreed principles for taking forward the preparations for the hybrid operation were communicated to President Al-Bashir in identical letters sent by the Secretary-General and the Chairperson of the African Union on 6 March. From 19 to 26 March, in Addis Ababa, African Union and United Nations multidisciplinary teams conducted joint planning for the hybrid operation in Darfur. The draft report is being reviewed by the United Nations Secretariat and the African Union Commission with a view to its being shared with the Security Council and the Peace and Security Council respectively.

IV. Implementation of the mandate of the United Nations Mission in the Sudan

Political support and reconciliation

26. Both at the level of the central Government and in the regions, UNMIS continued to provide good offices and mediation in support of the Comprehensive Peace Agreement. In Abyei, Mission staff worked actively and in close collaboration with local authorities and Misseriya community leaders to defuse persistent tension. In Malakal, UNMIS continued to engage all parties in support of the peaceful relocation of SAF and aligned groups from Phom al-Zeraf. Meanwhile, in Southern Kordofan, UNMIS, together with other United Nations agencies, actively supported local authorities in their efforts to reduce tension after clashes between local police and student demonstrators in Kadugli in February.

27. In Southern Sudan, UNMIS continued its work in support of efforts by local authorities to promote peace and reconciliation. In February, the Southern Sudan Peace Commission held a conference of governors and commissioners in Torit, Greater Equatoria, which was the first major region-wide peace conference. This event, held in collaboration with Pact Sudan, an international non-governmental organization, and in consultation with UNMIS, brought to light a number of local government concerns with the implementation of the Comprehensive Peace Agreement and laid important groundwork for further peace and reconciliation initiatives.

28. Simultaneously, UNMIS stepped up its engagement in efforts to reinvigorate the political process in Darfur in line with decisions taken at high-level consultations on Darfur held in Addis Ababa on 16 November 2006 and later confirmed by both the Security Council and the Peace and Security Council of the African Union. My Special Envoy for Darfur, Jan Eliasson, and the African Union Special Envoy, Salim Ahmed Salim, conducted two joint missions to the Sudan, meeting with all major stakeholders from the Government, opposition parties and rebel groups. Based on their contacts with key stakeholders, the Special Envoys are now developing a road map for the peace process in order to address the outstanding concerns raised by the non-signatories. UNMIS provided significant logistical and substantive support to the Envoys, as well as dedicated staff to the Joint Mediation Support Team.

Military deployment and activities

29. During the period under review, the UNMIS military component intensified its monitoring and verification activities in support of the ongoing redeployment process. In March the Mission's Force Commander convened special sessions of the Ceasefire Joint Military Commission to address discrepancies in data provided by the parties on the formation of

Joint Integrated Units and the alignment of other armed groups. UNMIS military personnel subsequently undertook an intensive verification of the composition and strength of the Joint Integrated Units.

30. As SAF forces continued to withdraw from Upper Nile State, UNMIS military personnel also played a significant role in fostering dialogue between military commanders and supervising confidence-building measures, particularly in Phom al-Zeraf. Tension in the area had eased noticeably by the end of the reporting period, following the successful redeployment of SAF forces and the incorporation of erstwhile other armed groups into the Joint Integrated Unit in Malakal.

31. The military component of UNMIS was active in undertaking civil-military cooperation tasks in local communities, including the provision of medical staff to clinics, the construction and grading of roads and the clearance of unexploded ordnance across all sectors. In a tragic incident on 26 January (see para. 3 above), an Indian peacekeeper was killed in a roadside ambush by unidentified attackers while providing protection to civilian demining contractors. While it appears that there is no regular threat in the area, the United Nations troops with armoured personnel carriers have since been redeployed to the area in order to increase security during demining operations.

32. Further progress was also made towards establishing new team sites in areas where a greater UNMIS presence is required. In this connection, suitable land was identified at Raga (Western Bahr Al Ghazal) and Baw (Blue Nile), and planning is under way to convert temporary team sites at Talodi and Jullud (Southern Kordofan) into permanent sites. Land has also been acquired in Al Fasher to accommodate staff officers associated with the light support package.

33. As at 10 April, 96.4 per cent of mandated UNMIS military personnel (9,363 out of a total of 9,706) had been deployed, including 595 United Nations military observers, 253 staff officers and 8,515 troops, in addition to 63 staff officers designated for deployment to AMIS under the light support package.

Disarmament, demobilization and reintegration

34. UNMIS, together with other United Nations agencies, continued to support the preregistration of 60,000 SAF soldiers nominated for disarmament, demobilization and reintegration in both the north and the south. Meanwhile, SPLA has identified 30,700 "non-essential" combatants to be preregistered for disarmament, demobilization and reintegration. UNMIS and its partners are already providing technical support to the northern and southern commissions responsible for planning disarmament, demobilization and reintegration programmes. However, the wider process remains hampered by a lack of meaningful engagement on the part of the parties in the principal disarmament, demobilization and reintegration mechanisms established by the Comprehensive Peace Agreement.

35. Coordination between the southern and northern disarmament, demobilization and reintegration commissions and the provision of direction to those bodies remain a major obstacle. The National Council for Disarmament, Demobilization and Reintegration Coordination, which is responsible for oversight, coordination and evaluation of the progress of the two commissions, had only its second meeting in March 2007, and it has made limited progress on strategic planning issues. This delay has hampered the functioning of

the commissions, which, despite support from UNMIS and other international partners, have yet to clarify the eligibility criteria and entitlements for the target groups.

36. Those factors have contributed to a disconnect in planning for disarmament, demobilization and reintegration and the process of SPLA transformation, as well as to problems with the demobilization of SAF-related militias in the south. More support, including international engagement with the National Council, will be required for the commissions to effectively implement their mandate.

37. Meanwhile, UNMIS has continued to provide assistance to the national and Southern Sudanese authorities on community security and arms control, including civilian disarmament efforts in Pibor County (Jonglei). Those issues pose challenges different from those of disarmament, demobilization and reintegration and need additional attention, including an integrated approach by which UNMIS, United Nations partners and local authorities can jointly tackle the intersection between arms control and livelihood issues.

Electoral assistance

38. In late January, the National Constitutional Review Commission confirmed its willingness to engage in a broad consultative process and established two subcommittees to liaise with political parties and other actors at the state level, while a third committee was recently formed to consider submissions from all stakeholders prior to preparing a draft election law. The Commission and the Presidency confirmed that the election bill would be submitted to the National Assembly in 2007, during either the April or October sessions.

39. The Mission continued to actively track legislative developments. Through various workshops, including on women's participation in elections, the Mission's election task force advocated for a fair and enabling environment for the electoral process. UNMIS also supported efforts aimed at legislative reform to promote an appropriate setting for the elections through regular meetings with the Secretary-General of the National Constitutional Review Commission and interaction with the chairpersons of the specialized committees of the Commission. It also provided an integrated approach and represented the Mission in external mechanisms such as the monthly election donor group meetings and informal parliamentary working group meetings.

Police

40. As at 10 April, UNMIS had deployed its 653 police officers, representing 91 per cent of the Mission's authorized strength.

41. In an attempt to address the pressing need for policing in camps for internally displaced persons, particularly with regard to crimes against women and children, UNMIS initiated a community policing programme, together with Government police at camps for internally displaced persons in Khartoum, Kauda (Southern Kordofan) and Kurmuk (Blue Nile). Training and workshops associated with this project began in March. Meanwhile, UNMIS also established special investigation units in its sector offices in Juba, Wau and Malakal to focus on improving conditions and reviewing the justification for the detention of prisoners in coordination with the Government of Southern Sudan.

42. UNMIS police consolidated and expanded its programme of co-location with the National Police and the Southern Sudan Police Service (SSPS). The Mission assisted the

two services in developing and seeking funding for approved training plans. In Southern Sudan, UNMIS continued the major undertaking of registering SSPS officers, with some 10,464 registered to date. UNMIS also assisted SSPS in identifying an organizational structure and supported the development of a draft Southern Sudan Police Service bill. The training programme and curriculum have been finalized with the leadership of SSPS. Recognizing the need to develop SSPS credibility as an alternative to the military in maintaining law and order, the Government of Southern Sudan Interior Ministry has also requested training in crowd control and maintenance of public order.

Human rights

43. In the area of human rights, the Mission continued its monitoring and capacity-building activities. In particular, with regard to the establishment of a national human rights institution, UNMIS supported broad-based discussions of the draft National Human Rights Commission act, including through a workshop for parliamentarians held on 20 January, and provided technical experts to the Southern Sudan Human Rights Commission as it prepared its enabling legislation and programmes.

44. While the members of the Southern Sudan Human Rights Commission have been appointed, the enabling law for the Commission has not been finalized. The Government of Southern Sudan needs to enact this important law, make available appropriate financial support and ensure the Commission's independence, in keeping with international standards. It will be important for United Nations agencies, donors and the wider international community to provide additional assistance to help implement the Commission's strategic plan.

45. UNMIS also facilitated workshops for the National Assembly's Human Rights Committee on the reform of laws concerning sexual violence and on parliamentary cooperation with civil society, and held a series of human rights training sessions for Government police in Khartoum.

Rule of law

46. UNMIS continued to support all parties involved in the development of new legislation related to the Comprehensive Peace Agreement, especially the Political Parties Act. The Mission organized workshops in Southern Sudan on the role of political parties in the electoral process and on good governance and the rule of law. In Khartoum, the Mission assisted in training organized by the Government of National Unity Ombudsman regarding administration oversight and supported workshops on juvenile justice.

47. UNMIS continued to advocate for corrections reform in the Sudan. In a welcome development, the national Interior Ministry agreed in principle to separate the prison system from the unified police force. In Southern Sudan, UNMIS completed the registration of prison staff in Central Equatoria and Lakes States and organized several training activities. The uncoordinated absorption of SPLA soldiers into the prison service remains a challenge, as do chronic gaps in capacity.

Public information

48. UNMIS radio (Radio Miraya-FM) further expanded its transmission network in an effort to transmit reliable and accessible information about the peace process to a wider audience in the Sudan. The Mission opened a new repeater station in Rumbek in January, and work is set to begin on four additional stations to enable Radio Miraya to broadcast in

remote areas of Western and Eastern Equatoria States. In addition to news and Comprehensive Peace Agreement-related programming, some primary educational programmes will begin broadcasting in April. In the absence of an agreement to air in the north, Radio Miraya is negotiating with Khartoum State radio to have it carry some of its programmes.

49. The Mission continued to deliver Comprehensive Peace Agreement workshops and outreach presentations at the community and government levels and to organize visits by journalists from northern Sudan to UNMIS and United Nations agency projects in the south and in transitional areas. UNMIS also continued to cooperate closely with AMIS in the sphere of public information and deployed two public information officers to Darfur under the light support package.

Humanitarian assistance

50. By mid-March, the United Nations workplan for the Sudan, which required $1.8 billion in funding for both humanitarian and recovery assistance in 2007, was 32 per cent funded, with over $580 million pledged. Donors had also pledged some $130 million to the Common Humanitarian Fund. The first tranche of $80 million was allocated to the regions with the most critical needs; Southern Sudan received the largest amount, to support the return of refugees and displaced persons before the onset of the rainy season, followed by Darfur.

51. An outbreak of meningitis reached epidemic levels, spreading to 8 of the 10 states in Southern Sudan as well as to Abyei. Returns of internally displaced persons and refugees were put on hold in several areas, including repatriations from Uganda. A vaccination campaign is ongoing, and the epidemic is now under control. The World Food Programme assisted 100,000 beneficiaries in Southern Sudan during the month of February. Although the annual needs and livelihoods assessment for Southern Sudan indicates that food security should improve in 2007, the United Nations estimates that 108,000 tons of food aid will still be required by 1.3 million people in the year, 60 per cent of which will be required by the chronically food-insecure households during the April to July "hunger season".

52. The humanitarian situation in Darfur has suffered from persistent violence and overall insecurity. Over 2 million people are now internally displaced, and their numbers continue to rise, while 1.9 million conflict-affected residents remain largely dependent on external aid. Approximately 107,000 civilians were newly displaced by insecurity and fighting between 1 January and 1 April. At the same time, humanitarian access in Darfur continues to be curtailed by a mixture of insecurity, targeted attacks on humanitarian workers and their assets and bureaucratic impediments. On 28 March the Government signed a joint communiqué with the United Nations, which represents a recommitment to the moratorium on restrictions for humanitarian access that entered into force in 2004. It is hoped that this will address the increasing bureaucratic delays experienced by non-governmental organizations working in Darfur. The communiqué also established a high-level committee to ensure proper implementation of the agreement.

53. In recognition of the serious humanitarian challenges in the Sudan, the recently appointed Emergency Relief Coordinator and Under-Secretary-General for Humanitarian Affairs, John Holmes, visited the country from 20 to 27 March, travelling to Khartoum, Juba and Government- and rebel-held areas in Darfur, and meeting with Government of National Unity and Government of Southern Sudan officials, humanitarian agencies and non-governmental organizations, affected populations and tribal leaders.

Protection of civilians

54. In recent months, some progress has been made with regard to the protection of civilians in Southern Sudan, including in Phom al-Zeraf, Tonga, Kaldak and surrounding areas prior to and following the SAF redeployment. However, conflict over land and cattle continues to generate serious protection challenges. UNMIS has verified reports of Murle raids in Jonglei State in which over 150 children were reported to have been abducted since January. During her visit to the Sudan in early February, my Special Representative for Children and Armed Conflict, Radhika Coomaraswamy, urged all parties to release children associated with armed groups.

55. UNMIS also identified protection concerns arising from the use of SPLA forces to enforce law and order. The normalization of civilian life and the strengthening of civilian authority were further complicated by insecurity associated with LRA in Equatoria.

Returns

56. The strong cooperation established between the Government of National Unity, the Government of Southern Sudan and United Nations agencies began to bear fruit, with the first organized returns of internally displaced persons from Khartoum to Southern Kordofan and Southern Sudan. By mid-April some 20,000 internally displaced persons had been assisted to return to their places of origin in five separate operations, and 25,000 refugees returned home from five neighbouring countries. While those movements started later than anticipated, they proceeded relatively smoothly. However, the total number of assisted returns are to date short of the target, owing partly to delays in establishing departure facilities in Khartoum, less than expected participation among registered internally displaced persons and delayed financing by the Government of National Unity and the Government of Southern Sudan.

57. The United Nations continued to monitor the living conditions of internally displaced persons in Khartoum through community-based mechanisms, assessments and dialogue with the relevant authorities. In Darfur, the current situation is not conducive to facilitated returns.

Mine action

58. UNMIS mine action teams have made considerable progress during the current dry season. To date, over 10 million square metres of suspected dangerous areas have been demined, and some 2,700 anti-personnel mines, 1,100 anti-tank mines and 590,000 pieces of unexploded ordnance and small arms ammunition have been cleared. UNMIS and the United Nations Children's Fund (UNICEF) have provided mine-risk education to over 1 million people in affected areas, as well as in camps and way stations for internally displaced persons, in an attempt to sensitize those returning to the risk of mines and unexploded ordnance. Over 1,300 kilometres of roads have been verified or cleared for emergency deployment and aid delivery, including several return routes.

59. In coordination with UNMIS mine action activities, the United Nations Development Programme (UNDP) trained five joint integrated demining unit teams, thus achieving the first benchmark for local mine action capacity development in the Sudan.

Recovery and reconstruction

60. The second meeting of the Sudan Consortium was held from 19 to 21 March in Khartoum and Juba. Donors made it clear that they would not be able to continue to finance

recovery and development efforts in the north unless there was progress in Darfur, which would have direct implications for support for the "three areas" (Abyei, Southern Kordofan and Blue Nile). It was recognized at the Sudan Consortium that the Government of Southern Sudan had made significant progress in 2006 in terms of the establishment of institutions at all levels, evidence of more active accountability and expanded capacity-building efforts. However, priorities will need to focus on building public institutions for good governance and establishing basic infrastructure links, enabling productive activities and delivering basic services. Donors also called for a review of aid mechanisms, including the establishment of new priorities and costing for the second phase of the original joint assessment mission.

61. Positive preliminary discussions were held with both the Government of National Unity and the Government of Southern Sudan on the establishment of "second windows" to the funds administered by UNDP, intended to speed up the disbursement and implementation of early recovery and reintegration initiatives through the multi-donor trust funds.

Gender

62. Pursuant to Security Council resolution 1325 (2000) and relevant provisions of the Comprehensive Peace Agreement, UNMIS provided technical support and capacity-building to the Government of National Unity and the Government of Southern Sudan ministries responsible for integrating gender perspectives into key legislation. In Khartoum, the Ministry of Social Welfare has submitted for adoption its final draft national gender policy to the Government. UNMIS also continued to support women's organizations seeking to achieve a 30 per cent target for women's representation in the Government of National Unity and a 25 per cent target in the Government of Southern Sudan. Within the Mission, UNMIS promoted gender mainstreaming through training for all staff and the establishment of a system of gender focal points in various Mission components.

HIV/AIDS

63. UNMIS continued to deliver peer HIV/AIDS training, graduating 104 new educators during the period under review, bringing the total to 359. Peer educator training targeted military, youth and women's associations, and the new batch of graduates will support SPLA and the Southern Sudan disarmament, demobilization and reintegration commission. HIV/AIDS sensitization among UNMIS peacekeepers was maintained at 90 per cent. In addition, UNDP, together with other United Nations agencies and non-governmental organizations, continued its efforts to address the HIV/AIDS problem, mainly as part of the Global Fund initiative.

Conduct and discipline

64. Since my previous report, 22 allegations of misconduct have been reported, including two serious cases, which were referred to the Office of Internal Oversight Services for investigation.

65. Following international media reports of alleged sexual exploitation and abuse by United Nations peacekeepers in Juba, UNMIS leadership re-energized the Mission's effort to enforce the United Nations zero-tolerance policy. In January and February, two workshops were organized with Government and civil society representatives in Khartoum and Juba to explain the prevention and reporting mechanisms as well as the disciplinary action

that would be taken against personnel found guilty of misconduct. In the meantime, a task force was established under the National Council for Child Welfare (Khartoum) with UNMIS, UNICEF and other national actors, which will undertake joint preventive and outreach activities. A similar body will be established in Juba with the Government of Southern Sudan.

Mission decentralization

66. As anticipated in the last report, in order to increase the effectiveness of the Mission's operations in Southern Sudan, UNMIS is moving forward with a phased programme of regionalization focusing on a further strengthening of its regional office in Juba. The aim of this process is to enable the office to deliver increased and more efficient support, services and programmes in Southern Sudan and to facilitate local decision-making. The need for this decentralization programme arises first from a series of logistical, administrative and operational challenges faced during the deployment phase in Southern Sudan and second from a growing need for closer daily interaction with the Government of Southern Sudan.

67. The delegation of substantial managerial, administrative and financial authority to the Juba office is well under way. The Mission has created a new post of head of sector 1 (Juba), within existing resources, to enable the Regional Coordinator to coordinate all Mission activities in Southern Sudan, focus on regional issues, represent the Head of Mission on a day-to-day basis with the Government of Southern Sudan and facilitate substantive and managerial oversight of sectors 1, 2 and 3. The Deputy Director of Administration has been relocated to Juba to head a strengthened support component, ensuring that sector offices 1, 2 and 3 are supported directly from the regional office in Juba. Over the next few months, the Mission will expand its office and living accommodation in Juba to cater to the additional staff being assigned there. Similarly, the Mission will continue the process of decentralization throughout its area of responsibility by delegating authority to transitional areas in sectors 4 (Kadugli), 5 (Blue Nile) and 6 (Abyei), as well as to the Darfur office. In Darfur in particular, decentralization will facilitate the deployment of the support packages to AMIS and help prepare the ground for the future deployment of the hybrid mission.

Civilian staffing

68. UNMIS has now substantially overcome its initial difficulty in recruiting and retaining well-qualified personnel. Civilian staff strength rose from 796 to 918 international staff (of a projected total of 1,139 posts), from 2,265 to 2,416 national staff (of a total of 3,342 posts) and 172 to 190 United Nations Volunteers (of a total of 231 posts).

V. Impediments in mandate implementation

69. The challenges described in my previous report persist, with the activities of the Mission hampered by both security constraints and logistical and bureaucratic impediments. The security environment in the Sudan continues to be very complicated, volatile and dependent on a variety of medium- to high-risk internal and external factors. In recent months, the Mission worked hard to enhance the security of its staff and installations through a range of additional and sustainable protective security measures. In Darfur, insecurity remains the major factor limiting the expansion of United Nations operations and support for AMIS. The ceasefire remains tenuous, and armed attacks and looting are on the increase.

70. On 19 January personnel from the United Nations, AMIS and international non-governmental organizations were arrested and detained by national security and local police while attending a gathering at a non-governmental organization guesthouse in Nyala (South Darfur). During the arrest and detention, several individuals, including five United Nations staff members, were physically assaulted with batons and rifles, and a female staff member was subjected to sexual harassment. Upon their release, criminal proceedings were initiated against the United Nations personnel but were later suspended pending review by the Government of National Unity Ministry of Justice. The United Nations has initiated its own board of inquiry to investigate the incident. While the Government had committed itself to cooperating with the United Nations in the investigation, no information has thus far been shared.

71. In the meantime, UNMIS and several agencies continued to face serious obstacles to their operations in Darfur, mainly in North Darfur, where personnel were regularly stopped when travelling, in contravention of the status-of-forces agreement.

72. UNMIS remains very concerned about breaches of the Government's commitments under the status-of-forces agreement. The reporting period saw an increase in interference with United Nations flight operations and customs clearance throughout the Sudan. In high-level meetings, the Government has pledged to address these recurring problems; however, there has not yet been any discernible change.

VI. Financial implications

73. The General Assembly, by its resolution 60/122 B, appropriated the amount of $1,079,534,400, equivalent to $89,961,200 per month, for UNMIS for the period from 1 July 2006 to 30 June 2007. Should the Security Council decide to extend the mandate of UNMIS beyond 30 April 2007, the cost of maintaining the Mission until 30 June 2007 would be limited to the amounts approved by the Assembly.

74. As at 31 December 2006, unpaid assessed contributions to the Special Account for UNMIS amounted to $283 million. The total outstanding assessed contributions for all peacekeeping operations as at that date amounted to $1.76 million.

75. Troop costs and contingent-owned equipment costs have been reimbursed for the period ending 31 January 2007 and 31 December 2006 respectively.

VII. Observations

76. As the members of the Security Council will recall, my previous report indicated that the implementation of the Comprehensive Peace Agreement was about to enter a critical phase. The two parties have weathered the first third of the interim period and have continued to make progress against considerable odds, including the untimely death of one of the Agreement's supreme architects, John Garang, continued mistrust and a still considerable number of spoilers. In addition, the ongoing conflict in Darfur remains a source of disagreement between the parties and has diverted the attention of the international community.

77. The implementation of the Comprehensive Peace Agreement has reached a delicate stage, at which either the point of departure or the destination could easily be lost. However, two critical reference points bind this middle phase of the interim period, namely, the full and verified redeployment of forces in 2007 and the holding of free and fair midterm

elections in 2009. Everything in reason should be done to successfully reach these important markers, which will help the parties to consolidate the gains made thus far and to embark on the final stretch of the peace process.

78. Until now, UNMIS has focused much of its attention and resources on assisting the parties to implement the Comprehensive Peace Agreement as well as on monitoring and observing the ceasefire, with measurable results. Although the parties have yet to agree on a shared strategic approach to security, including the development of Joint Integrated Units, they have so far acted to manage and de-escalate tensions on the ground. This process of cooperation and problem-solving will need to intensify as the two armed forces approach the larger strategic challenge of complete redeployment.

79. The completion of this vital redeployment process is likely to present several serious challenges in the months ahead. First, the parties must remain firmly committed to the details of the redeployment plans and accept the reality and far-reaching implications of their implementation. This process will require serious political engagement by both parties. Once completed, however, the redeployment will signify a historic end to a three-decade-old pattern of gross military interference and devastating hostilities.

80. With the assistance of the United Nations, the parties must now devote considerable attention to verification of the process. If and when disagreements emerge, they will need to be handled and resolved through the pertinent institutions without jeopardizing overall progress or compromising the integrity of the process. The conclusion of redeployment, which also requires transparency and progress in the integration of other armed groups and the development of Joint Integrated Units, will embody the parties' rejection of a military solution to the conflict that has divided them.

81. Fundamental to meeting all of these challenges is the parties' recognition that the destructive stalemate, which finally led to the momentous compromises reached in Naivasha, Kenya, two and half years ago, remains a lose-lose scenario. The full and irreversible implementation of the Comprehensive Peace Agreement is the only viable strategy for the Sudan and its peoples.

82. While the main responsibility for the completion of the security protocol lies with the two parties, they will require the full engagement and support of the international community. In this connection, I urge the Security Council and all concerned Member States to help the Sudanese honour their commitments under the Comprehensive Peace Agreement. Financial and other assistance from donors will be especially needed in the areas of Joint Integrated Unit development, disarmament, demobilization and reintegration programming and community security, based on meaningful security sector reform.

83. The second marker in this phase of the interim period—the preparation for and holding of democratic midterm elections in 2009—will require equal determination. The elections will be a crucial affirmation of the Naivasha promise to make the Comprehensive Peace Agreement an inclusive process, based on the will of the Sudanese people. The immediate focus of this endeavour should be on the long-overdue enactment of the elections law, to be followed by the prompt establishment of an independent National Election Commission. It is imperative that the National Constitutional Review Commission continue to drive the drafting process for those bills, based on broad and inclusive consultations. Other important prerequisites to effective planning and preparation for elections are an agreement on

the boundaries of Abyei and the 1 January 1956 border, the organization of a census and the repatriation of displaced persons.

84. It is equally important to recognize that free and fair elections do not begin at the ballot box; the time has come for tangible progress to be made on lifting restrictions on political opposition and civil society and in bringing the police and security services in line with the requirements of the Interim National Constitution. In this connection, I regret that the National Human Rights Commission has not yet been established. I urge the Government to do this quickly and in full compliance with the Paris Principles relating to the status of national institutions, as endorsed by the General Assembly in its resolution 48/134. In particular, I recommend that the composition of the Commission ensure the pluralistic representation of all social forces in civil society that contribute to the promotion and protection of human rights.

85. Support for the electoral process will also require a nimble adjustment of United Nations and international resources, allowing for the rapid build-up of technical assistance and monitoring capacity, as well as intensive engagement with civil society and political actors. In addition to the Government of the Sudan, I urge donors to plan now for the contributions they can make, including for the strengthening of the capacity of political parties, the media and civil society organizations, all of which have important roles to play in the process.

86. In preparing for the elections, the parties must also pay very close attention to the situations in Southern Kordofan, Abyei and Blue Nile and reach understanding on all outstanding issues related to those regions. I trust that the international community will lend its support to such efforts, mindful of the need for the eventual referendum for Abyei and the "popular consultation" for the other two areas, in accordance with the Comprehensive Peace Agreement.

87. Finally, I urge the Sudanese people, and particularly their leaders, to recognize that ultimately, peace in their country is indivisible. Without a resolution to the tragic and devastating conflict in Darfur, continued progress in and eventually a successful conclusion of the Comprehensive Peace Agreement will be hard to achieve. While troop redeployments can proceed without immediate impact on the situation in Darfur, the same is not true for the country-wide preparations necessary for successful midterm elections in 2009. Peace and stability throughout the country remain a fundamental requirement for elections. As the Security Council considers the future of the Sudan, I urge members to pursue an integrated approach in which an international strategy for peace in Darfur is reinforcing the implementation of the Comprehensive Peace Agreement. The paramount goal for international complementary efforts in the areas of security, political and humanitarian assistance must be to stabilize Darfur sufficiently so that its residents are able to participate in the 2009 midterm elections along with the rest of the country.

88. Peace in the Sudan will also require sustained attention to post-conflict recovery and development. Again, there can be little progress in the north, including the three areas, without an improvement in the situation in Darfur. In addition to supporting peace throughout the Sudan, donors will need to continue to meet the pledges they made at Oslo and prepare for additional commitments in 2008 and beyond to support the second phase of the joint assessment mission. Seeing those commitments through will be critical to realizing the joint pledge made at the meeting of the Sudan Consortium to make 2007 the year for the delivery of peace dividends.

89. For its part, the United Nations will do its utmost to contribute to the cause of peace throughout the Sudan, including through its full support to the implementation of the Comprehensive Peace Agreement, the Darfur Peace Agreement and other major decisions. In this connection, I would like to recommend that the mandate of UNMIS be extended for six months, until 31 October 2007.

90. In conclusion, I wish to express my gratitude to all United Nations personnel working in the Sudan for their determined effort to support the implementation of the Comprehensive Peace Agreement and to end the conflict in Darfur. I am also very appreciative of the efforts of the African Union—with whom the United Nations is cooperating very closely—as well as the invaluable assistance provided by Member States, including donors and troop- and police-contributing countries.

Annex
Military and police component as at 10 April 2007

	Military component									
	Observers		*Staff officers*		*Troops*		*Military subtotal*		*Civilian police*	
Country	*Male*	*Female*	*Male*	*Female*	*Male*	*Female*	*Male*	*Female*	*Male*	*Female*
Argentina	—	—	—	—	—	—	—	—	11	—
Australia	5	1	5	4	—	—	10	5	9	1
Bangladesh	20	—	31	—	1 503	—	1 554	—	27	—
Belgium	5	—	—	—	—	—	5	—	—	—
Benin	7	—	—	—	—	—	7	—	—	—
Bolivia	15	—	1	—	—	—	16	—	—	—
Bosnia and Herzegovina	—	—	—	—	—	—	—	—	2	—
Botswana	5	—	—	—	—	—	5	—	—	—
Brazil	24	—	—	—	—	—	24	—	3	—
Cambodia	10	—	1	—	134	—	145	—	—	—
Canada	23	—	7	—	—	—	30	1	1	1
China	14	—	11	—	424	11	449	11	7	2
Croatia	—	—	5	—	—	—	5	—	—	—
Denmark	10	—	6	—	—	—	16	—	2	—
Ecuador	20	—	—	—	—	—	20	—	—	—
Egypt	20	—	21	—	781	15	822	15	2	—
El Salvador	5	—	—	—	—	—	5	—	4	2
Fiji	7	—	—	—	—	—	7	—	4	3
Finland	—	—	2	—	—	—	2	—	2	—
Gabon	6	—	—	—	—	—	6	—	—	—
Gambia	—	—	1	—	—	—	1	—	4	—
Germany	33	—	5	—	—	—	38	—	5	—
Ghana	—	—	3	—	—	—	3	—	35	3
Greece	4	—	2	—	—	—	6	—	—	—
Guatemala	8	—	1	—	—	—	9	—	—	—
Guinea	10	—	—	—	—	—	10	—	—	—

Continued

	Military component									
	Observers		*Staff officers*		*Troops*		*Military subtotal*		*Civilian police*	
Country	*Male*	*Female*	*Male*	*Female*	*Male*	*Female*	*Male*	*Female*	*Male*	*Female*
India	20	—	27	—	2 577	4	2 624	4	20	2
Indonesia	10	—	—	—	—	—	10	—	—	—
Jamaica	—	—	—	—	—	—	—	—	3	2
Jordan	12	—	9	—	—	—	21	—	23	2
Kenya	6	1	10	—	776	32	795	33	18	2
Kyrgyzstan	5	3	—	—	—	—	5	3	2	—
Malawi	6	—	1	—	—	—	7	—	—	—
Malaysia	8	—	3	—	—	—	11	—	11	—
Mali	9	—	—	—	—	—	9	—	—	—
Moldova	2	—	—	—	—	—	2	—	—	—
Mongolia	2	—	—	—	—	—	2	—	—	—
Mozambique	1	—	—	—	—	—	1	—	—	—
Namibia	9	—	—	—	—	—	9	—	1	—
Nepal	6	2	6	—	—	—	12	2	55	2
Netherlands	14	—	3	—	—	—	17	—	14	1
New Zealand	2	—	1	—	—	—	3	—	—	—
Nigeria	10	—	5	1	—	—	15	1	29	2
Norway	16	—	11	—	—	—	27	—	4	—
Pakistan	20	—	26	—	1 538	—	1 584	—	36	2
Paraguay	10	—	—	—	—	—	10	—	—	—
Peru	17	—	—	—	—	—	17	—	—	—
Philippines	13	—	—	—	—	—	13	—	52	—
Poland	2	—	—	—	—	—	2	—	—	—
Republic of Korea	7	—	1	—	—	—	8	—	—	—
Romania	12	—	—	—	—	—	12	—	—	—
Russian Federation	15	—	3	—	120	—	138	—	11	—
Rwanda	15	—	8	—	254	—	277	—	24	—
Samoa	—	—	—	—	—	—	—	—	16	—
South Africa	—	—	4	—	—	—	4	—	—	—
Sri Lanka	3	—	—	—	—	—	—	—	22	1
Sweden	3	—	1	—	—	—	4	—	13	2
Thailand	12	—	1	—	—	—	13	—	—	—
Turkey	—	—	4	—	—	—	4	—	27	—
Uganda	9	—	—	—	—	—	9	—	17	3
Ukraine	4	—	—	—	—	—	4	—	23	—
United Kingdom	—	—	4	—	—	—	4	—	2	—
United Republic of Tanzania	15	—	2	—	—	—	17	—	2	—

	Military component									
	Observers		*Staff officers*		*Troops*		*Military subtotal*		*Civilian police*	
Country	*Male*	*Female*	*Male*	*Female*	*Male*	*Female*	*Male*	*Female*	*Male*	*Female*
United States	—	—	—	—	—	—	—	—	9	2
Uruguay	—	—	—	—	—	—	—	—	2	—
Vanuatu	—	—	—	—	—	—	—	—	6	—
Yemen	16	—	3	—	—	—	19	—	3	—
Zambia	10	2	11	—	306	39	327	41	21	1
Zimbabwe	12	2	2	—	—	—	14	2	22	11
Total pergender	**584**	**11**	**248**	**5**	**8414**	**101**	**9246**	**117**	**606**	**47**
Total	**595**		**253**		**8515**		**9363**		**653**	

9. Report of the Secretary-General on Darfur, 27 July 2007 (S/2007/462)

I. Introduction

1. The present report is submitted pursuant to paragraphs 6, 13 and 16 of Security Council resolution 1556 (2004), paragraph 15 of resolution 1564 (2004), paragraph 17 of resolution 1574 (2004) and paragraph 12 of resolution 1590 (2005). It covers the period from early January through July 2007. Some of the aspects of the situation in Darfur were covered in the report of the Secretary-General and the Chairperson of the African Union Commission on the hybrid operation in Darfur (S/2007/307/Rev.1), issued on 5 June.

II. Insecurity in Darfur

2. In recent months, the overall security situation in Darfur has been characterized by continual violence and insecurity. The nature of that insecurity, however, differed in the three states of the region. Western Darfur suffered from cross-border tensions between Chad and the Sudan, including direct hostilities in early April. Northern Darfur remained heavily affected by the conflict between the Government of the Sudan and the Darfur Peace Agreement non-signatory factions, particularly in the areas north of El Fasher and in Jebel Marra, while in Southern Darfur persistent tribal conflict also continued to result in violent attacks. In a disturbing development, elements of the two signatories to the Darfur Peace Agreement, namely the Government of the Sudan and the Minni Minawi faction of the Sudan Liberation Movement/Army (SLM/A), clashed on several occasions in March. The most significant security development of the reporting period, however, was the increasing violence against the African Union Mission in the Sudan (AMIS) and the United Nations Mission in the Sudan (UNMIS), as well as the broader United Nations and international non-governmental organization community in Darfur.

3. I am deeply saddened to inform the Council that the United Nations lost its first peacekeeper in Darfur on 25 May, when Lieutenant Colonel Ehab Nazih, an Egyptian military officer deployed to Darfur as part of the United Nations light support package, was murdered at his residence in El Fasher. The exact circumstances of the attack are still under investigation; however, it is known that late in the evening on 25 May, three armed men broke into the private house shared by Lieutenant Colonel Nazih and seven other UNMIS military, police and civilian staff, and took money and valuables from the occupants before shooting Lieutenant Colonel Nazih. He was rushed to the AMIS level II hospital, where he was pronounced dead on 26 May 2007. I wish to extend my deepest condolences to the family of Lieutenant Colonel Nazih as well as to the Government of Egypt, and to salute a peacekeeper who perished in the service of peace.

4. The UNMIS Coordinator in El Fasher, with the cooperation of the UNMIS Force Commander and the Department of Safety and Security of the Secretariat, is overseeing efforts to ensure a thorough investigation and tightened security measures for the safety of United Nations personnel.

5. In addition to the killing of Lieutenant Colonel Nazih, numerous attacks were launched against AMIS personnel during the reporting period, leaving a total of 11 peacekeepers dead. On 1 February, an AMIS staff member was shot dead by unknown men outside the

Kasab camp for internally displaced persons in Kutum, Northern Darfur. Three AMIS soldiers were killed in an attack on 5 March at an SLA-Minawi checkpoint in Gereida, Southern Darfur. On 31 March in Northern Darfur, a helicopter transporting a senior AMIS delegation, including the AMIS Deputy Force Commander, was shot at in the general area of Kurni, which is controlled by the Abdul Wahid faction of the SLM (SLM-Wahid). Furthermore, five AMIS peacekeepers were killed in an attack by SLA-Minawi forces on 1 April while guarding the water point in Umm Barru, Northern Darfur. On 10 April, an AMIS soldier died of injuries sustained in an attack by unidentified gunmen near Sortony, Northern Darfur. Four days later, on 14 April, the body of an AMIS officer was found near AMIS headquarters in El Fasher, his car having apparently been stolen. In addition, a total of 25 vehicles belonging to AMIS and its contractor, Pacific Architects and Engineers (PAE), have been carjacked since the beginning of the year, and an AMIS officer who was abducted on 10 December 2006 is still missing.

6. Additionally, AMIS continues to face serious impediments to the performance of its functions. On 27 May, for instance, the United Nations assisted AMIS in negotiating the release of one of its helicopters, which had been impounded by members of the national security force while on a reconnaissance flight in Umm Hosh, Western Darfur. There have been also impediments of a bureaucratic and administrative nature.

7. The humanitarian community in Darfur is also increasingly subject to violence. The incidents are too numerous to list, but a summary indicates the gravity of the situation: between January and mid-June 2007, 61 humanitarian vehicles were carjacked, 69 staff were temporarily abducted and 37 convoys were ambushed and looted, with assaults and injuries increasingly common during those ambushes. A particularly egregious incident occurred in Nyala in January, when five United Nations staff members, three AMIS personnel and 13 non-governmental organization workers were arrested and detained by Government security forces on charges of misconduct. All were physically assaulted, and one female staff member was sexually assaulted. To date, none of the officials involved in the incident has been brought to justice. Such incidents are seriously affecting the ability of humanitarian organizations to provide assistance.

8. There have also been disturbing reports of indiscriminate attacks causing civilian casualties. Earlier in 2007, the Government of the Sudan carried out several aerial bombardments of non-signatory strongholds in Northern and Southern Darfur, including Bamina; in Bahia in Western Darfur; and in Anka, Umm Rai and Birdik (Northern Darfur). Bombings were also carried out in the areas of Wadi Korma and Ein Siro in Northern Darfur, killing two civilians in addition to a large number of sheep, cattle and camels. In an interview with the BBC Arabic Service on 23 January, Sudanese President Omer al-Bashir confirmed that aerial bombardments against the non-signatories had taken place, but contended that rebel strongholds had been targeted, not civilians.

9. A lull in the Government's aerial bombardments followed, lasting until 19 April, but was broken by Sudanese Armed Forces (SAF) bombing raids in Northern Darfur. Between 19 April and 3 May, there were 13 days of confirmed bombardments of rebel positions by SAF. Several of those were in the Umm Rai area in Northern Darfur, at a time when the non-signatory factions of the SLA had extended invitations to the international community to attend a planned commanders' conference at that location. On 29 April, rebel factions near Umm Rai shot down an SAF Mi-24 attack helicopter. One pilot died in the crash and

another is still being held by the rebels. The Government of the Sudan confirmed the incident, but stated that the helicopter had been on a reconnaissance mission. On 28 May, a Government of the Sudan Antonov aeroplane conducted aerial reconnaissance over Umm Hosh, Anka and Umm Rai in Western Darfur. One day later, on 29 May, SAF conducted air strikes on the village of Wakhaim, asserting that they were acting in self-defence in reaction to the rebel groups' meeting to develop plans to attack the Government.

10. Ground attacks against civilian villages have also occurred on several occasions over the past few months. On 10 February, armed militiamen attacked approximately 20 people near Bala Firash (Western Darfur), killing 6 and injuring 7. On 13 February, armed militias attacked Fanga Shouk (Northern Darfur), considered an SLM-Wahid stronghold. The fighting resulted in 20 civilian casualties and the looting of around 2,000 heads of cattle. On 18 March, armed militiamen attacked Aro Sharo (Western Darfur). Three civilians were killed in the course of the attack and a large number of livestock was stolen.

11. The reporting period was also marked by a resurgence of intertribal clashes, predominantly between Rizeigat (primarily farmers) and Tarjem (primarily cattle herders) in Southern Darfur, which claimed hundreds of lives. Following severe clashes in January, fighting between the two tribes persisted in February and March. In late March, Tarjem representatives peacefully demonstrated in Nyala against the continuous attacks by Rizeigat. Large groups from both sides have been reported in the area since the incident.

12. To a lesser extent, fighting among other tribal groups also occurred. In January, the Habaniya tribe clashed with the Fallata, and on 4 February, two Arab tribes, the Mahaliya and the Jalul, clashed around the Kabkabiya area of Northern Darfur. The Zaghawa tribe, which is supported by the SLM-Minawi group, battled with the Mima and Maaliya tribes between January and April. In a related incident, on 12 March SLM-Minawi soldiers attacked Maaliya tribesmen in Al Muturwad, Southern Darfur. Ten civilians were killed in the fighting, and 14 others were injured. On 26 April, some 300 armed tribesmen attacked internally displaced persons in the Argo and Dabanera camps near Tawilla, Northern Darfur, committing acts of looting, physical assault and kidnapping.

13. In March 2007, tension and violence increased between Government forces and elements of Darfur Peace Agreement signatory SLM-Minawi on three separate occasions in both Northern and Southern Darfur. The most serious incident, however, took place on 24 March, when a gun battle erupted in Omdurman (Khartoum) in which nine people were killed, including eight SLM-Minawi members and one senior Government police officer.

14. In another incident, on 19 March, Government police officers and SAF soldiers exchanged fire in Nertiti (Western Darfur), which reportedly resulted in the death of several civilians. On the same day, a Government police vehicle was ambushed by suspected armed militiamen near Sirba (Western Darfur). In the course of the attack, eight policemen were seriously wounded, one policeman went missing, and several weapons, including a heavy machine gun, were stolen.

15. During the reporting period, tension also persisted between Chad and the Sudan. There were almost no attacks across the Chad-Sudan border in the first two months of 2007, but on 31 March Arab militia groups operating from Chadian territory attacked the two Sudanese villages of Tuiro and Moreina, located in Western Darfur close to the Chadian border. The attacks claimed the lives of about 300 persons, including civilians and

internally displaced persons. About 8,000 people are said to have fled the area. On 9 April, Chadian and Sudanese forces clashed directly for the first time, when the Chadian National Armed Forces entered Sudanese territory in pursuit of Chadian armed opposition groups that had launched an attack into Chad. Sixteen SAF soldiers were killed. The following day, the Government of Chad apologized for what were described as "unintentional clashes", and media reports indicated a similar reaction from the Minister for Foreign Affairs of the Sudan, who expressed his country's "determination" to seek a peaceful solution to the incident. Nevertheless, relations between Chad and the Sudan remained tense throughout April. Clearly, the incident resulted in a build-up of forces on both sides of the border.

16. Since the signing of the Riyadh agreement on 3 May, tensions between the Sudan and Chad appear to have decreased somewhat. In the last two weeks of May, more than 1,000 Sudanese rebels reportedly crossed into the Sudan from Chad following an ultimatum issued by President Deby for their withdrawal from Chadian territory under the terms of the Riyadh agreement. In addition, under the agreement, both countries have pledged to adhere to the provisions of the 8 February 2006 Tripoli Agreement and all subsequent agreements, including on the establishment of the joint military and security committee. Since June, the Government of Chad and leaders of the main rebel groups have been engaged in talks.

III. Human rights and protection

17. Human rights abuses continued in various forms during the reporting period. Among the major areas of concern were the aerial attacks on villages by Government aircraft, which are described above; attacks against internally displaced persons in and around camps; and sexual and gender-based violence against girls and women.

18. According to many reports, the aerial attacks on villages in Western and Northern Darfur were indiscriminate, as they failed to distinguish between military and civilian objects and used disproportionate means of warfare. The attacks on Umm Rai, located in Northern Darfur, which witnesses reported to UNMIS human rights monitors, resulted in civilian casualties; the destruction of houses, a school and other property; and the death of livestock.

19. Carrying out even the most basic daily tasks poses a serious security risk for most of the civilian population in Darfur. Whether in camps for internally displaced persons or in villages, men, women and children are under constant threat of arbitrary arrest, attack, rape and murder by armed groups. Relations between internally displaced persons in the Abu Shouk camp (Northern Darfur) and the local police deteriorated in the beginning of the year, when internally displaced youths seized the weapons of the police after the latter had attempted to take away their mobile telephones. In response, the police arrested the camp's tribal elders and 94 internally displaced persons. The detainees were subsequently released, but five of them were again detained by the authorities in February and held for almost a month without charges being brought. On 17 February, two armed men dressed in military fatigues entered the Krinding II camp for internally displaced persons, outside El Geneina, Western Darfur, and burned a shelter. When one of the persons present protested, he was fatally shot in the head.

20. On 4 March, SLM-Minawi soldiers and members of the National Intelligence and Security Service fired at each other in the Kalma (Southern Darfur) camp, killing one internally displaced person and injuring two others. On 18 March, a leader was shot and

injured by unidentified gunmen at the Hassa Hissa (Western Darfur) camp. In Western Darfur, on 3 April, a group of three armed men in green military-style uniforms opened fire in the Kondobe market, killing two civilians, including a 17-year-old boy, and injuring four others. In Southern Darfur, on 4 April, three female internally displaced persons were attacked and beaten by armed militia 10 kilometres east of the Sheria camp for internally displaced persons. One of the women was able to flee and reported the incident to other persons in the camp, but the other two were abducted by the men. A group of internally displaced persons went to search for the women and were fired at: one woman was killed and three others were severely injured. The two abducted women were later released.

21. During the reporting period, the female population of Darfur continued to be the target of systematic sexual and gender-based violence. In a single camp for internally displaced persons in Western Darfur, Massalit women and girls between the ages of 15 and 60 were involved in at least eight different reported incidents of sexual and gender-based violence between late January and early March 2007; in February alone, nine female internally displaced persons, including two girls under the age of 10, were raped in six separate incidents in various parts of Darfur, usually near camps for internally displaced persons; and, in a 14 April incident, a 10-year-old girl was physically assaulted and raped by an armed man on the outskirts of the Hamadiya camp in Zalingei (Western Darfur) while collecting firewood outside the camp with seven other women.

22. There were also reports that the SLM-Abul Gassim faction attempted to recruit adolescents in Menawashi and Mershing (Southern Darfur) in January. Villagers raised the issue with SAF, which ordered that all recruitment be stopped. SLM-Abul Gassim attempts to forcibly recruit adolescents in another camp also met with strong protests by residents. Those actions prompted many families and adolescents to flee Menawashi, Mershing and Dhuma to avoid recruitment. Despite SAF intervention, no significant return to the area has been witnessed to date.

IV. Humanitarian situation

23. I remain extremely concerned about the effects of the conflict on the civilian population, as the attacks and insecurity described in the present report continue to trigger civilian displacement. More than 150,000 people have been newly displaced since the beginning of the year. Those fleeing their villages are mostly seeking refuge in camps for internally displaced persons that in many cases are at or near capacity. That is the case in El Fasher (Northern Darfur), Zalingei (Western Darfur) and Nyala and Kass (Southern Darfur). The ongoing influx is further straining available resources and in some areas humanitarian indicators are once again deteriorating. A recent survey carried out at Otash camp (Southern Darfur) during the reporting period revealed a malnutrition rate above 15 per cent—the emergency threshold—with the highest rates among the newcomers.

24. I am also very concerned about the impact of the insecurity on the ability of the United Nations to deliver humanitarian assistance. Attacks on aid workers and their assets occur almost on a daily basis. In recent months, bombardments and general insecurity in North Darfur have forced humanitarian organizations to relocate their staff from several areas within the region. An estimated 83,000 internally displaced persons and conflict-affected residents in Tawilla and Tawilla Rural have lost access to medical support, while 200,000 beneficiaries are affected by the indefinite suspension of food distributions in Dar Zaghawa,

Umm Baru, Birmaza and Hashaba. The relocation of humanitarian personnel from Sirba and Abu Soroug to Geneina (Western Darfur) has left some 50,000 conflict-affected people temporarily without any humanitarian assistance. It is estimated that 566,000 of the 4.2 million conflict-affected persons in Darfur are currently cut off from humanitarian assistance.

25. Despite those daunting challenges, the humanitarian community has, by resorting to creative solutions, returned to many areas that were previously inaccessible. Newly accessed areas include eastern Jebel Marra, Thur and Umm Dukhum. The polio vaccination campaign of 26 to 28 March also reached many areas that had been previously inaccessible. In Goldo (Western Darfur), 14,422 children under 5 years of age were immunized for the first time.

26. Between 21 and 27 March, the new Under-Secretary-General for Humanitarian Affairs and Emergency Relief Coordinator, John Holmes, made his first trip to the Sudan. After meeting senior Government officials and non-governmental organization and donor representatives, and travelling to Darfur and Juba, he concluded his visit with the 28 March signing of the joint humanitarian communiqué by the Government of the Sudan and the United Nations. The communiqué details various measures to facilitate continued and timely assistance to the beneficiary population in Darfur and stipulates the establishment of a high-level committee and a tripartite joint technical committee to ensure the agreement's full implementation. The committees are made up of representatives of the Government of the Sudan, the United Nations and international non-governmental organizations.

27. To date, the high-level committee has met three times and has visited several field locations in Darfur, to ensure that the new procedures are followed at the field level. Notable progress in the implementation of the communiqué has been achieved, which has eased some of the considerable bureaucratic impediments created by the Sudanese Government that humanitarian organizations had experienced from January through March. Nevertheless, humanitarian organizations continue to encounter some administrative obstacles, including with regard to access to beneficiaries, hiring of national staff and the implementation of projects to address the issues of the protection of civilians and of sexual and gender-based violence. Close monitoring of the implementation of the communiqué will be essential in the coming months.

V. Implementation of the Darfur Peace Agreement

28. At the same time, some movement has been registered in the implementation of elements of the Darfur Peace Agreement, signed on 5 May 2006 in Abuja. Signatory movement representatives have been incorporated into newly created local governments, and the Transitional Darfur Regional Authority has been established. However, there remains keen dissatisfaction among the signatories of the Declaration of Commitment over allocation of posts as part of power-sharing arrangements.

29. The Transitional Darfur Regional Authority was officially inaugurated at a ceremony held on 24 April in Khartoum, which was followed by another ceremony in El Fasher. It is chaired by Minni Minawi, Senior Assistant to the President of the Sudan, with the Governors of the three states of Darfur serving as his deputies. There is concern, however, that the institution does not have the logistical support or the resources necessary to make it an effective and functioning body, and also that it is currently insufficiently representative of the people of Darfur. In addition, the relationship between the Chairperson of the Regional Authority and existing government structures in the three Darfur states requires clarification.

30. While some elements of the Darfur Peace Agreement appear to be gaining momentum, serious concerns have been raised over the selective implementation of power-sharing provisions, which has exacerbated the security situation in some areas. By adding six new localities, the local bureaucracy has stretched its meagre resources even thinner on the ground. Representatives of the signatory movements are also pointing to other critical aspects of the Agreement that have not been implemented, such as Janjaweed disarmament and full implementation of the security arrangements.

31. At the same time, progress has been made in mobilizing support for the political process, with the objective of making the Darfur Peace Agreement more inclusive while building consensus for the urgent deployment of a United Nations-African Union force on the ground, as envisaged in the joint African Union-United Nations report on the hybrid operation in Darfur (S/2007/307/Rev.1).

32. The African Union and United Nations Special Envoys for Darfur, Salim Ahmed Salim and Jan Eliasson, conducted three joint missions to the Sudan/Darfur and to the region (from 12 to 17 February; 23 to 29 March; and 6 to 10 May) during which they consulted with high-level Government officials, including President Al-Bashir, First Vice-President Salva Kiir and Senior Assistant to the President Minni Minawi, as well as other stakeholders, representatives of factions that are non-signatories to the Darfur Peace Agreement (including field commanders), civil society, opposition political parties, tribal leaders and internally displaced persons. The consultations were aimed at mobilizing support for an African Union/United Nations-led political process and at seeking views on how to make the Agreement more inclusive. During those initial consultations, all the parties consulted, including the Government of the Sudan, agreed that there could be no military solution to the crisis in Darfur and that a political solution was the only way forward to a lasting peace. Both the Government and the other parties largely accepted the fact that the support base for the Darfur Peace Agreement needed to be broadened so as to ensure its ownership by the people of Darfur, while acknowledging that the Agreement could not be renegotiated in its entirety. Within that framework, those consulted agreed to cooperate with the efforts of the Special Envoys. There are, however, still areas of divergence, as some leaders of the non-signatory movements refuse to accept the Agreement as a basis for renewed negotiations.

33. On behalf of the United Nations and the African Union, the Special Envoy of the Secretary-General for Darfur, Jan Eliasson, travelled to Asmara on 22 March to discuss with the Eritrean President, Isaias Afwerki, how to harmonize the joint African Union-United Nations mediation effort with the Eritrean initiative on Darfur. Special Envoy Eliasson travelled to Chad, also on behalf of both Envoys, to solicit the Chadian authorities' support for the African Union/United Nations-led political process and for meetings with some non-signatories.

34. On 28 and 29 April, the Libyan Arab Jamahiriya hosted a high-level meeting in Tripoli on the political process in Darfur. All key regional and international players participated, including the Sudan, Chad, Egypt, Eritrea and the Libyan Arab Jamahiriya, as well as the five permanent members of the Security Council. The Tripoli Consensus, which was adopted at that meeting, reaffirmed the importance of a comprehensive and sustainable political solution to the Darfur crisis and stressed the need for all national, regional and international peace initiatives to converge under African Union-United Nations leadership. It also urged the parties to accelerate preparations for negotiations, warned that those who

obstructed the political process would have to bear the consequences, and encouraged the Special Envoys to intensify consultations and finalize their road map on a strategy and timeline for renewed negotiations.

35. On 8 June, the joint African Union-United Nations road map for the Darfur political process was finalized. It consists of three phases: convergence of initiatives and consultations; pre-negotiations; and negotiations. As a point of departure for the implementation of the road map, the African Union and the United Nations expect all parties to declare their serious commitment to achieving a political solution to the Darfur crisis, creating a security environment in Darfur conducive to negotiations, participating in and committing to the outcome of the negotiation effort, and ceasing all hostilities immediately.

36. Meanwhile, the African Union-United Nations Joint Mediation Support Team (JMST) has been expanded to support the work of the Special Envoys. As part of that strengthening, Pekka Haavisto (Finland) was appointed Senior Adviser to Special Envoy Eliasson early in June. He will be based primarily in the Sudan and the region and will assist in preparing the ground for the renewed negotiations.

37. On 15 and 16 July, the second international meeting on Darfur was convened in Tripoli by African Union and United Nations Special Envoys Salim and Eliasson. In its final communiqué, participants noted that the initial convergence phase of the road map had ended and endorsed the beginning of the pre-negotiation phase. The Special Envoys also proposed to convene a meeting from 3 to 5 August with leading personalities of the non-signatory movements in Arusha, United Republic of Tanzania, in an effort to facilitate preparations for negotiations. That proposal was welcomed unequivocally. In addition, it was agreed at the meeting that invitations for the new round of negotiations should be issued by the Chairperson of the African Union Commission and the Secretary-General before the end of August 2007, requesting the Special Envoys to consult widely with all relevant stakeholders on the most appropriate date and venue for the talks.

38. At the same time, the African Union-led Preparatory Committee for the Darfur-Darfur Dialogue and Consultation (DDDC), inaugurated in November 2006, has made efforts to pave the way towards the projected DDDC. In the course of the reporting period, the Chairperson of the DDDC Preparatory Committee, who assumed charge earlier this year, completed a first round of consultations at the community level with stakeholders in Nyala (Southern Darfur), El Fasher (Northern Darfur), Zalingei and El Geneina (Western Darfur). A broad range of Darfurian stakeholders, including representatives of civil society, the native administration, political parties, Darfur Peace Agreement signatory and non-signatory factions, as well as internally displaced persons, have been consulted, with a view to identifying their main interests and concerns related to the conflict.

VI. United Nations support for the African Union Mission in the Sudan

39. The Tripartite Mechanism established to facilitate the speedy implementation of the United Nations light support package to AMIS has continued to meet regularly since its inception last December. At its 10th meeting, held in April, the Mechanism received an update on the progress achieved so far in the implementation of the light support package.

40. With respect to that package, of a total of 184 personnel, 154 have been deployed to the Sudan. That number includes 83 military officers, 34 police officers and 37 civilian staff

members. With respect to equipment, the main outstanding items are 36 armed personnel carriers. During the reporting period, the deployment of military and civilian personnel to Darfur has been hampered by continued insecurity and the scarcity of office and living accommodation that meet United Nations security standards. However, the construction of an additional 110 residential units for light package staff is expected to be completed soon, which will help to expedite deployment.

41. The heavy support package will entail the deployment of military, police and mission support personnel and equipment, as well as civilian staff to provide support in a range of areas, including civil affairs, humanitarian liaison, public information and support for the Darfur political process. Details of the package were communicated to the Government of the Sudan by the Secretary-General and the African Union Commission Chairperson in identical letters addressed to President Al-Bashir in January 2007.

42. In his response, dated 6 March 2007, President Al-Bashir expressed reservations and requested clarification with regard to some aspects of the package, and proposed that further discussions take place to address them. In order to provide clarity on those issues, a high-level African Union-United Nations team held a consultative briefing on 9 April in Addis Ababa with representatives of the Government of the Sudan. Comprehensive clarifications were provided by the African Union and the United Nations on the heavy support package as well as on the observations raised by the Government. On 16 April, the Government of the Sudan gave its agreement to the full heavy support package, the cost of which is estimated to be $287.9 million.

43. In addition to the urgently needed contribution by Member States of troops and police, deploying the heavy package will also require the agreement of the Government of the Sudan on land and water drilling in Darfur and its cooperation in clearing essential items currently held in Port Sudan; the deployment of two additional AMIS battalions with the equipment necessary to ensure protection for African Union and United Nations personnel; and the restructuring of AMIS from eight to three sectors. Deploying the heavy package will also require the immediate support of international partners for the expansion of seven AMIS camps to accommodate the deployment of the two additional AMIS battalions. Implementation teams have been established by the United Nations in Khartoum and El Fasher to expedite the deployment of the heavy package.

44. A budget of $68.6 million has been provided to the heavy support package by drawing from UNMIS resources to cater for expenses up to June 2007. I anticipate that almost all of the allocated resources will be directed towards the acquisition of assets that will be required to implement the heavy support package.

45. The United Nations and the African Union have agreed on troop contributors for all 11 military units included in the heavy package. As agreed, we have given preference to African troop contributors wherever possible, and, in our effort to proceed with full transparency, we have submitted to the Government of the Sudan a list of the selected troop-contributing countries and the units that they will be providing.

46. With respect to the police component of the heavy support package, 47 police-contributing countries have committed individual officers. As agreed, the United Nations will aim to ensure that the majority of those officers come from African Member States. Additionally, in close consultation with the African Union, the Department of Peacekeeping Operations

has selected Bangladesh, Nigeria and Pakistan to provide three formed police units to the heavy support package. As with the troop-contributing countries, the Secretariat has informed the Government of the Sudan of the selection.

VII. African Union-United Nations hybrid operation

47. Deliberations on the hybrid operation between the African Union and the United Nations began in Addis Ababa early in 2007. On the basis of those deliberations, a joint report was finalized detailing all aspects of the hybrid operation. As the Council will recall, I subsequently transmitted the joint report on the hybrid operation in Darfur (S/2007/307/Rev.1) to the Security Council on 5 June 2007. The report was also forwarded to President Al-Bashir through identical letters from the Chairperson of the African Union Commission and from me on the same day.

48. As with the heavy support package, the United Nations and the African Union jointly provided a technical briefing to the Government of the Sudan on the hybrid operation. The briefing, which took place on 11 and 12 June, provided the Government delegation with comprehensive clarifications on the hybrid operation, as detailed in the joint report. The consultations took place in a constructive atmosphere, and the Government delegation agreed to the deployment of the hybrid operation. President Al-Bashir confirmed his Government's acceptance of the hybrid operation during the 17 June visit of the Security Council to Khartoum.

49. It is also important to note that, in addition to accepting the hybrid operation, the Government delegation reconfirmed the need for an immediate and comprehensive cease-fire accompanied by an inclusive political process. I welcome this in view of the fact that a solution to the crisis in Darfur will require concerted action on both the peacekeeping and political tracks. While the Government delegation accepted the hybrid, it also outlined concerns and expressed the hope that the Council would take those concerns into account when developing a resolution authorizing the operation.

50. Now that the Government of the Sudan has reached agreement regarding the deployment of the hybrid operation, it will be important for the Council to provide a mandate for the operation as soon as possible. At its 79th meeting, on 22 June 2007, the African Union Peace and Security Council issued a communiqué authorizing the hybrid operation, which included elements for a mandate based on the joint African Union-United Nations report on the hybrid. A financial addendum (S/2007/307/Rev.1/Add.1) to the hybrid report with detailed cost estimates for the hybrid operation was issued on 5 July 2007. Given the complexity, magnitude and unique nature of this operation, it may be necessary to consider the establishment of another senior management post in addition to those reflected in the hybrid report (S/2007/307/Rev.1), at the level of Assistant Secretary-General, to manage all administrative and financial aspects of this enormous operation.

51. On 29 June, the Department of Peacekeeping Operations convened a meeting with potential troop- and police-contributing countries for the hybrid operation. As the United Nations continues to seek contributions for this massive undertaking, we will do our utmost to maintain the African character of the operation while also ensuring that all troops deployed are sufficiently equipped and up to United Nations standards in order to enable them to operate in such a challenging environment.

52. In order to ensure strong leadership in Darfur prior to the deployment of the hybrid operation, the African Union and the United Nations have appointed Rodolphe Adada, who has been the Minister for Foreign Affairs of the Congo since 1997, as the Joint Special Representative of the African Union and the United Nations for Darfur. Prior to the deployment of the hybrid operation, he will be the Head of AMIS. I have been in regular contact with the Joint Special Representative, who arrived in Khartoum on 4 July. The African Union has also appointed General Martin Agwai of Nigeria as the Force Commander of AMIS, with the understanding that he will be the Force Commander of the hybrid operation when it replaces AMIS. General Agwai, who was most recently the Nigerian Chief of Defence and who has significant United Nations experience, arrived in El Fasher in the second half of July.

53. During my consultations with the Chairperson of the African Union Commission on 13 July in New York, I welcomed the fact that the Government of the Sudan agreed with African Union-United Nations plans for the hybrid operation, and I noted the high expectations of the Security Council that an effective deployment would occur rapidly. I also stressed the importance of progress towards holding peace negotiations in late August or early September and the need for increased emphasis by the international community on development issues in Darfur. In our discussion, the Chairperson shared his view that a comprehensive ceasefire was within reach and stressed the importance of ensuring that those who would not join the African Union-United Nations led peace process faced serious consequences. The Chairperson and I further agreed on the importance of Security Council unity in supporting the authorization and implementation of the hybrid operation. We also agreed on the need for rapid progress in the implementation of the hybrid operation in Darfur, including, as immediate priorities, United Nations-African Union agreement on deployment plans and timelines, senior management, mission structure and personnel generation. These operational plans will be further developed by the United Nations and the African Union during a joint planning session to be held in Addis Ababa early in August.

VII. Observations

54. While the situation in Darfur remains very precarious, I am encouraged by the Government's agreement to the deployment of the hybrid operation. I intend to move forward expeditiously, in full cooperation with the African Union, with the implementation of this crucial peacekeeping initiative. The successful deployment of the hybrid operation will very much depend on the Government's cooperation and assistance, especially with regard to the provision of adequate land, permission to drill for water and the timely clearance of critical mission-support items through customs. In addition to the provision of critical support by the Government of the Sudan and the full deployment of the heavy support package, the international community should also work together towards finalizing the process of force generation within 30 days of the authorization of the mandate and deploying the headquarters and management elements of the hybrid operation as soon as possible. It will be vital to transfer authority from AMIS to the hybrid operation as soon as effective operating capability and command and control structures are on the ground.

55. Meanwhile, I am very concerned about the continuing violence and insecurity in Darfur. Although the humanitarian communities strive to provide protection and assistance to those affected by the conflict, violence against civilians has continued. This is especially true for girls and women, who are victims of widespread violence, including systematic rape. It is

imperative that all those involved be brought to justice, and I call on the Sudanese authorities to review their national laws and judicial procedures to ensure that they adequately address the deplorable violence against girls and women.

56. I reiterate my deep concern over the bombing by the Government of the Sudan of areas in Northern and Western Darfur. While the number of aerial bombardments by SAF decreased in February and March, they resumed in April and May. In addition, ground attacks by SAF and associated armed militias continued. Those indiscriminate attacks have brought death, displacement and prolonged suffering to Darfurian civilians. As I have noted on several occasions, as long as hostilities continue in Darfur, efforts to reach a political settlement and achieve durable peace will not succeed. It is imperative that the Government and all parties take effective steps to cease hostilities and act on their commitment to uphold the ceasefire without delay. At the same time, inter- and intra-tribal clashes, which have exacerbated the already fragile security and humanitarian situation since the beginning of the year, need to be urgently addressed.

57. Humanitarian organizations have been forced to curtail some of their programming owing to the continuing insecurity. That has led to the deterioration of the living conditions of the millions of conflict-affected people who depend on humanitarian agencies for their survival. I appeal to all parties to abide by the ceasefire in order to allow humanitarian organizations to carry out their mission of bringing succour to the war-ravaged population.

58. In a positive development, following the signing on 28 March of the joint humanitarian communiqué on humanitarian assistance in Darfur, cooperation between humanitarian organizations and the authorities with regard to facilitating humanitarian operations has significantly improved. Joint mechanisms established to ensure the full implementation of the Darfur Peace Agreement have been functioning successfully. I hope that the cooperation of the Sudan will continue to improve the operating environments for the United Nations and other organizations.

59. In addition, there is an urgent need for a comprehensive development strategy, supported by the Sudanese and the international community, to complement ongoing mediation and peacekeeping efforts. It is critical to mobilize support for recovery and rehabilitation in Darfur, especially with regard to the availability of water for the general population. I intend to explore that possibility with a view to alleviating the suffering of the population.

60. I am also extremely concerned that UNMIS and AMIS peacekeepers and United Nations and non-governmental organization aid personnel have increasingly become the target of violent attacks. Such attacks against African Union, United Nations and non-governmental organization personnel deployed in Darfur constitute serious violations of international law and of the relevant resolutions of the Security Council. I therefore call on all parties to respect the status of both organizations and to create an environment that enables those staff members to deliver life-saving assistance and help bring stability to Darfur. I also urge the Government of the Sudan and the movements to take the appropriate measures, in their respective areas of control, to identify those responsible for the attacks on AMIS and UNMIS personnel and to hold them accountable.

61. Meanwhile, with regard to the political process, my Special Envoy for Darfur continues to work with his African Union counterpart, Salim Ahmed Salim, to engage signatories and non-signatories to the Darfur Peace Agreement, as well as other stakeholders, in the

process of finding a political solution to the conflict. That process has included three joint missions to the Sudan and several trips to the region to meet with the leaders of Chad, Egypt, Eritrea and the Libyan Arab Jamahiriya as well as the 8 June issuance of a road map regarding the peace process in Darfur.

62. I was particularly encouraged by the outcome of the second international meeting on Darfur—a follow-up to the April Tripoli meeting—convened by the Special Envoys on 15 and 16 July in Tripoli in order to take stock of the progress made regarding implementation of the road map. The meeting noted that the first phase of the road map had been concluded, endorsed the beginning of the pre-negotiation phase and agreed that invitations for the projected peace talks should be issued before the end of August 2007.

63. I am appreciative of the initiative taken by Member States to bring renewed energy and commitment to the international community's efforts to take forward the process of resolving the Darfur crisis. In that context, the meeting of the Enlarged Contact Group for Darfur convened by France on 25 June gave additional momentum to African Union-United Nations efforts to reinvigorate the political process and strengthen peacekeeping in Darfur, and it focused international attention on the critical humanitarian situation and prospects for Darfur's reconstruction. I would like to acknowledge President Sarkozy and Foreign Minister Kouchner for having convened that timely meeting on the way forward in addressing the situation in Darfur. It demonstrated the international community's strong commitment to the resolution of that deteriorating crisis.

64. The coming weeks and months will be a crucial period in the quest for peace in Darfur. Joint African Union-United Nations efforts to achieve a political solution will gain momentum as the Special Envoys make every effort to commence negotiations. Meanwhile, implementation of the forthcoming Security Council resolution on the hybrid operation will be a major litmus test of the political will of all involved, including the parties, whose actions will be closely monitored by the international community.

65. As we enter this critical phase, it is essential that work on all four tracks of international engagement in Darfur continue in earnest. There must be substantial progress towards a political settlement and concrete action to strengthen peacekeeping through the hybrid operation. We must also ensure that the massive humanitarian assistance programme continues to sustain millions of people in Darfur. Finally, recovery, development and rehabilitation strategies must be put in place to ensure that these critical longer-term considerations are addressed.

66. This four-track strategy will require the full and sustained commitment of the international community. I count on the active support of all stakeholders as we continue to respond to the enormous challenges of restoring peace and prosperity to Darfur.

10. Report of the Secretary-General on Sudan, 20 August 2007 (S/2007/500)

I. Introduction

1. The present report is submitted pursuant to paragraph 11 of Security Council resolution 1590 (2005), in which the Council requested me to keep it regularly informed of progress in implementing the Comprehensive Peace Agreement and the mandate of the United Nations Mission in the Sudan (UNMIS). The report covers the period since my 17 April 2007 report (S/2007/213), including references to recent developments with regard to Darfur.

II. Implementation of the major elements of the Comprehensive Peace Agreement

2. During the period under review, the parties held intensive consultations aimed at resolving outstanding differences over implementation of the Comprehensive Peace Agreement. According to representatives of the Sudan People's Liberation Movement (SPLM) and the National Congress Party (NCP), these consultations resulted in progress on key issues, including the sensitive question of oil contracts. However, the parties have not yet settled their differences on the issue of Abyei, despite indications in April and May of significant progress on the issue. Nor were any significant advances made in the area of legislation related to the Comprehensive Peace Agreement. In the meantime, the parties, with the assistance of UNMIS, continued to work towards the full redeployment and verification of forces, in accordance with the Agreement; however, the important deadline of 9 July 2007, intended to mark the full redeployment of the Sudanese Armed Forces (SAF) to the north of the 1956 boundary line, was not met.

Security

3. The overall security situation remained calm as the 9 July 2007 deadline (see para. 4 below) approached, with no clashes associated with the redeployment. However, the security situation in the ceasefire zone deteriorated slightly during the reporting period, with localized violence, particularly in Southern Kordofan, Eastern Equatoria and parts of Upper Nile. Most incidents appeared to be related to clashes over natural resources, or were due to ill-disciplined soldiers or banditry. In the most serious incident of violence, which took place on 5 May 2007, armed members of the Toposa tribe attacked unarmed members of the Didinga tribe in Lauro, Eastern Equatoria, killing 54 people, mostly women, and stealing 800 head of cattle as well as agricultural equipment. In Equatoria, insecurity was compounded by the reported westward movement of Lord's Resistance Army (LRA) forces, presumably towards their designated assembly areas.

4. A major focus of the Mission's efforts during the reporting period was the monitoring of the redeployment by the Sudanese Armed Forces to the north of the1 January 1956 border between northern and southern Sudan, which was to have been completed by 9 July 2007. While much of the redeployment was carried out as required, the deadline was not met in full. SAF acknowledge that some 3,600 of their troops remain in southern Sudan, mainly in small concentrations in Upper Nile State, but claim that these forces are required to protect the oilfields pending full deployment of Joint Integrated Units. The Sudan People's Liberation Army (SPLA) does not agree with this argument. Meanwhile, some southern

civilian sources including the Governor of Unity State continue to assert that much larger numbers of SAF remain in the south. These issues are being addressed by the Joint Defence Board, which according to the Comprehensive Peace Agreement has the responsibility to coordinate between the two forces, command the Joint Integrated Units and address threats to the security of the oil installations.

5. As of 17 July 2007, both parties and UNMIS agreed that 66 per cent of the required reduction of SAF forces had been carried out (32,221 of an estimated 46,403 troops). This figure includes those redeployed north of the 1 January 1956 boundary (57 per cent) and those verified as redeployed to Joint Integrated Units, which are to be composed of personnel from both parties in the south (9 per cent). In addition, there have been some important symbolic steps, including the handover on 9 July of the SAF headquarters at Malakal to the local Joint Integrated Unit, commanded by SPLA.

6. However, the status of some SAF personnel in the south remains to be finalized. These troops include some 2,800 Joint Integrated Unit elements undergoing re-verification by UNMIS (6 per cent) as well as some 8,900 troops (19 per cent) "voluntarily demobilized" by SAF under article 19 of the Comprehensive Peace Agreement security protocol. SPLA argues that these demobilized groups still receive salaries from SAF, and should therefore be considered active soldiers until they go through the formal programme of disarmament, demobilization and reintegration. The Ceasefire Political Commission has determined that SAF will complete its payments to these forces by the end of 2007.

7. Both parties have taken steps to address the status of other armed groups. In May, SAF facilitated unilateral disarmament of SAF-aligned other armed group members in southern Sudan, collecting weapons in exchange for substantial payments. However, the exercise took place outside the framework of the national disarmament, demobilization and reintegration institutions, raising concerns about the lack of planning for reintegration of ex-combatants. While only 827 former combatants were formally disarmed in this process, SAF declared in a ceremony in Khartoum on 24 June that all SAF-aligned other armed groups in southern Sudan had been officially dissolved, and any remaining militiamen should henceforth be considered illegal. However, SPLA maintains that SAF should share responsibility for the remaining ex-militiamen pending their full reintegration into society.

8. For its part, SPLA has continued to make progress in the formal integration of those militias that had aligned themselves to SPLA under the 2006 Juba Declaration. In May, Salva Kiir, President of the Government of Southern Sudan and Commander-in-Chief of SPLA, announced that SPLA would formally incorporate some 34,000 combatants of former other armed groups, who used to be part of the South Sudan Defence Forces (SSDF). The full integration of SSDF and the overall restructuring of SPLA into a professional army remains one of the key challenges ahead.

9. The formation of Joint Integrated Units is significantly behind schedule. The number of troops assembled for inclusion into the Joint Integrated Units has reached 77 per cent of the expected total. However, the SPLA and SAF components of the Joint Integrated Units remain functionally separate and under different chains of command. The Joint Defence Board (JDB) and JIU High Command have made progress in agreeing on priorities for integration and development, including at a workshop of SAF and SPLA JIU Commanders held in Juba from 21 to 23 May, but JDB has yet to agree on a request for international assistance to support this process.

10. In July, SPLA began the redeployment of its remaining forces in Southern Kordofan and Blue Nile States, under verification by joint monitoring teams. SPLA asserts that some forces and heavy equipment cannot be moved immediately owing to poor road and weather conditions. Verification of the early stages of redeployment was hindered in a number of areas by non-cooperation of commanders on the ground. During the reporting period, both parties continued to restrict UNMIS movement in sector VI, which includes Abyei.

Political

11. NCP and SPLM convened high-level meetings throughout the reporting period, with the stated objective of resolving outstanding differences over the implementation of the Comprehensive Peace Agreement. The agenda included long-deadlocked disputes over oil contracts and the status of the Abyei area, which I have highlighted in previous reports.

12. In mid-April, the parties reported a breakthrough in negotiations over Abyei, announcing to the National Assembly that the Presidency had agreed, in principle, on an interim civil administration to be appointed for a period of six months pending final agreement on its administrative boundaries. However, this consensus later unravelled, as disputes emerged over the temporary boundaries of the interim administration. A decision from the Presidency on the Abyei issue is still awaited.

13. In the meantime, the parties announced progress on a range of other issues, mainly relating to the respective jurisdictions of the federal and southern Sudan levels of government. In June, they appeared to reach an agreement on arrangements for development of the disputed oil concession "Block 5B" in Jonglei State, for which each side had previously signed a concession with different commercial companies. However, one of the companies concerned later expressed dissatisfaction with the reported agreement, and said that it would take steps to protect the original terms of its licence.

14. Meanwhile, owing to active bilateral discussions between the parties, the Assessment and Evaluation Commission suspended its work during the month of May but reconvened in June. The Ceasefire Political Commission met only once during the reporting period, in late July.

15. The National Assembly ended its spring session on 27 June without having received drafts of pending legislation required for implementation of the Comprehensive Peace Agreement, including bills for the national security service, the police service and the elections. In addition, the National Electoral Commission and the commissions for both human rights and for land have yet to be established. In May, some SPLM and National Democratic Alliance parliamentarians expressed dissatisfaction with the slow pace of the review of existing legislation for its compatibility with the Comprehensive Peace Agreement, and asked the Ministry of Justice to explain the delays.

16. In a number of areas, implementation of the Agreement is being delayed by the slow disbursement of federal funds to relevant commissions and ministries. Fiscal decentralization, stipulated by the Agreement, has yet to take full effect. In May, the Chairman of the Fiscal and Financial Allocation and Monitoring Commission noted that states were currently receiving much less from the federal level than had been allocated by the Comprehensive Peace Agreement.

17. In a positive development, a pilot census was finally conducted in April in advance of the national population census, covering a wide range of sample regions including locations

in Darfur. Plans for the full census were delayed, however, from November 2007 to January 2008, owing to concerns about the preparedness of the Southern Census Commission, linked to slow disbursement of funds by the national Government. Of $30 million in federal funding originally requested by the Commission for 2007, only 56 per cent has been granted and only a small proportion of that amount has been disbursed. This has severely delayed mapping of the 79 southern counties, which is now further hampered by the onset of the rainy season.

18. Meanwhile, incremental progress was made on defining the demarcation of the 1 January 1956 border between northern and southern Sudan. The Technical Border Committee conducted field visits to the border regions, and Committee members visited London and Cairo to survey relevant maps available in the two capitals. The Committee has also begun to plan for an international workshop on best practice in border demarcation processes, which UNMIS intends to support. The Committee has indicated that it expects border demarcation to be conducted in the spring of 2008.

19. On 1 July, after a six-month delay, new governors were appointed for Southern Kordofan and Blue Nile States, in line with the requirements of the Comprehensive Peace Agreement for the rotation of posts between the parties. However, there was no significant progress in harmonizing the parties' respective police and civil administrations in either state. In Blue Nile, the creation of an additional locality, called "Al Tadamon", sparked political protests. SPLM supporters believe the creation of the locality was an attempt to manipulate the political geography of Blue Nile State at the expense of SPLM.

20. In the meantime, the Government of Southern Sudan made progress in developing and staffing its new institutions. The President of the Government continued to reorganize the states' administrations in a bid to improve efficiency and tackle corruption. On 3 July he announced a major cabinet reshuffle, including the appointment of several new presidential advisers. The President also appointed more than 200 legal counsellors and prosecutors. Meanwhile, the first group of human rights monitors from the Southern Sudan Human Rights Commission was deployed, and the United Nations Development Programme (UNDP) began training of police and prisons personnel with support from the Multi-Donor Trust Fund.

21. The budget shortfall facing the Government of Southern Sudan is likely to have a negative impact on many of the above activities. In May and June, payment delays related to the Government's shortage of financing triggered protests in different locations, including a teachers' strike in Rumbek. In Jonglei State, SPLA veterans blocked the main Juba-Bor road to protest their not receiving allowances. In addition, the ongoing integration of 34,000 former SSDF elements into SPLA will strain the already overstretched SPLA payroll.

22. As a countermeasure, the Ministry of Finance of the Government of Southern Sudan has sought ways to diversify non-oil revenues, including through the introduction of a new income tax bill which is currently before the Legislative Assembly. All ministries and governors have been instructed to revise their budgets downwards in order to address recent funding shortages. This, however, may hinder the efforts of the Government to put in place an effective civilian administration throughout the south.

23. On a positive note, the Southern Sudan Peace and Reconciliation Commission began to function as a body mandated to promote reconciliation in southern Sudan. The Commission played a role in launching the SPLM initiative on the Darfur political process, and although

still lacking in organizational capacity, has engaged in preliminary efforts to take forward reconciliation between rival ethnic groups in Eastern Equatoria and Jonglei.

III. Implementation of other peace processes in the Sudan

24. In eastern Sudan, after a long period of stagnation, steps were taken to begin implementation of the 14 October 2006 Eastern Sudan Peace Agreement. Following high-level bilateral discussions in Asmara, three leaders of the Eastern Front were appointed to senior-level posts in the Government of National Unity on 25 May: one as Assistant to the President, another as Adviser to the President and the third as State Minister of Transport and Roads. In June, eight members of the Eastern Front were appointed as deputies to the National Assembly, where they will occupy seats previously allocated to NCP. Meanwhile, former combatants of the Eastern Front began assembling at Kassala for disarmament, demobilization and reintegration organized by the Government of the Sudan with the support of UNDP.

25. With regard to Darfur, the adoption by the Security Council of resolution 1769 (2007) marks a major step forward in United Nations efforts to assist the Sudanese people in resolving the crisis in Darfur. Intensive preparations are ongoing to ensure that the African Union-United Nations hybrid operation is deployed as rapidly and as effectively as possible. Additional capable troops must be committed, support systems must be put in place and command structures must be established. The unequivocal and continuous support of both the Government of the Sudan and the rebel movements will be critical in this regard.

26. As we redouble our collective efforts to strengthen peacekeeping in Darfur, we must also acknowledge that it is only through a political process that we can achieve a sustainable solution to the conflict. My Special Envoy for Darfur, Jan Eliasson, and the Special Envoy of the Chairperson of the African Union for Darfur, Salim Ahmed Salim, convened a meeting of Darfur rebel groups who have not acceded to the Darfur Peace Agreement from 3 to 6 August, in Ngurdoto, near Arusha in the United Republic of Tanzania. The main objective of the Arusha meeting was to create an enabling environment for the movements to consult among themselves, with other participants, and with the United Nations and the African Union, and to facilitate the preparations for the forthcoming negotiations. All the major non-signatory movements were represented at the Arusha consultations (Justice and Equality Movement, Sudan Federal Democratic Alliance, National Movement for Reformation and Development, Sudan Liberation Movement-Unity, Sudan Liberation Movement-Abdul Shafi and Sudan Liberation Movement-Khamis), with the exception of Abdul Wahid, leader of one of the Sudan Liberation Movement factions, who boycotted the meeting. The meeting benefited from the presence not only of the political leaders of the non-signatory groups but also of some field commanders and representatives of Chad, Egypt, Eritrea and the Libyan Arab Jamahiriya.

27. The consultations focused on five key issues: (a) a common negotiation platform of the movements for the resumed talks; (b) the criteria for, and level of participation in, the final negotiations; (c) the agenda and venue for the renewed talks; (d) inclusion of the concerns of internally displaced persons, refugees, tribal leaders, women and other civil society groups; and (e) security and humanitarian matters.

28. After two days of intensive discussions, the representatives of the various movements presented a joint paper to the Special Envoys outlining their common platform on the main agenda items for the final negotiations (wealth sharing, power sharing, security, land issues

and humanitarian assistance). Considering that the movements had not been able to reach a common platform until then, the Special Envoys were impressed by their commitment to do so rapidly in Arusha.

29. At the end of the meeting, Special Envoys Eliasson and Salim consulted the movement leaders and the representatives of neighbouring countries and issued chairmen's conclusions highlighting the following key principles, which the movements had agreed to during the meeting: readiness to participate in a mediation process led by the African Union and the United Nations; preparedness to keep the platform open for others (rebel movements); readiness to respect a cessation of hostilities, provided that all other parties make similar commitments; assurances to allow unhindered humanitarian access in Darfur and to refrain from violence against the African Union Mission in the Sudan (AMIS) and humanitarian personnel; acceptance of Security Council resolution 1769 (2007) and support for its implementation; and endorsement of the inclusion of the concerns of all stakeholders (internally displaced persons, refugees, traditional leaders and women's groups) in the process of negotiations through an appropriate mechanism.

30. The movement leaders also recommended that the resumed talks should be held within two to three months from the conclusion of the Arusha talks, in "countries of the regional initiatives or at any other location determined appropriate by the Special Envoys provided the environment and facilities were adequate". Overall, both the chairmen's conclusions and the movements' common platform provide important benchmarks for the political process.

31. The Government of the Sudan subsequently welcomed the Arusha conclusions and reiterated a general willingness to enter into talks with the non-signatories in order to amend and augment the Darfur Peace Agreement. At the same time, it restated the Government's objection to wholesale renegotiation of the Agreement.

32. In the meantime, UNMIS continued to provide assistance to AMIS under the Light and Heavy Support Packages, as described in greater detail in my report on Darfur dated 27 July 2007 (S/2007/462). UNMIS and AMIS continue to apprise the Government of the Sudan of the details of the support packages through the Tripartite Mechanism.

33. The Government of Southern Sudan, along with my Special Envoy for the LRA-affected areas, Joaquim Chissano, continued to facilitate the peace talks between LRA and the Government of Uganda. After a five-month break, the parties resumed peace talks on 25 April and on 2 May signed an agreement on comprehensive solutions to the conflict which covers participation in national politics, security issues, the return of displaced persons and the reconstruction of war-affected areas. On 29 June, further agreement was reached on the principles of accountability for war crimes, to be addressed through a traditional justice and reconciliation mechanism. UNMIS continues to provide vital logistical support to the talks.

IV. Implementation of the mandate of the United Nations Mission in the Sudan

Political support and reconciliation

34. During the reporting period, my Acting Special Representative, Tayé-Brook Zerihoun, initiated a new mechanism for periodic high-level consultations with the parties to provide opportunities for UNMIS to discuss its priorities with NCP and SPLM, in an attempt to ensure transparency and streamline efforts regarding implementation of the Comprehensive

Peace Agreement. Through these high-level consultations, UNMIS intends to provide coordinated support to the parties and share with them its views on the objectives and concerns of the international community. The first of these high-level consultations is expected was held on 10 August.

35. In the transitional areas of Abyei, Southern Kordofan and Blue Nile, UNMIS continued to work actively with politicians and local communities to promote the Comprehensive Peace Agreement and invigorate local peace initiatives. In southern Sudan, UNMIS supported the Security Committee of the South Sudan Legislative Assembly in its efforts to resolve the Mundari-Bari and the Toposa-Didinga tribal conflicts by addressing land and resource issues. In Jonglei State, UNMIS staff worked with the administration and tribal leaders to address tension between the Murle tribe and its neighbours, as violent cattle raiding prompted calls from the community for immediate forcible disarmament of the Murle.

United Nations military deployment and activities

36. As at 17 July 2007, 97 per cent of the mandated UNMIS military personnel (9,415 of a total of 9,706) were deployed, including 591 United Nations military observers, 280 staff officers and 8,544 troops.

37. The reporting period saw enhanced monitoring and verification activity as the Mission's military component worked with the parties to support the redeployment of SAF in advance of the 9 July 2007 deadline. The Ceasefire Joint Military Committee, headed by the UNMIS Force Commander, met eight times to monitor progress, resolve disputes and help the parties consolidate trust and confidence. The Committee continued to provide an effective forum for keeping the process on track. Area Joint Military Committees also met regularly in each of the six sectors. In addition, United Nations military observers and the parties' national monitors conducted hundreds of joint monitoring patrols, accounting for military movements and verifying forces assigned to Joint Integrated Units. However, full verification in some areas was complicated by limitations of logistics and terrain, while in others the lack of cooperation by the parties or political sensitivities precluded progress.

38. As the parties move towards full implementation of the security protocol, the monitoring and verification of their forces on the ground remains vital to the building of trust as the parties make the transition from war to peace. Full implementation of the security arrangements mandated by the Comprehensive Peace Agreement—including redeployment, the Joint Integrated Units' assumption of their mandate to protect the oilfields, the integration and demobilization of other armed groups and the gradual downsizing of the parties' armed forces—is a key element of the vital first phase of peace consolidation, which will pave the way for the wider stabilization of the Sudan.

39. In the early part of the reporting period, there was a spike in violence in sectors I and III and in the transitional areas. UNMIS military contingents intensified their patrolling and ceasefire investigations to help improve security and build confidence among the local population. However, in some areas, such activity was hampered by restrictions imposed on the movement of United Nations monitors. Allegations of activity by other armed groups in UNMIS sector VI (which includes Abyei and borders Darfur) could not be verified owing to continued restrictions on the movement of United Nations military observers across the sector by both parties.

40. In view of local logistical constraints, the Mission also revised earlier plans to establish team sites at Raja (Western Bahr el Ghazal) and Baw (Blue Nile). A more visible UNMIS presence in these areas will be achieved by intensified patrolling and use of temporary operating bases. In addition, as mentioned above, the arrival of the rainy season in southern Sudan, making many roads impassable, is already having an impact on military operations. The UNMIS riverine unit stationed in Malakal suffered considerable storm damage during the reporting period, and on 10 May a major tornado wrought substantial destruction at sector IV headquarters in Kadugli.

Disarmament, demobilization and reintegration

41. The coordination of a national disarmament, demobilization and reintegration process gained momentum during the reporting period with the convening of the National Disarmament, Demobilization and Reintegration Coordination Council and the establishment of a national technical subcommittee. UNMIS is providing technical assistance to the subcommittee, which oversees the drafting of a national strategic framework for disarmament, demobilization and reintegration. However, UNMIS has no formal relationship with the National Council, which impedes policy dialogue between the United Nations and the national body as well as planning related to disarmament, demobilization and reintegration in both the north and south. In order to support the process in the Sudan efficiently, there is a need for UNMIS and the donor community to understand the National Council's policy guidance on key issues, such as the eligibility criteria for entry into the programme and implementation arrangements in the transitional areas. In addition, several critical issues need to be urgently considered by the Council, in particular the Sudanese Armed Forces' unilateral disarmament and discharge of members of other armed groups in Upper Nile, Western Bahr el Ghazal and across Eastern Equatoria. This unilateral disarmament and discharge process remains a source of concern as it is not part of the formal disarmament, demobilization and reintegration programme.

42. Meanwhile, preparations are under way for the voluntary disarmament and demobilization of ex-combatants in Southern Kordofan and Blue Nile State. SAF and the northern Sudan Disarmament, Demobilization and Reintegration Commission have pre-registered 25,000 combatants for this process, and the demobilization of a first group of some 13,000 is expected to begin as soon as a national strategy is ready. UNMIS will monitor compliance with agreed standards for personnel and weapon verification and will also provide reinsertion assistance. SPLA also submitted a list of some 25,000 pre-registered candidates for disarmament, demobilization and reintegration. However, owing to the late start of the programme, the respective target caseloads for 2006/07 have been rolled over to 2007/08.

43. UNMIS, UNDP and partners continued to coordinate and support Southern Sudan's voluntary civilian disarmament initiative in Jonglei State. Some 1,200 light weapons have been collected there so far, and efforts for the demobilization of children are ongoing. In northern Sudan, 25 children were demobilized and reunited with their families, while in southern Sudan over 250 demobilized children are participating in reintegration programmes.

Electoral assistance

44. UNMIS continued to monitor progress in developing the draft elections law and related legislative developments. Stakeholders, including political parties and civil society, presented

further submissions to the National Constitutional Review Commission on the draft law, which is expected to be tabled in the October session of the National Assembly. The UNMIS electoral task force continued to track developments on the census and to engage with international partners on planning for electoral assistance activities. The Mission has initiated measures to establish electoral capacity in southern Sudan within the next few months, including through the establishment of the Juba regional office, to be followed by expansion into the sectors. Capacity will also be strengthened at UNMIS headquarters in order to be prepared for the run-up to elections, subsequent to the enactment of the elections law and establishment of the national elections commission.

Police

45. As at 9 July 2007, UNMIS had deployed 686 police advisers, representing 96 per cent of the authorized strength. In a significant development, the Mission began delivery of the new United Nations police training assistance package in southern Sudan, designed to improve local capacity and compliance with principles of democratic policing and international best practices. The package focuses on basic police skills and on special training in crisis response, which will strengthen the credibility of the police as an alternative to the military in maintaining law and order. United Nations police conducted the first crisis response training in Juba in June 2007; a first group of 29 officers has graduated and is expected to form the nucleus of a local formed police unit in Juba. Meanwhile, five northern states have also requested United Nations police training support.

46. In addition, United Nations police continue to promote community policing practices in all sectors and to monitor and address human rights abuses by the police, particularly in the area of unlawful detention. During the reporting period, the new gender and child protection and special investigation units of the United Nations police component intervened to secure the release of 75 persons unlawfully held in local police and prison custody.

47. United Nations police also continued to advise the Southern Sudan Police Service on strategic development, including on command and communications structures. United Nations officers are now co-located with local police at six out of 10 State commands and at 36 local stations. During the reporting period, a registration database and identity card scheme for the Southern Sudan Police Service, established by UNMIS, was transferred to the control of the Service. This will aid them in planning and in the effective management of authorized officers.

48. Meanwhile, UNMIS continued to promote community policing in camps for internally displaced persons, completing a fifth workshop at the Al Baraka camp near Khartoum which resulted in the establishment of a local joint action programme for community policing with relevant stakeholders. The Mission also provided community policing training for national police officers from Darfur to enable them to initiate their own projects on return to the region.

Human rights

49. UNMIS continued to promote the urgent establishment of the human rights institutions mandated by the Comprehensive Peace Agreement, in cooperation with Government officials and representatives of civil society. In this context, UNMIS organized two preparatory workshops on the structure and competencies of the projected national human rights commission.

In the south, the Mission continued to assist the Southern Sudan Human Rights Commission by providing two short-term technical advisers who are to train the newly selected southern Sudanese human rights monitors.

50. In Khartoum, the UNMIS human rights component closely coordinated with the National Assembly's human rights committee in organizing a workshop on harmonizing existing laws with international human rights standards. Following the suspension of Al-Sudani newspaper and the detention of two journalists in violation of the right to freedom of expression, UNMIS monitored and attended court hearings while at the same time advocating for the adoption of the draft law on press and publications to grant greater freedom of the press. While UNMIS worked towards strengthening cooperation and information-sharing with the Khartoum State police, it continued to closely monitor developments affecting internally displaced persons in camps, including recent police raids on the Mayo and Soba camps located near Khartoum.

51. In this context, UNMIS has engaged an international expert on human rights training for police forces, who will help to develop a comprehensive strategy and manual on human rights training for national police forces. Meanwhile, UNMIS staff delivered human rights and rule of law training for police, prosecutors and legal advisers newly appointed in southern Sudan.

Rule of law

52. In Khartoum, on 10 May, the Government, UNMIS and UNDP signed a memorandum of understanding relating to the reform of the prison system in the Sudan. A prison development committee will now be established, and the Government has requested that 15 international corrections officers be deployed across the Sudan to provide technical assistance. Twenty-five advisers are already being placed in prisons in southern Sudan. In Juba, training began for 532 ex-SPLA soldiers assigned to the Southern Sudan Prison Service. Through UNMIS facilitation, a group of new southern Sudan prison personnel are being trained in prison management in Kenya.

53. However, across southern Sudan, the shortage of infrastructure and facilities for the courts continues to hinder judicial activities. Prosecutors and judges have no office space or staff support to sustain a functioning court system. In addition, the interface between customary law courts and statutory courts remains a contentious issue pending the adoption of relevant legislation.

Public information

54. UNMIS radio (Radio Miraya-FM) continues to expand its broadcast network into remote areas of the south. Work is ongoing to build repeater stations in Torit, Yambio and Maridi in Western and Eastern Equatoria. Miraya journalists are now permanently based in Malakal, Wau and Rumbek. Miraya-FM broadcasts on a dedicated internet site can also be heard by audiences, including the Sudanese diaspora. Negotiations with the Government to secure approval for UNMIS to broadcast in the north continue. Miraya-FM is closely cooperating with AMIS in preparing weekly programmes and public service announcements which are broadcast by state radio stations in Nyala, Geneina and El Fasher. UNMIS also holds regular weekly press briefings, including presentations on activities by substantive units and members of the United Nations country team. In the south and transitional areas,

the Mission continues to reach out to the community with workshops on the Comprehensive Peace Agreement and the role of UNMIS.

Humanitarian assistance

55. By June, the United Nations and partners workplan for Sudan was 62 per cent funded, with some $780 million pledged towards the total of $1.26 billion in humanitarian requirements for 2007. Funding for food aid, which represents just over half of the total workplan, was particularly strong, whereas other sectors including basic infrastructure, health and support for returns remain significantly underfunded.

56. The second instalment of $45 million from the 2007 Common Humanitarian Fund was allocated in early April. In southern Sudan, $10 million was divided between Warrap, Eastern Equatoria, Jonglei, Upper Nile and Northern Bahr el Ghazal—five states which are prime destinations of the majority of internally displaced persons and refugees returning to their areas of origin in southern Sudan, but are generally underserved in terms of basic social services and key sectors. Meanwhile, United Nations agencies and implementing partners have nearly completed the distribution of vital seeds and tools to target beneficiaries in southern Sudan, mainly returnees from the north. Some 82 per cent of the targeted beneficiaries have received agricultural inputs and started planting.

57. In Darfur, the humanitarian situation and operations continued to be characterized by forced movement of civilians, increasing the number of internally displaced persons to 2.2 million and raising the level of tensions in camps. All in all, while a major humanitarian crisis is being averted, providing humanitarian assistance in Darfur continues to be an uphill struggle with decreasing assets and staff available to maintain the aid operations. There are now 12,300 aid workers active in Darfur. Access to populations in need has dropped from 78 per cent to 68 per cent during the reporting period, owing largely to security concerns arising from an increase in banditry. At the same time, the caseload of conflict-affected populations has increased by more than half a million, to 4.2 million people, which is an increase of 15 per cent.

Protection of civilians

58. UNMIS continues to monitor and work with relevant actors to address issues of civilian security. The Mission and agency partners succeeded in obtaining the agreement of the Khartoum State government to a set of guiding principles for the relocation of displaced persons, which will open the door to addressing the shelter needs of this vulnerable population.

59. In southern Sudan, the activities of some regular armed forces and local militias, the exploitation of oil resources and tribal insecurity continue to pose challenges for the protection of civilians. In Eastern Equatoria, UNMIS facilitated the investigation into the killing of over 50 women and children in Lauro following the eruption of violence mentioned in paragraph 3 above. In Unity State, an UNMIS assessment mission observed serious problems associated with oil development, including lack of consultation and failure to compensate communities for environmental damage and loss of land. In particular, new roads have changed water courses and have adversely affected grazing and farming. UNMIS continues to advocate for respect of the provisions of the Comprehensive Peace Agreement, which calls for natural resources to be developed with regard for sustainable development and with due consultation and compensation for affected individuals and communities.

60. Across the Sudan, UNMIS, in coordination with the United Nations Children's Fund (UNICEF), continues to monitor and advocate for the release of children associated with armed groups. As a result of efforts by the Special Representative of the Secretary-General for Children and Armed Conflict, UNICEF and UNMIS, Sudan Liberation Army leader and Presidential Assistant Minni Minawi agreed to release minors associated with his forces. Another breakthrough occurred in Unity State, southern Sudan, when 26 boys affiliated with SPLA were demobilized in May. However, it is estimated that thousands of children still remain to be demobilized.

Returns

61. The current return season saw a dramatic increase in the number of organized returns compared to 2006. Some 85,000 internally displaced persons and refugees have been transported back to their homes by the United Nations as part of the joint plan agreed between the national and Southern Sudan authorities and the United Nations. The main areas of return have been Central Equatoria, Northern Bahr el Ghazal and Blue Nile. With the onset of the rains, return operations have decreased but will continue, utilizing road networks that remain open from Kenya and Uganda as well as air and river corridors to otherwise inaccessible areas. As expected, the rate of spontaneous returnees has decreased this quarter as more people take advantage of organized transport provided by the United Nations. This description of returns does not cover Darfur, which is dealt with in my separate reports to the Council.

Mine action

62. UNMIS mine action teams continued to make good progress during the final weeks of the dry season. Of 2,080 dangerous areas identified in 2003, 814 have been cleared. During the reporting period, UNMIS also began work to assess the needs of mine survivors and mine-affected communities in southern Sudan. UNMIS and UNICEF continue to provide mine-risk education to people living in or returning to affected areas, as well as to all incoming United Nations personnel.

63. During the reporting period, the National Mine Action Centre opened an office in Kassala, while the Southern Sudan De-mining Commission has been establishing regional offices in Yei and Malakal. These are positive steps towards the development of a self-sustaining indigenous mine action capacity in the Sudan that will be able to tackle the problems associated with landmines and explosive remnants of war after the departure of UNMIS.

Economic recovery and reconstruction

64. The March 2007 Sudan Consortium identified three tasks to be completed before the next meeting of donors in October: a detailed review of the Joint Assessment Mission and plans for the 2008-2011 phase, to be fully integrated with the planning of the Government of National Unity and the Government of Southern Sudan; establishment of a Government of National Unity-Government of Southern Sudan task force to review and address constraints to aid delivery; and preparations for the October Consortium, including a review of the Consortium's mandate. During the reporting period, the Government of National Unity established a high-level committee to pursue these recommendations, including representatives of the World Bank, the United Nations and donors. Field visits by the committee are under way in northern Sudan, assessing challenges to aid delivery.

65. Proposals for creating a second window to the multi-donor trust funds were officially presented to the Government of National Unity and the Government of Southern Sudan in May 2007. Initial indications reflect that the two Governments view the proposal positively; however, they are yet to provide a formal response.

Gender

66. During the reporting period, UNMIS partnered with the Ministry of Social Welfare, Gender and Child Affairs to formulate a workplan for the implementation of the Sudan's national policy for women's empowerment. The policy covers six thematic areas derived from the Millennium Development Goals and the Beijing Platform for Action. In addition, the Mission's gender unit continued to provide technical support and capacity-building to other government institutions at national and state levels, focused on the prevention of gender-based violence and recognition of women's role in peacebuilding. Internally, UNMIS continued to ensure gender awareness within the military, police and civilian components of the Mission.

HIV/AIDS

67. UNMIS maintained its training of peer educators and HIV/AIDS counsellors, including a new initiative for training by HIV/AIDS regional committees. A total of 503 peer educators had been trained by the end of June. In addition, over 20,000 members of the armed forces, police and general public across the Sudan received HIV/AIDS sensitization training. In a special initiative with UNDP and the southern Sudan authorities, 39 HIV/AIDS local counsellors were trained to support SPLA and the Southern Sudan Disarmament, Demobilization and Reintegration Commission.

Conduct and discipline

68. During the reporting period, some 30 allegations of misconduct in UNMIS were reported, including two allegations of serious misconduct which were referred to the Office of Internal Oversight Services. One allegation of sexual exploitation and abuse, published by a local newspaper in Wau (sector II), was found to be false and was officially retracted. The Mission continued to work actively with staff members and in the local community to raise awareness of conduct and discipline issues and my policy of zero tolerance of sexual exploitation and abuse.

V. Observations

69. In this progress report, I had hoped to be able to inform the Security Council of the completion of redeployment by the Sudanese Armed Forces out of southern Sudan, and to register this as a major achievement of the parties. Regrettably, despite some hard work by all concerned and frequent assurances by the Government of its commitment, the 9 July 2007 deadline has not been fully met. I call upon SAF immediately to remove all remaining regular military elements from southern Sudan, with the exception of those earmarked for Joint Integration Units. I welcome recent progress in the Ceasefire Political Commission to establish timelines and mechanisms for resolving the status of voluntarily demobilized troops and trust that these arrangements will be implemented without delay. Meanwhile, UNMIS will continue its efforts to complete full verification of the redeployment, which requires the cooperation of the parties.

70. While redeployment is a major stepping stone towards full implementation of the Comprehensive Peace Agreement's security protocol, several other elements of this key agreement still need to be pursued in earnest by both parties in the months ahead, and closely monitored and verified by UNMIS, as mandated in resolution 1590 (2005).

71. As I previously stressed to the Council, the development of the Joint Integration Units remains an issue of central importance. According to the timelines provided in the Comprehensive Peace Agreement, the formation of these units is a prerequisite for full redeployment of SPLA forces from Southern Kordofan and Blue Nile States. The Joint Integration Units are also mandated to protect the Sudan's oilfields, while oil installations themselves are to be demilitarized under the Agreement. Given the importance of this process, I strongly urge the parties to complete the assignment of troops to the Joint Integration Units, which is already some nine months overdue. In the meantime, the efforts of the Joint Defence Board and the Unit leaders to develop plans for integration and training of the Units are welcome, and UNMIS stands ready to assist in this process. In this context, I also encourage Member States concerned to consider what assistance they may be able to provide to establish effective Joint Integration Units.

72. Another key issue facing the implementation of the Comprehensive Peace Agreement is the reintegration of former members of other armed groups. I welcome the recent progress made by both parties in this area. The formal dissolution of the Southern Sudan Defence Force and the incorporation of its members into SPLA or their absorption into disarmament programmes is a positive step. Declarations of incorporation or demobilization, however, must be followed up by transparent action. The parties should be encouraged to continue cooperation on this issue and ensure that the process is indeed completed, with a view to achieving comprehensive peace and stability.

73. These concerns, together with the uncertainty about the status of Abyei, agreement on the 1 January 1956 boundary and management of the oil sector, will be key issues for the parties and the United Nations to deal with in the coming months. Indeed, Abyei needs to become a real "bridge between north and south", as envisaged in the Comprehensive Peace Agreement. In this regard, the parties will have to establish a functioning interim executive as provided for in the Agreement, and resolve their differences on the boundary issue as soon as possible. For this reason, I have assured the parties that I will make available to them United Nations expertise and/or mediation support, if they believe this would help their discussions. Once again, I strongly urge them to lift all restrictions they have imposed on the movement of UNMIS personnel in the area around Abyei.

74. I welcome the progress in the efforts to resolve outstanding disputes over wealth sharing, particularly in the face of budgetary pressure over falling oil revenues. The parties are expected to cooperate in the sharing of resources, as provided for in the Comprehensive Peace Agreement, and in particular to make good use of the Stabilization Fund, in order to minimize the impact which future oil price fluctuations might have on national revenue. I appeal to the parties to continue close cooperation aimed at achieving a transparent regime for the management and sustainable development of oil resources, and to protect the population from the negative effects of resource exploitation.

75. The international community expects the parties to support the early technical demarcation of the 1 January 1956 border between the north and the south, which should be based

on the principles agreed by the NCP and the SPLM and informed by due consultation with local communities, as well as best international practice. In the meantime, the United Nations is taking steps to provide expertise to the Technical Border Committee in support of this important process.

76. The intensive contacts and negotiations by the parties in their joint executive institutions are a welcome reaffirmation of their commitment to address critical issues related to the Comprehensive Peace Agreement, to strengthen partnership and to overcome mistrust. The two parties should be congratulated on the progress they have made, but be mindful that the real value of the results of negotiations will be in their implementation on the ground. Meanwhile, every effort should be made to use the institutions created by the Comprehensive Peace Agreement, in particular the Assessment and Evaluation Commission, to ensure that all key matters are addressed and disagreements resolved.

77. With regard to elections, the pace of their preparation has so far been disappointing, and both parties have to accelerate work dramatically on the necessary legislative reforms. UNMIS remains ready to assist in that effort.

78. In southern Sudan, the Government of Southern Sudan is making commendable efforts to transform wartime structures into a civilian administration capable of building long-term peace. However, daunting challenges in this crucial area remain. Civilian structures, including the police and judiciary, continue to be weak, mainly because of scarcity of resources and capacity. In this context, I urge both the Government of Southern Sudan and donors to expand and accelerate the training and development of the Southern Sudan Police Service.

79. Law and order aspects also remain a major pillar of a broader social transformation challenge. To achieve stability, the Government of Southern Sudan needs to tackle fundamental issues of land and natural resources, manage its relationship with traditional authorities and facilitate reconciliation among tribes and factions in southern society. Donors are encouraged to seek additional ways to support the south in these major challenges, including through the provision of financial or technical assistance to the Southern Sudan Peace and Reconciliation Commission.

80. With the completion of SAF redeployment, the focus of Comprehensive Peace Agreement implementation efforts will naturally turn to the required redeployment of SPLA from Southern Kordofan and Blue Nile. I welcome the recent moves by SPLA to begin this process and urge it to take forward redeployment in a timely manner, with monitoring and verification conducted through the Ceasefire Joint Military Commission. At the same time, I strongly encourage the civilian authorities of both parties in the transitional areas to support the process through the integration of administrations stipulated by the Comprehensive Peace Agreement.

81. In recent months, the parties have made welcome progress in supporting the return of refugees and displaced persons, and in planning for the disarmament, demobilization and reintegration of ex-combatants. These are two essential components of the search for durable peace in the Sudan. I urge both signatories of the Comprehensive Peace Agreement to rapidly complete the national disarmament, demobilization and reintegration strategy, and hope that the international community will promptly identify funding to support implementation, including plans for the reintegration of ex-combatants. I welcome the excellent cooperation

between the Government of National Unity and the Government of Southern Sudan related to the return of the displaced, facilitated by the United Nations, and encourage the parties to continue their joint efforts. While work to meet return targets continues, there is also a pressing need to ensure that returns are sustainable. The reintegration and rehabilitation of war-affected communities, a key principle of the Comprehensive Peace Agreement, will require sustained support by both parties and the international community.

82. In conclusion, I wish to express my gratitude to all United Nations personnel working in the Sudan for their sacrifices and determined effort to support the implementation of the Comprehensive Peace Agreement and to end the devastating conflict in Darfur. I am also appreciative of the efforts of the African Union—with whom the United Nations is cooperating very closely—as well as the invaluable assistance provided by many Member States, including donors and troop- and police-contributing countries.

Annex
Military and police component as at 17 July 2007

	Military component									
	Observers		*Staff officers*		*Troops*		*Military subtotal*		*Civilian police*	
Country	*Male*	*Female*	*Male*	*Female*	*Male*	*Female*	*Male*	*Female*	*Male*	*Female*
Argentina									11	—
Australia	6	—	7	2			13	2	8	2
Bangladesh	20	—	34	—	1 523	—	1 577	—	32	—
Belgium	5	—					5	—		
Benin	6	—					6	—		
Bolivia	15	—	1	—			16	—		
Bosnia and Herzegovina									2	—
Botswana	5	—					5	—		
Brazil	24	—					24	—	3	—
Burkina Faso	6	—					6	—		
Cambodia	8	—	1	—	135	—	144	—		
Canada	24	—	7	1			31	1	2	1
China	14	—	8	—	424	11	446	11	8	—
Croatia			5	—			5	—		
Denmark	10	—	6	—			16	—	1	—
Ecuador	20	—					20	—		
Egypt	18	—	21	—	781	15	820	15	7	—
El Salvador	5	—					5	—	3	2
Fiji	7	—					7	—	4	3
Finland			1	—			1	—	2	—
Gabon	8	—					8	—		
Gambia			1	—			1	—	19	1
Germany	35	—	5	—			40	—	4	—
Ghana			3	—			3	—	40	4

	Military component									
	Observers		Staff officers		Troops		Military subtotal		Civilian police	
Country	Male	Female	Male	Female	Male	Female	Male	Female	Male	Female
Greece	4	—	2	—			6	—		
Guatemala	8	—	1	—			9	—		
Guinea	5	—					5	—		
India	18	—	28	—	2 575	4	2 621	4	19	2
Indonesia	10	—					10	—	1	—
Jamaica									5	4
Jordan	12	—	10	—			22	—	21	2
Kenya	6	1	11	—	775	45	792	46	18	2
Kyrgyzstan	8	—					8	—	2	—
Malawi	6	—	1	—			7	—		
Malaysia	8	—	4	—			12	—	11	—
Mali	5	—					5	—		
Moldova	2	—					2	—		
Mongolia	2	—					2	—		
Mozambique	1	—					1	—		
Namibia	7	2					7	2	1	—
Nepal	6	2	7	—			13	2	58	1
Netherlands	14	—	4	—			18	—	8	1
New Zealand	2	—					2	—		
Niger			1	—			1	—		
Nigeria	13	1	7	1			20	2	47	4
Norway	13	—	12	2			25	2	6	—
Pakistan	19	—	29	—	1 539	—	1 587	—	40	2
Paraguay	10	—					10	—		
Peru	17	—					17	—		
Philippines	13	—					13	—	52	1
Poland	2	—					2	—		
Republic of Korea	7	—	1	—			8	—		
Romania	12	—					12	—		
Russian Federation	12	—	3	—	120	—	135	—	11	—
Rwanda	15	—	8	—	253	—	276	—	21	—
Samoa									15	—
Senegal			5	—			5	—		
South Africa			4	—			4	—		
Sri Lanka	3	—					3	—	23	1
Sweden	3	—	3	—			6	—	12	2

Continued

	Military component									
	Observers		*Staff officers*		*Troops*		*Military subtotal*		*Civilian police*	
Country	*Male*	*Female*	*Male*	*Female*	*Male*	*Female*	*Male*	*Female*	*Male*	*Female*
United Republic of Tanzania	15	—	6	—			21	—	1	—
Thailand	12	—	2	—			14	—		
Turkey			3	—			3	—	14	—
Uganda	8	1					8	1	11	3
Ukraine	6	—					6	—	13	—
United Kingdom			4	—			4	—	1	—
United States									8	2
Uruguay									2	—
Yemen	16	—	4	—			20	—	3	—
Zambia	12	2	13	—	328	16	353	18	15	3
Zimbabwe	12	2		—			12	2	22	9
Total per gender	**580**	**11**	**274**	**6**	**8453**	**91**	**9306**	**108**	**606**	**50**
Total	**591**		**280**		**8544**		**9414**		**656**	

H. West Africa

1. Twelfth Progress Report of the Secretary-General on the United Nations Mission in Liberia, 12 September 2006 (S/2006/743)

I. Introduction

1. By its resolution 1667 (2006) of 31 March 2006, the Security Council extended the mandate of the United Nations Mission in Liberia (UNMIL) until 30 September 2006 and requested me to present further recommendations for a drawdown plan for UNMIL. These recommendations were provided in my report of 9 June 2006 (S/2006/376). The present report provides an update on major developments in Liberia and contains broad benchmarks for the first phase of the consolidation, drawdown and withdrawal of UNMIL.

II. Major political developments

2. I visited Liberia from 3 to 5 July to witness the progress being made in rebuilding the country and to consult with the Government on how best the United Nations could continue to support its efforts to consolidate peace and advance the recovery process. I met with President Ellen Johnson-Sirleaf, members of her Cabinet and other senior public officials and had the privilege of addressing a joint session of the Liberian Legislature. I was impressed by the commitment and dedication to peace and democratic governance demonstrated by the leaders and people of Liberia and was reassured by the progress made in recent months notwithstanding the severe economic and financial limitations.

3. On 20 June, former Liberian President Charles Taylor was transferred from the Special Court for Sierra Leone to The Hague, Netherlands, pursuant to Security Council resolution 1688 (2006). Mr. Taylor's transfer elicited mixed reactions from the Liberian public. Most civil society and human rights organizations, as well as political figures supported the transfer as necessary to ensure stability in Liberia and the subregion. Others expressed concern that the victims of war crimes allegedly committed by Mr. Taylor would be denied the opportunity to witness the trial in the country where serious crimes were committed. However, the predominant view expressed was that Mr. Taylor should have a fair and transparent trial.

4. Despite some delays caused by tensions between the executive and legislative branches, the Government's first national budget for the fiscal period 2006/07 was unanimously passed by the Legislature on 22 August and signed into law by President Johnson-Sirleaf on 28 August. The budget, which is based on a base revenue projection of $120.9 million and a contingent revenue projection of $9 million, focuses on the Government's national reconstruction and development priorities for Liberia. Revenues are expected to be generated from taxes on income, profits, property, domestic services, international trade and cellular phone companies, while contingent revenues will be dependent on income from sources such as timber, diamonds, iron ore and rubber.

5. In the aftermath of the fire on 26 July that destroyed part of the Executive Mansion, President Johnson-Sirleaf made changes within her Cabinet and in the leadership of the State security structures. The Minister of State for Presidential Affairs and Chief of Staff

was replaced and a new Director of the Special Security Services was appointed. The President indicated that these changes were aimed at strengthening the efficiency of the Executive Mansion staff with respect to security, administration and other responsibilities.

6. On 18 August, the Supreme Court rejected the writs of prohibition filed by some human rights and democracy organizations, as well as by two Senators, against the induction and seating of former leader of Liberians United for Reconciliation and Democracy and National Transitional Government of Liberia Minister of Justice, Kabineh Ja'neh, as Associate Justice of the Supreme Court. This cleared the way for Mr. Ja'neh's induction on 29 August.

7. The President continued her anti-corruption campaign during the period under review. The President dismissed a number of senior government officials for corruption, including a deputy minister, an assistant minister, a chief medical officer, a deputy director of the Liberian National Police and a chairman of a public corporation. She also terminated the appointments of three revenue collectors, a senior economist and a supervisor of the foreign travel section for financial improprieties.

8. The long-awaited report on economic crime in Liberia, which was prepared by the Economic Community of West African States (ECOWAS) during the tenure of the National Transitional Government of Liberia, was publicly released by the Government in July. It may be recalled that ECOWAS did not release the report while the Transitional Government was still in office. The report had recommended the immediate dismissal of four senior officials in the Transitional Government for misappropriation and mismanagement of public funds. Several civil society groups and media outlets have since called for the prosecution of the individuals named in the report.

9. The President has reconstituted the task force on recovery of public assets. The previous membership had failed to recover government assets from former officials of the National Transitional Legislative Assembly of Liberia. These assets include vehicles, furniture and computers, which were allocated to them for use in their official capacity. In addition, the President has instructed the Ministry of Justice to conclude action on several audit reports of different government entities and to identify, for the purpose of prosecution, individuals who have abused the public trust. In the meantime, 12 former employees of the National Social Security and Welfare Corporation who were being prosecuted for misappropriating public funds, were acquitted by the Supreme Court on 23 August.

10. During the reporting period, the 17-member ad hoc presidential commission established to investigate the inter-ethnic dispute in Nimba County concluded hearings in Sanniquillie and Saclepea after obtaining verbal assurances from the conflicting parties that they would peacefully settle future disputes. The commission is still conducting hearings in Ganta and has established a technical committee to investigate land and property claims in that city. In the meantime, UNMIL has continued to work closely with the Ministries of Internal Affairs, and Lands, Mines and Energy and with civil society organizations, to address other inter-ethnic, religious, community and land and property disputes in other parts of the country.

11. On 20 August, the Cabinet approved a draft anti-corruption policy paper prepared by the Governance Reform Commission, which sets out a framework to tackle impunity and promote a sustainable system of accountability and public integrity. The Governance

Reform Commission also submitted a draft code of conduct and draft declaration of income, assets and liabilities form for public servants, which are both designed to ensure transparency, efficiency and effectiveness of public servants in the performance of their duties. In the meantime, the Government has submitted, for adoption by the Legislature, acts to ratify the United Nations Convention against Corruption and the African Union Convention on the Prevention and Combating of Corruption.

III. Security situation

12. The security situation in Liberia has remained generally stable, but there are continuing serious threats to stability that require careful and robust management. Although the transfer of Mr. Taylor's trial from the region has considerably reduced tensions in Liberia, concern remains over the activities of his associates and supporters.

13. During the reporting period, UNMIL conducted military operations aimed at reassuring the populace and underlining the Mission's resolve to maintain peace and stability throughout the country. The operations involved robust patrolling within the Mission's area of operations and the deployment of the Mission's quick reaction force to the border areas and to Freetown to reinforce security at the Special Court for Sierra Leone.

14. Demobilized personnel from the former Armed Forces of Liberia, the Liberian National Police and the Special Security Service staged several demonstrations to demand severance payments and other benefits. Some of these demands were met when retired Armed Forces of Liberia personnel were honoured at a ceremony attended by the President during the Independence Day celebrations and when former personnel of the Anti-Terrorist Unit (a militia group established and controlled by former President Charles Taylor) received payments from the Government, albeit on humanitarian grounds. Many of these demobilized personnel have limited access to employment opportunities and are susceptible to manipulation by various interest groups.

15. Incidents of armed robbery within Monrovia and its environs also increased during the reporting period, leading to calls by the public for the arming of the Liberian National Police and the adoption of more extensive security measures to curb the activities of criminal gangs. UNMIL police, in cooperation with the Liberian National Police, increased their patrols in high crime areas within Monrovia and continued to develop community-based approaches to crime prevention. In addition, on 16 August, UNMIL troops and formed police units commenced joint night foot patrols throughout Monrovia. UNMIL has also continued to conduct joint cordon and search operations to recover firearms. These operations will actively continue in the weeks and months ahead.

16. Several incidents of armed robberies and killings involving management, workers, residents and ex-combatants were reported at the Cocopa and Guthrie rubber plantations. On 15 August, with the assistance of UNMIL, the Government officially re-established its control over the Guthrie rubber plantation. UNMIL has also increased its patrolling activities at Cocopa and other rubber plantations. In the meantime, efforts are being made to accelerate the establishment of interim management teams at contested or abandoned rubber plantations, as recommended by the joint Government/UNMIL task force on rubber plantations.

17. There were also shooting incidents within Monrovia involving officials of the Special Security Service, which provides close protection to the President. On 3 and 5 August,

separate shooting incidents occurred at the residence of the Director of the Special Security Service. The latter incident resulted in the death of the Director's personal bodyguard from gunshot wounds allegedly inflicted by a second security officer. The investigations into the causes of these incidents and of a third shooting incident on 8 August at the residence of the Deputy Director of the Special Security Service are ongoing.

18. As mentioned in paragraph 5 above, on 26 July, during Liberia's 159th Independence Day celebration, a fire broke out in the Executive Mansion where President Johnson-Sirleaf was hosting a luncheon for some 300 people, including the Presidents of Ghana, Côte d'Ivoire and Sierra Leone. Although no injuries were reported, significant damage was done to the Executive Mansion. An investigation into the fire was conducted with the assistance of UNMIL and South African forensic experts. On 3 September, the Government released the investigation report, which attributed the cause of the fire to an electrical fault.

19. No significant military activity that could threaten the stability of Liberia was observed on Liberia's borders with Sierra Leone, Côte d'Ivoire or Guinea. However, the unstable situation in Côte d'Ivoire continues to present a serious potential threat to stability in Liberia. In particular, there are concerns about the possible movement of armed groups from Côte d'Ivoire into Liberia; the recruitment of former Liberian combatants, including children, by Ivorian militia groups and Liberians to fight in Côte d'Ivoire; and an influx of Ivorians seeking refuge in Liberia in the event of violence in that country. To counter these potential threats, UNMIL has positioned additional forces in the eastern and southern border areas and strengthened its aviation capability in the southern part of the country.

20. In order to increase the presence of the United Nations in the border areas, establish cross-border liaison and reassure the local population, UNMIL and the United Nations Operation in Côte d'Ivoire (UNOCI) conducted concurrent patrols along the Liberian-Ivorian border from 26 to 30 June in "Operation Mayo". Similar patrols were undertaken from 7 to 11 August with the Sierra Leonean forces in "Operation Loko".

IV. Status of implementation of the mandate of the United Nations Mission in Liberia

A. Rehabilitation and reintegration of ex-combatants

21. As at 15 August, some 39,000 ex-combatants had not yet benefited from the reintegration programme. It is expected that 19,409 of these ex-combatants will be absorbed by projects sponsored by the United Nations Development Programme (UNDP) Trust Fund, while the remaining caseload will be covered by bilaterally funded programmes.

22. In the meantime, UNMIL continued to collect and destroy residual weapons and ammunition that were voluntarily surrendered or discovered through search operations. Since the end of the disarmament and demobilization programme in 2005, 632 weapons, 70,454 rounds of small arms ammunition, 941 pieces of unexploded ordnance and 11,550 assorted spares have been collected and destroyed by UNMIL.

23. A coordination group comprising representatives from UNMIL, the United Nations Children's Fund (UNICEF), UNDP, the Liberian National Police and the Liberian National Commission for Small Arms and Landmine Action (an international non-governmental

organization) has been established to streamline efforts to eliminate small arms and light weapons from Liberia. The coordination group has prepared a common strategy, which includes modalities for the collection and disposal of unexploded ordnance and explosive remnants of war, and mine risk education. The group's work is complemented by the UNDP Community Arms Collection for Development programme. Since its launch in January, over 7,000 small arms ammunitions, 100 guns and 100 unexploded ordnances and rocket-propelled grenades have been collected through the Community Arms Collection for Development programme. As at August, the programme was being implemented in Lofa, River Gee, Maryland, Nimba, Grand Gedeh and Bong Counties.

B. Reform of the Liberian National Police

24. The reform and restructuring of the Liberian National Police continues to make good progress. As at 1 September, 2,073 Liberian National Police, 392 Special Security Services and 155 Seaport Police officers had been trained and deployed. Some 295 new Liberian National Police recruits are currently undergoing field training, while 419 are receiving basic training. In order to reach the target of 3,500 fully trained Liberian National Police personnel by July 2007, the field training programme has been compressed from 26 to 16 weeks. Moreover, to address the serious shortfall in the mid-level ranks of the Liberian National Police, the United Nations police has developed a basic management course for 300 Liberian National Police officers and a senior leadership qualification programme for 50 officers.

25. At the same time, the presence of the Liberian National Police in the interior of the country remains far below acceptable levels. This is partially due to the unavailability of suitable housing, vehicles and communications equipment needed to sustain the deployment of the police in the counties. To date, the Liberian National Police has deployed only 454 officers throughout the 15 counties in Liberia. Immediate priority has been given to providing reinforcements for the Liberian National Police county headquarters and the Guthrie rubber plantation. Of the remaining 1,577 trained police officers, 208 are assigned to zones and depots within Monrovia, 49 are assigned to Roberts International Airport, 300 are assigned to the Liberian National Police Support Unit, 174 are assigned to the Monrovia Central Patrol Division, and the remaining 731 are assigned to the Liberian National Police headquarters in Monrovia. The United Nations police is working with the Liberian National Police to rationalize the high number of officers currently assigned to the Monrovia headquarters.

26. The Government urgently needs funds to complete the basic training programme for new recruits, to conduct specialized management and thematic police training programmes and to provide vehicles, communications equipment and accommodation allowances to sustain the deployment of the Liberian National Police in the interior of the country. UNMIL is assisting the Government to prepare an appeal to Member States for assistance in these critical areas. I urge Member States to respond favourably to this request.

27. As at 1 September, 2,035 out of a targeted 2,351 Liberian National Police officers had been deactivated with funds provided by the United Kingdom of Great Britain and Northern Ireland. Those remaining to be deactivated include officers who have either disputed their deactivation or who cannot be located.

C. Reform of the Armed Forces of Liberia

28. The United States of America continues to assist the Government in building a new Armed Forces of Liberia. To date, 7,050 recruits have applied to be enlisted in the Armed Forces of Liberia, of whom 6,327 have passed the literacy tests, 2,510 have passed the physical fitness test and 1,050 have passed all medical tests. However, as at 1 September, only 563 applicants had been recommended for training. The first group of 110 recruits for the new army began training at the Barclay Training Centre in Monrovia on 22 July. However, the first fully trained battalion is expected to be operational only in 2008.

29. The Government is also in the process of formulating a national security policy and has tasked the Governance Reform Commission with leading the public dialogue on security sector reform.

D. Consolidation of State authority throughout the country

30. Steady progress continued to be made in the restoration and consolidation of State authority throughout the territory of Liberia, with UNMIL facilitating the return of government officials to their duty stations in the counties. However, the work of county officials and government line ministries in the interior of the country continues to be constrained by the lack of communications equipment, transportation and office and residential accommodations. In the meantime, special support teams jointly established by UNMIL and the United Nations country team to assist county superintendents in strengthening coordination and to develop community recovery and development priorities have become operational in the counties.

31. Three additional Central Bank payment centres, constructed with the assistance of the Mission's quick-impact projects, were opened in Kakata, Margibi County, Gbarnga, Bong County and Buchanan, Grand Bassa County to facilitate salary payment to government officials stationed in remote locations. The number of Central Bank payment centres in the counties is now six. The Central Bank has carried out assessments in Barclayville, Grand Kru County, Harper, Maryland County and Greenville, Sinoe County with a view to opening payment centres in those locations, and is also encouraging commercial banks to expand their operations outside Monrovia.

32. Another important step in the restoration of State authority was the election of a new nine-member National Traditional Council of Paramount Chiefs and Elders. In addition, initial steps have been taken by the National Elections Commission, in collaboration with the Ministry of Internal Affairs, to prepare for municipal and chieftaincy elections, which are scheduled for October 2007, in which city mayors, paramount chiefs, clan chiefs and town chiefs are to be elected.

E. Restoration of proper management of natural resources

33. The Government is making progress in its efforts to regain control over the country's natural resources. In compliance with Security Council resolution 1689 (2006), a national forestry reform law, which was drafted with the assistance of UNMIL, is in the process of being enacted. Moreover, the Government's policy on the movement of timber within the country is being strictly implemented at the joint UNMIL/Forestry Development Authority checkpoints in Monrovia, which has led to an increase in public revenues. Efforts are being made to extend this arrangement to other parts of the country. The Government is also in

the process of developing an environmentally sustainable pit-sawing policy with the assistance of UNMIL.

34. The President has extended the mandate of the joint Government/UNMIL task force established to undertake a comprehensive assessment of Liberia's rubber plantations. The task force is now mandated to oversee the implementation of the recommendations contained in its 23 May report to the President, including the repossession of illegally occupied plantations, review of concession and management agreements and establishment of interim management teams for contested or abandoned plantations.

35. UNMIL is assisting with the installation of the interim management teams. The Mission has constructed a campsite and structure on the Guthrie rubber plantation, which will house the Liberian National Police, the Magistrate Court and other relevant government agencies. In addition, Liberian National Police personnel have been deployed to the plantation to conduct night and day patrols with the support of the United Nations police, and an interim management team has been created to manage the plantation pending the establishment of a permanent management team in accordance with the Public Procurement and Concessions Act.

36. The Government has accepted the recommendations of the Kimberley Process assessment team that visited Liberia in May, including the need to establish an inter-ministerial task force and a steering committee on Kimberley Process compliance and to suspend all large-scale mining activities. The United States of America is assisting with the construction of the Liberia Diamond Authority building, which will house the Government's Kimberley Process Certification Scheme diamond appraisers and administrators. In the meantime, UNMIL has temporarily provided containers that are being used as diamond certification offices. In June, with the support of UNMIL and UNDP, the Government hosted a West Africa subregional conference on the harmonization of taxation, border controls, law enforcement and issues related to alluvial diamond mining. The conference decided that civil society organizations should participate in the future establishment of diamond mining policies and artisanal alluvial miners should be provided with funding and training assistance.

37. Despite these efforts, illegal artisanal mining continues to be reported, mainly in the western parts of the country and in Nimba and Sinoe counties. In that regard, UNMIL will continue to assist the Government, to the extent possible, with its surveillance, mapping and inspection activities.

F. Promotion of human rights and the rule of law

1. Promotion of human rights

38. During the reporting period, UNMIL continued to carry out human rights promotion, protection and monitoring activities throughout the country. The Mission also intensified its capacity-building activities by conducting comprehensive legal education and training programmes for members of the legal profession and judicial system. A series of workshops was held for magistrates and justices of the peace from all 15 counties. In addition, with the support of the Office of the United Nations High Commissioner for Human Rights and Penal Reform International, a non-governmental organization, UNMIL conducted a three-day workshop on best practices, strengthening the rule of law and human rights protection for 120 participants drawn from the police, corrections, judiciary and local

administration across the country. The aim of the workshop was to improve and strengthen the criminal justice system and justice delivery in the country. Despite these activities, there has been an increase in reported cases of sexual and gender-based violence, in particular, rape and sexual abuse of women and girls.

39. During the reporting period, UNMIL released its fourth report on the human rights situation in Liberia. The report, which covers the period from February to April 2006, highlights human rights violations by law enforcement and judicial personnel, the human rights situation on rubber plantations and issues related to the protection of child rights. It also reports on the impact of the interference of government officials in the judicial system, corruption, high rates of sexual and gender-based violence, particularly involving child victims, and the use of harmful traditional practices on the enjoyment of human rights. The report contains a number of recommendations aimed at helping the Government with the implementation of its international human rights obligations.

40. The Truth and Reconciliation Commission commenced operations following the nationwide launching of its programme of public activities on 22 June. However, the Commission is still beset by financial and logistical constraints. While the Commission has requested $10 million for its two years of operations, it has only received $150,000 out of $600,000 pledged by UNDP; €84,000 out of €300,000 pledged by the European Commission; and $180,000 out of $278,000 promised by the Open Society Initiative for West Africa. In the meantime, the Government has earmarked $300,000 in the 2005/06 budget and office space and vehicles for the Commission's operations. UNMIL continued to support the Commission's public outreach programme and to make its air assets available for access to remote parts of the country.

41. The Independent National Commission on Human Rights is still in the process of appointing its members. On 10 August, the independent committee of experts, which was established to vet the nominees and applicants for the posts of Chairman and Commissioners, conducted interviews of 12 prospective candidates. Interviews for the remaining 13 candidates will be conducted shortly, after which the committee will conduct an assessment of all candidates on the basis of their human rights experience and prepare a shortlist to be examined by the Chief Justice. The final selections will be made by the President and confirmed by the Senate.

2. Support for the judicial system

42. Reform of the justice sector is continuing, albeit at a slow pace. The administration of justice continues to be constrained by the lack of court buildings in many counties and the dearth of qualified judicial and legal officers. UNMIL has funded a number of court construction and renovation projects across the country through its quick-impact project scheme. To date, six projects have been completed in Kakata, Tubmanburg, Gbarnga, Greenville, Bensonville and Careysburg and another seven projects are ongoing in Buchanan, Zwedru, Harper, Ganta, Sanniquellie, Bopolu and Cestos City.

43. UNMIL has also assisted the Government with the hiring of 12 national prosecutorial consultants and 11 public defence consultants for an initial period of six months. This has resulted in more cases being heard by the courts, which has contributed to a reduction in the backlog of pending cases; greater access to justice; improved adherence to fair trial standards; and increased public trust and confidence in the judicial system. Arrangements are under way to hire an additional seven public defence consultants.

44. The Mission's legal and judicial system support division continued to expand its capacity-building activities in the counties. The division is providing advice and assistance to legal and judicial officers in the counties in order to enhance their practical and procedural capacities to administer justice.

45. A task force constituted by the Minister of Justice to facilitate the establishment of the law reform commission commenced work in July. The draft law for the establishment of the commission is expected to be finalized and submitted to President Johnson-Sirleaf later this year. The success of this initiative will depend on the provision of adequate funding and support by the Government and the international community.

3. Support for the corrections system

46. UNMIL continued to assist the Bureau of Corrections and Rehabilitation in improving the conditions of correctional facilities in the country. The refurbishment programme, which is being funded by the United States of America and Norway, is continuing. Work has been completed at Kakata prison, while the rehabilitation of the Monrovia, Gbarnga, Buchanan and Harper prisons and the Zwedru Palace of Corrections is at varying stages of completion. The Firestone Company has also commenced rehabilitation of the Bondiway prison, which had been closed due to its dilapidated condition. Most correction facilities still rely heavily on UNMIL, the World Food Programme (WFP), the International Committee of the Red Cross and other partners for water, food, medical and other essential supplies to prisoners.

47. The Government has absorbed all the graduates of the first corrections officers' training class into the civil service. In the meantime, the recruits of the third corrections officers' training class have completed their 12-month induction training and the recruitment and training of qualified candidates for the fourth training class has been approved. The Government has also agreed to the deactivation of corrections personnel who do not meet civil service recruitment criteria.

G. Economic governance

48. Since my previous report, further progress was made in the implementation of the Governance and Economic Management Assistance Programme. The concessions and contracts expert, who was recruited for the technical secretariat of the Contracts and Concessions Review Committee, assumed duties. In addition, the European Commission commenced the recruitment exercise for an auditor general who will head the General Auditing Commission. On 16 June, the Government signed a memorandum of understanding for the consolidation of operational bank accounts for State-owned enterprises.

49. The Economic Governance Steering Committee continued to meet regularly to monitor progress in the implementation of the Governance and Economic Management Assistance Programme. The Steering Committee's technical team is working with the internationally recruited experts to ensure that they focus on improving financial management and transparency and on building the capacity of Government institutions and personnel through the proper transfer of skills and knowledge. The Steering Committee has asked the internationally recruited experts to provide monthly status reports on their activities. In the meantime, as part of the capacity-building process, the Government, in collaboration with UNDP, has convened a knowledge-building seminar to discuss how Liberia's State-owned enterprises can best utilize the international experts.

50. On 26 June, UNMIL, in collaboration with the Steering Committee technical team's public information subcommittee, launched an information campaign to raise public awareness of the progress being made in the implementation of the Governance and Economic Management Assistance Programme. The campaign will include daily interviews with government officials, civil society and international partners on UNMIL Radio. A website on the implementation of the Programme has also been created. In addition, the World Bank has agreed to provide a grant for public communication and sensitization efforts related to the Programme.

51. The Government continued to undertake initiatives aimed at improving controls over the granting of contracts and concessions and implementing a basic procurement system through its Public Procurement and Concessions Committee. During the reporting period, the Committee, in collaboration with the European Commission, convened a meeting of the Contracts and Concessions Review Committee, which was established to undertake an independent review of all contracts and concessions entered into by the National Transitional Government of Liberia.

H. National recovery, reconstruction and development

52. A partners' meeting was held in Monrovia on 12 and 13 July to assess the Government's performance during its first six months in office and to agree on the way forward for Liberia's recovery, reconstruction and development. The meeting provided an opportunity for the Government to meet with its international partners to address several policy issues prior to the partners' forum scheduled for early next year in Washington, D.C. At the meeting, the Government highlighted the severe capacity and implementation constraints that it faces in achieving its reconstruction and development objectives and presented a compelling case for targeted budget support and early debt relief. International partners acknowledged the positive achievements already made by the Government and urged it to continue to adhere to its reform programmes so as to ensure compliance with the Heavily Indebted Poor Countries Initiative and eventual debt relief.

53. During his visit to Liberia on 21 and 22 July, the President of the World Bank, Paul Wolfowitz, pledged the Bank's commitment to the economic development of Liberia and agreed to provide assistance for labour-intensive public works schemes aimed at building key infrastructure and generating employment. The Secretary of State for International Development of the United Kingdom of Great Britain and Northern Ireland, Hilary Benn, and the President of the African Development Bank, Donald Kaberuka, also paid a joint visit to Liberia on 18 and 19 July to review areas in which the United Kingdom and the African Development Bank could assist Liberia.

54. The Government has continued to highlight the urgent need for job creation. On 15 July, it launched the Liberia Emergency Employment Programme and the Liberia Employment Action Programme. The Liberia Emergency Employment Programme is aimed at creating short-term employment opportunities, while the Liberia Employment Action Programme is intended to provide long-term sustainable employment. Sources of short-term employment will include the labour-intensive rehabilitation of roads and critical infrastructures across the country. Over 5,000 local community members, including returnees and ex-combatants, have benefited from this initiative, which is supported by the WFP "Food support for local initiatives" programme. UNMIL's quick-impact projects have also enhanced the process of

employment creation, with nine projects providing short-term employment to some 900 ex-combatants and local community members in the south-eastern part of Liberia. In addition, UNMIL has continued to assist in the distribution of donated tools, as well as seed rice and other agricultural commodities provided by China.

55. The Government and the World Bank signed an agreement for the first part of a $68 million grant to conduct emergency rehabilitation and repair of critical infrastructure, including the rehabilitation of the Monrovia-Buchanan and Monrovia-Ganta highways, repairs to 65 bridges and construction of six bridges. The second part of the grant will be used to increase the Government's capacity to carry out road maintenance functions, build the capacity of the Liberia Water and Sewer Corporation and construct ports, airports, schools and health clinics. The grant is aimed at creating short-term jobs and providing a basis for economic development.

56. UNMIL and Liberia's international partners continued to support the Government's efforts to implement its 150-day action plan, which was designed to address some of the most urgent needs of the population, such as the partial restoration of electricity, road repairs and the rehabilitation of Government infrastructure. The Government estimates that more than 60 per cent of the action plan was successfully completed on schedule. As part of the 159th independence anniversary celebration of Liberia and in fulfilment of the promise made at her inauguration ceremony, President Johnson-Sirleaf switched on the Monrovia emergency electricity supply on 26 July, which was made possible with assistance from Ghana, the United States of America and the European Commission.

57. A team from the International Monetary Fund visited Monrovia from 20 to 28 July to assess progress under the Fund's staff-monitored programme. The team was impressed with the considerable progress made in the implementation of key policies under the staff-monitored programme and with the fact that revenues exceeded the programme target.

V. Humanitarian activities

58. The humanitarian situation continued to improve during the reporting period. To date, 77,523 refugees have returned to their places of origin with the assistance of the Office of the United Nations High Commissioner for Human Rights (OHCHR). In order to accelerate the return of the refugees, OHCHR has contracted a vessel to repatriate Liberian refugees residing in Ghana. The first group of 300 refugees from Ghana arrived in Liberia on 28 July. Although the camps for internally displaced persons have been officially closed since 20 April, some 13,000 internally displaced persons continue to reside in and around the camps.

59. There are several humanitarian challenges that require urgent attention in the communities of return. These include the provision of health care, water and sanitation, education, shelter, food and livelihood opportunities for returnees. The 2006 United Nations consolidated appeal for Liberia has only received 34 per cent of the estimated requirements for 2006, as per the mid-year review, which was launched on 19 July. I appeal to donors to generously provide the assistance required to meet these needs.

VI. Gender

60. The Mission's Gender Affairs Unit continued to build the Mission's capacity to implement Security Council resolution 1325 (2000) by conducting a training programme for middle and senior management in the Mission. The Unit also collaborated with the United

Nations Development Fund for Women and the Ministry of Gender and Development to organize a sensitization workshop for 100 women on the challenges and lessons learned from their participation in the 2005 national elections. In addition, the Unit actively supported the Truth and Reconciliation Commission process by providing training to the newly appointed commissioners aimed at facilitating outreach to women and girls. It facilitated a one-week consultative visit to Liberia by the Committee on the Elimination of Discrimination against Women, during which Committee members met with President Johnson-Sirleaf, who assured them of her Government's political support for the implementation of the Convention on the Elimination of All Forms of Discrimination against Women. The Unit also participated in training organized by UNDP and the World Bank for legislators and government agencies involved in the preparation of the budget.

VII. HIV/AIDS

61. The Mission's HIV/AIDS Unit continued to collaborate with the Mission's Integrated Training Cell to carry out HIV/AIDS awareness, training and sensitization as part of the induction training for military, police and civilian personnel. The Unit also continued to promote HIV/AIDS awareness through its participation in an UNMIL Radio live phone-in programme. In addition, it organized workshops for HIV/AIDS peer educators drawn from non-governmental organizations and UNMIL's military, police and civilian components. It also facilitated a training workshop organized by the Liberian Council of Churches for 28 church and youth leaders and, in collaboration with UNICEF, facilitated another workshop for 60 Montserrado video club owners.

VIII. Personnel conduct and discipline

62. The UNMIL Personnel Conduct and Discipline Team focused on developing strategies to prevent, identify, report and effectively respond to all categories of misconduct through training and awareness-raising. In addition to standardized training for all United Nations personnel, the Mission designed a training module for focal points for the prevention of sexual exploitation and abuse in the Mission area, which is aimed at strengthening reporting mechanisms, responding effectively to reported allegations and providing support to victims of abuse.

63. Some 31 "Category 1" offences, including 24 cases of sexual exploitation and abuse, and 95 "Category 2" offences have been reported since January 2006. All cases are under investigation.

IX. Public information

64. The public information component of the Mission continues to support a number of priority programmes of the Mission, the United Nations agencies, the Government and civil society. The component organized several sporting activities to promote peace among communities. UNMIL Radio also increased its programming on the activities of the three branches of Government and introduced a new programme, in Liberian English, entitled "Talk with the President", which focuses on the activities of the Government. In addition, the radio station introduced three programmes in the Bassa, Lorma and Kpelle local languages. In the meantime, the Mission has established a new radio station studio at its headquarters in Monrovia to provide increased access to the radio.

65. The public information component conducted training for several community radio practitioners, newspapers publishers and Ministry of Information personnel. In addition, the component established a press club in one of the high schools in Gbarma, Gbarpolu County, to teach interested students basic journalism skills, including how to create a school newsletter and basic reporting on the community radio station.

X. Adjustment of the Mission

A. Military component

66. As at 1 September, UNMIL troop strength stood at 14,827 out of an authorized strength of 15,125. In my previous report, I indicated that, given the relative stability that has prevailed since the inauguration of the new Government and based on the detailed assessment provided in my tenth progress report (S/2006/159), which remains valid, one infantry battalion would be withdrawn by the end of 2006. Accordingly, the Mission will repatriate one battalion, without replacement, in November 2006. As I have proposed in my previous reports, further adjustments, including the withdrawal of another infantry battalion in early 2007, will be considered if the security situation permits.

67. UNMIL continued to provide security to the Special Court for Sierra Leone in accordance with Security Council resolution 1626 (2005). In view of the high-profile nature of the detainees at the Special Court, security protection at the Court's premises remains a top priority. The 250-strong military unit from Mongolia charged with responsibility for guarding the Court's premises was rotated in July.

B. Police component

68. As at 1 September, the Mission's police strength stood at 1,056 officers, out of an authorized ceiling of 1,240 officers, which includes four United Nations police immigration officers, 605 officers in five formed police units and 18 corrections officers. The fifth formed police unit will be deployed to the Mission in September to support the efforts of the Liberian National Police in containing threats to public order in Monrovia and other urban centres, as well as on rubber plantations.

69. In order to support the efforts of the Liberian National Police to re-establish police primacy throughout the country, the United Nations police has increased its presence in five locations, including Bo Waterside, Foya, Pleebo, Toe Town and the Guthrie rubber plantation. Plans are under way to establish United Nations police team sites at Weebo, River Gee County and Kungbor forest, Gbarpolu County, where illegal mining activities have continued. In addition, an increased number of United Nations police have been assigned to the criminal investigation department and patrol section of the Liberian National Police headquarters in Monrovia and in the counties.

70. As training priorities for the Liberian National Police have shifted towards institutional capacity-building and operations support, efforts are now focused on deploying skilled United Nations police personnel to the Mission to fill specialized training positions. The strength of the United Nations police component will be reviewed as the reform and training programmes progress, and further recommendations will be provided in my future reports.

XI. Benchmarks

71. In my June report (S/2006/376), I indicated that UNMIL was developing benchmarks to guide the consolidation, drawdown and withdrawal of UNMIL. In that regard, the benchmarks covering the consolidation phase are set out in annex I of the present report.

72. The benchmarks are divided into four categories, including security; governance and the rule of law; economic revitalization; and infrastructure and basic services. The security benchmarks, including the training and deployment of the Armed Forces of Liberia and Liberian National Police, development by the Government of a national security strategy and architecture, reintegration of ex-combatants and return and reintegration of refugees, are critical in determining the pace and timing of the drawdown and eventual withdrawal of the Mission. The Mission will continue to elaborate on these key benchmarks and further details will be provided in my subsequent reports. Although the benchmarks covered under governance and rule of law, economic revitalization and infrastructure and basic services are critical for the consolidation of peace and stability, these are primarily long-term tasks that are expected to be fully accomplished after the departure of UNMIL.

XII. Observations

73. Liberia has continued to make tangible progress in a number of areas. The three branches of Government are functioning; the reform and restructuring of the security sector is gradually progressing; the resettlement of internally displaced persons has been completed; an increasing number of Liberian refugees have returned home; the Government is taking active measures to fight corruption; and the Truth and Reconciliation Commission has begun its work.

74. Progress has also been made in implementing a number of important structural reforms. The Government has commenced the review of concessions, contracts and licences, and international financial experts have been deployed to most of the key revenue-generating agencies under the Governance and Economic Management Assistance Programme. Measures have also been taken to strengthen the management and operations of the Central Bank and to boost revenue collection and control government expenditure. The efforts of the Government to meet the goals set out in the 150-day action plan are yielding some results, such as the partial restoration of electricity and pipe-borne water to some parts of Monrovia.

75. The progress made in Liberia was warmly welcomed by the African heads of State and Government at the last summit of the African Union, held in Banjul in July 2006. Liberia, which was once at the centre of conflict in the subregion, now serves as an example of hope and of what can be achieved when leaders and citizens work together and are committed to peace.

76. Nevertheless, Liberia still faces enormous challenges in several areas. The country is heavily dependent on UNMIL for the provision of security, given that the new police service is still in its formative stages and the training of the new armed forces is only just beginning. The Government and UNMIL will need to remain vigilant to carefully manage the internal threats to stability, especially those emanating from spoilers who may be adversely affected by the Government's reform processes. Close monitoring of Liberia's borders will also continue to be essential, in the light of the volatile situation in the

subregion, particularly in Côte d'Ivoire. In addition, a number of other tasks that are critical to the sustainability of peace in the country have yet to be completed, including the reintegration of ex-combatants, the resettlement of internally displaced persons and returning refugees and the consolidation of State authority.

77. The large number of unemployed youth concentrated in urban centres is a serious source of concern, especially given that the increase in criminal activities in Monrovia and other city centres has been linked to their presence. Unless economic activity is rapidly revived and employment opportunities created in the near future, these unemployed youths and frustrated former combatants will continue to constitute a source of major instability. It is gratifying to note that the Government has recently launched a number of programmes aimed at providing employment opportunities. I encourage international partners to fully support these very important initiatives.

78. While the progress that has been made in restructuring the Liberian security sector is encouraging, the Government still needs to rapidly develop a national security policy and architecture, which will enable it to set out a coherent road map for assuming security responsibility for the country. Since the Mission's drawdown will be linked to this road map, the Government should work expeditiously towards finalizing this policy.

79. The transfer of former President Charles Taylor from the region to stand trial before the Special Court for Sierra Leone sitting in The Hague was an important development. Not only did it signal that the world will not accept impunity, it also demonstrated the recognition by the Government of Liberia, regional leaders and the Security Council that Mr. Taylor's continued presence in Freetown was a threat to peace and stability in the subregion. In this regard, I wish to express my deep appreciation to all the Member States who collaborated to make possible the holding of Mr. Taylor's trial in The Hague.

80. In the light of the security issues outlined above, and in view of the planning for the drawdown of UNMIL, I recommend the extension of the mandate of UNMIL for a period of one year, until 30 September 2007.

81. The Government has taken further steps to reform the judicial sector and enhance the rule of law. However, there are a number of major structural challenges that will require the generous assistance of the international community if they are to be effectively addressed. At the same time, support will be needed for the work of the Independent National Human Rights Commission and the Truth and Reconciliation Commission. It is important for donors to provide funding for these critical areas.

82. Efforts to consolidate peace in Liberia are already bearing fruit, including the cultivation of good relations with its neighbours. The attendance of the Presidents of Côte d'Ivoire and Sierra Leone at the 159th Liberian Independence Day celebrations was a highly commendable gesture, which will have a positive impact on relations among the Mano River Union member States and Côte d'Ivoire. The leaders of these countries are encouraged to build on this development and continue to take measures that will enhance subregional dialogue and revitalize the Mano River Union.

83. In conclusion, I would like to commend the people and Government of Liberia, my Special Representative, Alan Doss, and all UNMIL military and civilian personnel for the progress accomplished during the reporting period. I would also like to thank all troop- and

police-contributing countries, ECOWAS, the African Union, the International Contact Group on the Mano River Basin, United Nations agencies, funds and programmes, humanitarian organizations, multilateral and bilateral donors and international and local non-governmental organizations for their important contributions and support to the peace consolidation process in Liberia.

Annex I
Benchmarks for phase I of the consolidation, drawdown and withdrawal of UNMIL
Consolidation phase—2006-2007

Benchmark	*Indicators of progress*
Security	
Armed Forces of Liberia training and deployment	• Armed Forces of Liberia training commences • Ministry of Defence fully staffed • Armed Forces of Liberia concept of operations produced • First Armed Forces of Liberia battalion operational
Liberian National Police training and deployment	• Deactivation of Liberian National Police personnel completed • 3,500 Liberian National Police personnel recruited and trained • Liberian National Police support unit trained and equipped • All county police stations fully staffed and operational
National security strategy and architecture	• Complete national security review • Produce and adopt national security strategy and commence implementation • National Security Council and local structures in place and functioning
Reintegration of ex-combatants	• Remaining ex-combatants enrolled in reintegration programmes • Small arms collection and control programme extended to all counties
Return and reintegration of refugees	• Organized refugee returns concluded
Governance and rule of law	
Strengthen administration of justice	• Law Reform Commission established and comprehensive review of laws commenced • Comprehensive review of court administrative procedures completed and being implemented • All Circuit Court houses and magistrates courts constructed or renovated, equipped and staffed • Legal aid clinics available in each county • Reduction in pre-trial detention period

Benchmark	*Indicators of progress*
Strengthen human rights	• Independent National Commission on Human Rights functioning effectively • National human rights action plan developed and being implemented • Truth and Reconciliation Commission process ongoing in all counties
Conflict management	• County-level reconciliation and conflict management processes established to address longstanding grievances, including property and housing committees
National institutions	• Local authorities at county level established • County superintendents' offices established and equipped
Anti-corruption	• Anti-corruption strategy approved and implemented
Civil service reform	• Implementation of civil service code of conduct
Corrections reform	• National policy framework for Corrections Bureau formulated and approved • Corrections staff trained and deployed • Revised penal legislation adopted and any necessary changes implemented • Correction facilities in each county fully operational
Economic revitalization	
Implementation of the Governance and Economic Management Assistance Programme[a]	• Establishment of financial management and budgeting procedures in line with International Monetary Fund (IMF) recommendations (staff-monitored programme) • Government revenue increased in line with IMF projections • Transparent procedures for granting of concessions implemented as recommended by Economic Governance Steering Committee
Revival of economic production	• Increase in economic growth in line with IMF (staff-monitored programme) projections—between 3.8 to 8 per cent in 2007
Strengthen Government's management of natural resources	• Forestry legislation enacted • Environmental Protection Agency staffed and deployed in all counties • Sanctions on diamonds lifted
Infrastructure and basic services	
Rehabilitation of the transport network	• Main strategic routes repaired and maintained (interim poverty reduction strategy target)[b] • Emergency work at Monrovia Freeport completed

Continued

Benchmark	*Indicators of progress*
Rehabilitation and expansion of health services	• Rehabilitation of health facilities in each county (interim poverty reduction strategy) • Increase in health workers employed and deployed in each county (interim poverty reduction strategy) • Construction and rehabilitation of water and sanitation facilities in each county (interim poverty reduction strategy)
Rehabilitation and expansion of education services	• Rehabilitation of public schools across country (interim poverty reduction strategy) • Increased school enrolment, particularly of girls, across the country (interim poverty reduction strategy)

[a] GEMAP will terminate after 36 months (September 2008) unless the Completion Point under the Heavily Indebted Poor Countries Initiative has not been reached.

[b] The specific indicator will be based on the goals identified in the Government's interim poverty reduction strategy.

Annex II
United Nations Mission in Liberia: military and police strength as at 1 September 2006

Component	*Military*				*Police*
Country	*Military observers*	*Staff officer*	*Troops*	*Total*	*Civilian police*
Argentina					
Bangladesh	17	11	3 188	3 216	28
Benin	4	1		5	
Bolivia	3	1		4	
Bosnia and Herzegovina	17				9
Brazil		1		1	
Bulgaria	2			2	
China	5	7	558	570	23
Croatia		3		3	
Czech Republic	3			3	5
Denmark	2			2	
Ecuador	3	1		4	
El Salvador	3			3	2
Ethiopia	17	8	2 536	2 561	
Egypt	10			10	
Fiji					30
Finland		2		2	
France		1		1	
Gambia	4			4	32
Germany			13	13	5
Ghana	11	7	846	867	41
Indonesia	3			3	

Component	Military				Police
Country	Military observers	Staff officer	Troops	Total	Civilian police
Ireland		3	352	355	
Jamaica					8
Jordan	7	8	115	130	138
Kenya	3	4		7	27
Korea	1	1		2	
Kyrgyzstan	4			4	3
Malawi		2		2	18
Malaysia	10	0		10	
Mali	4	1		5	
Mongolia		2	248	250	
Montenegro	2			2	1
Namibia	3	4	609	616	6
Nepal	3	2	40	45	256
Niger	3			3	
Nigeria	18	13	1 951	1 982	136
Norway					10
Pakistan	16	11	2 738	2 765	31
Paraguay	3	1		4	
Peru	3	2		5	
Philippines	3	5	165	173	34
Poland	2			2	3
Portugal					
Republic of Moldova	3	1		4	
Romania	3			3	
Russian Federation	6			6	13
Rwanda					15
Samoa					16
Senegal	3	3	600	606	
Serbia	4			4	5
South Africa					
Sri Lanka					11
Sweden		3	230	233	11
Togo		1		1	
Turkey					33
Uganda					21
United Kingdom of Great Britain and Northern Ireland		3		3	
Ukraine	3	1	298	302	13
Uruguay					
United States of America	6	6		12	10

Continued

Component	*Military*				*Police*
Country	*Military observers*	*Staff officer*	*Troops*	*Total*	*Civilian police*
Yemen					4
Zambia	3			3	27
Zimbabwe					31
Total	**220**	**120**	**14 487**	**14 827**	**1 056**

2. Tenth Progress Report of the Secretary-General on the United Nations Operation in Côte d'Ivoire, 17 October 2006 (S/2006/821)

I. Introduction

1. The present report is submitted pursuant to Security Council resolution 1603 (2005) of 3 June 2005, by which the Council requested me to keep it regularly informed of developments in Côte d'Ivoire and on the implementation of the mandate of the United Nations Operation in Côte d'Ivoire (UNOCI). The report covers developments since my report of 17 July 2006 (S/2006/532).

II. Political developments

2. During the reporting period, Prime Minister Charles Konan Banny, supported by the United Nations, regional leaders and other international partners, made commendable efforts to use the last three months before the 31 October 2006 deadline for the elections to accelerate the implementation of the key tasks relating to the disarmament of combatants, the identification of the population and the re-establishment of State authority throughout the country. To that end, the Prime Minister focused on achieving the benchmarks agreed upon during the high-level meeting of Ivorian and regional leaders, which I convened in Yamoussoukro on 5 July 2006. However, as indicated in paragraphs 5 to 19 below, implementation of the decisions of the Yamoussoukro meeting encountered deliberate obstruction resulting in a new stalemate.

3. The impasse emanated mainly from major disagreements among the Ivorian parties on fundamental issues concerning the procedures for issuing certificates of nationality and the related preparation of the voters' list. These disagreements also stalled the implementation of the pre-cantonment phase of the disarmament, demobilization and reintegration process, which was to be implemented concomitantly with the initial phase of the identification process. At the same time, the dismantling of militias was suspended on account of the low number and poor quality of the weapons and ammunitions surrendered.

4. In the meantime, the Prime Minister continued to face constraints in exercising his authority under Security Council resolution 1633 (2005). In particular, he lacked authority over the Defence and Security Forces and did not have full control over public funding for the key aspects of the transition process, especially disarmament, identification, the re-establishment of State authority throughout the country and the electoral preparations.

A. Implementation of the Yamoussoukro benchmarks

Identification of the population

5. The Yamoussoukro high-level meeting, which I convened on 5 July, had agreed that 50 mobile courts were to be deployed by 15 July, public hearings would be conducted and birth certificates and certificates of nationality would be issued to those eligible. Implementation of that decision started on 17 July. However, the total number of operational mobile courts never exceeded 25. In the southern part of the country, the mobile courts were immediately disrupted by supporters of the ruling Front populaire ivoirien (FPI) party. The President of the party, Affi N'Guessan, called upon its followers to oppose the operations of the mobile

courts "by all means", claiming that the issuance of certificates of nationality by such courts was inconsistent with the law. In addition, despite the joint monitoring mechanism put in place by UNOCI and the High Representative for the elections, Gérard Stoudmann, President Laurent Gbagbo and his party, FPI, insisted that the mobile court hearings could be used fraudulently to grant Ivorian citizenship to those who were not eligible.

6. The attempts by FPI supporters, in particular the Young Patriots, to disrupt the operations of the mobile courts, led to violent clashes with the opposition parties. In Divo and Grand-Bassam, the clashes resulted in the death of at least eight Ivorians on 22 and 23 July. The violent disruption campaign continued until early August, when the Prime Minister announced new guidelines, based on a strict interpretation of the nationality law, which prohibited the mobile courts from issuing certificates of nationality. According to the law, there are only 34 designated courts in the country that can issue certificates of nationality. Such a small number of courts would be inadequate to handle the estimated caseload of some 3 million Ivorians expected to apply for certificates of nationality. Furthermore, the courts are inaccessible to the vast majority of the potential applicants and they are unevenly distributed between the northern and southern parts of the country. The opposition parties rejected the new guidelines, arguing that the public hearings conducted by mobile courts had been legally used to issue certificates of nationality prior to the conflict and that no law expressly prohibited the practice.

7. After the proclamation of the new guidelines, the number of persons appearing before the mobile courts dropped precipitously. By mid-September, the operations of the mobile courts, which were initially scheduled to run for two months, had completely stopped in all areas. Between 17 July and 15 September, only 933 mobile court hearings were held (327 in the southern part of the country, 583 in the northern part of the country and 23 in the zone of confidence), and some 74,000 birth certificates and 70,000 certificates of nationality were issued. UNOCI provided logistical support for the operation, including transporting préfets and sous-préfets to the areas controlled by the Forces nouvelles.

Disarmament, demobilization and reintegration

8. With regard to disarmament, the Yamoussoukro meeting had decided that a monitoring group, comprised of the National Armed Forces of Côte d'Ivoire (FANCI), the Forces nouvelles, UNOCI and the French Licorne force, would be established by 15 July, and that the pre-cantonment of combatants would be completed by 31 July. Although the monitoring group was established on 13 July, the Forces nouvelles suspended its participation in the group and in the dialogue on military issues in reaction to the proclamation of the new guidelines on the operations of the mobile courts. They argued that the guidelines violated the agreed principle of conducting the initial phases of the disarmament and identification processes concomitantly. The monitoring group has therefore not been able to verify the claims by the Forces nouvelles and FANCI that they had completed the pre-cantonment of their respective combatants (24,000 FANCI personnel and 13,000 Forces nouvelles elements).

9. With the breakdown of the military dialogue, many combatants were reported to have left the pre-cantonment sites and returned to their deployment areas. In addition, despite UNOCI efforts, the two sides have not yet submitted the lists of their combatants and weapons. Furthermore, the Forces nouvelles are now insisting that the restructuring of the national army must be implemented immediately, as part of the disarmament, demobilization and

reintegration process. To that end, they have called for the establishment of an integrated command under the authority of the Prime Minister.

Dismantling and disarmament of militias

10. The Yamoussoukro high-level meeting had also envisaged that the dismantling and disarming of the militias would be completed by 31 July. The process started in the western part of the country on 26 July. The National Programme for Disarmament, Demobilization and Reintegration (PNDDR) registered 981 combatants who surrendered only 110 mostly unserviceable weapons and some 6,975 assorted rounds of ammunitions before the process was suspended on 4 August on account of the low number and poor quality of the surrendered weapons. Efforts to resume the process in a more credible fashion have not yet succeeded, and the militia leaders are demanding that an additional 3,000 individuals be allowed to join the programme. UNOCI provided logistics support to the PNDDR Operational Centre, as well as technical expertise to PNDDR on disarmament procedures and on the storage of weapons and ammunitions.

Preparations for the elections

11. The Yamoussoukro meeting also took a number of decisions related to the preparation of elections. First, it decided that President Laurent Gbagbo would issue a decree to allow the Independent Electoral Commission to make any technical adjustments to the electoral code of 2000 deemed necessary, in order to facilitate the transitional elections. On 29 July, the President signed a decision empowering the Commission to submit to the Prime Minister its proposed amendments to the electoral code. The Prime Minister would, in turn, assess the proposed amendments and refer them to the President for promulgation.

12. The leader of the Parti démocratique de Côte d'Ivoire (PDCI), Henri Konan Bédié, and the leader of the Rassemblement des Républicains (RDR), Alassane Ouattara, wrote to me on 17 August to convey their concern that President Gbagbo had not been following the consultative process established by the African Union mediator, President Thabo Mbeki of South Africa, for issuing such decisions, which have crucial implications for the electoral process. They also contended that the decision gave the President the final say on matters governing an election in which he would be a candidate.

13. On this question, the High Representative for the elections noted that the decision retained the essential need for the Independent Electoral Commission to initiate proposals and contained safeguards against abuse, which included the Prime Minister's assessment and certification by the High Representative.

14. The Yamoussoukro decisions also called upon the Independent Electoral Commission to establish countrywide structures by 31 July. Under its operational plan, the Commission intended to establish 24 regional commissions, 48 departmental commissions and 358 local commissions. So far, 19 regional commissions have been established. From the outset, the deployment of the regional and local commissions has been hampered by several factors, including inadequate funding and organizational capacity, as well as security concerns. An additional constraint is the electoral law, which provides that each subnational commission must have the same membership composition as the central commission, which has 31 members. This would require a total of some 33,000 commissioners, most of whom must be members of political parties signatory to the Linas-Marcoussis Agreement, which makes

it impracticable. The High Representative for the elections has suggested that the extraordinary procedures for changes to the electoral law should be used to reduce the size of local commissions.

15. The Yamoussoukro high-level meeting also reaffirmed the validity of the Pretoria Agreement of 29 June 2005, including its paragraph 6, which referred to the respective roles of the Independent Electoral Commission and the National Institute of Statistics in the electoral process. President Gbagbo and his supporters are adamantly opposed to the preparation of a new voters' roll and maintain that the voters' list used during the 2000 elections should simply be updated by the Institute. The opposition parties, for their part, have rejected the voters' list used in 2000 and insist that a new voters' roll must be prepared by the Commission, and not the Institute, on the basis of the identification process.

16. On 19 July, in response to a formal request from President Gbagbo, President Mbeki, in his capacity as the African Union mediator, clarified the disputed roles of the two institutions, reaffirming the exclusive responsibility of the Independent Electoral Commission for organizing the elections and indicating that the National Institute of Statistics should report directly to the Commission. The opposition parties are, however, concerned that the top posts at the Institute are dominated by officials who also have formal roles in the leadership of the ruling party. This stalemate could be resolved by replacing the identified FPI-affiliated officers with non-partisan individuals.

17. The Yamoussoukro meeting also decided that a donors' conference would be convened to mobilize funding for the elections as soon as the electoral preparations had made sufficient progress. The operational budget for the elections is approximately $74 million and there is still a funding gap of some $39 million. However, the progress made in the technical preparations for the elections has not been adequate to warrant the convening of the envisaged conference.

Redeployment of State administration

18. With regard to the re-establishment of State administration in the northern part of the country, which was one of the benchmarks set in Yamoussoukro, the Prime Minister reported on 8 September to the International Working Group established by the Security Council under resolution 1633 (2005), that 92 mayors' offices had been reopened as of 24 August, and that 61 officials had been redeployed to their prefectures by 31 August. To date, some 12,000 displaced civil servants are yet to return to the areas controlled by the Forces nouvelles.

Establishment of a compulsory code of conduct for the media

19. With regard to the incitement of violence through the media, the Yamoussoukro meeting decided that there should be a code of conduct for the media. UNOCI has assisted the media regulatory bodies in preparing a draft code of conduct, but it has not yet been implemented.

B. Efforts to break the political stalemate

20. On 5 September, Prime Minister Banny convened in Yamoussoukro a further meeting of the main Ivorian political leaders (President Gbagbo, former President Bédié, former Prime Minister Ouattara and Forces nouvelles leader Guillaume Soro) in an effort to reach

agreement on measures to break the stalemate in the peace process. Their discussions focused on proposals by the Prime Minister for the adoption of extraordinary measures to allow the issuance of certificates of nationality to eligible Ivorians. The meeting, however, failed to secure an agreement on this crucial issue, and the political leaders requested Prime Minister Banny to continue his search for alternative solutions.

21. The impasse in the peace process was further compounded by the dissolution of the transitional Government by Prime Minister Banny on 6 September, following a scandal created in late August by the dumping of toxic waste in Abidjan by a foreign vessel. Although the Prime Minister announced a new Government on 16 September, in which he replaced the Ministers of Transport and Environment, the toxic waste crisis sidetracked the efforts to break the impasse in the peace process. For several weeks, the Ivorian youth held demonstrations, which at times turned violent, in the commercial capital against the dumping of the toxic waste.

22. On 8 September, the International Working Group met in Abidjan and adopted a communiqué (S/2006/738, annex) in which it concluded that it was no longer possible to meet the 31 October 2006 deadline for the elections. The Working Group identified the main obstacles to the peace process and recommended that, in view of the expiration of the transition period on 31 October, the Security Council adopt a new resolution on Côte d'Ivoire that would eliminate the ambiguities in the current transition arrangements and reinforce the powers of the Prime Minister.

23. The Chairman of the African Union, President Denis Sassou-Nguesso of the Congo, visited Côte d'Ivoire on 11 and 12 September and discussed with President Gbagbo, Prime Minister Banny, Mr. Bédié, Mr. Ouattara and Mr. Soro further possible measures to resolve the stalemate over the procedures for issuing certificates of nationality. However, the compromise solution proposed by President Sassou-Nguesso was not accepted by one of the parties.

24. On 20 September, I convened a follow-up meeting of the Ivorian and regional leaders, in the margins of the sixty-first session of the General Assembly, in New York, as agreed during the 5 July high-level meeting in Yamoussoukro. One week before the meeting, by which time all the other leaders had confirmed their participation, I received a letter from President Gbagbo informing me that he would not attend the meeting. He stated that he intended to present his own proposals on the Ivorian peace process at a meeting of the African Union. The letter followed a number of public statements by the President rejecting the communiqué issued by the International Working Group on 8 September and asserting that the time for negotiations was over.

25. In my letter of reply, I expressed regret at President Gbagbo's decision not to attend this important meeting and reminded him that the decision to convene the follow-up meeting in New York had been taken with his full consent. I also pointed out that the views emerging from the follow-up meeting would be conveyed to the Economic Community of West African States (ECOWAS), the African Union and the Security Council, so that those bodies would take them into account when they meet to decide on the way forward on Côte d'Ivoire. As such, the follow-up meeting was not intended to replace the envisaged meetings of ECOWAS, the African Union and the Security Council.

26. Prime Minister Banny, Mr. Bédié, Mr. Ouattara and Mr. Soro, as well as the African Union Chairman, President Sassou-Nguesso of the Congo, President Blaise Compaoré of Burkina Faso, President John Agyekum Kufuor of Ghana, President Mbeki of South Africa, the Foreign Ministers of Mali, the Niger and Nigeria, the Chairman of the African Union Commission, Alpha Oumar Konaré, and the Executive-Secretary of ECOWAS, Mohammed Ibn Chambas, participated in the meeting. In opening the meeting, I stressed the special significance of its timing, noting that, with only six weeks before the end of the transition period in Côte d'Ivoire, the peace process was at a stalemate, and it was no longer technically feasible to hold elections by 31 October 2006. I therefore proposed that, in addition to taking stock of progress towards meeting the benchmarks agreed upon in Yamoussoukro and discussing measures needed to break the political stalemate, the meeting should discuss the way forward after 31 October and the measures to be taken to ensure that a new transition period would not end without elections again.

27. Prime Minister Banny, my Special Representative Pierre Schori and the High Representative for the elections, Gérard Stoudmann, provided an assessment of the implementation of the decisions of the Yamoussoukro meeting of 5 July, along the lines indicated in paragraphs 5 to 19 above. In their statements, the participants recognized that it was no longer technically feasible to organize and conduct elections in Côte d'Ivoire by 31 October 2006. The Ivorian political leaders provided their views on the fundamental causes of the current stalemate in the peace process. They and many of the participating regional leaders acknowledged that an extension of the transition period was necessary, and that a new transition process should guarantee the holding of credible elections.

28. Prime Minister Banny stressed the need for urgent measures to resolve the impasse on the procedures for issuing certificates of nationality, in order to enable the Government to make as much progress as possible in the remaining weeks before the end of the transition period on 31 October. President Mbeki, however, expressed the view that it would not be appropriate for the meeting to decide on those crucial issues in the absence of President Gbagbo and FPI. The participants agreed that it was important for ECOWAS, the African Union and the Security Council to decide, without delay, on measures to break the impasse and on the extension of the transition period with arrangements that would guarantee the holding of elections. The Executive Secretary of ECOWAS announced that he intended to propose the convening of an extraordinary summit of ECOWAS to discuss those issues. The ECOWAS summit was subsequently held in Abuja on 6 October.

29. In a further effort to resolve the political impasse, on 25 September, President Mbeki travelled to Abidjan, where he met with President Gbagbo and Prime Minister Banny. On 26 September, Presidents Mbeki and Gbagbo proceeded to Ouagadougou for consultations with President Compaoré. Meanwhile, in separate letters addressed to the Chairman of the African Union, President Sassou-Nguesso, the Forces nouvelles, RDR, and PDCI demanded the termination of President Mbeki's role as the African Union mediator in the Ivorian crisis, alleging that his mediation efforts had not been impartial. The stalemate in the peace process remained unresolved up to the time of the ECOWAS summit on 6 October.

30. The ECOWAS summit issued a final communiqué in which it reaffirmed that, for ECOWAS, Security Council resolution 1633 (2005) remained an ideal framework for resolving the Ivorian crisis. It also recommended that the Security Council take all necessary

measures to address the obstacles to the implementation of the resolution. In a closed session, the ECOWAS leaders agreed on specific recommendations that were not made public. These important proposals will be considered by the Peace and Security Council of the African Union at a meeting scheduled to take place in Addis Ababa on 17 October. The African Union will, in turn, present its decisions to the Security Council.

III. Security situation

31. During the period under review, the security situation in Côte d'Ivoire remained unpredictable, mainly as a result of the tension created by the disruption of the operations of the mobile court hearings, the conditions facing the combatants who had assembled at pre-cantonment sites that had no adequate facilities, the disagreements between PNDDR and militia leaders over the implementation of the programme for dismantling and disarming militias, the toxic waste scandal, inflammatory statements by political leaders, posturing by the political parties as the end of the transition period approached with the peace process at an impasse and a series of strikes and protests by public servants and personnel from the gendarmerie.

32. Several violent incidents in the zone of confidence led to new displacements of populations in the area during the reporting period. The impartial forces have increased efforts to curb violent crime in the zone, in order to facilitate the return of the displaced persons. The deficiencies of the Ivorian judicial system have however impeded the efforts to stabilize the area. In the western part of the country, the presence of armed militiamen and persistent land disputes perpetuated a climate of insecurity.

33. Violent crime has spread beyond Abidjan to other areas, mainly Bouaké, Korhogo and the western part of the country. Armed burglaries and street robberies as well as checkpoint racketeering are now relatively common in the southern and northern parts of the country, while highway robberies by so-called "*coupeurs de route*" are endemic in the western part of the zone of confidence and in the northern part of the country.

34. UNOCI and the French Licorne force continued to face obstructions to their operations, in particular their arms embargo and monitoring activities. In addition, recent inflammatory statements by the President of the ruling party, Mr. N'Guessan, calling for the departure of the French Licorne force from Côte d'Ivoire, as well as public calls by President Gbagbo for the "lifting" of the zone of confidence, could exacerbate tensions and lead to an increase in the obstruction to the freedom of movement of the two forces.

35. On 2 October, Mr. N'Guessan issued another inflammatory statement threatening violence against ECOWAS nationals living in Côte d'Ivoire, if the ECOWAS summit of 6 October failed to take a decision to force the Forces nouvelles to disarm. The former Speaker of the erstwhile National Assembly, Mamadou Koulibaly, reiterated that threat on 6 October. In a statement released on 5 October, I deplored the inflammatory remarks made by Mr. N'Guessan and called upon all Ivorian political leaders and their followers to exercise the utmost restraint at this critical juncture. ECOWAS issued a similar statement on 4 October.

IV. Deployment of the United Nations Operation in Côte d'Ivoire

A. Military component

36. As of 6 October 2006, the strength of UNOCI stood at 8,045 military personnel against the authorized ceiling of 8,115. The deployment of the 1,025 additional military personnel, approved by the Security Council in its resolution 1682 (2006), has been completed. In this regard, a mechanized infantry battalion from Jordan was deployed in Abidjan to enhance the operational capabilities of UNOCI in the city. An infantry company from Benin was deployed in the western sector to reinforce the Benin battalion's positions in that highly volatile region.

37. The Sous-Groupement de sécurité, which provides security to members of the Government, was strengthened by an additional 73 gendarmes from Benin, Ghana, the Niger, Senegal and Togo. Ghana also provided the long-awaited aviation unit, which is stationed in Bouaké.

38. Although the deployment of these reinforcements has enhanced UNOCI force capabilities, there is still a significant shortfall, as mentioned in my previous reports, in the number of troops required to support effectively the implementation of the road map for peace, should the peace process make sustained progress. This troop deficit could also become critical in the near future, should there be a major deterioration of security situation in Côte d'Ivoire. In this regard, I urge the Security Council to keep the troop strength of UNOCI under review, with a view to authorizing the deployment of the remaining three battalions, out of the four recommended in my report of 3 January 2006 (S/2006/2).

39. UNOCI has also made substantial progress towards enhancing the efficiency of its troops. To that end, most components of the UNOCI force have received basic training in crowd control in order to enhance their ability to protect United Nations personnel and property and to support the formed police units in the event of widespread violent actions by unarmed civilians. All the new units inducted in the Operation during the reporting period comprise elements equipped and trained to face hostile crowds with non-lethal force.

40. At the inter-mission Force Commanders Conference, which took place on 9 June 2006, the Force Commanders of the United Nations Mission in Liberia (UNMIL) and UNOCI decided to conduct concurrent patrols along the Côte d'Ivoire-Liberia border in order to increase the United Nations security presence, monitor and deter cross-border movements, establish cross-border liaison and reassure the local population. Coordinated patrols in border areas were temporarily suspended in September owing to troop rotation but resumed in early October.

41. The military leadership of UNOCI has maintained close contacts with the command of the Ivorian Defence and Security Forces and the Forces nouvelles to secure their continued commitment to the military dialogue and their cooperation in stabilizing the overall security situation. As a result of several meetings of the UNOCI Force Commander with the Minister of Defence and the chiefs of Staff of FANCI and the Forces nouvelles, the latter have agreed, in principle, to resume the military dialogue by the end of October 2006.

B. Police component

42. As of 9 October 2006, the strength of the UNOCI police component stood at 949 personnel, including five formed police units totalling 625 police personnel, against an authorized

strength of 1,200 police personnel. The temporary shortfall is primarily due to a delay in the deployment of one of the three additional formed police units authorized by the Security Council under resolution 1682 (2006). Two additional formed police units, from Jordan and Bangladesh, arrived in Côte d'Ivoire in August and September and have been deployed, respectively, to Abidjan and Yamoussoukro. The third additional formed police unit should arrive by mid-November.

43. The remainder of the United Nations police officers are deployed in 18 sites nationwide, including nine locations in the areas controlled by the Forces nouvelles, two in the zone of confidence and seven in the Government-controlled areas. They continue to train gendarmes and police officers, as well as mentor and advise local security forces. In Abidjan, joint patrols with Ivorian Defence and Security Forces are undertaken on a daily basis, and allow United Nations police officers to mentor and provide technical advice to the local law enforcement agencies. In the northern part of Côte d'Ivoire, measures are being taken to deploy the security auxiliaries trained by the United Nations police in 2005 to newly constructed police stations, funded by the European Union, where United Nations police officers will continue to mentor them.

V. Judicial system

44. During the period under review, UNOCI continued to monitor the performance of the judicial system in Côte d'Ivoire. On 5 August, President Gbagbo issued a decree nominating judges nationwide. The decree exacerbated political tensions, as the opposition argued that the President had not followed the law in making the appointments. The appointment of judges is a particularly sensitive issue in the Ivorian context given their role in delivering certificates of nationality.

45. In August 2006, UNOCI published a major report on the functioning of the prison system nationwide, providing a detailed evaluation of the conditions of detention in all prisons in Côte d'Ivoire. The report makes recommendations for immediate and structural improvements in the corrections system. UNOCI is currently training 12 local trainers as part of the implementation of these recommendations. A project developed with UNOCI assistance to refurbish eight prisons, including two in controlled areas by the Forces nouvelles, will be funded by the European Union for 1 million euros. UNOCI also developed a prison farm project with the non-governmental organization Prisoners without Borders and local prison administration authorities, which was submitted for donor funding.

VI. Humanitarian situation

46. In mid-August, over 580 cubic metres of toxic petrochemical waste from a foreign cargo ship were dumped at 18 sites in Abidjan. The resulting contamination caused the death of eight people, while some 100,000 others received medical treatment. The United Nations system assisted the Government in providing an emergency response to this environmental and public health crisis, supplying drugs to 32 health centres, treating affected people, testing the quality of drinking water and providing basic equipment to secure the dumping sites.

47. The United Nations Children's Fund (UNICEF) and the World Health Organization (WHO) provided medicines worth over $150,000 to health facilities treating the affected populations, while the United Nations Development Programme donated protective gear

and cordoning material, and WHO deployed a team of highly specialized staff, including a chemical toxicologist and an environmental health expert. The United Nations Industrial Development Organization sent an expert to determine whether the chemicals were recognized as dangerous under the Basel Convention on the Control of Transboundary Movements of Hazardous Wastes and Their Disposal and the United Nations Environment Programme announced that it would investigate the legal aspects of the incident through the secretariat of the Basel Convention.

48. The Office for the Coordination of Humanitarian Affairs deployed a disaster assistance and coordination team, comprising environmental and chemical experts, to provide technical assistance and support coordination efforts, while a private French company launched a cleaning-up operation. Although the immediate threat has been reduced, the contamination of soil and water sources might have long-term effects. Several investigations are ongoing under the auspices of the Government.

49. The internally displaced population in Côte d'Ivoire is still estimated at 700,000 persons. Most have now been displaced for four years and live in dire social and economic conditions. The humanitarian community continues to provide protection and assistance to the displaced population under the leadership of the Office of the United Nations High Commissioner for Refugees (UNHCR). However, humanitarian access in western areas continues to be impeded by the presence of armed elements, in particular between Guiglo and Bloléquin. Nonetheless, an estimated 5,000 displaced persons have returned to 53 villages in the Toulépleu area.

50. By the end of September 2006, Côte d'Ivoire was still host to some 40,000 refugees, more than 98 per cent of whom are of Liberian origin. UNHCR expects to repatriate about 22,000 of the Liberian refugees by the end of 2006. Many have requested to be resettled in third countries.

51. From 28 August to 24 September 2006, school examinations were held in all school districts in the areas controlled by the Forces nouvelles. The examinations were organized by the Ministry of Education with the support of United Nations agencies, UNOCI and non-governmental organizations. In a positive development, during 2006 several examination centres were under the direct supervision of the staff of the Minister of Education and elements of the Forces nouvelles.

52. Humanitarian assistance continues to be seriously underfunded in Côte d'Ivoire. In 2005, the humanitarian community appealed for $43.7 million under the Consolidated Appeal Process, but received only $13.6 million to implement projects under the Consolidated Appeal Process and $8.4 million through other channels. An additional $4.9 million have been allocated through the new Central Emergency Response Fund grant under "neglected underfunded emergencies", to finance critical projects in the areas of health, water and sanitation, and for the protection of internally displaced persons. The funding shortfalls affect not only humanitarian sectors but also recovery and reconciliation aspects of the road map. The 2007 Consolidated Appeal Process will seek $50 million to address humanitarian emergencies in Côte d'Ivoire.

VII. Impact of the crisis on the economic and social situation

53. The crisis has had a significant economic, social and regional impact. Its ripple effects are felt throughout the West African subregion, stifling trade and transportation, investment

and growth, and regional integration. Nonetheless, Côte d'Ivoire remains a cornerstone of the regional economy, constituting about 40 per cent of the gross domestic product of the West African Economic and Monetary Union. Neighbouring countries, such as Burkina Faso, Mali and the Niger, continue to depend very heavily on the transport facilities of Côte d'Ivoire for imports and exports and on remittances from migrant nationals.

54. The recent increase in oil exports from Côte d'Ivoire has helped mitigate the considerable macroeconomic impact of the crisis. In 2005, oil exports earnings for the first time exceeded proceeds from cocoa/coffee as a result of high oil prices and new production capacity achieved in late 2005. Nevertheless, the negative political and security environments continue to impede the recovery of investments and economic activity. Inflation reached 4 per cent in 2005, compared with 1.5 per cent in 2004. A modest recovery began in 2004/05, with real annual growth averaging 1.8 per cent, owing to higher cocoa exports and a rise in petroleum output. A modest 2 per cent growth is anticipated for 2006. Meanwhile, foreign direct investments have decreased significantly and many foreign businesses have closed down or scaled down operations considerably pending the resolution of the crisis. The crisis has also resulted in the expansion of the informal economy and in an increase in smuggling, in particular of cocoa and diamonds, to neighbouring countries.

55. The conflict has also halted most structural reforms, leading to the deterioration of economic governance and transparency. Efforts have been made to maintain sound fiscal management; however, military and other expenditures are often financed and executed outside regularized fiscal channels.

56. On the social front, the crisis has increased the poverty rate, accounting for an estimated 44 per cent of the population. Youth unemployment remains extremely high. The delivery of basic social services has deteriorated, HIV/AIDS is endemic and the achievement of most Millennium Development Goals is seriously jeopardized. There has also been significant deterioration in Côte d'Ivoire's human development index: the country now ranks 163 of 177 countries rated.

57. As of the end of September 2006, the country's arrears to the World Bank reached about $350 million. Since November 2004, the Government has been in a non-accrual status vis-à-vis the World Bank, precluding any financial activity from the Bank, including funding for the disarmament, demobilization and reintegration programme. The agreement reached between the Government and the World Bank on the clearance of the arrears has not yet been implemented.

VIII. Human rights

58. The peace and reconciliation process in Côte d'Ivoire continues to be threatened by serious human rights violations committed with impunity by members of the Defence and Security Forces in the southern part of the country, members of the armed forces of the Forces nouvelles in the north, and members of armed and unarmed militia in both regions. The pattern of violations is still characterized by summary and extrajudicial killings, enforced disappearances, torture and other inhumane and degrading treatment, sexual violence and exploitation, including trafficking of women and children, interference with freedom of movement and freedom of expression, arbitrary arrests and detention and intercommunity violence. In Abidjan, during the period under review, several incidents involving the Young Patriots, sometimes armed, and members of the Fédération estudiantine et scolaire

de Côte d'Ivoire (FESCI), resulted in serious violations of human rights, which were not prevented by law enforcement authorities.

59. Clashes over land disputes among different communities, respectively in Divo, Alepé and Yamoussoukro, led to killings, raping and burning of houses and plantations of the different communities. Other incidents of intercommunity violence were also reported in the zone of confidence and in the western part of the country. Restriction of freedom of movement continues to be a matter of concern in some regions. Several individuals suspected of being infiltrators or spies from the southern part of the country were arrested in Bouaké, Korhogo and Odienné. Meanwhile, UNOCI pursued its human rights advocacy and awareness-raising campaign, including through television programmes and periodical reports documenting human rights violations.

Child protection

60. UNOCI and UNICEF are in the process of ascertaining the claim of the Forces nouvelles that no more child combatants are associated with its forces in Bouaké and Katiola. The Forces nouvelles also sought UNOCI assistance in identifying and demobilizing children in other areas under their control. Advocacy efforts by UNOCI and PNDDR have resulted in four militia groups operating in the western part of the country (Front de libération du grand-ouest, Mouvement ivoirien pour la libération de l'ouest de la Côte d'Ivoire, Alliance patriotique-Wé and Union patriotique pour la résistance du grand-ouest) considering subscribing to a regional action plan to end the association of children with their fighters, in application of Security Council resolutions 1539 (2004) and 1612 (2005).

IX. Role of the media in the crisis

61. UNOCI continues to monitor the media closely and has introduced a new media-monitoring programme on its radio station, ONUCI-FM. In collaboration with media monitoring bodies, it has also designed and elaborated a media road map aimed at improving the political environment through ONUCI-FM, UNOCI television programmes and the UNOCI website.

62. Segments of the local media continued to broadcast inflammatory statements. Some newspapers spread rumours of violence by the militias or alleged plans to attack and kill political leaders. Others called for mobilization against foreign nationals. During the period under review, UNOCI continued to monitor and report on hate media.

63. In August, President Gbagbo signed two decrees related to the mandates and powers of the National Press Council and the National Council on Audio-Visual Media and the institution of a press identification card. These measures are expected to contribute towards improving the media sector's legal framework, as the laws mandate sanctions against offenders, including the temporary closures of media houses. Meanwhile, UNOCI and the Office of the High Representative for the elections are working on the elaboration and adoption of a compulsory code of conduct for the media during the electoral period.

X. Gender issues

64. During the reporting period, UNOCI carried out gender awareness and induction training programmes for 26 male and 4 female police officers. UNOCI also assisted the Ministry of Family and Social Affairs in drafting a national gender policy, and in training the

Ministry's personnel on gender issues. All UNOCI components are working to mainstream gender into their workplans.

XI. HIV/AIDS

65. In accordance with Security Council resolution 1308 (2000), UNOCI continued activities aimed at discouraging HIV/AIDS conducive behaviour among peacekeepers. Some 400 United Nations staff members received HIV/AIDS awareness training during this period, while 85 staff members underwent voluntary confidential counselling and testing. UNOCI also continued to foster strategic partnerships in the field of HIV/AIDS prevention, notably through the consortium of an HIV/AIDS network of non-governmental organizations in Côte d'Ivoire and with the Network of People Living with HIV/AIDS, the Alliance of Religious Leaders for the Fight against AIDS and with United Nations agencies.

XII. Conduct and discipline of United Nations personnel

66. During the reporting period, UNOCI remained proactive in implementing measures aimed at preventing sexual exploitation and abuse. In this regard, UNOCI is looking into cases of specific conditions that could lead to potential acts of misconduct, such as access to UNOCI military compounds and command responsibilities related to such access. Regular training on conduct and discipline issues is being provided to United Nations personnel.

67. The Conduct and Discipline Unit continued to receive allegations of misconduct and worked with the Office of Internal Oversight Services on investigations into allegations involving UNOCI personnel. A UNOCI hotline has been established to facilitate better access to the reporting mechanism.

XIII. Observations and recommendations

68. For the past four years, the international community has invested a considerable amount of resources to help the Ivorian parties take their country out of crisis. Despite these efforts the first transition period prescribed in the Linas-Marcoussis Agreement in January 2003, ended in October 2005 without elections and with no progress on the key issues of disarmament, dismantling of the militia, identification and reunification of the country. The extension of the transition period for an additional 12 months in October 2005 had created initial hope, in particular because of the commendable efforts of Prime Minister Banny to cultivate confidence and forge dialogue among the Ivorian political leaders as he set out to implement the mandate given to him under Security Council resolution 1633 (2005).

69. Thanks to Prime Minister Banny's political skills and perseverance, as well as the tremendous amount of time and energy exerted by the leaders of the region, in particular Presidents Mbeki, Olusegun Obasanjo and Sassou-Nguesso, with whom I have closely worked in the efforts to keep the peace process on track, the initial phases of the disarmament process, the dismantling of the militia, the identification of the population and the restoration of State authority throughout the country, were launched earlier in 2006. Thus, for the first time since the start of the conflict in Côte d'Ivoire, concrete steps have been taken to implement the core processes that are critical to the resolution of the crisis.

70. Regrettably, events have taken a negative and disappointing turn over the past three months. The manifest lack of political will by the main Ivorian political leaders, in particular their

inability to transcend narrow personal and political interests, and to put the national interest first in addressing the core issue of the identification of the population, have created yet another major stalemate. At every critical turn of the peace process, some of the main political leaders have resorted to calculated obstruction of the peace process, exploiting loopholes in the peace agreements, using legal technicalities and often inciting violent acts by their followers. Consequently, the second transition period, like the first, is coming to a close without elections.

71. However, despite understandable frustrations, the international community should not abandon the Ivorian people. They deserve continued support in their quest for a lasting peace in their country and in the entire subregion. I therefore welcome the initiative taken by the ECOWAS leaders, who have developed important recommendations concerning the way forward after the current transition period expires on 31 October. It is imperative for the African Union and the Security Council to capitalize and build upon the proposals of the ECOWAS leaders, in order to put in place the requisite measures to accelerate the peace process and guarantee the success of the anticipated new transition arrangements. This time, ECOWAS, the African Union and the United Nations can ill afford a transition period that again ends without elections.

72. In this context, it is my strong belief that the duration of the anticipated new transition should be determined strictly on the basis of the time required to complete the disarmament, demobilization and reintegration process, to conduct effective identification, to dismantle the militias, to re-establish State authority and to finalize the technical preparations for the elections. The lack of political will on the part of the Ivorian political leaders should not be allowed to impede progress again. To that end, it would be important to make it clear to those leaders that the envisaged further extension of the transition period should be the last. Should they again fail to move towards elections, ECOWAS, the African Union and the Security Council should consider putting in place transitional governance arrangements comprising eminent, non-partisan personalities from civil society to complete the remaining transition processes and conduct the long overdue elections, and thus address the aspirations of the Ivorians and the States of the region to bring lasting stability to the country.

73. As the Security Council considers the envisaged new transition arrangements, based on the recommendations of ECOWAS and the African Union, it is important to be mindful of the need to preserve and build upon the gains made so far, in particular on the delicate disarmament and identification processes. In this regard, the Council should consider preserving the agreed principle of concomitant implementation of disarmament and identification, and insisting on the resumption of the implementation of the pre-cantonment phase of the disarmament programme and the dismantling of the militia, on the basis of the already agreed procedures, with adequate resources and clear weapons criteria for the admission of individuals into the programme for dismantling the militia.

74. Without specific unambiguous guidance on the core issues concerning the issuance of certificates of nationality and the preparation of voters' lists, which are at the centre not only of the current impasse, but also of the conflict itself, the anticipated new transition process will, like the previous one, go through the same vicious cycles of endless stalemates. I therefore urge the Security Council to consider ways of addressing these crucial issues, taking into account the recommendations of ECOWAS and the African Union.

75. In addition, in order to eliminate the existing loopholes and avoid previously encountered obstacles, it would be essential for the Security Council to consider setting the following ground rules and safeguards: (a) international instruments that set out the special arrangements for the transition period (past and future Security Council resolutions, African Union and ECOWAS decisions, and peace agreements) should take precedence where there may be a divergence with the Ivorian Constitution and national laws; (b) the Prime Minister should have the necessary authority over all relevant public offices, as well as the Defence and Security Forces, for all issues pertaining to the implementation of the road map. He should also have control over the appointment of senior public officials and the high command of the Defence and Security Forces; (c) all commanders of the Defence and Security Forces, as well as political leaders, should be held personally responsible for activities that disrupt the implementation of the road map, and should be subject to the imposition of individual sanctions by the Security Council in this regard, with the more serious cases referred to the International Criminal Court; (d) all parties should allow the Ivorian population and the impartial forces complete freedom of movement throughout the country; and (e) the Prime Minister should have full and unfettered authority to implement the disarmament programme, the identification process, the dismantling of the militia and the earliest re-establishment of State authority throughout the country and to commit the necessary funds to ensure the implementation of those key processes. It is also obvious that for the peace process to succeed, articles 35 and 48 of the Constitution should not be invoked during the transition period in respect of these key processes.

76. With regard to the transition institutions, it would be important to establish, under the Prime Minister's authority, two task forces, respectively, on the restructuring of the defence and security force, and on the identification process. Both task forces would comprise representatives of the Ivorian parties, the Prime Minister's office and the impartial forces, as well as other relevant partners. It is also important to ensure that the Independent Electoral Commission has the final authority on the electoral process during the transition period, and that the National Institute of Statistics operates under the direct oversight of the Independent Electoral Commission. The composition of these bodies should be reviewed by the Prime Minister, who should take the final decision on the new appointments, in order to ensure their total impartiality. This process would be certified by the High Representative for the elections.

77. With regard to the role of the international community, I recommend that the United Nations have an enhanced role in supporting and implementing the key processes of disarmament, identification, the re-establishment of State authority, the dismantling and disarmament of the militias and the technical preparations for the elections. In this context, it would be necessary for the Council to review the mandate of UNOCI and to augment its resources. It is also important for the Security Council to closely monitor the implementation of the road map during the new transition period, in particular, with a view to imposing targeted sanctions against those obstructing the peace process, or seizing the International Criminal Court.

78. Concerning the electoral process, it is imperative to ensure that the High Representative for the elections has the authority to make binding determinations on all issues pertaining to the electoral process, including those aspects of the peace agreements relating to electoral matters. Each stage of the electoral process should be certified by the High

Representative. In this regard, I regret to report that, despite generous contributions received from the European Commission, France, Norway, Spain, Switzerland and the United Kingdom of Great Britain and Northern Ireland during 2006, the available resources remain inadequate to sustain the Office of the High Representative. Considering the crucial role of the High Representative in the peace process, in particular in the next phases, it is my intention, as indicated in my eighth report on UNOCI (S/2006/222), to seek the approval of the General Assembly for the use of assessed contributions to fund his office.

79. The role of ECOWAS and the African Union in supporting the new transition process will be equally critical. It is important for these two regional bodies to forge unity among the regional actors and mediators. In this regard, I urge the Chairmen of ECOWAS and the African Union to ensure that all mediation efforts are harmonized and properly coordinated.

80. I am pleased to note that at the extraordinary summit held on 6 October 2006 in Abuja, the ECOWAS leaders came up with concrete recommendations on the way forward in Côte d'Ivoire, which have already been conveyed to the African Union. It is my fervent hope that in reviewing those recommendations, the planned summit of the Peace and Security Council of the African Union will come up with clear decisions that would meet the imperatives outlined above for effective and expeditious implementation of the peace process.

81. In conclusion, I would like to commend my Special Representative, Pierre Schori, the High Representative for the elections, Gérard Stoudmann, and the civilian and military staff of UNOCI for their continued efforts in support of sustainable peace in Côte d'Ivoire. Similarly, I would like to express my gratitude to the United Nations country team, the humanitarian and development organizations and the bilateral donors and the countries that are contributing troops and police personnel to UNOCI, as well as to the African Union and the Economic Community of West African States, for their invaluable contributions to the peace process.

Annex
United Nations Operation in Côte d'Ivoire: military and civilian police strength as at 6 October 2006

Country	*Military observers*	*Staff officers*	*Troops*	*Total*	*Formed police unit*	*Civilian police*
Argentina						4
Bangladesh	11	9	2 738	2 758	250	
Benin	7	7	421	435		27
Bolivia	3			3		
Brazil	4	3		7		
Cameroon						61
Canada						2
Central African Republic						7
Chad	3			3		5
China	7			7		
Croatia	3			3		
Djibouti						39
Dominican Republic	4			4		
Ecuador	2			2		
El Salvador	3			3		1
Ethiopia	2			2		
France	3	14	171	188		10
Guatemala	5			5		
Ghana	6	7	529	542		1
Gambia	3			3		
Guinea	3			3		
India	8			8		
Ireland	2			2		
Jordan	7	11	1 050	1 068	375	4
Kenya	4	5		9		
Madagascar						6
Morocco	1	3	732	736		
Namibia	3			3		
Nepal	3			3		
Niger	6	3	372	381		71
Nigeria	7			7		11
Pakistan	10	9	1 110	1 129		2
Paraguay	9	2		11		
Peru	3			3		
Philippines	4	3		7		6
Poland	2			2		
Republic of Moldova	4			4		
Romania	7			7		

Continued

Country	Military observers	Staff officers	Troops	Total	Formed police unit	Civilian police
Russian Federation	11			11		
Rwanda						15
Senegal	7	8	319	334		18
Serbia	3			3		
Switzerland						2
Togo	6	4	314	324		1
Tunisia	5	2		7		
Turkey						19
Uganda	4	3		7		
United Republic of Tanzania		1		1		
Uruguay	1	1		2		6
Vanuatu						4
Yemen	6			6		2
Zambia	2			2		
Total	**194**	**95**	**7 756**	**8 045**	**625**	**324**

3. Eleventh Progress Report of the Secretary-General on the United Nations Operation in Côte d'Ivoire, 4 December 2006 (S/2006/939)

I. Introduction

1. The present report is submitted pursuant to Security Council resolution 1603 (2005), by which the Council requested me to keep it regularly informed of developments in Côte d'Ivoire and in the implementation of the mandate of the United Nations Operation in Côte d'Ivoire (UNOCI). The report covers developments since my report of 17 October 2006 (S/2006/821).

II. Political developments

2. While it was welcomed in the subregion as a major step forward, Security Council resolution 1721 (2006) received mixed reactions from the Ivorian parties. On 2 November, President Laurent Gbagbo delivered an address to the nation in which he welcomed the resolution, but added that those of its provisions that were "inconsistent with the Constitution" of Côte d'Ivoire would not be implemented. Subsequently, the President announced that he was conducting a series of consultations with various segments of Ivorian society, including religious and traditional leaders, youth and women's organizations, and the business community, with a view to developing an "alternative framework" for resolving the Ivorian crisis. In that regard, the President expressed the view that all the peace plans devised by the international community since the conflict started had failed and that the Ivorian people therefore had the responsibility to find "their own solution". This course of action was generally perceived as an attempt to walk away from resolution 1721 (2006).

3. On 3 November, the Chief of Staff of the National Armed Forces of Côte d'Ivoire (FANCI), General Philippe Mangou, made a radio/television broadcast in which he assured President Gbagbo of the support of the Defence and Security Forces. General Mangou also welcomed the President's initiative to hold consultations with the various segments of the population and called upon the Forces nouvelles to return to the negotiation table. On 18 November, supporters of President Gbagbo, united under the umbrella group, the National Resistance Council for Democracy (CNRD) issued a statement presenting their views on the resolution of the crisis. The statement called for the appointment of a new prime minister by the President; the separation of the identification process from the preparation of the electoral rolls; the lifting of the zone of confidence; and the withdrawal of the French Licorne force.

4. For their part, the Forces nouvelles issued a statement on 2 November 2006 in which they welcomed resolution 1721 (2006), saying that it addressed their major concerns. The coalition of the opposition parties, Rassemblement des Houphouëtistes pour la démocratie et la paix, similarly welcomed the resolution and called on its supporters to boycott the consultations initiated by President Gbagbo.

5. In an address to the nation on 8 November, Prime Minister Charles Konan Banny expressed his determination to implement resolution 1721 (2006) and stated that there was no need for another framework to resolve the Ivorian crisis. He also announced that he

intended to focus on the outstanding tasks assigned to him, in particular disarmament, demobilization and reinsertion; identification of the population; dismantling of the militia; restructuring of the army; redeployment of state administration; and preparations for the elections. In that regard, the Prime Minister indicated that he would take all necessary measures to relaunch as soon as possible the disarmament programme and to establish a new structure for the military dialogue between the Forces nouvelles and FANCI.

6. The opposition parties and the Forces nouvelles commended the resolve shown by the Prime Minister in his 8 November statement and pledged their full support to him in the implementation of his peace mission. Similar sentiments were expressed by several civil society groups, who urged the Prime Minister to move expeditiously to implement resolution 1721 (2006).

7. On 7 November, I sent letters to President Denis Sassou-Nguesso of the Republic of the Congo and President Mamadou Tandja of the Republic of the Niger, the current chairmen of the African Union and the Economic Community of West African States (ECOWAS), respectively, requesting them to intervene personally in order to secure the acceptance of the resolution by all the parties and avert the new developing stalemate. I also emphasized that it was imperative for the Ivorian political leaders to immediately open a dialogue aimed at reaching consensus on a flexible way to implement resolution 1721 (2006).

8. My Special Representative, Pierre Schori, along with the High Representative for the elections, Gérard Stoudmann, and the Special Representative of the African Union Mediator, General Jean-Marie Mokoko, engaged in extensive consultations with the main Ivorian parties and the local media to impress upon them the need to implement resolution 1721 (2006) in good faith and in full. They also met with the Prime Minister in Yamoussoukro on 12 November to discuss the next steps. The Prime Minister reaffirmed his determination to implement the resolution, but stressed that this required the necessary political will from all the parties. The Prime Minister also requested UNOCI and other international partners to assist the Government to develop a plan for the implementation of the new transition process. President Gbagbo and Prime Minister Banny held a private meeting on 23 November, facilitated by the Special Representative of the International Organization of la Francophonie, Lansana Kouyaté, to discuss the way forward in setting the new transition process into motion.

9. In keeping with paragraph 21 of resolution 1721 (2006), the day-to-day mediation group met on 8 November, under the chairmanship of the Special Representative of the African Union Mediator and with the participation of my Special Representative, the High Representative for the elections, the Special Representatives of the ECOWAS Executive Secretary and of the Chairperson of the African Union Commission, and a representative of the International Organization of la Francophonie. The mediation group has so far held four meetings since the adoption of resolution 1721 (2006). The meetings discussed how best to assist the Prime Minister in preparing a road map for the new transition period. To that end, the mediation group decided to develop a new draft implementation schedule, which will be presented to the Prime Minister and the next ministerial meeting of the International Working Group established by the Security Council under resolution 1633 (2005), scheduled to take place on 1 December.

10. Despite the efforts to encourage the Ivorian leaders to open a constructive dialogue and work together to relaunch the implementation of the identification and disarmament

processes and the re-establishment of state authority throughout the country, the political atmosphere appeared to be deteriorating, with deepening disagreements between the President and the Prime Minister. On 23 November, the national commission of inquiry into the toxic waste scandal submitted its final report, in which it confirmed that the Minister of Transport, the General Manager of the Port of Abidjan, the Director-General of Customs and the Governor of the District of Abidjan, should be held accountable for the dumping of toxic waste from a foreign vessel in July 2006. Those officials had already been suspended from their respective posts by the Prime Minister on 6 and 14 September.

11. However, on 26 November, President Gbagbo issued presidential decrees limiting the suspension of the officials to three months, until 16 December. On 27 November, the Office of the Prime Minister broadcast a statement on national television stating that the Prime Minister had not been consulted on the decrees, that the matter should have been discussed within the Government and that the President's decisions were contrary to the principles of good governance, transparency and justice and would represent a major impediment in the fight against impunity. On 26 November, President Gbagbo also dismissed the Director-General and the entire board of the government newspaper Fraternité Matin, after the newspaper printed an article expressing the view that resolution 1721 (2006) was the only way out of the crisis.

12. In the early hours of 28 November, elements of the Defence and Security Forces entered the premises of the state-owned Radio Télévision Ivorienne (RTI) by force and prevented a repeat broadcast of the Prime Minister's statement. On the same day, in a major confrontational step, President Gbagbo issued a decree dismissing the Director-General and the management board of the RTI. The situation deteriorated, with demonstrations organized in several towns to protest against the President's decisions. In addition, on 1 December, the Republican Guard blocked the UNOCI unit in charge of the Prime Minister's security from access to the Prime Minister's compound.

13. The International Working Group met in Abidjan on 1 December. The Group noted with deep concern the delays in implementing resolution 1721 (2006). It also condemned the dismissals at the RTI, noting that they were contrary to the Pretoria Agreement, as undermining the neutrality and impartiality of the public media as well as freedom of expression. It considered indispensable the reinstatement of the officials.

14. The Working Group also set out the main timelines for relaunching the disarmament and identification processes, the preparations for the elections, as well as the commencement of the reform of the security sector. It further condemned obstructions to the freedom of movement of the impartial forces, in particular the refusal by the Republican Guard to grant the UNOCI unit in charge of the Prime Minister's security access to his compound. Reacting to the communiqué of the Working Group on 3 December, President Gbagbo said that it strengthened his resolve to develop an alternative solution to the Ivorian crisis. He added that he would inform me and the Security Council of the "dangerous stance" taken by the Working Group.

III. Security situation

15. The security situation has remained relatively calm following the adoption of Security Council resolution 1721 (2006). However, violent clashes, unrelated to reactions to the

resolution, occurred in Yopougon, near Abidjan, on 1 and 3 November 2006, when the local population reacted to criminal harassment by the Groupement des patriotes pour la paix (GPP) militia and the support the militia was receiving from the Defence and Security Forces. At least five people were killed during the clashes, including two militiamen who were burned alive by Yopougon residents. The situation calmed down after the Defence and Security Forces relocated the militia elements, numbering about 200, to the gendarmerie barracks in another part of Abidjan.

16. On 10 November, in Yamoussoukro, a group of youth affiliated with the Rassemblement des Houphouëtistes pour la démocratie et la paix blocked a convoy of supporters of the presidential camp en route to Abidjan to attend President Gbagbo's consultations. Clashes broke out and two people were wounded. The Defence and Security Forces used tear gas to disperse the crowd. On 20 November, a few days before the release of the report of the national commission of inquiry into the toxic waste scandal, elements of the Young Patriots blocked the access to the Abidjan autonomous port, demanding that the Director-General of the port, suspended by the Prime Minister in September, be reinstated. The Defence and Security Forces dispersed the group.

17. On 6 November 2006, in the western town of Duékoué, militias who were demonstrating to demand payment of the first instalment of their disarmament benefits (safety net allowance) from the National Programme for Disarmament, Demobilization and Reintegration (PNDDR), seized a UNOCI vehicle. The incident was resolved following the intervention of UNOCI and the local authorities. Obstruction to the freedom of movement of the impartial forces by militias in the west was reported during the period under review. Meanwhile, in the north, a significant rise in the crime rate was reported, in particular in Bouaké and Korhogo, while ethnic tensions rose in the zone of confidence and in the southwest of the country, leading in particular to the killing of five persons around the village of Blodi during clashes between Burkinabé and Géré, prompting increased patrolling by UNOCI and the French Licorne force in those areas.

IV. Deployment of the United Nations Operation in Côte d'Ivoire

Force deployment and activities

18. As at 20 November, the troop strength of UNOCI stood at 8,042 military personnel, consisting of 11 battalions (5 in Sector West, 4 in Sector East and 2 in Abidjan), one aviation unit, three engineering companies and one transport company providing support to the battalions. In order to minimize the risk of escalation of the prevailing political tensions in the country, in particular in Abidjan, the force is actively engaged in extensive operational activities, in close cooperation with the French Licorne force. The force conducts an average of 120 patrols per day over the entire theatre of operations, as well as large-scale operations in Abidjan and in the western part of the country, aimed at dominating their areas of responsibility and monitoring the security situation. The force has also undergone a training programme aimed at enhancing its crowd control capacity, in close coordination with the Operation's formed police units. The UNOCI and Licorne force commanders continue to hold monthly meetings with the Chief of Staff of the FANCI, General Mangou. In the meantime, UNOCI and the United Nations Mission in Liberia (UNMIL) continue to conduct simultaneous patrols of the border areas in order to prevent illegal cross-border movements of arms and combatants.

19. Enhanced cooperation between the UNOCI and French Licorne forces in the whole theatre, and notably Abidjan, has culminated in several quick reaction force rehearsals conducted with the Licorne force, which were repeated after each rotation of contingents. At the end of October, as part of the tripartite monthly meetings involving representatives of UNOCI, the Licorne force and the Defence and Security Forces of Côte d'Ivoire, the Chief of Staff of the FANCI agreed, in principle, to resume joint patrols in Abidjan.

20. During the new transition period, it will be essential to adjust the overall posture of the UNOCI military component. In particular, the Force will gradually reduce its presence in the zone of confidence, as appropriate, shift from the current emphasis on separating the armed groups and increase its presence and mobility throughout the country, with a view to enhancing its role in providing security for the resumption of the mobile courts and to the cantonment, demobilization and disarmament sites, securing the electoral process, providing technical assistance to the restructuring of the armed forces, strengthening the protection of civilians and facilitating freedom of movement, especially between the north and the south. To that end, and for the reasons provided in my eighth report, of 3 January 2006 (S/2006/2), I once again urge the Security Council to authorize the deployment of the remaining three battalions out of the four recommended in that report. In addition, the Sous-Groupement de sécurité, which provides security to the signatories of the Linas-Marcoussis Agreement and members of the Government will be required to provide security for the members of the Electoral Commission and for the High Representative for the elections. It is therefore imperative to reinforce this unit by 250 additional gendarmes.

Police deployment

21. As at 20 November, the strength of the police component of UNOCI stood at 1,004 personnel, including 379 United Nations police officers and 625 personnel from five formed police units, against an authorized police effective of 1,200 personnel. The shortfall is due to the delayed deployment of one formed police unit, which is expected to arrive in the area in January 2007. The United Nations police officers are deployed throughout the country at 22 team sites, in the north and south of the zone of confidence, and within the zone. Two formed police units are deployed in Abidjan, one in Bouaké, one in Daloa and one in Yamoussoukro, while the fifth will be deployed in Guiglo.

22. During the period under review, the joint patrols conducted between United Nations police and the internal security forces (police and gendarmerie) of Côte d'Ivoire, which resumed in June 2006, have been gradually extended to the entire area controlled by the Government, south of the zone of confidence. In the near future, UNOCI intends to launch similar patrols in the area controlled by the Forces nouvelles jointly with the auxiliaries of police who have been trained by UNOCI. During the period ahead, the United Nations police will also continue to interact with the internal security forces of Côte d'Ivoire involved in police training at the various police and gendarmerie schools and academy centres and will be involved in the restructuring of the security sector.

23. With the anticipated resumption of the mobile court hearings, the United Nations police will continue to provide assistance to the UNOCI Electoral Division, including by participating in UNOCI observer teams deployed at the mobile court sites. The formed police units will also continue to provide security at mobile court sites in their five main areas of deployment in Abidjan, Daloa, Guiglo, Yamoussoukro and Bouaké. Formed police units

will also continue to provide enhanced security for UNOCI personnel and premises and to conduct joint training and exercises on crowd control management with the mission's military contingents, in close collaboration with elements from the mobile gendarmerie unit of the Licorne force.

V. Steps needed to relaunch the key processes under the road map

24. Security Council resolution 1721 (2006) provided a sound framework for the relaunching of the key processes that had been stalled since August 2006, including the disarmament process, the dismantling and disarmament of the militias, the mobile court hearings, the re-establishment of state authority and the technical preparations for the elections. In this regard, the parties should focus, in a pragmatic manner, on resolving the outstanding issues in order to facilitate the resumption of the key processes without any further delay.

Concomitant resumption of identification and disarmament processes

25. The resumption of the identification and disarmament processes should build upon the experience gained during the pilot project launched by Prime Minister Banny in May 2006 and the subsequent initial concomitant operations of the mobile courts and the pre-cantonment process in July 2006. That experience demonstrated the feasibility of the approach developed during this important phase. In order to relaunch the mobile courts, the outstanding disagreements on the procedures for issuing certificates of nationality must be resolved expeditiously. In this regard, the decree issued by President Gbagbo on 5 October, which increased the number of jurisdictions competent to deliver certificates of nationality to 147, should form the basis for resolving this matter. The final call for bids for the operator who will be responsible for implementing the technical aspects of the identification process (data collection and sorting, production of identification cards and voter cards) is also an encouraging step towards relaunching the identification process.

26. However, further steps are necessary. For instance, it should be recalled that, with only 23 courts currently functioning, the Government is facing the daunting task of organizing the work of the new courts. Technical delays have already put a tight timeline under further stress. It is unfortunate, for example, that the selection of the operator mentioned above has still not been made. It will also be essential to provide adequate funding and the requisite logistical resources to ensure sustained operation of the mobile courts and other aspects of the identification process, once they resume. In this regard, UNOCI could contribute to the successful conduct of the identification process by providing limited logistical support, as appropriate and within currently available resources, especially for the operation of the mobile courts.

27. In order to ensure that the identification process is conducted in a transparent, credible and coordinated manner and is consistent with international standards, the working group on the identification of the population and the registration of voters provided for in resolution 1721 (2006) should be established without delay under the authority of the Prime Minister. The participation of representatives of all the Ivorian parties, as well as UNOCI and the High Representative for the elections in this important working group will be critical to ensuring the transparency of the identification process.

28. The principle of conducting the disarmament and identification processes concomitantly, agreed upon by the Ivorian parties, should be preserved. In order to expedite the

disarmament process and in view of the assurances given by the respective forces that the pre-cantonment of their troops was completed in July 2006, it has been proposed that the disarmament process should be relaunched at the cantonment phase. In this regard, the verification, screening and profiling of combatants and the listing of their weapons would now be carried out during the cantonment phase of the programme. This proposal is aimed at avoiding the logistical difficulties that plagued the implementation of the pre-cantonment phase in July 2006. The cantonment operations would be conducted at 17 cantonment sites, including 9 in the area controlled by the Forces nouvelles and 8 in the area controlled by the Government. The PNDDR had planned to complete the physical rehabilitation of the facilities at the cantonment sites by the end of December. However, the Programme is facing a shortfall of approximately $10 million for the procurement of the necessary equipment for those sites.

29. The initial pilot phases of the disarmament process, which were conducted between May and August 2006, exposed capacity and resource constraints in the PNDDR, which could be addressed by strengthening UNOCI's role in the implementation of the Programme. I therefore recommend that UNOCI be authorized to provide direct assistance to the PNDDR in refurbishing and equipping the cantonment sites. Such assistance would ensure the timely relaunching of the Programme and thus preserve the politically sensitive principle of conducting the disarmament of combatants and the identification of the population concomitantly. The proposed enhanced role of UNOCI would have financial implications for the mission. In addition, as indicated in my ninth progress report on UNOCI (S/2006/532), the World Bank continues to withhold the $80 million it had pledged to contribute towards the cost of the reintegration of demobilized combatants, because of the Government's unpaid arrears. This issue has been outstanding for some time and is not likely to be resolved in the foreseeable future. I therefore appeal to Member States to contribute individually the funds required to meet that shortfall, which could jeopardize the effective implementation of the Programme. In this regard, it should be noted that any delays in the implementation of the disarmament and identification processes could have a negative impact on the election schedule.

30. In order to facilitate the timely resumption of the disarmament process, it is also imperative that the PNDDR and UNOCI receive the lists of combatants and weapons from the Forces nouvelles and the FANCI before the resumption of the disarmament programme. To that end, Prime Minister Banny should set a deadline for the submission of this critical information, to be followed by a quick verification phase, conducted by the parties together with the impartial forces. Work on reintegration opportunities to be provided to ex-combatants should also begin without delay, so as to ensure that there is no gap between the disarmament and reintegration programmes. In this regard, the PNDDR should pursue its plan to establish a network with local authorities and civil society, which would enhance the sustainability of the reinsertion process.

Dismantling and disarmament of militias

31. As reported in my tenth progress report on UNOCI (S/2006/821), the dismantling and disarmament of the militias was suspended in early August by the PNDDR as a result of a low weapon-to-combatant ratio and the high number of unserviceable weapons surrendered by the 981 disarmed militia members. In addition, the leaders of the militias in the

west were demanding the inclusion of 3,000 additional individuals in the disarmament programme, under which they would be entitled to receive a safety net allowance of $900. However, the PNDDR rejected that demand, stressing that the eligible 2,000 militias should surrender a credible number of weapons, in keeping with the established weapons-to-combatant ratio. Once these outstanding issues are resolved and if the outstanding caseload of eligible militia members remains at 1,000, based on the previously agreed framework, it would take only two weeks to disarm the militias in the west. The establishment of two additional disarmament sites in Toulépleu and Bloléquin, as proposed by UNOCI, would help expedite this process.

32. In order to facilitate the early relaunching of the process, the PNDDR, in consultation with UNOCI, should expeditiously issue clear criteria and procedures for the disarmament of the remaining armed militias. In addition, the status of the militias in Abidjan, in particular the GPP, whose command and control structure remain intact, despite claims that they were dismantled by the Defence and Security Forces in 2005, needs to be clarified by the PNDDR and subsequently verified. Effective sensitization on the criteria for dismantling the militias should be conducted for all concerned groups and adequate measures, involving in particular the Defence and Security Forces, should be envisaged to prevent the re-emergence of the militia groups. The early establishment of the military unit intended to provide direct support to the Office of the Prime Minister for this purpose would also contribute to progress on the issue.

Restructuring of the Defence and Security Forces

33. As envisaged in resolution 1721 (2006), the disarmament programme should be placed in the broader context of the restructuring of the armed forces. The Prime Minister has yet to announce the establishment of the working group provided for in resolution 1721 (2006) to prepare the plan for the restructuring of the Defence and Security Forces. The envisaged plan is expected to address such issues as the overall role and strength of the armed forces and their deployment throughout the country, criteria for recruitment and assignments, career development and entitlements for soldiers and their families, as well as the integration of elements from the Forces nouvelles. The restructuring programme should also include other components of the Defence and Security Forces (gendarmerie, police and intelligence services), while a review of the legislative and executive framework governing the security sector should be addressed in a holistic and transparent manner. UNOCI is expected to provide technical assistance to the restructuring programme. I urge Member States in a position to do so to offer the Government assistance in developing and implementing its plans in this vital area.

Redeployment of state administration

34. The National Committee for the Restoration of State Authority (CNPRA) has indicated that at least half of the 24,437 civil servants displaced by the crisis had been redeployed by October 2006, with 3,962 civil servants redeployed in the west and 8,424 civil servants in the central, eastern and northern parts of the country. The redeployment of the remaining 12,091 civil servants was impeded in part by the funding gap of $30 million needed for the rehabilitation of infrastructure and the payment of allowances to the civil servants concerned. In addition, the Forces nouvelles should not place any preconditions for the return of civil servants to the north and should guarantee their security. In this connection, the

CNPRA is expected to submit a revised redeployment plan. During preliminary consultations, the Minister for Territorial Administration submitted a provisional $25 million budget to support the redeployment of civil servants to the north.

35. To be sustainable, the redeployment of state administration should also include the redeployment of the judiciary in the zone of confidence and in the north. UNOCI intends to increase the presence of civil affairs and rule of law officers throughout the country to support this process.

Technical preparations for the elections

36. The Chairman of the Independent Electoral Commission has informed UNOCI and the High Representative for the elections of his intention to establish all 430 local structures of the Commission (24 regional, 48 departmental and 358 local) as soon as possible, regardless of whether all parties eligible will be in a position to nominate their representatives to those bodies as currently envisaged. He has also created 10 technical subcommissions within the central electoral commission in order to begin detailed planning for the elections, with the support of 10 experts from UNOCI.

37. Within a short time frame, the Chairman of the Independent Electoral Commission is also expected to determine the dates for the holding of the first round of presidential elections. In the meantime, UNOCI and the High Representative for the elections will continue to assist their Ivorian counterparts in the efforts to streamline the processes leading to the elections, in particular with regard to the number of commissioners in the local commissions to be established by the Independent Electoral Commission throughout the country. UNOCI and the High Representative for the elections will also support the fund-raising efforts of the Government in order to ensure that adequate resources are made available for the preparations for the elections in Côte d'Ivoire. The budget for the elections is estimated at $95 million.

38. In view of the inadequate resources received from donors for the office of the High Representative for the elections, I had indicated in my tenth progress report on UNOCI (S/2006/821) my intention to seek the approval of the General Assembly to fund his office from assessed contributions. I am pleased to report that an alternative source of funding has been identified, through the United Nations Trust Fund for Peacekeeping and Peacemaking Activities. However, continued support to the activities of the High Representative will be needed from donors through contributions to the Trust Fund.

VI. Humanitarian situation

39. The humanitarian situation continues to be a source of concern. The health situation continues to be deteriorating, with new reports of cholera and yellow fever outbreaks as well as continued shortages of water and sanitation in the northern part of the country. In addition, a census conducted by the United Nations Population Fund and the Government concluded that 710,000 internally displaced persons lived in five regions of the area controlled by the Government, putting the overall numbers of internally displaced persons in the country at approximately 800,000.

40. During the period under review, UNOCI and the United Nations country team continued to provide coordinated assistance to the Government's efforts to mitigate the humanitarian and health consequences of the dumping of toxic waste from a foreign ship, in Abidjan, at

the end of August. As at 23 October 2006, 10 people were reported to have died, 64 persons had been hospitalized and 104,000 patients had sought health consultations. Following the deployment of a United Nations disaster assistance and coordination team in response to a request by the Government for international assistance, a joint mission was fielded by the Office for the Coordination of Humanitarian Affairs, the United Nations Development Programme, the United Nations Environment Programme and the United Nations Human Settlements Programme, from 22 to 29 November 2006, to identify the support needed by the Government in establishing a toxic waste contingency plan and an action plan.

41. On 12 and 13 October 2006, a workshop on the protection of civilians took place in Abidjan, with the participation of 80 representatives of the Government of Côte d'Ivoire, UNOCI, entities of the United Nations system, humanitarian organizations, donors and civil society, to take stock of the key protection challenges and to agree on action to be taken. Participants agreed on the urgent need to develop coherent and complementary protection strategies, taking into consideration the regional dimension of protection challenges, such as small arms, and to take immediate action in priority areas, such as the establishment of security in the west, in particular in the zone of confidence, introducing justice systems to end impunity and improving assistance to vulnerable groups.

42. The protection network, composed of United Nations entities and non-governmental organizations, has since established working groups to address: (a) protection of refugees, internally displaced persons and host families; (b) protection of children and gender-based violence; (c) physical protection of civilians, humanitarian staff and humanitarian access; (d) justice and the rule of law; and (e) disarmament, demobilization, reinsertion of ex-combatants and rehabilitation of infrastructures. I encourage UNOCI, the French Licorne force, United Nations entities and the humanitarian community to jointly develop a comprehensive operational plan for the protection of civilians.

VII. Financial aspects

43. By its resolution 60/17 B, the General Assembly appropriated a total amount of $420.2 million for the maintenance of UNOCI for the period from 1 July 2006 to 30 June 2007. I am requesting an additional amount of $52.7 million in the revised budget for the Operation for the period ending 30 June 2007 in response to the increase by 1,500 in the strength of the military and police components of the Operation authorized by the Security Council in its resolution 1682 (2006). It is expected that the General Assembly will take action on my proposal during the main part of its sixty-first session. The total resources approved for the mission would support 8,115 military personnel, 450 United Nations police personnel and 750 formed police personnel, authorized by the Security Council in its resolutions 1609 (2005) and 1682 (2006).

44. Should the Council decide to endorse my recommendations in paragraphs 29, 35 and 54, as well as to increase the military and police strength of UNOCI as recommended in paragraph 55, I shall seek additional resources for the Operation from the General Assembly.

45. As at 30 September 2006, unpaid assessed contributions to the special account for UNOCI amounted to $186.6 million. The total outstanding assessed contributions for all peacekeeping operations at that date amounted to $2,080.2 million. As at 30 September 2006, amounts owed to the UNOCI troop and formed police contributors totalled

$17.9 million. Reimbursement of troop and contingent-owned equipment costs has been made for the period up to 31 July 2006.

VIII. Observations

46. Although the Ivorian parties have failed to meet the election deadline for the second time, the successful launching of the initial phases of the PNDDR, the identification of the population and the restoration of state authority in the north provided a practical basis for meaningful progress. The experience in the operation of the mobile courts, including the consensus on the principle of conducting identification and disarmament concomitantly, as well as the lessons drawn from the pre-cantonment phase, the dismantling of militias in the west, the return of civil servants to the north and the reunification of the school examinations system, have all demonstrated the feasibility of the road map adopted by the Prime Minister.

47. Recent Security Council decisions provide a sound framework for carrying forward these initial, but precious gains, in order to bring the peace process to a successful conclusion in the coming 12 months. Resolution 1721 (2006) offers the necessary tools and safeguards that should make it possible to overcome the technical issues that have hitherto impeded progress. Most of these obstacles and the resultant series of stalemates witnessed in the past 12 months were clearly contrived. I am convinced that the main Ivorian political leaders can rise above narrow partisan and personal interests and make the compromises needed to take their country out of crisis. They have already demonstrated this at the two meetings in Yamoussoukro on 28 February and 5 July 2006. I therefore appeal to President Gbagbo, Henri Konan Bedié, Alassane Ouattara and Guillaume Soro to muster the necessary political will, seize the opportunity offered by the final extension of the transition period and work together with Prime Minister Banny to build on the initial positive steps they have taken on disarmament, identification and the restoration of state authority.

48. The framework offered by Security Council resolution 1721 (2006) must be complemented by efforts from both Ivorian and international stakeholders to nurture a security and political environment in which trust can take root among the main Ivorian political leaders. Sustained dialogue can play a crucial role in building confidence among the leaders. I urge President Gbagbo and Prime Minister Banny to provide the necessary leadership in this regard, eschew confrontation and maintain a constructive working relationship. International mediators, in particular regional and other leaders, should also assist in building confidence among the Ivorian parties. As recognized by the Security Council, Ivorian civil society, which has so far been marginalized, must be brought into the mainstream of the peace process. At the same time, if civil society is to play a credible role, it too must eschew political agendas and put the national interest first.

49. Ivorian political leaders and civil society should together take a hard and honest look at Côte d'Ivoire's political dispensation, with a view to addressing the factors that underlie the inclination to maintain the status quo. They must together cultivate a culture of political accommodation and tolerance, fight impunity, tackle the hate media, rid the nation of xenophobia, pay attention to the insidious local land and ethnic conflicts in the west and contribute, as called for by the international community, including the African Union and ECOWAS, to put in place a mechanism to guarantee the credibility and transparency of the crucial identification of the population. Above all, for Côte d'Ivoire to emerge from conflict, all Ivorian stakeholders

must recognize and accept the need for exceptional measures during and immediately following the transition period, including the possibility of power-sharing arrangements.

50. In the meantime, the most pressing task is to relaunch the implementation of the key outstanding tasks. Regrettably, the Ivorian parties have already lost precious time. Moreover, some of them are pursuing actions that could further polarize political discourse, exacerbate current tensions and lead to widespread violence. Considering that the current 12-month extension of the transition process is final, the situation brooks no further delay. I therefore appeal to all Ivorian parties to extend full cooperation to the Prime Minister in the implementation of the road map for the new transition.

51. This is particularly needed in view of the current political stalemate, which could easily lead to a deterioration of the situation and possibly develop into a long-term stand-off that would be very damaging to the resumption of the key processes. I am, however, pleased to note that some technical preparations for the disarmament and identification processes have continued in spite of the stalemate. The PNDDR is refurbishing cantonment sites, the Prime Minister has drafted ordinances on the hearings in the mobile courts and the establishment of the working groups called for in resolution 1721 (2006). The Ivorian stakeholders now need to open urgent dialogue and consultations among the Ivorian stakeholders should focus on the resumption of disarmament, the hearings in the mobile courts, the dismantling of the militia and the restoration of state authority, within the framework established by Security Council resolution 1721 (2006). There is ample room for the necessary flexibility and accommodation as regards the concerns of each party. All Ivorian stakeholders should therefore avoid courses of action that depart from the existing and already tested frameworks, discard the gains already made, exacerbate divisions and tensions and risk the renewal of hostilities.

52. For its part, the international community should act in unity in supporting the peace process. It must offer appropriate incentives to the parties, while at the same time it should be ready to act against individuals and parties who deliberately obstruct the peace process, as well as the operations of the impartial forces, and those who commit crimes against the civilian population. In this connection, it is my fervent hope that regional leaders will remain fully engaged with the Ivorian parties, including by impressing on them the need to fulfil, in good faith, all their obligations under the various peace agreements, as well as the decisions and resolutions of the African Union and the Security Council.

53. The peace process cannot succeed without adequate resources. I therefore appeal to Member States to contribute generously the funds needed to support the peace process, in order to ensure sustained implementation of the key processes once they are relaunched. The costs of the key processes are estimated at $24 million for the operation of the mobile courts, $25 million for the redeployment of state administration, $76 million for the elections, $150 million for the PNDDR and $2.5 million for the dismantling and disarmament of the militias. In addition, the costs of the identification process and the restructuring of the Defence and Security Forces are yet to be determined.

54. In the light of the above and mindful of the fact that the current transitional period is expected to be completed by 31 October 2007, I recommend that the Security Council authorize the renewal of the mandate of UNOCI for an additional year, until 15 December 2007. Furthermore, in order to enable UNOCI to effectively support the key tasks in the transition process, I urge the Council to approve the recommendations contained in

paragraphs 21-34 of the present report, related to the United Nations contribution in support of the key processes. In addition, I seek the Council's support for an expanded presence of the civil affairs, political affairs, human rights and the rule of law components of UNOCI in the northern and western parts of the country, to support the restoration of state administration, which is expected to gather momentum during this final transition period. UNOCI's public information component also plans to develop a robust sensitization campaign in close collaboration with relevant counterparts (Government, the media, civil society and so on) and in coordination with the office of the High Representative for the elections, in its continuing efforts to combat hate media and to sensitize the population on the key processes, including the elections. To that end, the Operation will expand the coverage of its radio to allow widest possible access by the Ivorian people especially those in such remote areas as Aboisso, Bouna, Korhogo and Odienné.

55. The conduct of the politically sensitive identification of the population, as well as the preparations for the elections, will require effective security from the impartial forces. For this reason, and in view of the need to adjust the overall posture of the UNOCI military component and to enhance its role in facilitating freedom of movement and protecting civilians, I once again appeal to the Security Council to approve the remaining three battalions for UNOCI, out of the four recommended in my seventh progress report (S/2006/2). In that regard, and pursuant to Security Council resolution 1609 (2005), the Council may wish to consider taking advantage of the adjustment in the strength of UNMIL, in particular the envisaged departure of one battalion at the end of 2006, to reinforce UNOCI.

56. The activities of the office of the High Representative for the elections are expected to expand, as this final transition period is expected to yield the long-awaited elections. Although an alternative funding mechanism has been identified, which should go a long way towards addressing some of the difficulties mentioned in my letter to the Security Council dated 16 October 2006 (S/2006/820), the funding of his office from voluntary contributions continues to pose significant challenges. I therefore, once again, appeal to potential donors to urgently provide the resources required to sustain the critical work of the High Representative.

57. In conclusion, I would like to commend my Special Representative, Pierre Schori, and the High Representative for the elections, Gérard Stoudmann, as well as the civilian and military staff of UNOCI for their continued efforts in support of sustainable peace in Côte d'Ivoire. Similarly, I would like to express my gratitude to the United Nations country team, humanitarian and development organizations and bilateral donors and the countries that are contributing troops and police personnel to UNOCI, as well as to the African Union and ECOWAS, for their invaluable contribution to the peace process.

4. Thirteenth Progress Report of the Secretary-General on the United Nations Mission in Liberia, 11 December 2006 (S/2006/958)

I. Introduction

1. By its resolution 1712 (2006), the Security Council extended the mandate of the United Nations Mission in Liberia (UNMIL) until 31 March 2007 and requested me to provide information on progress made in meeting the broad benchmarks laid out in my report of 12 September 2006 (S/2006/743). The present report provides an update on major developments in Liberia, including the progress made in meeting the key benchmarks for the first phase of the Mission's consolidation, drawdown and withdrawal.

II. Major political developments

2. The overall political situation remained generally stable during the period under review. The relationship between the legislative and executive branches of government improved, allowing for the relatively smooth passage of the national forestry reform law in compliance with Security Council resolution 1689 (2006).

3. In furtherance of the spirit of national reconciliation, President Ellen Johnson-Sirleaf hosted a celebratory dinner to mark the end of Ramadan, which was attended by Muslim leaders, members of the Mandingo ethnic group and former warring faction leaders, including Sekou Damate Conneh of the former Liberians United for Reconciliation and Democracy and Alhaji Kromah of the former United Liberation Movement for Democracy in Liberia. During the event, the President reaffirmed her Government's commitment to religious freedom and tolerance. On 21 November, the President convened a meeting of political stakeholders, which brought together the leaders of registered political parties, many of whom had contested the 2005 presidential elections. The party leaders expressed appreciation for the President's initiative and exchanged views on several issues of national importance, including national security and the country's draft interim poverty reduction strategy.

4. The Presidential Commission that was established to investigate inter-ethnic land and property disputes in Nimba County and to make recommendations for the resolution of disputes that could impede the peaceful coexistence of ethnic communities in the County has completed its work and is in the process of finalizing its report. UNMIL is working closely with the Government and civil society organizations to address other inter-ethnic, religious, community and property disputes in various parts of the country. In this regard, the Mission has completed the mapping of potential conflict areas and is in the process of establishing district peace and reconciliation committees that will focus on conflict resolution.

5. The 29 August by-election to fill the House of Representatives District Number 2 seat in Margibi County, left vacant by the death of a representative from the ruling Unity Party, resulted in no candidate securing the required "50 per cent plus one" majority vote. As a result, on 12 September the National Elections Commission held a run-off election between the two candidates who had received the most votes. The candidate from the Congress for Democratic Change obtained 52 per cent of the votes, while the Unity Party candidate won 48 per cent of the votes. The winning candidate was inducted to the House of Representatives on 21 September, bringing the House back to its full membership of 64 members.

However, another seat fell vacant shortly thereafter, following the death of the Unity Party representative for District Number 6 in Nimba County on 15 October. The National Elections Commission is currently organizing a by-election to fill this vacant seat.

6. During the reporting period, the President continued her efforts to combat corruption. In this regard, the President signed into law two acts ratifying the African Union Convention on Preventing and Combating Corruption and the United Nations Convention against Corruption. In addition, the Government has approved the Governance Reform Commission's anti-corruption policy statement and is currently considering a draft national anti-corruption strategy. A major proposal in this draft is the establishment of an anti-corruption commission, which would have investigative and prosecutorial powers. The Government is also considering draft legislation to grant the Governance Reform Commission full autonomy. In the meantime, the United Nations Democracy Fund has awarded the Government a $360,000 grant to support its anti-corruption initiatives.

7. As part of its efforts to curb corruption, the Ministry of Finance has improved the process for the payment of civil servant salaries, resulting in the removal of over 4,700 "ghost" workers from the Government's payroll. With the support of the international community, the Government is also streamlining its administrative structures and procedures. At the same time, in order to deal with the dearth of management capacity in the public sector, the Government, in collaboration with its development partners, is pursuing the establishment of a "senior executive service", which will be composed of qualified Liberians for senior administrative and technical positions.

8. The sixteenth session of the Ministerial Council of the Mano River Union was held in Monrovia on 18 and 19 October 2006. The meeting, which was attended by the ministers of economic planning of Liberia, Sierra Leone and Guinea, recommended a new organizational and salary structure for the Union's operations. It is hoped that this would assist in revitalizing this subregional organization, which has remained dormant for over 10 years owing to security and economic constraints. The budget is expected to be approved at the summit meeting of the Heads of State of the Mano River Union in January 2007.

III. Security situation

9. The security situation in Liberia remained generally calm during the reporting period, although there were minor disturbances caused by deactivated security service personnel who staged a series of demonstrations to demand benefits they claim are outstanding, including salary arrears. In this regard, President Johnson-Sirleaf directed her Cabinet, as well as the Inspector General of the Liberian National Police and the Director of the Special Security Services to carry out a comprehensive assessment of the total remaining salary arrears and pensions due to these deactivated personnel and to develop a plan for the liquidation of the arrears and the payment of pensions.

10. Operation "Sweeping Wave", which was launched on 8 September by President Johnson-Sirleaf in response to public concerns about the increase in reported criminal activities, especially armed robberies and rapes, has resulted in a significant reduction in violent crime in Monrovia and its environs. The exercise involved the conduct of cordon-and-search operations, as well as day and night patrols in high crime areas by the Liberian National Police and other security agencies, together with UNMIL. A National Joint

Operations Centre, composed of representatives of UNMIL, the Ministry of Defence and national security agencies, was established to coordinate the operation.

11. UNMIL conducted a successful operation, referred to as "Exercise Tight Grip", on 27 and 28 October, to evaluate the Mission's capabilities and operational readiness to respond to a possible major deterioration in the security situation in Monrovia. The exercise also served to reassure residents of Monrovia of the Mission's active support of the security needs of the country.

12. The security situation along Liberia's borders with Sierra Leone, Côte d'Ivoire and Guinea remained stable during the reporting period. However, potential threats to the stability of Liberia include the possible movement of armed groups from Côte d'Ivoire into Liberia, recruitment of former Liberian combatants, including children, by Ivorian militia groups and Liberians to fight in Côte d'Ivoire, and an influx of Ivorians seeking refuge in Liberia in the event of renewed hostilities in that country. UNMIL has, therefore, strengthened security along Liberia's borders to mitigate possible threats, including trafficking of arms. In addition, UNMIL and the United Nations Operation in Côte d'Ivoire (UNOCI) conducted concurrent patrols along the Liberian-Ivorian border in "Operation Mayo" between 9 and 14 October, as well as from 27 November to 2 December. Similar patrols were undertaken during the same period with the Sierra Leonean forces along the Liberian-Sierra Leonean border in "Operation Loko". In addition, the first coordinated exercise between UNMIL and Guinean forces, referred to as "Operation Seskin", began along the Liberia-Guinea border. These exercises were aimed at demonstrating the presence of United Nations security forces in the border areas, establishing cross-border liaison and reassuring the local populations.

IV. Status of implementation of the mandate of the United Nations Mission in Liberia

A. Rehabilitation and reintegration of ex-combatants

Reintegration of war-affected populations

13. At 15 November, some 39,000 ex-combatants had not yet been absorbed into reintegration programmes. However, it is expected that by July 2007, 16,624 of these former combatants will benefit from projects sponsored by the United Nations Development Programme (UNDP) Trust Fund, and a further 22,544 will benefit from bilaterally funded programmes.

14. The Joint Implementation Unit, which consists of the National Commission on Disarmament, Demobilization, Reintegration and Rehabilitation, UNMIL and UNDP, recently approved 10 new vocational skills training projects, which should absorb some 8,000 ex-combatants. So far, 3,000 ex-combatants have registered for these projects. In addition, former combatants have the option of enrolling in several formal education schemes.

15. UNMIL continued to collect and destroy residual weapons and ammunition that were voluntarily surrendered or discovered through search operations. Since the end of the disarmament and demobilization programme in November 2004, 632 weapons, 74,403 rounds of ammunition, 1,002 pieces of unexploded ordnance and 11,622 assorted spares and miscellaneous parts have been collected and destroyed. In addition, 230 rifles and guns, 19,935 rounds of ammunition, 457 magazines, bayonets and spares and 289 pieces of unexploded

ordnance have been collected under the UNDP community arms collection for development programme, which was launched in January 2006.

B. Reform of the Liberian National Police

16. The restructuring and training of the Liberian National Police continued to make progress, although efforts to equip the police force and rehabilitate police infrastructure throughout the country continues to lag behind. At 1 December, 2,214 Liberian National Police had been trained and deployed, while 358 Special Security Services personnel and 155 Seaport Police officers had graduated from the National Police Academy. Currently, 566 police recruits are receiving field training, while 454 recruits are undergoing basic training. In order to reach the target of 3,500 trained Liberian National Police personnel by July 2007, the United Nations police, in collaboration with the Liberian National Police, has intensified the country-wide recruitment drive. The drive is also targeting civil society leaders and educational institutions in an effort to identify and attract young recruits. Some 300 candidates will need to be recruited by the end of December if the training programme is to be completed by the target date.

17. As part of its efforts to strengthen senior leadership capacities within the Liberian National Police, the United Nations police conducted a seven-week senior leadership training programme, which was attended by 31 senior Liberian National Police officers. The United Nations police conducted a similar course for 18 Bureau of Immigration and Naturalization officers and also provided in-service basic training for 71 of these officers. In addition, 50 Liberian National Police officers received specialized training in different aspects of policing in Ghana and Egypt, and another 3 officers are currently undergoing a six-month cadet programme in Ghana. The United Nations police have also launched a refresher firearms training programme for the 300 police support unit personnel who underwent training in Nigeria in 2005. The firearms authorized by the Security Council Committee established pursuant to resolution 1521 (2003) concerning Liberia to be imported from Nigeria for use by the Liberian National Police in the conduct of their duties arrived in the country and were officially handed over to the Government of Liberia on 1 December.

18. The deployment of the Liberian National Police to the interior of the country continues to be hampered by the absence of basic infrastructure and the lack of police equipment, including vehicles and communications. However, UNDP, with the support of Japan, recently provided 22 motorcycles to the Liberian National Police for use in the interior of the country. In addition, with bilateral assistance provided by the Netherlands, Norway, the United Kingdom of Great Britain and Northern Ireland, the United States of America, as well as through the UNMIL quick-impact projects, police stations are being reconstructed or rehabilitated in Zorzor, Vahun, Foya and Voinjama in Lofa County; Ganta and Tappita in Nimba County; Soul Clinic Internally Displaced Persons Camp Community and Arthington Town in Montserrado County; Robertsport and Sinje in Grand Cape Mount County; Greenville, Sinoe County; Bopolu, Gbarpolu County; and Unification Town, Margibi County. The Liberian National Police headquarters in Monrovia is also being refurbished. At the same time, classrooms, dormitories and office space for training staff are being constructed at the National Police Training Academy. Despite these efforts, there are many police facilities in urgent need of rehabilitation.

C. Reform of the Armed Forces of Liberia

19. The United States continued to assist the Government with the recruitment and training of the new Armed Forces of Liberia. On 4 November, the first group of 106 recruits for the new army graduated from basic training at the Barclay Training Centre in Monrovia. These soldiers are currently undergoing further specialized training, which will end in December. Some 500 recruits for the next basic training class have been selected and are in the process of being notified. They will commence training in early 2007.

20. In line with the Ministry of Defence restructuring plan, about 130 middle-level personnel are undergoing a 17-week training programme funded by the United States at the Barclay Training Centre in Monrovia. The training is scheduled to end in March 2007, at which time 91 trainees will have been selected to occupy posts at the Ministry of Defence.

D. Consolidation of State authority

21. During the reporting period, limited progress was made in the restoration and consolidation of State authority throughout the country. Although some 74 district and township commissioners were selected for 8 of the 15 counties, the work of the county officials and government line ministry representatives continued to be hampered by a lack of communications, office equipment, accommodation and vehicles, as well as delays in the payment of salaries. As a result of these constraints, many officials continued to commute from Monrovia to their duty stations.

22. The county support teams, which were jointly established by UNMIL and the United Nations country team to assist the local authorities in strengthening coordination mechanisms and in developing community recovery and development priorities, have continued to function effectively. In this regard, representatives of UNMIL, the United Nations country team, non-governmental institutions, the Ministry of Internal Affairs, county administration and government line ministries have been meeting on a monthly basis in each of the 15 counties to assess the priority needs of each county and to develop action plans to address these needs.

E. Management of natural resources

23. Steady progress was made by the Government in its efforts to regain control over and efficiently manage the country's natural resources. Following the full lifting of sanctions on timber exports on 20 October 2006, the Government took immediate steps to finalize regulations for the effective management of the timber industry. In addition, technical, institutional and financial reforms are being implemented at the Forestry Development Authority to ensure efficiency, effectiveness, transparency and accountability. UNMIL is also working closely with the Authority in the establishment of a national pit-sawing policy. In the meantime, unregulated pit-sawing continued to be conducted in several parts of the country.

24. The Forestry Development Authority, with the technical and logistical support of UNMIL, has been issuing permits for the transportation of timber in order to generate public revenue. Between April and November, the Authority issued 1,873 permits for the transportation of 695,480 pieces of timber resulting in public revenue of US$ 423,321, compared with US$ 62,262 for the same period in 2005.

25. In an effort to ensure that the conditions for the lifting of the Security Council sanctions on diamonds are met, President Johnson-Sirleaf established a National Diamond Task Force, which is being co-chaired by my Special Representative, Alan Doss, and the Minister of Land, Mines and Energy, to work on implementing the Kimberley Process Certification Scheme. In addition, on 12 and 13 October, the Government convened a stakeholders' forum to prepare a national mineral policy for Liberia. The office of the Liberian Diamond Authority is currently being constructed with the support of the United States and UNMIL, while De Beers and other international partners are assisting in the training of Liberia's Diamond Authority personnel. In the meantime, illegal artisanal mining continued to be reported in the western part of the country and in Nimba and Sinoe counties.

26. UNMIL continued to oversee the implementation of the recommendations contained in the report of the joint Government of Liberia/UNMIL Rubber Plantation Task Force that was presented to the President on 23 May. The recommendations include the repossession of illegally occupied plantations by the Government, review of existing concession and management agreements and establishment of interim management teams for contested or abandoned plantations. In this regard, UNMIL provided support to the Government in re-establishing its authority over the Guthrie Rubber Plantation. UNMIL also deployed military and police resources to support the Liberian National Police personnel stationed at the plantation. The interim management team, which was appointed by the Government, began commercial operations and is providing employment for more than 1,500 workers on the plantation. At the same time, some 200 registered ex-combatants and residents at the plantation have signed up to participate in reintegration and rehabilitation programmes, while many others have expressed their intention to seek employment on the plantation.

27. The Environmental Protection Agency is now fully operational, following the appointment of the board of directors and the executive director by the President. UNMIL, together with the United Nations Environment Programme, UNDP and other partners, is providing technical and logistical support to this important agency.

F. Promotion of human rights and the rule of law

1. Human rights

28. UNMIL continued its human rights promotion, protection and monitoring activities throughout the country. However, during the reporting period, respect for fundamental human rights continued to be impeded by weak rule of law structures. In this regard, the few operational county circuit courts in the country are either applying legal rules and procedures in an inconsistent manner or are failing to observe minimum human rights standards. Incidents of corrupt practices involving magistrates and judicial officials, inefficiency in trial processes and prolonged pretrial detention periods have also been reported. In some remote areas of the country, communities continued to practice trial by ordeal, in part owing to the absence of courts and police services.

29. The problems in the area of juvenile justice are yet to be fully addressed. There is only one functioning juvenile court in Monrovia. In a number of counties, juveniles are held in long-term pretrial detention with adults, without being indicted or tried, while in other locations they are sometimes tried by magistrates' court or released without trial.

30. More than 10 months after the enactment of the Rape Amendment Act, very little progress has been made in stemming the high incidence of sexual violence, including rape of

women and girl children. The relevant provisions of the Act have not been uniformly applied by the magistrates and judges when trying rape cases and many cases are either not being investigated or brought before competent courts. In the few cases where rape trials took place, minimum sentences were handed down.

31. Detention conditions are still below minimum human rights standards. Some correction facilities, including the Monrovia Central Prison, remain overcrowded. In four facilities in Bong, Grand Bassa, Bomi and Margibi counties, detainees cited prolonged pretrial detention without adequate sanitation as reasons for prison riots. During the period under review, there was also increase in the number of jailbreaks, including by persons accused or convicted of rape. On 27 November, 57 inmates escaped from the maximum security prison in Monrovia. While eight of them have been recaptured, the remainder are still at large. An investigation is being conducted into the circumstances surrounding the escape.

32. During the reporting period, a consultant engaged by UNMIL conducted a human rights audit of key Liberian legislation to determine whether the laws conformed with international human rights standards and instruments that have been ratified and signed by the Government. The consultant concluded that there were several laws, including some provisions of the Constitution that were not in compliance with international human rights standards and instruments ratified by Liberia and recommended, inter alia, that the applicable laws be amended to comply with these standards.

33. UNMIL also released its fifth report on the human rights situation in Liberia. The report, which covered the period from May to July 2006, highlighted human rights violations by law enforcement and judicial officers, the human rights situation on rubber plantations and issues related to the protection of child rights. It also addressed corruption, the high rate of sexual and gender-based violence, in particular incidents involving child victims, and the use of harmful traditional practices. In addition, the Mission released a report on the human rights situation in 48 orphanages, which concluded that the conditions essential for the healthy development of children were not being met in many orphanages. The two reports contain a number of important recommendations, including on the need for the Government to take concrete steps to ratify all human rights treaties to which it is signatory, and to ensure the harmonization of domestic legislation with international human rights commitments.

34. The Truth and Reconciliation Commission commenced taking statements in the counties on 10 October. UNMIL assisted in training more than 200 statement-takers on the promotion and protection of fundamental human rights prior to their deployment. In addition, UNMIL continued to provide logistical support to the Commission and launched a programme on UNMIL Radio called "TRC in Action" to enhance public awareness of the activities of the Commission. Unfortunately, the Commission's operations are still hampered by financial and logistical constraints, as well as by inadequate management support. On 28 November, the Commission announced that it was suspending its statement-taking work because it had insufficient funds to pay the salaries of statement-takers. In this regard, I appeal to members of the international community to assist the Commission by generously providing the funds urgently required for it to complete its work.

35. Since my previous report, no further progress was made towards the establishment of the Independent National Commission on Human Rights. The Independent Selection Panel,

which was established to vet nominees and submit a shortlist of nine candidates to serve as members of the Commission, agreed on 3 names out of 15 finalists for inclusion on the final shortlist. UNMIL has advised the Panel to submit the names of all finalists to the President for her consideration and appointment.

2. Support for the judicial system

36. During the reporting period, court activities increased throughout the country, in particular trials for serious offences, such as murder, rape and armed robbery. One reason for the increased activity was the engagement of national lawyers, with UNMIL support, to serve as prosecutorial and public defence consultants for indigent defendants. However, the justice system continues to be constrained by the lack of court buildings and a dearth of qualified judicial and legal personnel.

37. UNMIL continued to expand its capacity-building activities in the counties by providing training for legal and judicial officers. The Mission also conducted workshops to enhance the practical and procedural capacities of legal and judicial officers. In addition, some 261 magistrates were trained by UNMIL between May and November 2006. UNDP has also funded the recruitment of a Liberian expert to support the Governance Reform Commission's work on rule of law and the strengthening of the judiciary.

38. In September, the Mission launched a radio programme entitled "Community Court" to sensitize the public on the operations of the justice system and fundamental rights. The radio programme has already addressed the issues of domestic violence, payment of child maintenance, landlord and tenant disputes and trial by ordeal.

39. Significant progress was made in the establishment of the Law Reform Commission. The task force constituted by the Minister of Justice to facilitate the establishment of the Commission organized a series of stakeholders' symposiums and public interactive forums, following which a draft law for the establishment of the Commission was finalized and submitted to the Minister of Justice on 25 September. The Commission will require funding and the sustained support of the Government and the international community in order to be effective.

3. Support for the corrections system

40. UNMIL continued to assist the national Bureau of Rehabilitation and Corrections in improving the conditions of correctional facilities throughout the country. The refurbishment work on the facilities, which is being funded by Norway and the United States, is at various stages of completion. While the refurbishment of the Harper and Buchanan prisons has been completed, the rehabilitation of the Monrovia and Bondiway prisons, as well as the Zwedru Palace of Corrections, is still ongoing. The contract to refurbish the Gbarnga prison had to be terminated owing to the inability of the contractor to implement the project. UNMIL is also utilizing its quick-impact project funds to improve the facilities in Voinjama and Sanniquellie. While, the Government has made occasional contributions of foodstuff and medical supplies to the Monrovia Central Prison, prisoners continued to receive food and other supplies from the World Food Programme (WFP), the International Committee of the Red Cross and other partners.

41. Since the training programme for corrections officers commenced in February 2005, UNMIL has trained a total of 79 corrections officers. During the reporting period, 20 corrections

officer recruits graduated from the Police Academy, while 25 recruits are currently in the first phase of basic training. The Mission's corrections and prison advisory service conducted a training-the-trainers course for 12 national correction officers, who will subsequently carry out training programmes for corrections officers at the National Police Academy.

42. Owing to budgetary constraints, the Government has been able to absorb only 25 out of the 79 newly trained correction officers into the civil service. Moreover, because of low salaries many trained officers have left the corrections service to join the Liberian National Police and the Armed Forces of Liberia, which offer higher wages. This loss of trained personnel has severely hampered the effectiveness of the corrections service. In the meantime, the criteria for the retrenchment of serving officers who do not meet the civil service requirements have been developed and submitted to the Government for consideration and approval.

G. Economic governance

43. Steady progress continued to be made in the implementation of the Governance and Economic Management Assistance Programme. The Economic Governance Steering Committee met regularly to monitor progress in the implementation of the Programme and the internationally recruited experts submitted monthly status reports of their activities to the Steering Committee. There are currently eight international experts with co-signatory powers working with Liberia revenue-generating entities. During the period under review, a Liberian national was selected for a position funded by the World Bank of communications coordinator assigned to the Presidency to assist the Government in enhancing public awareness of the Programme. A consultant sponsored by the European Commission also commenced his assignment with the Bureau of Customs. The Government, in collaboration with international partners, is currently conducting a self-evaluation review on the implementation of the Programme after its first year of operation.

44. The Contracts and Concessions Review Committee of the Public Procurement and Concession Commission continued to review contracts and concessions entered into by the National Transitional Government of Liberia. Although the Review Committee has suffered some setbacks owing to operational and logistical constraints, as at 23 November 2006 it had completed the initial review of 79 out of 186 contracts, and was in the process of reviewing a further 21 contracts. In response to concerns that further delays in concluding the reviews could adversely affect Liberia's economic and investment climate, the President has stated that the review process must be completed by 31 December 2006. In the meantime, with the support of UNMIL, a local and international lawyer have been engaged to work with the Review Committee, while the European Commission has deployed experts to facilitate the review process.

H. National recovery, reconstruction and development

45. The Government continued to treat employment generation as a major priority. With the support of international stakeholders, the Government is creating short-term employment opportunities, including for ex-combatants, through the labour-intensive rehabilitation of roads and other critical infrastructure throughout the country. In October 2006, UNDP, UNMIL and the World Bank launched a joint initiative to rehabilitate critical roads, to which UNMIL is contributing technical expertise and engineering assets and the World

Bank is providing funding through UNDP. The first project to be implemented under this initiative was the rehabilitation of the Voinjama-Zorzor road in the north-western part of the country. A total of 1,200 community members and ex-combatants have already benefited from this initiative. In addition, the Mission's military engineers are rehabilitating secondary and feeder roads with the support of the WFP "Food support to local initiatives" programme and the Ministry of Public Works. This initiative has provided short-term employment for over 5,000 ex-combatants and members of their communities. UNMIL has also used its quick-impact projects to enhance employment creation.

46. Under the Liberia Employment Action Programme, which is intended to provide long-term sustainable employment, the Government, together with its international partners, is focusing on creating long-term employment opportunities, particularly in the agricultural sector, through the distribution of seeds and tools to farmers, and agricultural skills training.

47. An International Monetary Fund mission visited Liberia from 5 to 17 November 2006 to assess the progress made under the Fund's staff-monitored programme for 2006 and to discuss with the Government the design of the successor programme for 2007. The mission projected that there would be an 8 per cent increase in the real gross domestic product in 2006 and reiterated its support for finding a solution to Liberia's external debt problem.

48. The Government is in the process of finalizing its interim poverty reduction strategy, which will be presented at the Partners Forum planned for 13 and 14 February 2007 in Washington, D.C. The Forum, which will be co-sponsored by the European Commission, the United Nations, the United States and the World Bank, will bring together the Government of Liberia and its partners to discuss the country's reconstruction and development strategy as defined in the interim poverty reduction strategy paper, and to confirm the resource requirements to implement that strategy.

V. Humanitarian activities

49. To date, 81,000 refugees have voluntarily returned to their places of origin with the assistance of the Office of the United Nations High Commissioner for Refugees (UNHCR). The repatriation of the remaining 139,000 refugees continued to be hampered by poor road conditions, which were made worse by the rainy season. The repatriation efforts are expected to increase at the start of the dry season in November. Meanwhile, the Government, with the support of UNHCR, has repatriated more than 3,000 of the 5,500 internally displaced persons who had continued to reside in and around camps after their official closure on 20 April.

50. During the reporting period, there was tangible progress in the health sector. The country achieved almost 100 per cent immunization for early childhood diseases, and reproductive health care also improved. Cholera, however, was a serious public health concern, with 3,127 persons reported to have been infected by the disease in various parts of the country. There was also a national awareness campaign to prevent the outbreak of Lassa fever. Although no single case of Avian Influenza has been reported, the World Health Organization, with the support of the United Nations country team and UNMIL, has prepared a contingency plan for responding to the disease.

51. To date, the 2006 United Nations consolidated appeal for Liberia has received 45 per cent of the estimated US$ 145 million required for humanitarian activities. In order to address the funding shortfall, the Emergency Relief Coordinator provided Liberia with a

US$ 4 million grant, through the Central Emergency Response Fund, to support life-saving projects, including water and sanitation, health, food and agriculture. I renew my request to donors to generously provide the required assistance to meet the needs set out in the consolidated appeal.

VI. Gender

52. The Mission's Gender Adviser Unit facilitated the development of a mission-wide action plan, with benchmarks, for the implementation of Security Council resolution 1325 (2000) on women, peace and security. The Unit also continued to deliver gender analysis training to UNMIL personnel. In addition, UNMIL collaborated with and provided technical support to the Ministry of Gender and Development to ensure that gender considerations inform the mechanisms that guide the early recovery and reconstruction process. The Mission also supported the efforts of the Government and women's organizations to prepare a national action plan to prevent and respond to sexual and gender-based violence.

VII. HIV/AIDS

53. The Mission's HIV/AIDS Unit continued to collaborate with the Mission's integrated training cell to conduct HIV/AIDS awareness, training and sensitization, as well as personal risk assessment sessions, as part of induction training for military, police and civilian personnel. The Unit also collaborated with the Mission's gender component to provide training to female uniformed personnel on women's vulnerability to HIV infection. In addition, the Unit continued to promote HIV/AIDS awareness through its participation in an UNMIL Radio phone-in programme. In order to meet the rise in demand for voluntary counselling and testing by UNMIL personnel, another voluntary counselling and testing centre has been opened at the Jordanian Level III Hospital.

VIII. Personnel conduct and discipline

54. The UNMIL Conduct and Discipline Team continued to focus on developing strategies to prevent, identify, report and effectively respond to all categories of United Nations personnel misconduct. It also focused on strategies to ensure the implementation of the Secretary-General's zero tolerance policy against sexual exploitation and abuse through training, awareness-raising and attention to welfare concerns of all categories of United Nations personnel. Outreach programmes for local civil society organizations and communities living in close proximity to United Nations facilities are also being developed and implemented. On 4 November, with the support of the United Nations In-Country Network, the Government launched a one-year national awareness campaign aimed at strengthening advocacy to combat sexual exploitation and abuse throughout Liberia.

55. Some 40 "Category 1" offences, including 28 cases of sexual exploitation and abuse, and 155 "Category 2" offences have been reported since January 2006. All cases are under investigation.

IX. Public information

56. The public information component continued to support several of the Mission's priority programmes, the United Nations agencies, the Government and civil society aimed at consolidating the peace process, encouraging reconciliation and promoting national recovery. The component also organized several community sporting events to promote national reconciliation.

A nationwide sporting event is being planned for February 2007 with US$ 75,000 worth of sports equipment and materials donated by the International Olympic Committee. The Mission held a nationwide talent competition for Liberian youth under the age of 20 years to sensitize them about HIV/AIDS and sexual and gender-based violence. In addition, through the employment of groups of traditional communicators, it conducted awareness-raising campaigns about Lassa fever control in Nimba County, and about voter and civic education for the Margibi County by-election. The Mission has also established a media centre, equipped with research and Internet facilities, as well as a conference room for media practitioners.

X. Adjustment of the Mission

A. Military component

57. As at 1 December 2006, UNMIL's troop strength stood at 14,311 out of an authorized strength of 15,125. The discrepancy between the authorized and actual troop strength emanates from the delayed arrival of the advance company of the quick reaction force from Pakistan, which is expected to be deployed by the end of December. Also, UNMIL had earlier repatriated a company from Namibia in accordance with Security Council resolution 1626 (2005). Given the relative stability that has prevailed since the inauguration of the new Government and based on the detailed assessment provided in my tenth progress report (S/2006/159), which remains valid, on 28 November the Mission commenced the repatriation of one infantry battalion, which it does not intend to replace. As proposed in my previous reports, further adjustments, including the withdrawal of another infantry battalion in 2007, will be considered if the security situation in the country permits.

58. UNMIL continued to provide security to the Special Court for Sierra Leone in accordance with Security Council resolution 1626 (2005). During the reporting period, the 250-strong Mongolian military guard unit responsible for guarding the Special Court's premises completed a series of exercises aimed at ensuring the Court's security.

B. Police component

59. As at 1 December, the Mission's police strength stood at 1,098 officers, out of an authorized ceiling of 1,240 officers, which includes 6 United Nations police immigration officers, 479 officers in 4 formed police units and 15 corrections officers. A fifth formed police unit, comprising 125 personnel, is expected to arrive in the Mission by January 2007 to support the efforts of the Liberian National Police in containing threats to public order in Monrovia and other urban centres, as well as on rubber plantations. Owing to the urgent need to strengthen the capacity of the Liberian National Police, all efforts are being made to ensure the expeditious deployment of qualified United Nations police officers and coordinators to the Mission.

XI. Benchmarks for the first phase of the consolidation, drawdown and withdrawal plan

60. In my September report (S/2006/743, para. 72), I set out a series of benchmarks against which progress would be measured during the first phase of the consolidation, drawdown and withdrawal of UNMIL, which is currently under way. Some progress has been made in meeting these broad benchmarks, which include security, governance and the rule of law, economic revitalization, and infrastructure and basic services.

61. With regard to the security benchmark, as indicated in paragraphs 16 to 18 above, the recruitment target of 3,500 trained police officers by July 2007 is likely to be met. However, the effective deployment of these officers continues to be hampered by logistical and management constraints. With respect to the new armed forces, while the basic training has commenced, only 106 recruits out of the targeted 2,000 strong army have so far received basic training. It is expected that the new army will not be fully operational until 2008 at the earliest. Moreover, the Government is yet to take a final decision on the country's complete security architecture. In the case of ex-combatants, some 39,000 out of an initial caseload of 101,495 ex-combatants have yet to access reintegration programmes.

62. Progress in meeting the governance and rule of law benchmarks has been slow, owing primarily to the funding and capacity constraints explained in paragraphs 28 to 42 above. Corrections facilities have been established in only 7 of the 15 counties in Liberia. In addition, the county superintendents and assistant superintendents for development are also not fully operational in all 15 counties owing to capacity and human resource constraints. There is also a marked absence of critical line ministries, including health, education and public works in many of the counties, for which external funding is urgently required.

63. The progress made in meeting the economic revitalization benchmarks as described in paragraphs 23 to 27 and paragraphs 43 and 44 is very encouraging. There was a marked improvement in financial management and revenue administration in the public sector, as well as an increase in custom and excise duties as a result of the effective implementation of the Governance and Economic Management Assistance Programme. However, additional steps will need to be taken to improve procurement practices and to complete the review of concessions and contracts by the 31 December deadline given by the President. It will be important for international partners to expedite the deployment of promised specialist expertise to assist in the completion of these tasks. While the progress made in the Government's management of the timber sector is encouraging, much work remains to be done in order to meet the conditions for the lifting of diamond sanctions.

64. The restoration of street lighting and piped water in parts of Monrovia have been the most visible indicators of progress in meeting the benchmarks identified under the infrastructure and basic services pillar. As referred to in paragraph 45, the World Bank/UNMIL joint infrastructure and employment programme is also helping with the development of critical infrastructure. However, the limited extension of public health services to the counties remains a critical concern. Currently, the country is heavily dependent on non-governmental organizations, which provide about 90 per cent of the primary health care and hospital services.

65. A full update on the progress made in meeting each of these benchmarks will be provided in the next progress report on UNMIL, and subsequently on a six-monthly basis at the time of each mandate renewal.

XII. Observations

66. The Government of President Johnson-Sirleaf has continued to make encouraging progress in consolidating peace, promoting national reconciliation and stimulating economic recovery. The three branches of Government functioned in relative harmony; the reform and restructuring of the security sector is progressing; more Liberian refugees have returned home; and the Government has continued to take robust measures to fight corruption.

67. The successful adoption of the forestry reform law, through sustained negotiations between the Senate and the House of Representatives, is a positive indication that the Government of Liberia can overcome partisan positions in the national interest. I wish to encourage the executive and legislative branches of Government to continue to employ constructive dialogue to resolve policy differences that may arise.

68. I would like to commend President Johnson-Sirleaf for her initiatives in bringing together members of various religious and ethnic groupings, as well as political party leaders. I encourage the President to continue to work towards involving all Liberians in the country's recovery process and appeal to all political and civil society leaders to continue their constructive engagement in the reconstruction and reform processes currently under way.

69. As indicated in paragraphs 60 to 64, some progress has been made in meeting the Mission's consolidation, drawdown and withdrawal benchmarks. While these developments are promising, serious challenges persist that must be addressed if progress is to be sustained. I call upon the Government to expeditiously finalize its national security strategy and policy and prepare a comprehensive national security architecture that will allow Liberian security agencies to sustain the stable security environment currently ensured by the presence of UNMIL. This is also a crucial element in the planning and management of the drawdown of UNMIL forces. At the same time, I urge Liberia's international partners to urgently provide assistance in addressing the outstanding logistical and infrastructure needs of the security sector, particularly those of the national police.

70. The management and operational capacities of the national police force still need to be strengthened to enable the Liberian National Police to effectively assume security responsibilities prior to UNMIL withdrawal. With this critical objective in mind, a review team from the Department of Peacekeeping Operations will travel to Liberia in early 2007 to assess the impact of the work of the UNMIL police component on the capacity development of the Liberian National Police. In the meantime, everything possible should be done to operationalize the new police and to expedite the deployment of the Liberian National Police to the countryside.

71. The presence of large numbers of unemployed youth in the urban centres, ex-combatants still awaiting reintegration opportunities, and deactivated police and army personnel, remains a very serious source of tension. I encourage the Government to intensify its efforts to revive economic activity and to create job opportunities for the unemployed, including former combatants, without which the security of the country will be undermined. In that regard, I reiterate my earlier appeal for donor support to the Government's employment generation initiatives. I also urge international partners to continue to work closely with the Government to ensure that the remaining former combatants who have not yet entered rehabilitation and reintegration programmes are provided with opportunities to do so in an expeditious manner.

72. Although the Government has continued to make progress in the consolidation of its authority throughout the country, much remains to be done to enhance its capacity to deliver public services, including judicial and legal services, to all parts of the country. In the meantime, it is gratifying to note that the efforts of the Government to take control of natural and mineral resources, especially in the forestry and rubber sectors, are beginning to bear fruit, as demonstrated by the increase in public revenues. In this regard, I commend the

Government for the timely passage of the forestry reform law. The establishment of the National Diamond Task Force is also a welcome development that will assist in ensuring that the conditions necessary for the lifting of the Security Council sanctions are met.

73. The reform of the judicial sector and the promotion of the rule of law continue to present major structural challenges that will require the generous assistance of the international community. The effective countrywide administration of justice is not only a prerequisite for the people of Liberia to fully enjoy their basic rights, but is also essential for economic growth. I appeal to donors to provide the funding required for the Truth and Reconciliation Commission and the Independent National Human Rights Commission to become fully operational.

74. I am deeply concerned by the high incidence of sexual violence, including rape committed against women and girl children in Liberia, as well as by the spate of violent crime in Monrovia and elsewhere in the country. In that regard, the swift action taken by the Government in establishing operation "Sweeping Wave" aimed at curbing criminal activities is commendable. Every effort must be made to ensure that criminal justice is rapidly and fairly addressed and that widespread violence against women and children is brought to an end.

75. In conclusion, I would like to commend the people and Government of Liberia, my Special Representative, Alan Doss, and all UNMIL military, police and civilian personnel for the progress accomplished during the reporting period. I would also like to thank all troop and police-contributing countries, the Economic Community of West African States, the African Union, the International Contact Group on the Mano River Basin, United Nations agencies, funds and programmes, humanitarian organizations, multilateral and bilateral donors, as well as international and local non-governmental organizations, for their important contributions and support to the peace consolidation process in Liberia.

Annex
United Nations Mission in Liberia: military andcivilian police strength (at 1 December 2006)

Component	*Military*				*Police*
Country	*Military observers*	*Staff officer*	*Troops*	*Total*	*Civilian police*
Argentina					8
Bangladesh	17	11	3 181	3 209	29
Benin	3	1		4	
Bolivia	4			4	
Bosnia and Herzegovina					11
Brazil					
Bulgaria	2			2	
China	5	8	558	571	23
Croatia		3		3	
Czech Republic	3			3	5
Denmark	4			4	
Ecuador	1	1		2	

Continued

Component	Military				Police
Country	Military observers	Staff officer	Troops	Total	Civilian police
El Salvador	3			3	2
Ethiopia	19	8	2 301	2 328	
Egypt	8			8	
Fiji					30
Finland		2		2	
France		1		1	
Gambia	4			4	32
Germany			14	14	7
Ghana	13	7	849	869	41
Indonesia	3			3	
Ireland		1	325	326	
Jamaica					8
Jordan	7	8	119	134	140
Kenya	5	3		8	27
Kyrgyzstan	4			4	3
Macedonia					1
Malawi		2		2	19
Malaysia	10			10	
Mali	3			3	
Moldova	3	1		4	
Mongolia		2	248	250	
Montenegro	2			2	
Namibia	2	2	609	613	6
Nepal	5	2	40	47	256
Niger	3			3	
Nigeria	19	14	1 949	1 982	162
Norway					10
Pakistan	16	10	2 737	2 763	28
Paraguay	3			3	
Peru	1			1	
Philippines	3	5	165	173	34
Poland	2			2	3
Portugal					
Republic of Korea	1	1		2	
Romania	3			3	
Russian Federation	6			6	11
Rwanda					15
Samoa					16
Senegal	3	3	599	605	
Serbia	4			4	7
South Africa					

Component	*Military*				*Police*
Country	*Military observers*	*Staff officer*	*Troops*	*Total*	*Civilian police*
Sri Lanka					11
Sweden		3		3	13
Togo	2	1		3	
Turkey					33
Uganda					20
United Kingdom of Great Britain and Northern Ireland		3		3	
Ukraine	3	1	300	304	13
Uruguay					3
United States of America	5	6		11	10
Yemen					4
Zambia	3			3	26
Zimbabwe					31
Total	**207**	**110**	**13 994**	**14 311**	**1 098**

5. Twelfth Progress Report of the Secretary-General on the United Nations Operation in Côte d'Ivoire, 8 March 2007 (S/2007/133)

I. Introduction

1. The present report is submitted pursuant to Security Council resolution 1603 (2005), by which the Council requested me to keep it regularly informed of developments in Côte d'Ivoire and in the implementation of the mandate of the United Nations Operation in Côte d'Ivoire (UNOCI). The report covers developments since my report of 4 December 2006 (S/2006/939).

II. Political developments

2. During the period under review, the political stalemate in the Ivorian peace process remained unresolved with no significant progress towards implementing Security Council resolution 1721 (2006). An initiative announced by President Laurent Gbagbo on 19 December 2006, by which he offered to open direct dialogue with the Forces nouvelles, opened up a fresh opportunity to resolve the protracted political impasse. As indicated in paragraphs 7 to 18 below, the dialogue culminated in the signing of a new peace agreement by President Gbagbo and the Secretary-General of the Forces nouvelles, Guillaume Soro, in Ouagadougou on 4 March 2007, under the facilitation of the President of Burkina Faso, Blaise Compaoré.

3. Prior to the dialogue and until the signing of the new peace agreement, the Prime Minister, Charles Konan Banny, made efforts to reinvigorate the peace process by implementing the schedule proposed by the International Working Group at its ministerial meeting of 1 December 2006. The schedule, presented in the Working Group's communiqué, which the Security Council endorsed in its presidential statement of 21 December (S/PRST/2006/58), proposed specific timelines for implementing the main tasks set out in Council resolution 1721 (2006). However, the efforts to implement those key tasks achieved limited results.

4. One of the main steps taken by the Prime Minister was the establishment of a working group on security sector reform on 12 December, as called for by the Council in resolution 1721 (2006). In addition, UNOCI, Licorne and the National Programme for Disarmament, Demobilization and Reintegration continued to work on the technical preparations for the implementation of the disarmament programme, including development of modalities for the deployment of joint verification teams (Ivorian defence and security forces, Forces nouvelles, United Nations and Licorne) to all pre-cantonment areas, and arrangements for the provision of security. However, as indicated in my previous report, the Programme continues to face a shortfall of approximately $10 million for the rehabilitation of cantonment sites.

5. With regard to the identification of the population, the International Working Group proposed the deadline of 5 December 2006 for establishing a working group on identification called for in resolution 1721 (2006). The Prime Minister established the working group on 5 December 2006. In addition, on 30 January 2007, the Government selected a technical operator for the registration of the population. The Prime Minister also pressed ahead with the gradual resumption of the public hearings for the identification process in functioning

court jurisdictions, setting a target of 25 sites by the first week of February 2007. Operations started on 19 January in two courts located in the Adjamé and Attécoubé districts of Abidjan. On 16 February, mobile courts were deployed to conduct the hearings at four additional sites in the Government-controlled area; as at 20 February, the courts had issued 1,094 birth certificates out of 1,186 applications submitted.

6. With regard to preparations for the elections, the International Working Group had proposed 15 December 2006 as the deadline for the nomination of political party representatives on the local structures of the Independent Electoral Commission, to be followed immediately by the opening of the local structures and the announcement of an electoral timetable by the Independent Electoral Commission. However, on 18 January, President Gbagbo wrote a letter to the Chairman of the Commission asking him to suspend all technical preparations for the elections and to await the outcome of the dialogue with the Forces nouvelles. Although the Commission did not announce a timetable for the electoral process, on 19 January, it informed President Gbagbo of its intention to deploy 24 regional electoral commissions. Subsequently, the first regional electoral commission was opened in Abidjan on 22 February, and four others were established at Abengourou, Bondoukou, Bouaflé and Koumassi on 27 February.

Dialogue between President Gbagbo and the Forces nouvelles

7. In a radio address on 19 December 2006, President Gbagbo announced a new initiative, offering to open direct dialogue with the Forces nouvelles under the auspices of the President of Burkina Faso, Blaise Compaoré. President Gbagbo also called for the removal of the zone of confidence that divides the country; proposed the enactment of a new amnesty law; indicated his intention to launch a national civilian service for young people and an assistance programme for resettling displaced persons; and suggested that elections be held by July 2007. The President explained that his initiative was aimed at finding a "home-grown" solution to the Ivorian crisis, as none of the solutions proposed by the international community had brought peace to the country.

8. On 1 January 2007, the Secretary-General of the Forces nouvelles, Guillaume Soro, welcomed President Gbagbo's proposal to open dialogue with his group, but stressed that such dialogue should lead to the implementation of Security Council resolution 1721 (2006). Mr. Soro also urged the coalition of Ivorian opposition political parties, the Group of Seven, to urgently work towards reaching a unified position on President Gbagbo's proposals. Subsequently, Mr. Soro met with the leaders of the Group of Seven in Abidjan on 18 January 2007. After intensive consultations, the Group issued a communiqué accepting President Gbagbo's offer to open dialogue with the Forces nouvelles. The communiqué, among other things, stressed that the dialogue should seek to accelerate the peace process within the framework of resolution 1721 (2006).

9. On 12 January 2007, Mr. Soro participated in the twelfth ministerial level meeting of the International Working Group, together with Prime Minister Banny, and informed the Working Group of his intention to accept President Gbagbo's proposal for direct dialogue. In a communiqué issued after the meeting, the Working Group reaffirmed its support for sustained consultations among the Ivorian parties. It also stressed that the direct dialogue proposed by President Gbagbo should focus on achieving concrete and precise solutions to the issues concerning identification, the disarmament process, the restructuring of the

armed forces and the holding of credible elections throughout the national territory. On the same day, during a meeting with the co-chairs of the International Working Group, in Abidjan, President Gbagbo explained that the first stage of the dialogue would address military issues and therefore participation would be limited to the Forces nouvelles only, while the other political leaders would be involved at a later stage.

10. The Heads of State of the Economic Community of West African States (ECOWAS) expressed their support for the dialogue between President Gbagbo and the Forces nouvelles during their thirty-first summit, held in Ouagadougou on 19 January. They also entrusted President Compaoré, the incoming Chairman of ECOWAS, with facilitating the dialogue. In a communiqué issued at the summit, the Heads of State invited all Ivorian parties to cooperate in implementing resolution 1721 (2006). Furthermore, the Heads of State proposed that the Security Council consider sending a special mission to Côte d'Ivoire to assist in giving fresh impetus to the peace process. They also undertook to dispatch a high-level ECOWAS mission to Côte d'Ivoire to prevail on the Ivorian leaders to embrace and implement resolution 1721 (2006) in good faith, and to send a similar mission to the capitals of the five permanent members of the Council.

11. On 25 January, Mr. Soro invited members of the day-to-day mediation group to the Forces nouvelles headquarters in Bouaké to brief them on the outcome of the various meetings he had had with President Compaoré regarding the planned talks. At the briefing, Mr. Soro expressed the view that the international community should closely monitor and witness the dialogue in order to ensure that it was transparent and inclusive and that it remained within the framework of resolution 1721 (2006). Mr. Soro travelled to Burkina Faso on 23 January to discuss the final preparations for the dialogue with President Compaoré. President Compaoré and President Gbagbo held a similar meeting on 24 January.

12. On 17 January, I wrote to President Sassou-Nguesso and President Compaoré, in their respective capacities as Chairpersons of the African Union and ECOWAS, welcoming their efforts to help the Ivorian parties to resolve the prolonged impasse in the peace process and assuring them of the continued engagement of the United Nations in cooperative efforts to find a lasting solution to the crisis in Côte d'Ivoire. I conveyed to them my view that only an inclusive dialogue could secure a comprehensive political settlement that would address the underlying concerns of all parties and chart a clear and unambiguous path for disarmament, identification and the elections.

13. I also met President Gbagbo during the African Union summit held in Addis Ababa from 28 to 30 January. I urged President Gbagbo to harmonize his initiative with resolution 1721 (2006). I also assured him of the continued support of the United Nations for the peace process in his country. President Gbagbo assured me that the dialogue would eventually include all the political forces in Côte d'Ivoire and that his plan for the resolution of the Ivorian crisis was not an "enemy" of resolution 1721 (2006), but rather complementary to it.

14. Representatives of President Gbagbo and the Forces nouvelles began discussions with the facilitator, President Compaoré, in Ouagadougou, on 5 February. The two delegations, led by President Gbagbo's spokesman, Désiré Tagro, and the Deputy Secretary-General of the Forces nouvelles, Louis Dakoury-Tabley, developed a draft comprehensive agreement for consideration by the two leaders. Alassane Ouattara, leader of the Rassemblement des républicains (RDR), and Alphonse Djédje Mady, Secretary-General of the Parti démocratique

de Côte d'Ivoire (PDCI) led by Henri Konan Bédié, travelled to Ouagadougou on 21 February for consultations with the facilitator on issues arising from the working-level discussions. Prime Minister Banny's representatives also were present at the talks.

15. President Compaoré invited both the High Representative for the elections, Gérard Stoudmann, and the Officer-in-Charge of UNOCI, Abou Moussa, to Ouagadougou on several occasions, to seek their views on a number of electoral, political and military issues arising from the talks. The UNOCI Force Commander and the Licorne Deputy Force Commander participated in the consultations held on 20 February, to provide advice on military issues.

16. On 14 February, I sent another letter to President Compaoré, in which I conveyed the appreciation of the United Nations for his facilitation role and informed him of my readiness to assist, as appropriate, with technical advice on issues relating to the dialogue. I also thanked the President for the contacts he has maintained with UNOCI and the High Representative for the elections during the talks, and stressed the need to establish channels of communication, in the light of the key role that UNOCI will be expected to play in supporting the implementation of the expected agreement.

17. On 4 March, President Gbagbo and Mr. Soro signed the new agreement in Ouagadougou, under the facilitation of President Compaoré. The agreement builds upon Security Council resolution 1721 (2006) and previous peace agreements. It addresses key issues that had blocked the implementation of the identification of the population, the disarmament process, the restructuring of the armed forces, the restoration of State authority throughout the country and the preparation of the voters list. The agreement also envisages new institutional arrangements, which are expected to be agreed upon within a month. An annex to the agreement sets out an implementation schedule, which envisages the completion of the key process within a period of 10 months. The parties requested the facilitator to submit the agreement to the Security Council, through the African Union, for endorsement.

18. The role of the United Nations in supporting the implementation of the agreement will need further clarification, especially with regard to the deployment of United Nations troops in the zone of confidence, as will the support of the Organization for the implementation of the disarmament process and the provision of security for the various key processes, including the elections. The role of the United Nations in the follow-up mechanisms and that of the High Representative for the elections will also need to be clarified, while urgent discussions should be undertaken with the facilitator and the parties on the implementation of the proposal to deploy more African troops in UNOCI.

III. Security situation

19. During the period under review, the overall security situation in Côte d'Ivoire remained relatively calm but unpredictable and often tense owing to the political and social difficulties deriving from the prolonged crisis. Frequent strikes by public servants from the health and education sectors, as well as protests in 22 prisons in the south of the country, created disturbances, which gradually subsided following assurances that the Government would look into the grievances. The strikes were in protest at the poor conditions of service. Crime in the economic capital is rife.

20. In the zone of confidence, several cases of murder and attacks against the civilian population were reported. In the absence of law enforcement agencies and the judiciary, the

rule of law continued to be violated, in spite of enhanced patrolling by UNOCI and Licorne. Ethnic tensions also remain a serious concern. On 16 January, heavily armed elements of the defence and security forces escorting the wife of the President on a visit to Yetrobi village, in the eastern part of the country, deliberately entered the zone of confidence, despite strict measures taken by UNOCI to ensure the safety of Mrs. Gbagbo during her visit. UNOCI sent a letter of protest to the Chief of the Defence Staff of Côte d'Ivoire, General Philippe Mangou. On 19 January, the Young Patriots organized a demonstration in Duékoué, demanding the immediate removal of the zone of confidence to enable the Ivorian armed forces to take over security responsibility from the impartial forces.

21. In the western part of the country, the security situation remained volatile, with several reports of clashes between members of the Guéré ethnic group and Burkinabé immigrants, which claimed the lives of several people. Criminal activities were also reported in several villages and along the road between Duékoué and Bangolo. The eastern part of the country remained calm, except for an armed attack perpetrated by unidentified elements in Noé, on the border between Côte d'Ivoire and Ghana, on 12 January. The attack left five persons dead, including two gendarmes and one customs officer. The motive of the attack remains unclear.

22. In the northern part of the country, the lack of functioning law enforcement agencies engenders volatility and Forces nouvelles elements sometimes allegedly contribute to crime. The lack of security continues to affect negatively the living conditions of most of the population.

23. In response to the deterioration of the situation in neighbouring Guinea in February, UNOCI increased its patrols along the border to closely monitor any displacement of civilians and prevent the movement of armed groups. As at 26 February, no significant cross-border movement had been reported.

IV. Deployment of the United Nations Operation in Côte d'Ivoire

Military component

24. As at 21 February 2007, the military strength of UNOCI stood at 8,052 personnel, comprising 7,760 troops, 198 military observers and 94 staff officers, against an authorized ceiling of 8,115. The force comprises 11 battalions, 9 of which are deployed in the two sectors (East and West), and 2 in Abidjan for urban security and contingency tasks. One aviation unit, three engineering companies, one transport company and one special force company are providing enabling capacity and an operational reserve to the force. A total of 14 light infantry companies and three mechanized companies are deployed in Sector West, the most challenging; 10 light infantry companies, one armoured company and the aviation unit, are deployed in Sector East.

25. During the reporting period, the UNOCI military component continued to conduct regular operations to demonstrate its state of preparedness. It also conducted highly visible rehearsals of contingency plans and reinforced joint patrols with Licorne units. Initially limited to Abidjan, these joint operations have been extended to all areas in which ONUCI forces are deployed. The operations complement activities aimed at dominating the areas of responsibility through the establishment of random checkpoints and temporary camps in hot spots and the conduct of special patrols. UNOCI has also significantly increased its

patrols within the zone of confidence in order to curb the escalation of armed attacks and roadside robberies in this area.

26. UNOCI military units also continued to initiate and participate in regular confidence-building meetings with local communities and ethnic groups to facilitate the peaceful settlement of disputes, in particular in the west. In addition, UNOCI maintains close cooperation and liaison with the Licorne force, both at the headquarters level and in theatre, particularly inside the zone of confidence. All UNOCI units conduct regular exercises with the Licorne force, which also serves as the quick reaction force for UNOCI. The exercises are repeated after each rotation of contingents.

27. In addition, UNOCI military units continued to conduct regular patrols along the Liberia border to monitor the situation and to prevent movements of weapons or armed groups. Joint operations between UNOCI and the United Nations Mission in Liberia (UNMIL) along the common border resumed after the completion of the rotation of the Pakistani battalion stationed in that area in October 2006. In keeping with Security Council resolution 1721 (2006), contingency plans are regularly updated to enhance cooperation between the two missions, including possible mutual reinforcements in the event of serious deterioration of the security situation, as envisaged by resolution 1609 (2006).

28. The Ouagadougou agreement signed envisages adjustments in the role, deployment and composition of UNOCI troops. Urgent consultations with the parties and the mediator will therefore be required.

Police component

29. The role of the UNOCI police component under the new peace agreement will also need to be discussed with the parties and the mediator. As at 21 February, the strength of the police component stood at 1,150, comprising 400 police officers and 750 personnel in six formed police units, against an authorized ceiling of 1,200. The shortfall is due to continuing difficulties in identifying qualified francophone police officers capable of providing technical advice to the local authorities in the area of policing and security, and of interacting with the local population.

30. The arrival in Côte d'Ivoire of a sixth formed police unit on 20 February 2007 completed the deployment of all authorized formed police units to the country. Formed police units are now operational in Abidjan, Bouaké, Daloa, Guiglo and Yamoussoukro. The primary tasks of the formed police units focus on providing security to United Nations personnel, facilities and equipment, as well as to United Nations police officers in the zone of confidence. They also continue to conduct regular crowd control exercises in collaboration with UNOCI military contingents and the Licorne force. Formed police unit personnel also provided specialized training courses on crowd control and civil unrest management to 600 ONUCI military personnel in five different units.

31. The rest of the UNOCI police personnel are deployed at 20 sites throughout the country, where they perform monitoring and mentoring tasks to enhance the professional conduct of the Ivorian national police and gendarmerie personnel. However, joint activities are often hampered by the limited human and logistic resources at the disposal of the Ivorian security forces.

32. In anticipation of the start of the disarmament process, 535 security auxiliaries, trained by UNOCI in 2005 and 2006 in the northern part of the country, will be deployed to

54 police stations in that area to maintain law and order as Forces nouvelles elements are cantoned. The police stations to which the auxiliaries will be deployed were refurbished with funds provided by the European Commission. An official graduation ceremony was organized for the auxiliaries in Bouaké on 15 December 2006. Prime Minister Banny and several Ministers attended the ceremony. United Nations police officers will be deployed alongside the security auxiliaries to provide continuous technical support, mentoring and monitoring of day-to-day activities in the field. Mentoring has commenced as a pilot project in Bouaké, and will continue with the expected deployment of 54 auxiliaries to Man.

33. United Nations police officers continued to participate actively in inter-mission cooperation, in particular in the joint patrolling of Liberia-Côte d'Ivoire border areas with military units. A dedicated liaison office has also been established in both UNOCI and UNMIL to facilitate the exchange of information between the police components of the two missions.

V. Humanitarian situation

34. The humanitarian situation in Côte d'Ivoire remains primarily a protection crisis. In the west, militias from the south and armed groups from the north, including traditional hunters (*dozos*), continued to attack both local and foreign civilian populations in the zone of confidence. The atmosphere of insecurity and fear led to the displacement of thousands of persons to Duékoué and undermined efforts of the humanitarian community to assist vulnerable populations and to facilitate the return of more than 10,000 displaced persons in Duékoué, as well as the 6,000 displaced who had found refuge in Bangolo since June 2006.

35. To address the serious humanitarian issues in the west and questions relating to the return of internally displaced persons, the United Nations country team and representatives of the donor community undertook a mission to Duékoué, Guiglo, the Zou area and Man from 14 to 16 December 2006. The mission recommended the reinforcement of protection activities by local authorities and United Nations troops, the increase of coordination activities among all actors and the need for an in-depth evaluation of humanitarian, security and development issues, in particular with a view to facilitating the return of internally displaced persons. The situation has deteriorated in recent weeks, as increased banditry and militia activities have severely hampered humanitarian operations in the western part of the country. Since 26 February, militia elements of the Front de libération du grand-ouest have erected barricades on the Guiglo-Bloléquin axis and prevented vehicular traffic in the area. This obstruction to freedom of movement disrupted the repatriation of Liberian refugees from Toulepleu, which the Office of the United Nations High Commissioner for Refugees had scheduled for 27 February. On the same day, the International Organization for Migration was forced to suspend the return of some 900 internally displaced persons from Toulepleu to 14 villages around Péhé. These incidents were brought to the attention of the Minister for Territorial Administration and to that of the local administrative authorities in Guiglo.

36. On 23 January 2007, a mission was undertaken to Bouaké to assess the humanitarian situation in the north, focusing on security, child protection, access to basic social services and the return of internally displaced persons. The Forces nouvelles leaders, including Mr. Soro and the head of their armed forces, General Bakayoko, requested the assistance of the humanitarian partners, in particular in support of the young.

37. In January and February, a total of 31 people and an undetermined number of cattle and poultry died as a result of the outbreak of a mysterious disease in the village of Diobala in

the centre-west of the country. As at 28 February, the World Health Organization and the Ministry of Health had dispatched investigation teams to the area to investigate the illness, which remains unidentified.

38. During the period under review, there was a setback in the education sector. Several teachers' strikes paralysed primary school activities in December 2006, affecting 1,668,623 children throughout the country. After the Government promised the payment of accommodation fees for teachers, the strike was suspended on 4 January 2007 for three months.

39. The Consolidated Appeal Process was launched nationally on 31 January 2007 in Abidjan. The Process highlighted the increases in poverty and vulnerability in Côte d'Ivoire, showing that 50 per cent of the rural population in the north and west do not have regular access to clean drinking water and 60 per cent of basic medical services are not delivered. A total of $56.3 million is sought to assist more than 4 million vulnerable persons.

VI. Economic impact of the political crisis

40. The uncertainty relating to the peace process continued to have a negative impact on the economic situation. The sector most damaged is the processing industry, which has lost nearly half of its manufacturing potential and workforce in the past five years. Since the outbreak of the crisis, productive investments, from both domestic and foreign investors, have virtually dried up. The production sector continued to be burdened with hidden costs because of racketeering and extra transport and insurance costs. Without immediate measures on taxation, support to the better-performing sectors, vocational training for the workforce and a greater effort in the fight against smuggling, there is a risk that the industry will lose its competitiveness to a level at which recovery will be lengthy and difficult.

41. Without progress in the peace process, the country is unable to capitalize on its natural resources and considerable human capital to realize its vision of economic growth and integration into the global economy. Consequently, the country is unable to generate enough employment for its active population, in particular for the young. Efforts to promote youth employment have not been systematic and would benefit from an overall national economic plan that has yet to be formulated.

VII. Human rights situation

42. Although no widespread human rights violations were observed during the reporting period, the general human rights situation continues to raise concern. Routine cases of intimidation, arbitrary arrest, detention, racketeering at checkpoints and frequent interethnic conflicts in the west continue to be monitored by UNOCI nationwide.

43. In the Government-controlled areas, cases of widespread violence on university campuses and schools perpetrated or instigated by members of the Fédération estudiantine et scolaire de Côte d'Ivoire were reported. On 25 January, during a wave of strikes and demonstrations organized by the union throughout the country to demand public funding of school fees, union militants attacked, ransacked and destroyed private property belonging to local traders and sympathizers of opposition political parties. To address the widespread violence on campuses and schools, the Ligue ivoirienne des droits de l'homme launched a 10-month pilot project to sensitize students on human rights at the University of Cocody in Abidjan.

44. In the western region of the country, cases of ethnically motivated attacks, sometimes resulting in killings, were reported in Daloa, Duékoué and Guiglo, and the zone of confidence. The insecurity in the zone of confidence, which is due to the absence of any law enforcement authority, continues to have a negative impact on the overall human rights situation. The cases of abuse witnessed in the zone range from banditry to ethnically motivated, targeted killings and attacks. In addition, freedom of movement continues to be affected by frequent attacks by bandits in the western part of Côte d'Ivoire and by the activities of *dozos* and pro-government militias (*cocotaillés*).

45. In the area controlled by the Forces nouvelles, there have been increasing reports of Forces nouvelles elements offering their services to settle private disputes, resorting sometimes to punishment and ill-treatment against the parties concerned. The Forces nouvelles also continue to detain several people in Bouaké and Korhogo, including some who were arrested as long ago as 2005, after being accused of supporting President Gbagbo or spying for the Young Patriots.

46. With funding from the Office of the United Nations High Commissioner for Human Rights, UNOCI conducted awareness-raising campaigns on various human rights issues in Abidjan, Bouaké, Daloa, Korhogo, Odienné and Yamoussoukro. To strengthen the capacity of civil society organizations, ONUCI launched, on 18 January, the Cercle des ONG des droits de l'homme, a forum for regular exchanges among non-governmental human rights organizations. In this context, UNOCI and the Coalition for the International Criminal Court defined a common strategy for advocacy in favour of the ratification by Côte d'Ivoire of the Rome Statute; on 25 January, ONUCI and the Association pour le développement du droit launched a campaign to harmonize the legislation of Côte d'Ivoire with international human rights instruments.

47. The inauguration of the National Human Rights Commission by Prime Minister Banny on 11 January 2007 was a positive development. The Commission, the creation of which was called for in the Linas-Marcoussis Agreement, is expected to play a key role in promoting long-term national reconciliation and respect for human rights.

48. ONUCI continued to discuss the report of the Secretary-General on children and armed conflict in Côte d'Ivoire (S/2006/835) with the leaders of the Forces nouvelles and pro-Government militia groups, bringing to their attention the many concerns expressed by the Secretary-General, as well as his appreciation for their commitment to the implementation of the action plans to end the use of child soldiers. While UNOCI has no evidence of any ongoing active recruitment of children by militia groups or the Forces nouvelles, the continuing association of children with fighting forces is generally acknowledged by those groups. The United Nations Children's Fund (UNICEF) continued to support a prevention, demobilization and reintegration programme for children associated with armed groups and children at risk of being recruited, benefiting a total of 2,208 children.

49. Cases of human trafficking were reported in the northern cities of Korhogo and Odienné and in the area of Aboisso in the south. Despite the efforts of ONUCI and other organizations, well-organized networks continue to be used to bring young girls from neighbouring countries into Côte d'Ivoire to work as prostitutes. UNOCI investigated, in particular, cases of trafficking of children from Mali and Burkina Faso, smuggled through the Ouagadougou-Bouaké-Dimbroko-Abidjan railway line, to work in Côte d'Ivoire as domestic servants or

plantation labourers. On 21 December 2006, 27 children of Malian nationality were repatriated from Bouaké to Mali by local authorities and UNICEF.

VIII. Media monitoring

50. In order to better promote the peace process and expand its outreach, UNOCI set up four new sub-offices in Man, San Pedro, Yamoussoukro and Bondoukou and is seeking to establish a presence in four other regions. Moreover, a series of forums and a peace caravan were organized in various parts of the country. In Yamoussoukro, a plan of action was developed with the Convention de la societé civile to enhance the participation of civil society actors, such as women, youth, the media and the economic sector, in the peace process. Similarly, a children's forum brought together some 500 vulnerable children as a precursor to the children's caravan that will be visiting schools in all communes of Abidjan before touring the country.

51. UNOCI also continued to advocate for the creation of an improved media environment. In this regard, the mission provided support to the Ministry of Communication for the establishment of an early-warning unit on hate media that would include representatives of the Government, media regulatory bodies, the national journalists' association and UNOCI. The mission also strengthened its collaboration with media regulatory bodies such as the National Press Council, the National Council on Audio-visual Media and the Observatoire pour la liberté de presse, de l'ethique et de la déontologie. It should be noted, however, that the effectiveness of the first two bodies is severely hampered by the fact that their governing councils have still not been established. In accordance with resolution 1721 (2006), UNOCI also provided the Government with samples of codes of conduct from different countries to assist in the formulation of an Ivorian code of conduct for the media. The code, which was due to be published by 15 December 2006 according to the schedule proposed by the International Working Group, has yet to be finalized.

52. In collaboration with the National Council on Audio-visual Media and the Embassy of Canada in Côte d'Ivoire, UNOCI has initiated a partnership with a network of local radios with a view to helping them promote peace. The partnership will entail joint productions, supplying the stations with ONUCI FM programmes that they can rebroadcast, and training. The mission has developed a code of ethics to which each participating radio station will be required to adhere.

IX. HIV/AIDS

53. Pursuant to Security Council resolution 1308 (2000), UNOCI continues to mainstream HIV/AIDS awareness in the mission's activities through the promotion of HIV risk-free behaviour. Since October 2006, 1,501 United Nations personnel have participated in HIV/AIDS-awareness workshops and 62 peer educators have been trained in two training sessions. In that time, voluntary counselling and testing services were reinforced and 488 personnel presented themselves for voluntary HIV-testing.

54. In addition, in collaboration with Vidri Canal, a local organization, UNOCI conducted a trainers' workshop on HIV/AIDS, gender and human rights for 25 women members of various local associations from Abidjan. During the commemoration of the nineteenth World AIDS Day, a psychosocial centre for the care of people infected or affected by HIV/AIDS, financed by UNOCI quick-impact project funds, was opened in the northern part of the country.

X. Gender issues

55. In the pursuit of gender mainstreaming, UNOCI conducted gender awareness and training programmes for 523 new staff members and 146 soldiers during the period under review. The mission also trained 15 regional electoral officers on gender- and elections-related issues. UNOCI also contributed, in collaboration with the United Nations Population Fund (UNFPA), to the training of 25 members of the Ministry of Family and Social Affairs on gender issues and development, as well as 60 women leaders of local non-governmental organizations and 15 representatives from various ministries on Security Council resolution 1325 (2000) as an advocacy tool to address gender issues affecting women during and after the conflict.

56. The mission and the country team continued to receive reports of sexual violence in the northern and western parts of the country, as well as reports of alleged systematic harassment of women and young girls in rural areas and at checkpoints. UNICEF, in collaboration with UNFPA, has undertaken a study to assess the scope of the problem in order to provide a coherent response. In the meantime, a large part of the UNICEF protection programme is committed to providing assistance to the victims of sexual violence.

XI. Conduct and discipline of United Nations personnel

57. During the period under review, two allegations of sexual exploitation and abuse by United Nations personnel were reported and are under investigation. UNOCI continues to work closely with all mission components and the United Nations country team to strengthen training initiatives and prevention measures for all peacekeepers, as well as monitoring and reporting mechanisms. As at 31 December 2006, 4,242 personnel had undergone mandatory training on sexual exploitation and abuse. Over 45 per cent of UNOCI senior managers have received additional targeted training on their obligation and responsibility to prevent acts of sexual exploitation and abuse by personnel under their supervision. UNOCI also continues to encourage external partners, including national and international non-governmental organizations, to share information on allegations of abuse by United Nations personnel through the established mechanisms in the mission.

XII. Observations

58. I welcome the successful conclusion of the dialogue on the Ivorian peace process and the signing of a peace agreement between President Gbagbo and Mr. Soro on 4 March. This is an important achievement, for which I commend the two leaders. I also congratulate President Compaoré for his effective and even-handed facilitation role, and I assure him and the Ivorian political leaders of the commitment and readiness of the United Nations to assist in the implementation of the agreement. I also wish to assure him that Côte d'Ivoire will remain among my top priorities this year.

59. The Ouagadougou agreement promises to resolve the current impasse and pave the way for a lasting political settlement in Côte d'Ivoire, particularly because it builds upon previous peace agreements and Security Council resolutions and addresses many of the key issues that have impeded progress. However, the agreement will be judged by the political will of the parties to implement it. The agreement also carries special significance, because it was drawn up by the Ivorian leaders themselves, which places on them a special responsibility to implement it in full. I therefore urge the parties to begin the implementation process

immediately. In the meantime, I will initiate discussions with the facilitator and the parties on the role UNOCI and the High Representative for the elections are expected to play in supporting the implementation of the agreement, including in the follow-up mechanisms.

60. In its resolution 1721 (2006), the Security Council stressed that the current extension of the transition period was final. The new agreement reaffirms the commitment of the parties to all relevant Council resolutions, and declares that its objective is to facilitate the implementation of resolution 1721 (2006). It also sets out an ambitious agenda and a tight implementation schedule in an effort to meet the deadline set in the resolution. Despite a number of technical and other issues that may require further elaboration, the effort made to build upon Council resolutions and previous peace agreements is commendable. It may therefore be timely for the Council to consider favourably the recommendation by the ECOWAS leaders to visit Côte d'Ivoire. Such a visit would provide an opportunity to reach a common understanding with the parties and the facilitator not only on the role of the United Nations in the implementation process, but also on a pragmatic implementation process that is consistent with both the agreement and Council resolutions and recognizes the mutual concerns of the parties and the international community.

61. Prior to the conclusion of the dialogue, it was necessary to continue the efforts to move forward with the technical preparations for the eventual implementation of disarmament, identification and security sector reform, and the electoral process. I commend the determination shown by the Prime Minister to press ahead with these tasks. The initial progress made during 2006, albeit very limited, provides a good basis on which to build further progress that would ensure timely and full implementation of the Ouagadougou agreement. The international community should be prepared to provide the assistance necessary for the implementation of key processes, in particular disarmament, security sector reform and the preparation of the elections. The United Nations stands ready, and continues to prepare and assist the Ivorian parties in implementing rapidly and in a comprehensive manner the many key tasks related to those processes. In the meantime, I look forward to continuing to work with the Chairmen of ECOWAS and the African Union in assisting the Ivorian political leaders to secure a lasting political settlement.

62. The support of the international community for the political process should be complemented by commensurate efforts to address the humanitarian situation in the country. While recognizing the significant contribution of a number of key partners, such as the European Union, I urge donors to contribute generously to the Consolidated Appeal Process for Côte d'Ivoire in 2007.

63. I wish to extend my deep appreciation to Pierre Schori, who completed his assignment as my Special Representative for Côte d'Ivoire on 15 February 2007. He made a significant contribution to the efforts to move the peace process forward during his two-year tour of duty. I also wish to commend the current Officer-in-Charge of UNOCI, the High Representative for the elections, as well as the military and civilian personnel of UNOCI and members of the United Nations country team for their continued commitment to the peace process. I also express my gratitude to the humanitarian and development organizations, bilateral and multilateral donors and the countries that are contributing military and police personnel to UNOCI for their invaluable contribution to peace in Côte d'Ivoire.

Annex
United Nations Operation in the Congo: military and civilian police strength as at 21 February 2007

Country	*Military observers*	*Staff officers*	*Troops*	*Total*	*Formed police units*	*Civilian police*
Argentina						4
Bangladesh	11	10	2 725	2 746	250	9
Benin	7	7	421	435		28
Bolivia	3			3		
Brazil	4	3		7		
Cameroon						62
Canada						3
Central African Republic						7
Chad	3			3		5
China	7			7		
Croatia	3			3		
Djibouti						39
Dominican Republic	4			4		
Ecuador	2			2		
El Salvador	3			3		1
Ethiopia	2			2		
France	3	12	173	188		10
Guatemala	5			5		
Ghana	6	7	531	544		1
Gambia	3			3		
Guinea	3			3		
India	8			8		11
Ireland	2			2		
Jordan	7	12	1 048	1 067	375	4
Kenya	5	4		9		
Madagascar						6
Moldova	3			3		
Morocco	1	3	733	737		
Namibia	3			3		
Nepal	3			3		
Niger	6	3	379	388		71
Nigeria	8			8		17
Pakistan	8	9	1 114	1 131	125	2
Paraguay	9	2		11		
Peru	3			3		
Poland	2			2		
Philippines	4	3		7		11

Continued

Country	Military observers	Staff officers	Troops	Total	Formed police units	Civilian police
Romania	7			7		
Russian Federation	12			12		
Rwanda						15
Senegal	7	8	321	336		58
Serbia	3			3		
Switzerland						2
Togo	6	4	315	325		1
Tunisia	5	2		7		
Turkey						21
United Republic of Tanzania	1	2		3		
Uruguay	2	1		3		6
Uganda	5	2		7		
Vanuatu						4
Yemen	5			5		2
Zambia	2			2		
Zimbabwe	2			2		
Total	**198**	**94**	**7 760**	**8 052**	**750**	**400**

6. Fourteenth Progress Report of the Secretary-General on the United Nations Mission in Liberia, 15 March 2007 (S/2007/151)

I. Introduction

1. By its resolution 1712 (2006), the Security Council extended the mandate of the United Nations Mission in Liberia (UNMIL) until 31 March 2007 and requested me to provide information on progress made in meeting the broad benchmarks outlined in my report of 12 September 2006 (S/2006/743). The present report provides an update on major developments in Liberia and of the progress made towards meeting the key benchmarks for the consolidation and drawdown of UNMIL since my report of 11 December 2006 (S/2006/958).

II. Major political developments

2. The overall political situation in Liberia remained relatively stable during the period under review. On 16 January 2007, in an address to mark the anniversary of her administration's first year in office, President Ellen Johnson-Sirleaf highlighted the restoration of peace, the progress made in economic recovery, the growth in public revenue, the partial restoration of health services, the increase in school enrolment and the provision of electricity and pipe-borne water to some parts of Monrovia as the main achievements of her Government to date. She also identified the many challenges ahead, including the creation of employment opportunities, the rehabilitation of roads and the strengthening of national capacities to implement her Government's reform agenda. On 29 January, in her annual address to the Legislature on the state of the nation, the President expressed her intention to submit 10 concessions and acts for legislative approval, including the governance reform commission bill, the national defence bill and the draft anti-corruption statute.

3. The work of the Legislature was hampered by divisions in the House of Representatives over calls for the removal of Edwin Snowe from the post of Speaker of the House. The group of legislators calling for his removal claimed that he no longer enjoyed the confidence of members of the House and accused him of bringing the House into disrepute through activities that were inconsistent with legislative practice. The divisions within the House resulted in two groups of legislators meeting at separate venues.

4. On 18 January, 43 members of the House of Representatives at a meeting in Virginia, just outside Monrovia, passed a resolution to remove Mr. Snowe from the position of Speaker. In response, on 22 January, Mr. Snowe filed a petition for a writ of prohibition in the Supreme Court, arguing that the procedure adopted in the passage of the resolution denied him due process, and that the sitting parliament had passed the resolution in a venue that breached article 40 of the Constitution, which provides for both Houses of the Legislature to sit in the same city. Mr. Snowe also alleged that members of the House of Representatives had been bribed by the Executive to remove him from office. Although the Supreme Court granted Mr. Snowe's petition, he eventually resigned on 15 February, as the number of legislators demanding his removal continued to increase. The Deputy Speaker was designated to act until the election of a new Speaker.

5. The events leading up to the resignation of the Speaker affected proceedings in both the House and the Senate, in particular the passage and enactment of draft legislation. It also increased tensions between the three branches of Government. In the meantime, the International Contact Group on Liberia, some legislators and members of civil society have called for an independent and transparent investigation into the allegations of bribery made by the Speaker.

6. On 6 February, the National Elections Commission organized a by-election to fill the vacant House of Representatives seat for District Number 6 in Nimba County. No candidate obtained the absolute majority required to be declared the winner. As a result, on 20 February, a run-off by-election was held between two candidates from the ruling Unity Party and the Liberian Action Party, which had both secured the highest votes. On 21 February, the Unity Party candidate was declared the winner.

7. As part of the Government's anti-corruption campaign, the former Chairman of the now defunct National Transitional Government of Liberia, Charles Gyude Bryant, together with several former ministers and deputy ministers who were implicated in the report on economic crimes prepared by a team of investigators from the Economic Community of West African States (ECOWAS) during the transitional period, were charged with financial malfeasance during the period under review. The former Vice-Chairman of the Transitional Government, Wesley Momo Johnson, was also interrogated by the Liberian National Police in connection with findings in the same report. On 17 February, the Supreme Court ordered the execution of a search warrant to secure the financial records of six former Finance Ministry personnel from the Transitional Government, who are being prosecuted for embezzlement of public funds. On 2 March, the former Speaker of the House of Representatives, Edwin Snowe, was also questioned by the police in connection with allegations that he misappropriated some US$ 1 million from the Liberia Petroleum Refinery Company while serving as managing director during the transitional period.

8. The risk of localized inter-ethnic conflicts resulting from property and land disputes remains a major source of concern. On 22 January, some 50 members of the Mandingo ethnic group from Nimba County staged a demonstration in front of President Johnson-Sirleaf's office in Monrovia, demanding to talk to the President about land disputes between them and members of the Gio and Mano ethnic groups. The President received the group's leadership to discuss their concerns. In the meantime, the Presidential Commission that was established to investigate the inter-ethnic land and property disputes in Nimba County submitted its report to the President. The Commission recommended, inter alia, the urgent institution of mechanisms to reconcile feuding communities. The President subsequently requested the Commission to share its recommendations with the residents of Nimba County, during which the key recommendations were accepted. The President has since ordered the restitution of contested properties in Nimba County to their rightful owners and requested UNMIL to assist in repairing roads designated for commercial activities in the area.

9. The political and economic tensions in Guinea have been a source of concern. On 14 and 15 December 2006, President Johnson-Sirleaf and President Alhaji Ahmed Tejan Kabbah of Sierra Leone visited Conakry to meet with President Lansana Conté to discuss subregional issues, including the revitalization of the Mano River Union. On 20 February, the two Presidents returned to Conakry where they discussed with President Conté the political crisis in Guinea, including reports about the possible involvement of Liberian ex-combatants in

the disturbances in Guinea. The Presidents agreed to reactivate the Mano River Union security units in all three countries to facilitate information-sharing and to ensure border security. Following her return to Monrovia, President Johnson-Sirleaf made a statement to the press advising that any Liberian who crossed the border to take part in the conflict in Guinea would be in violation of Liberian laws.

III. Security situation

10. The overall security situation in Liberia has remained generally calm and stable. However, deactivated security personnel and retrenched employees of the National Ports Authority staged demonstrations to protest the non-payment of outstanding benefits, including salary arrears. In one such incident, on 8 February, some 500 deactivated army, police and security personnel organized a violent demonstration in Monrovia, which disrupted the flow of traffic and normal business activities. They demanded to meet with President Johnson-Sirleaf regarding the payment of benefits. The Liberian National Police, supported by the United Nations police and formed police units, brought these incidents under control.

11. Criminal activities, including armed robbery, decreased significantly in Monrovia and its environs, while the number of reported cases of rape increased during the reporting period. The reduction in reported criminal activities was due to "Operation Sweeping Wave", which was mounted by UNMIL, the Liberian National Police and other national security agencies to address the problem of violent crime in Monrovia. The operation involved the conduct of cordon and search activities, and increased day and night patrols in high crime areas. In a separate joint operation named "Spider Web", which was launched in December to curb criminal activities during the festive period, several checkpoints were set up in strategic locations throughout Monrovia to conduct random checks on vehicles.

12. On 10 December, UNMIL carried out the second phase of "Exercise Tight Grip" to test the Mission's capabilities and operational readiness to respond to a possible serious deterioration in the security situation in the country. The first phase of the exercise was carried out in Monrovia in October 2006.

13. The security situation along the borders with Sierra Leone, Côte d'Ivoire and Guinea remained stable with no visible threat to the stability of Liberia, despite rumours about the possible involvement of Liberian ex-combatants in the disturbances in Guinea and unconfirmed reports about cross-border movements of Liberian ex-combatants into Côte d'Ivoire. However, the continuing uncertainty in Côte d'Ivoire and Guinea continues to present a potential threat to stability in Liberia. UNMIL has continued to coordinate with the United Nations Operation in Côte d'Ivoire (UNOCI) and with the Guinean military forces to monitor the security situation in border areas. UNMIL conducted concurrent patrols with the Guinean authorities along the Liberian-Guinean border in "Operation Seskin 2" from 22 to 30 January and, without the Guinean authorities, in "Operation Seskin 3" from 19 to 23 February. Similar concurrent patrols along the Liberian-Sierra Leonean border were conducted with the Sierra Leonean authorities in "Operation Loko 3". These exercises were aimed at demonstrating the presence of United Nations security forces in the border areas, deterring illegal cross-border movements, establishing cross-border liaison and reassuring the local populations while fostering better coordination among the security agencies deployed in the border areas.

IV. Deployment of the Mission

A. Military component

14. As at 1 March, UNMIL troop strength stood at 14,832 out of an authorized strength of 15,125. A company of the quick reaction force from Pakistan comprising 250 personnel arrived in the Mission on 23 December 2006 to replace the Swedish quick reaction force, which departed in October 2006. In addition to the activities described in paragraphs 11 to 13 above, UNMIL continued to provide security throughout the country. The Mission undertook several additional cordon and search operations to retrieve weapons, extended support to the United Nations Development Programme (UNDP) community arms collection for development programme, carried out air and ground patrols, especially along Liberia's borders, and assisted in the rehabilitation of roads and bridges. It also provided security support to the Special Court in accordance with Security Council resolution 1626 (2005). In addition, the UNMIL quick reaction force conducted "Exercise Green Horizon" from 22 to 28 January, which was aimed at reinforcing the security of the Special Court.

B. Police component

15. As at 1 March, the Mission's police strength stood at 1,201 officers out of an authorized ceiling of 1,240 officers, and included 574 United Nations police advisers, 604 officers in 5 formed police units, 17 corrections officers and 6 immigration officers. The fifth formed police unit, from India, comprising 105 women and 20 men, arrived in the Mission on 30 January. This unit is the first predominantly female police unit deployed in the history of the United Nations. During the reporting period, the UNMIL police component continued to mentor, monitor, advise, train and support the Liberian National Police. It supported the efforts of the Liberian National Police to contain threats to public order in Monrovia and other urban centres, as well as on rubber plantations. It also provided basic and specialized training for Liberian National Police personnel and immigration and naturalization officers.

C. Adjustments of the Mission

16. Given the relative stability that has prevailed since the inauguration of the new Government and based on the detailed assessment provided in the tenth progress report on UNMIL (S/2006/159), which remains valid, one infantry battalion from Ethiopia was withdrawn from UNMIL on 17 December 2006. Following the departure of this battalion, the operational boundaries between sectors 1, 2 and 3 were realigned, which affected the deployment of troops in Margibi, Bong and Nimba Counties. Further adjustments, including the withdrawal of another infantry battalion, will be considered in 2007, security conditions permitting. Any further drawdown will be guided by progress made in the implementation of the UNMIL mandate and in meeting the benchmarks for consolidation, drawdown and withdrawal, which are set out in section V.

V. Status of implementation of the mandate of the Mission and the benchmarks for the consolidation, drawdown and withdrawal of the Mission

A. Training, restructuring and reform of the Liberian National Police

17. The restructuring and training of the Liberian National Police continued to make steady progress. To date, 2,610 Liberian National Police have been trained and deployed while 358 Special Security Services personnel and 210 Seaport Police officers have graduated from

the National Police Academy. As at 1 March, 736 police recruits were receiving field training, while 184 were undergoing basic training. The Mission has intensified its recruitment efforts in order to achieve the target of 3,500 fully trained Liberian National Police personnel by July 2007.

18. In order to ensure the recruitment of qualified women into the police force, an educational support programme for female police candidates, funded by the Netherlands, was launched on 20 January. The programme, which is a joint initiative of the Government of Liberia and UNMIL, aims at improving the educational qualifications of women under the age of 35 years who are interested in joining the police force. Successful applicants will attend an intensive three-month programme to achieve a high school equivalency diploma. As at 1 March, 309 applications had been received.

19. In continuing efforts to further enhance the capacity of the Liberian National Police, the United Nations police are conducting in-service driver certification training for national police personnel, as well as job specific training for 32 officers of the Bureau of Immigration and Naturalization and senior management courses for 39 officers.

20. The Government of Liberia has decided to establish, over the next five years, a 500-strong police quick-reaction force in addition to the 3,500 police personnel referred to in paragraph 17. This specialized unit, whose personnel will be drawn initially from the 200-strong Liberian National Police Support Unit, will have the capacity to respond quickly, efficiently and robustly to major breaches of internal security. A team of Liberian National Police officers and United Nations police visited Sierra Leone on 26 January and Ghana on 8 February to draw lessons from the police quick reaction force in those countries.

21. The deployment of the Liberian National Police to the interior of the country continues to be hampered by the absence of basic infrastructure and the lack of police equipment, including vehicles and communications. Currently, 537 newly trained Liberian National Police personnel have been deployed to Bomi, Grand Cape Mount, Gbarpolu, Bong, Nimba, Lofa, Sinoe, Grand Gedeh, River Cess, Maryland, Grand Kru and River Gee Counties. In addition, plans are under way to deploy police officers to all county headquarters and newly constructed police stations before December.

22. International partners continue to assist the Government in addressing the logistical challenges facing the police force, but further support from donors is required. On 11 December 2006, UNDP provided nine vehicles to the Liberian National Police. In addition, with bilateral assistance provided by the Netherlands, Norway, the United Kingdom of Great Britain and Northern Ireland, the United States of America and, through UNMIL quick-impact projects, three police stations at Zorzor in Lofa County, Greenville in Sinoe County and Zone 5/Depot 6 in Montserrado County were constructed and handed over to the Liberian National Police. The rehabilitation of the police stations at Bopolu in Gbarpolu County, Voinjama in Lofa County and Robertsport in Grand Cape Mount County are at advanced stages of completion. Some refurbishment work was also carried out at the Liberian National Police Headquarters in Monrovia. Furthermore, police stations are being reconstructed and rehabilitated in Kolahun and Foya in Lofa County, Yekepa and Tapeta in Nimba County, Arthington Town and Schefflin in Montserrado County, Sinje in Grand Cape Mount County, Unification Town in Margibi County, Morweh in River Cess County, Krowroeken in River Gee County, Owensgrove in Grand Bassa County, Salala in Bong

County and Toe Town in Grand Gedeh County. In the meantime, the bids for the construction of new police stations at Buchanan in Grand Bassa County, Harper in Maryland County and Zwedru in Grand Gedeh County have been awarded. Notwithstanding these efforts, many more police facilities still need urgent rehabilitation.

B. Training, restructuring and reform of the armed forces of Liberia

23. The United States continues to lead the international support for the training and restructuring of the armed forces of Liberia. The first batch of 106 soldiers who graduated from basic training at the Barclays Training Centre in Monrovia in November 2006 is now undergoing advanced individual training, with 44 attending the basic non-commissioned officer course, 23 undergoing medical training and another 38 scheduled to begin other military occupational speciality training courses. Training for the second batch of recruits has been postponed from January to April. This delay is a cause for concern given that the rebuilding of Liberia's armed forces is a critical benchmark for the Mission's exit strategy. It would, therefore, be important to accelerate this programme.

C. Development of a national security strategy and architecture

24. President Johnson-Sirleaf has requested the Governance Reform Commission to conduct comprehensive national consultations on developing a national security strategy and architecture. The Commission has held several rounds of consultations with security agencies, Government bodies, international partners and civil society. The Commission's report is expected to be issued in early 2007, following which the Government will articulate its national security policy and architecture. In the meantime, UNMIL is working with the Government to establish a county network for security coordination and reporting.

D. Reintegration of ex-combatants

25. Completing the reintegration of the remaining caseload of ex-combatants remains a key factor in the UNMIL exit strategy. As at 1 March, some 75,000 out of 101,874 demobilized former combatants have either completed, are currently participating in or are registered for reintegration programmes. This includes 11,000 ex-combatants who signed up for formal education courses that started in November 2006, and 3,500 beneficiaries who registered for 8 new vocational skills training projects. Five of the training projects have commenced, while another three are expected to begin shortly. However, some 23,000 ex-combatants are still waiting to be provided with reintegration opportunities under bilaterally funded programmes, while 911 are waiting to be covered under the Disarmament, Demobilization, Rehabilitation and Reintegration Trust Fund managed by UNDP. The reintegration programme for children associated with the fighting forces, which is coordinated by the United Nations Children's Fund (UNICEF), has so far provided reintegration opportunities to 9,704 of the 11,000 child beneficiaries. This includes 4,967 children who have graduated or are currently participating in the community education investment programme and 4,737 beneficiaries who are undergoing or have graduated from vocational training.

26. UNMIL continued to actively collect and destroy residual weapons and ammunition that were voluntarily surrendered or discovered through search operations. Since the end of the disarmament and demobilization programme in 2005, 632 weapons, 77,504 rounds of ammunition, 1,187 pieces of unexploded ordnance and 11,674 assorted spares and miscellaneous parts have been collected and destroyed. In addition, the UNDP community arms

collection for development programme has collected 240 rifles and guns, 20,830 rounds of ammunition, 598 magazines, bayonets and spares and 294 pieces of unexploded ordnance since its launch in January 2006.

E. Consolidation of State authority

27. Progress in the consolidation of State authority throughout the country remains slow. The county support teams, which were established by the international partners and the Government in each county, continue to assist in building the capacities of local authorities to assess, plan, coordinate and deliver basic services. The teams, which comprise representatives from UNMIL, the United Nations country team, the Ministry of Internal Affairs, county administration, Government line ministries and non-governmental institutions, meet on a monthly basis in each of the 15 counties to develop action plans to address the needs of each county. The teams have developed long-term capacity-building strategies for all superintendents and assistant superintendents for development, and have agreed to assist in the rehabilitation of seven and construction of four administrative buildings in the counties, in collaboration with the United States Agency for International Development. In the meantime, UNDP has donated vehicles to each county superintendent and assistant superintendent for development. Notwithstanding these efforts, the work of the county officials and Government line ministry representatives continues to be seriously hampered by a lack of communications, office equipment, accommodation, vehicles and good roads.

F. Management of natural resources

28. The Government continued to take action to regain control over and efficiently manage the country's natural resources for the benefit of the people of Liberia. Since the enactment of the new national forestry reform law, the Government has further developed legislation required for restarting large-scale commercial logging and, with the support of UNMIL, has embarked on a vigorous public sensitization campaign about this legislation. It is also in the process of recruiting a private company to manage the chain of custody system for forestry logs in accordance with the provisions of the new law. In the meantime, the United Kingdom Department for International Development has provided funding for the development of comprehensive legislation on community forestry, which should enable the Government to address the issues of community rights and benefits.

29. As part of its efforts to meet the requirements for the lifting of sanctions, the Government has applied to join the Kimberley Process Certification Scheme and requested that a Kimberley Process review mission visit Liberia as soon as possible. With the support of UNMIL, the Government has completed the construction of a diamond office in Monrovia and regional diamond certification offices in six counties. Canada, South Africa, the United Arab Emirates and the United States, as well as the De Beers diamond company are assisting the Government with the training of Liberia Diamond Authority personnel. The Government has also finalized an iron ore mining concession agreement with Acelor-Mittal, valued at $1 billion, which will pave the way for the reopening of the iron ore mines in Nimba County, as well as the rehabilitation of the Yekepa-Buchanan railroad and the Buchanan port.

30. UNMIL collaborated with the Ministry of Lands, Mines and Energy to finalize a sand mining policy, which provides for the establishment of sites that are suitable for sustainable sand mining. The policy is aimed at preventing coastal erosion, in particular in Monrovia,

where illegal and indiscriminate sand mining has been taking place. UNMIL also assisted the Government in identifying and assessing potential sites for sand mining, while its force engineers are assisting in the rehabilitation of roads leading to these sites.

31. UNMIL continued to support the Government in re-establishing security in disputed rubber plantations within the framework of the joint Government of Liberia/UNMIL rubber plantation task force. Since the Government took control of the Guthrie Rubber Plantation in August 2006, the security situation on the plantation has remained stable, with UNMIL and the Liberian National Police providing security for the management of the plantation. At Cocopa plantation, security remains a source of serious concern as conflicts persist between the plantation management and the local communities. UNMIL has deployed military and police personnel to support the Liberian National Police stationed at the plantation, where the use of shotguns is commonplace. In the meantime, the appointment by the Government of an interim management team for the Cocopa plantation in January has been legally challenged. The Government, in consultation with UNMIL, is also taking measures to address the security problems at the Sinoe rubber plantation.

G. Promotion of human rights and the rule of law

1. Promotion of human rights

32. During the reporting period, UNMIL continued its human rights promotion, protection and monitoring activities throughout the country. Although the overall human rights situation in the country continues to improve, major challenges remain, in particular in the area of prisons, the judiciary and the juvenile justice system. The work of the Truth and Reconciliation Commission also continues to be hampered by mismanagement and financial constraints.

33. Very weak rule of law institutions continue to impede the administration of justice. The judicial system lacks qualified personnel, infrastructure, logistic support and basic office supplies. Court officials often apply legal rules and procedures in an inconsistent manner or fail to observe minimum human rights standards. In addition, corrupt practices involving some magistrates and judicial officials, inefficiency and prolonged pre-trial detention continued to be observed throughout the country. Despite denunciations by the Ministry of Justice, the practice of trial by ordeal remains common in some remote areas of the country, in part because of the absence of courts and police services. In an effort to strengthen the capacity of the judiciary, the Government has provided 20 vehicles for the use of circuit court judges across the country.

34. Detention conditions are still below minimum human rights standards. Some correction facilities, including the Monrovia Central Prison, are overcrowded because of delays in bringing cases to trial. As a result of staff shortages and poor working conditions, the number of jailbreaks increased during the reporting period.

35. Although there has been an increase in the number of rape cases tried by the circuit courts, the relevant provisions of the Rape Amendment Act are still not being uniformly applied by magistrates and judges. In addition, many cases are not being investigated or brought before competent courts.

36. The juvenile justice system remains a source of serious concern. In several counties, juveniles continued to be held in long-term pre-trial detention with adults without indictment or trial, while in other counties, juveniles have been tried by the magistrate courts.

37. The orphanages that were declared illegal and listed for closure by the Ministry of Health and Social Welfare in 2006 continued to operate. Conditions in these unaccredited homes are below the minimum standard required for the healthy development of children and their protection from exploitation.

38. Since my previous report, the Truth and Reconciliation Commission has not made much headway in implementing its mandate. Although some progress was made in the identification and recruitment of key staff, a numbers of posts remain vacant. In addition, the only member of the International Technical Advisory Committee who was resident in Liberia resigned his appointment. The Commission's operations are hampered by financial and logistical constraints, as well as by shortcomings in its management. Donors recently rejected the draft budget prepared by the Commission because of concerns about lack of transparency in the previous disbursement of funds. In an effort to resolve these problems, on 23 January, the International Contact Group on Liberia wrote to the Chairman of the Truth and Reconciliation Commission to recommend the establishment of a working group, to be composed of representatives, of the Contact Group, including the United Nations, and the Commission. The Chairman has since agreed to the establishment of the working group, but with a larger membership. The first meeting of the working group was to take place on 8 March. In the meantime, the Commission's plans to commence public hearings in Monrovia have been suspended.

39. During the reporting period, some progress was made towards the establishment of the Independent National Commission on Human Rights. On 17 January, the Independent Selection Panel, which was established to vet nominees, submitted a short-list of candidates to the President for consideration. Owing to the delay in the vetting and selection process, UNMIL was unable to proceed with planned activities, including training of the Commissioners and staff members in human rights law and investigation.

2. Support for the judicial system

40. During the reporting period, the number of trials for serious offences such as murder, rape and armed robbery increased. The first rape case to be tried since the end of the conflict was concluded in Tubmanburg, Bomi County, and several high-profile corruption cases involving several former senior Government officials were prosecuted. This increase in judicial activity was partially due to the engagement of national lawyers, with UNMIL support, to serve as prosecutors and public defenders. The Minister of Justice and the Chief Justice have since requested that the lawyers be engaged for a further six months. Despite these developments, the justice system continues to be constrained by the lack of court buildings and a dearth of qualified judicial and legal officers, which have resulted in serious delays in the processing of criminal cases.

41. UNMIL continued its capacity-building activities by providing training for legal and judicial officers. Since May 2006, 330 magistrates have been trained by UNMIL. The Mission is currently assisting the Chief Justice in identifying the training needs of circuit court judges and other judicial personnel. Meanwhile, the Governance Reform Commission has prepared a draft paper on legal and judicial reforms required in the justice sector.

3. Support for the corrections system

42. UNMIL continued to assist the Bureau of Rehabilitation and Corrections to improve the conditions of correctional facilities throughout the country. The refurbishment work on

the facilities, being funded by Norway and the United States, is at various stages of completion. The construction of a new cell block at the Monrovia Central Prison is also in the final stages of completion, while the first phase of the refurbishment of the National Palace of Corrections in Zwedru and the rehabilitation of the Bondiway Prison have been completed. In collaboration with UNMIL, the Government is in the process of reviewing the security and logistical needs of the Zwedru facility. In addition, with the assistance of the UNMIL quick-impact project funds, the refurbishment of the Buchanan Prison has been completed while the rehabilitation of the facilities in Voinjama and Sanniquellie is ongoing. The World Food Programme (WFP), the International Committee of the Red Cross and other partners continued to provide foodstuff and other supplies to the prisoners.

43. Since the training programme for corrections officers commenced in February 2005, UNMIL has trained 79 corrections officers. During the reporting period, 25 correction officers completed their basic training at the Police Academy and are currently undergoing practical training at correctional facilities. UNMIL has also provided these officers with training in HIV/AIDS, gender mainstreaming, fire safety and equipment and first aid.

44. Owing to budgetary constraints, the Government has only absorbed 25 of the 79 newly trained corrections officers into the civil service. However, in response to the frequent incidents of escape from prisons, which have been attributed to an acute shortage of trained corrections officers, President Johnson-Sirleaf has recently committed to absorbing 55 corrections officers into the civil service in 2007, and to ensuring better conditions of service for corrections staff. The Government has also procured new uniforms for these officers.

H. Economic governance

45. The Government continued to make steady progress in the implementation of the Governance and Economic Management Assistance Programme. The Economic Governance Steering Committee met regularly to monitor progress in the implementation of the Programme. It also continued to review the monthly status reports on the activities of the internationally recruited experts. During the period under review, the Senate confirmed the Government's nominee for the position of Auditor-General at the General Auditing Commission, which is being funded by the European Commission. A non-governmental organization was selected to conduct a nationwide campaign, sponsored by the World Bank, to raise awareness about the Programme. In addition, the Government, in collaboration with international partners, completed an internal review of the implementation of the Programme after its first year of operation and released a status report, which was published on the Programme's website (www.gemapliberia.org). The progress highlighted in the report includes improvements in Government financial management and expenditure, as well as increased transparency in the management of State-owned enterprises.

46. The Contracts and Concessions Review Committee of the Public Procurement and Concessions Commission completed its review of 186 contracts and concessions entered into by the National Transitional Government of Liberia by the 31 December 2006 deadline established by President Johnson-Sirleaf. A local lawyer and an international lawyer provided by UNMIL conducted legal reviews of 23 of these contracts. Of the 186 contracts reviewed, the Committee recommended the acceptance of 52, the renegotiation of 14 and the cancellation of 29. The Committee was unable to examine 3 telecommunications agreements and 44 lease agreements because of the absence of technical experts, while another

44 contracts from different sectors could not be comprehensively reviewed because of missing documentation. At a meeting of the Steering Committee on 24 January, the President instructed that the three telecommunications agreements should be nullified for violating Government procurement procedures and laws.

47. The Government's commitment to improving economic governance continued to yield positive results. According to the Ministry of Finance, the Government realized $114 million in revenue in 2006, which represented a 48 per cent increase from the $77 million collected in the previous year. This marked improvement resulted from the fiscal reforms and regulatory measures adopted by the Government.

I. National recovery, reconstruction and development

48. On 13 February, the Government of Liberia convened a Liberia Partners' Forum to review progress made on its recovery and reconstruction agenda, as well as to solicit feedback on the strategic priorities outlined in its interim poverty reduction strategy and discuss financing requirements and mechanisms. The Forum, which took place in Washington, D.C., was sponsored by the African Development Bank (ADB), the European Commission, the International Monetary Fund, the United Nations, the World Bank and the United States. During the Forum, Germany and the United States pledged to forgive Liberia's bilateral debt, while the United Kingdom agreed to provide 10 per cent of the funds needed to clear Liberia's arrears with ADB. Other international partners promised to support the Government's efforts to eliminate its external debt. I encourage the international community to translate the tremendous goodwill expressed at the Forum into tangible resources that could be used to address the priority needs of the country.

49. During a one-day visit to Liberia, on 1 February, President Hu Jintao of China signed a number of bilateral economic agreements with the Government and announced the cancellation of Liberia's US$ 10 million dollars debt. In addition, President Hu gave Liberia a $1.5 million cash grant and pledged $25 million to the country over the next two years.

50. Employment generation remains a key priority of the Government. A joint initiative of UNDP, UNMIL and the World Bank, aimed at rehabilitating critical roads, has so far provided short-term employment opportunities for some 5,700 workers, including ex-combatants. In addition, some 768 community members and ex-combatants have benefited from the rehabilitation of secondary and feeder roads by UNMIL military engineers. With the support of the WFP food support to local initiatives programme and the Ministry of Public Works, UNMIL has also facilitated the employment of some 3,000 local community members in roadside brushing and other basic road repair works. Moreover, the Mission has facilitated the establishment of three manual quarry projects for the production of stones used for road rehabilitation, which has provided jobs for about 350 people. UNMIL also continues to use its quick-impact projects to enhance employment creation.

VI. Humanitarian situation

51. Further improvement was recorded in the humanitarian situation during the reporting period. As at 1 March, 89,344 refugees had voluntarily returned to their places of origin with the assistance of the Office of the United Nations High Commissioner for Refugees, while some 36,000 were reported to have returned spontaneously. This leaves some 107,348 refugees still to be repatriated from various countries in the subregion. There are also

16,168 refugees residing in Liberia from Sierra Leone, Côte d'Ivoire and other countries. Meanwhile, the humanitarian community has reviewed its contingency plans for responding to any possible humanitarian emergency that may arise as a result of the fragile political and security situation in Guinea and Côte d'Ivoire.

52. During the period under review, the number of functioning health facilities increased from 280 to 389. Despite this improvement, access to basic health care remains inadequate, in particular in remote counties. The majority of health-care facilities are being operated by non-governmental organizations, some of which plan to cease operations in Liberia later in 2007. The Government's efforts to deliver adequate health care have continued to be constrained by limited resources and the dearth of qualified health personnel.

53. To date, the 2006 United Nations consolidated appeal for Liberia has received 50 per cent of the estimated $145 million required for humanitarian activities. Some $117 million will be needed to address humanitarian needs in 2007, including the delivery of basic social services, the provision of security and productive livelihoods for returnee communities and strengthening the capacity of civil society and local authorities. I appeal to donors to generously provide the required assistance to meet these needs, which are outlined in the 2007 Common Humanitarian Action Plan for Liberia.

VII. Gender

54. The Mission's Gender Adviser Unit continued to facilitate the development of a mission-wide action plan, with benchmarks, for the implementation of Security Council resolution 1325 (2000) on women, peace and security. Through its membership in various committees and working groups, the Unit gave technical, logistical and financial support for the implementation of a national action plan in the areas of rule of law, the protection of human rights and the promotion of women in decision-making. During the reporting period, the United Nations Gender Theme Group, which is comprised of representatives of the United Nations country team, including UNMIL, developed an action plan to support the Government in elaborating its national strategy on the implementation of resolution 1325 (2000), the development of a gender policy and the preparation of a report on the implementation of the Convention on the Elimination of All Forms of Discrimination against Women in Liberia. The Unit also conducted gender analysis training for UNMIL personnel.

VIII. HIV/AIDS

55. The UNMIL HIV/AIDS Unit collaborated with the Mission's integrated training cell to conduct awareness training and sensitization, as well as personal risk assessment sessions, as part of the induction training for military, police and civilian personnel. The Unit also continued to promote HIV/AIDS awareness through its participation in a live UNMIL Radio phone-in programme. In addition, it collaborated with UNICEF, the Foundation for International Dignity, the Young Men's Christian Association and the Right to Play organization to conduct awareness workshops on HIV/AIDS for youths residing in Montserrado County.

IX. Personnel conduct and discipline

56. The Mission's Conduct and Discipline Unit continued to focus on developing strategies to prevent, identify, report on and effectively respond to all categories of United Nations personnel misconduct. It also focused on strategies to ensure the implementation of the

Secretary-General's zero tolerance policy on sexual exploitation and abuse through training, awareness-raising and attention to welfare concerns of all categories of United Nations personnel. In 2006, the Mission trained 3,360 personnel in conduct-related issues, including prevention of sexual exploitation and abuse. During the reporting period, UNMIL hired a local consultant to conduct awareness training for 30 national non-governmental organizations, which are expected to participate in the implementation of the Mission's outreach programmes to local communities close to United Nations facilities. The Unit has also continued to participate in coordinating the national sexual exploitation and abuse awareness campaign launched by the Government in December 2006.

57. During the period under review, seven allegations of sexual exploitation and abuse were reported. All reported cases are being investigated by the Office of Internal Oversight Services. UNMIL will continue to publicize the outcome of completed investigations.

X. Public information

58. The public information component of UNMIL continued to support the priority programmes of the Mission, as well as those of the United Nations agencies, the Government of Liberia and civil society, which are aimed at consolidating peace and stability, encouraging reconciliation and promoting national recovery. The Mission also organized several sports and cultural events to promote national reconciliation. The sports for peace programme, which is expected to bring Liberians throughout the country together to play football, volleyball and kickball, was launched on 2 March by my Special Adviser on Sports for Development and Peace, Adolf Ogi. UNMIL also organized a musical concert in Tubmanburg, Bomi County, to sensitize the populace about sexual exploitation and abuse. The Mission has also continued to work with other partners in developing the capacity of the national media by providing training for print and electronic media personnel.

XI. Observations

59. Liberia continues to make steady progress in consolidating peace, stability and democracy, as well as in promoting economic recovery, with the sustained support of its international partners. I am pleased to note that the Government remains focused on the important priorities of ensuring economic recovery; fighting corruption; implementing the Governance and Economic Management Assistance Program; reforming the security sector; regaining control and efficient management of its natural resources; strengthening the capacity of its institutions, parastatals and agencies; and consolidating its authority. In addition, the Government has implemented structural and fiscal reforms; drafted critical legislation; and transparently reviewed contracts and concessions entered into by the former National Transitional Government of Liberia.

60. Notwithstanding these encouraging developments, Liberia still faces significant reconstruction and development challenges arising from 14 years of civil strife, including pervasive poverty, food insecurity, high unemployment, massive illiteracy, debilitated infrastructure and the inadequate delivery of basic services, including potable water, health services and education. In addition, a number of tasks that are critical to the consolidation of peace in the country have yet to be completed, including the reintegration of ex-combatants, the resettlement of returnees, the reform of the judiciary and the extension of the rule of law throughout the country.

61. The Government also needs to accelerate the development of a national security strategy and framework, as well as the training and restructuring of the new army. While some progress has been made in restructuring and training the police, vehicles, communications equipment and accommodation are needed to sustain their deployment to the interior of the country. I trust that donors will contribute generously towards these pressing requirements, which will help the Government to strengthen the rule of law.

62. The potential threat to stability presented by the unemployed, including former combatants and deactivated security personnel, remains a source of serious concern. To address this threat, labour-intensive employment opportunities must be provided in the short term, while sustainable employment opportunities generated through a revitalized economy will need to be created in the long term. I appeal to donors to assist the Government in generating these employment opportunities. I also urge international partners to intensify efforts to provide former combatants, who have not yet participated in reintegration programmes, with reintegration opportunities.

63. The positive expressions of support by international partners during the Liberia Partners' Forum were very encouraging. I was particularly gratified by the commitment made towards helping the Government find solutions to clear its debts with international financial institutions. It is hoped that the partners will follow through on these commitments so that Liberia's multilateral debt arrears can be cleared in a timely manner.

64. In my address to the Liberia Partners' Forum, I stressed the importance of assisting the Government in building the capacity of its State institutions and in restoring effective State administration of the country's natural resources so that the remaining sanctions may be lifted. In providing our collective support to meet these and other urgent priorities, it will be important to protect the fundamental human rights of every Liberian, promote gender equality and foster national reconciliation.

65. It is a matter of concern that the work of the Truth and Reconciliation Commission is progressing rather slowly owing to a number of management, personnel and budgetary challenges. These problems need to be resolved on an urgent basis so that the Commission can continue its valuable work of ensuring lasting peace in Liberia. I would like to express appreciation to the international partners who have so far provided assistance to the Truth and Reconciliation Commission and appeal to them to continue to work closely with the Commission in the implementation of its mandate.

66. The recent tensions in the House of Representatives have diverted the attention of legislators away from the very crucial national reconstruction and recovery work of the country. Members of the House should work constructively together to overcome these difficulties and to settle all disputes within the appropriate legal frameworks.

67. At the same time, it is important to continue to pay attention to the potential external threats to peace and stability in Liberia. In particular, the unpredictable situations in Côte d'Ivoire and Guinea create an environment that poses additional challenges to efforts to build sustained stability in Liberia. The ongoing cooperation between UNMIL and UNOCI, as well as with the Sierra Leonean and Guinean armed forces, in patrolling the border areas needs to be complemented by commensurate policies at the highest political levels to promote good neighbourly relations and build mechanisms for stability in the border areas and the wider subregion. I am therefore greatly encouraged by the growing cooperation among the Governments of Guinea, Liberia and Sierra Leone in addressing these border issues.

68. In the light of the challenges outlined above, and given the limited progress made in meeting the benchmarks for the consolidation and drawdown of the Mission, I recommend the extension of the mandate of UNMIL for a period of 12 months, until 31 March 2008.

69. In conclusion, I would like to commend the people and Government of Liberia, my Special Representative, Alan Doss, and all UNMIL military and civilian personnel for the progress made in the country during the reporting period. I would also like to thank all troop- and police-contributing countries, ECOWAS, the African Union, the International Contact Group on the Mano River Basin, United Nations agencies, funds and programmes, humanitarian organizations, multilateral and bilateral donors, as well as international and local non-governmental organizations, for their important contributions and support to the peace consolidation process in Liberia.

Annex

United Nations Mission in Liberia: military and civilian police strength (at 1 March 2007)

	Military				
Country	*Military observers*	*Staff officers*	*Troops*	*Total*	*Civilian police*
Argentina					8
Bangladesh	17	12	3 183	3 212	29
Benin	4	1		5	
Bolivia	1	1		2	
Bosnia and Herzegovina				0	11
Brazil		1		1	
Bulgaria	2			2	
China	5	8	557	570	18
Croatia		3		3	
Czech Republic	3			3	5
Denmark	2			2	
Ecuador	4	1		5	
El Salvador	3			3	2
Ethiopia	14	7	2 536	2 557	
Egypt	8			8	4
Fiji				0	30
Finland		2		2	
France		1		1	
Gambia	5			5	32
Germany			18	18	5
Ghana	10	4	847	861	40
India					125
Indonesia	3			3	
Ireland		6	396	402	
Jamaica				0	8

Continued

Country	Military				Civilian police
	Military observers	Staff officers	Troops	Total	
Jordan	8	7	115	130	140
Kenya	1	3		4	26
Kyrgyzstan	4			4	3
Malawi		2		2	19
Mali	2	1		3	
Moldova	3	1		4	
Malaysia	10			10	
Namibia	3	3	857	863	6
Nepal	3	2	40	45	256
Niger	1			1	
Nigeria	19	14	1 943	1 976	157
Norway				0	10
Pakistan	16	9	2 732	2 757	28
Paraguay	3	1		4	
Peru	3	3		6	
Philippines	3	5	164	172	28
Poland	2			2	3
Republic of Korea	1	1		2	
Romania	3			3	
Russian Federation	6			6	10
Rwanda					15
Samoa				0	14
Senegal	3	3	600	606	
Serbia	6			6	7
Sri Lanka				0	10
Sweden	0	4	231	235	12
The former Yugoslav Republic of Macedonia					1
Togo	2	1		3	
Turkey				0	33
Uganda				0	21
United Kingdomof Great Britain and Northern Ireland		3		3	
Ukraine	3	1	300	304	13
Uruguay				0	3
United States of America	7	6		13	7
Yemen				0	4
Zambia	3			3	27
Zimbabwe				0	31
Total	**196**	**117**	**14 519**	**14 832**	**1 201**

7. Thirteenth Progress Report of the Secretary-Generalon the United Nations Operation in Côte d'Ivoire, 14 May 2007 (S/2007/275)

I. Introduction

1. In its presidential statement (S/PRST/2007/8), issued on 28 March 2007, the Security Council welcomed the agreement signed by President Laurent Gbagbo and Mr. Guillaume Soro in Ouagadougou on 4 March 2007 (S/2007/144), under the facilitation of the Chairman of the Economic Community of West African States (ECOWAS), President Blaise Compaoré of Burkina Faso. The Council also expressed its readiness to take further steps to help the parties in implementing the agreement and requested me to submit, by 15 May 2007, recommendations on the role that the United Nations should play in that regard. The present report, which is based on the findings of a multidisciplinary technical assessment mission that visited Côte d'Ivoire from 10 to 22 April 2007, provides therequested recommendations.

II. The Ouagadougou agreement

2. The Ouagadougou agreement seeks to resolve the crisis in Côte d'Ivoire by merging the Forces nouvelles and the national defence and security forces through the establishment of an integrated command centre; replacing the zone of confidence with a green line marked by UNOCI observation points that would be dismantled gradually; deploying mixed Forces nouvelles and national police units to maintain law and order in the area formerly covered by the zone of confidence; re-establishing State administration throughout the country; dismantling the militias; disarming combatants and enrolling them in a civic service programme; granting amnesty for all crimes relating to national security committed between September 2000 and the date of signing of the agreement; simplifying and accelerating the identification of the population and the registration of voters; and organizing a free, fair, open and transparent presidential election, in accordance with the Linas-Marcoussis and Pretoria agreements. The agreement also provides for the creation of new institutional arrangements to implement these tasks, including a new transitional Government.

3. In order to facilitate monitoring of the peace process, the agreement created two new follow-up mechanisms. The first is a standing consultative mechanism comprising President Gbagbo, Prime Minister Soro, former President Henri Konan Bedié, former Prime Minister Alassane Ouattara and the facilitator, President Compaoré. This mechanism will address all arising issues pertaining to the agreement. The second mechanism is an evaluation and monitoring committee, to be chaired by a representative of the facilitator, which will comprise three representatives each from the two signatory parties. The two parties may decide to include other Ivorian parties in the committee, while the facilitator may also call upon any member of the international community to participate in the committee, as he deems appropriate. The monitoring and evaluation committee's role is to assess the implementation of the agreement and offer recommendations on measures to facilitate the peace process. Any disagreements relating to the interpretation or implementation of the agreement will be settled through arbitration by the facilitator.

4. The schedule of implementation of the Ouagadougou agreement sets out the following key timelines: setting up of the integrated command centre beginning on 18 March 2007

(two weeks after the signing of the agreement); establishment of the institutional framework for implementing the agreement starting on 1 April (four weeks after the signing of the agreement); formation of the new interim government by 8 April (five weeks after the signing of the agreement); removal of the zone of confidence and creation of the mixed police and military units beginning on 15 April (one week after the formation of the new government); dismantling and disarmament of the militias starting on 23 April (two weeks after the formation of the new government), to be completed within two weeks (by 7 May); cantonment of the former fighting forces, storage of their weapons under the supervision of the impartial forces (United Nations Operation in Côte d'Ivoire (UNOCI) and the Licorne troops) and the re-establishment of State administration throughout the country and the launching of mobile court hearings, all starting by 23 April (seven weeks after the signing of the agreement); voter registration and identification beginning on 21 May (one month after the beginning of the mobile courts hearings); unification of the two forces and enrolment of ex-combatants into the civic service programme starting on 5 June (15 days after the beginning of the voter registration process); and preparation and issuance of identity cards and voters' cards beginning once the voters register is officially adopted. The schedule envisages completion of all these tasks within a period of 10 months, that is by 4 January 2008, followed by the organization of a presidential election. The agreement does not, however, set the date for the elections.

5. On 26 March 2007, President Gbagbo and Guillaume Soro signed a supplementary agreement designating Mr. Soro as the new Prime Minister of Côte d'Ivoire. The supplementary agreement stipulated that Mr. Soro will remain in office until the holding of the presidential election. It also barred him from standing as a candidate for that election. The agreement further stated that the new Prime Minister would be accorded specific powers for the purpose of implementing the Ouagadougou agreement. Both the Ouagadougou agreement and the supplementary agreement were endorsed by ECOWAS in its communiqués of 16 and 28 March, and by the Peace and Security Council of the African Union in its communiqués of 19 and 29 March. The African Union transmitted the agreements to the Security Council, with a recommendation to endorse them and to consider a gradual drawdown of the impartial forces.

III. Status of implementation of the Ouagadougou agreement

6. Implementation of the Ouagadougou agreement started on schedule with the signing of a presidential decree establishing the integrated command centre on 16 March 2007. President Gbagbo and Prime Minister Soro subsequently inaugurated the headquarters of the command centre in Yamoussoukro, on 16 April.

7. Pursuant to chapter V of the agreement, on 7 April Prime Minister Soro announced a 33-member cabinet comprising 11 members from the ruling Ivorian Popular Front populaire ivoirien (FPI), seven from the Forces nouvelles and five each from the Rassemblement des Républicains (RDR), the Parti democratique de Côte d'Ivoire (PDCI), smaller political parties and civil society. Four members of the cabinet are women, compared to six in the previous Government.

8. On 12 April, President Gbagbo, in keeping with chapter VI of the Ouagadougou agreement, issued an ordinance granting amnesty for crimes relating to national security committed between 17 September 2000 and the date of the signing of the agreement.

Economic crimes, as well as war crimes and crimes against humanity were excluded from the amnesty.

9. In order to facilitate the lifting of the zone of confidence, on 11 April the Chiefs of Staff of the national defence and security forces and the Forces nouvelles, General Philippe Mangou and General Soumaila Bakayoko, as well as the Force Commanders of UNOCI and Licorne, signed an agreement nullifying "code 14" of 31 July 2005, which had provided the legal basis and security arrangements for the zone. At the request of the two Chiefs of Staff, UNOCI and Licorne subsequently assisted the integrated command centre to define the coordinates of the green line that will replace the zone of confidence.

10. The removal of the zone of confidence started as scheduled, on 16 April, with the dismantling of the UNOCI checkpoints at Tiebissou and Djébonoua, the installation of the first UNOCI observation post along the green line at Ngatta Dolikro, and the deployment of the first mixed police unit. Two more mixed units were deployed at Bangolo and Zeale, in the west, on 30 April. The lifting of the zone of confidence will be conducted progressively, based on the pace at which the integrated command centre puts together and deploys the mixed police units responsible for maintaining law and order in the area. In the meantime, UNOCI will continue to maintain check points and to conduct patrols in areas where the mixed police units have not yet been deployed.

11. The parties were unable to meet the 23 April deadline for starting the implementation of the more complex cluster of tasks consisting of the dismantling of the militias, the cantonment of combatants, the redeployment of State officials throughout the country and the launching of the mobile court hearings for the identification of the population. These tasks required more detailed technical planning than envisaged by the tight timelines set in the agreement.

12. The Prime Minister's office has initiated a series of workshops with the participation of relevant Government ministries, national implementing institutions and international partners, including UNOCI, the United Nations country team, the office of the High Representative for the elections, the World Bank, the International Monetary Fund (IMF), the African Development Bank and the European Union, to develop the operational plans and budgets for these processes, as well as for the electoral process and security sector reform. A national workshop chaired by Prime Minister Soro in Yamoussoukro on 2 May determined the cost and funding gaps of these processes, as follows: disarmament, demobilization and reintegration, approximately \$100 million (funding gap: \$78 million); the civic service programme, \$41 million (fully funded by the Government); identification of the population, \$37 million (shortfall: \$33 million); elections, \$72 million (funding gap: \$56 million); redeployment of State officials throughout the country, \$41 million (shortfall: \$29 million), national reconciliation, \$4 million (shortfall: \$4 million); and public information campaign, \$825,000 (shortfall: \$825,000). The Yamoussoukro workshop also designated the various national institutions that will be responsible for implementing these tasks and decided that a working group to be established by the Government would finalize the operational plans.

IV. Issues arising from the Ouagadougou agreement

13. The Ouagadougou agreement assigned most of the military tasks related to the peace process to the integrated command centre. The agreement was silent, however, on some major police and civilian tasks performed by the United Nations, including the United

Nations role in the electoral process and the certification and arbitration role of the High Representative for the elections. It nevertheless mentioned a specific role for the United Nations in the following areas: overall supervision of the implementation of the disarmament and demobilization process; supervision of the cantonment of units of the former fighting forces and the storage of their weapons; and maintaining observation posts along the green line. The new follow-up mechanisms created by the agreement did not include the United Nations.

14. These aspects of the agreement, coupled with the ECOWAS and African Union recommendation to the Security Council to consider a gradual drawdown of the impartial forces (UNOCI and Licorne), as well as the announcement of Licorne's plans to downsize by one battalion by mid-May, created a widespread impression that the signatories to the Ouagadougou agreement were seeking a limited role for the United Nations in the peace process and expected a UNOCI drawdown. Furthermore, the ECOWAS and the African Union recommendation for a drawdown appeared to contradict the call in the agreement for the inclusion of more African troops in UNOCI. The purpose of the proposed additional troops therefore required clarification, since the agreement assigned all key military tasks to the integrated command centre.

15. The agreement was also silent on the important issue of promoting and monitoring human rights, which is crucial to the normalization of the political situation in Côte d'Ivoire. In addition, it did not explain the expected role of the International Working Group, established by the Security Council through its resolution 1633 (2005), and its relationship with the new follow-up and monitoring mechanisms.

16. In the light of the ambiguities emanating from these issues, the Security Council, in a press statement issued on 14 March 2007, encouraged me to discuss with President Compaoré and the Ivorian parties, the role they expected that the United Nations should play in the peace process. To that end, on 26 March 2007, I sent a letter to President Compaoré, seeking his views on these issues. In addition, I sent a technical assessment mission, led by the Assistant Secretary-General for Peacekeeping Operations, Hédi Annabi, to Côte d'Ivoire and Burkina Faso to consult with the facilitator and the parties and to gather the information required to develop the recommendations requested by the Security Council.

17. In a letter dated 27 March 2007, President Compaoré informed me that the signatories to the Ouagadougou agreement expected the United Nations and the international community to continue to play an important role in the Ivorian peace process, in particular to support the implementation of the key tasks set out in the agreement. He also stated that the impartial forces were expected to work in collaboration with the integrated command centre to implement the tasks leading to the removal of the zone of confidence and to assist in providing security in the area. President Compaoré's letter further indicated that the United Nations should help to provide security for the elections and, in particular, observe the electoral process and provide technical advice to the Ivorian institutions.

V. Technical assessment mission

18. The technical assessment mission visited Côte d'Ivoire from 10 to 22 April 2007. Participants in the assessment mission included representatives of the Department of Peacekeeping Operations, the Department of Political Affairs, the Office for the Coordination of Humanitarian Affairs, the Office of the United Nations High Commissioner for Human

Rights (OHCHR), the Department of Public Information, the Office of the United Nations High Commissioner for Refugees (UNHCR), the Department of Safety and Security and the United Nations Development Programme (UNDP).

19. The assessment mission received detailed briefings from representatives of UNOCI, the United Nations country team, the World Bank, IMF, the African Development Bank and the Licorne force and consulted with a wide spectrum of national and international stakeholders, including President Gbagbo, Prime Minister Soro, the Chiefs of Staff of the Forces nouvelles and the national defence forces, the heads of the police forces on both sides and representatives of opposition political parties and national institutions responsible for implementing the key tasks set out in the Ouagadougou agreement. Consultations were also held with members of the diplomatic community, civil society and national and international non-governmental organizations.

20. The mission travelled to Daloa, Duékoué and Guiglo, in the volatile western part of the country, where it visited one of the newly established UNOCI observation posts along the green line and a camp for internally displaced persons. In addition, on 14 April, Mr. Annabi travelled to Ouagadougou for consultations with President Compaoré and his facilitation team. During a visit to South Africa on 19 April, Mr. Annabi used the opportunity to consult with President Thabu Mbeki's legal counsel and, on his way back to New York, met with senior French officials in Paris on 23 April, at their request.

VI. Findings of the technical assessment mission

21. The technical assessment mission's consultations with the parties and the facilitator helped to clarify the issues identified in section IV above. All national stakeholders, including the President, the Prime Minister and the facilitator, stressed that continued United Nations assistance for the peace process was essential. President Gbagbo publicly reaffirmed that view on 16 April when he officiated at the ceremonies marking the beginning of the removal of the zone of confidence.

22. The President and the Prime Minister explained that while the Ivorian parties have assumed ownership and leadership of the peace process, they expected the United Nations and other international partners to join the Ivorian institutions in carrying out the tasks set out in the agreement, providing the requisite resources, technical advice and logistical support and observing the implementation process. Prime Minister Soro emphasized that the Ivorian parties were just beginning to build mutual confidence and cautioned that a premature withdrawal of the impartial forces could precipitate a resumption of hostilities. The two leaders further confirmed that during the Ouagadougou talks the continued presence of the impartial forces in Côte d'Ivoire was not at issue and that neither they nor any other Ivorian leader had called for the withdrawal of UNOCI. This view was echoed by the facilitator during his meeting with Mr. Annabi on 14 April.

23. The Ivorian parties, including the President and the Prime Minister, presented a common view on the nature of the assistance they expect the United Nations to provide in specific areas, including the lifting of the zone of confidence, the restoration of law and order institutions in the north and west, the re-establishment of State administration and basic social services throughout the country, the disarmament of combatants and militias, the identification of the population, the protection of vulnerable populations, support for economic and social recovery and addressing the security and humanitarian situation, particularly in

the western part of the country. President Gbagbo emphasized that, in accompanying, advising and assisting the Ivorian institutions as they carry out these tasks, the United Nations and other international partners should avoid substituting for, or imposing decisions on, the national institutions.

24. At the same time, the Ivorian authorities recognized the challenges emanating from the limited capacity of the key national institutions mandated to implement the tasks set out in the agreement. The newly formed integrated command centre and the mixed police units, which have the responsibility for performing crucial security tasks, face serious capacity constraints. While the two Chiefs of Staff have demonstrated commendable determination in providing effective and professional leadership to the integrated command centre and in pressing ahead with the implementation of the military tasks assigned to the centre, the requisite planning capacity, logistics, personnel and financial resources are not yet in place. Building the capacity of these key institutions will take time.

25. The President and the Prime Minister also called for an increased role for the development and humanitarian agencies of the United Nations in addressing the needs identified by the Government in the areas of economic recovery, resettlement of internally displaced persons, protection of vulnerable groups, restoration of basic services, rehabilitation of the infrastructure in the northern part of the country and support for the civic service programme. In addition, all Ivorian stakeholders, including the President and the Prime Minister, appealed to the United Nations to increase the presence of its civilian personnel outside Abidjan and to reinforce its troop deployments in the western part of the country in order to effectively assist the local authorities in addressing the humanitarian and security challenges in that volatile region. The Chiefs of Staff from the two forces also emphasized the need to maintain and reinforce United Nations patrols in the areas along the border with Liberia and requested assistance in training and building the capacity of the police in the north and with their integration into the national police, within the context of security sector reform and the reunification of the country.

26. Both the Chief of Staff of the national defence and security forces and the President have drawn attention to the parties' request to the Security Council, contained in paragraph 6.1.2 of the Ouagadougou agreement, that it consider granting an exception to the arms embargo in order to allow the importation of riot control equipment and side arms for the national police. The Chief of Staff indicated that the exception should also include spare parts for the Government's military transport helicopter to facilitate travel throughout the country by personnel involved in the implementation of the Ouagadougou agreement. The assessment mission advised them on the established procedure for requesting exceptions to the arms embargo from the sanctions.

27. Concerning the challenges facing Government officials who must travel around the country in connection with the implementation of the agreement, Prime Minister Soro requested that the United Nations should consider allowing such officials to travel on its aircraft and vehicles. In a related request, civil society groups and national relief organizations suggested that UNOCI should use its engineering assets to assist in rehabilitating roads, bridges, schools and clinics in the communities in which they are deployed, especially in the western part of the country.

28. All national stakeholders, especially civil society organizations, were very concerned about the lack of adequate information among the population in the countryside on the

Ouagadougou agreement. They emphasized that, in some areas, this had created unfounded anxieties about the security implications of lifting the zone of confidence. In this context, President Gbagbo requested the United Nations to assist the Government to expand the coverage of the national radio and television (RTI) throughout the country in order to enable the Government to sensitize the population on the reunification and reconciliation process. The office of the Prime Minister informed the technical assessment mission that it was developing a public information campaign to ensure that the population was fully informed about the peace process. The assessment mission stressed the need for Radio télévision ivorienne and Radio ONUCI-FM not only to expand their coverage, but also to enhance their collaboration and disseminate factual information about the peace process, where possible in the main local languages, and to work together with the more than 100 community radio broadcasters in the country.

29. On the same issue, national non-governmental organizations and civil society groups emphasized the importance of placing the state media under the management of professionals without political affiliations to ensure that they can objectively promote national unity and reconciliation. Furthermore, these organizations requested the United Nations and other international partners to help empower women, including through providing advice to the Government on gender mainstreaming in various national institutions. They also called on the United Nations to pay particular attention to the special needs of women and children associated with the former fighting forces when supporting the implementation of the disarmament, demobilization and reintegration programme and the envisaged civic service programme.

30. Reports from civil society groups about cases of misconduct by some UNOCI troops in Abidjan have been a major source of concern. The assessment mission was also informed that there were instances when UNOCI troops in the western part of the country had failed to intervene when civilians in their areas of deployment were under attack, including cases of gender-based violence. In that regard, they echoed the call to reinforce the United Nations military and civilian presence in the west. Mr. Annabi discussed these issues at a debriefing meeting with the heads of all components of UNOCI and stressed the need to take immediate action to ensure full compliance with the Secretary-General's zero tolerance policy. The leadership of the mission has initiated an investigation into the allegations of misconduct.

31. The only issue on which the Ivorian parties initially expressed divergent views was the role the United Nations should play in the electoral process and, in particular, the certification and arbitration roles of the High Representative for the elections. While Prime Minister Soro and the opposition parties expressed the view that, since the issue had not been addressed by the Ouagadougou agreement, the role of the United Nations in the electoral process remained unchanged, the President initially objected to the certification and arbitration roles of the High Representative for the elections. In a letter addressed to Mr. Annabi dated 18 April, the President contended that the role of the United Nations in the electoral process should be limited to observation and technical advice. The President also cited a letter dated 27 March 2006 addressed to me by the facilitator, in which he had expressed the same view. The opposition parties, however, expressed very strong views in support of the certification role of the High Representative, pointing out that that role was provided for in the Pretoria agreement and was based on a delicately negotiated compromise after the parties had failed to agree on the demand of the opposition parties that the elections should be organized and conducted by the United Nations.

32. When he met with the facilitator on 14 April, Mr. Annabi brought to his attention the differences among the Ivorian parties on this important issue and requested him to help them to reach a common view. During a second round of consultations with President Gbagbo, the assessment mission provided a detailed explanation of the importance of maintaining an international certification mechanism to guarantee the transparency and credibility of the electoral process and to ensure that all parties accept the results. The mission stressed that such international certification would not replace but rather would be in addition to the role to be played in this regard by the Constitutional Council of Côte d'Ivoire. It also emphasized that it was important for the parties to reach a common view on this important issue in order to enable the Security Council to decide on any necessary adjustments to the role of the United Nations.

33. Ultimately, President Gbagbo informed the assessment mission that he had consulted the Prime Minister and that a consensus had been reached on this issue. In this regard, he confirmed that, based on the explanations provided by the mission, he accepted that the United Nations should retain responsibility for international certification of the electoral process. However, he maintained his objection to the arbitration role and other functions of the High Representative for the elections as defined in Security Council resolution 1721 (2006), insisting that they were too intrusive. With regard to arbitration, it should be noted that President Compaoré, in his capacity as the facilitator, is expected to act as arbitrator on all aspects of the Ouagadougou agreement.

34. The assessment team's consultations with the facilitator and his team in Ouagadougou helped to clarify the request that additional African troops be included in UNOCI and the issue of United Nations participation in the new follow-up mechanisms. With regard to the latter, President Compaoré was amenable to the inclusion of the United Nations, the African Union and ECOWAS in the Evaluation and Monitoring Committee and he undertook to consult the Ivorian parties on this issue. Meanwhile, during the fourteenth meeting of the International Working Group, which took place on 13 April, members of the Group were divided over its future. Some maintained that the Group should be dissolved to avoid a proliferation of competing monitoring mechanisms, others proposed streamlining the Group to make it smaller and less formal, while several other members insisted that the Group still had a useful monitoring role because the peace process was still fragile and vulnerable to possible reversals. The co-chairs of the Working Group (UNOCI and Ghana, in its capacity as Chairman of the African Union) were therefore requested to consult ECOWAS and the African Union and submit recommendations for consideration by the Security Council.

35. Concerning the deployment of additional African troops in UNOCI, Prime Minister Soro and the Burkinabé facilitation team explained that the purpose of the request was to reassure key political leaders who were concerned about their personal security. They advised, however, that in the light of the positive political and security climate emerging in Côte d'Ivoire, there was no longer a need to deploy those troops at the present stage.

36. UNOCI continues to depend on the Licorne force for quick reaction support. The Licorne presence also complements the role of UNOCI in providing security for key processes. During the consultations with the Licorne Force Commander, the assessment mission received assurances that the planned adjustments to the force would be tailored to support the redeployment of UNOCI troops from the zone of confidence and that the quick

reaction force capabilities provided by Licorne to UNOCI, under the memorandum signed on 29 December 2005, are likely to remain unchanged.

37. On the whole, the assessment mission returned with the feeling that the signing of the agreement and the determination shown by the parties to respect the implementation schedule had created a more relaxed political atmosphere in the country. An encouraging trend in this regard is the significant decrease in the dissemination of messages from the hate media and in other messages inciting violence, which had become the hallmark of Côte d'Ivoire's political discourse. The agreement has also engendered a new spirit of consensus, which was highlighted by the information by the opposition parties that they were consulted by the facilitator and the signatories before, during and after the Ouagadougou talks and that they fully supported the agreement.

38. However, beyond the optimism and high expectations generated by the significant improvement in the political climate, there was a widespread acknowledgement of the enormity of the challenges still facing the country. In particular, it was noted that the agreement is yet to have a commensurate impact on the humanitarian situation. All international and national stakeholders who met with the assessment mission, including President Gbagbo and Prime Minister Soro, were very concerned about the host of humanitarian and security challenges in the western part of the country, where internally displaced persons remain in camps, militias maintain an ambivalent attitude towards the agreement and land disputes, ethnic tensions and possible cross-border movement of combatants could reignite violence. Most of the internally displaced persons are still hesitant to return to their places of origin, citing the uncertainty of the security situation, concerns that returning may render them ineligible to receive humanitarian assistance without the provision of alternative aid and the lack of clarity regarding the recovery of their property. The absence of basic public services for the population in the north is causing equal concern.

39. Nonetheless, the agreement is expected to create an environment in which international organizations can continue to provide humanitarian aid while recovery and developmental partners help to build the capacity of national partners and institutions. At present the United Nations and other international organizations are assisting some 4 million persons affected by the conflict at some 23 locations nationwide. These organizations plan to provide support for the various aspects of the Ouagadougou agreement that have implications for the overall humanitarian situation, such as the national programme to assist persons affected by the conflict, the implementation of the disarmament, demobilization and reintegration programme and the dismantling of the militias, the provision of assistance to and protection of vulnerable groups during cantonment and reintegration, the removal of the zone of confidence and the re-establishment of State administration. The humanitarian community will also accompany and observe the identification process, including the development of modalities to ensure that the process takes into account the special situation facing internally displaced persons seeking access to the identification and voter registration processes. They will also provide assistance to Ivorian returnees and refugees who may decide not to be repatriated.

40. Representatives of the World Bank, IMF and the African Development Bank explained to the assessment mission the heavy toll the crisis has taken on the economy of Côte d'Ivoire. Most macroeconomic and social indicators have declined. Since the onset, economic growth has averaged 0 per cent. The industrial sector has suffered the most, owing to the

lack of investment. In addition, Côte d'Ivoire has seen its role as a regional trading hub diminish. Fiscal performance and transparency have also declined. Tax revenues have fallen below the convergence criteria set by the West African Economic and Monetary Union of 17 per cent of gross domestic product (GDP) and the composition of spending has shifted towards more sovereignty outlays at the expense of social and investment needs. Overall, fiscal deficits have risen, financed increasingly through higher domestic and external arrears and debt. Governance and bank prudential indicators have deteriorated. On the social front, the low farm-gate prices offered to coffee and cocoa producers during the period from 2004 to 2006, the depressed private sector climate, very high unemployment, especially among the young, and the delay in economic recovery have particularly affected the most vulnerable groups. Poverty has grown from an estimated 38 per cent before the crisis to about 44 per cent, while access to health care and education has decreased. Delays in the restoration of Government services in the northern part of the country have also contributed to the increasing gap in service delivery between war-affected regions and the rest of the country. The crisis has resulted in a significant deterioration in Côte d'Ivoire's human development index. The country now ranks 164 out of 177 countries and per capita GDP dropped from $1,242 in 1980 to $839 in 2005.

VII. Recommendations

41. Based on the common view and requests conveyed to the technical assessment mission by the Ivorian authorities, and taking into account the advice provided by the main national and international stakeholders and the assessment mission's overall findings, it is recommended that the United Nations should adjust its role in Côte d'Ivoire to effectively support the new phase of the peace process as set out below.

A. Support to the integrated command centre

42. The Ouagadougou agreement assigns the lead role in the implementation of all military and security tasks relating to the peace process to the integrated command centre. However, in view of their capacity constraints, the parties have requested the support of the United Nations for the implementation of those tasks, which include the integration of the Forces nouvelles and the national defence and security forces, the lifting of the zone of confidence, the deployment of mixed police units, implementation of the disarmament, demobilization and reintegration programme and the provision of security for all key processes, such as the identification of the population, the restoration of State administration throughout the country and the elections. As it performs those military tasks which the Ouagadougou agreement specifically assigns to the impartial forces, such as the maintenance of observation posts along the green line, UNOCI will also work in close coordination with the integrated command centre and the Licorne force.

1. Setting up the integrated command centre

43. At the request of the Chiefs of the Defence and Security Forces of Côte d'Ivoire and the Forces nouvelles, UNOCI and the Licorne force have provided assistance to the two forces in defining the structure and functions of the command centre and setting up the headquarters of the integrated command centre in Yamoussoukro. The command centre will comprise seven functional sections as follows: human resources; operations, short-term planning and intelligence; logistics, including finance, transport and operations; long-term planning,

including for disarmament, demobilization and reintegration; security sector reform; communications and information systems; and civil-military cooperation. The centre will also have a secretariat, including a public information adviser.

44. A service support company comprising about 120 soldiers and 10 gendarmes, with each party providing a half of these personnel, will provide administrative and logistics support for the integrated command centre. In addition, the centre will include a gendarmerie liaison detachment, whose size is yet to be determined, with personnel drawn from both parties. The military chiefs have also agreed on the methodology to be followed in appointing the members of the command centre, ensuring an equitable division of key posts between the two parties. The commander of the centre will report directly to the two Chiefs of Staff. The total strength of the command centre is subject to further discussion by the parties, but it is estimated that the two forces will collectively provide some 230 personnel, most being military.

45. The two Chiefs of Staff have requested UNOCI and the Licorne force to assign two military liaison officers each, and have also requested one United Nations police liaison officer, for the integrated command centre. The parties have further requested the impartial forces to deploy a platoon each to provide security to the integrated command centre headquarters in Yamoussoukro. It is recommended that the Security Council approve the liaison and security support tasks requested of UNOCI by the parties as described above. In addition to those tasks, it is recommended that UNOCI continue to provide technical advice to the integrated command centre, extend to it the necessary logistical support within its capabilities and assist in developing its operational capacity.

2. Lifting the zone of confidence and establishing the green line

46. As indicated, in paragraph 4 above, the process of lifting the zone of confidence and replacing it by a green line started as scheduled, on 16 April. UNOCI will establish 17 observation posts at designated axes of infiltration along the green line. Half of these observation posts are to be deactivated every two months, until all are removed. As of 16 April, UNOCI had started setting up the observation posts at the designated 17 sites. However the removal of the zone of confidence and the dismantling of UNOCI checkpoints in the zone will be conducted progressively as the integrated command centre establishes and deploys mixed police units that will be responsible for maintaining law and order in the area. A total of six such mixed units will be deployed in the area formerly covered by the zone of confidence. The two parties have requested UNOCI to assign four United Nations police officers to each mixed unit to provide with advice and support in the performance of their law enforcement responsibilities.

47. Each mixed unit will comprise 25 personnel (10 each from the two parties, 4 from UNOCI and one medical assistant) and will be assigned to a particular civilian administration jurisdiction. Two units will operate in each of the three zones sub-dividing the green line, which will be called the west, centre and east zones. In addition, one joint military support unit will provide immediate security support for the two mixed units operating in each zone. The three joint military support units will each comprise about 70 military personnel (one platoon from each party). Leadership of the three joint military support units has been divided between the two parties, with an officer from the Forces nouvelles commanding the west zone unit and officers from the defence and security forces commanding the remaining two units in the centre and east zones.

48. It is recommended that the Security Council approve the assignment of United Nations police officers to support the mixed police units and the integrated command centre, as requested by the parties. Furthermore, the police personnel that would come from the Forces nouvelles would require training and mentoring. With the consent of the two parties, UNOCI would support the national police and gendarmerie in providing training for these police personnel. In addition, the UNOCI battalions operating adjacent to the green line will each provide a company sized quick reaction force to support their subordinate units and green line observation posts.

3. Security sector reform and deployment of the new defence and security forces throughout the country

49. As the removal of the green line and the reunification of the country progresses, the mixed police and gendarmerie units deployed in the area formerly covered by the zone of confidence would eventually be replaced by the security arrangements envisaged in the framework of the country-wide deployment of the new restructured defence and security forces. If requested by the parties, UNOCI could provide advice on the reform and restructuring of the new army and police, in particular on the development of the country's new defence and security policy and architecture. However, it would be advisable for the Government to seek assistance from bilateral partners who have the capacity to provide support for the training and restructuring of the new armed forces. The United Nations could assist the Government in identifying such bilateral partners.

50. United Nations police could also provide training to the police personnel from the Forces nouvelles and advice on the integration of such personnel into the national police force. It is recommended that, in addition to assisting in the training of the police and providing advice on the reform of the security sector, United Nations police also accompany, advise and provide logistical assistance for the deployment of national police throughout the country, within its capabilities.

4. Reinforcement of UNOCI deployment in the west

51. The capacity of the integrated command centre and the envisaged integrated police and armed forces to tackle the security challenges in the volatile western part of the country will take some time to develop. The Ivorian authorities have therefore requested UNOCI to reinforce its military and police deployments in that area, including the regions along the border with Liberia. It is therefore recommended that, as it redeploys from the zone of confidence, UNOCI should conduct a careful troop-to-task analysis with a view to determining the level to which it could reinforce its presence in the west and in the areas along the border with Liberia. However, as requested by the parties, the role of UNOCI in this sensitive area should not substitute for the national institutions. In this regard, as the development of the envisaged new armed forces progresses, the integrated command centre should be encouraged to give priority to deploying national defence and security personnel to this area. In the meantime, the anticipated reinforcement of the UNOCI military and police presence in the west should be complemented by increased assistance from UNOCI and United Nations country team to the Government and Ivorian civil society in developing initiatives for the promotion of social cohesion and national reconciliation, as well as the restoration of basic social services in that area. Radio ONUCI-FM coverage would also be strengthened correspondingly in the west. In addition, UNOCI will continue to conduct coordinated patrols with the United Nations Mission in Liberia (UNMIL) in the border areas.

5. Implementation of the disarmament, demobilization and reintegration programme

52. Prime Minister Soro confirmed that, in keeping with the Ouagadougou agreement, the integrated command centre will assume the lead role in the implementation of the disarmament and demobilization phases. The National Programme for Disarmament, Demobilization and Reintegration is expected to continue to play a key role in the implementation of the programmes for the reintegration of ex-combatants and rehabilitation of communities. Both the Prime Minister and representatives of the National Programme informed the technical assessment mission that they expected UNOCI, the United Nations country team, the World Bank and the European Union to assist the national institutions in the planning and implementation of the disarmament, demobilization and reintegration programme. They also indicated that the reintegration aspect would be modified to take into account the civic service programme. The Chiefs of Staff of the two forces indicated that they expect to establish a disarmament, demobilization and reintegration planning and implementation cell, to be co-chaired by the two forces, in which they expect UNOCI to participate.

53. A new concept of operations for the implementation of the disarmament, demobilization and reintegration programme was developed at a coordination meeting convened by the Prime Minister's office on 25 April, which was attended by representatives of the National Programme for Disarmament, Demobilization and Reintegration, UNOCI, the Licorne force, the World Bank, the European Commission and UNDP. Under the revised concept, the defence and security forces will be cantoned in eight sites in the southern part of the country and the Forces nouvelles in nine sites in the north, beginning on a date to be determined by the integrated command centre. The parties have agreed that, while the defence and security forces will be cantoned and their weapons placed in storage, there are no longer any armed forces personnel that will be eligible for disarmament and demobilization because all the 3,000 irregular armed forces personnel recruited after the events of September 2002 have been integrated into the armed forces through a presidential decree. Within the framework of the integrated command centre, the Chiefs of Staff of both forces will propose, for approval by the President and the Prime Minister, the number of Forces nouvelles personnel to be integrated into the unified army. Only those Forces nouvelles personnel who will not be integrated into the new army will be disarmed and enrolled into the civic service programme and other reintegration projects.

54. The National Programme for Disarmament, Demobilization and Reintegration and UNOCI confirmed that 25 disarmament, demobilization and reintegration sites have been refurbished and are ready for the cantonment of combatants. However, the Forces nouvelles have asked for an additional four sites and the defence and security forces for another two sites in order to reduce the distance the combatants would have to travel to the nearest site. The Government and the National Programme for Disarmament, Demobilization and Reintegration have asked UNOCI to assist in constructing these additional sites. In addition, the impartial forces will be expected to provide security for the disarmament sites, supervise the overall disarmament, demobilization and reintegration programme, in keeping with the Ouagadougou agreement, and assist the integrated command centre in destroying the unserviceable weapons and ammunition surrendered, while ensuring storage of those that are serviceable.

55. The disarmament and dismantling of the estimated 1,100 remaining armed militias will be conducted on the basis of the same process that was applied in August 2006: the armed groups will be identified and then disarmed. Profiles of the ex-militia personnel will be prepared in order to facilitate their inclusion into rehabilitation activities. Unarmed militias will be dismantled and will have the benefit of reinsertion programmes, but will not be entitled to the safety net package provided to armed elements.

56. In the light of the above requests, it is recommended that UNOCI support the implementation of the disarmament, demobilization and reintegration programme by, inter alia, constructing the additional disarmament, demobilization and reintegration sites, continuing to provide strategic planning and logistical assistance to the integrated command centre and the National Programme for Disarmament, Demobilization and Reintegration, helping the integrated command centre to provide security at the cantonment sites, assisting in the destruction of collected weapons, coordinating the assistance provided by international partners and overseeing the cantonment, disarmament and demobilization processes and the storage of weapons collected from the cantoned military units. As indicated in my report of 4 December 2006, the cost of constructing the additional six disarmament, demobilization and reintegration sites is estimated at $10 million (S/2006/939, para. 28). If requested by the integrated command centre, UNOCI could also assist in establishing a database on the combatants and the weapons collected.

57. The United Nations agencies, together with the World Bank and the European Commission, will assist the Ivorian authorities to formulate and implement equitable reintegration programmes that take into account similar programmes for internally displaced persons, former militia members and those joining the youth reinsertion and civic service programmes. They will also assist the Government in mobilizing the resources needed for the reintegration and civic service programmes. Furthermore, UNOCI and the agencies will work with humanitarian organizations to assist the Ivorian authorities in developing appropriate rehabilitation and reintegration programmes for the estimated 4,000 children associated with the former fighting forces, as well as other vulnerable groups affected by the disarmament, demobilization and reintegration process, such as women combatants and women associated with the fighting forces. UNDP will continue to assist with the procurement of equipment for the disarmament, demobilization and reintegration sites and will work with UNOCI to help the Government in the preparation of information campaign strategies in support of the collection of small arms and light weapons.

58. In order to ensure effective and integrated support for the disarmament, demobilization and reintegration programme, it is also recommended that the United Nations system in Côte d'Ivoire set up an integrated implementation support cell, which would be co-located with the integrated command centre's disarmament, demobilization and reintegration cell in Yamoussoukro. The United Nations integrated disarmament, demobilization and reintegration implementation support cell would include all relevant UNOCI military, police and civilian components, including logistics and public information, and all concerned United Nations agencies, funds and programmes. It is further recommended that UNOCI establish an additional disarmament, demobilization and reintegration field office in the west, which is currently covered by only one officer based in Daloa. In addition, UNOCI intends to deploy a disarmament, demobilization and reintegration logistics officer at each of the 17 cantonment sites.

B. Support for the restoration of State administration throughoutthe country

59. The Executive-Secretary of the Comité national de pilotage du redéploiement de l'administration informed the technical assessment mission that, based on the Ouagadougou agreement, the Government has decided to put in place new institutional arrangements to implement the restoration of State administration throughout the country. Under these arrangements, the Prime Minister will oversee the work of the Comité national, with the support of the Minister of Public Service and the Minister of Home Affairs and Local Administration. According to the Comité, to date, out of the 24,437 civil servants who were displaced during the crisis, a total of 12,343 have already returned to their posts, including 3,962 to the west and 8,381 to the north. The Government is currently focusing on appointing préfets and sous-préfets, who are expected to be deployed to the north and west. The Prime Minister indicated that the two parties have already agreed on 90 per cent of the candidates for the posts of préfets. The 600 police auxiliaries from the Forces nouvelles, who were trained by UNOCI, are expected to provide security for the return of the préfets and civil servants.

60. The Comité national de pilotage du redéploiement de l'administration has requested specific assistance from the United Nations to support the redeployment of the remaining 12,094 civil servants, which is scheduled to take place between 23 April and 22 July 2007. The requested support includes sensitization campaigns through Radio ONUCI-FM and funding workshops to train préfets and sous-préfets in post-crisis management. The Comité also indicated that, until the Ivorian financial institutions re-establish their branches throughout the country, the Government will need logistical and security support from UNOCI to transport funds for the payment of salaries to civil servants in the field. The Comité also requested the United Nations to assist in mobilizing funding for the rehabilitation of public administration infrastructure in the north, the cost of which is estimated at $22 million.

61. It is recommended that UNOCI support the sensitization programme for the redeployment of State administration to the north, as requested by the Ivorian authorities. UNOCI would also assist in the training of préfets in post-conflict crisis management. The relevant United Nations funds, agencies and programmes should support the rehabilitation of public administration infrastructure in the north and west. In addition, the United Nations will work with other partners to support the provision of basic services during the return of local state administrators and law enforcement authorities. The United Nations will also support the restoration of rule of law institutions in the north and west, in particular the judicial system and police, as part of overall restoration of state authority and administration throughout the country.

62. As indicated earlier, the United Nations police would provide mentoring and training assistance to Ivorian police and gendarmerie personnel deployed to the north to support the delivery of professional and democratic law enforcement and police services and gain the trust and confidence of the population. Initial efforts would focus on the 600 security auxiliaries, to be deployed at 54 locations within the former zone of confidence and throughout the northern part of the country. In the southern part of the country, United Nations police will continue to accompany, support and advise Ivorian law enforcement personnel, including by helping the authorities to conduct a comprehensive needs analysis, formulate strategies and develop and implement programmes.

C. Supporting the identification and voter registration processes

63. The Ouagadougou agreement sets out detailed procedures for the general identification of the population in Côte d'Ivoire, which are linked to the registration of those eligible to vote. These procedures include the deployment of some 208 special mobile courts throughout the country to issue judgements, in lieu of birth certificates, to persons who do not have them. The judgements will record the birth place and the nationality of the individual's parents, which would determine the citizenship of the individual. The parties also made a commitment to reconstitute destroyed or lost civil registers.

64. In addition, in order to facilitate the holding of the presidential election, the agreement seeks to accelerate the process by which Ivorian citizens of voting age can obtain the documents they need in order to register to vote. To that end, the parties agreed that Ivorians of voting age can register to vote based on birth registration documents (birth certificates or court judgements in lieu of birth certificates, to be issued by the mobile courts). Upon registration, eligible voters will receive a receipt with a unique number, which would enable them to obtain both a voters card and a national identity card.

65. The final electoral roll will be prepared on the basis of the electoral lists established in 2000. Thus, individuals who are already on the 2000 voters list will be automatically enrolled on the new voters' list upon presentation of a valid identity card. Eligible Ivorians who are not on the 2000 voters list will be registered if they present the requisite birth registration documents.

66. In order to help enhance the transparency and credibility of the crucial identification process, it is recommended that UNOCI and relevant United Nations agencies accompany and support the National Commission for the Supervision of Identification and participate in observing the operations of the hearings of the mobile courts. With the consent of the Ivorian authorities, United Nations agencies should also assist the national implementing institutions to formulate practical arrangements that would ensure access to the identification process by internally displaced persons and by refugees who choose to remain as permanent residents. They would also support the reconstitution and establishment of updated civil registries and help develop systems to update data for future census exercises. In addition, in keeping with its mandate to prevent and reduce statelessness, UNHCR would provide support and advice to the Ivorian authorities in implementing the identification process. The dissemination of information on the process, including the criteria and procedures, will be of crucial importance to the integrity of the process. UNOCI and United Nations agencies will assist the Ivorian authorities in developing and implementing a nationwide sensitization campaign for the identification process. It is also recommended that UNOCI assist the integrated command centre in providing security for the mobile courts operations.

D. Support to the electoral process

67. The Independent Electoral Commission has completed setting up its central and regional structures and will soon deploy its local commissions throughout the country. The Chairman of the Commission stressed that the security of the electoral process before, during and after the elections was crucial. He therefore requested UNOCI to provide security for the 13,400 central and local commissioners of the Independent Electoral Commission, the 90,000 polling personnel, 430 local offices of the Commission, the 11,000 polling stations and the electoral observers. In addition, he requested the United Nations to assist in

mobilizing funding for the elections and proposed that UNDP should manage the funds contributed by the international community. Furthermore, he expressed concern about the role of the media in the electoral process and requested the United Nations to support the Commission's public information programme. The Chairman also requested the United Nations to provide the necessary logistical support for the electoral process.

68. In its resolution 1528 (2004), the Security Council mandated UNOCI to contribute, within its capabilities and areas of deployment, to the security of the areas where voting is to take place and to provide technical assistance to the electoral process. It is recommended that UNOCI should maintain this role in support of the integrated command centre with regard to security.

69. It is also recommended that UNOCI maintain its current electoral mandate as defined in Security Council resolution 1739 (2007). In addition, the mandate should be adjusted to include coordination of international observers. The coordination of long- and short-term observation of the electoral process would require UNOCI to establish a small unit in its electoral component, which would be dedicated to that task.

70. It is further recommended that UNOCI technical support include assistance to the Independent Electoral Commission in reviewing its operational plans, budgets and calendar, conducting cartographic and logistical surveys of sites selected for the mobile courts and polling centres and planning how the public information, logistics and security components of the mission can assist in a broad civic education campaign. In this regard, UNOCI should enhance coordination between the military, police, logistics, gender, civil affairs, political and public information components of the mission, as well as with United Nations agencies that have a role in providing support for the identification and electoral processes.

71. Considering the constraints still facing the integrated command centre and the limited UNOCI troop levels, UNOCI would help to develop security plans that identify high risk areas where security arrangements would be put in place to protect the 208 mobile courts, the 24 regional, 48 departmental and 358 local electoral commissions and the envisaged 11,000 polling stations, in order to ensure the establishment of a secure environment for the election and its preparatory phases. United Nations police would assist Ivorian law enforcement agencies by providing technical advice and training on operational planning and elections security. If requested by the Ivorian authorities, UNOCI formed police units could provide training to the national police in crowd management and conduct joint exercises with Ivorian police and gendarmerie units on providing security for the elections.

72. United Nations agencies and programmes intend to support the electoral process by helping to mobilize resources to finance additional technical assistance to the Independent Electoral Commission, the procurement of electoral material and data processing equipment, and the updating of voters lists and communication. UNDP is well positioned to mobilize additional resources for the elections and has taken steps to formulate a technical assistance project in close collaboration with UNOCI to support the Commission.

E. Role of the High Representative for the elections

73. All the Ivorian parties recognize the importance of and accept the need to maintain the United Nations responsibility for international certification of the electoral process, based on the Pretoria agreement, in order to ensure the transparency and credibility of the

elections and to minimize the risk of a political crisis in the event that the electoral process is challenged by some parties. It was acknowledged that the United Nations certification role should not replace but should rather be in addition to the prerogatives of national institutions to certify the various aspects of the electoral process.

74. In the light of the above, and taking into account the wish of the parties to exercise greater ownership of the peace process and the difficulties which have arisen regarding the role of the High Representative for the elections, it is recommended that the Security Council consider entrusting the certification role to my Special Representative. In order to ensure that my Special Representative receives independent advice and support in performing this certification role, a small unit, separate from UNOCI's electoral component and consisting of up to three staff, would be set up in his office. In addition to his certification role, my Special Representative would also perform the original mandate of the High Representative as spelled out in Security Council resolution 1603 (2005).

F. Support to persons affected by the conflict

75. United Nations agencies and programmes will assist the Government in formulating a national strategy for providing assistance to vulnerable persons affected by the conflict, including a plan of action outlining areas of support by the United Nations and other international partners. They will also provide support for the dissemination of information on international humanitarian law and the United Nations Guiding Principles on Internal Displacement to the public and to the civilian and military authorities. Other areas in which the development and humanitarian agencies will provide support include the formulation of a national legal framework for the protection and return of internally displaced persons, building the Government capacity to undertake humanitarian advocacy and contributing to the formulation of a comprehensive strategy that will outline immediate and longer-term investments in key service areas such as water, health and education. The overarching goal is to ensure that an agreement is reached with the Ivorian authorities and donors to provide a comprehensive response that concurrently addresses the needs of internally displaced persons, host families and receiving communities. It is equally important to support the authorities and displaced communities in identifying and implementing the most appropriate durable solutions for internally displaced persons.

76. Humanitarian activities will also continue to give priority to mitigating epidemic outbreaks and facilitating access of the population to potable water in order to prevent diseases such as diarrhoea, cholera, measles and guinea worm. The humanitarian community will also advocate the restoration of the social fabric and the rule of law, including the rapid return of the judiciary. In addition, they will assist the Ivorian authorities to create access for the youth, who constitute 42 to 48 per cent of the total Ivorian population, to education and employment opportunities.

77. UNOCI's HIV/AIDS Unit, in partnership with the United Nations Population Fund (UNFPA), will assist in the training of peer educators, assure HIV/AIDS sensitization and provide voluntary counselling and testing services. UNOCI would also deploy voluntary counselling and testing mobile clinics to disarmament, demobilization and reintegration sites.

78. While the agreement does not explicitly address the issue of access to land and housing rights, this issue will come to the fore in the context of the return of internally displaced persons foreseen in the agreement. The international community, including the United

Nations country team and its partners, would be prepared to support the Government to put in place appropriate mechanisms to deal with the recovery of land and property by returnees. Where such recovery is not deemed feasible, the Government would be encouraged to put in place appropriate compensation or another form of reparation mechanisms.

G. Supporting efforts to create a positive political environment

79. In the Ouagadougou agreement, the Ivorian parties expressed their commitment to organize a wide campaign of information and sensitization of the population to support the peace and reconciliation process and to refrain from any type of propaganda that might jeopardize national cohesion and unity. In order to address the lack of information among the population about the peace process, it is recommended that UNOCI and relevant United Nations agencies work with the Ivorian authorities and other partners to assist in the development and implementation of an effective public information plan that would make full use of the available national and UNOCI communications capacities, including Radio ONUCI-FM, Radio télévision ivorienne and the network of community radio stations. The Ivorian authorities will continue to have access to Radio ONUCI-FM to disseminate information on the agreement and the peace process in general. It is essential for the Government and UNOCI to discuss and agree on how Radio ONUCI-FM and Radio télévision ivorienne can play complementary roles in supporting the peace process, promoting national reconciliation and helping to cultivate a positive political environment throughout the country. Additional resources will be required for the expansion of Radio ONUCI-FM coverage where it is most needed.

H. Supporting efforts to promote and protect human rights

80. The Ouagadougou agreement does not expressly address the human rights situation in Côte d'Ivoire. Nonetheless several public national and international stakeholders, in particular civil society organizations consulted by the technical assessment mission, stressed that serious human rights violations are one of the root causes of the Ivorian crisis. They requested the United Nations and other international partners to continue to monitor and promote human rights in the country and to assist the Government to fight impunity in order to ensure a lasting solution to the crisis.

81. It is therefore recommended that UNOCI continue to support the promotion and protection of human rights, as well as monitor, investigate and report on human rights abuses committed in the country. In addition, the mission should also assist the Government in the formulation and implementation of a national human rights action plan, in preparation and submission of outstanding country reports to United Nations human rights treaty bodies and in the effective functioning of the newly established National Human Rights Commission.

82. With regard to the protection of children, UNOCI and the United Nations Children's Fund (UNICEF) will continue to advise the Ivorian authorities on addressing issues pertaining to the juvenile justice system, the rehabilitation of children associated with fighting forces, street children and child prostitution, as well as to monitor and report on violations perpetrated against children in application of Security Council resolution 1612 (2005).

I. Supporting the economic recovery process

83. The operations of IMF and the World Bank are being scaled up in Côte d'Ivoire. Since early 2007, the two institutions have designated country representatives, marking the beginning

of a re-engagement with the country. Nevertheless, further development of relations will be tied to fundamental structural reform, such as transparency in the management of cocoa, coffee and oil revenues, the development of a detailed plan of action for clearance of arrears and concrete progress in the peace process. The World Bank is preparing a pre-arrears grant of some $120 million in order to support reintegration of ex-combatants, the identification process and community rehabilitation. In the meantime, UNOCI and other United Nations agencies have begun preliminary work with the World Bank on the appropriateness and the timing of a post-conflict needs assessment, which would feed into steps for recovery and reconstruction.

VIII. Adjustments to the United Nations presence

A. Military component

84. As at 20 April 2007, the military strength of UNOCI stood at 8,050 personnel, comprising 7,758 troops, 193 military observers and 99 staff officers, against an authorized ceiling of 8,115. These troops make up 11 battalions, nine of which are deployed in the two sectors (East and West), and two in Abidjan. One aviation unit, three engineering companies, one transport company and one special force company are providing enabling capacity and an operational reserve to the force. A total of 14 light infantry companies and three mechanized companies are deployed in Sector West, the most challenging area; 10 light infantry companies, one armoured company and the aviation unit, are deployed in Sector East. The military component also includes the Sous-Groupement de sécurité, comprising 279 personnel, who provide security to the signatories to the Linas-Marcoussis Agreement, members of the Government, members of the Electoral Commission and the High Representative for the elections.

85. Based on the views expressed by the Ivorian authorities, it is recommended that UNOCI should not begin its drawdown at this stage. As the zone of confidence is progressively lifted, the troops deployed in the area will be redeployed to support the integrated command centre in performing the key tasks set out in the Ouagadougou agreement, as described in section VII above. In this regard, the priority is to deploy troops, as requested by the parties to the agreement, to each of the 17 cantonment sites, with up to a maximum of one company, as appropriate (some cantonment sites contain more than one disarmament site), to supervise and support the disarmament and demobilization process and the storage of weapons. In addition, the request of the parties that six additional disarmament, demobilization and reintegration sites be established may require UNOCI to establish temporary military bases in Kani and Ouangolodougou in the north-west. The remaining troops will be assigned to help the integrated command centre to secure other key processes, such as the identification process, the redeployment of State officials throughout the country and the electoral process, and to provide security for the command centre headquarters in Yamoussoukro and reinforce current UNOCI deployments in the west. The troops remaining in the area formerly covered by the zone of confidence will include a platoon (35 personnel) at each of the 17 observation posts along the green line and six companies (600 personnel) that will be deployed in the vicinity of the green line to serve as a quick reaction force.

86. The plans for the redeployment to the west and throughout the country in support of the key tasks are being developed in consultation with the integrated command centre and the

Licorne force, based on a troop-to-task analysis. UNOCI is also reviewing the security protection priorities for the Sous-Groupement de sécurité, in consultation with the parties, to reduce their current range of tasks in order to provide more effectively protection support to those members of the current Government who request it and to respond to other mission related priorities.

87. It is recommended that, once the disarmament, demobilization and reintegration process and the restoration of State administration throughout the country are completed, possibly within the coming three months, UNOCI would conduct a review of its troop level and determine the military resources required to support the completion of the remaining tasks. However, any troop reductions based on that review should take into account the need to retain sufficient troop levels to effectively secure the electoral process. The completion of the presidential election and the installation of the elected Government will be the next key benchmarks that should trigger the beginning of the withdrawal of UNOCI. In the meantime, I recommend the extension of the mission's mandate for a further period of six months, until December 2007. My next report, which will be submitted in September 2007, will take stock of the progress made towards completing disarmament, demobilization and reintegration and restoration of State administration throughout the country and will provide recommendations concerning the mission's troop and police levels.

B. Police component

88. The current strength of the police component of UNOCI stands at 1,157, including 408 individual police officers and 749 members of six formed police units, against an authorized strength of 1,200 police personnel. United Nations police personnel are deployed at 19 locations throughout the country. Two formed police units are deployed in Abidjan and four in Bouaké, Daloa, Guiglo and Yamoussoukro. The primary task of the formed police units is to provide security for United Nations personnel, equipment and facilities. Formed police units conduct regular joint exercises in crowd control management with United Nations and Licorne military forces.

89. In order to provide support to the implementation of the Ouagadougou agreement, in particular to assist in the training of the national police in the north, the UNOCI police component will deploy to two new locations in the north. In addition, one formed police unit will be redeployed from Abidjan to Boundiali, in the north-west, to provide security for the increased number of United Nations police as well as other UNOCI personnel and equipment to be deployed to the north. Up to 72 United Nations police officers will be deployed to the area formerly covered by the zone of confidence to advise and support the mixed police units in performing their law and order maintenance functions. Although the integrated command centre has requested only one United Nations police liaison officer, UNOCI plans to assign five officers to the centre, given the tasks involved, which go beyond liaison and include providing advice on policing issues. The United Nations police officers deployed to the northern part of the country will provide further training and mentoring to the 600 police auxiliaries deployed at 54 locations and will also provide training for newly recruited police cadets from the Forces nouvelles, as requested by the parties.

C. Civilian component

90. With respect to the civilian component, the mission will deploy more personnel in the north and west to support the disarmament, demobilization and reintegration programme

and the restoration of State administration in those areas. In addition, an integrated disarmament, demobilization and reintegration implementation support cell will be co-located with the integrated command centre's disarmament, demobilization and reintegration planning cell in Yamoussoukro.

91. In order to ensure that the organizations of the United Nations system in Côte d'Ivoire support the peace process in a more efficient manner, UNOCI will coordinate its relevant civilian functions with those of the United Nations country team, with a view to ensuring integrated planning. Significant progress has already been achieved in the alignment of activities between UNOCI's human rights section and the country team. Key areas that require urgent synchronization include identification, gender, HIV/AIDS and public information.

92. The Ouagadougou agreement creates an environment in which partnerships between relief and development organizations can be strengthened to ensure coherence and the maximization of resources. Priority areas in which such partnerships could be forged include the rehabilitation of homes, roads, bridges and public infrastructure and the provision of technical support to local state administrators and civil society. UNDP and other United Nations agencies are also harmonizing their approaches to humanitarian assistance and post-crisis early recovery as a basis for operational partnerships to support the electoral process, disarmament, demobilization and reintegration and community rehabilitation.

IX. Mission support issues

93. Ongoing and planned integrated mission support activities will be assessed and adjusted as required to ensure a (United Nations system-wide) coordinated and optimal tasking and response to additional and changed operational priorities. Major support challenges include the dismantling of checkpoints in the former zone of confidence, the establishment of observation points along the green line and the establishment of disarmament, demobilization and reintegration camps and related operational support activities. Additionally, the planned reinforcement of deployments to the western part of the country, the provision of logistics support to the electoral process and the continued expansion of the mission's radio coverage in support of sensitization campaigns remain key support priorities.

94. Detailed resource implications and implementation plans will be determined on the basis of still-developing concepts of operations and implementation timelines for the respective programmes. It is important, however, to note that, based on current tentative timelines, the United Nations system may be expected to respond to major concurrent and resource-intensive support activities that may require short- to medium-term operational surge capacity.

X. Financial aspects

95. By its resolutions 60/17 B and 61/247, the General Assembly appropriated the total amount of $472.9 million for the maintenance of UNOCI for the period from 1 July 2006 to 30 June 2007. The total resources approved for the mission would support 8,115 military personnel, 450 United Nations police personnel and 750 formed police personnel authorized by the Security Council in its resolutions 1609 (2005) and 1682 (2006).

96. Should the Security Council approve my proposals made in paragraph 56 above, the resulting resource requirements would be met through the use of the mission's existing resources and resources that will be appropriated by the General Assembly for the period from 1 July 2007 to 30 June 2008.

97. As at 31 December 2006, unpaid assessed contributions to the special account for UNOCI amounted to $90.4 million. The total outstanding assessed contributions for all peacekeeping operations at that date amounted to $1,760 million. Reimbursement of troop- and contingent-owned equipment costs has been made for the period up to 28 February 2007 and 31 December 2006, respectively.

XI. Observations

98. Prior to the Ouagadougou dialogue, the Ivorian parties had signed a total of five peace agreements since the outbreak of the conflict in 2002. Each of those agreements significantly contributed towards resolving some important aspects of the crisis. In addition, within the framework of those agreements, the impartial forces helped to prevent the parties from returning to full scale hostilities. The advent of the Ouagadougou agreement, however, takes the Ivorian peace process to a unique turning point. For the first time since the beginning of the crisis, the Ivorian parties have undertaken a dialogue at their own initiative, with a facilitator of their choice. Furthermore, the parties have themselves drawn up the framework for resolving key issues that had hitherto impeded progress in the peace process. The opposition parties, which were not directly involved in the dialogue, have confirmed that they fully support the agreement and that they have mandated Prime Minister Soro to represent them. Prime Minister Soro and the facilitator consulted them throughout the dialogue. Accordingly, the Ivorian parties wish to assume full ownership of the process set out in the Ouagadougou agreement and to see national institutions take the lead in implementing it.

99. I congratulate the Ivorian parties for mustering the necessary political will to assume full responsibility for resolving the crisis in their country and I commend President Compaoré for his effective facilitation role. I also thank President Olusegun Obasanjo of Nigeria, President Thabo Mbeki of South Africa and President Sassou Nguesso of the Republic of the Congo for their mediation role over the past four years.

100. Ownership of the peace process imposes a unique responsibility on the Ivorian parties to implement the Ouagadougou agreement in full and in good faith. They have made a good beginning in this regard, meeting the first crucial deadlines set out in the implementation schedule. However, as in all peace processes, unforeseen events will test their will at every critical turn. I urge them to remain steadfast and keep the peace process on track. In this regard, it is imperative to nurture and sustain the spirit of consensus engendered by the Ouagadougou agreement and to forge national cohesion and promote genuine national reconciliation in order to underpin the emerging positive political environment. Furthermore, addressing the main sources of insecurity among the population, including human rights violations, the activities of militias and incitement to violence, inter alia, by the media, will also be crucial to the preservation of a healthy political climate and confidence among the parties.

101. The political will of the parties alone will not sustain the peace process. Already, the delays in launching the dismantling of militias, the cantonment of the former fighting forces, the redeployment of State authority and the mobile courts hearings, which were all scheduled to begin on 23 April, have underscored the challenges that the capacity limitations of national institutions can present for the implementation of the agreement. The Ivorian authorities will need the assistance of the United Nations and other international partners to develop the capacity of the main national institutions involved in the implementation of the Ouagadougou agreement, especially the newly formed integrated command centre.

102. Needless to say, the ultimate test for the Ouagadougou agreement lies in its ability to resolve the fundamental issues that lie at the heart of the Ivorian crisis, in particular the identification of the population, the disarmament of combatants, the reunification of the country and the re-establishment of State authority throughout the country. Failure to effectively address these issues could lead to a breakdown of the peace process, with dire consequences, not only for Côte d'Ivoire, but also for the subregion.

103. The Ouagadougou agreement provides an opportunity for both the Ivorian parties and their international partners to turn a new page. For the parties, this agreement could well be the last chance for a peaceful solution to the crisis. The setbacks and prolonged stalemates of the past should therefore be avoided. With the prevailing ideal situation, where the parties now own and lead the peace process, the international community should adjust its role and relationship with the Ivorian parties accordingly. In particular, it is important to respect and sustain the spirit of consensus among the parties, which is the critical factor propelling the peace process forward. At the same time, the considerable amount of resources already invested in Côte d'Ivoire imposes on the international partners on the ground the obligation to help the parties to ensure that all key processes are conducted in a transparent, balanced and credible manner. Accordingly, in accompanying the national institutions as they implement the agreement, the international partners cannot be mere passive observers, they should provide the necessary support and advice, with a view to ensuring that the peace process is conducted in accordance with internationally accepted standards. This requires regular consultations with the parties. I therefore urge the parties and the facilitator to involve the international partners in the monitoring and evaluation mechanisms.

104. For its part, the United Nations system is ready to provide the support requested by the Ivorian authorities. The capacity of UNOCI and the United Nations country team to support the implementation of previous peace agreements will remain to provide support to the new phase of the peace process, as outlined in section VII above. In providing such support, the United Nations system will also help to reinforce the capacity of national institutions, enhance the credibility and transparency of such crucial processes as the identification of the population, disarmament and the elections and assist in preventing the process from sliding back. The United Nations system will also coordinate and work closely with other international partners. I therefore invite the Security Council to approve the recommendations in section VII above.

105. In conclusion, I would like to express my gratitude to the Officer-in-Charge of UNOCI, Mr. Abou Moussa, the High Representative for the elections, Mr. Gérard Stoudmann, and the military and civilian personnel of UNOCI and members of the United Nations country team for their continued commitment to the peace process. I would also like to express my gratitude to the humanitarian and development organizations, bilateral and multilateral donors and the countries that are contributing military and police personnel to UNOCI for their invaluable contribution to peace in Côte d'Ivoire.

Annex
United Nations Operation in Côte d'Ivoire

Military strength as at 7 May 2007

Country	*Military observers*	*Staff officers*	*Troops*	*Total*	*Formed police units*	*Civilian police*
Argentina						4
Bangladesh	11	10	2 722	**2 743**	250	9
Benin	8	9	420	**437**		28
Bolivia	0			**0**		
Brazil	4	3		**7**		
Burkina Faso				**0**		
Cameroon				**0**		62
Canada				**0**		3
Central African Republic				**0**		7
Chad	3			**3**		5
China	4			**4**		
Congo	0			**0**		
Croatia	3			**3**		
Djibouti				**0**		39
Dominican Republic	4			**4**		
Ecuador	2			**2**		
El Salvador	3			**3**		1
Ethiopia	4			**4**		
France	2	11	173	**186**		10
Guatemala	5			**5**		
Ghana	6	7	531	**544**		1
Gambia	3			**3**		
Guinea	3			**3**		
India	6			**6**		11
Ireland	2			**2**		
Jordan	7	11	1 049	**1 067**	375	4
Kenya	5	3		**8**		
Lebanon				**0**		0
Madagascar				**0**		6
Moldova	3			**3**		
Morocco	1	3	733	**737**		
Namibia	3			**3**		
Nepal	3			**3**		
Niger	6	3	379	**388**		71
Nigeria	8			**8**		17
Pakistan	10	11	1 113	**1 134**	125	2
Paraguay	9	2		**11**		

Continued

Country	*Military observers*	*Staff officers*	*Troops*	*Total*	*Formed police units*	*Civilian police*
Peru	0			**0**		
Poland	2			**2**		
Portugal				**0**		
Philippines	5	3		**8**		11
Romania	7			**7**		
Russian Federation	11			**11**		
Rwanda						15
Senegal	8	8	322	**338**		58
Serbia	3			**3**		
Spain				**0**		
Switzerland						2
Sri Lanka				**0**		
Togo	6	4	315	**325**		1
Tunisia	5	2		**7**		
Turkey				**0**		21
United Republic of Tanzania	1	2		**3**		
Uruguay	2	0		**2**		6
Uganda	5	2		**7**		
Vanuatu				**0**		4
Yemen	5			**5**		2
Zambia	2			**2**		
Zimbabwe	2			**2**		
Total	**192**	**94**	**7 757**	**8 043**	**750**	**400**

8. Fifteenth Progress Report of the Secretary-General on the United Nations Mission in Liberia, 8 August 2007 (S/2007/479)

I. Introduction

1. By its resolution 1750 (2007) of 30 March 2007, the Security Council extended the mandate of the United Nations Mission in Liberia (UNMIL) until 30 September 2007 and requested me to present, no later than 45 days prior to the expiration of the mandate, a detailed drawdown plan for the Mission, including specific recommendations on force levels. In order to collect the information required to prepare the plan, an interdepartmental technical assessment mission led by the Department of Peacekeeping Operations visited Liberia from 11 to 22 June. The present report provides an update on major developments since my report of 15 March 2007 (S/2007/151) and sets out the drawdown plan and recommendations on force levels.

II. Major developments

Political situation

2. During the reporting period, the Government of Liberia continued to implement its agenda for peace consolidation, governance reform and economic recovery. As part of the efforts to improve governance, President Ellen Johnson-Sirleaf undertook an extended visit to Nimba, Grand Gedeh, River Cess, Sinoe, Grand Kru and Maryland Counties in April to conduct a first-hand assessment of the economic, social and infrastructural conditions in these areas and to hold "town hall" meetings with local communities. In Harper, Maryland County, the President convened the first-ever cabinet meeting held outside Monrovia.

3. In furtherance of the Government's efforts to foster national reconciliation and ensure inclusiveness in the decision-making process, President Johnson-Sirleaf began a series of "executive consultations" to solicit the views of national stakeholders on the country's development and recovery process. On 24 June, she met with the Inter-religious Council of Liberia, the Liberian Business Association, and the Liberian Council of Chiefs. On 6 and 10 July, she met with opposition political parties and the Liberian National Bar Association.

4. During the period under review, the Government continued its anti-corruption campaign. On 22 March, the Deputy Minister and an assistant minister in the Ministry of Lands, Mines and Energy were relieved of their posts for allegedly granting bogus mining licences. The trials of the former Chairman of the National Transitional Government of Liberia, Gyude Bryant, who was indicted on charges of economic sabotage, and the former Speaker of the House of Representatives, Edwin Snowe, who was indicted on charges of theft of US$ 1 million from the Liberia Petroleum Refining Corporation during his tenure as Managing Director, are ongoing.

5. However, on 12 and 18 June, the independent Auditor General, who is funded by the European Commission, publicly alleged that the current Government of Liberia was "three times more corrupt" than its predecessor, without providing the evidence to support this allegation, and that "millions of dollars were unaccounted for" in the 2007/08 draft budget.

During a public hearing on the draft budget on 26 June, the Auditor General informed the legislature that the draft budget did not "measure the true financial position of Liberia". The President requested the Auditor General to initiate dialogue with the relevant ministries to discuss those areas concerning which he had expressed concerns. In the meantime, the draft budget, amounting to US$ 199 million, was approved by the Senate on 24 July.

6. The crisis in the legislature that followed the resignation of the former Speaker of the House of Representatives, Edwin Snowe, has been resolved. It will be recalled that Mr. Snowe resigned amid expressions of lack of confidence in his leadership by members of the House. Thereafter, the work of the legislature was paralysed by a dispute over the issue of succession. On 5 April, Alex Tyler of the Liberian Action Party was elected as the new Speaker. During the reporting period, the legislature passed several important bills, including the National Census Act, and ratified a number of agreements, including the renegotiated Mittal Steel Agreement.

Security situation

7. The overall security situation in Liberia has remained generally calm and stable. However, on 17 July, George Koukou, a former Speaker of the National Transitional Legislative Assembly, and Major General Charles Julu, a former Army Chief of Staff and commander of the Special Anti-Terrorist Unit during President Samuel Doe's administration, were arrested and charged with treason for planning to destabilize the Government. The arrests were made after local authorities in Côte d'Ivoire detained a third Liberian, Colonel Dorbor, who had allegedly attempted to purchase and transport arms to Liberia.

8. Other significant security-related developments during the reporting period included violent protests by disgruntled groups and incidents relating to land disputes. On 7 April, a land dispute between the citizens of Blebo and Karbwlaken in Grand Kru County resulted in the burning of houses in Blebo. On 28 April, the death of a five-year old boy in Bong Mines, Bong County, led to a violent disturbance following allegations that the police were involved in the child's death. A newly constructed police station was burned down, while the residences of the Liberian National Police and the house of the city mayor were vandalized during the disturbance. The joint intervention of UNMIL and the county superintendent brought the situation under control.

9. There were also several violent demonstrations involving university students, including a two-day protest in mid-April at the Cuttington University in Gbarnga, Bong County over inadequate facilities on the campus. On 19 June, the Liberia National Police sought the support of the UNMIL formed police units to control a violent protest at the University of Liberia by students expressing solidarity with their lecturers, who had been on strike over the non-payment of salary arrears and benefits. The disturbances occurred in front of the President's Office at the Ministry of Foreign Affairs in Monrovia.

10. On 20 June, former combatants protesting delays in the payment of subsistence allowances held simultaneous demonstrations in Buchanan, Ganta and Gbarnga. The situation deteriorated in Buchanan when ex-combatants forcibly entered the United Nations Development Programme (UNDP) office and damaged property. On 16 July, a group of ex-combatants assembled outside the UNDP headquarters in Monrovia demanding inclusion in reintegration programmes and payment to them of outstanding allowances. The UNDP senior management met with the group and explained to them the plans to provide reintegration opportunities for the remaining caseload of ex-combatants.

11. Meanwhile, on 9 July, during a visit by the Inspector General of Police to the Freeport in Monrovia to investigate reports about the theft of fuel, violent clashes broke out between the Liberia National Police and the Liberia Seaport Police, which resulted in injuries to 50 persons. On the same day, the President directed that a board of inquiry be convened to investigate the incident. The board has since submitted its report to the President for her review and appropriate action.

12. Incidents of armed robbery and rape continued to increase during the reporting period, prompting President Johnson-Sirleaf to launch "Operation calm down fear", which has increased the number of security patrols and spot-checks on vehicles in Monrovia. This is in addition to the ongoing "Operation sweeping wave", which involves cordon and search activities, and increased day and night patrols in high crime areas.

13. The security situation along the borders with Sierra Leone, Côte d'Ivoire and Guinea remains stable. However, the incident referred to in paragraph 7 above underscores the need for effective policing of the border areas. UNMIL continues to conduct several operations to deter the possible cross-border movement of weapons and recruitment of mercenaries, as well as to reassure the local populations and foster better coordination among security agencies deployed in the border areas. In this regard, the Mission conducted concurrent patrols with the Guinean armed forces along the Liberian-Guinean border in "Operation Seskin 4 and 5" from 9 to 13 April and from 27 to 30 May. Similar concurrent patrols were conducted along the Liberian-Sierra Leonean border with the Sierra Leonean armed forces in "Operation Loko 7, 8 and 9" from 26 to 28 April, 28 to 30 May and 27 to 29 June. UNMIL also continued to conduct coordinated patrols with the United Nations Operation in Côte d'Ivoire (UNOCI) to monitor the security situation along the Liberian-Ivorian border.

III. Technical assessment mission

14. The technical assessment mission led by the Department of Peacekeeping Operations, which visited Liberia from 11 to 22 June to collect the information required in order to develop the plan for the drawdown of UNMIL, was comprised of representatives of the Department of Political Affairs, the Office for the Coordination of Humanitarian Affairs, the Department of Safety and Security, UNDP and the Office of the United Nations High Commissioner for Human Rights (OHCHR). The assessment mission met with a broad cross-section of stakeholders, including UNMIL, the United Nations country team, Government ministers and members of the donor and diplomatic community, including the Economic Community of West African States (ECOWAS) and the African Union, as well as political parties, non-governmental organizations and civil society groups. The assessment mission also visited Bomi and Grand Cape Mount Counties, where it specifically assessed the challenges and operational capabilities of the newly trained Liberian National Police deployed in these two counties. Prior to its departure from Liberia, the assessment mission discussed its findings with President Johnson-Sirleaf, the International Contact Group on Liberia and the United Nations country team.

Findings

A. Security situation and threat assessment

15. Liberia has become a generally stable country in a volatile subregion. However, the prevailing peace is very fragile and Liberia is still susceptible to lawlessness. The most

immediate threats to sustained peace and stability in Liberia at this stage include increasing violent criminal activities, especially armed robbery and rape; the limited capacity of the security sector to curb violent crime; the weak justice system; the limited capacity of key national institutions to deliver on the promised peace dividend; the proliferation of disaffected groups such as unemployed ex-combatants, deactivated soldiers and police personnel, and elements from the dismantled irregular militias; economic insecurity, in particular youth unemployment; resurfacing ethnic and social cleavages; and the perception by some opposition political parties that the Government is not genuinely pursuing national reconciliation.

16. There is still a risk of the possible resurgence of armed groups, which may be easily organized to cause political instability. Some Liberian stakeholders expressed concern that elements whose interests are threatened by the Government's reform agenda, as well as individuals loyal to former President Charles Taylor, could attempt to instigate political instability. These factors, as well as the risk of a possible spillover from the unstable situation in Guinea, Sierra Leone and Côte d'Ivoire, underscore the country's continued vulnerability. Nonetheless, Liberia's relations with its neighbours have improved to the extent that potential insurgents would find it difficult to use a neighbouring country's territory to destabilize the country.

17. Prior to the arrival of the technical assessment mission, four joint security assessment teams, co-led by UNMIL and the Government, conducted a comprehensive evaluation of the security situation in the country. The teams, which included representatives of UNMIL, the United Nations country team and the Ministries of Internal Affairs, Defence and National Security, as well as the National Security Agency, the National Bureau of Investigation, the Bureau of Immigration and Naturalization and the Liberian National Police, concluded that security, State administration and the rule of law in the counties were extremely limited. While the security situation in Bomi, Grand Cape Mount and Margibi Counties was assessed as relatively benign, Sinoe and Lofa Counties were assessed as relatively high risk areas.

18. The joint security assessment teams also determined that the weak presence of State authority in some counties, aggravated by poor communications and the lack of livelihood opportunities, have contributed to the movement of ex-combatants, youth and foreigners into areas that are rich in natural and mineral resources. In some of these areas, the tension between the local residents and the "enclaves" who are engaged in these illegal activities is very high. In addition, larger communities of ex-combatants tend to maintain liaison with their former factional commanders. The joint security assessment teams concluded that the security cover provided by UNMIL remains a critical guarantee of peace and stability in Liberia.

B. Status of implementation of the Mission's mandate

19. Following the installation of an elected Government in January 2006, UNMIL redefined its strategic goal to focus on peace consolidation and helping Liberia to attain a steady state of security with police and armed forces that can stand on their own. To that end, the priorities of UNMIL emanating from its mandate include assisting the Government to rebuild its security and rule of law sectors, re-establish functioning administrative structures throughout the country, complete the reintegration of ex-combatants, restore proper administration of the country's natural resources, resettle returnees and internally displaced

persons, promote and protect human rights, and forge national reconciliation. Working in cooperation with the United Nations country team and other international partners, UNMIL has made considerable progress in implementing these key aspects of its mandate over the past year. However, the remaining tasks and the new challenges that are emerging are overwhelming.

1. Rebuilding the Liberian National Police

20. UNMIL has achieved the initial target of providing basic training for 3,500 police officers by 30 June. To date, 3,522 police officers have graduated from the National Police Academy. The first all-female class, comprising 110 police recruits, began training on 4 June after completing the special Ministry of Education/Liberian National Police/United Nations police educational support programme. In addition, several advanced programmes designed to strengthen the supervisory and specialized capacities of the national police are ongoing.

21. However, the deployment of the Liberian National Police to the counties continues to be hampered by lack of funding, basic infrastructure and police equipment, including vehicles and communications. To date, only 676 police personnel have been deployed to the 15 counties. The Inspector General of the Liberian National Police informed the assessment mission that the most pressing needs of the police are adequate funding; equipment, especially communications equipment, vehicles, vehicle maintenance facilities and forensic laboratory equipment; training of specialists; police infrastructure in the counties; development of managerial capacity and elimination of corruption.

22. On 20 June, the technical assessment mission visited the Liberian National Police county headquarters in Bomi and Grand Cape Mount Counties, where it witnessed first-hand the administrative and logistical challenges facing the police. Owing to a lack of communication facilities in these county headquarters, police officers use their personal mobile phones to meet their reporting responsibilities to their commanders and to communicate among themselves, as well as to police headquarters. In Grand Cape Mount County, where the police have only one vehicle and a motorbike for use by 42 officers, the county commander pays for the fuel and maintenance of the vehicle from his own salary. He also provides the fuel for a donated generator and food for detainees from his personal resources.

23. The Government, with the support of its international partners, is addressing some of the infrastructure challenges facing the police force. Through bilateral support provided by Norway and the Netherlands, the renovation, construction and equipping of police stations are under way in Buchanan in Grand Bassa County, Zwedru in Grand Gedeh County, Harper in Maryland County, Tubmanburg in Bomi County, Kakata in Margibi County, Gbarnga in Bong County and Sanniquellie in Nimba County. The construction of the police headquarters in Grand Kru, River Gee and River Cess Counties is ongoing.

24. The construction of police stations in Webbo, River Gee County and Morweh, River Cess County are also under way. Through UNMIL quick-impact projects, the reconstruction and rehabilitation of police stations in Owensgrove in Grand Bassa County, Salala in Bong County, Unification Town in Margibi County, Schefflin Town in Montserrado County and Robertsport in Grand Cape Mount County have been completed. The rehabilitation of the police stations in Bopolu in Gbarpolu County, Voinjama in Lofa County, Bo-Sinje in

Grand Cape Mount County, Foya and Kolahun in Lofa County, Tapeta and Yekepa in Nimba County and Toe Town in Grand Gedeh County is also under way.

25. The further training and equipping of the 450-strong Police Support Unit is ongoing. Some 300 of these officers were already trained in 2005 by the Government of Nigeria. An additional 150 officers will begin training shortly at the National Police Academy. Some members of the Unit have been equipped with firearms and ammunition, as authorized by the Security Council sanctions Committee. The United Nations police are working closely with instructors from the Liberian National Police to ensure that officers who use firearms receive refresher and requalification training in accordance with the firearm policy of the Liberian National Police.

26. Given the small size of the envisaged Armed Forces of Liberia, the Government has decided to establish a 500-strong Police Quick Reaction Unit. The training curriculum and terms of reference for trainers and advisers of the unit are being developed and the selection of recruits is under way. It is envisaged that 200 of these officers will become operational by July 2008 and that the training and equipping of the full unit will be completed by July 2009. The United States and Ireland have agreed to contribute to this project.

2. Training, restructuring and reform of the Armed Forces of Liberia

27. The United States continues to support the building of a new 2,000-strong Armed Forces of Liberia. It has contracted two private companies, DynCorp and Pacific Architects and Engineers (PAE), to implement this project. DynCorp is responsible for the recruitment and the provision of basic training of the recruits at the Barclay and Camp Ware training centres, while PAE is responsible for providing advanced training of the recruits and the construction of the barracks, as well as the battalion and brigade headquarters, at Camp Kessely near Monrovia.

28. The technical assessment mission visited Camp Kessely and the Camp Ware training facility where it noted the very impressive and well-equipped barracks, training facilities and battalion and brigade headquarters constructed by PAE and DynCorp for the new armed forces. The private contractors informed the assessment mission that most of the $20 million already spent in restructuring the new army has been invested in the construction of these facilities.

29. However, so far, only 105 recruits have completed basic training. Nine of these recruits were commissioned as second lieutenants on 8 May after graduating from the Officers' Candidate School in March. On 21 July, basic training for the second batch of 525 recruits commenced at Camp Ware. The new Armed Forces of Liberia will be comprised of two infantry battalions, an engineering unit, a military police unit, a military band and medical personnel.

3. Development of a national security strategy and architecture

30. The Government is still in the process of elaborating a national security strategy and architecture, which are expected to define the respective roles of the Armed Forces of Liberia, the Liberian National Police, the Liberian Seaport Police, the Police Quick Reaction Unit, the Special Security Service, the Bureau of Immigration and Naturalization, Customs and other key security agencies, as well as provide for a national policymaking and crisis-management capacity and an intelligence-gathering agency. It is envisaged that these

security agencies will have clear mandates, which will complement each other. The overall security architecture should ensure that Liberia's security sector has the capacity to anticipate and deal with security threats before they materialize.

4. Disarmament, demobilization, reintegration and rehabilitation

31. A verification exercise carried out earlier this year by a technical working group comprised of UNMIL, UNDP, the United Nations Children's Fund (UNICEF), the European Commission, the United States Agency for International Development (USAID) and the National Commission on Disarmament, Demobilization, Reintegration and Rehabilitation concluded that some 90,000 ex-combatants have benefited from the reintegration and rehabilitation programme, some 2,000 ex-combatants (2 per cent) have spontaneously reintegrated into communities and some 9,000 eligible ex-combatants are still awaiting reintegration opportunities. UNDP informed the assessment mission that it had provided reintegration opportunities for some 63,000 ex-combatants and planned to close its trust fund at the end of June. It is envisaged that other international partners will provide training opportunities to the remaining caseload of ex-combatants within ongoing programmes.

32. Many Liberians, however, informed the assessment mission that the reintegration programme has failed to provide sustainable alternative livelihoods for ex-combatants. The majority of ex-combatants are still unemployed and thousands have regrouped for the purpose of illegally exploiting natural resources in diamond and gold mining areas, as well as on rubber plantations.

33. UNMIL continues to collect and destroy residual weapons and ammunition voluntarily surrendered or discovered through search operations. Since the end of the disarmament and demobilization programme in 2005, a total of 748 weapons, 1,390 pieces of unexploded ordnance, 99,980 rounds of ammunition and 11,790 assorted spares and miscellaneous parts have been collected and destroyed by UNMIL. The UNDP community arms collection programme has collected 320 rifles, 36,593 rounds of ammunition, 938 assorted spare parts and 706 pieces of unexploded ordnance since its launch in January 2006.

5. Supporting the consolidation of State authority

34. Progress in the consolidation of State authority throughout the country remains slow, owing to the lack of financial resources, office and residential accommodation, logistics and passable roads, as well as capacity constraints. Only 10 of the 15 county administration buildings are expected to be completely rehabilitated by October 2007, while the remaining five will be rehabilitated during the next fiscal year. County support teams, comprised of representatives of UNMIL, the United Nations country team, the Ministry of Internal Affairs, county administrations, government line ministries and non-governmental organizations, are assisting in building the capacities of local authorities to assess, plan, coordinate and deliver basic services. These teams meet on a monthly basis to report on progress and challenges in each county.

35. The United Kingdom's Department for International Development has agreed to provide a grant of US$ 2.5 million to the Civil Service Agency, the Governance Reform Commission and the Liberian Institute for Public Administration, in support of the Liberian public service capacity-building programme, while the World Bank has provided a grant of US$ 900,000 under the low income countries under stress programme, to assist reform activities.

In addition to these initiatives, the Government of Liberia is establishing, with the assistance of international partners, a Senior Executive Service designed to attract qualified Liberians to public service.

36. Municipal and chieftaincy elections have been delayed owing to a lack of resources. According to the Minister of the Interior, US$ 19 million is needed to organize these elections. In the meantime, elections for county branches of the National Traditional Council of Liberia are ongoing.

6. Promotion of human rights and the rule of law

(a) Human rights

37. The human rights situation in the country continues to improve. However, deficiencies in the justice system are posing serious challenges to efforts to promote and protect human rights. There are recurring reports of court officials who continue to apply rules and procedures in an inconsistent manner, fail to observe minimum human rights standards and engage in corrupt practices. In addition, trial by ordeal is still practised in some areas, partially because of the absence of functioning courts and police in remote areas.

38. The enactment of the Rape Amendment Act in 2006 has had little impact on stemming the high incidence of sexual violence, including rape of women and girls. In support of the Government's efforts to address this situation, UNMIL and the United Nations country team established a joint task force, which reviewed the processes involved in the handling of rape cases and made recommendations on the way forward.

39. The Independent National Commission on Human Rights has still not been fully established owing to the delay in the appointment of its commissioners. As a result, a national human rights action plan has not been developed.

(b) Support for the judicial and corrections system

40. The development of the judicial and corrections system has been very slow. The judicial system is constrained by limited infrastructure, shortage of qualified personnel, lack of capacity to process cases, poor management and lack of the necessary will to institute reforms. As a result of these shortcomings, many Liberians have little confidence in the justice system.

41. Although State prosecutors are now assigned to every circuit court and most magistrates' courts, there are still insufficient public defence counsels assigned to the counties. As a result, many indigent defendants do not have access to legal counsel.

42. The state of the juvenile justice system is a source of deep concern. The sole juvenile court in Monrovia, as well as those county magistrates' courts which are authorized to exercise juvenile jurisdiction, lack qualified personnel. In addition, juveniles are often held for long periods in pre-trial detention with adults, or are either tried by magistrates' courts or released without trial.

43. UNMIL has continued to provide training for legal and judicial officers. Since May 2006, 336 magistrates, 220 justices of the peace, 226 prosecutors, 147 magistrates' court clerks and 53 circuit and Supreme Court clerks have been trained. In addition, UNMIL has provided legal training to 351 immigration officers. Nine quick-impact projects for courthouses have been completed and work is ongoing on four other courthouses.

However, considerable additional funding will be required to renovate all the courthouses in the country.

44. A bill to establish a law reform commission has been drafted with the support of UNMIL and the United States Institute of Peace. Once established, the commission is expected to undertake a comprehensive review of the laws of Liberia. UNMIL is assisting the Ministry of Justice in identifying laws to be repealed or reformed, including those that do not conform to international standards. In addition, the Mission is helping the Government to elaborate a policy framework for judicial reform.

45. With respect to the corrections system, UNMIL is training personnel of the Bureau of Corrections and Rehabilitation and providing security at correctional facilities. So far, UNMIL has recruited and trained 104 corrections officers and intends to train another 125 officers in 2007. In addition, the Mission will need to provide intensive training and mentoring to corrections officers at three new facilities which will open shortly in Gbarnga, Bong County, Tubmanburg, Bomi County and Greenville, Sinoe County. In the meantime, the United States has agreed to fund the deactivation of some 60 correction officers.

46. Most of the correction facilities, including the Monrovia Central Prison, are overcrowded. Due to the acute shortage of staff and the poor working conditions at these facilities, jailbreaks and disturbances are a regular occurrence. Two new facilities in Monrovia and Zwedru are due to open later this year, which should help to partially alleviate the problems of overcrowding. In addition, UNDP and the Office of the United Nations High Commissioner for Refugees (UNHCR) have agreed to renovate the old prison and build a new facility in Gbarnga. Currently, the Bureau of Corrections and Rehabilitation has 10 operational corrections facilities in 9 of the 15 counties in the country.

7. Promoting national reconciliation

47. The mandate of the Truth and Reconciliation Commission is due to expire in September 2008. Thus far, the Commission has only recorded 5,000 out of an estimated 30,000 statements. In addition, it has received only $2.2 million out of a projected initial operating budget of US$ 14 million. The work of the Commission was suspended earlier this year owing to management and transparency problems. In March, a joint working group comprised of representatives of the Commission and the International Contact Group on Liberia was established to assist the Commission in overcoming these challenges. So far, the working group has proposed revisions to the budget, provided policy guidelines, developed a work plan and revised the staffing strength and personnel policies of the Commission.

48. With respect to the Government's efforts to foster political and ethnic reconciliation, the opposition political parties expressed the view that genuine national reconciliation is yet to begin and accused the Government of pursuing policies that could revive old ethnic and social cleavages. President Johnson-Sirleaf acknowledged that the Government needed to do more to engage with the opposition parties and to promote national reconciliation, while pointing out that her Government was inclusive. She informed the assessment mission that she intended to conduct a consultative process to solicit the views of Liberian political groups and civil society on issues of national importance. The President has since commenced these consultations, as indicated in paragraph 3 of the present report.

8. Promoting efficient management of natural resources

49. Following the enactment of the National Forestry Reform Law in August 2006, and the lifting of sanctions on the export of Liberian timber, the Government of Liberia established the Forestry Reform Monitoring Committee to develop a forestry reform package and to monitor the implementation of 29 forestry regulations.

50. With the termination of sanctions on diamonds on 27 April, Liberia was admitted to the Kimberley Process Certification Scheme on 4 May. On 28 July, the Government removed the country's self-imposed ban on diamond mining, which paves the way for the official export of diamonds. In the meantime, the widespread illegal mining of diamonds by ex-combatants, foreigners and unemployed youth continues to pose serious challenges to the Government's efforts to re-establish its authority in the areas concerned.

51. UNMIL is supporting the Government in its efforts to revive Liberia's rubber industry by assisting in the recovery of plantations, including those that are illegally occupied by ex-combatants. The Mission continues to provide security at the Guthrie rubber plantation, which was recovered and placed under the management of an interim team established by the Government. The security situation on the Cocopa rubber plantation, another illegally occupied property, has improved significantly following the collection of single-barrel shotguns from the plantation's residents. As a result, the Government was able to transfer the management of the plantation to the concession owner in April. The Government's re-possession of the Sinoe rubber plantation has been delayed owing to the poor state of the roads in Sinoe County. The plantation is currently being occupied by ex-combatants, who are exploiting the lack of State authority in the area to extract rubber illegally.

9. Supporting implementation of the Governance and Economic Management Assistance Programme

52. The implementation of the Governance and Economic Management Assistance Programme (GEMAP) continues to make progress. The Government's financial management practices have improved considerably, especially in the areas of budgeting, expenditure controls, cash management and procurement planning. The Government has established a Technical Secretariat for the Cash Management Committee and an integrated financial management information system. It has also instituted policies and guidelines to improve procurement practices and the granting of concessions.

53. On 28 April, the President attended a retreat with international partners to review progress made in the implementation of GEMAP. Pursuant to recommendations made at the retreat, which were subsequently accepted by the GEMAP Steering Committee, the GEMAP technical team is now being co-chaired by the Government and international partners. In addition, government agencies hosting internationally recruited GEMAP experts are now expected to submit joint expert/government quarterly reports to the technical team, highlighting the issues resolved, results achieved and plans to address ongoing problems.

IV. Economic recovery, reconstruction and development

54. Liberia's economy has begun to rebound. The growth rate, which was 5.3 per cent in 2005, has increased to 7.9 per cent in 2007. The gross domestic product (GDP) at current prices is estimated at US$ 574.5 million, with a per capita income of US$ 163. The sectoral performance of the economy showed some signs of recovery last year, with the agricultural

sector, including forestry, accounting for 95.4 per cent of export earnings. By the end of 2006, Liberia's external debt portfolio was estimated at US$ 3.7 billion, which is about 800 per cent of GDP and 3,000 per cent of exports. The country's domestic debt, including salary arrears, is estimated at US$ 700 million.

55. Employment generation is still a major challenge and a key priority of the Government. A joint initiative of the Ministry of Public Works, UNMIL, UNDP, UNHCR, the World Food Programme (WFP) and the World Bank, aimed at rehabilitating critical roads, has so far provided short-term employment opportunities for some 9,000 workers, including ex-combatants. In addition, some 4,000 community members and ex-combatants have benefited from the rehabilitation of roads by UNMIL military engineers. With the assistance of the WFP "Food support to local initiatives" programme and the Ministry of Public Works, UNMIL has facilitated the employment of some 8,000 local community members in roadside brushing and other basic road repair works, and over 9,000 community members have been employed through labour-intensive infrastructure projects supported by USAID, the European Commission, the Swiss Development Corporation and international non-governmental organizations. Despite these achievements, more efforts are needed to encourage massive private-sector investments in order to generate employment.

V. Humanitarian situation

56. The humanitarian situation in Liberia continues to improve. However, the country still faces serious challenges, particularly in the health, education, food, and water and sanitation sectors. In this regard, the Central Emergency Response Fund (CERF) provided US$ 4 million through the World Health Organization (WHO), the United Nations Children Fund (UNICEF), the Food and Agriculture Organization of the United Nations (FAO) and their implementing partners to improve access to health facilities and essential drugs, construct and rehabilitate water and sanitation facilities and enhance food security.

57. So far only 21.1 per cent of the US$ 117 million needed to address high-priority humanitarian needs, including the delivery of basic social services, the provision of productive livelihoods for returnee communities and the strengthening of civil society and local authorities, as outlined in the 2007 Common Humanitarian Action Plan for Liberia, has been received.

58. On a positive note, the UNHCR-supported voluntary repatriation programme was completed on 30 June. Through this programme, UNHCR has assisted the voluntary repatriation of some 110,000 refugees, while some 50,000 refugees are reported to have returned spontaneously. There are now approximately 80,000 refugees remaining to be repatriated from various countries in the subregion. There are also 16,253 refugees from Sierra Leone, Côte d'Ivoire and other countries residing in Liberia.

VI. Gender

59. The Mission's Gender Adviser Unit has developed an action plan, with benchmarks, for the implementation of Security Council resolution 1325 (2000) on women, peace and security. The Unit also continues to conduct gender training for UNMIL personnel and for corrections officers. Through its membership of various committees and working groups, the Mission is providing technical, logistical and financial support for the implementation of a national action plan in the areas of the rule of law, the protection of the rights of women and girls and the promotion of women in decision-making areas.

VII. HIV/AIDS

60. The UNMIL HIV/AIDS Unit is collaborating with the Mission's integrated training cell to conduct awareness training and sensitization, as well as personal risk assessment sessions, as part of the induction training for military, police and civilian personnel. It also promotes HIV/AIDS awareness in Liberia through its participation in an UNMIL live phone-in programme.

VIII. Personnel conduct and discipline

61. In the first half of the year, seven cases of sexual exploitation and abuse were reported in UNMIL, as compared to 21 cases in the same period last year. In addition, four "category 1" cases and 70 "category 2" disciplinary cases were reported. Investigations of two of the seven cases of sexual exploitation and abuse have been completed, while investigations into the remaining five cases are continuing.

62. The Mission's conduct and discipline team is focusing on developing and implementing strategies to prevent, identify, report and effectively respond to all categories of misconduct by United Nations personnel. The Mission continues to emphasize the Secretary-General's zero tolerance policy on sexual exploitation and abuse in its training and awareness raising campaigns. UNMIL also assists in the coordination of the Government's national sexual exploitation and abuse awareness campaign.

IX. Public information

63. The UNMIL public information unit continues to support the priority programmes of the Mission, as well as those of the United Nations agencies, the Government of Liberia and civil society. The Mission organized a series of public outreach events and radio programmes, including a five-week nationwide "sport for peace" tournament in March. UNMIL Radio introduced five new programmes to provide more coverage of social and human rights issues. In addition, the Mission is conducting training for local media, supporting the Ministry of Information in the training of public information personnel and conducting media and public relations/information training for members of the Liberian National Police.

X. Adjustment and drawdown of the Mission

64. As indicated in my previous reports, UNMIL repatriated one company (250 military personnel) in March 2006 in compliance with Security Council resolution 1626 (2005) of 19 September 2005. The Mission also repatriated one battalion (750 military personnel) in December 2006 as a result of the relative stability that had prevailed since the inauguration of the new Government. The current UNMIL troop strength stands at 14,141 out of the authorized strength of 15,125, while its police strength stands at 1,180 (including 18 corrections officers) out of the authorized maximum of 1,240 officers.

65. The technical assessment mission and UNMIL have determined that notwithstanding the remaining challenges facing the country and the security risks identified in section III of the present report, sufficient progress has been made in the implementation of the Mission's mandate and in stabilizing the security situation in the country to allow for further adjustments to be made to the military and police components of UNMIL.

Benchmarks

66. The assessment mission proposed that the pace of the drawdown process should be linked to the following core benchmarks: (a) completion of the basic training of 3,500 personnel of the Liberian National Police by July 2007; (b) completion of police operating procedures by December 2008; (c) completion of the formation of the 500-strong Police Quick Reaction Unit by July 2009; (d) equipping of police personnel and their deployment to the counties, as well as building of police infrastructure by December 2010; (e) finalization of the national security strategy and architecture and their implementation throughout the country by December 2008; and (f) training and operationalization of the first and second Armed Forces of Liberia battalions by September 2008 and September 2009, respectively.

67. In addition, the restoration of the rule of law and the strengthening of State administration and authority in all of Liberia's 15 counties, along with the elections scheduled to take place in Sierra Leone in 2007 and in Guinea and Côte d'Ivoire in 2008, are important contextual benchmarks that need to be taken into account when deciding on the timing of adjustments to UNMIL troop deployments.

XI. Recommendations

A. Military component

68. UNMIL and the technical assessment mission developed a concept which provides for the drawdown of the military component of the Mission in three stages. During the first stage, 2,450 troops (three infantry battalions and three infantry companies) would be repatriated, leaving the Mission's troop strength at 11,691. There would be no significant change in the Mission's deployment locations and smaller units would be redeployed to locations left by the repatriated troops.

69. The second stage of the drawdown would focus on restructuring the existing four military sectors into two. This would involve the repatriation of some 500 military personnel from two sector headquarters, including staff officers, military observers and two medical units, as well as some Force Headquarters staff officers. At the end of this stage, the Mission's troop level would stand at 11,191.

70. In the third stage, a further two battalions and some sector units (2,191 personnel) would be repatriated, reducing the overall troop strength of UNMIL to 9,000 personnel. These reductions would be assessed against the remaining core benchmarks.

71. After the repatriation of each major unit, adjustment periods of three months would follow to provide UNMIL with time to realign its logistic support arrangements and prepare for the next repatriation. In addition, technical assessments would be conducted during the three drawdown stages to assess the progress made in meeting the benchmarks and to make specific recommendations on the further adjustments to the Mission.

72. It is assumed that the 250-strong Mongolian military guard force deployed at the Special Court for Sierra Leone would be retained throughout the drawdown period, unless the Special Court completes its work. Moreover, it is expected that UNMIL capacity to reinforce UNOCI on the basis of Security Council resolution 1609 (2005) would decrease to an infantry company of approximately 150 troops during the drawdown phase.

73. The technical assessment mission and UNMIL considered several options for implementing the concept described in paragraphs 68 to 70 above. However, following consultations with the Government of Liberia, they recommended only one option. Under this option, stage one (repatriation of 2,450 troops) would start in October 2007 and end in September 2008. It would be followed by a three-month review period (until December 2008) to assess the overall stability of the new force structure and to evaluate progress made in strengthening State administration and authority in all 15 counties, as well as developments in the subregion, including the anticipated elections in Côte d'Ivoire and Guinea. It was determined that this review period would be critical, given the fragile situation in Liberia and the unpredictability of developments in the subregion. Stage two (repatriation of 500 military personnel and streamlining of the sectors) would start in January 2009 and end in August 2009. A crucial benchmark that would be assessed during this period is the formation of the Police Quick Reaction Unit, which is expected to be completed by July 2009. Stage three (repatriation of 2,191 troops) would then run from September 2009 until December 2010.

74. It is too early to determine when the final withdrawal of UNMIL should take place and to plan for successor arrangements. It is therefore recommended that a technical assessment mission be dispatched to Liberia in mid-2010 to conduct a detailed review of the progress made in stabilizing the country and in the development of the national security sector, with a view to developing a plan for the period beyond December 2010. The important national elections due to be held in Liberia in October 2011 would also need to be taken into account in making the final decision on the Mission's withdrawal.

B. Police component

75. The technical assessment mission, in consultation with UNMIL, recommended a gradual reduction of 498 police advisers in seven stages between April 2008 and December 2010. There will be no drawdown of the 18 corrections officers who are part of the Mission's police strength. Moreover, it will be essential to include an additional six corrections officers to reinforce support for the strengthening of the corrections system. These officers will be deployed to provide training at the new correctional facilities opening shortly in Bong County, Bomi County and Sinoe County. Appropriate "hold and review periods" to assess the security situation in the country and the development of the operational capability of the Liberian National Police would be built into the drawdown process. The proposed reduction would bring the police strength to 742 personnel by December 2010. The five formed police units (605 police personnel), which provide support to the Liberian National Police in controlling riots and civil disturbances, would remain in the Mission area throughout the drawdown period. In addition, police advisers with specialist policing skills, especially in forensics, criminal investigation, management, intelligence, operations, organized crime, professional standards, drug enforcement, airport security and the protection of women and children, will be deployed to the Mission during routine rotations to provide the national police force with advanced training and appropriate mentoring. The adjustments in the level of the UNMIL police component will also be tied to the core benchmarks referred to in paragraph 66 above.

C. Civilian component

76. UNMIL will continue to adjust its civilian component, as appropriate, to adapt to evolving priorities. The Mission has already started making adjustments to its Reintegration,

Rehabilitation and Recovery Section, as well as to its Humanitarian Coordination Section, in the light of the progress made in the reintegration of ex-combatants and in the transition from the emergency humanitarian phase to early recovery.

XII. Observations

77. President Johnson-Sirleaf's Government has made great strides in consolidating peace and promoting economic recovery in the country. The main achievements of the Government include completing the implementation of the measures required to lift timber and diamond sanctions; increasing public revenues by 48 per cent; completing the staff-monitored programme of the International Monetary Fund; preparing and implementing an interim poverty reduction strategy; restoring electricity and water supply to some parts of Monrovia for the first time in 15 years; increasing school enrolment by 40 per cent; improving the human rights situation and cultivating mutually beneficial relations with Liberia's neighbours. In addition, the Government has remained focused on the important priorities of consolidating its authority, fighting corruption, implementing the Governance and Economic Management Assistance Programme, reforming the security sector, regaining control and regulation of its natural resources and strengthening the capacity of its institutions.

78. These are remarkable achievements for a country that is emerging from a situation of complete lawlessness and whose State institutions and infrastructure had crumbled. However, the remaining challenges are formidable. The process of consolidating peace and rebuilding State institutions is still in its formative stage. Until the army and police can stand on their own and the justice system is rehabilitated and accessible to all Liberians, the country will remain vulnerable to the risk of a return to lawlessness. Moreover, providing alternative livelihoods for ex-combatants and deactivated security sector personnel, creating employment opportunities, ensuring genuine national reconciliation, addressing the needs of the victims of the conflict, alleviating poverty and delivering basic social services to the population are critical tasks that must be accomplished to ensure durable stability in Liberia. In order to meet these challenges, appropriate measures to promote economic growth must be implemented in order to generate the requisite public revenues.

79. The slow progress in strengthening the security sector is a source of great concern. The training of the Armed Forces of Liberia has faced considerable delays, which has resulted in the postponement of the operationalization date of its units. Meanwhile, although significant progress has been made in meeting the training benchmarks for the Liberian National Police, its operational effectiveness is constrained by the lack of adequate funding, vehicles, communication equipment and accommodation. These deficiencies are a major obstacle to the full deployment of the police throughout the country. The management of the Liberian National Police will also need to be strengthened. I appeal to the international community to generously support the equipping and deployment of the Liberian National Police and to assist in completing the training of the new Armed Forces of Liberia expeditiously. I also call on the Government of Liberia to finalize its national security strategy and architecture in the coming months.

80. Although illegal diamond mining continues to pose serious challenges and remains a potential source of instability, it is gratifying to note the commendable efforts of the Government to curb these activities, which have resulted in the lifting of the sanctions on diamonds and Liberia's admission into the Kimberley Process Certification Scheme.

I encourage the Government to further strengthen its regulation of this important sector and to ensure, in particular, that Liberia becomes fully compliant with the Kimberley Process.

81. President Johnson-Sirleaf is to be commended for the positive steps that she has taken to foster national reconciliation and political inclusiveness in the country. However, the ethnic and social cleavages that have plagued the country in the past could still resurface. I therefore call on the Government of Liberia to intensify its efforts to promote national and local reconciliation in the interest of sustaining peace and stability in the country.

82. The uncertain situation in Côte d'Ivoire and Guinea poses additional challenges to stability in Liberia. I am encouraged however by the continuing efforts to strengthen cordial relations among the countries of the Mano River Basin.

83. Considering the many challenges that still face Liberia, in particular its complex and fragile security environment, I recommend that the Security Council approve the drawdown concept set out in section XI above, as well as the force levels described in paragraph 73 and the plan for the adjustment of the UNMIL police component set out in paragraph 75. The proposed plan allows UNMIL to adapt to evolving priorities and to conduct a gradual, phased and deliberate transfer of responsibility for the security of Liberia to the Government in a manner that gives the Government the opportunity to build its capacity, while the Mission continues to help to maintain the prevailing stability. The plan emerged from a careful analysis of the existing security situation, as well as a thorough threat assessment and evaluation of the unfinished tasks under the UNMIL mandate. The plan is also the product of close consultations with the Government of Liberia, national stakeholders and Liberia's partners.

84. The drawdown process will need to be continually assessed in the context of the specific benchmarks identified in the present report. The Government and the international community are therefore strongly encouraged to make a timely and effective investment in the accomplishment of these benchmarks. Should the Council approve these proposals, I intend to submit regular updates on the implementation of the drawdown process. This would provide the Security Council, the Government and UNMIL with the opportunity to take stock of the security situation and to evaluate the progress made in accomplishing the benchmarks. In the meantime, I recommend that the Mission's mandate be extended for a further period of one year, until September 2008.

85. In conclusion, I wish to express my deep appreciation to the Security Council and to troop- and police-contributing countries, as well as to ECOWAS, the African Union and donor countries, for their continued support in consolidating peace in Liberia. I also wish to pay tribute to my Special Representative, Alan Doss, and all UNMIL military and civilian personnel, and humanitarian and development agencies, as well as non-governmental organizations, for their important contributions to the continued progress of peace consolidation in Liberia.

United Nations Mission in Liberia: military and civilian police strength (as at 1 August 2007)

Component	*Military*				*Police*
Country	*Military observers*	*Staff officer*	*Troops*	*Total*	*Civilian police*
Argentina				0	8
Bangladesh	17	11	3 187	3 215	28
Benin	3	1		4	
Bolivia	3	1		4	
Bosnia and Herzegovina				0	11
Brazil		2		2	
Bulgaria	2			2	
China	6	7	558	571	18
Croatia		5		5	
Czech Republic	3			3	5
Denmark	2			2	
Ecuador	2	1		3	
El Salvador	3			3	2
Ethiopia	19	8	1 798	1 825	
Egypt	8			8	4
Fiji				0	30
Finland		2		2	
France		1		1	
Gambia	4			4	30
Germany				0	5
Ghana	12	8	849	869	40
India					125
Indonesia	3			3	
Ireland		1		1	
Jamaica				0	7
Jordan	7	8	115	130	140
Kenya	3	4		7	19
Kyrgyzstan	4			4	2
Malawi		2		2	20
Malaysia	10			10	
Mali	4	1		5	
Moldova	3	1		4	
Mongolia		2	248	250	
Montenegro	2			2	
Namibia	3	4	608	615	5
Nepal	3	2	40	45	256
Niger	3			3	
Nigeria	17	12	1 944	1 973	163

Continued

Component	*Military*				*Police*
Country	*Military observers*	*Staff officer*	*Troops*	*Total*	*Civilian police*
Norway				0	10
Pakistan	16	12	3 389	3 417	32
Paraguay	3	1		4	
Peru	3	1		4	
Philippines	3	5	165	173	33
Poland	2			2	3
Portugal				0	
Republic of Korea	1	1		2	
Romania	3			3	
Russian Federation	6			6	8
Rwanda				0	12
Samoa				0	13
Senegal	3	2	598	603	
Serbia	4			4	3
South Africa				0	
Sri Lanka				0	1
Sweden				0	14
The former Yugoslav Republic of Macedonia				0	1
Togo	2	1		3	
Turkey				0	23
Uganda				0	21
United Kingdom		3		3	
Ukraine	3	1	300	304	13
Uruguay				0	3
United States	7	6		13	8
Yemen				0	4
Zambia	3			3	27
Zimbabwe	2			2	30
Total	**207**	**117**	**13 799**	**14 123**	**1 177**

INDEX

INDEX

(References are to roman numerals volume: page number)

A

B

C

D

F

G

M

N

O

P

R

T

U

The manufacturer's authorised representative in the EU for product safety is Oxford University Press España S.A. of El Parque Empresarial San Fernando de Henares, Avenida de Castilla, 2 - 28830 Madrid (www.oup.es/en or product.safety@oup.com). OUP España S.A. also acts as importer into Spain of products made by the manufacturer.
Printed and bound by CPI Group (UK) Ltd, Croydon, CR0 4YY
14/09/2026
02216290-0017